Advanced GNVQ
BUSINESS

Advanced GNVQ
BUSINESS

Stan Golab
Peter Horton
Michael Leake
Tony Magee
Peter Rooney
Graham Wood

PITMAN PUBLISHING
128 Long Acre, London WC2E 9AN

A Division of Pearson Professional Limited

First published in Great Britain 1995

© Pearson Professional 1995

ISBN 0 273 61067 8

British Library Cataloguing in Publication Data
A CIP catalogue record for this book can be obtained from the British Library.

All rights reserved; no part of this publication may be reproduced, stored in a retrieval system, or transmitted in any form or by any means, electronic, mechanical, photocopying, recording, or otherwise without either the prior written permission of the Publishers or a licence permitting restricted copying in the United Kingdom issued by the Copyright Licensing Agency Ltd, 90 Tottenham Court Road, London W1P 9HE. This book may not be lent, resold, hired out or otherwise disposed of by way of trade in any form of binding or cover other than that in which it is published, without the prior consent of the Publishers.

10 9 8 7 6 5 4 3 2 1

Typeset by Pantek Arts, Maidstone, Kent.
Printed and bound in Great Britain.

The Publishers' policy is to use paper manufactured from sustainable forests.

CONTENTS

Preface   xi

Unit 1: BUSINESS IN THE ECONOMY

Element 1.1 Analyse the forces of supply and demand on businesses   3

Introduction ■ The demand for goods and services ■ The supply of goods and services ■ The interaction of supply and demand ■ Classification of businesses ■ Self assessment questions ■ Assignment

Element 1.2 Analyse the operation of markets and their effects on businesses and communities   30

Introduction ■ Types of market ■ Wealth and welfare ■ Self assessment questions ■ Assignment

Element 1.3 Examine the effects of government policies on markets   43

Introduction ■ The reasons for government intervention ■ How governments can influence markets ■ Economic systems ■ Government approaches to economic management ■ Fiscal policy ■ Privatisation ■ The European Union ■ Exchange rates ■ Self assessment questions ■ Answers to self assessment questions

Unit 2: BUSINESS ORGANISATIONS AND SYSTEMS

Element 2.1 Investigate business organisations   77

Introduction ■ The objectives of business organisations ■ Business ownership in the private sector ■ Public sector organisations ■ Organisation structures ■ Self assessment questions ■ Assignment

Element 2.2 Investigate administration systems   100

Introduction ■ The management structure and its role within the organisation ■ The effect of information technology on administration systems ■ Evaluation of administration systems and planning for change ■ Systems description and documentation ■ Health and safety ■ Self assessment questions ■ Assignment

Element 2.3 Analyse communication in a business organisation 120

Introduction ■ Communication channels ■ Types of communication ■ Communication equipment ■ The effects of changes to communication equipment ■ Self assessment questions ■ Assignment

Element 2.4 Analyse information processing in a business organisation 142

The purposes of information processing ■ Computers ■ Data protection ■ Health and safety ■ The use of an integrated business computer system ■ The effects of computer technology ■ Self assessment questions ■ Assignment ■ Answers to self assessment questions

Unit 3: MARKETING

Element 3.1 Investigate the principles and functions of marketing in organisations 163

Introduction ■ Marketing principles ■ Marketing objectives ■ Customer focus and the marketing concept ■ Marketing functions and activities ■ Managing change ■ Growth of organisations ■ Self assessment questions ■ Assignment

Element 3.2 Propose and present product developments based on analysis of marketing research information 200

Introduction ■ Secondary data ■ Primary data ■ Ensuring suitability of information ■ Analysing marketing research information ■ Marketing research and its contribution to marketing decisions ■ Self assessment questions ■ Assignment

Element 3.3 Evaluate marketing communications designed to influence a target audience 227

Advertising ■ Public relations ■ Sales promotion ■ Segmentation and targeting ■ Product performance ■ Direct marketing ■ Guidelines and controls ■ Self assessment questions ■ Assignment

Element 3.4 Evaluate sales methods and customer service to achieve customer satisfaction 253

Sales distribution channels ■ Duties and responsibilities of sales staff ■ Customer service and sales staff's role ■ Sales communication methods ■ Sales administration ■ Self assessment questions ■ Assignment ■ Answers to self assessment questions

Unit 4: HUMAN RESOURCES

Element 4.1 Investigate human resourcing — 269

Introduction ■ The responsibilities of human resourcing ■ The rights of employers and employees ■ Grievance procedures ■ Disciplinary procedures ■ Redundancy ■ Industrial relations ■ Methods of gaining employee co-operation ■ Self assessment questions

Element 4.2 Investigate job roles and changing working conditions — 299

Job roles within business organisations ■ The human resource responsibilities of job roles ■ Changes to working conditions ■ Self assessment questions

Element 4.3 Evaluate recruitment procedures, job applications and interviews — 317

Recruitment and selection procedures ■ Job descriptions ■ Person specifications ■ Letters of application ■ The curriculum vitae ■ Interviews ■ Interviewee technique ■ Legal obligations ■ Ethical obligations ■ Self assessment questions ■ Answers to self assessment questions

Unit 5: PRODUCTION AND EMPLOYMENT IN THE ECONOMY

Element 5.1 Analyse production in business — 343

Introduction ■ The purpose of organisations ■ The value-added method ■ Added value as a measure of performance ■ Self assessment questions

Element 5.2 Investigate and evaluate employment — 355

Introduction ■ Business sectors ■ Causes of decline in industrial output and employment ■ Women and employment ■ Effects of changes in contracts of employment ■ Flexibility and society ■ Self assessment questions

Element 5.3 Examine the competitiveness of UK industry — 367

Introduction ■ Government economic policies ■ Government growth policies ■ Other government economic objectives ■ Business strategies to improve competitiveness ■ Europe's top companies ■ International comparisons of 'competitiveness' ■ UK unemployment 1984–90 ■ Revision questions ■ Additional activities ■ Assignments ■ Self assessment questions ■ Answers to self assessment questions

Unit 6: FINANCIAL TRANSACTIONS, COSTING AND PRICING

Element 6.1 Explain added value, distribution of added value and money cycle 397

Considerations for the seller ■ Considerations for the buyer

Element 6.2 Explain financial transactions and complete supporting documents 401

Purposes of financial transactions and documentation ■ Purchases and sales documents ■ Payments and receipts documents ■ Processing cash and cheques ■ Recording sales ■ Recording purchases ■ Statements and remittance advices ■ Maintaining petty cash records ■ Self assessment questions ■ Additional activities ■ Assignment

Element 6.3 Calculate the costs of goods or services 460

Introduction ■ Direct and indirect costs ■ Fixed and variable costs ■ Marginal costing ■ Self assessment questions ■ Assignment

Element 6.4 Explain basic pricing decisions and break-even 481

Pricing considerations ■ Marginal cost pricing ■ Drawing a break-even chart ■ Analysis of the break-even chart ■ Reasons for using a break-even chart ■ Self assessment questions ■ Additional activities ■ Assignment ■ Answers to self assessment questions

Unit 7: FINANCIAL FORECASTING AND MONITORING

Element 7.1 Explain sources of finance and financial requirements of business organisations 499

Introduction ■ Asset types ■ Current liabilities ■ Working capital ■ Sources of business finance ■ The balance sheet ■ Sources of asset finance ■ Self assessment questions ■ Assignment

Element 7.2 Produce and explain forecasts and a cash flow for a small business 516

Introduction ■ Working capital ■ Capital budgets ■ Trading forecasts ■ Cash budgets ■ Computer spreadsheets ■ Self assessment questions ■ Assignment

Element 7.3 Produce and explain profit and loss statements and balance sheets 536

Introduction ■ Double-entry bookkeeping ■ Accounting documentation ■ The trial balance ■ Final accounts and balance sheets ■ Year-end adjustments ■ Self assessment questions ■ Assignment

Element 7.4 Identify and explain data to monitor a business 562

Users of accounting information ■ Reasons for monitoring a business ■ Key components of accounting information ■ Ratio analysis ■ Self assessment questions ■ Assignment

Unit 8: BUSINESS PLANNING

Element 8.1 Prepare work and collect data for a business plan 597

Introduction ■ Introduction to planning ■ Business objectives ■ Legal implications ■ Insurance implications ■ The feasibility study ■ External support ■ Resource requirements ■ The new business proposal ■ Assignment

Element 8.2 Produce and present a business plan 608

Introduction ■ The purposes of producing a business plan ■ The marketing plan ■ The production plan ■ Forecasting ■ Departmental budgets and the business plan ■ Assignment

Element 8.3 Plan for employment and self-employment 631

Types of employment and self-employment ■ Statutory requirements ■ Opportunities for employment and self-employment ■ The skills required ■ An action plan for employment ■ An action plan for self-employment ■ Sources of information ■ Assignment

Index 647

PREFACE

Although this book is intended to be used by students of the BTEC Advanced GNVQ in Business it can be used for similar Advanced Level courses offered through either the RSA or City and Guilds. Additionally it can be of use to any student of business studies at 'A level', BTEC National, or Higher National levels.

The authors have attempted to keep the text as concise as possible and to use simple, non-technical language throughout. The text is intended to be read and used by students rather than as an academic text for teachers. The book has been written to cover the unit specifications published by NCVQ and the three awarding bodies in 1995. Each of the eight mandatory units forms a 'chapter' in the book. Each unit is also further broken down into its constituent elements.

At the end of each element is a series of self testing or assessment questions, answers to which are given at the end of each unit. These are written in the format of the external tests that have to be passed by each student in each unit. These questions allow the student to test their understanding of the content of the element and to gain an insight into the format of the external test. As seventy per cent is the mark necessary to pass these tests students should be given as much practice as possible in answering these questions.

The performance criteria for each element is listed at the start of the respective element. Within the elements the student is required to undertake 'activities' which are intended to reinforce learning. All of the activities are linked to the performance criteria (PCs) and teachers may use these activities to form part of the assessment system of the course. These activities are not intended to form part of the grading system used on the course, and should be used on a 'competent or not yet competent' basis.

In addition to the activities at the end of each element, there is an 'assignment' which is also linked to the performance criteria. These assignments are intended to be graded and should be undertaken while that particular element is being taught. All the PCs are covered at least once throughout the activities or the assignment and are clearly marked with an icon in the margin. Whenever possible the relevant skills PCs have also been listed with C for Communication, IT for Information Technology and AN for Application of Numbers. It is not the intention of this book to cover all of the skills areas and course teaching teams are recommended to assess skills in separate activities and workshops.

The normal duration of an advanced course is two years and the authors recommend that four units are taken in each year. Many centres have adopted a semester system whereby two mandatory units and one optional unit are taken in each half year, the first semester finishing at the January test date. This system allows maximum attempts at the external tests by the students.

Unit 8, Business Planning, is not tested by an external test and is best assessed by the production of a written business plan produced by each individual student and presented to a 'bank manager'. This unit effectively combines the content of each of the other seven units and allows the student to put into practice the knowledge and skills developed in the other parts of the course. It should, therefore, be scheduled as the last activity in the course at the end of year two. As there is no test associated with Unit 8 the elements in this book for this unit have no self assessment questions.

Acknowledgements

The authors wish to thank their colleagues and families for their forbearance during the writing of this book. In particular Michael Leake acknowledges the involvement and help in the writing of Units 2, 7 and 8 given by his wife Margaret who contributed substantial parts of the text.

Every effort has been made to trace and acknowledge ownership of copyright. The Publishers will be glad to make suitable arrangements with any copyright holders whom it has not been possible to contact.

UNIT 1

BUSINESS IN THE ECONOMY

This unit provides the student with an understanding of the forces of supply and demand and their impact on businesses in the real world. The different types of market conditions are discussed, from the very competitive markets to restrictive monopoly markets, as are the obvious implications for individual consumers and businesses. This unit also examines current environmental concerns by looking at the social costs and social benefits of businesses.

Any unit which examines the economy would not be complete without significant investigation into the role of government. The government's role in the economy is crucial and has enormous implications for business.

Throughout this unit the emphasis is on how we can apply economic theory to the real world. We need to understand some key economic tools but the real importance lies in the understanding of their application – how they can help individuals, businesses and the government reach the correct conclusions concerning economic decisions.

Element 1.1
ANALYSE THE FORCES OF SUPPLY AND DEMAND ON BUSINESSES

Performance criteria

1. **Explain demand for goods and services.**
2. **Explain how businesses decide about what goods and services to supply.**
3. **Analyse the demand and supply interaction and how it influences business.**
4. **Explain the effects on business decisions caused by changes in demand and supply.**
5. **Report research findings about demand and supply interaction and the price and sales for a particular product.**
6. **Suggest future changes in demand and supply of particular products and suggest how these may affect business decisions about which products to supply and in what quantity.**

Introduction

All businesses need to be aware of the demand and supply for their products and services. If they fail to take account of consumer demand then their profits will decline. The success of a business often depends on its ability to maintain a 'unique selling proposition' – to convince the consumer that what the business offers is unique and totally different to other competitors.

The ability of producers to satisfy consumer demand in a market economy depends on good market research regarding consumer behaviour and a good knowledge of the pricing strategies of competing firms.

Before we examine different businesses in the market place we need to understand the fundamental principles behind supply and demand. In this element we analyse the effects of supply and demand on businesses.

Unit 1   Business in the economy

THE DEMAND FOR GOODS AND SERVICES

Demand can be defined as:

> The quantity of goods or services that the consumer is prepared to buy at a given price in a given time period.

The *market demand* for a product is the total amount that will be bought in a specific market in a specified time period. Producers are more concerned with the total demand or market demand for their products rather than the individual levels of demand. The market demand is the summation of all individual demand levels for any given product or service. For example, the market demand for motor vehicles bought each month in the UK would include the demand for the products of all the motor manufacturers supplying the UK market, such as Vauxhall, Ford, Nissan, Fiat, Renault, BMW, Rover, etc.

ACTIVITY 1.1.1

List five other examples of market demand. Make them as varied as possible.

Demand is not the same thing as desire. You may desire to own a Rolls Royce, but not have the £120 000 cash to buy it. In economics demand is often referred to as 'effective demand' which simply means that a person must have the ability to buy the good or service.

The law of demand

When economists are studying demand, they assume that consumers are rational. This means that consumers will normally seek to maximise their satisfaction from their purchases. They make decisions which aim at maximising their pleasure (in economics, the term used is *utility*) from the goods or services purchased. The rational consumer will only purchase goods and services, if the pleasure expected from consuming them is at least equal to the sacrifice of money used in purchasing them. For example, it follows that a non-smoker will not pay £2.40 for a packet of cigarettes because he or she will not receive any satisfaction from smoking them. The smoker may even pay more than £2.40 for them, if they are in short supply and he or she needs a smoke.

If we consume up to the point where the price we pay and the pleasure we receive are equal, then any subsequent reduction in price will result in an increase in the quantity of goods that we purchase.

The law of demand states:

> As the price of the good falls, more will be demanded.

Table 1.1. shows a demand schedule for personal computers.

Element 1.1   Analyse the forces of supply and demand on businesses

Table 1.1. Demand for personal computers

Price	Quantity demanded (000s)
£5000	100
£4000	200
£3000	400
£2000	600
£1000	900

In Table 1.1 we see that more consumers will buy computers, if the price falls. When the price falls to £1000 for a computer, considerably more people wish to purchase, i.e. 900 000. This data can now be plotted on a graph (see Fig. 1.1).

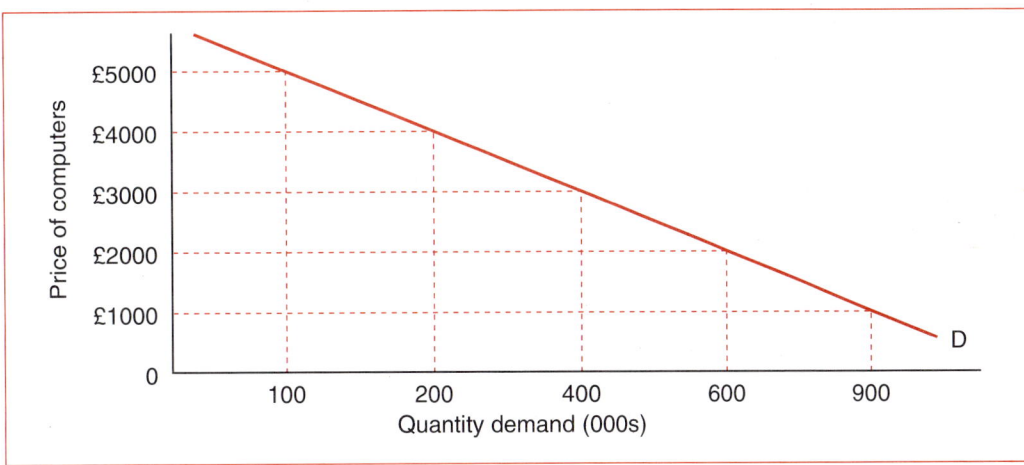

Fig 1.1 Demand schedule for personal computers

From Fig. 1.1, we can see that the downward sloping demand curve is inversely related to price. Economists make a number of assumptions when looking at price changes on demand curves. They assume that all other factors remain constant or unchanged, that is *'ceteris paribus'*.

The conditions of demand

The assumption of *'ceteris paribus'* is a highly unrealistic in the real world because there are a number of variables which can influence consumer choice other than price. These include:

- substitute goods
- complement goods
- quality of the good
- advertising
- income of the consumer
- taste and fashion
- expectations
- distribution of income.

Economists refer to these variables as the *conditions of demand*.

Price

Changes in demand caused by changes in price are represented by movements along the demand curve. This is dependent on the assumption *'ceteris paribus'* (other things being equal). In other words, the only change in the conditions of demand is a price change (*see* Fig. 1.2). There is a movement in demand from A to B.

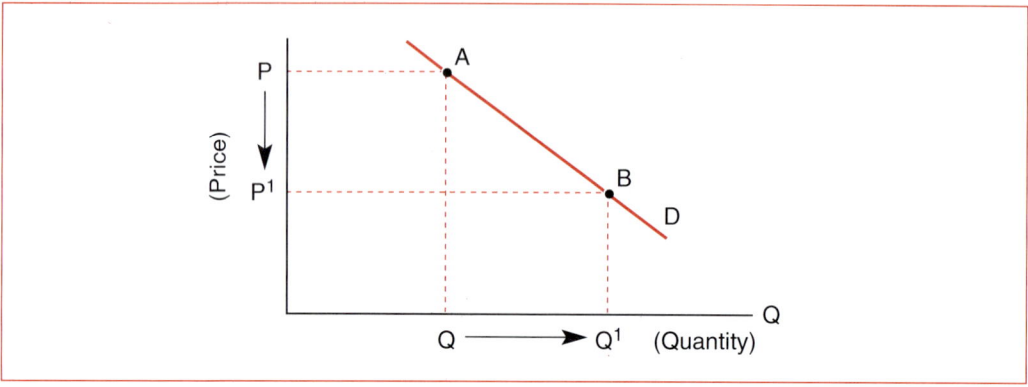

Fig 1.2 Price changes from A to B

Note that the lower the price, the greater the quantity demanded. An increase in demand due to factors other than price would move the curve upwards from D to D1, and a decrease in demand would move the curve downwards from D to D2 (*see* Fig. 1.3).

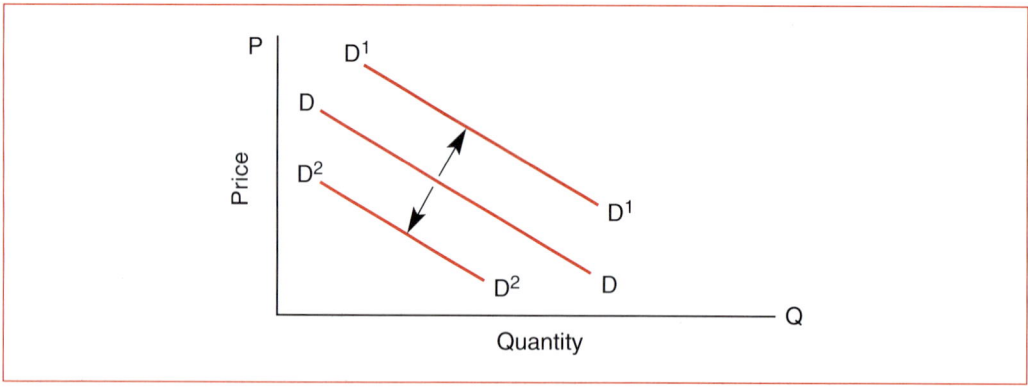

Fig 1.3 Movement of the demand curve

Price of other products

Substitute goods are in competition with one another, so a price change in one will affect the demand for the other. For example, if Ford decided to reduce the price of its Mondeos by 10 per cent and Vauxhall kept the price of its Cavaliers at the same price many consumers would buy Ford rather than Vauxhall and Vauxhall would lose some of its market share (*see* Fig. 1.4).

Element 1.1 Analyse the forces of supply and demand on businesses

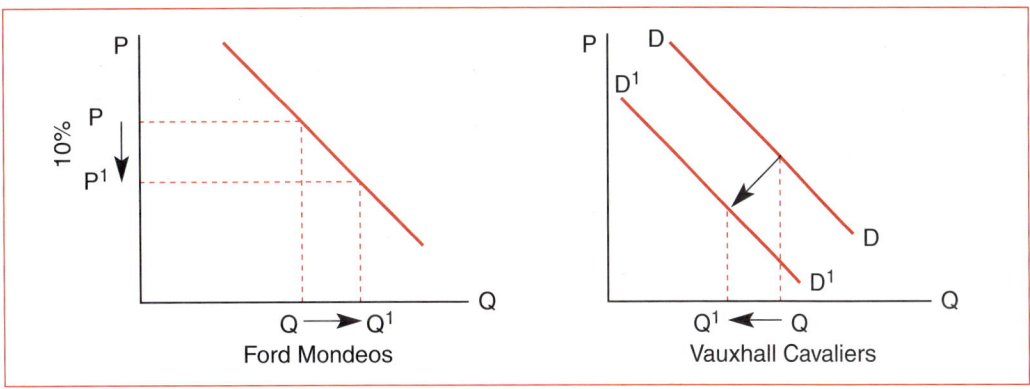

Fig 1.4 Substitute goods: Ford versus Vauxhall

Complement goods are in joint demand and so a price change in one will automatically affect demand for the other. Petrol and cars are a good example. If there is an increase in the price of petrol, this will have an effect on the demand for cars, i.e. it will fall. This arose in the 1974 oil crisis when petrol increased by some 300 per cent and demand for motor vehicles fell (*see* Fig. 1.5).

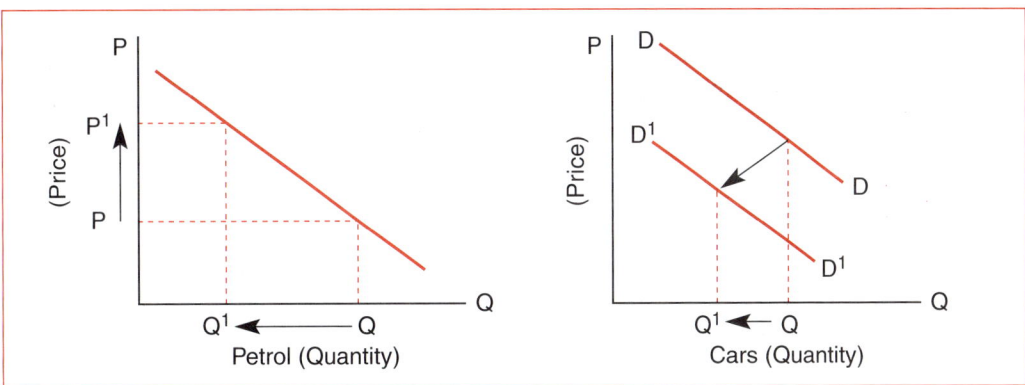

Fig 1.5 Complement goods: petrol and cars

ACTIVITY 1.1.2

Task 1. List five examples of substitute goods.

Task 2. List five examples of complement goods.

Task 3. If the price of coffee increased, what would happen to the demand for tea? Use two diagrams to illustrate your answer.

Task 4. If the price of tyres fell by 100 per cent, what would happen to the demand for motor vehicles? Use two diagrams to illustrate your answer.

Crunch time for the crisp companies

Rather than continue to fight own-label brands on price, snack manufacturers must take the humble potato crisp upmarket in the search for profits, writes **John Waples**

RICHARD CLOTHIER, chief executive of Dalgety, the food conglomerate, had an unsavoury message to deliver to the stock market last Monday: the fierce price war in the crisp market had taken a big bite out of his group's profits.

Figures from Dalgety's crisp-and-snack arm Golden Wonder, had been hit in the battle being waged by the supermarkets and the food discount chains. Clothier chose his words carefully: "The bottom end of the crisp market is certainly much less profitable than it should be."

Dalgety has become one of the bigger victims in the British crisps war, its products caught up in the onslaught of the cheap, own-label products that have slashed the profit margins on the branded crisps.

The own-label phenomenon has been building momentum in the past two years and has resulted in a highly competitive market for the nation's favourite snack. Some stores charge just 29p for a six-pack of crisps, half of what was charged a few years ago. "It's a tough battle all round in the food sector at the moment," says one City analyst, "and crisps are in the thick of it."

The own-labels have created turmoil in the £1.8 billion British salty-snacks market, of which crisps account for 60%. While manufacturers such as Dalgety and United Biscuits have been happily churning out own-label crisps for the large chains, they have at the same time been damaging sales of their own products for the sake of overall volumes.

Cut-throat pricing has also forced Britain's crisp manufacturers into expensive promotional campaigns to maintain market share. "In the future, the biggest influence on margins will be marketing investment," says Eric Nicoli, chief executive of United Biscuits. "Marketing initiatives funded by cost savings will drive future growth."

The crisp business is dominated by three players: Walkers Smiths, the market leader and the British arm of PepsiCo Foods International (the world's largest snack-foods company with annual retail sales of more than $4 billion); United Biscuits with its KP division; and Dalgety's Golden Wonder. More than 30m bags of crisps and snacks are sold every day in this country, with crisps alone generating sales of £1 billion a year.

The price war has sliced into the main players' profits.

United Biscuits, Europe's number one snacks giant, like Dalgety, showed that competition had pulled back profits growth when it reported its half-year figures last week.

In short, while Britain's crisp-loving munchers have never had it so good, the manufacturers have never had it as tough. "Manufacturers have nothing more to give," says Anthony Fiddian, the finance director at Bensons Crisps, a quoted snack company that provides own-label supplies to supermarkets. "Margins for crisps have fallen 5% in the past 15 months. I don't think we can absorb any more pain – and the same must be true of all manufacturers."

Bensons, says Fiddian, is being squeezed by rising raw materials costs, including edible oil and film wrapping, and has, as yet, failed to pass on this increasing burden to the retailer or consumer.

Analysts believe it is the small companies, like Bensons, that are most exposed to the price squeeze. "Everybody, with the exception of Walkers, which continues to trade strongly, has been hurt by the low prices. But the greater the reliance on the standard crisp, the greater the pain," says John Parker at BZW.

Industry experts are anticipating a big realignment in the crisps market, with the main players increasingly concentrating on premium product lines and avoiding competition with own-label brands.

Golden Wonder is expected to jettison the production of its cheap brands and reposition its products as premium crisps with a premium price. KP is hoping that McCoy's and Brannigans, the thick potato chip, will increase its strength at the premium end of the market.

Jack Rowell, the executive director of Dalgety's food consumer division, said: "You've got to reposition your business for the new era. What is important is that you fall out the other side healthier and more robust than before."

But it is Walkers Smiths, which produces 5.5m crisps packets daily, that has proved to be the shrewdest player so far. Its more to higher quality packaging and expensive promotions is paying dividends. In the summer it launched Walkers Doritos, a corn tortilla chip, as an upmarket product. It quickly became one of the big winners in the snack market.

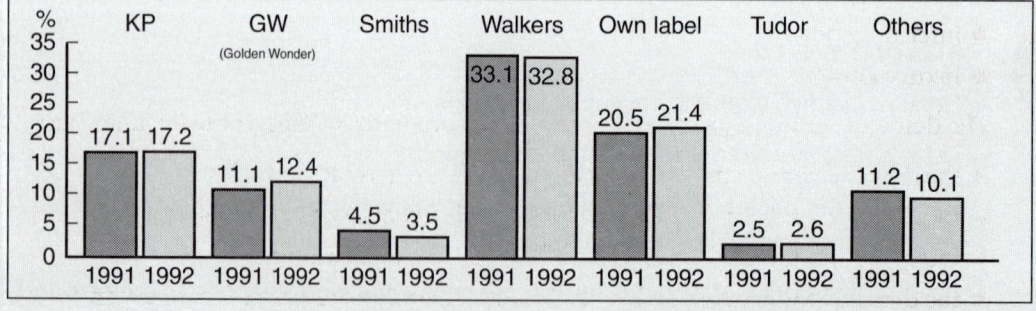

Fig 1.6 Crunch time for crisp companies
Source: The Sunday Times, Sept 1994

Element 1.1 Analyse the forces of supply and demand on businesses

ACTIVITY 1.1.3

Read the article in Fig. 1.6 and answer the following tasks.

Task 1. Why has the share price of the food conglomerate Dalgety gone down on the Stock Market?

Task 2. What does the author mean by the 'British Crisp War'?

Task 3. Using supply and demand diagrams show what has happened to the market price of crisps given the fierce competition within the industry.

Task 4. Suggest why Walkers have not been so badly affected by the fierce price war.

PC
1.1.1
1.1.2
1.1.3
1.1.4
1.1.5

Quality of the good

Many consumers are willing to pay a little bit extra for a good, if they know that the good purchased is of superior quality, for example, Sony televisions, VW cars, Marks and Spencer clothes, Sainsbury's food, etc. They see they are getting value for money i.e. 'you get what you pay for'.

Advertising

In many industries competition is so intense that a firm cannot differentiate its products from that of its competitors by price, quality, etc. It uses advertising and its related disciplines of public relations and promotion to establish its 'brand' in the minds of its customers, to inform customers of the benefits of its product and to encourage loyalty to its product.

Income

As household income rises, the consumer can afford to buy more goods or services or better quality goods or services. Goods can be classified as:

- normal goods
- basic goods
- inferior goods
- luxury goods.

The demand for these goods will change as income rises or falls. If the income rises:

- the demand for normal goods will tend to rise, e.g. motor vehicles;
- the demand for inferior goods will fall, e.g. black-and-white televisions;
- the demand for basic goods, e.g. milk, will reach a maximum;
- the demand for luxury goods will rise e.g. expensive designer clothes, expensive cars such as Mercedes and Rolls Royce.

ACTIVITY 1.1.4

Task 1. List five basic goods.

Task 2. List five normal goods.

Task 3. List five inferior goods.

Task 4. List five luxury goods.

Tastes and fashion

Taste and fashion can change for psychological, social or economic reasons. It is therefore difficult to predict their effect on demand. For example, a *psychological effect* on demand might be the desire by some people to be seen as Yuppies – that is, to drive the right type of car (a BMW, but never a LADA), to buy the right type of designer clothes and shoes and to go on the right type of holidays.

Social factors can affect tastes and fashion. For example, there is now a trend towards more ecological awareness with a move to buy 'green products' and producers and retailers have taken note of these changes and adjusted their production techniques and product range accordingly.

Economic factors will affect consumers' tastes and fashion. For example, in recent years there has been a trend for more married women to join the labour market which has obviously affected the household budget. Today, more and more people are taking foreign holidays and more and more households have two or more cars.

ACTIVITY 1.1.5

Task 1. Think of three products where demand has increased due to changes in taste and fashion.

Task 2. Think of three products where demand has decreased due to changes in taste and fashion.

Task 3. Consider your own psychological, social and economic reasons for buying a product and list them.

Expectations

The things that people expect to achieve or acquire throughout their lives affect their demand for particular products. Expectations change due to social and economic conditions. For example, in the UK, home ownership has become an expectation in the last 20 years along with car ownership. If consumers expect a price increase for the product, they will attempt to buy it before the price increases; hence their expectations of a price increase change their demand. For example, if the Chancellor announces a rise in petrol duties in the Budget, consumers immediately go out and fill up with petrol.

Element 1.1 Analyse the forces of supply and demand on businesses

ACTIVITY 1.1.6

Task 1. List some of your life expectations.

Task 2. How do these affect the products that you demand.

Distribution of income

A society in which the majority of the population have a middle income will demand different quantities of certain products to a society where the majority of the population are on lower incomes. In this way the distribution of wealth affects demand. People on low incomes tend to buy more inferior goods than normal goods (for example, white bread rather than wholemeal bread), whereas people on high incomes tend to buy only normal goods and luxury goods, for example, exotic foreign holidays, Porsche cars, etc.

ACTIVITY 1.1.7

Task 1. Consider Table 1.2.

Table 1.2 Demand for potato crisps

Price (p)	Quantity demanded (QD) per annum (million packets)
18	100
20	90
23	80
25	70
30	60
35	50
39	40
42	30
48	20
55	10
64	5

Task 2. Using graph paper, plot the demand curve for crisps, remembering to label the axes correctly.

Task 3. Explain in your own words why only 5 million packets are demanded at a price of 64p, whereas 100 million packets are demanded at a price of 18p?

Task 4. If demand for crisps increased by 25 per cent what would be the new demand curve at existing prices. Plot the new demand curve on your graph against the old demand curve.

Task 5. What effect might a relative price decrease in a substitute for crisps have on the demand curve for crisps. Identify a possible substitute product for crisps.

PC
1.1.1
1.1.3
1.1.6
AN
3.1.1
3.1.2
3.1.3
3.1.4
3.3.1
3.3.2
3.3.3

Unit 1 Business in the economy

PC
1.1.1
1.1.2
1.1.3
AN
3.1.3
3.2.2
3.2.4
3.3.1
3.3.3

ACTIVITY 1.1.8

Rate of interest	Supply of mortgage funds £ million	Demand for mortgages £ million
1	16	210
2	19	200
3	20	190
4	30	170
5	40	160
6	52	150
7	61	139
8	75	129
9	81	120
10	95	110
11	100	100
12	110	98
13	130	89
14	180	66

Task 1. Plot the rate of interest on the vertical axis and £ million on the horizontal axis.

Task 2. Draw the supply and demand conditions for mortgages and mark off the equilibrium rate of interest.

Task 3. Mark off the excess supply and excess demand positions at:
a) Rate of interest 13%
b) Rate of interest 4%

Task 4. The Commercial Banks enter the market for mortgage funds which affects the Building Societies. This causes a 20% drop in the demand for mortgages from Building Societies.

Calculate and plot the new demand course and show the new equilibrium rate of interest.

Price elasticity of demand

The price elasticity of demand (PED) for a product can be defined as follows:

a measure of the responsiveness of demand to a given change in price.

Elasticity determines the gradient or slope of the demand curve. If demand is elastic, the demand curve will be fairly flat, whereas, if demand is inelastic, the demand curve will have a steep slope. (*See* Fig. 1.7.)

Price elasticity of demand can be calculated using the following formula:

$$\text{PED} = \frac{\% \text{ change in } Qd}{\% \text{ change in } P}$$

Element 1.1 Analyse the forces of supply and demand on businesses

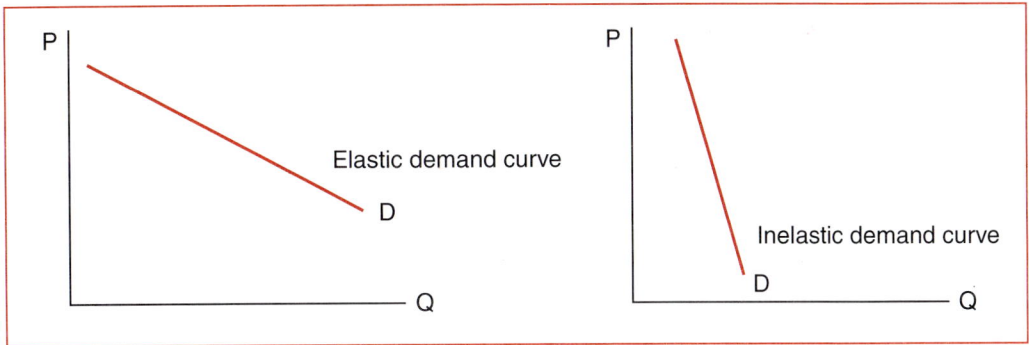

Fig 1.7 Elastic and inelastic demand curves

i.e. $\dfrac{\dfrac{\Delta Q}{Q}}{\dfrac{\Delta P}{P}}$

Where Qd = quantity demanded
P = price

The calculation of price elasticity of demand can best be illustrated by an example. Consider the demand schedule in Table 1.3

Example of PED calculation:

Table 1.3 Demand for a product

Price (pence)	Quantity (units)
20	60
18	80
16	100
14	120
12	140
10	160
8	180
6	200

If the manufacturer reduced his price from 20p to 18p we can calculate the PED for the product, using the equation already mentioned:

$$\text{PED} = \dfrac{\% \text{ change in } Qd}{\% \text{ change in } P}$$

ACTIVITY 1.1.9

Task 1. Calculate the price elasticity of demand (PED) if price falls from 10p to 8p.

Task 2. Calculate the PED, if price increases from 14p to 20p.

Task 3. Calculate the PED, if price increases from 6p to 10p.

PC
1.1.1
1.1.2
AN
3.1.2
3.1.3
3.2.2
3.2.3
3.2.4

PED is of major importance to a manufacturer because he can calculate whether the market is elastic or inelastic and link this to his total revenue or sales.

- If PED is calculated and demand is *greater* than 1, demand is elastic. (>1)
- If PED is calculated and demand is *less* than 1, demand is inelastic. (<1)
- If PED is calculated and demand is *equal to* 1, demand is unity. Elasticity = ∞

If the market is elastic, this means a small change in price will have a more than proportionate effect on demand. If the market is inelastic, however, a small change in price will have a less than proportionate effect on total demand.

We can examine this more clearly in Fig 1.8. With total revenue equal to price (p) × quantity (Q), we can see from the two diagrams that in an elastic market, if the manufacturer lowers his price, he will make an overall increase in total revenue. In an inelastic market, however, if he lowers his price, there will be an overall decrease in his total revenue.

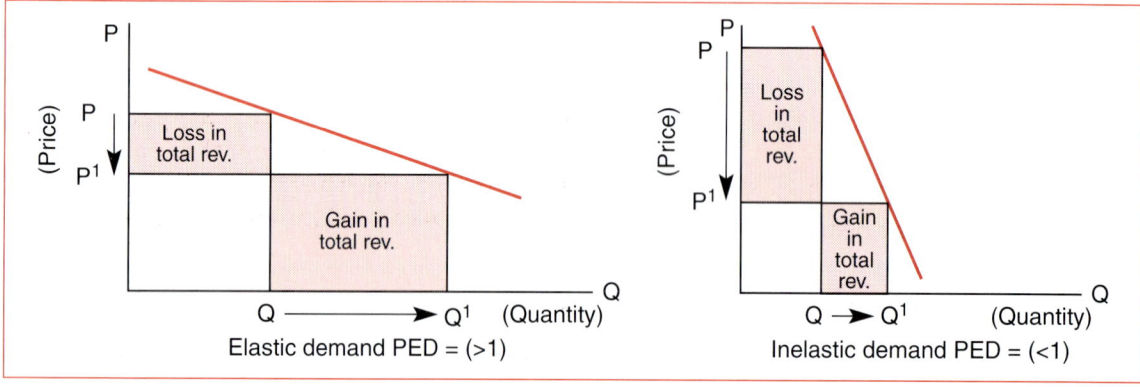

Fig 1.8 Elastic and inelastic markets

ACTIVITY 1.1.10

Task 1. After studying Fig 1.7, suggest the pricing strategy the manufacturer should adopt.

Task 2. Draw two diagrams to explain what would happen to total revenue if the manufacturer increased prices substantially in both the elastic market and inelastic market.

Factors influencing price elasticity of demand (PED)

The following conditions will affect the price elasticity of demand.

1 *Availability of substitutes.* If there are few substitutes available, the consumer is unlikely to switch products; this would make the demand for the product inelastic. If there is a large number of substitutes available, however, the consumer can switch easily and PED for the product will be elastic.

2 *Consumer loyalty.* If consumers have built up loyalty to the product they are less likely to switch to an alternative, which explains the importance of manufacturers branding their products, i.e Heinz Beans, Coca-Cola, etc. This would make demand for the product inelastic.

3 *Absolute price.* If a good is inexpensive a large percentage change in price represents only a few pence. For example, if the price of matches were to double from 12p to 24p, smokers would still buy the product despite the 100 per cent price increase, hence making the good inelastic.

4 *Proportion of income.* If the good takes up only a small proportion of a consumer's income, then consumers will not react significantly to a price change, hence making the product inelastic in demand. Examples include Mars bars, newspapers, etc.

4 *Complements.* If the good has many complements, then it will be needed when the other products are used. This will tend to make demand for the product inelastic.

Cross elasticity of demand

Most products do not have the same elasticity of demand throughout their price range; generally, as the price of the product rises, the demand becomes more elastic as consumers consider switching to alternative products which may be cheaper. This switch in demand from one good to another can be measured through *cross elasticity of demand*.

Cross elasticity of demand (XED) can be defined as:

a measure of the responsiveness of demand for good A to a given change in price of good B.

The equation for the calculation of cross elasticity of demand is:

$$\text{XED} = \frac{\%\text{ change in } qd\text{A}}{\%\text{ change in } p\text{B}}$$

$$\text{i.e.} = \frac{\frac{\Delta Q}{Q} \text{ good A}}{\frac{\Delta P}{P} \text{ good B}}$$

where $qd\text{A}$ = quality demanded of good A
$p\text{B}$ = price of good B

It is worth noting that, since XED can be negative, it is important to include minus signs.

- If XED is *positive*, the two goods are in competitive demand, i.e. they are substitutes for each other.
- If XED is *negative*, the two goods are in joint demand, i.e. they are complements.
- If XED is *zero*, the two products are unrelated, i.e. independent goods.

Unit 1 Business in the economy

Income elasticity of demand

Income elasticity of demand can be defined as:

a measure of the responsiveness of demand to a change in income.

The equation for the calculation of the income elasticity of demand is:

$$\text{Income elasticity of demand} = \frac{\% \text{ change in quantity demanded}}{\text{change in income}}$$

$$= \frac{\frac{\Delta Qd}{Qd}}{\frac{\Delta y}{y}}$$

The value of income elasticity of demand can either be positive, negative or zero.

- If a rise in income results in a fall in demand for the product (income elasticity of demand is *negative*), the good in question is termed an inferior good. Examples include black-and-white televisions, white bread and margarine.
- If the income elasticity of demand for the good is *positive*, the good is considered a normal good or a luxury good. With a rise in income, people tend to buy more of the product or service. Examples include foreign holidays, good wine, luxury cars, camcorders, etc.
- Some goods have *zero* income elasticity of demand; this means that whatever happens to a person's income his or her consumption of the product is unlikely to change. An example of such a product would be salt.

It is important to note that income elasticities measure something quite different to price elasticities. Price elasticities show the responsiveness of demand to a change in price, whereas income elasticity measures the responsiveness of demand to a change in income. Price elasticity is always negative whereas income elasticity can be positive, negative or zero.

PC
1.1.3
AN
3.1.2
3.1.3
3.2.2
3.2.3

ACTIVITY 1.1.11

Table 1.4 relates to the income and expenditure of a household.

Table 1.4

	Weekly earnings (£s)	Quantity of meat (kilos)
Jan	160	180
Feb	200	260

Task. Calculate the income elasticity of demand for meat.

Element 1.1 Analyse the forces of supply and demand on businesses

ACTIVITY 1.1.12

This activity examines the market conditions for a commodity.

Market conditions for commodity X in the U.K.

Retail Prices	Tons per day	
Pence per kilo	Supply	Demand
5	0	280
10	100	278
15	120	275
20	160	271
25	240	266
30	400	260
35	720	253
40	1560	245
45	2840	236
50	5400	226

Task 1. Can you suggest a name of a commodity which will have these market characteristics? (Justify your choice.)

Task 2. Calculate the price elasticity of demand for this product when there is an increase in price from 25 to 30 pence.

Task 3. Calculate the price elasticity of supply:
(a) when price drops from 25 to 20 pence.
(b) when price drops from 40 to 35 pence.

Task 4. Can you suggest reasons for the difference between the elasticities in (a) and (b)?

Task 5. What will be the total revenue from sales of this commodity for the whole industry?

Task 6. How could an individual producer increase his turnover?

THE SUPPLY OF GOODS AND SERVICES

Businesses will supply goods and services for the market provided they can make a profit. Their profit margins depend not only on their costs of production, but also on the prices they can charge for their goods and services. This means they need to be aware of the market price of their goods and services. If the market price is too low, the suppliers may not enter the market until the market price rises.

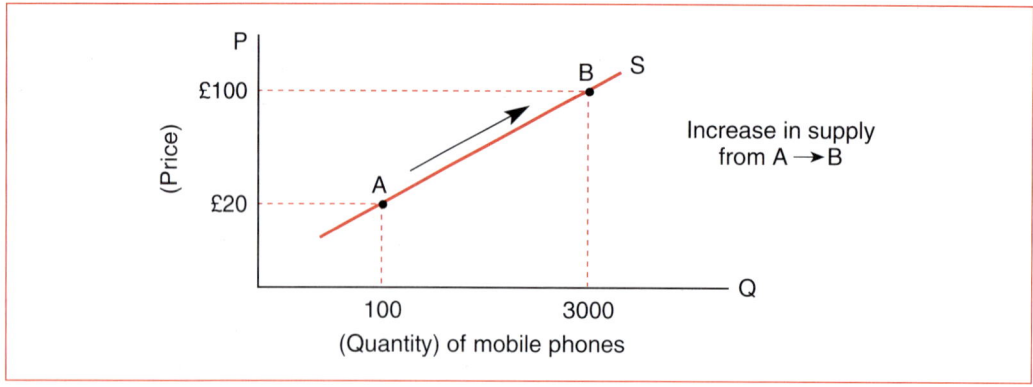

Fig 1.9 The supply curve: the supply of mobile phones

Suppliers take into account the costs of production when they produce a good. These costs include both variable and fixed costs. *Fixed costs* would include the cost of the factory and the cost of the capital machinery needed for production. *Variable costs* include the cost of labour needed for production and the necessary raw materials required.

Market prices are set or market equilibrium is reached when demand and supply meet.

The supply curve takes the opposite shape to a demand curve because as prices rise, more firms enter the market attracted by the higher prices. The higher the price of the good, the more profit can be made. Figure 1.9 shows a supply curve for mobile phones. At point A only a certain number of firms are willing to supply to the market at a price of £20 (i.e. 100 phones). If the price of the phones is increased to £100 at point B, more suppliers enter the market, (i.e. 3000 phones). We can see that the total market supply increases substantially.

What determines supply?

Price

The price of the product has a major influence on supply. The higher the price that consumers are willing to pay, the more producers will supply, as illustrated by the move from A to B in Fig. 1.9. This is referred to as an *extension of supply*. We can see from Fig. 1.9 that the supply of mobile phones increases from 100 to 3000 when the price rises from £20 to £100. Conversely, if the price fell from £100 to £20, there would be fewer suppliers willing to enter the market at the lower price so the total market supply would fall.

Costs of production

The producer will set a price related to costs of production. For example, if the cost of producing a mobile phone was £20, and the producer wanted a 100 per cent mark-up, the price would be set at £40. If the costs of production fell to £10, however, then to achieve the same mark-up, the producer can afford to lower the price to £20.

A supplier will only be able to change the price significantly if the demand for the good being supplied is strong or the supplier is the only supplier to the retailers. If there are a large number of mobile phone manufacturers, the producer will not be able to change the price, as it will result in a loss of market share.

Technology

The level of technology influences the level of supply, if suppliers employ the very latest technology they can afford to reduce the cost per unit significantly. This price reduction can then be passed on to the consumer (*see* Fig. 1.10).

The introduction of new technology reduces the suppliers' costs of production and means more phones can be produced at a cheaper price. For example, in Fig. 1.10 6000 phones were produced at a price of £60. We can see a movement in supply from S to S_1. This is known as a *shift in supply*.

- When there is an *increase* in supply, the supply curve shifts to the right.
- When there is a *decrease* in supply, the supply curve shifts to the left.

Over the last five years there has been a dramatic increase in new technology in many manufacturing industries. In the motor industry there has been a development in computer-aided design, robot welding and automated paint spraying. This new technology has influenced the supply of motor vehicles on to the market (*see* Fig. 1.11). Motor vehicles today are cheaper in real terms than they were five years ago. Because of the new technology they are also far more reliable and manufacturers offer longer guarantees.

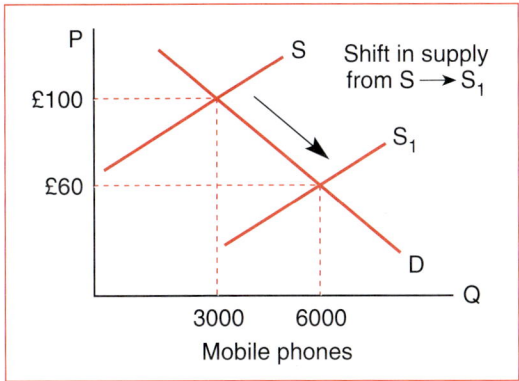

Fig 1.10 The increase in technology used in the production of mobile phones

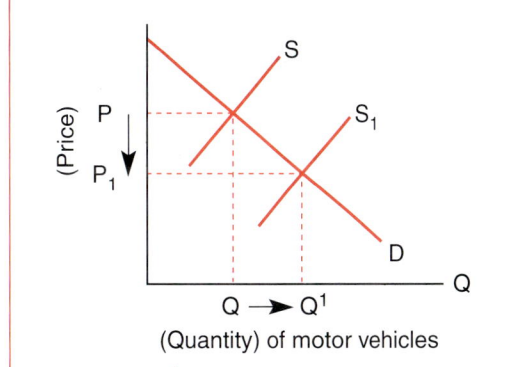

Fig 1.11 The increase in the supply of vehicles brought about by new technology

Government influence

The influence of government can affect the supply curve for a product. For example, if the government increases the rate of VAT on goods and services, this immediately affects their price. Any form of government tax increases the price of the good or service (for example, car tax, petrol duty, tobacco duty, excise duties on alcohol, etc.).

Figure 1.12 shows a decrease in the supply of mobile phones caused by the government increasing the rate of VAT on mobile phones.

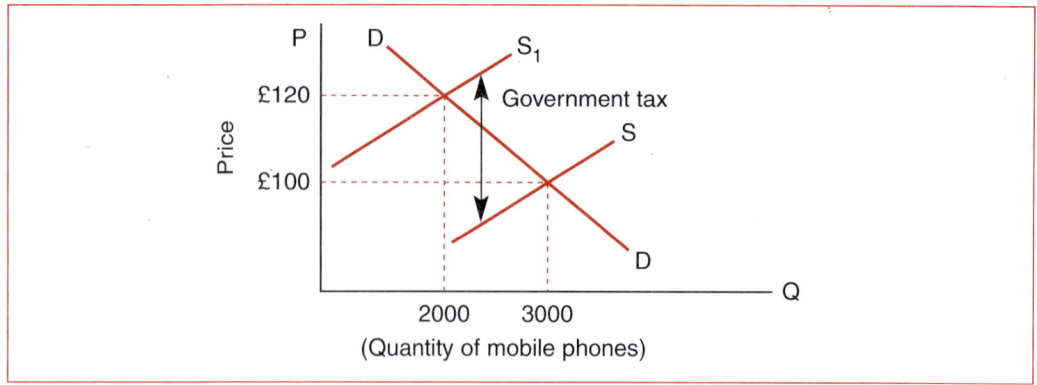

Fig 1.12 The decrease in the supply of mobile phones caused by the government increasing the rate of VAT on mobile phones

Costs of production: economies of scale

When more of a good is produced, economies of scale have the effect of reducing the average cost per unit of production.

Technical economies of scale

The larger the firm, the more opportunity there is to make technical economies of scale. Large firms have greater scope for the division of labour and more specialisation. This in turn enables more capital machinery to be employed which raises productivity and reduces the cost per unit. As output increases labour costs per unit of output decline. This principle of 'increased dimensions' applies in manufacturing and in distribution. For example, the running costs of a 40 tonne lorry will not be much more than a 3 tonne lorry; the volume of goods carried will be considerably more, however. Running a double decker bus is no more expensive than running a single decker bus and it can take twice as many passengers. An oil tanker, twice as big as another tanker in terms of its length and breadth, can carry eight times as much volume, but certainly does not require any more crew or eight times more power to propel it through the water.

Indivisibility

Many production processes are not financially viable on a small scale; they are indivisible (i.e., they cannot be broken down into small-scale production). For example, in the manufacture of motor vehicles, there is a minimum efficient scale of production (MES). This is effectively a break-even point. If the firms operate below this level, they do not achieve economies of scale. In the case of motor vehicles, the MES is one million cars per annum. This explains why the motor industry is dominated by such large multinational companies as Ford, General Motors, BMW, VW, etc.

Purchasing economies of scale

Large firms such as Marks and Spencer's buy their raw materials in huge quantities and as a result can demand big discounts from their suppliers. These suppliers are willing to reduce their margins because they know that the retailer will be selling large quantities to a mass market. Small firms are not able to take advantage of such discounts and therefore pay considerably more for their raw materials.

Marketing economies of scale

Large firms can make more effective use of their salesforce. For example, a salesman can negotiate an order for 5000 units in the same way as an order for 50 units. The administrative costs will not be much more for the bigger order. Large firms can afford to pay for the best advertising media and, more often than not, have already established a well-known branded product on the market and have a good brand image (for example, IBM, BMW, McDonald's, Heinz, Sony, etc.).

Managerial economies of scale

Large firms can afford to employ the very best managers, paying high salaries and offering numerous fringe benefits. Many of the best people try to work for large established companies to gain valuable experience and enhance their future career prospects.

Financial economies of scale

Large firms are able to raise capital more easily and cheaply than small firms. They have substantially more assets and a sound trading record. Most lenders see them as a lower degree of risk and charge them much lower rates of interest for loans.

THE INTERACTION OF SUPPLY AND DEMAND

The market price is determined by the interaction of supply and demand. In Fig. 1.13 we can see that at a price of £10 000, General Motors is willing to supply 70 000 Vauxhall Cavaliers and at that price all the consumers are willing to buy. In other words, there is no excess demand or excess supply we have an equilibrium position.

Supply = Demand.

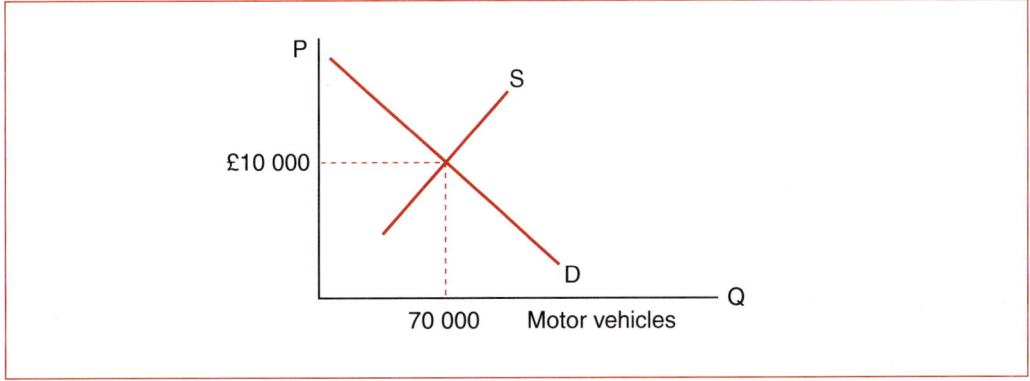

Fig 1.13 The interaction of supply and demand

Excess demand

Suppose that General Motors misjudged the correct market price for Cavaliers and set a price too low. Clearly there would be a healthy demand but General Motors would have more customers than it was willing to supply at that price. In short, there would be an *excess demand* situation (*see* Fig. 1.14).

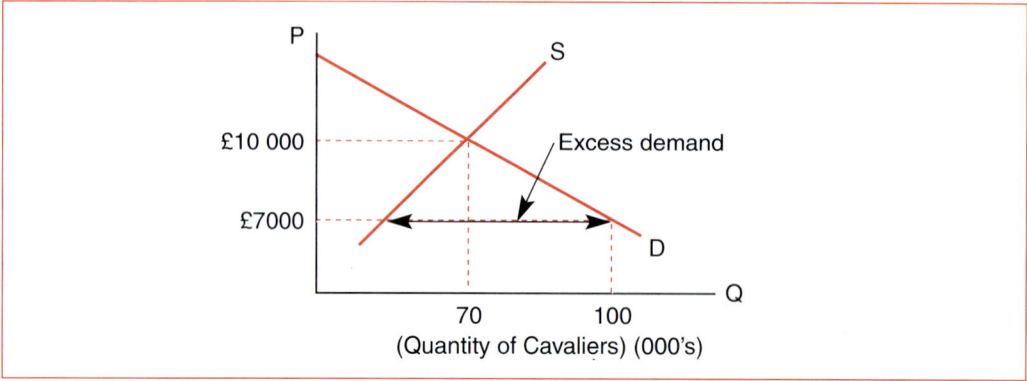

Fig 1.14 **Excess demand**

Excess supply

If the producer sets a price higher than the market equilibrium price, then an excess supply situation would arise. For example, if General Motors sets a price of £17 000 rather than the market price of £10 000 then it will not be able to sell all of the Cavaliers. The consumers will not buy at that price so General Motors will have an excess supply of Cavaliers (*see* Fig. 1.15).

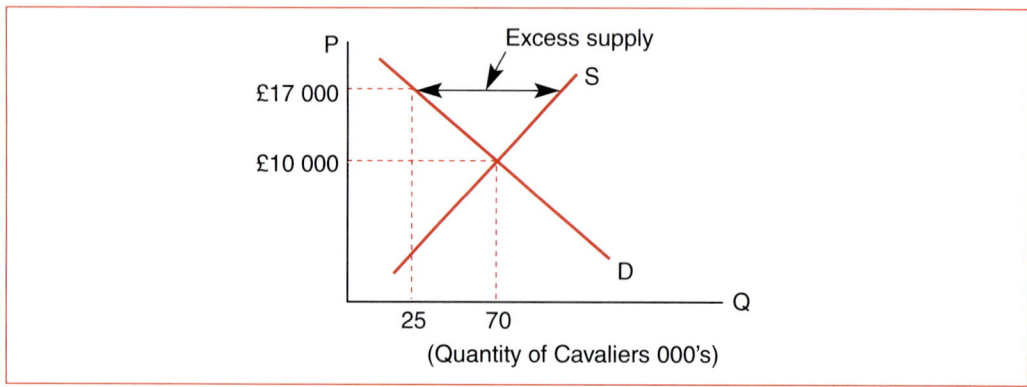

Fig 1.15 **Excess supply**

The price mechanism

The price mechanism under market conditions allocates resources automatically through supply and demand. It determines what goods will be produced, how they will be produced and how they will be allocated to the consumer.

In *market economies*, the levels of output and consumption of products and services are the result of the varied decisions of households and firms being put into operation through the price mechanism.

Recent events in the Soviet Union and the Eastern Europe during the period 1989–90 have shown how *planned economies* have moved towards becoming market economies, relying on the price mechanism to allocate resources. Millions of Russians and Eastern Europeans have supported the move towards market economics. They have felt that their lives would be improved under free-market conditions.

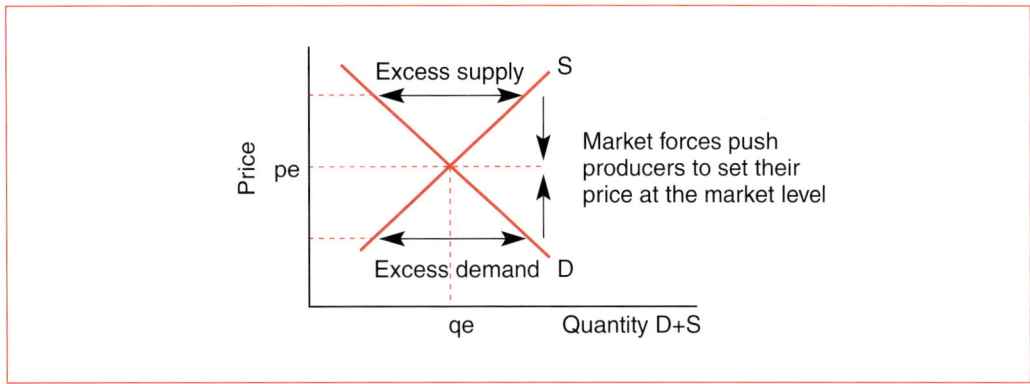

Fig 1.16 The functions of the price mechanism rationing of goods and services

As we can see from Fig. 1.16, if the producer sets a price above the market equilibrium, there will be an excess supply situation and the only way to sell the goods quickly in the market will be to reduce the price back down to the market equilibrium point. We can see that if the producer sets a price below the market equilibrium then this creates an excess demand situation. Again the only way to maximise profits would be to increase the price back up to the market equilibrium position, i.e. pe.

Price rewards the factors of production

It is possible to think of the rewards to the factors of production as being a price, that is:

- rent for land
- interest for capital
- wages for labour
- profits for enterprise.

When the price of a good rises, rewards to the factors of production also rise. When demand for an industry's output is rising, workers in that industry tend to see an increase in their wages. Conversely, when demand for an industry's output is falling there is pressure to reduce wages for workers in the declining industry.

Price acts as a signalling function

Price acts as a signal to producers of what to produce – it acts as a motivator. The higher the price obtainable for a good or service, the more likely that more producers will enter the market encouraged by the high prices and resulting profit potential.

Price indicates changes in demand

Consumers can indicate to producers whether they demand the product or not through the price mechanism. Price allows them to dictate their tastes and preferences. If nobody wants a particular product, the producer will be forced to drop the price to sell the product. For example, look at the housing market at the present time: sellers have to lower their prices substantially to attract potential buyers. We hear the phrase: 'a buyer's market'.

Price indicates changes in supply

Price can also be used by producers to tell consumers when there are changes in the conditions of supply. For example, if raw material costs rise, more often than not the producer will pass on these increased costs to the consumer in the form of increased prices. Obviously, the elasticity of demand will play an important part here. If there are few competitors and the market demand is inelastic, the producer will be able to pass on all of the increased costs to the consumer. If demand is elastic, however, and there is healthy competition in the market, the producer will have to absorb most of the increased costs.

The price mechanism fails to reflect social costs and benefits, that is externalities and the provision of public and merit goods.

Externalities

Externalities are costs (*negative externalities*) or benefits (*positive externalities*) which are not reflected in the normal market mechanism. For example, if a farmer decided that the cheapest method of disposing of straw left after harvesting fields was to burn it, the externality would be the pollution of the surrounding area with black smoke and ash. People who had to pay for cleaning their carpets and curtains would bear the full cost, not the farmer.

Today smoking is considered a major externality. When a person smokes, he or she immediately pollutes the surrounding physical environment. There is now strong evidence on the health risks associated with passive smoking, so much so that many large employers now completely ban smoking on their premises.

An example of a positive externality is staff training. If a firm provides good training for its workforce, this has a positive effect for society as a whole. The greater skill of the workforce improves its productivity which in turn increases overall production and improves the standard of living for everybody.

ACTIVITY 1.1.13

Task 1. Thinks of three positive externalities and give a brief description of each.

Task 2. Thinks of three negative externalities and give a brief description of each.

Public goods

Public goods, as the name implies, are goods that are provided for public consumption, for example, defence, street lighting, public roads, lighthouses. Public goods are:

- Non-excludable. This means it is impossible to stop someone enjoying the benefits even if he or she has not paid; prices cannot be attributed to specific individuals.
- Non-rivalrous. This means that one person's use of the public good does not deprive any other person from using the good. For example, the use of street lighting by one person does not stop someone else from using and benefiting from the good or service.
- Non-marketable. It is the non-excludability of public goods that makes them non-marketable. If private providers cannot specify who pays for the good, they will be reluctant to provide it. This is referred to as the 'free rider effect'; referring to consumers who use the good without paying for it directly. This is why the main method of financing public goods is through general taxation. This means payment for the good is averaged out over the whole community.

Merit goods

Merit goods are goods that confer benefits on society in excess of the benefits conferred on individual consumers. For example, health care and education benefit the individuals who receive them, but there are also benefits to society from having a healthy, well educated workforce. If merit goods were provided through the market system, only certain sections of society would be in a position to afford them. This is why the government encourages consumption of them by subsidising them to lower their market price, or by providing them free of charge to consumers.

It is important to note that, unlike public goods, merit goods could be produced by the private sector. This happens in the case of private education and private health care. If these goods were produced entirely through the market, however, they would be underconsumed.

CLASSIFICATION OF BUSINESSES

At this point it is necessary to introduce some common classification of businesses as these will be referred to regularly throughout the book. The sectors are outlined here and covered in greater detail later in the book.

Industrial sectors

All productive organisations, whether privately or publicly owned, form part of industry and contribute to the UK's total output or production, defined as *Gross National Product* or *GNP*. This is the total amount of goods and services produced in the UK per annum. Generally the higher a country's GNP, the wealthier the country is because it means there are more goods and services available for the total population, i.e. a higher standard of living. This GNP is made up of three sectors of the economy, each contributing to the economy in different ways, i.e. in terms of total output or in terms of total employment.

- *The primary sector* comprises all those industries that extract the raw materials used in production process at the next stage (hence the secondary sector). Primary sector industries include agriculture, forestry, fishing, farming, mining and mineral extraction.
- *The secondary sector* industries are those that actually produce goods i.e. the manufacturing process. Such industries would include manufacturing, construction and public utilities such as water, gas and electricity.
- *The tertiary or service sector* industries include distribution, retailing, wholesaling, financial services, insurance services, travel and tourism and public services such as education and health.

Public and private sectors

Private sector organisations

Private sector organisations can be:

- sole traders;
- partnerships;
- private limited companies;
- public limited companies;
- charities (non-profit making organisations).

The main long-term aim of the organisations in the private sector is to make as much profit for their owners as possible. This primary objective can be overridden in the short term, however, by such objectives as financial survival whereby cash flow becomes more important when the firm cannot pay its debts, or when it tries to develop new products or enter new markets, or fight off take-overs by other companies.

Not all companies seek to maximise their profits as their prime objective. The managers and owners of some firms are quite content to let the firm jog along and underachieve because perhaps any changes to their existing work patterns are too much trouble, or they themselves do not have the skills to make the required changes, or they lack the finance to fund the changes and are unwilling to risk the borrowing required.

Charities are non-profit making organisations, whose main objective is to provide a quality service for their customers. Their principal objective is for their output to reach as many people as possible, e.g. Oxfam, Cafod, NSPCC, RSPCA, etc.

The objectives of private sector organisations are: profit maximisation, survival, market domination and satisficing. These are examined in greater detail in Element 2.1.

Public sector organisations

Public sector organisations are all those organisations that are owned and controlled by government. Services can be provided at national level by central government (e.g. defence, NHS, social security, etc.) or at local level by local government (e.g. local government trading enterprises such as libraries, parks, museums, refuse collection, leisure centres, etc.).

Element 1.1 Analyse the forces of supply and demand on businesses

ACTIVITY 1.1.14

Make a list of ten public sector organisations.

The objectives of public sector organisations vary according to whether they are providing a service (e.g. National Health Service) or whether they are selling a product (British Nuclear Fuels). Public sector organisations that provide a service are nearly always provided at zero cost to the consumer, with the taxpayer bearing the burden of the total cost. One important objective of public sector organisations providing a service is to improve the welfare of citizens and provide the best service possible given the financial constraints. Today many public sector organisations are run along similar lines to private sector organisations.

Self assessment questions

1 Consider the following statements.
   (i) Mining for coal is primary sector employment.
   (ii) Refining oil is primary sector employment.
   Which option best describes the two statements:
   a (i) True   (ii) True
   b (i) True   (ii) False
   c (i) False   (ii) True
   d (i) False   (ii) False

2 Which of the following organisations is in the private sector?
   a BBC
   b Post Office
   c Bank of England
   d British Aerospace

3 Which organisation's principal objective is to make a profit?
   a British Nuclear Fuels
   b British Petroleum
   c Oxfam
   d NHS

4 A limited company is in the retail business. This company is in the:
   a primary sector
   b public sector
   c private sector
   d secondary sector?

5 Price elasticity of demand is defined as:
   a responsiveness of demand to a change in supply
   b responsiveness of demand to a change in income
   c responsiveness of demand to a change in price
   d responsiveness of price to a change in demand?

6 Examine Fig. 1.16 on page 23 and identify which of the following statements is true.
   a The change in demand is caused by a decrease in price.
   b The change in demand is caused by an increase in price.
   c The change in demand is caused by an increase in income.
   d The change in demand is caused by a decrease in the price of a substitute good.

7 There is a decreased demand for oranges. This change can be explained by:
   a a fall in the price of oranges
   b a fall in the price of apples
   c more efficient orange production
   d a fall in the price of a substitute?

8 Table 1.5 relates to the income and expenditure of a household.

   Table 1.5

	Average weekly earnings (£)	Weekly consumption of wine (bottles)
Month 1	100	3
Month 2	300	10

   The income elasticity of demand for wine in this household can be said to be:
   a elastic
   b inelastic
   c unit elasticity
   d zero elasticity?

9 The market for a product is said to be inelastic if:
   a total revenue rises with an increase in price
   b total revenue falls with an increase in price
   c total revenue neither falls nor rises with an increase in price
   d total revenue falls proportionately with the increase in price?

10 The following factors shift the demand curve to the right except for one of the following:
   a Income
   b Price
   c Price of substitutes
   d Price of complements?

11 There is an increase in demand for oranges. This can be explained by:
   a a fall in the price of apples
   b a successful advertising campaign to eat more oranges
   c better storage of oranges
   d an increase in imports of oranges from South America?

12 If the price of butter increased, the sale of which of the following would be most likely to increase?
   a Margarine
   b Eggs
   c Cream
   d Milk

13 Privatisation has produced an economy which is less
   a free-market
   b competitive
   c planned
   d open?

Assignment

Read the article and complete the following tasks:

Geest shares slip on banana storm

BANANA prices in the shops are set to rise after Geest, the fresh produce group, reported that a tropical storm has devastated its Windward Islands' crop. The group has turned to alternative supplies from Latin America (Colin Narbrough writes). A statement about damage caused by the September 10 storm sent Geest's shares tumbling 30p to 211p.

Geest, which harvested 55 per cent of its bananas from the Windwards in the first half of this year, said initial estimates suggest losses of some 40 per cent of Windward production for 1994 and that production would continue to be affected for the whole of next year. The loss of tariff-free fruit from the Windwards means that Geest will have to use supplies from Central America, which do not enjoy similar tariff advantage.

Equities slipped on a banana skin, along with Geest, which is one of the largest banana suppliers. Its shares slid 30p to 211p, on thin volume of 693,000 traded, after the fresh fruit group reported extensive flooding at its plantations in the Windward Isles after the onset of tropical storm Debbie.

The group, where David Sugden is chief executive, said that Windward banana production is expected to be about 40 per cent below normal levels for the remainder of 1994 and will also affect 1995. Geest, which is due to announce its interim results next Thursday, confirmed it has alternative sources of supply and is looking at reconfiguring shipping schedules.

Fyffes, its fellow banana group, reacted to the news with a 2p fall to 98p.

PC
1.1.3
1.1.4
1.1.5
AN
3.1.1
3.1.2
3.1.3
3.1.4
3.2.2
3.2.3
3.2.3
3.2.4
3.3.3.
3.3.4

Task 1. Draw a supply and demand curve for bananas at a market price of 60p.

Task 2. Draw a new supply curve showing the shift in supply caused by the storm.

Task 3. What will be the effect on the price of bananas? You need to show this on your diagram.

Task 4. Explain what the 'loss of tariff-free fruit' means.

Task 5. Explain why the effect on Geest's share price was so immediate.

Element 1.2
ANALYSE THE OPERATION OF MARKETS AND THEIR EFFECTS ON BUSINESSES AND COMMUNITIES

Performance criteria

1 **Explain types of markets.**

2 **Compare competition within markets.**

3 **Analyse behaviour of businesses in different markets.**

4 **Evaluate the social costs of market operations.**

5 **Evaluate the social benefits of market operations.**

Introduction

In this element we examine the different types of market condition, by looking at competitive and non-competitive markets such as monopolies and oligopolies. We examine their different pricing strategies: for example, monopoly pricing or perfect competition with the consumer enjoying maximum benefits in terms of choice and prices. It is important that students develop an understanding of the role of competition in markets and the different pricing strategies that develop. We also examine how supplying the market can generate costs that affect not only the organisation concerned, but also society as a whole, i.e. not only private costs but social costs. For example, a business polluting a lake would affect the health of people using it for leisure purposes, such as swimmers and windsurfers. Students must also appreciate the fact that a social cost to one person could conceivably be a social benefit to another. For example, roads and airports could be seen as infrastructure which benefits individuals and businesses but could also be seen as increased noise and air pollution increasing environmental damage.

Element 1.2 Analyse the operation of markets and their effects on businesses and communities

TYPES OF MARKET

In any particular market, the number of firms which make up the market (what economists call the *degree of concentration*) will be an important influence on the behaviour we can expect to find in the market.

Economists categorise market structures as:

- Perfect competition
- Imperfect competition
- Oligopoly
- Monopoly

The characteristics of the particular market structure will determine whether the consumer has sovereignty or is faced with a given price structure which has to be accepted. In other words, is the supplier a *price maker* or a *price taker*?

Perfect competition

The interaction between supply and demand, which we have examined in Element 1.1, depends on the right market conditions. In order for supply and demand to move freely, there must be no imperfections in the market. In other words, no single supplier should dominate the market. Consumers should be free to choose between a variety of producers, which means there should be healthy competition with many buyers and sellers. This form of free competition is known as *perfect competition*, which is based on the concept of the consumer is king. This is known as *consumer sovereignty*. Consumers indicate to the manufacturer what they want through the market mechanism. If the consumers do not like the good, they 'vote with their feet' and refuse to buy. If the price is too high, the consumers will not purchase the good until the price falls.

A good example of consumer sovereignty in the 1990s is the market for owner-occupied houses. Because there is a surplus of houses and buyers are still hesitant about buying, it is a buyers' market and the consumer is king. The cash buyer can force down the price of a house for a quick sale. Sellers who set their price too high can have their property up for sale for years.

Perfect competition exists when the following conditions are present:

- a large number of buyers and sellers;
- perfect knowledge;
- homogeneous products;
- no barriers to entry.

With a large number of buyers and sellers, there is no danger of a monopoly situation arising. No single buyer or seller is large enough to influence the market price; buyers and sellers are price takers not price makers. If consumers have perfect knowledge of the market, this means that they know what prices are being set for the goods and who and where the manufacturers are. If the goods are homogeneous, this means that the goods on offer to the consumer are the same; no single good is different from any other. If there are no barriers to entry, it means that no single supplier can stop another supplier from entering the market and offering the good to the consumer.

Perfect competition is an ideal market condition because it ensures that there is consumer sovereignty and plenty of healthy competition without any monopoly practices. In reality, however, it is not always possible for all the conditions necessary for perfect competition to be met.

- If we examine the market for most manufactured goods, we see that the manufacturers attempt to differentiate their product through 'branding' and advertising. For example, Sony televisions are seen as being superior in quality to Ferguson televisions and this is reflected in the price. The price of televisions is not homogeneous.
- The assumption that the consumer has perfect knowledge of the market is also false. Perfect knowledge implies that the consumer knows all the manufacturers and knows all about their product specifications and prices. This would involve considerable research time and involve travelling to the different retailers who offered the products. Most consumers do not spend a great deal of time researching the product because it involves additional costs. Evidence on buying patterns suggests that consumers prefer to shop in one big location (hence the growth of superstores and mail-order shopping).

Despite the fact that perfect competition rarely exists in the real world, it is still a useful model of market conditions. This is because it can act as a benchmark for the comparison of competitiveness between the different types of market condition. Clearly the more a market moves towards perfect competition, the better the position for the consumer. There is more competition and therefore more competitive prices and products available. This also tends to bring better quality and value for money for the consumer.

The more efficient producers will do better under perfect competition; those who keep their costs down will make the best profits and can afford the best staff and resources. Higher profits also mean the firms can afford to pay higher rents and can therefore get the best business locations (for example, Marks and Spencer's). Less efficient producers will make less profits and lose their market share to the more efficient producers. Eventually they will be forced out of business and taken over by the more efficient producers. Holding companies, such as Hanson, specialise in take-overs of smaller less efficient companies.

Imperfect competition

Imperfect competition is also known as *monopolistic competition*. An imperfect competitive market is similar to a perfectly competitive market in that a large number of buyers and sellers supply the market. However, unlike perfect competition where the products are homogeneous, under imperfect competition the products supplied are different. Suppliers attempt to differentiate their product in some way. This product differentiation is partly real and partly imaginary. For example, there are real differences between the various brands of soap powder supplied on to the market but these differences are not as great as the advertisers would have us believe.

Element 1.2 Analyse the operation of markets and their effects on businesses and communities

Oligopoly

In the UK economy, most markets for manufactured goods are oligopolies. An *oligopoly* exists when only a few suppliers dominate the market. For example, in banking, the 'big four' – Barclay's, Lloyd's, Midland and National Westminster – dominate the industry. In the motor industry, Ford, Vauxhall, Nissan and Rover (now part of BMW) dominate the market. In telecommunications, British Telecom and Mercury hold the market. In the fiercely competitive detergent market with a multitude of washing powders (such as Ariel, Persil, Daz, Radion, Bold, Surf, etc.), we find the industry dominated by two giant companies: with the American multinational, Procter & Gamble, holding over one third of the total market and the Anglo-Dutch company, Unilever, holding a quarter of the total market. The European market for soap powder is currently worth over £6 billion annually.

Concentration ratios

The degree of concentration of particular industries can be measured using *concentration ratios*. The five-firm concentration ratio, C5, shows the proportion of the market for a particular good supplied by the five firms in the industry. The five-firm concentration ratio is the most common measure used to determine the degree of concentration and hence the possibilities for consumer exploitation. Table 1.6 shows the five-firm concentration ratios for selected industries in 1990.

Table 1.6 C5 concentration ratios (1990) (%)

Flour	86.0
Blended whisky	87.1
Detergents	82.8
Telephone installations	98.9
Washing machines	100.0
Trailers & caravans	34.6
Wool sorting etc.	72.3
Hosiery etc.	40.2
Wallpaper	74.1
Woven carpets	57.5
Vehicles	87.0
Tobacco	99.0
Chemicals	53.0
Timber wooden furniture	21.0
Paper printing other	30.0

ACTIVITY 1.2.1

Task 1. Examine the concentration ratios in Table 1.6 and identify the five most concentrated industrial sectors?

Task 2. Suggest possible reasons why these industries should be so concentrated?

Oligopolies prefer to compete through 'non-price competition' rather than through direct price changes. They are very aware that the fellow oligopolist has similar resources to their own so would simply retaliate to a price change causing a price war. For example, a multinational company such as BT has a market capitalisation of over £23 billion, so clearly has considerable resources to compete with a rival oligopolist such as Mercury. Each knows that if the two companies entered a price war, each has abundant resources to fight, making a price war futile. In 1991 BT spent over £29.7 million on advertising. The top spending advertiser in 1991 was Procter and Gamble spending £71 million on advertising.

A price war may benefit the consumer but would simply reduce the oligopolist's profits. The oligopolist would then operate 'non-price competition' as a method of winning consumer loyalty. For example, branding its goods, offering free gifts and even holidays! Remember Hoover's infamous offer, 'Spend over £100 on a vacuum cleaner and get a free holiday to the USA'.

Most oligopolists spend millions of pounds on advertising and special offers all aimed at capturing consumer demand and maintaining their market share. For example, Unilever recently allocated over £250 million for the launch of 'Persil Power'. An oligopolist, such as Unilever, will defend its market share by 'brand proliferation', offering the consumer a variety of different branded goods. If Unilever can offer some 15 different branded washing powders, any potential new entrant to the market has to compete with 15 established brands rather than one. Brand proliferation is particularly evident in the tobacco industry where the two dominant companies – Imperial Tobacco and Gallaghers – supply the market. They advertise a multitude of brands through sports advertising and other sponsorship deals, for example, Benson and Hedges (cricket), Rothmans (snooker), etc. In 1992 Gallaher Tobacco spent over £27 million on sports and advertising and other sponsorship deals.

Monopoly

Monopoly literally means 'single seller'. A monopoly occurs when one firm is the sole supplier of the industry or as defined by the Monopolies and Mergers Commission when it controls 25 per cent of the market. Since the monopolist is the sole supplier of a particular good or service, then its demand curve will in fact be the market demand curve. Examples of UK monopolies include British Rail (which has a monopoly in rail transportation), The Post Office (which has a monopoly in mail distribution), British Nuclear Fuels (which has the monopoly in the provision of nuclear energy).

Monopolists have an inelastic demand curve because there are no close substitutes available. This means that they could exploit the consumer by charging high prices and still keep their market share. Recently the privatised water companies have been criticised for increasing water prices for domestic consumers, making record profits and paying their chief executives enormous salaries. In the case of water, the consumer has no choice; if the price increases, the consumer must pay or face being cut off. This is equally true for other recently privatised utility industries, such as gas and electricity.

We can see from Fig. 1.19 on page 36 that if British Gas increased its prices by 50 per cent, because the demand for gas is very inelastic, the company would only see a small change in quantity demanded. In fact its total revenue would actually increase.

Element 1.2 Analyse the operation of markets and their effects on businesses and communities

ACTIVITY 1.2.2

Read the article from *The Times* of 24 September 1994 in Fig. 1.18.

Task. Answer the following questions:
a Is the claim by Procter & Gamble that Unilever's product is unsatisfactory backed up by empirical evidence?
b If Unilever spent £25 million promoting the new product, why did it not ensure that it was suitable for the consumer?
c Unilever spent over £250 million on the new product and invested over £100 million in three new factories. The company's aim was to overtake Ariel as the number one branded washing powder. Do you think that they succeeded? State your reasons clearly.

PC
1.2.1
1.2.2
1.2.3
C
3.2.1
3.2.2
3.2.3
3.2.4
3.4.1
3.4.2
3.4.4

Soap powder rival throws cold water on Persil pledge

BY NIGEL HAWKES AND JON ASHWORTH

CLAIMS by Unilever that it has removed the clothes rotting element from Persil Powder were disputed by its main rival yesterday.

Procter & Gamble, the maker of Ariel, leapt on an admission by the Unilever co-chairman Morris Tabaksblat that the first version of Persil Power had been launched with insufficient preparation. "We made a mistake," he told journalists in Peking. "We launched a product which had a defect which we had not detected."

P&G welcomed Unilever's acknowledgement that the earlier version damaged fabrics but claimed that the new version did too. "Persil should come clean to consumers on fabric damage," P&G said. "All our research and the findings of independent test institutes and consumer organisations in Europe show that the reformulated Persil products continue to cause unacceptable levels of fabric damage."

Mr Tabaksblat is the most senior Unilever manager to have conceded that the original version of Persil Power had faults. But the company says the defective version, called Mark 4, has been replaced by Mark 5, which contains far less of the ingredient, a manganese catalyst, which caused the trouble.

A Unilever spokesman said yesterday: "All Mr Tabaksblat was doing was reflecting the company position. This defect only shows up under laboratory conditions, and not in the two-year trial we conducted with 60,000 users. The new formulation meets all the industry standards."

But the Consumers' Association said yesterday that thousands of consumers were still using the old version and that its test had shown "there can be substantial damage to some clothes". Derek Prentice, the association's assistant director, said: "Any claim that the original Persil Power causes damage to cloths only under extreme conditions is nonsense . . . [Consumers] deserve a little more plain speaking from Unilever." He said that the association's tests on the new version were incomplete. Marks and Spencer is conducting tests too.

P&G said that if Unilever had acknowledged sooner that it had made a mistake, "It would have helped avoid unnecessary consumer confusion and concern". Unilever's campaign had begun on a note of high optimism. Its scientists discovered that manganese compounds could act as catalysts at low temperatures, improving the oxidation process by which clothes are bleached.

Conventional bleaches such as hydrogen peroxide work best above 60C but many modern fabrics need to be washed at lower temperatures. The answer appeared to be a manganese catalyst to enhance the bleaching power. Unilever, confident of success, guarded the new catalysts with 35 patents began investing £100 million in three new factories. The company allocate more than £250 million for the Europe-wide launch of Persil Power.

Then a Dutch newspaper reported claims that Unilever's new product destroyed clothes. A war of words with P&G followed and off the record both sides talked of dirty tricks. Lawsuits winged to and fro and in Britain a range of "knocking" advertisements by P&G in July was followed up by an "anti-knocking" campaign by its opponent.

Unilever sent 11 million free samples of Persil Power to homes across Britain, part of a campaign that cost the company close to £25 million.

In the first three weeks after its launch in May, Persil reputedly overtook Ariel to become Britain's concentrated brand leader. P&G responded by parading photographs of clothes allegedly ruined by the new brand. The reports wiped 10 per cent off Unilever's share price. Persil Power is reportedly down to about half the market share it achieved immediately after launch.

Now the companies are beating each other about the head with reports from consumer organisations across Europe. The Dutch consumer organisation Consementenbond has found for P&G while its Austrian counterpart has given comfort to Unilever.

The effect of the manganese is to react with the dyes in the fabric, causing fading and weakening the fabric. The issue now is whether the much lower levels of the agent in the latest formulation still has this effect.

Much is at stake. American-based P&G claims about a third of Europe's £6 billion annual soap power sales. Unilever, an Anglo-Dutch conglomerate, commands 23 per cent of the market.

Fig 1.18 Powder war   *Source: The Times*

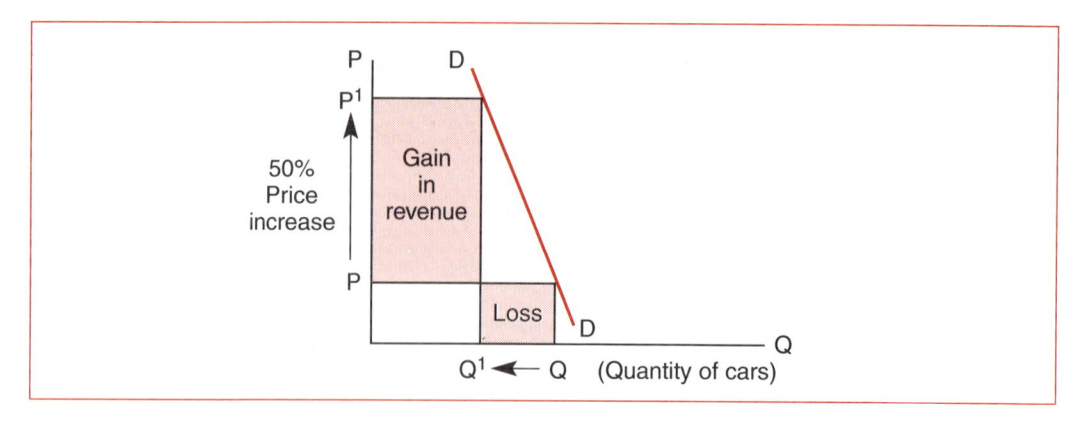

Fig 1.19 British Gas increases prices by fifty per cent

The Monopolies and Mergers Commission

The Monopolies and Mergers Commission (MMC) was established in 1948 as an independent body to investigate the behaviour of monopolies and report on any restrictive practices. The Commission is made up of industrialists, trade unionists and academics. It is supported by a full time team of economists, accountants and civil servants. The MMC assesses whether monopolies and potential monopolies and mergers are operating against the 'public interest'. It reports to the Director General of Fair Trading and the Secretary of State for Trade.

The MMC has been criticised for being too prone to political interference and too slow in its investigations and reports. For example, in 1991 the MMC investigated the UK motor industry and concluded, after a long investigation, that the car manufacturers were not exploiting the consumers by profiteering and keeping their prices artificially high. This report received fierce criticism particularly from the respected Consumers' Association (*Which?* magazine).

With the introduction of the EU Single Market and the free competition which it involves, it is likely that the major impetus for the regulation and restriction of monopolies in the UK will increasingly come from the European Union.

ACTIVITY 1.2.3

Task 1. British Gas is a monopoly. Why then does it spend so much on television advertising?

Task 2. Find out what the following organisations do and write a short paragraph on each one:
a OFTEL
b OFWAT
c OFT

Task 3. British Rail was created in 1948 as a statutory monopoly to provide rail transportation across the UK. It was controlled by the state to avoid any possible exploitation of the consumer. Why then has the government now privatised it?

Task 4. Find out the names of four monopolies and four oligopolies operating in the UK?

WEALTH AND WELFARE

Wealth and welfare are not the same thing even though they are closely related.

Wealth

Wealth refers to a country's total resources – in other words, the factors of production. From these factors of production we derive our standard of living (i.e. our clothes, houses, food, roads, schools, hospitals, cars, computers, etc.). Countries' factors of production and hence wealth vary. For example, the USA has more wealth than the UK because of its vast size and resource base. Some countries are small but have considerable wealth because of the nature of their resources. For example, Middle Eastern countries, such as Kuwait, have large supplies of oil.

Economists measure wealth by calculating the total Gross Domestic Product (GDP) produced each year. GDP measures the total of all economic activity which takes place in the various industrial sectors (for example, manufacturing, chemicals, agriculture, services, etc.). This can then be compared between countries once exchange rate adjustments are made.

In 1994 the UK GDP totalled £628 billion. If we then divide this by the total UK population, we can calculate a crude measure of wealth per person or per capita – that is, £628 billion/57.6 million which equates to £10 902 per person.

International comparisons can be made to indicate the relative wealth of each country's inhabitants. If we compared the UK per capita GDP figure with other countries, we can see that the UK is not as wealthy as our main competitors (*see* Table 1.7).

Table 1.7 per capita GDP figures (1994) (£s)

France	13 357
Germany	14 896
Japan	15 077
USA	13 575
UK	10 902

This is only a crude comparison between countries. If we examined UK male average earnings for the same period the figure is much higher at £342.7 per week or £17,820 p.a. Like any average, however, there will be many people earning much higher amounts and equally many earning much lower amounts.

Welfare

Welfare although obviously linked to wealth, refers to something quite different – the well-being of all the citizens of a country. It is not only concerned with economic goods (wealth), but also with public health, hours of work, law and order, maternity provision, suitable housing, education and healthcare, etc. Welfare to the unemployed would mean the adequate provision of social security and other benefits. Generally speaking, as a society becomes richer it can improve the welfare of its citizens. The country is better able to afford improved healthcare for the sick and more social security benefits for the poor and less fortunate members of society. In 1994 the UK government spent over £66 billion on social security payments. This represented nearly 30 per cent of all government public expenditure. Many Conservative ministers have questioned the high levels of government expenditure and have argued for reductions. Ministers who believe in free enterprise argue that the unemployed should not receive such support; a reduction in benefits would, they believe, encourage the unemployed to search harder for work. Moral questions arise from such a stance. How much should we as a society provide for those less fortunate? Should a civilised society provide adequate resources to ensure the welfare of its people? If the answer is positive, then how much should it provide?

Wealth versus welfare

While it is true to say that with economic growth an increase in overall wealth and welfare can be achieved, much depends on the form of economic growth. For example, a country could increase its overall wealth by making its labour force work longer hours, but this would not lead to an increase in welfare because the workers would be sacrificing their leisure time. In short, economic growth may bring an increase in a country's wealth but not necessarily an increase in its welfare.

Externalities

Externalities arise when the actions of producers and consumers affect not only themselves but also others. An example of a 'negative externality' would be pollution and congestion from cars. Motorists, when they consider a journey in their car, do not consider the extra cost involved to others in terms of the pollution they cause or the fact that they add to the congestion on the road. We can see here that there is a welfare benefit to the car owners in terms of a better standard of living but unfortunately there are welfare costs to non-users in terms of pollution, danger and added congestion.

An example of a 'positive externality' would arise where the actions of one individual benefit a third party. For example, a beekeeper indirectly provides a source of pollination to market gardeners.

The Pareto optimum

In order to establish an objective criterion of social welfare, economists use the notion of '*Pareto optimality*' (named after the Italian economist, Vilfredo Pareto) (1848–1923). A Pareto optimum allocation of resources is said to exist if:

It is not possible to reallocate resources so as to improve the well-being of one person without making at least one person worse off.

When such a situation occurs there will be a maximisation of the economic welfare of the community.

The problem with Pareto efficiency is that it is too theoretical: it relies on certain assumptions which only exist under perfect competition. In the real world, prices do not

Element 1.2 Analyse the operation of markets and their effects on businesses and communities

ACTIVITY 1.2.4

Study the article in Fig. 1.20.

Task 1. How do countries compare their relative wealth?

Task 2. What factors do you think would be good indicators of a country's standard of living? Explain your answer.

Task 3. The report shows that high levels of human development can be achieved at even modest income levels. Explain why?

Task 4. Explain the following terms used in the article:
- 'real national wealth per head'
- 'literacy rates'
- 'purchasing power'
- 'basic necessities'.

PC
1.2.4
1.2.5
C
3.2.1
3.2.2
3.2.3
3.2.4
3.3.1
3.3.2
3.4.1
3.4.2
3.4.4

Britain's top ten spot for the quality of life

By JACKI DAVIS, Consumer Affairs Correspondent

THE quality of life in Britain is tenth best in the world and better than in West Germany and America, according to a United Nations report.

Japan tops the list, followed by Sweden and Switzerland, while West Germany is two places behind the UK and the US is in 19th position. Niger in west central Africa is in last place.

The report was compiled by a group of leading economists from around the world led by the former finance minister of Pakistan, Mahbub ul Haq.

Its authors say the index is most useful for measuring differences between developing countries, because levels of purchasing power, literacy and life expectancy in most industrialised countries are well above basic levels.

'Industrialised countries tend to cluster together, with only five years' difference in life expectancy and four per cent difference in literacy rates among the 19 highest ranked countries,' says the report.

Literacy

The index shows Britain – with a life expectancy of 76, a 99 per cent literacy rate and real national wealth per head of population of £7,347 – in tenth place, but little separates it from the top country, Japan.

The report points out that there is no automatic link between a country's wealth and its people's well-being. America's real national wealth per head of population is £10,547, the highest of the top 20 countries, but it comes only 19th in the index.

The report's authors say America's low ranking is explained by the large number of different ethnic communities in its population, with lower health, nutritional and education levels than average.

'The USA is not one society, but several societies. For instance, among the black community in Harlem and New York the life expectancy is just 46 years, lower than Bangladesh and Africa and 30 years lower than the national average in the USA,' said Mr ul Haq.

West Germany's large population of immigrant Turkish workers, with much lower standards of living than average, helps push it below Britain on the index.

'It is also partly because Germany has devoted far less to human development levels and social security systems,' added Mr ul Haq.

He said Japan's place at the top of the index was achieved not only because of its huge economic success, but also because it is virtually a one-race nation with no ethnic minorities, due to a strict immigration policy.

The Soviet Union is in a lowly 26th place on the index. Its life expectancy of only 70, real national wealth per head of population of £3,592, and a much higher than average level of military spending combine to put it below regimes including East Germany and Czechoslovakia.

Modest

The report shows that high levels of human development can be achieved at even modest income levels, so long as people are placed at the centre of policies. But in some Third World countries money is poured into the military at the expense of basic necessities, with soldiers outnumbering physicians eight-to-one and the ratio of soldiers to teachers is as high as five-to-one.

Military expenditure in developing countries has increased three times as fast as in industrialised nations over the last 30 years, and in some of the poorest countries, military spending is two to three time larger than their spending on education and health.

But Costa Rica, which abolished its army in 1948, ranks 28th in the index with a life expectancy of 75 years, a literacy rate of 93 per cent and its national wealth per head of population of £2,251. The report says most developing countries could do more for their people by cutting military spending, inefficient state enterprises, unnecessary government controls and social subsidies which benefit the rich.

But it says significant progress has been made in developing countries in the last 30 years, with life expectancy up from 46 to 62 years, adult literacy up from 43 per cent to more than 60 per cent, a halving of child mortality rates and nutrition levels up by 20 per cent.

*Human Development Report 1990, published for the UN Develop-ment Programme by the Oxford University Press.

How we were judged

THE list produced by the United Nations Development Programme ranks 130 countries according to a human development index. This goes much further than previous studies which concentrated on a country's wealth. The index combines factors such as life expectancy, adult literacy and purchasing power into a simple measure to show how economic growth translates into human well-being.

Fig 1.20 Source: The Guardian

reflect their true social costs of production and consumption. For example, a manufacturer would only take into account its private costs and not consider the social costs. Motor manufacturers do not take into account the social costs their cars can create (such as accidents, pollution, congestion, etc.). It is only through government intervention with pollution controls that they consider these social costs.

ACTIVITY 1.2.5

Professor JK Galbraith, an American economist once stated that we now live in an 'effluent society rather than an affluent society'. What did Professor Galbraith mean by this? How is it relevant to our examination of wealth and welfare?

Self assessment questions

1 An oligopoly exists where there are:
   a few firms dominating the industry
   b many firms dominating the industry
   c few buyers in the market place
   d one firm dominating the industry

2 Perfect competition exists when the following conditions are met:
   a there is a large number of buyers and sellers
   b there is a homogeneous product
   c firms set their own prices
   d there are no barriers to entry

3 Imperfect competition exists when there are:
   a few sellers
   b few buyers
   c few buyers and sellers
   d many buyers and sellers

4 The term 'non price' competition is used to describe an
   a oligopoly
   b monopoly
   c perfect competition
   d monopoly

5 The following organisation is an example of an oligopoly:
   a Unilever
   b BBC
   c Post Office
   d British Rail

Element 1.2 Analyse the operation of markets and their effects on businesses and communities

6 Economists define welfare as:
   a the well being of all the citizens
   b the overall wealth of all the citizens
   c the average per capita income of all citizens
   d the total GNP of a country

7 A Pareto Optimum situation arises when:
   a it is not possible to reallocate resources without making someone worse off
   b it is possible to reallocate resources without making someone worse off
   c it is possible to reallocate resources and only make a few people worse off
   d it is not theoretically possible to obtain a maximisation of economic welfare in any given society

8 A situation of consumer sovereignty exists in the following market conditions:
   a monopoly
   b oligopoly
   c imperfect competition
   d perfect competition

9 One of the tasks of the National Rivers Authority is:
   a to protect the environment for everyone
   b to minimise prices for water charges
   c to encourage more consumer awareness of the water boards
   d to maximise government investment in the water industry

10 A monopoly firm is faced with an:
   a elastic demand curve
   b inelastic demand curve
   c perfectly elastic demand curve
   d perfectly inelastic demand curve

Unit 1   Business in the economy

C
3.2.1
3.2.2
3.2.3
3.2.4
3.4.1
3.4.2
3.4.4

Assignment

Task 1. Study the article from *The Times* of 27 July 1994 in Fig. 1.21.

Task 2. What evidence is there in the article that commercial business objectives only account for private costs, not social costs?

Task 3. What is the European Union doing to take account of these social costs?

World's fishing fleets face ruin as catches disappear

BY NICK NUTTALL ENVIRONMENT CORRESPONDENT

COMMERCIAL fishermen and their communities face extinction as pollution, habit destruction and over-exploitation deplete the world's fish stocks, an international research group has claimed.

A report by the Worldwatch Institute estimates that nine out of ten fishing jobs, or the livelihoods of up to 19 million people, will have disappeared within 20 years unless governments act to curb the destruction of fish stocks.

The group is calling for an end to the mismanagement and subsidies that are fuelling the destruction of the marine environment and endangering the food supplies of millions of people.

The Washington-based think-tank blames a doubling in the size of the world's fishing fleet since 1970.

Modern fishing vessels, able to travel further and process catches at industrial rates, are also denuding the seabed by trawling up the plants and tiny sea creatures that live there. The report shows that all but two of the world's 15 big fishing areas, including those in the Atlantic, Pacific, Mediterranean and the Black Sea, are suffering a serious decline in catches.

Some countries, including members of the European Community, have schemes to cut the number of trawlers but other nations plan to expand. Vietnam, for example, aims to double its boats.

The report, written by the Peter Weber of the institute, says pollution and bad management of coastal areas have accelerated the decline. In Indonesia the destruction of coastal habitats has eliminated up to 80 per cent of important fish species.

But the impact of over-fishing is the key, Mr Weber claims. Atlantic cod, traditionally the British staple fish, may now be commercially extinct, the report says.

In 1968 3.9 million tons were caught but the catch fell to 1.2 million tons by 1990.

Similar falls are being logged for herring, pilchards, haddock, mackerel and other fish. The biggest percentage fall is in catches of polar cod, down 94 per cent from its peak of 350,000 tons in 1971. Species such as blue and yellow fin tunny are becoming rare.

Mr Weber claims the decline in numbers is increasing the likelihood of conflict as nations compete for stocks.

The report says a moratorium is needed on the fishing of many species to allow stocks to improve and the huge subsidies which fuel the factory fishing industry must be cut.

The world marine fish catch in 1989 sold for $70 billion but catching the fish cost $124 billion, with the shortfall coming from subsidies.

FISHERY DECLINES OF MORE THAN 100,000 TONS, PEAK YEAR TO 1992

Species	Peak year	Peak catch (million tons)	1992 catch (million tons)	Change per cent
Pacific herring	1964	0.7	0.2	−71
Atlantic herrring	1966	4.1	1.5	−63
Atlantic cod	1968	3.9	1.2	−69
Southern African pilchard	1968	1.7	0.1	−94
Haddock	1969	1.0	0.2	−80
Peruvian anchovy	1970	13.1	5.5	−68
Polar cod	1971	0.35	0.02	−94
Cape hake	1972	1.1	0.2	−82
Silver hake	1973	0.43	0.05	−88

*The catch of Peruvian anchovy hit a low of 94,000 tons in 1984, less than 1 per cent of the 1970 level, before climbing up to the 1992 level
Source: FAO

Fig 1.21   Source: *The Times* 27 July 1994

Element 1.3
EXAMINE THE EFFECTS OF GOVERNMENT POLICIES ON MARKETS

Performance criteria

1 **Explain the reasons for government intervention in markets.**

2 **Explain the means by which governments can influence markets.**

3 **Evaluate the effects on markets of UK government policies and EU policies.**

Introduction

In this element we examine the reasons for government intervention in the economy. This can be to regulate monopoly practices, to ensure fair competition, to protect employees through health and safety legislation or to protect consumers through consumer protection legislation. The government can also stimulate demand in the economy to generate more employment through 'Keynesian demand management' or control inflation through monetary and fiscal policies. The Conservative government in the UK, in power since 1979, has been concerned that the economy operates through market forces with the minimum amount of impediments and has placed greater emphasis on supply-side economics, therefore.

The means by which governments can influence markets are also covered, including subjects such as deregulation, monopoly controls, monetary and fiscal policies, public ownership and privatisation.

We then look at UK government policies which involve the use of interest rates, personal income tax, corporation tax, VAT and the use of government spending in the economy. Finally, we discuss European Union policies, examining briefly the role of the EU and the various institutions. We also examine key European legislation such as the Single European Act and the Maastricht Treaty.

THE REASONS FOR GOVERNMENT INTERVENTION

The government intervenes in the economy for a number of reasons.

- *To protect consumers from uncompetitive actions by monopolies or oligopolies* which often operate against the public interest. This is becoming increasingly important with the large number of foreign multinational firms operating in the UK. In this case the UK operates as the host country, but the multinational's allegiance (if it has one) is to its own home country where the main parent company head office is situated.

- *To improve employment opportunities* by increasing total demand in the economy. In this case the objective might be to obtain a high level of employment (often referred to as 'full employment' with 98 per cent of the workforce in employment) – a situation which few governments have been able to achieve in recent years.

- *To control the level of inflation in the economy.* The government aims to do this so that consumers and businesses do not suffer. Since the Conservative government was elected in 1979 it has been one of the government's key aims. It firmly believes once inflation is controlled economic growth will follow.

- *To encourage economic growth.* This will lead to better job opportunities and improved wealth for all members of the community. For example, if the unemployed get a job when the economy improves, this has two benefits for the government. The first benefit is that it no longer pays out unemployment benefit to those newly employed; the second is that those now employed pay income tax so the government's tax receipts increase.

- *To encourage greater degrees of competition.* We have seen this recently with the deregulation of many traditional public/local government services. The government deregulates the economy so that more and more private businesses operate via the forces of supply and demand. The Conservative government believes that many of the old nationalised industries, which have operated at a loss, should be sold off and since its election in 1979 the Conservative government has adopted such a strategy. A large number of industries have been privatised (for example, British Telecom, which was privatised in 1984).

Even though British Telecom is now a PLC operating in the private sector, the government still has an influence over its business activities through its regulation process. BT needs to conform to the 1984 Telecommunications Act and is required by law to report to OFTEL, the office of telecommunications, such things as its pricing policy, public service obligations and its competitive approach. In BT's case it was a condition of its 25-year licence, granted on privatisation in 1984, that it followed a strict pricing policy of RPI–*x* with *x* set at 3 per cent for the first five years of operation. This effectively meant that BT was required to set a pricing policy of 3 per cent below the current rate of inflation in each year.

- *To protect employees from exploitation by their employers* particularly regarding safety at work. The Health and Safety at Work Act 1974 states that employers have a duty of care towards their employees: to ensure a safe working environment as far as possible; to provide information and training regarding the health and safety of workers; to ensure the safe use, handling, storage and transportation of articles and substances;

and to provide adequate facilities for the welfare of their workers. The government strictly enforces its legislation through the Health and Safety Executive which covers four areas: factories, agriculture, railways and nuclear installations.

- Employers need to ensure that their employees are adequately trained to use machinery and equipment. The penalties for failing to comply with health and safety legislation can be severe with fines of up to £20 000 and/or six months' imprisonment.

HOW GOVERNMENTS CAN INFLUENCE MARKETS

Economic policies

All governments, whether they are politically left wing or right wing, face the same economic problem: that is, one of allocating scarce resources which have alternative uses. For example, should the government spend more money on the National Health Service and less on defence? More on education and less on transport? The list of political choices is never ending because, just like any individual, the government has a given budget.

In 1993 total UK government expenditure for key services, such as education, health, defence, social security, and transport, was £286 billion – well above what the government received in tax revenue and other forms of government revenue. The government effectively overspent by some £37 billion and needed to borrow to balance its budget. This form of borrowing is known as the *public sector borrowing requirement* (PSBR); it is used to balance the deficit between total government expenditure and total government income.

The government can have a major influence either directly or indirectly.

Direct influences

A direct influence would be government policy regarding taxation. For example, if the government increased the rate of corporation tax (a tax on company profits), this would affect company profit margins. Conversely, if the government decreased the rate of corporation tax this would benefit businesses.

Government spending can have a direct effect on the economy and generate favourable conditions for businesses. For example, government spending on defence, education, health and transport will affect all businesses involved in these areas. For example, Vickers' survival in Leeds was directly linked to a Ministry of Defence contract for Challenger tanks.

The government can also influence businesses by offering financial support. As part of its regional policy, the government offers various inducements to businesses to relocate or locate in depressed areas of the UK. There are a variety of schemes such as enterprise zones, grant aid in assisted areas, regional selective assistance, business expansion schemes, etc.

Government can also introduce legislation to cover areas of concern such as health and safety, consumer protection, control of monopolies, etc.

Indirect influences

A form of indirect government influence would be its policy over interest rates. If the government increases the rate of interest, this adds to the company's costs in the form of increased overdraft payments. Moreover, a sharp increase in interest rates could affect public confidence and consumers could reduce their expenditure and this would indirectly affect the company's sales.

Social policies

The government should be aware of social forces in the economy, because these can have important effects on business. Social forces are dynamic because societies' values and attitudes change over time. The Conservative 'Back-to-Basics' policy of the early 1990s was aimed at reviving traditional values, such as the importance of the family and moral responsibility. Traditionalists argue that the record increase in crime, vandalism and drugs in the UK in the 1990s is due to the fact that many individuals have lost their respect for the rule of law. They argue that it is the fault of too many liberal 'do-gooders' and that we need to tighten up the judiciary.

ACTIVITY 1.3.1

Task 1. Do you agree with the traditionalists that we are too soft on criminals? What effect does this have on consumers and businesses?

Task 2. If you do agree with the traditionalists, what steps would you take to tighten up on criminals? If you disagree, state some of your main points of disagreement.

Social changes affect organisations in many ways. We have seen a sharp increase in criminal activity over the last ten years and this has led to one of the fastest growing service industries: crime prevention. Many businesses now exploit the 'fear culture' (for example, car phones for women, burglar alarms, security windows and doors, car alarms, security coded cassettes, etc.).

Many businesses are now more socially aware and appreciate that the economic pressure to make a profit can no longer nowadays be considered in isolation from the social responsibility of the business. This includes the responsibilities of the business to its employees as well as to the public at large. One of the major social trends in recent years has been the concern for our environment.

Environmental policies

The government is much more concerned today with the environment and, even though we live in a free-market economy, it will intervene to protect the environment and society.

Many environmental pressure groups, such as Greenpeace, have made the public more aware about the need for environmental protection. Rapid economic growth and technological change can affect finite resources and damage the environment. The environment is subject to exploitation because it is a free resource. In most cases it is impossible to charge for its use. You cannot charge people for the fish in the ocean or the air that they breathe. Because of this there has been an inevitable increase in the pollution of our rivers and oceans, overfishing, destruction of the rain forests, etc. The main problem posed for the environmentalists is that the environment lies outside national boundaries – it is an international issue. In law it is almost impossible for one country to take another country to court seeking damages for pollution.

The Norwegians have long complained about UK industries causing pollution by acid rain and have sought compensation. Concern about acid rain first arose in the 1960s in Scandinavia. The Scandinavians conducted scientific tests and discovered that sulphur dioxides and nitrogen oxides produced by burning fossil fuels in UK power stations caused acid rain in Sweden, Norway and Germany. Further studies in the late 1980s and early 1990s showed that 60 per cent of the Black Forest was affected with over one third of the trees dying. Tests in Sweden at the same time found that most of Sweden's lakes were dying with some 90 per cent of lakes and rivers in South Norway having no fish in them.

The solution to the problem is relatively simple. If UK firms reduced their sulphur dioxide emissions by using 'de-sulphurisation technology', then most of the acid rain would disappear. The technology is expensive, however, and British firms are reluctant to pay for it. In Britain it would increase average consumers' electricity bills by 25 per cent.

ACTIVITY 1.3.2

Task 1. Why have 'green' issues become more important over recent years?

Task 2. If you were in political power in Sweden, what would you attempt to do about pollution from British companies?

ECONOMIC SYSTEMS

To solve the problem of the allocation of scarce resources, certain decisions have to be taken:

1. What goods should be produced?
2. What quantities should be produced?
3. How should these goods and services be distributed?

Unit 1   Business in the economy

Three types of economic system have developed over the years, with differing approaches to how these decisions should be taken:

1 the command economy or planned economy (Socialism, Communism)
2 the free market or free enterprise (capitalism, private enterprise);
3 the mixed economy (mixed system).

The command economy

Under a command economy, the state decides what goods to produce, how to produce them and how to distribute them.

Command economies are based on Marxism or Socialism and they existed in the Soviet Union and Eastern Europe for over 40 years up until the late 1980s.

In March 1985, when Michail Gorbachev became the Soviet leader, he introduced a more open system in the USSR known as *'perestroika'* and the Soviet economy moved away from Communism to a more capitalist model. In 1990 the one-party Communist system in Russia was laid to rest and Gorbachev encouraged further reforms under *'Glasnost'* (openness). President Yeltsen, who succeeded Gorbachev in 1991, has moved Russia further towards the Western free-market approach.

Although many Eastern countries have moved towards the Western free-market model, there are still planned systems in the world, for example, China, North Korea, Vietnam and Cuba.

Advantages and disadvantages of a planned economy

Advantages	Disadvantages
■ The state can ensure that essential public goods and merit goods are provided.	■ Consumer choice is limited to the range of goods and services decided by the state.
■ The government owns land and capital and controls the labour which means in theory there is no unemployment.	■ Command economies can lead to overproduction of certain commodities and underproduction of other commodities.
■ Wasteful competition can be eliminated and the ensuing monopolies controlled by the state.	■ Command economies are less efficient than the free-market systems, and there tends to be a lot more bureaucracy. Without the profit-making opportunity, inefficiency and complacency can arise.
■ The elimination of private profit and large wage differentials can reduce economic and social disadvantages.	■ Individual and total production of goods and services tend to be lower than under the free-market system.
■ Command economies do not appear to be subject to the periodic recessions which occur in Western economies.	■ The political system under a planned system can become autocratic and repressive and reduce individual freedom.

Element 1.3 Examine the effects of government policies on markets

The free-market economy

Under a free-market system, the ownership of the means of production and distribution of goods and services is by individuals and companies. Capitalism is based on the understanding that individual consumers will seek to maximise their personal satisfaction by demanding goods and services which will give them the greatest level of satisfaction for the money they have available. The distribution of resources is through the market or price mechanism, i.e. through the forces of supply and demand.

A pure free-market economy is difficult to find since most developed economies are mixed, i.e. they employ both the free-market and government intervention. Hong Kong is the closest country to a free-market system.

Advantages and disadvantages of the free-market system

Advantages	Disadvantages
■ The right type and the right quantity of goods and services are produced.	■ The free-market system takes no account of those who cannot afford to pay for the goods and services produced.
■ There is no need for a large bureaucratic planning system.	■ The system fails to provide public goods and merit goods for society.
■ There is freedom for consumers to buy the goods and services they desire.	■ Private producers, in their search for profits, can damage the environment, e.g. water pollution, noise and chemical pollution.
■ The individual acting for reasons of self-interest can benefit other members of the community.	■ The free-market system is subject to the trade cycle which creates periods of inflation and periods of high unemployment.

The mixed economy

The mixed economy, as the name suggests, is a mixture of both the planned system and the free-market system. The mixed economy system has been adopted by almost all major developed countries in the world. This system is better than the other two because it eliminates many of their disadvantages but adopts all their advantages. For example, it adopts the efficiency of the free-market system via supply and demand but eliminates some of the weaknesses with the government intervening in the market to provide public goods and merit goods free to all individuals. This is paid for through taxation.

The UK and nearly all of Europe, America, Australia and Japan incorporate features of both free-market and command economies.

Unit 1 Business in the economy

PC
1.3.1
1.3.2
1.3.3
C
3.2.1
3.2.2
3.2.3
3.4.1
3.4.2

ACTIVITY 1.3.3

Examine the information below which looks at the advantages and disadvantages of the different economies and fill in the missing words.

Command economy
Command economies are often known as c_____ or s_____. This theory is based on Marxism here the s_____ decides what to produce, h_____ to produce and how to a_____ resources. The c_____ political system existed in the U_____ and E_____ E_____ for over 40 years until the system was overthrown in the late 1980s. However c_____ systems still exist in C_____, N_____ K_____, V_____ Cuba and other countries. The government through a central body identifies what to produce and how much of it to produce. The state also decides on the a_____ of resources i.e. How g_____ and s_____ are distributed.

The state is the main p_____ and e_____. It controls the factories and the farms, railways and the shops. The question of who gets such g_____ is determined by a rigorously enforced incomes policy which gives higher incomes to those workers who the government regard as most i_____. Individual consumers then have the f_____ to spend their i_____ as they wish.

Market economy
In a market economy each consumer is free to spend as he or she wishes. The price mechanism through supply and demand allocates resources. The market economy indicates consumer wants and needs to producers. It also encourages competition between producers and leads to a greater e_____. The market economy tends to encourage more c_____ which leads to lower p_____ and more consumer ch_____.

One of the big problems with the market economy is that it fails to take account of m_____ goods and p_____ g_____. There is also a danger that the economy can experience business cycles of boom and slump which can mean high levels of u_____ in the s_____ and high levels of i_____ in the b_____. For example, unemployment in the former East Germany rose from zero per cent to over forty per cent in 1991 as uncompetitive old state subsidised industries closed down.

Over recent years under the Conservative government the British economy has moved towards a more m_____ orientated e_____. This is because the government believe that the market m_____ is the most e_____ means of allocating resources.

Mixed economy
In a mixed economy the g_____ does take some part in the economy. This normally takes the form of attempting to respond to the failings of the m_____ system. One form of failure is that the market system does not provide p_____ goods or m_____ goods. Private companies working in a market orientated economy tend to produce ne_____ ex_____ which causes problems for society as a whole. These ne_____ ex_____ are produced because private firms only take account of their private c_____ and not p_____ costs. Another problem which the mixed economy deals with is that of unemployment. In a mixed economy the g_____ will attempt to control the levels of u_____ normally by de_____ management techniques. In practice most economies are mixed with some resources being owned by the g_____ and some r_____ being owned by p_____ individuals.

Element 1.3 Examine the effects of government policies on markets

PC
1.3.1
1.3.2
1.3.3
C
3.2.1
3.2.2
3.3.3
3.3.4
3.3.5
3.3.1
3.3.2
3.4.1
3.4.2
3.4.2
3.4.3
3.4.4

ASSIGNMENT 1.3.4

You are employed as a research assistant in a large multinational company. The company's Chief Economist, Clive Johnston, is addressing a business conference involving over 25 large public limited companies, many of which are also multinational. The theme of the conference is 'Political change in Europe'.

Clive has asked you to research the following:

- the recent collapse of the Eastern European Communist system;
- the key characteristics of the free-market economic system;
- the main advantages of the free-market system.

He has requested the information as an informal report using the above as the headings. Clive is rather concerned that there will be a number of journalists present who have in the past been critical of the capitalist system. For this reason he wants you also to identify some of the problems associated with the free-market system and what businesses can do to improve the system.

GOVERNMENT APPROACHES TO ECONOMIC MANAGEMENT

The government intervenes in the market because it has a number of economic objectives. These objectives would not be met if the government left them to market forces. Businesses are concerned about full employment, for example, but they are more concerned with making a profit for their shareholders and minimising their costs of production.

The UK government has four main objectives:

- full employment;
- control of inflation;
- economic growth;
- balance of payments equilibrium.

Figure 1.22 illustrates these objectives and the alternative approaches to achieving them.

Unfortunately not all of these objectives can be achieved at once. In fact the pursuit of one objective can have an adverse effect on the other. For example, a policy aimed at curbing inflation would attempt to depress consumer demand and force prices down. This would lead firms to lay off workers and unemployment would rise, defeating the government's objective of full employment.

Different political parties have different views on how to achieve these objectives. The labour party believes in full employment and argues for more government intervention in the economy. This is known as *'demand management'* or demand side economies. The Conservative party believes in a more *'laissez faire'* approach (leave it alone); they attach more importance to supply-side economics, that is to ensuring that supply conditions are right in the market and firms are producing goods and services for consumers efficiently without bureaucratic government intervention.

Unit 1 Business in the economy

```
                    UK Government objectives
                    ↙      ↓      ↓      ↘
  Full employment   Controlling   Economic    Balance of payments
                    inflation     growth      equilibrium
```

Demand side economics

Government spending

Budget deficits

Fiscal Policy (taxation)

Supply side economics

Monetary policy

Control of the money supply

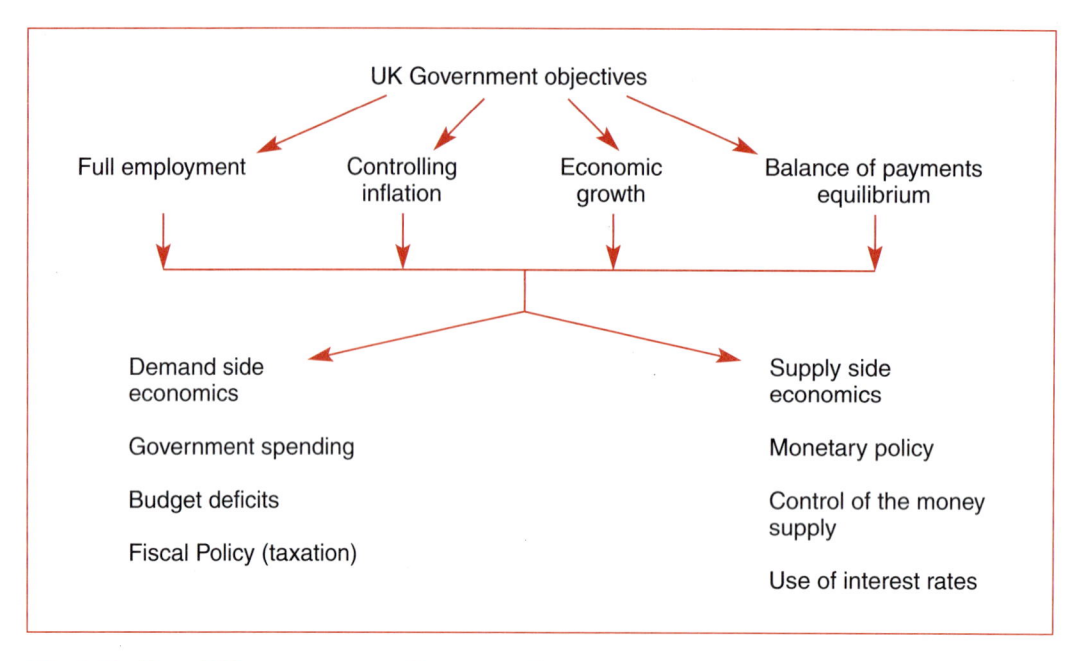

Use of interest rates

Fig 1.22 How UK governments intervene in markets

Demand-side economics

Demand management in the economy was developed by John Maynard Keynes as far back as 1936 in his famous book, *The General Theory of Employment, Interest and Money*. His views dominated economic policy for over 30 years and were followed up until the early 1980s.

Keynes introduced the concept of the *circular flow of income* (see Fig. 1.23). In his simple model he introduced two sectors of the economy: *the householder* (H) who was both consumer and worker and *the firm* (F) who paid the householder for his labour and produced goods and services for consumption.

The householder was paid a wage (Y) – income for his factor service (FS) (his labour) – and then he bought goods and services from the firm (C) – consumption. Providing the

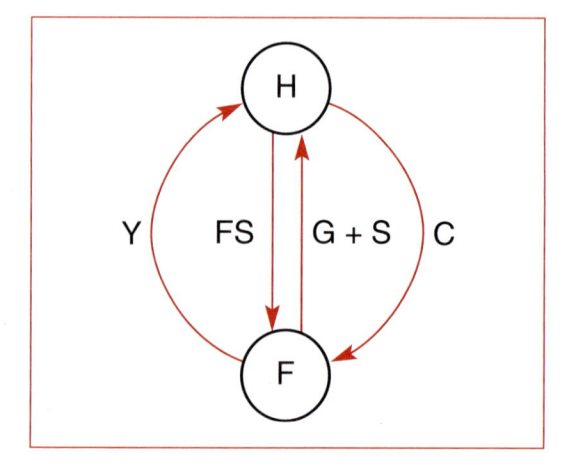

Fig 1.23 Simple circular flow of income

householder spent all of his income on the firm's goods and services the firm could continue to employ him, thus creating a circular flow of income.

We all know that in the real world the economy is far more complicated than Keynes' simple model shows. In the real world the householder does not spend all his income but may try to save some in a bank or building society. In the real world the government takes taxes directly from our incomes (PAYE) or indirectly through expenditure taxes (e.g. VAT). In the real world we do not restrict ourselves to only buying British goods; we also buy foreign goods – whatever represents good value for money.

The real world is taken into account in the Keynes' model by incorporating:

- *leakages* from the circular flow through savings (S), taxation (T) and imports (M); and
- *injections* into the circular flow through investment (I), government spending (G) and exports (X).

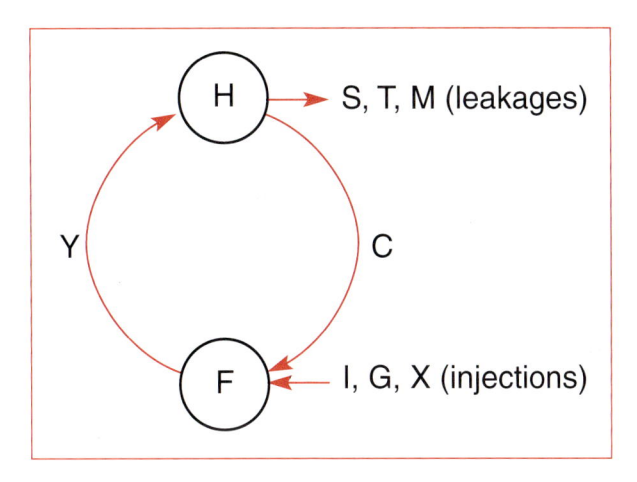

Fig 1.24 Complex circular flow model

Figure 1.24 illustrates Keynes' more complex circular flow model. Keynes pointed out that the economy would be in balance or equilibrium if:

$$S + T + M = I + G + X$$

If the economy was not in equilibrium, it would move into recession and high levels of unemployment would arise. He argued it was up to government to make sure equilibrium would arise, hence the term *'Demand Management'*. If for any reason total demand in the economy did not match total supply the government needed to step in to make up the deficit.

The simplest way to explain this mechanism is to consider the diagrams in Fig. 1.25. It follows that, if demand was deficient by £10 billion, the government would need to step in and inject more money into the circular flow to stimulate total demand (called *aggregate demand* (AD)).

$$AD = C + I + G (X-M)$$

where C = consumption
       I = investment
       G = government spending
       X = exports
       M = imports

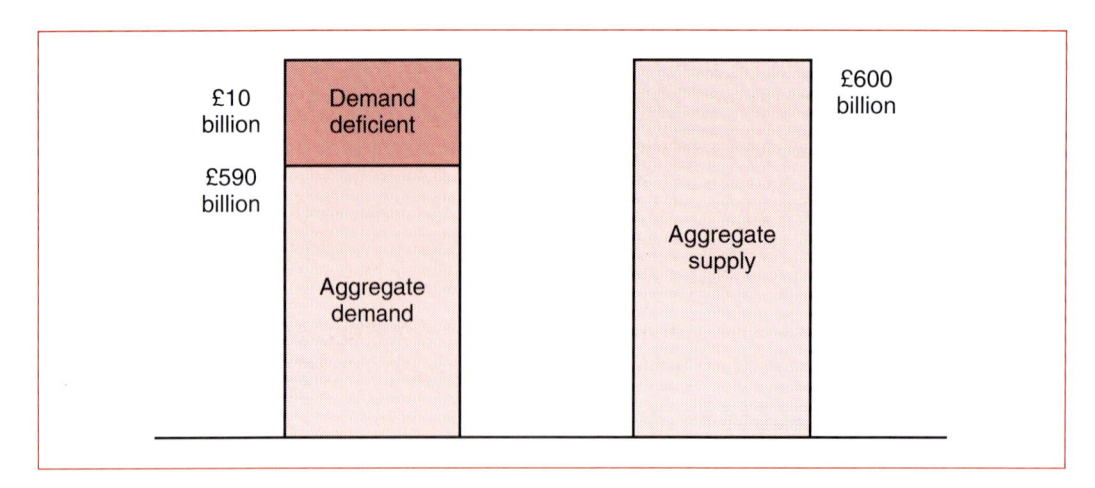

Fig 1.25 Aggregate demand and aggregate supply

The quickest and most effective method of stimulating total demand would be through government spending, for example, injecting money into public sector programmes such as schools hospitals, motorways, etc. This would generate a *multiplier effect* in the economy and lead to an overall increase in total demand. The multiplier effect means that the government does not have to inject very large sums of money into the economy, because once the money is in the circular flow it creates an income for somebody else. One person's income, when spent, becomes another person's income.

Government increases expenditure by building a new motorway. The building industry spends the money on raw materials and labour. More people are employed reducing unemployment and they spend their income on consumer goods and services, thus creating more income for other members of the economy, e.g. retailing, banking, leisure, manufacturing, etc.

```
Government increases expenditure by building a new motorway
                        ↓
Building industry spends the money on raw materials and labour
                        ↓
More people are employed reducing unemployment
                        ↓
These spend their income on consumer goods and services thus
creating more income for other members of the economy e.g.
retailing, banking, leisure, manufacturing etc.
```

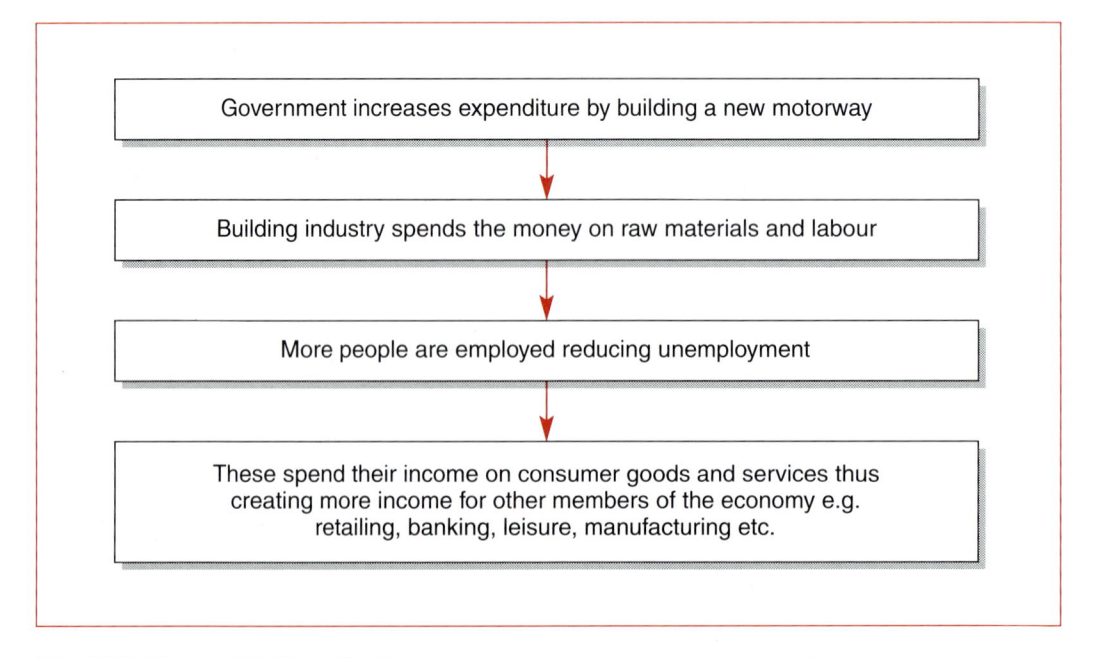

Fig 1.26 The multiplier effect

In the case of the example in Fig 1.25 and 1.26 if all those people employed spent 90 per cent of their income and saved 10 per cent, the government would only need to inject £1 billion because the multiplier effect would increase this tenfold. (i.e. £16)

$$\text{Multiplier} = \frac{1}{\text{MPS}} = \frac{1}{10\%} = \frac{1}{1/10} = \frac{10}{1} = 10$$

Note: Marginal Prosperity to Save i.e. extra inclination to save from an increase in income. If a person received an increase of £1.00 and saved 10p then the MPS = 0.1.

Supply-side economics

Since 1979, the Conservative party has had the control of inflation as its number one objective. The Conservative government believes in a *'laissez faire'* (leave it alone) approach and that the role of government is to set the right level of free-market conditions so that businesses can grow and prosper. If business confidence is good then levels of unemployment will be reduced.

The government believes that if inflation gets too high, business confidence will suffer and British goods will become uncompetitive. Consumers will switch to foreign goods, e.g. Japanese electronics etc. Moreover, overseas buyers will be reluctant to buy British goods. Once demand for British goods falls, firms employ less people and the spiral of depression develops.

Inflation adversely affects those on fixed incomes or those workers who are unable to secure pay increases in line with inflation. This has been the case with public sector workers recently.

Fig 1.27 Inflation destroys the value of money

There are three main causes of inflation:

- *Cost push inflation* arises from increases in business costs which can be through wage increases not linked to productivity or increases in raw material prices which are then directly passed on to the consumer, fuelling inflation.
- *Demand pull inflation*, as the name suggests occurs when there is excessive demand in the economy which is not matched by total supply, i.e. 'Too much money chasing too few goods'.

  If overall demand in the economy (*aggregate demand*) exceeds total supply (*aggregate supply*), the prices will be 'pulled' upwards. Demand pull inflation is often evidenced by low levels of employment, numerous job vacancies, abundant overtime working and shortages of goods and services. Such conditions enable skilled workers to press for higher wages which their employer concedes because he or she can pass the price rise on to the consumer whilst consumer demand is buoyant.

- *Monetarist (money supply) inflation*. The Monetarist view of inflation originates from the work by Milton Friedman at the Chicago Business School. He argued that excessive increases in the money supply would cause inflation. In order to control inflation, the government needed to control the money supply. Friedman advised Margaret Thatcher in the early 1980s that the British money supply should only be allowed to grow in line with British output of goods and services, i.e. aggregate supply. The Monetarist view took over from the Keynesian view of demand management from 1979 onwards. Since 1985, however, hardline Monetarist policy has been abandoned in favour of supply-side economic policies. It fell out of favour because empirical evidence showed that the direct link between the money supply and price rises, which Friedman claimed, did not occur. For example, during the period 1985–6 the target rate of growth for the money supply (£M3) was 5–9 per cent but the actual rate of growth was 14.8 per cent and yet UK inflation fell from 6.1 per cent in 1985 to 3.4 per cent in 1986. Friedman and other Monetarists had always claimed that any increase in the money supply would increase inflation and any decrease in the money supply would therefore reduce inflation.

FISCAL POLICY

The Chancellor's budget

In the UK, the budget is the announcement by the Chancellor of the Exchequer of the government's income and expenditure plans for the coming year. Until 1994, the budget took place in the spring and the autumn each year; in 1994, the government announced both income and expenditure plans at the same time in the autumn budget.

The Chancellor can aim for one of three types of budget:

1. *a balanced budget*, where income and expenditure are the same;
2. *a budget deficit*, where government expenditure is greater than government income;
3. *a budget surplus*, where government income is greater than government expenditure.

The government can use the budget as a form of 'demand management'. Most of the recent budgets have tended to be budget deficits, where government expenditure has been greater than government revenue.

In the Autumn 1994 budget, the Chancellor Kenneth Clarke announced his intentions to reduce government spending by over £28 billion over the coming three years. He intends to reduce government borrowing, i.e. the PSBR (public sector borrowing requirement) which makes up the difference between government spending and government income. For example, if government expenditure was £250 billion and government income was £200 billion then the PSBR would be £50 billion to make up the shortfall.

The PSBR for 1994/95 is £34.4 billion and the government plans to cut it to £5 billion by 1997/98. The Chancellor argued that a cautious budget advocating fiscal restraint was the best course of action for sustained economic growth. Low inflation was the key.

Taxation

A government operates a system of taxation for the following reasons:

1 *To raise government revenue* to finance government expenditure, e.g education, health, etc.

2 *To redistribute incomes*, to ensure that those without income receive some form of state benefit, e.g. pensions, social security, unemployment benefits, etc.

3 *To use as a method of 'demand management' in the economy.* Taxation can be used to reduce consumer spending to decrease aggregate demand if there are inflationary pressures in the economy. It can also be used as a means of influencing the location of industry in the UK. For example, Japanese companies such as Nissan have been offered various government grants and tax advantages to locate in the UK. Nissan was offered over £200 million to locate in Sunderland.

There are two forms of taxation: direct and indirect.

Direct taxation

Direct taxation, as the name suggests, comes directly out of income. For example, with pay as you earn (PAYE), an employer deducts the tax from income before the employee receives it. For the tax year 1994–5, there are three bands of income tax:

20%   up to £3000
25%   £3201–£24 300*
40%   over £24 301*

* includes increases in line with the rise in the Retail Price Index adjusted in the autumn 1994 budget.

Everybody receives a personal allowance before tax is deducted. In the autumn budget, personal tax allowances were increased in line with inflation so for the tax year 1994–5 the personal allowance is:

Single person   £3525
Married Couple £1720*

(*relief at 20 per cent unchanged in autumn 1994 budget)

Businesses also pay direct taxation: *corporation tax* – a tax on company profits. For the tax year 1994–5, corporation tax is set at two rates:

Small companies   25%
(up to £300 000 profits per annum)

Large companies   35%
(more than £300 000 profits per annum)

The Conservative government does not like increasing taxes too much because it is an interference with the operation of the free market. If tax rates were too high, businesses would not be motivated to make profits and generate the necessary wealth in the economy. It is rather ironic, however, that taxes have increased significantly in recent years. The government needs to balance the level of taxation with the need to obtain the necessary finance for its ever increasing government spending.

Indirect taxation

Indirect taxes are forming an increasing part of government revenue. These are taxes on expenditure rather than income, for example, VAT, Motor Vehicle Tax, tobacco duties, alcohol taxes, Capital Gains Tax, Stamp Duty, TV Licence, etc.

These are called indirect taxes because in theory they can be avoided. A non-smoker will not pay any taxes on tobacco. In the 1994 budget, however, the Chancellor introduced VAT on domestic fuels. Clearly this tax would be unavoidable for people using electricity and gas.

Because of increasing pressure regarding VAT on fuel bills, the Chancellor increased cold weather payments for the elderly in his autumn 1994 budget. From 1995 there will be an extra annual £52 for single pensioners and £73 for couples as a compensation for VAT on fuel.

PRIVATISATION

When the Conservative government gained power in the UK in 1979, the then Prime Minister, Margaret Thatcher, vowed to make the economy less reliant on government interference and more in line with the free-market approach of the United States. An important method of achieving this was to free the economy from the large state-controlled nationalised industries.

In 1979 nationalised industries contributed almost a quarter of the UK gross national output and employed nearly two million people. They were also responsible for 20 per cent of all investment in the economy. The government was against nationalisation and a new term was introduced – *privatisation* – which meant the selling off of public corporations to the private sector.

The governments argued for privatisation on the following grounds.

1 The government believed that these industries would operate more efficiently under the private sector because the directors would be directly accountable to their

shareholders and would be able to make more effective use of given resources. This argument was supported by the American economist, Milton Friedman, who regularly gave Margaret Thatcher advice at that time. He took the Classical view that optimality would be brought about by 'Adam Smith's invisible hand of self-interest' where the price system would bring about the optimum allocation of resources.

2 The government believed that most of the state-nationalised industries were far too bureaucratic which again led to inefficiencies because they were too far removed from the consumer.

3 The government maintained that nationalised industries were a drain on the economy by wasting taxpayers money. They argued that these loss making industries could be made into profitable ones, once they were privatised. A private industry would attack the problems in these large declining industries through rationalisation and a more positive market-oriented approach.

For these reasons the government embarked on a vigorous privatisation programme:

National Freight	1982
British Steel	1988
British Telecom	1984
British Gas	1986
Rolls Royce	1987
British Airways	1987
British Airports Authority	1987
British Petroleum	1987
Water boards (in England and Wales)	1989
Electricity boards	1991
National Bus Company	1991
British Rail	1994

The privatisation of many of the large public utility industries (e.g. British Gas, the electricity boards and the water boards) has led to heated debate and considerable press coverage. The government has used industries such as British Telecom to highlight the success of its privatisation programme. Recently, the massive profits of the privatised utilities and the excessive pay awards given to their chief executives have dampened the success of the government's programme.

A 1995 BBC Panorama programme was highly critical of the privatised water boards. The programme pointed out that the new privatised water boards were exploiting their customers by charging excessive prices and failing to provide the large amounts of capital investment which were promised when they were privatised. The regulator, OFWAT, was also criticised for failing to tackle the problem and not regulating the industry effectively.

The key critisicm is that privatisation of the main utility industries has failed to generate a more competitive situation; it has only replaced a state monopoly with a private monopoly.

It is rather ironic that one of the main reasons for nationalisation is to prevent the abuse of monopoly power. The argument is that where an industry has control over the market, nationalisation would ensure that the industry is administered in the public interest and not just for private profit, thus gaining the benefits of large-scale production without the abuses of monopoly.

Unit 1 Business in the economy

PC
1.3.1
1.3.2
C
3.2.1
3.2.2
3.2.3
3.3.4
3.4.1
3.4.3
3.4.4

ACTIVITY 1.3.5

Task 1. Study the newspaper article from the *Yorkshire Evening Post* of 1 April 1994 in Fig. 1.28.

Task 2. Answer the following questions:
a What is Railtrack?
b What are the government's arguments for the privatisation of British Rail?
c What arguments do the critics of privatisation of BR advocate?

Task 3. Write a short letter to the newspaper explaining your own views on the privatisation of BR?

The biggest every changes have been undertaken in the history of the railways were today under way. Transport Reporter VANESSA BRIDGE puts them under the microscope, and assesses their likely impact on our region.

END OF THE LINE FOR BR

BRITISH RAIL was today being broken up into some 60 or more businesses but the public, it is promised, will see no differences – for a few months at least.

The new Government-owned body, Railtrack, takes over the running of the system but until lines are officially passed to private companies to run, BR will continue at the helm.

What is certain is that no lines will be in private hands before 1995 and only six of the 25 lines envisaged will be operated privately by the end of 1995 – including the east coast main line. State-aid for the railways will continue, but for how long, it is not yet known.

The Government has promised that railcard schemes for the elderly, young people and disabled passengers will continue and through tickets to any destination will remain available under privatisation. Season tickets will still be valid after a particular line has been privatised.

In addition, private operators will be asked to participate in schemes like the "go-anywhere" Travelcard.

Stations or lines cannot be closed without "rigorous" statutory closure procedures, says BR. And train operators have to submit a safety case for approval before taking on services, as well as publishing a passengers' charter explaining the complaints procedure and how compensation will be paid.

Critics of privatisation see it as "a leap in the dark". According to one passenger group, rail users could find themselves travelling in discomfort on a deteriorating system if privatisation flops.

Major General Lennox Napier, chairman of the Central Transport Consultative Committee, said that despite the great determination to pull the trick off it will only work if two things happen.

"High levels of investment must be maintained – but I have no indication that that will happen. Second, we must keep the advantages that came from one, co-ordinated network and we have not had full assurances of that," he said.

Transport Secretary John MacGregor, who has had to spearhead the passage of privatisation legislation through Parliament, remains optimistic. But Murray Hughes, editor of *Railway Gazette International* said April Fool's Day marked "a leap into the dark".

ONE TO BECOME SIXTY

BRITISH Rail has finally embarked on the free-market express with its fragmentation into about 60 businesses.
Key groups in the new structure include:
- Railtrack – A Government-owned body owning and running the infrastructure – more than 10,000 miles of track, 2,500 passenger stations, nearly 1,000 tunnels and about 90,000 bridges. It will levy access charges totalling about £2.2 billion a year.
- Shadow franchises – 25 companies which will eventually be sold to the private sector will be running specified train services; local services will be run by Regional Railways North East train operating company (TOC). The East Coast main line (TOC) will be among the first to be sold, by the end of 1995.
- The regulator – The role of John Swift, QC, will be to defend passengers' interests, ensure operators meet operational, financial and safety standards, approve access agreements between Railtrack and the operators, and ensure that fares are kept at "reasonable levels".

LEASING
- Stations – Most stations will be leased by Railtrack to train-operating companies with the exception of 13, including Leeds city station, which have large commercial potential and are being set up as "independent" stations. They will eventually be leased on a long-term basis to independent companies.
- Passenger trains – three rolling stock companies (Roscos) are being set up to lease BR's 11,000 vehicles to train operators. These companies will be privatised.
- Goods trains – FreightBR's Trainload Freight business and Railfreight distribution are being transformed into three geographically-based companies which will also be privatised.

Fig 1.28   *Source*: Yorkshire Evening Post

Element 1.3 Examine the effects of government policies on markets

THE EUROPEAN UNION

The UK is very much a part of Europe. Many UK businesses trade heavily within the single European market. Since 1960 Britain's trade with the EU has doubled. In 1969 29 per cent of Total UK visible exports went to the EU. In 1995 that figure is 65 per cent. Millions of jobs in the UK rely on our future development with Europe. Supporters of the Single Market and the Maastricht Treaty argue that this is the final step towards economic and political union for all member countries.

The Conservative government, although committed to the UK being a major part of the European Union (EU), has some reservations. The Conservative leadership is not without its critics regarding some key aspects of European Union policy, and has to balance its actions between pleasing European member countries and appeasing vociferous European sceptics at home. For example, successive Conservative leaders have been very critical about the European Social Charter arguing that it was simply a form of 'backdoor socialism'. At the 1991 European Council meeting in Maastricht, the UK was the only member state to vote against the Social Charter. The UK governments believes that it would only lead to job losses in the UK because it includes minimum wage regulations.

Supporters of the Social Charter argue that it protects the welfare and social rights of all European workers. They point out that a basic minimum wage is essential to stop exploitative manufacturing businesses from investing in those countries where labour laws are lax. They also point out that, unless labour laws are brought into line, manufacturers will move away from the more affluent European member countries, such as Germany, France and Italy, to the poorer European member countries, such as Greece, Spain and Portugal. At the time of writing Britain stands alone as the only member country not to be a part of the Social Charter.

The development of the European Union

In order to understand the current debate between member countries and the various European issues which affect British businesses, we need to have some knowledge of the background to our present position in the European Union. We also need to understand the broader objectives behind the European Union and how they might affect the UK. For this reason the following section outlines a brief history of the European Union

The Treaty of Rome 1957

The key to the origins of the European Union was the Treaty of Rome which established the European Economic Community (EEC). The original members were Belgium, France, Italy, Luxembourg, Netherlands and West Germany. The aims of the Treaty of Rome were to establish:

1 *A free trade area*. The six countries abolished all tariffs and quotas to trade but kept their own tariffs and quotas on goods imported and exported to countries outside of the EEC.

2 *A customs union*. This is one stage further than a free trade area, with the imposition of a common tariff on all goods exported to and imported from outside the EEC.

3 A *common market*. The Common Market was one step further and combined both the external tariff and a free trade area along with an attempt to harmonise economic policies in certain key areas. For example:

- free movement of goods between members;
- free movement of labour between members;
- free movement of capital between members;
- free movement of services between members;
- harmonisation of laws between all member states, etc.

European Free Trade Association (EFTA)

EFTA was formed in 1959; members included the UK along with Austria, Switzerland, Portugal, Norway, Sweden and Finland. EFTA shared some of the aims of the EEC, i.e. free trade between member countries, but the aims of EFTA were limited. EFTA did not aim for greater political and economic harmonisation, as did the EEC. There was no common external tariff in EFTA or common policy towards farming, fishing, transport and social affairs. EFTA was always seen as a second best alternative to the EEC because it did not include the more powerful European countries, like Germany, France and Italy.

Britain joins the EEC

In 1973, Britain joined the EEC along with Denmark and the Irish Republic making a total of nine members. Britain originally applied to join in 1961 and later still in 1967, but this was rejected by the French President, Charles de Gaulle. A third attempt was made in 1973 and this time Britain was successful. The Conservatives were in power at the time and Edward Heath was the Prime Minister. At the time there was not a consensus in the party or the country about joining the EEC and many felt that Britain would be faced with more disadvantages than advantages.

Heath lost the 1974 general election and the Labour Party were elected under the leadership of Harold Wilson who promptly called for a referendum over the issue of Britain's membership. The majority view was that Britain should stay in the EEC.

The community continued to develop and grow in economic strength. In 1981 Greece joined, and in 1986 Portugal and Spain joined bringing the total membership to 12. With the unification of Germany in 1990, over 18 million former communist citizens joined the community from the former East Germany.

The Single European Act (SEA) 1987

The SEA came into operation on 1 July 1987. The SEA aimed to provide a single market:

an area without internal frontiers in which the free movement of goods, people, services and capital is ensured.

To speed up the four freedoms – free movement of labour, goods, services, and capital – there were significant changes in the decision-making process. Majority voting took over from unanimous agreement for most major areas of the single market programme which meant that certain member countries could not use delaying tactics to slow down European unity and Common Market harmonisation. The European Economic Community became the European Community (EC) emphasising the wider nature of the market, than merely dealing in economic matters. The EC was seen as a single domestic market. By the end of 1992 all barriers would be removed and to a large extent they have been removed.

Element 1.3   Examine the effects of government policies on markets

The European Union in the 1990s

Now called the European Union, the economic bloc created by the 12 countries has grown significantly as a major economic power with a population of over 324 million people. With the end of communist rule in Eastern Europe and a move towards free-market economic policies there has been a sharp increase in countries wishing to join the EU (e.g. Austria, Sweden, Finland, Cyprus, Norway, Switzerland, Czechoslovakia, Hungary and Turkey).

The opening of the Channel Tunnel in 1994 marked a historic step towards a closer European Union. By 1995 the European Union is expected to include 16 members rather than the present 12 encompassing over 375 million people. Finland, Austria and Sweden have voted to join but to the acute embarrassment of the Norwegian government the Norwegians narrowly voted not to join in November 1994.

Maastricht Treaty Feb 1992

The Masstricht Treaty represented a major advance towards total European Union. It took the EU from being merely an economic institution towards full political economic and social union. Its three main aims were:

- To create economic and social progress through an area without internal frontiers and through economic and monetary union (EMU).
- To develop a common foreign, security and defence policy.
- To introduce citizenship of the union.

There aims were to be achieved in three stages. The final stage involved the establishment of a European System of Central Banks (ESCB) which would hold and manage the official reserves of all the member states. Exchange rates would be fixed and the European Currency Unit (ECU) would have full status as the main European currency. Because of UK objections the UK was allowed not to proceed to Stage 3 if it did not wish to. One of the governments main arguments against Stage 3 was that it involved the Social Charter with included 'citizens rights to fair pay' (minimum wage legislation).

The main institutions of the EU

The Council of Ministers

This is the Union's major decision-making body, equivalent to our Cabinet of senior government Ministers. It is made up of one minister from each of the 12 countries (normally the Foreign Secretary). When specific matters are raised, the relevant minister is normally called (e.g. for transport, the Transport Minister, for agriculture, the Agricultural Minister, etc.).

The Council meets monthly, normally in the country which holds the Presidency, which is rotated between members every six months. Britain held the Presidency at the end of 1992. All decisions are taken by majority vote and member countries are allocated votes according to their population size. Britain along with Germany, France and Italy get ten votes, Spain gets eight, Belgium, Greece, the Netherlands and Portugal get five each, while Denmark and Eire get three each and tiny Luxembourg gets two. The headquarters of the Council is in Brussels.

The European Council

The meetings of the European Council take place twice a year and take the form of a European Summit. This often provides a valuable forum for major initiatives, which can often be proposed by the member country which holds the Presidency. Even if agreement is reached at this meeting, however, and a decision is taken, it still needs to be approved by the individual countries' parliaments – a process known as *ratification*.

The European Commission

This is equivalent to Britain's Civil Service. It is headed by a team of 17 commissioners chosen from member states. The UK appoints two commissioners, but they are under the control of the President of the Commission and are not expected to act for Britain or for any political party. Commissioners deal with major policy areas such as competition policy or agriculture.

The European Parliament or European Assembly

The European Assembly is elected every five years with a total of 518 MEPs. The number of MEPs from each country is determined by population size. The UK, like Germany, France and Italy, has 81 seats, Spain has 60, the Netherlands 25, Belgium, Greece and Portugal 24, Denmark 16, Eire 15 and Luxembourg 6. Each member country uses its own political system to elect its MEPs with the UK using the 'first-past-the-post' system. The majority of member countries use a form of proportional representation. The parliament sits for five years. Meetings are held in Strasbourg and most of the sittings are open for public viewing. MEPs sit in political groups, not in national groups. There are six different political groups: Communists, Socialists, Christian Democrats, Liberals, Democrats, and European Progressive Democrats.

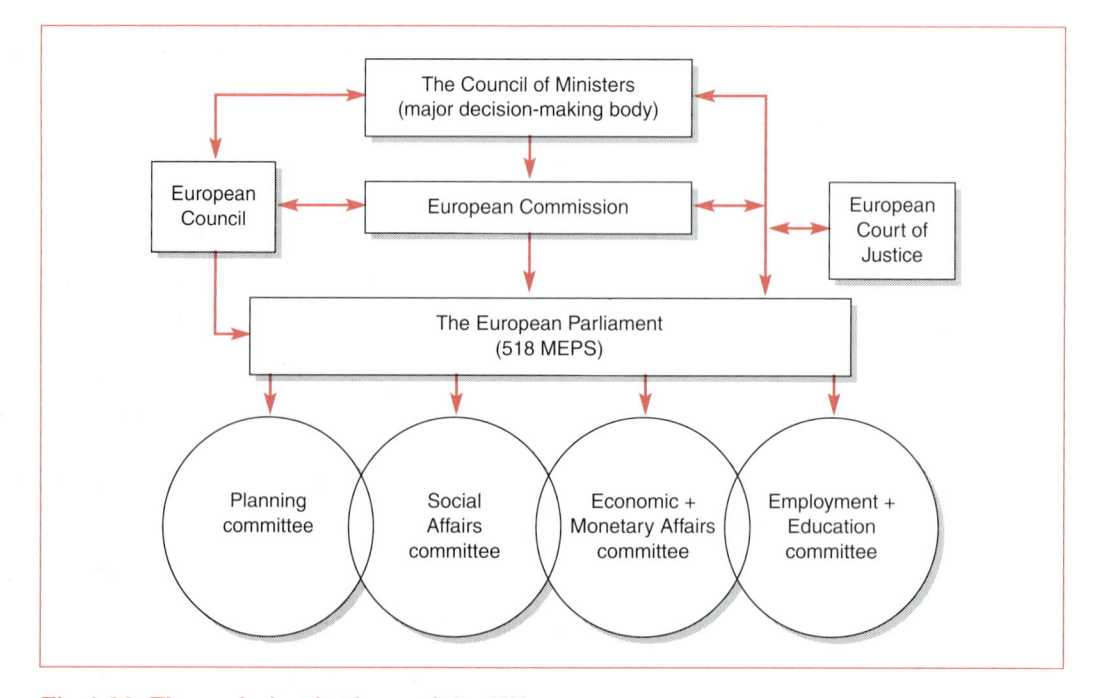

Fig 1.29 The main institutions of the EU

Element 1.3 Examine the effects of government policies on markets

The majority of parliamentary work is carried out by committees and the largest political group can choose the chairperson for the committees. Committees cover a range of community areas such as planning, transport, economic and monetary affairs, regional policy, social affairs and employment and education. The European Parliament gives opinions on and suggests amendments to legislation made by the Commission.

The European Court of Justice

As a member of the European Union, the UK is subject to EU law and British companies need to comply with European legislation, no matter how bureaucratic it may appear. European Union law consists of union legislation and judgements that have been referred to the European Court of Justice. It is mainly concerned with customs duties, agriculture, the free movement of labour, goods and capital, restrictive trade practices and the regulation of coal, steel and nuclear energy industries. European law must be obeyed by all member countries; anyone breaking it may be taken before either his or her own national courts or to the Union's Court of Justice in Luxembourg.

The European Court makes rules and gives judgements on the interpretation and application of Union law. Its judgements are binding in all member countries and as such it is the final court of appeal. It is Europe's supreme judicial body, comprising of 13 judges, one from each member state plus one.

The European Court has wide powers of jurisdiction. It can hear actions brought against a member state by either the Commission or by any member country that wishes to bring an action. Even individuals can appeal to the European Court, if they feel aggrieved.

ACTIVITY 1.3.6

You are currently employed for a large multinational business in the Marketing and Public Relations Department. The business relies heavily on trade within Europe. The Public Relations Manager has read the article in Fig. 1.30 overleaf and feels it gives a totally unbalanced view of the European Union. She has asked you to draft a letter to the author, Richard Littlejohn, to attack his article and present a favourable picture of the European Union. The letter should not be more than 200 words long. (It might then stand a chance of being printed in the newspaper!)

You need to concentrate on the beneficial effects for British businesses. There are a number of reports produced by the Department of Trade and Industry which point to all the benefits that Europe offers British businesses. Don't forget the *Cecchini Report (1988)* which identified a number of economic benefits of the Single Market, estimating savings of over £140 billion per year and the creation of millions of jobs.

Task 1. Write a paragraph explaining why the author criticises the European Union (use empirical data).

Task 2. What does the author mean by the 'European adventure ending in tears'?

Task 3. Write a paragraph explaining some of the benefits of being in Europe.

Task 4. Why is the author so critical of the ex-Chancellor, Norman Lamont?

PC
1.3.1
1.3.2
1.3.3
C
3.2.1
3.2.2
3.2.3
3.2.4
3.3.2
3.4.1
3.4.2
3.4.3
3.4.4

We knew John Major did us a favour when he sacked Norman Lamont. Until now, we didn't realise quite how big a favour.

Freed of the chains of cabinet responsibility, Lamont has at last told the truth about Britain's disastrous and expensive European adventure.

He has admitted the government is deliberately deceiving us into believing there will never be a single currency or a European superstate.

And he has rightly scoffed at John Major's absurd claims that Britain is at the heart of Europe.

The truth is that Britain has no future within the European Union. Sooner or later we will have to contemplate complete withdrawal. Preferably sooner.

As Lamont put it in his speech in Bournemouth: "As a former Chancellor, I cannot pinpoint a single economic advantage that comes to this country as a result of our membership."

He could have gone even further and spelt out the real cost of Britain's participation in the great European folly.

Membership of the EU has cost us £295billion since 1973 – £4,000 for every man, woman and child in Britain. And that is set to double over the next decade.

We have absolutely nothing to show for it. Quite the opposite, in fact.

The Common Agricultural Policy adds £15billion a year to our food bills. A pound of butter costs 69p within the EU, only 29p outside.

Billions are spent paying inefficient foreign farmers to grow food no one wants to eat. Billions more goes to farmers to grow nothing at all. Still further billions are wasted destroying surplus crops.

Regulations spewing from Brussels seem intentionally designed to wreck British industry and put up prices.

Once-profitable firms, providing thousands of jobs and contributing to the export derive, are forced to close by the cost of complying with unnecessary European rules.

The glasshouse industry is about to become the latest casualty, because of Italian and Spanish inspired legislation on the level of nitrates in lettuces.

This has nothing to do with dangerous chemicals. It is simply that lettuces grown under glass produce more nitrates than lettuces grown in the open air.

In Britain, because of our climate, most lettuces grow under glass. In Italy and Spain – surprise, surprise – they grow in the open air.

So we shall have to shut all our greenhouses, sack thousands of British workers, and import lettuces from Spain and Italy at whatever price they choose to sell them to us.

That's just one instance of the lunacy detailed every week in the *Sunday Telegraph* by Christopher Booker, co-author of *The Nad Officials* – a frightening catalogue of bureaucratic vindictiveness and incompetence, carried out in the name of "Europe".

I've written time and again of the damage being done to this country of membership of the EU, from the hounding of WIs for producing home-made jam without a licence to the obscenity of British fishermen being forced to watch as Spanish trawlers hoover up our fish stocks. Two-thirds of our fishing catch was surrendered to

'If Lamont had the courage of his convictions then... thousands of people would not have lost their homes'

Europe by Traitor Heath to bribe them into letting us join the club.

(To borrow a phrase from Groucho Marx: I don't want to belong any club which would have Heath as a member.)

Politicians in both parties know all this. But they are not only unwilling, but increasingly unable to do anything about it.

John Major is like a petrified rabbit caught in the headlights of the European juggernaut. Douglas Hurd seems to see the job as Foreign Secretary as representing the interests of foreigners.

For all Major's talk of opt-out, the truth is that Brussels always gets its own way, by hook or by crook. Labour and the Liberals are ten times worse.

The politicians try to scare us with bankruptcy, financial ruin and unemployment if we withdraw from Europe.

What the hell do they think we've got now?

There is no reason why we should not retain free-trade links with the Continent, without any political union.

To say we would be cast into the wilderness is absolute cobblers. Britain is one of the biggest markets in Europe. They want to sell us their goods, so they would have to buy ours.

If the Germans and French cut up rough, there are plenty of others willing to trade freely with us, most notably the Japanese and the emerging Pacific Rim countries. And the Commonwealth.

The Americans have never been know to turn their backs if there's a buck in it, either.

The European adventure is destined to end in tears. Soon it will dawn on other countries, particularly the Danes and even the Germans, that they are being taken for the most expensive ride in history.

You can't force diverse peoples to conform to an artificial norm. You can't have British chip shops run from Strasbourg, or Spanish commissioners deciding whether or not Scottish housewives are allowed to make butterscotch for jumble sales.

More importantly, you can't have German bankers setting British mortgage rates. Or French generals deciding British defence policy.

If it doesn't end in tears, it may end in blood and bullets. Look at the former Yugoslavia.

If we don't get out, it will certainly end in ruin and oppression.

The best we can hope is that we write it all off to experience. Then some day we'll look back on this and it will all seem funny.

Norman Lamont may be bitter and twisted and his outburst this week may well be a splenetic venting of resentment at his sacking. But that doesn't make it any less valid.

It's just a pity that he didn't tell us all this a couple of years ago when he was voting for the Maastricht Treaty and spending billions of our money propping up the European Monetary System, in which he now says he never believed.

If he'd had the courage of his convictions then, hundreds of thousands of people would still be in a job.

Perhaps, even including him.

Fig 1.30 Floating Exchange Rate
Source: The Sun, 13 October 1994

Element 1.3 Examine the effects of government policies on markets

EXCHANGE RATES

Exchange rates affect not only businesses trading abroad, but also individuals travelling abroad and the prices of goods imported. Since 1971, the UK has operated a *'Floating'* exchange rate system. This means that the value of the pound is determined by the forces of supply and demand. Figure 1.29 illustrates pound sterling floating against the US dollar.

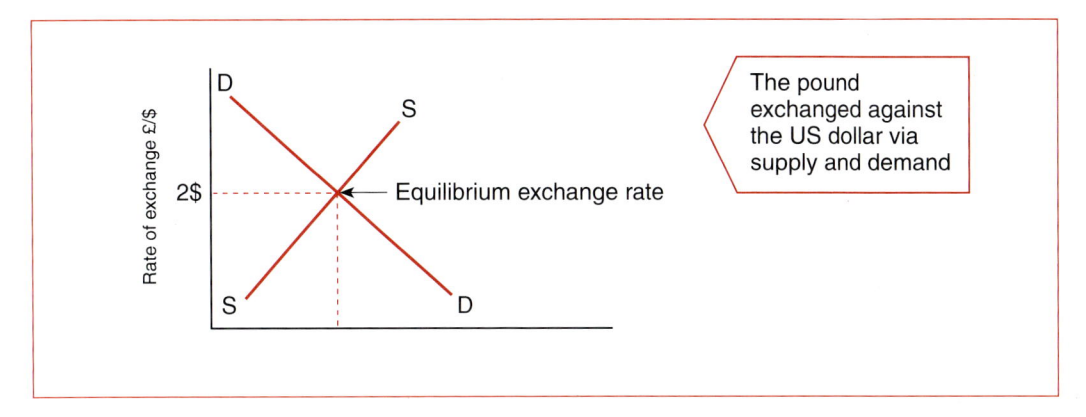

Fig 1.29 Floating exchange rate

When the demand for pounds is equal to the supply of pounds, the equilibrium exchange rate is reached. Under a floating system, the exchange rate can change very quickly. For example, if there was an increase in demand for British goods by US citizens, this would increase the demand for pounds sterling. The US citizens would need more pounds in exchange for dollars to pay for the British goods (*see* Fig. 1.30).

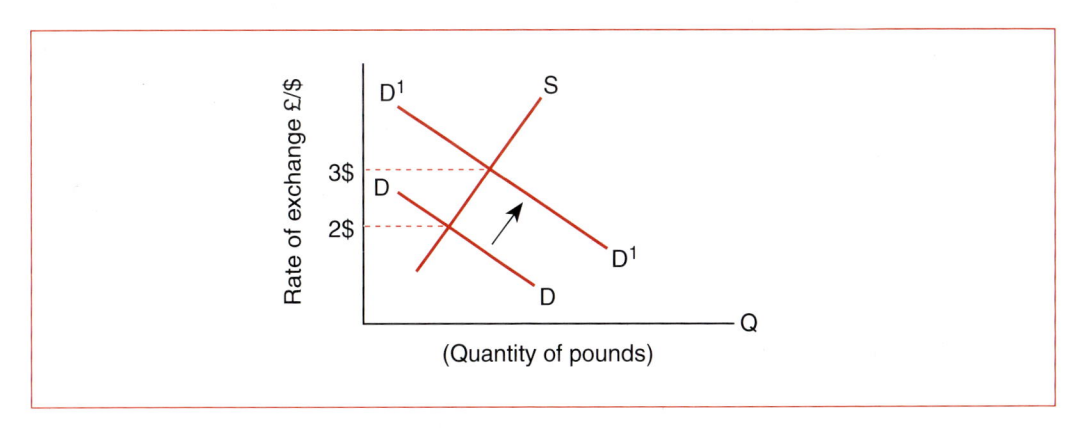

Fig 1.30 Increased demand for pounds

This increased demand for pounds would shift the demand curve for sterling to the right increasing the exchange rate, i.e. from £1 = $2 to £1 = $3.

Conversely, if the demand for British goods from the pound would decrease against the dollar (*see* Fig. 1.31). Demand for pounds would fall on the foreign exchange markets and the demand curve would shift to the left. The pound would depreciate against the dollar.

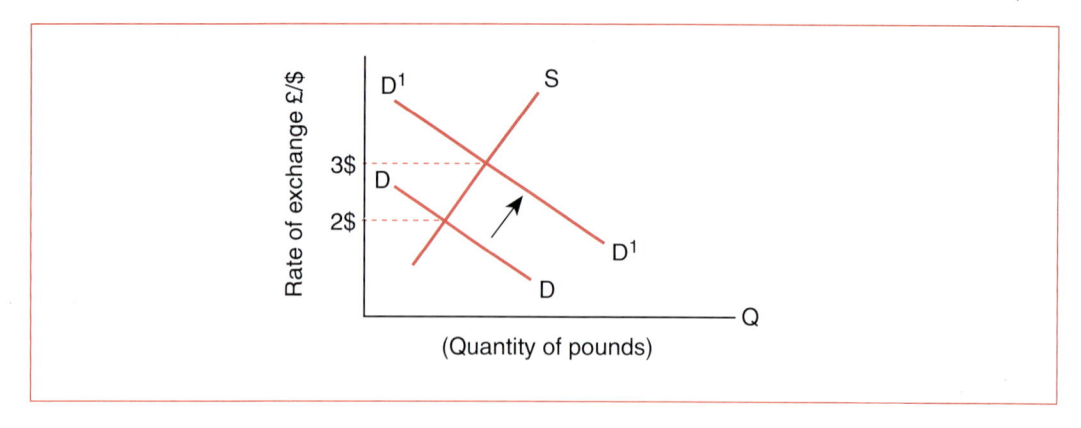

Fig 1.31 Decreased demand for pounds

The implications of a floating exchange rate for businesses

The obvious problem with a floating exchange rate is that it can fluctuate either up or down. Businesses who enter a contract with overseas buyers for goods with future delivery dates are uncertain as to what the exchange rate will be (and hence how much they have to pay). This has led to many businesses buying ahead on the forward exchange market in order to safeguard their interests. Businesses prefer stability; they do not like the uncertainty of the floating exchange system.

Changes in the exchange rate affect their business. For example, a fall in the value of the pound will:

- raise the price of imports and hence the firm's raw material costs;
- reduce the price of exports and hence benefit businesses involved in exporting.

An increase in the value of the pound will:

- reduce the price of imports and hence reduce the firm's costs if it imports raw materials from abroad;
- raise the price of exports which will adversely affect businesses trading abroad.

Let us examine the implications of an increase in the value of the pound to a company like BT.

If BT signed a contract to sell £3 million of telecommunications equipment to an American importer in three months' time and at the time of the contract the exchange rate was £1 = $2, the cost to the American importer at the time of the contract would be £2 million.

If the pound increased in value from $2 to $3 during the three months between the signing of the contract and the date of delivery, the importer is faced with increased costs, i.e. £3 million to pay instead of £2 million. Clearly, if the importer was concerned about an increasing exchange rate, it might buy elsewhere. The increasing exchange rate would threaten BT's sales in the American market.

Many British companies rely on importing raw materials from abroad. If the pound depreciates against other currencies, they find that their costs increase. Many firms operate in a very competitive market and may not be able to pass on the increased costs to their customers.

Government influences on the exchange rate

If the government is faced with a continual declining exchange rate, it may decide to intervene in the foreign exchange market by buying sterling which would shift demand to the right forcing the exchange rate back up. This is known as 'dirty floating' and can be a very expensive.

In September 1992, the then Chancellor of the Exchequer, Norman Lamont, tried to keep the value of the pound at its agreed rate in the European Exchange Rate Mechanism

THE EXCHANGE RATE MECHANISM

EMS established 13th March 1979 ... Britain joined the ERM 8th October 1990 ... and left on 'Black Wednesday', Sept 1992

THE Exchange Rate Mechanism (ERM) is simply an agreement between European governments to limit movement in their currencies. But it has far-reaching implications for the way our economies are run – and for Britain's future in Europe.

WHAT DOES THE ERM DO TO THE ECONOMY?
A FIXED exchange rate against countries with lower inflation rates imposes a painful discipline. No longer can the pound be devalued – an escape route from competitive failure that has persistently added to our inflation rate. Instead, industry has to restrain costs – or lose business. If pay rises faster in Salford than Stuttgart, the Germans will cream off still more of Europe's business. The outcome depends on how quickly we adjust.

The ERM is not a totally fixed system. We had entered with wide bands – and we can seek agreement to a change in our central rates. This give us some leeway. But it will hurt. Other counties' experiences (notably that of the French) suggest that the ERM does squeeze inflation – but squeezes industry at the same time.

WHO INVENTED THIS THING, ANYWAY?
IN THE 1970s, European governments became increasingly disillusioned with the experience of floating exchange rates. Businessmen say that wild currency movements hinder trade and investment decisions. Many European countries reckoned that linking their currencies to the German mark would force their inflation rates down.

WAS 1990 A GOOD TIME TO JOIN?
IT WOULD have been much easier to join in 1985, when Nigel Lawson first tried to persuade Mrs Thatcher. Inflation was lower – closer to German levels, making the adjustment so much easier. We were not in recession. And we were still in surplus on our external trade.

HOW DO REALIGNMENTS WORK?
BECAUSE everybody is involved, these are hard to negotiate, and have to be thrashed out over a weekend, when the currency markets are closed. In the first four years of the ERM, there were six realignments. But since 1983, there have been only four – the most recent in January, 1987.

WILL BRITAIN REJOIN THE ERM?
Britain is unlikely to join the ERM before the next election even though it has satisfied the Maastricht Treaty but a decision will have to be made before the end of the decade about rejoining the ERM.

WHY DID WE JOIN ERM
SINCE monetarism ran into trouble, we have lacked a clear economic discipline. The Government's shilly-shallying over the ERM was causing difficulty in European negations. It was also causing us trouble in the currency markets. The economy was sliding into recession, and the Prime Minister wanted lower interest rates. Industry had been pressing for early membership; the Opposition parties were committed to membership. The markets were getting impatient with delay. A bleak party conference was looming – and the Chancellor said we could not cut interest rates safely until we were in the ERM.

WHAT ARE THE REWARDS?
WHEN entry was announced in 1990, share prices boomed, and the pound bounced. By Monday's close, the Stock Market was $7\frac{1}{2}$ per cent higher than before the announcement. This euphoria reflected the fact that, inside the ERM, we have been able to cut interest rates without weakening the pound. That lessens the danger of recession turning into slump, without increasing the danger of importing inflation. Interest-rate cuts feed through to retail prices, which help bring down the published rate of inflation; while a firm pound will help keep the lid on industrial prices.

WHERE DOES ERM LEAD TO?
MEMBERSHIP of the ERM is "stage one" of central bankers' plan for monetary union – a single Euro-currency. Britain remains opposed to the final objective; but now has greater weight in the talks between government heads on a new Treaty of Rome that will start in December. The president of the European Commission, Jacques Delors, has already expressed anxiety that Britain will use its ERM membership to delay progress. In one sense, at least, it certainly will. It will take time for the system to absorb sterling. It will be several months, at least, before we move to the narrow $2\frac{1}{4}$ per cent bands adopted by other EC countries.

WHAT ABOUT OTHER EXCHANGE RATES?
EUROPE cannot control exchange rates between its currencies and others outside the system – the dollar, say, or the yen. So the pound can still move sharply against the US currency. But managing internal European exchange rates means that European currencies move up and down against the dollar in close formation.

Fig 1.32 The Exchange Rate Mechanism

(ERM), but speculators in Britain and overseas lost confidence in the pound and sold sterling on the market which forced the pound downwards. Lamont instructed the Bank of England to maintain its value by using foreign currency and borrowing from abroad. Because of the sheer size of speculation and the cost to the country (millions of pounds), however, Lamont was forced to accept defeat and let the pound devalue. This forced Britain to leave the ERM. This day was named 'Black Wednesday'.

Self assessment questions

1 The government has four main economic objectives. Which of the following is not one of the government's main objectives?
   a Economic growth
   b Low taxation
   c Low inflation
   d Balance of payments equilibrium

2 The following list breaks down total UK production into different UK industries:

Manufacturing	35%
Distribution	13%
Finance	13%
Public services	16%
Agriculture	3%
Mining	3%
Other services	17%

   The total share of UK production for tertiary industry is:
   a 17%
   b 35%
   c 46%
   d 59%?

3 A free-market economy is one where:
   a the price mechanism allocates resources
   b the government sets price levels
   c consumers have little choice
   d the government allocates resources?

4 If the government wanted to help the car industry directly it could:
   a increase spending on roads
   b reduce duty on petrol
   c increase the cost of the MOT
   d increase the cost of driving lessons?

5 If the government wanted to reduce demand pull inflation it could:
   a increase taxes
   b reduce taxes
   c increase government expenditure
   d increase the money supply?

Element 1.3 Examine the effects of government policies on markets

6 If the government wanted to reduce unemployment it could:
   a increase income tax
   b decrease income tax
   c increase the rate of VAT
   d increase interest rates?

7 What is a progressive tax?
   a A tax on low-income earners
   b A tax on overseas exporters
   c A tax on domestic importers
   d A tax which takes more from the rich than the poor?

8 An oligopoly differs from a monopoly because:
   a there are few buyers
   b a few firms dominate the market
   c several firms dominate the market
   d there are few buyers and few sellers?

9 Which of the following is not an aim of the Single European Act?
   a To achieve a common foreign policy
   b To remove all physical barriers to trade
   c To remove all technical barriers to trade
   d To remove all anti-European members

10 A tariff is defined as:
   a a tax on imported foodstuff
   b a tax on imported alcohol and tobacco
   c a tax on imported goods
   d a maximum limit placed on imports?

Assignment

PC
1.3.1
1.3.2
1.3.3
C
3.2.1
3.2.2
3.3.3
3.3.4
3.4.1
3.4.2
3.4.3
3.4.4

Scenario

You are employed by a small, local manufacturing company. Your boss is interested in the government's management of the economy. Ultimately she would like to know how it affects the company. She is also aware of the increasing influence of the European Union (the EU) on national economies. To help her understand these complex issues she has asked you to conduct some preliminary research.

As preliminary research complete all of the following tasks and submit to your tutor in report form.

Task 1. Governments in EC manage mixed economies. However, the Eastern European countries have applied to join and they run their economies along lines closer to a command economy model. There are advantages and disadvantages to both approaches of economic management. Outline the advantages/disadvantages of both systems.

AN	Also give two examples of countries in Europe using each type of economic management system (a. command style economy b. mixed economy)
3.1.1	
3.1.2	
3.1.3	***Task 2.***
3.1.4	a. Briefly explain the purpose of the Budget.
3.1.5	b. In late November the Chancellor holds the Budget, list the main effects, both positive and negative, on businesses of this year's Budget.
3.1.6	
3.3.1	
3.3.2	***Task 3.***
3.3.3	a. How has the EC encouraged competiton within the European Union in terms of the Single European Act?
3.3.4	b. Prepare a factsheet on the history, aims and purposes of GATT that would be of use and interest to a business. The design and layout is up to you, bearing in mind that the information you present in your factsheet should be relevant but concise.

Answers to self assessment questions

Element 1.1	Element 1.2	Element 1.3
1. b	1. a	1. b
2. d	2. c	2. d
3. b	3. d	3. a
4. c	4. a	4. b
5. c	5. a	5. a
6. c	6. a	6. b
7. d	7. a	7. d
8. a	8. d	8. b
9. a	9. a	9. d
10. b	10. b	10. c
11. b		
12. a		
13. c		

# UNIT 2

BUSINESS ORGANISATIONS AND SYSTEMS

The aim of this unit is to investigate different types of business organisational structure in the private and public sectors at a national and local level. The different purposes, liabilities, use of profit, control systems and legal obligations will be considered. In addition to this the unit will cover individual organisations, their functions and their day-to-day activities.

Element 2.1
INVESTIGATE BUSINESS ORGANISATIONS

Performance criteria

1 **Explain the objectives of business organisations.**

2 **Explain the differences between types of ownership.**

3 **Compare organisational structures.**

Introduction

This element first identifies the different types of business organisation and then describes the types of structure that can exist within them.

THE OBJECTIVES OF BUSINESS ORGANISATIONS

Business organisations in the UK can take a variety of forms but are usually either in the public or private sector of the economy. *Private sector* organisations are owned by private individuals, or groups of them. *Public sector* organisations are owned by central or local government. Table 2.1 shows the form organisations take in each of the two sectors.

Table 2.1 Private and public sector organisations

Private sector	Public sector
Sole traders	Local government
Partnerships	Central government departments
Private limited companies	Public corporations
Public limited companies	Quasi-autonomous agencies
Co-operatives	
Franchises	

In the UK economy each of the many different types of organisation has its own set of objectives. Indeed, different organisations in the same sector of the economy may adopt different aims and objectives. The public sector organisations are government run or controlled organisations that exist to provide services that are non-profit making and are usually funded from taxation. Private sector organisations are firms that are set up in order to make profits for their owners.

There are subdivisions of these sectors that fit neither definition. Part of the private sector is made up of non-profit making organisations such as building societies, co-operative organisations, some types of housing association, etc. Their prime objective is to provide a service to their members or clients rather than make profits. In order to do so, they may need to accumulate quite large surpluses of cash to provide stability and fund future activities. They do not distribute profits or dividends, however, and do not have any owners as such other than their members.

Another subsector is the *voluntary sector* which includes organisations like charities, clubs, societies, and some types of housing association that offer a social service to the community, etc.

Objectives of public sector organisations

The aims and objectives of all public sector organisations other than central government are contained in the Act of Parliament that created them.

The National Health Service (NHS) was created in the late 1940s but was totally reorganised in the 1974 Act that created the basis of the current structure. Various amendments have been introduced since then that have produced the system described later in this element.

Local government was inherited by the Normans from the former Saxon and Viking organisations following the Conquest. By the Middle Ages it had developed into a patchwork of councils that provided services in the major cities. In 1603 the first local rating system of taxation allowed the councils to raise their own income to pay for services that were provided by employees. In the 1800s many new services were needed and new powerful local councils were formed to provide them. By the end of that century the modern system of local government and local government finance had been established. All of these developments were initiated by the various Local Government Acts, the last major Act being the 1973 Act.

In the UK central government has evolved since 1066 with a number of major changes over the years, the most important being the change of power from the monarchy to parliament after the Civil War in the 1640s, and the creation of the Civil Service in the 1830s. Over the years the way in which government has developed has been a piecemeal process that has never been written down in any charter or document. It constantly changes to meet new circumstances which are often forced on the government of the day by political expediency.

All these organisations have clear objectives which they set out for the public. There may be a need to balance some of the objectives, however. For example, one objective would be to provide a wide ranging service for the needs of the population but this needs to be set against the important objective of all public sector organisations – to run the most efficient and cost-effective service in line with central government budget constraints.

Today many public sector organisations are organised and run on very similar lines to private sector organisations; the argument is that private sector organisations are more accountable in that if the directors get their policies wrong, they can be dismissed by their shareholders. Recent examples include NHS trusts, the Benefit Agency, local management of schools and colleges, etc.

ACTIVITY 2.1.1

Obtain an information leaflet from your local town hall on the services that your local council offers (every town hall has one), and from your study of this information write a list of what you consider to be the council's objectives and how it tries to achieve them.

PC 2.1.1

The objectives of private sector organisations

The aims and objectives of the organisations in the private sector are much easier to define in that the main long-term aim is to make as much profit for their owners as possible.

The most common objectives of private sector organisations are summarised below.

Profit maximisation

Most business organisations aim to maximise their profits. This is particularly important to business which are owned by shareholders who expect a good dividend payment at the end of the year, which in turn depends on good profits. Good profits mean that the directors or owners can 'plough back profits' into the business and help it expand and grow larger and become more secure.

It also gives a good indication to external investors, trade creditors and other creditors to the business. If the business is making healthy profits the bank manager will look more favourably towards lending capital to the business because he or she knows the money will be secure. Most importantly, good profits mean the owners can obtain a return on all their hard work and effort and on their initial capital outlay.

Survival

Many people believe this is the main objective because if the business cannot survive, no other objectives can be achieved. Many people are happy not to maximise their profits but to achieve a satisfactory level of profits – sufficient to keep them in business and provide the owners and workers with a reasonable standard of living. Such people enjoy good holidays and reasonable working hours rather than killing themselves by working very long hours and destroying their family life.

The nature of the market might also dictate a survival strategy. If the market is very competitive and there is a lot of fierce price competition, the business may not be in a position to adopt a profit maximisation policy; it may only be able to set its prices at the break-even level and survive on a day-to-day basis. The hope is that such fierce competition will eventually drive some of its competitors out of the business.

Market domination

A firm may adopt a strategy of market domination which may be pursued for the purposes of profit maximisation but not necessarily so.

In a large company, managers may be rewarded on the total number of sales, i.e. total revenue, and adopt the appropriate strategies to achieve this. For example, a business may cut prices to undercut competitors and gain an increased market share. It may even adopt a loss-leadership policy. This will often be a short-term strategy to undercut rival firms and once they are out of the market the firm will have the monopoly situation and can then increase its prices substantially.

Operating at a satisfactory level

Some business owners or managers will want to operate at a level they consider satisfactory, that is to achieve certain sales and profits which are not at the optimum level. The business is underachieving and not making maximum profits. Managers may be happy to achieve a certain level of profits and once this is achieved they will adopt different policy objectives which may be counter to their organisational goals.

The desire to achieve more power and status by getting a better office or company car or other company perks is a good example. To achieve this objective, part of the organisation's profits, which would have been paid to shareholders, is diverted to the managers. Since managerial satisfaction pushes up the costs of production and ultimately the price charged, it is usually associated with businesses which operate in a less competitive area.

Non-profit maximising objectives

Charities are non-profit making organisation and they aim to provide a quality service for their customers. They are regulated by the state: all charities must be registered with the

Registrar of Charities who will decide whether they are a genuine charity and whether they are being run satisfactorily. All genuine charities enjoy tax benefits both for charities and for those who donate to the organisations. For example, under the 1996 Finance Act, those who wish to give to charities can donate as a tax-free deduction from pay.

> **ACTIVITY 2.1.2**
>
> Using, as an example, a private sector firm that you either work for or have worked for, write a description of what you see as its business objectives and explain how it attempts to achieve them. If you have never worked in such an organisation, you must interview someone who has.

PC 2.1.1

BUSINESS OWNERSHIP IN THE PRIVATE SECTOR

Sole trader

A business that is described as a sole trader is a business that has one owner – the sole trader. This does not mean that the firm has only one worker; the sole trader can employ as many people as he or she requires or, for that matter, can afford. This form of ownership is the most common form of business ownership in the UK. The sole trader benefits from all the profits the business makes but has to put up the capital to start the business and is also personally responsible for any debts that the business may incur.

Many small businesses trade as sole traders. Most sole traders tend to be in the construction and retail industries. Examples of sole traders include plumbers, electricians, bricklayers, market traders and grocers, florists, butchers, hairdressers, off-licences, window cleaners and restaurants.

The sole trader's business can trade under the owner's name or the owner can choose a business name, (for example, Peter Horton could trade as Horton Enterprises). Although this name does not have to be registered, a business is not allowed to use a business name which is registered to someone else, and it is advisable, therefore, for a business to register a name if it is different from the owner's name in order to protect the position of the business.

If you are operating as a sole trader, the benefits are that it is a simple form of business to establish and there are no formal legal restrictions. You can enjoy all the profits and there is no legal requirement to keep accounts other than to inform the tax inspector of the tax liability of the business (which will in fact be your personal income tax liability). The Inland Revenue will require acceptable accounts and taxation computation, however, and this will usually mean that you have to pay an accountant to draw up the final accounts and audit the books in order to avoid paying too much taxation and to satisfy the tax inspector at the Inland Revenue. As a sole trader there is nothing to stop you carrying out this work yourself if you have the required skills.

Fig 2.1

Being a sole trader also brings problems – mainly your difficulty in finding the necessary capital to start the business and the requirement on you if you do borrow from the bank, to put up some form of collateral such as your house and other personal possessions. Furthermore, you have unlimited liability, which means that if the business goes into receivership you will not only lose all of the money you have invested in the business but could, if the business owes more than its asset value, lose your own personal assets. A sole trader could be made personally bankrupt due to the failure of the business. You will probably have to work very long, and in many cases unsocial hours. If you become ill or want to go on holiday you will have to pay someone to look after the business. Can you put trust in such hired help? Running your own business can be very stressful.

Advantages and disadvantages of sole traders

Advantages	Disadvantages
■ They are easy to set up and require little paperwork.	■ One person takes all the decision-making responsibility.
■ All profits accrue to the sole trader.	■ One person is responsible for providing all the capital.
■ Decisions are made quickly.	■ Working long hours is necessary.
■ Close contact is kept between owner, employees and customers.	■ Unlimited liability for debts.

Partnerships

A partnership is a way of sharing the risk, skills and the workload involved in running a business. Many partnerships tend to be in the retail industries but there is also a high proportion of partnerships in agriculture, catering and the construction industry. Partnerships consist of between two and twenty partners but firms of partners within the various professions can be larger. Indeed, partnerships tend to be most common in the professional services where there is a legal barrier to most of them forming limited companies; examples include firms of solicitors, accountants, stockbrokers, doctors and dentists.

Although oral partnership agreements are legally binding it is necessary to draw up a formal partnership agreement. This involves writing out a deed of partnership drawn up with the help of a solicitor or an accountant. This document sets out the details of the partnership agreement and includes important items such as the amount each partner has put into the business, the responsibilities of each partner and how profits and losses are to be distributed between them.

Partnerships can trade under their own names or under a business name subject to the same restrictions as sole traders. If the partnership chooses a business name such as the Bradford Estate Agency, all of the partners must be shown on all business stationery.

There are two types of partnership: ordinary and limited. Under the *ordinary* partnership all partners must have unlimited liability and can take a full part in the running of the business. Under a *limited* partnership the sleeping partner can enjoy limited liability but he must not take an active role in the running of the business – hence, the name. The sleeping partner can provide the business with a valuable injection of capital, however. This can be particularly important when the business is growing.

The benefits of running a partnership are that more capital is available than with a sole trader and there are relatively few legal restrictions. The provisions of the Partnership Act 1894 still apply, however. There is also the opportunity for individual partners to specialise and gain more expertise than would be possible under a sole trader – one person cannot be an expert in everything. For example, individual partners in a firm of accountants could specialise in specific areas such as taxation, investment advice, property, etc. The responsibilities and stress involved in running the business are shared

Fig 2.2 Ernst & Young

among partners. There is a greater possibility of borrowing more money from the bank because each partner could put up some form of security as collateral.

The main problems running a partnership are that each partner must be consulted and there is obvious scope for disagreement which can affect the smooth running of the business and can even close the business down. All profits are shared between partners according to their partnership agreement. One partner, however, may not be as good or as hard working as the other partners yet receive a similar share of the profits. Even worse, one partner may be dishonest or negligent and cause problems in the partnership and all the other partners will then have to share the resulting liability. All partners (other than a sleeping partner) have unlimited liability so, if the partnership incurs debts, all partners are liable including their own personal assets.

Advantages and disadvantages of partnerships

Advantages	Disadvantages
■ The responsibilities are shared.	■ Disagreements between partners can occur.
■ Capital, skills and workload are shared.	■ Unlimited liability.
	■ Business decisions take longer.
	■ Large amounts of capital are difficult to raise.

Fig 2.3 'Disagreements between partners can occur'

ACTIVITY 2.1.3

You want to go into business as a manufacturer of paper bags. You have a definite market in mind – a number of local market traders who have been complaining about the poor service they receive from current suppliers. Recently, one of these suppliers was made bankrupt and you could purchase all of the required machinery cheaply and install it in your garage. A friend wants to join you in this enterprise. Write down all of the advantages and disadvantages of forming a partnership for this business as opposed to operating as a sole trader.

Limited liability companies

When a business with unlimited liability goes into liquidation because it is unable to repay its debts, the owners of the business may have to give up their personal possessions in order to repay any money that is owed. Sole traders and partners can usually have only unlimited liability. If a business has limited liability then the owners of the organisation have their personal possessions legally protected in the event of bankruptcy and they will only be liable for the amount of capital they have risked in the organisation. Private limited companies, public limited companies and co-operatives normally have the protection of limited liability.

The reason for starting up a company is to run a business for a profit. The owners of a company are its shareholders. The shareholders have each bought a piece of the company and own a certificate which states that they are part owners of a business. Some shareholders may own more shares in the company than others. The shareholder with the largest number of shares will have a controlling interest and be able to control the company's management. There must be at least two shareholders but there is no legal maximum.

Once it is set up, a company exists as a legal entity in its own right. Anyone wishing to deal with the company addresses 'the company' rather than the shareholders who own it. Shareholders are protected by limited liability and only risk their shares in the event of the company becoming insolvent. A limited company is defined as a corporate body which means it has its own legal identity and can sue or be sued in its own name. All limited companies must register with the Registrar of Companies at Companies House to whom the company must send certain information every year to comply with the Companies Acts.

A sole trader or partnership is controlled and run by the owners but a limited company is owned by the shareholders but run by a board of directors who make the major policy decisions and request the shareholders to approve their actions at the Annual General Meeting. These annual general meetings are often attended by only a small percentage of the total shareholders. This is particularly the case with a large public limited company which may have a million shareholders!

There are two forms of limited companies: (Ltd) and (PLC).

Private limited companies (Ltd)

As the name suggests, a private limited company can only have a private issue of shares. Shares in this type of company cannot be sold on the stock exchange but in most cases may be traded with the consent of the board of directors. Private companies can be any size but are normally smaller than public companies. They are often family concerns with the family owning enough of the shareholding to maintain overall control of the business. This means that the shareholders of private limited companies are usually family and friends.

Private companies are controlled by the board of directors which is a body set up to protect the interests of the shareholders. The Managing Director is responsible for running the business and is appointed by the rest of the board. The shareholders are allowed to address the board of directors over its running of the business at times such as the Annual General Meeting. If the shareholders do not agree with the actions of the board of directors they can vote it out of office at a general meeting. It is, therefore, in the directors' interest to run the company in accordance with the shareholders' wishes.

Many private limited companies are small in size and their shares cannot be sold on the Stock Exchange. Many people are tempted to establish a private limited company rather than trade as a sole trader or partnership because they enjoy limited liability status, so if the business fails they only lose the amount of their investment in the business and not their own personal assets. In the UK economy private companies outnumber public companies in a ratio of about 20 to 1.

The main advantages of private limited companies include being able to raise cash through issuing shares and the protection of limited liability for shareholders. The main disadvantages include being costly to set up, having to keep proper accounts and pay auditors, having to produce reports and hold meetings in accordance with the Companies Acts and having to share out profits as dividends among shareholders.

Public limited companies (Plc)

Public companies are similar to private companies but are usually larger and are quoted on the Stock Exchange. The owners of public limited companies, as the name suggests, are shareholders who can be members of the general public or financial institutions such as banks, pension fund managers and insurance companies, or even other companies. The company shares can be freely bought or sold on the stock market. This means that public limited companies are able to raise large amounts of capital quickly and relatively easily, and this gives them a large amount of financial power.

In order to become a public limited company the business must raise a minimum of £50 000 in share capital and obtain a Certificate of Incorporation (which a private limited company also needs) and a Certificate of Trading. Most of the familiar household names are PLCs, e.g. Marks & Spencer, Sainsbury's, BP, British Gas, British Telecom, BHS, British Airways.

The advantages of forming a PLC are that shareholders enjoy limited liability status and a limited company can often obtain additional capital more easily, particularly in the case of a large PLC. It can issue more shares on the stock market, for example.

Large PLCs can afford to employ the best managers with the necessary expertise to analyse the market and make the best and most informed business decisions possible. Shareholders are free to sell their shares or buy more shares in the company when they wish. The demand or lack of demand from potential purchasers of a company's shares determines the share price on the stock exchange computer. The higher the demand the higher the share price. The disadvantages of forming a limited company are the number of legal requirements needed when forming such a business, particularly if it is a PLC. There are also ongoing legal and financial requirements under the Companies Acts that make the accounts of the business far less private than either a partnership or a sole trader. All financial records and the directors' report must be audited and made available to the Registrar of Companies at Companies House. Additionally these documents must be freely available for anyone to inspect and scrutinise.

A further disadvantage of being a PLC is that the original shareholders can lose control of the organisation if large numbers of shares are bought by a rival organisation wishing to take over control. Such take-overs usually start when another company buys up a substantial amount of the company's shares. It must then make a final offer to the existing shareholders for the remaining shares. The directors of the company under threat of take-over will advise shareholders whether or not to accept the offer. If it is a hostile bid they will do their best to fight it off. At the end of the day, however, it is up to the shareholders to decide whether to accept or reject an offer from the take-over company.

ACTIVITY 2.1.4

Research a recent take-over bid and write a short report stating why it was successful/unsuccessful. What steps did both companies take to win their argument with the shareholders? Make notes on your research and use them as a basis of a class discussion on company take-overs.

Co-operatives

The number of businesses taking the form of co-operatives has increased in the UK in recent years but still remains small in number relative to other business types. There are three basic types of co-operative: consumer, worker and marketing co-operatives.

Consumer co-operatives

This type of co-operative operates High Street retail outlets which offer consumers a share of the profits in the company in return for their loyal custom. This can take the form of traditional dividend on purchases or a range of other member benefits.

Worker co-operatives

This type of organisation is actually owned, controlled and run by the employees themselves. This is achieved by each employee becoming a stakeholder in the business. All employees are given the opportunity of membership and issued with a single vote.

Fig 2.4

Profits are distributed equally among the members and major decisions relating to the running of the business are decided democratically at meetings where all the members can be present. Some worker co-operatives have been formed by the redundant employees of manufacturing businesses that have been forced to close down (for example, Norton, who manufacture motorcycles). Other workers may join together to produce a particular product or service (for example, a baby-sitting service or hand-crafted goods).

Marketing co-operatives

This type of co-operative consists of separate producers of similar or identical products who join together to market their produce. The most common type of marketing co-operative consists of farmers who set up a marketing board, for example, to advertise, promote, sell and distribute their product. This category also includes organisations such as the Spar shops at the other end of the distribution line. These are small independently owned retail shops who band together in order to take the advantages of bulk purchasing and the branding and marketing of both the shops and their products.

Fig 2.5 Shops which band together, like the Spar chain, enjoy the benefits of bulk purchasing and advertising

Franchising

Many new firms are set up as franchise operations where an owner can purchase a business idea, the product or service and marketing expertise from another business. The best example of this type of business is McDonald's where the business is locally owned and run but the owner is contracted to McDonald's for the supply of shop fittings and equipment and the fast food products themselves.

Business organisations, such as McDonald's, are so successful that they are able to expand by selling rights to market their own product or service to others. These organisations are known as franchisers and the organisations they sell rights to are known as franchisees. Other examples of well known franchise networks include The Body Shop, Prontaprint and Benetton.

Fig 2.6 Prontaprint – an example of a well known franchise

For a fee the franchiser allows the franchisee to sell its product or service, trade under the same name and use exactly the same business image. In some cases the franchisee may also have to pay a proportion of profits back to the franchiser. In return for these arrangements the franchisee usually gets the right to be the sole provider of the product or service in a locality.

Advantages and disadvantages of franchises

Advantages

- The certainty of knowing the product or service is a proven success.
- Membership of a network of organisations all engaging in the same activity.
- Advice on the selection and purchase of stock.
- Training given by the franchiser.
- Use of the franchiser's greater advertising and bulk purchasing power.
- Benefits from the franchiser's research and development efforts.
- Assistance and direction with setting up businesses.
- Greater credibility with financial institutions when seeking capital.

Disadvantages

- Less independence and freedom to make own decisions.
- The success of the franchisee depends on the continuing success of the franchiser.
- If a single franchisee acts in a disreputable way then this reflects on all the other franchisees in the network.

> **ACTIVITY 2.1.5**
>
> Your father has just been made redundant after working 30 years as a coal miner. He intends to use his redundancy money and his savings to open a new pizza franchise restaurant in your area. List the problems and benefits that will apply to this proposal.

PUBLIC SECTOR ORGANISATIONS

The main public sector organisations in the UK are:

- the central government, its departments of state and their various agencies;
- the National Health Service (NHS);
- the various local authorities.

Even after the privatisation and public sector cutbacks of the 1980s and 1990s the public sector still represents almost one half of the country's economic activity. The National Health Service is the largest single employer in the European Union. The various local authorities are usually the largest employer in their own locality, employing teachers, social workers, road maintenance and building workers, etc. Today central government

Fig 2.7 Central government, located in the House of Commons, is a large public sector organisation

controls the activities of all public sector organisations through the allocation of finance and the detailed regulations that it issues to other organisations.

The public sector consists of organisations that are owned or controlled by the government or local authorities. It can be argued that there are some services to which every UK citizen is entitled, for example, health care and education. Other services can only be provided for properly if the government carries out this provision, such as policing and defence. These arguments provide justification for the existence of the public sector.

Government ownership of organisations on behalf of the nation has diminished greatly since 1979 through the pursuit of the policy of *privatisation*. Privatisation means that a government-owned industry is sold off to private individuals, usually by the sale of shares via a major issue. Nearly all large public sector companies have been privatised since 1979, including British Telecom, British Gas, British Steel, Rolls-Royce, Cable and Wireless, the water utilities in England and Wales and the electricity companies. (When an organisation is taken out of private ownership and into public sector ownership, this is referred to as *nationalisation* – no longer a favoured policy in the UK and other European countries.) The remaining public sector activities can be categorised broadly into four types: public corporations, central government departments, the health service and local government authorities.

Public corporations

Some important institutions are owned by the government on behalf of the people. A public corporation is an organisation established by the government through an Act of Parliament to run and control a particular public service or industry. Industries that exist as public corporations are known as nationalised industries. As public corporations are in the public sector their managers are accountable to the government rather than shareholders.

Although the state owns public corporations their managers are given a great deal of freedom of control of the organisation. In the past public corporations were expected to contribute towards government policies such as maintaining full employment and the provision of public services in the interests of social responsibility rather than profit. They were assisted in these provisions by large financial subsidies from government. Today public corporations are encouraged to concentrate on objectives such as profitability or other financial targets and subsidies from government are no longer available.

Examples of public sector corporations are becoming harder to find as most have been transferred to the private sector through the operation of the government policy of privatisation. The BBC is an example of an existing public corporation at the time of writing. Prior to the privatisation programme the nationalised industries formed a substantial part of the public sector. Most of these have now become very large PLCs; indeed most of the largest private sector firms are former public sector utilities.

Central government

The UK central government is formed by the political party that has the largest number of members elected to the House of Commons. The leader of that party becomes the Prime Minister who appoints other members of parliament and members of the House of Lords to be ministers in the government. The most senior ministers are the various Secretaries of State, the Home Secretary and the Chancellor of the Exchequer. A committee of about twenty of the most important ministers form the Cabinet which is chaired by the Prime Minister and is the senior policy-making unit of government.

Ministers are supported by senior Civil Servants who give advice and arrange for the implementation of government policy. Other Civil Servants in the various departments of state carry out these policies. Government departments have a reputation for being large, bureaucratic, slow moving organisations. In order to help dispel this image, some government departments are being partly privatised by having contracts for their services put out to tender. Many of these departments have recently been formed into agencies, such as the Benefits Agency for the provision of social services. These reorganisations are a government attempt to update the way that the Civil Service operates, to make the management more accountable and to increase the efficiency of the service.

Examples of government departments include the Department of Trade and Industry which regulates all UK business activity and the Inland Revenue which collects some UK taxes.

Control over the spending of the Civil Service is exercised by the Chancellor with the help of the Treasury. Expenditure plans for each department are approved in the budget. No other expenditure is lawful. The income needed to finance the costs of the spending departments is raised from general taxation such as VAT and Income Tax. The levels of taxation are also approved in the budget. The budget for both income and expenditure is completed in November and relates to the financial year that starts in the following April.

The National Health Service

The National Health Service (NHS) is effectively controlled by the central government Department of Health, headed by the Health Secretary. The actual provision of services is delegated to the Regional Health Authorities. These in turn contract and finance the various District Health Authorities or the new NHS Trusts that can be established by the major hospitals. The service also finances the doctors, general practitioners' practices, dentists, prescriptions, the blood transfusion service and a range of community care services.

Other than prescription and dental charges, most NHS provision is free. The bulk of the cost of the service is financed through the central government's budgetary system, in that the Department of Health allocates part of its budget to the Regional Authorities, who in turn finance the services in their areas. Thus, the service is paid for with the receipts from general taxation.

There are two main problems that are currently affecting the NHS, and together these are causing a great deal of friction within the service. The first is the imposition of new management systems, whereby a new level of senior managers is attempting to introduce new managerial and financial practices into the service which are challenging the traditional autonomy of the senior doctors who are known as consultants. The second problem relates to the need to change the level of the current provision of services, particularly hospitals, from areas of declining population to areas of increasing population. This is particularly noticeable in the London areas where the decline in the population of inner London has been very dramatic, while the areas just outside the London boundaries have seen a large increase. This means closing some very well-known hospitals in order to transfer their resources to other centres.

Local government

We have over 400 different local authorities, each of which is controlled by a council of elected councillors who form themselves into committees to oversee the provision of council services. Councillors are elected representatives of the localities (wards) under the control of the authority. Councillors usually belong to one of the political parties and as in the House of Commons the party with the largest number of councillors will control the actions of the council. The councillors in turn employ officers to manage or work in the various departments (for example, planning or the environmental health department).

The councils generate part of their own income through charges for some of their services and from the imposition of local business rates for business properties and the Council Tax for domestic properties. Most of their income, however, comes from the Department of the Environment through the government grant. Local authorities are responsible for providing services to the local communities (for example, car parks, leisure centres, parks and social services provision). Many local authorities contract out some of their services to private sector organisations (for example, refuse collection or park maintenance). The process of 'contracting out' services is usually carried out on a tender basis with the organisation offering the best service for the best price eventually winning the contract. The tendering local authority or council normally allows its own employees to enter bids for contracts.

The local authority budgetary process starts each September and is completed by the following March when the council approves the amount of the Council Tax. The biggest influence on the budget is the amount of government grant that the authority will receive and this is notified to the authority about Christmas time. As with central government, once the council approves the budget the spending departments have the approval to spend the money on the purposes agreed in the budget. Any other expenditure is unlawful.

ACTIVITY 2.1.6

This is a group activity for the whole class. Each group must prepare a five-minute explanation of one of the following organisations in the public sector. You must explain to your colleagues what the organisation is, what it does, why it is needed and how it is financed.

- central government
- public corporations
- the NHS
- local government.

ORGANISATION STRUCTURES

All organisations are usually divided up into different departments, each having an important role to play within the organisation. Most sole traders have simple organisation structures in that there is the owner–manager who often undertakes the marketing and selling functions, plus a few production workers, a van driver and a part-time secretary to do the administration and bookkeeping.

It is only when the firm grows to a certain size that it needs different departments and departmental managers to run them. When this size is reached, communications within the firm and the co-ordination of the firm's activities become a major management problem.

The different types of business organisation that exist in the UK have already been described. This section explains the various structures that can exist within an organisation. An organisational structure can describe a variety of features applicable to an organisation including its size, functions, levels of authority, span of control and relationships. There are different kinds of structural 'models' that summarise the different ways in which these features can be arranged.

As outlined above, very small organisations may not be greatly concerned about structure. As organisations grow, however, the various functions become more clearly defined (for example, Finance, Sales, Marketing, Administration, etc.). A structure based on a more formal model begins to develop in order for management to gain control over activities, increase efficiency and identify areas of responsibility and accountability. An organisation may choose to follow one particular structural model rather than another or, alternatively, its structure may be less well planned and simply the result of adapting to circumstances over time. The main models of organisational structure that exist are summarised below.

Models of organisational structure

The design or plan of an organisation's structure varies according to the business activity or sector in which it operates.

In the real world no organisation will conform exactly to a description or 'model' of an organisational structure. Most will approximate, or look similar to, any given model rather than be identical to them. In this section several models of organisational structure are described in the context of how they affect the job roles of the employees in that structure. It is important to remember that the models are based on observations of different real-life organisations rather than the other way around!

When a firm is large and employs hundreds or thousands of employees, these problems of management become crucial to its success. How the firm's managers organise its departments and activities can affect its performance.

Hierarchical and flat structures

Hierarchies relate to levels or 'layers' of authority within organisations. A layer of authority relates to a position or post which has a management responsibility. For example, lower, middle and senior management represent three layers of authority. Some organisations may need many layers of management between the top and bottom jobs within the organisation; others need far fewer. Those organisations with many layers are commonly classified as having 'tall' or *hierarchical* structures as they have many layers making their organisation chart look relatively high. See Fig. 2.9. Organisations with fewer layers have a short or *flat* structure; they will tend to be less hierarchical in nature and have a shorter, squatter organisation chart. See Fig. 2.8.

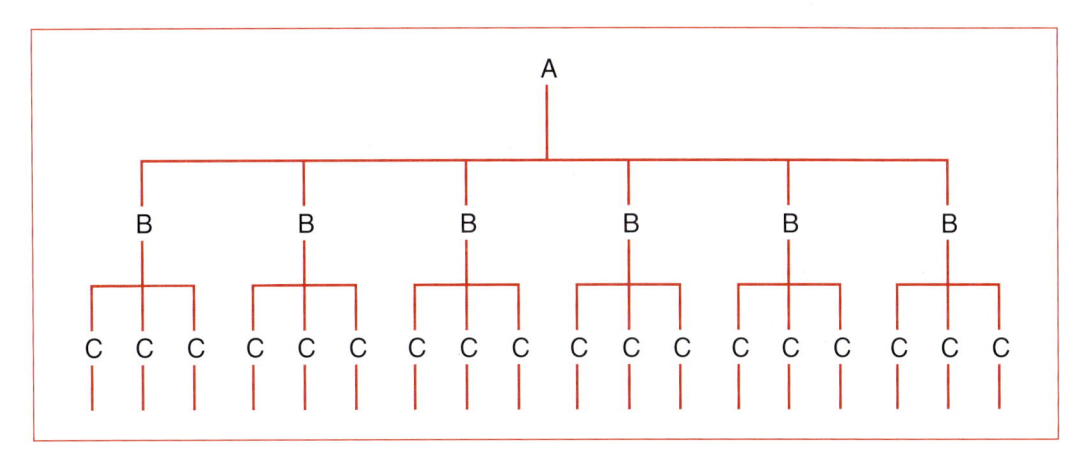

Fig 2.8 A 'flat' organisation structure

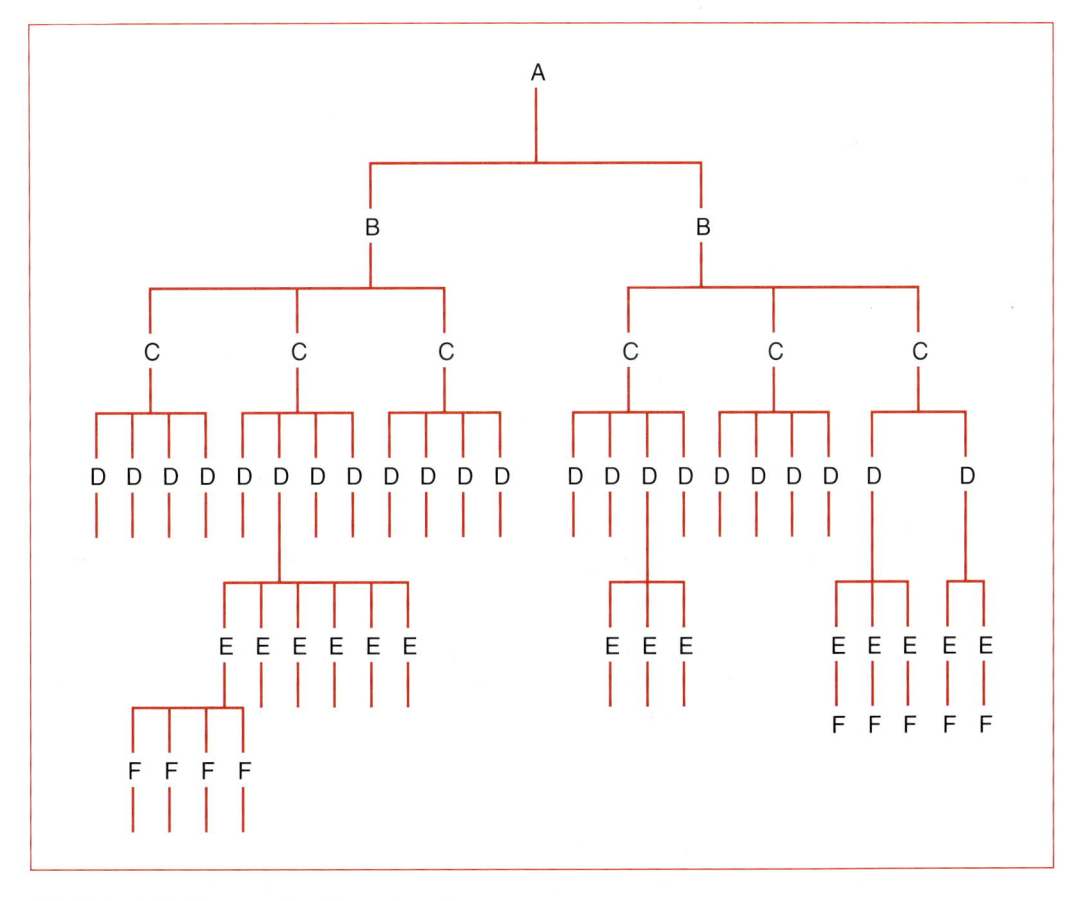

Fig 2.9 A 'tall' organisation structure

There will be other differences between tall and flat organisations that result from having relatively more or less layers of authority. These differences are explained below.

Span of control of managers

The span of control a manager has depends on the number of people that manager is responsible for and the number of different areas under his or her control. In an organisation with a tall structure managers will have a relatively narrow span of control compared to a manager in an organisation with a flatter structure. In Fig. 2.8 manager A has six subordinates. While in Fig. 2.9 manager A has just two.

The degree of delegation

Delegation within organisations involves passing down responsibility and authority for carrying out tasks or duties to those at a level lower down the structure. In an organisation with a tall structure there is certain to be a higher degree of delegation as there are more levels across which tasks and duties may be delegated down. As flat structures have relatively fewer layers the opportunities for delegation are diminished. Therefore less delegation can take place.

Length of communication lines

The length of communication lines has obvious implications for the speed at which messages can be passed through an organisation. Organisations with taller structures have a higher number of levels across which messages have to be passed. This means that communication lines will tend to be longer in tall than they are in flat organisational structures.

The degree of functional specialisation

Functional specialisation describes the extent to which the work an organisation carries out is broken down to provide clearly defined areas of specialisation. This usually follows natural lines – for example, the finance function deals only with work related to financial matters, the personnel function only with personnel/human resource matters, etc. Organisations with tall structures tend to have a high degree of functional specialisation among functions. For example, the finance function may be further subdivided into other smaller specialist functions. On the other hand, organisations with flatter structures will tend to have a lower degree of functional specialisation and, as a result, their employees will tend to be more flexible between job roles and be 'generalists' rather than 'specialists'.

Centralised and devolved structures

In addition to the number of layers of authority, organisations can be characterised by the structure of the power relationships within them. The majority of the power can be held centrally in one place (usually at the top layers of the organisation) or shared out, that is, devolved down to the layers further down the organisation. Hierarchical organisations have a tendency to be more centralised than devolved, whereas flat organisations are more likely to have a more devolved structure of power relationships. The main differences between centralised and devolved structures are explained below.

Co-ordination and control

The operations of a centralised structure will be co-ordinated from a centralised administration. The various divisions or functions of the organisation will be under the control of the central administration and will use it as a common centre from which to receive direction and to report back. In a devolved structure the divisions or functions of the organisation will be more autonomous and each will be responsible for its own co-ordination and administration.

There are advantages and disadvantages to both structures. A centralised administration has the advantage of saving on duplication of effort as all the administration for the organisation is carried out in one place, requiring no further co-ordination. A devolved structure may require additional co-ordination among the divisions or functions to ensure the efficient operation of the whole organisation. This will mean more demands on resources.

A large, centralised administrative centre may tend to be bureaucratic and its control and co-ordination of divisions compromised by ineffective communication links. The organisation's response to changing circumstances will be slower as a result. Devolved co-ordination gives the opportunity for a more 'hands-on' approach to control and more effective communication links. The organisation will therefore be able to respond to changing circumstances far more quickly.

Motivation of managers

It can be argued that centralised power structures will tend to weaken the motivation of managers. As the majority of the important decisions are made centrally, the managers may feel less personally responsible or accountable for the success of the division or function they have in their charge. Managers may also experience frustration in dealing with a slow moving bureaucratic centre. On the other hand, it can be argued that a devolved power structure acts to motivate and strengthen managers. All the responsibility and accountability for the success of their division or function rests to a much greater extent on their own shoulders. This can provide a much greater incentive to improve performance and efficiency. The frustration managers experience through dealing with a bureaucratic centre is likely to be reduced or absent as control is far more direct and communication links far shorter in a devolved structure. (It should be noted that motivation is not purely dependent on work environment. Many other factors, both internal to the individual concerned and external to the place of work, can also affect motivation levels (for more information on what motivates employees to perform well *see* Element 4.1).)

Static and dynamic structures

Some organisations are more responsive to change over time than others and this can be due, in part at least, to their structure. Organisations that evolve and adapt quickly in response to changing circumstances can be said to have a 'dynamic' structure. At the other end of the spectrum, organisations that remain consistent and adapt only very slowly in the face of changing circumstances can be said to have a more 'static' structure.

Whether an organisation's structure tends to be closer to a static or dynamic model will greatly depend on the activity it is involved in. For example, some business activities are strongly traditional and operate on a basis of convention such as a barrister's chambers or a firm of stockbrokers. Other business activities are more subject to periods of rapid evolution such as the creative or media industry. If the business activity itself is subject to dynamic change then the organisation will have a structure that is able to respond promptly to that change. Where the activity the organisation is involved in changes far more slowly, perhaps only in a quite gradual manner, the organisational structure will have a far more static nature.

The differences between job roles of employees will be dependent to some extent on what form the prevailing culture of the organisation takes. Organisations with a static structure will tend to have a higher respect for procedure and convention. Job roles will tend to be quite rigid and formal relationships and functional differences between job roles will be recognised. Managers are likely to take a specialist approach within their functional areas. Within this culture the emphasis will tend to be on the individual efforts and achievements of employees. Differences in status and privilege between employees will also be respected and valued. Communications in a static structure will tend to be formalised with information flowing vertically, up and down the organisation. Drawing up an organisation chart for a static structure is fairly easy to do due to the mechanical way in which this kind of organisation operates.

By comparison, organisations with a dynamic structure will conform far less to procedure and convention, the focus being on evolving processes and responding to change. Job definitions will be more flexible, with informal relationships and flexibility across functions. Managers are likely to take a generalist rather than specialist approach to their role. Within this culture the emphasis will tend to be on team rather than individual efforts of employees. Differences in status and privilege between employees will be suppressed and devalued. Communications in a dynamic structure will tend to be open and informal with more information flowing laterally within the organisation. Drawing up an organisation chart for a dynamic structure is more difficult to do due to the organic way in which this kind of organisation operates.

ACTIVITY 2.1.7

Using your school or college as an example, write about 500 words explaining the model that best fits its structure.

Self assessment questions

1 Which of the following organisations is in the public sector of the economy?
   a The Bradford Hospital Trust
   b The Bradford and Bingley Building Society
   c The West Yorkshire Co-operative Society
   d Yorkshire Cable PLC

2 Which of the following organisations is in the private sector of the economy?
   a The City of Bradford Metropolitan Council
   b Yorkshire Bank PLC
   c Bradford & Ilkley Community College
   d The British Heart Foundation

3 Consider the following statements.
   (i) Sole traders and partnerships have limited liability.
   (ii) If you are a shareholder in a company you may be liable for the company's debts.
   Which option best describes the two statements?
   a (i) True, (ii) True
   b (i) True, (ii) False
   c (i) False, (ii) True
   d (i) False, (ii) False

Element 2.1 Investigate business organisations

4 Which of the following organisations is responsible for the employment of secondary education teachers?
   a central government
   b the Educational Supply Association PLC
   c the local education authority
   d the Benefits Agency

5 Consider the following statements.
   (i) Anyone can buy shares in a private limited company.
   (ii) Shares in PLCs are bought and sold on the stock exchange.
   Which option best describes the two statements?
   a (i) True,   (ii) True
   b (i) True,   (ii) False
   c (i) False, (ii) True
   d (i) False, (ii) False

6 Consider the following statements.
   (i) The Managing Director of a PLC can be voted out of office at the AGM.
   (ii) Anyone can inspect the directors' report and accounts for a PLC.
   Which option best describes the two statements?
   a (i) True,   (ii) True
   b (i) True,   (ii) False
   c (i) False, (ii) True
   d (i) False, (ii) False

7 Which type of organisation structure best describes the local police force?
   a centralised
   b decentralised
   c flat
   d devolved

Assignment

PC
2.1.1
2.1.2
2.1.3

You are required to research the administrative structure of three organisations that you either work for or have some contact with. One should be a public sector organisation such as a school or college or your own or your parents' work-place. The other two should be different types of organisations in the private sector.

You must write comments on each of the three organisations directing your comments to the following:

1 an explanation of the organisations' broad financial objectives explaining profit and not-for-profit motives;

2 an explanation of any area of conflict between commercial, industrial or service objectives;

3 an explanation of how financial, legal and controlling differences can influence the objectives of the organisation;

4 a simple organisation chart for each organisation.

Element 2.2
INVESTIGATE ADMINISTRATION SYSTEMS

Performance criteria

1 **Identify administration systems which support functions of business organisation.**

2 **Explain suitability of one administration system in supporting functions in an identified business organisation.**

3 **Identify information technology developments changing administration systems.**

4 **Explain how administration systems can support change in business organisations.**

5 **Suggest improvements to an administration system.**

Introduction

Most organisations need a range of administration systems that are necessary to run the organisation. If you employ people, you obviously have to pay them, and in a larger organisation this will involve the interaction of the payroll department, the personnel department and the cashiers' office. Similarly, if goods are bought on credit, we need systems for receiving them and checking that they are correct and a system for paying the bills. This could involve the stores department, the buying department and the creditor payments department.

These functions are routine administrative functions. Some functions carried out in the organisation may not be of a routine nature such as research and development and product planning. All organisations should be capable of administering both routine and other functions even though most of their attention will inevitably be concentrated on their routine operations.

The following notes relate to a medium-sized firm that is large enough to require most of the normal administrative and production departments of a limited company in the private sector.

THE MANAGEMENT STRUCTURE AND ITS ROLE WITHIN THE ORGANISATION

An organisation is usually divided up into different departments, each having an important function to play within the organisation. The structure of the organisation will depend on its size and its type of business. The organisation chart in Fig. 2.10 shows a typical organisation structure for a company.

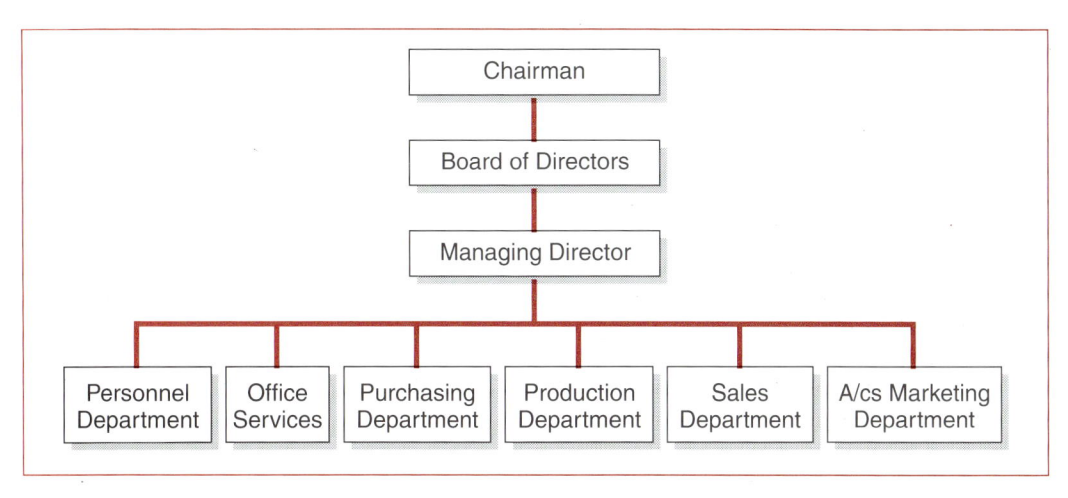

```
                        Chairman
                           │
                    Board of Directors
                           │
                    Managing Director
                           │
    ┌──────────┬──────────┼──────────┬──────────┬──────────┐
 Personnel   Office   Purchasing  Production   Sales    A/cs Marketing
 Department  Services Department  Department   Department Department
```

Fig 2.10 **A typical organisation structure for a company**

The Chairman and the board of directors

The Chairman is usually elected by the board of directors or is appointed by the majority shareholders. The Chairman is directly responsible to the shareholders for the direction of company policy and the performance of the company. His primary function at board meetings is to oversee the conduct of the meeting and provide leadership to the other board members. When voting on company matters, the Chairman usually exerts great influence over the other board members and in the event of a tied vote the Chairman will have the casting vote.

As all board members are appointed by the shareholders, the shareholders who own the majority of the shares in the company control the election of the Chairman and the board of directors. The Chairman's main task is therefore to ensure that the majority shareholders' interests and policies for the company are implemented in its policies. The Chairman and the board of directors appoint the company's management. The Managing Director is therefore responsible to the Chairman.

Quite often there are two types of company directors who serve on the board of directors. One type represents the management of the company (i.e. the Managing Director, Marketing Director, etc.) – these are direct employees with specialist knowledge or expertise. The other type of director is called a 'non-executive' director. These people are appointed for their advice and influence in the general business community. Some non-executive directors are in fact directors of many different companies. Their knowledge of the workings of other companies is regarded as a great benefit to the company. Obviously these people would not be appointed on to the board of directors if they were seen to have a conflict of interest between the various directorships. Many 'non-executive' directors are part-time appointments. The benefit of having 'non-executive' directors lies in their objectivity. They are not responsible for the day-to-day management of the company's departments, which quite often leads to a very narrow approach to decision making.

The board of directors' duties include:

- the introduction of a mission statement of the company;
- implementing a strategic plan;
- overseeing all capital expenditure;
- implementing suitable administration systems for the running of the company.

Managing Director

The Managing Director is appointed by the board of directors to oversee the smooth running of the departments within the organisation. In many companies, particularly the smaller limited companies rather than the larger PLCs, the Chairman of the board and the Managing Director are one and the same person. Often in small family firms this person is also the principal shareholder and has outright control over all aspects of company management. Most of our large nationally known companies are PLCs and most of these companies split the role of Chairman and Managing Director between two people.

When decisions are made at board level, it is the Managing Director's responsibility to see that these decisions are carried out. To do this effectively the Managing Director must liaise closely with all departmental managers. The Managing Director is responsible to the board for the effective execution of the policies set by the board and is seen as the main channel of communication between the company's senior employees and the board.

The duties of the Managing Director include the following.

- The Manging Director is responsible for the welfare of the staff in respect of their motivation and high morale.
- It is the responsibility of the Managing Director to promote the company both nationally and internationally by overseeing the advertising of the company/product and arranging trade fairs, etc. (in conjunction with the Marketing Department).
- The Managing Director creates up-to-date reports or statements to ensure that the board of directors is kept fully in touch with what is happening at the grassroots level.
- The Managing Director is responsible for the effective running of the departments in terms of meeting the aims and objectives of the company.

The Company Secretary

The Company Secretary takes care of all the legal matters of the company and is usually responsible for the administrative systems. Quite often in small and medium-sized companies that are not large enough to employ their own company accountant the Company Secretary also has responsibility for the accounting system. In such companies the Company Secretary may also act as the companies' personnel manager.

The duties of the Company Secretary include the following:

- to keep shareholders fully informed of what is going on in the company and give them up-to-date information relating to their shares;
- in companies that do not have a separate accountant, to keep records of financial matters (e.g. profit and loss accounts, etc.);
- to keep records of minutes of meetings;
- to deal with all legal and insurance matters;
- to keep a register of shareholders and issue new certificates when shares are bought and sold;
- to pay dividends to shareholders and interest to debenture holders or other external lenders;
- to keep personnel records and operate the payroll system in companies that are not large enough to employ their own Personnel Manager.

ACTIVITY 2.2.1

PC 2.2.1

This activity requires you to research the administrative structure of the organisation that you either work for or have some contact with, such as a school or college or your parents' work-place. You are required to produce an organisation chart for the organisation that shows how the functions of the organisation are carried out. (Note that Activity 2.2.2 also relates to your research and you are advised to read it prior to undertaking your research.) See Fig. 2.8 and 2.9 for an outline of organisation charts.

Executive directors and departmental managers

As explained above, some departmental managers are also board members and have titles like Marketing Director, while in other companies the same departmental managers may not have seats on the board and may have titles such as Marketing Manager. It is up to each company to organise itself as it requires. The roles of each type of executive will be the same – the difference being the access to the major decision-making committee which is the board of directors.

Each manager will be responsible for the running of his or her department. Some departments may be directly involved with production, while others may provide a service such as administration or finance. The activities of all departments should be integrated and controlled so that the organisation can achieve the objectives set by the board of directors and ultimately the organisation's owners.

The Personnel Department

The Personnel Manager is responsible for the organisation's personnel policy and its effective implementation. The Personnel Manager has to attempt to achieve the organisation's goals and objectives through the recruitment, motivation, organisation and training of the work-force. In addition most personnel managers are responsible for the organisation's manpower planning and the provision of sufficient skilled workers to meet the organisation's planned future needs. This may involve the recruitment and training of new workers or the planned reduction in the number of workers who conduct certain tasks that are no longer required. Personnel management is concerned with the development and maintenance of human relationships and the physical well-being of the workers in order to allow them to contribute most effectively to the company's profitability. The functions of the Personnel Department are listed below.

- *Employment* — Recruitment, selection, promotion, transfers, termination of employment and employee records.
- *Education and training* — Induction, apprentice schemes, on-the-job training, organising and supporting education and training courses for all types of employees.
- *Remuneration* — Job analysis, job evaluation, merit rating, bonus schemes, fringe benefits, salary scales and pay levels.
- *Industrial relations* — Policy, grievance procedure, joint consultation with unions and workers' representatives.
- *Staff welfare* — Canteen, social facilities, pensions, etc.
- *Health and safety* — Implementing the Health and Safety at Work Act.

Office services

The responsibility for providing clerical support services rests with the Office Manager, but in small firms this role may well be linked with that of the Company Secretary or the Company Accountant. The Institute of Administrative Management defines office management as 'that branch of management which is concerned with the services of obtaining, recording and analysing information, of planning, and of communicating, by means of which the management of a business safeguards its assets, promotes its affairs, and achieves its objectives'.

Further definitions are useful when considering office management and support services. The following are extracts from the Office, Shops and Railway Premises Act 1963.

Office premises means a building or part of a building the sole principal use of which is an office for office purposes.

Office purposes include the purposes of administration, clerical work, handling money and telephone and telegraph operating.

Clerical work includes writing, bookkeeping, sorting papers, filing, typing, duplicating, machine calculation, drawing and editorial preparation of matter for publication.

One of the main problems facing office managers is that of keeping pace with new technology as it affects office work, particularly in the areas of electronic equipment and communication systems. These areas of work are examined in more detail in the other two elements of this unit.

The Purchasing Department

Only when an organisation is large and specialist enough are the economies of scale sufficient to justify a separate purchasing department. In smaller organisations the purchasing functions will be carried out jointly by the office staff and the production staff. In some companies the Purchasing Department will also have responsibility for the stores records and storage facilities. The objectives of the Purchasing Department are:

- to buy materials at the lowest cost;
- to agree with the Production Department the quality and specification of materials purchased;
- to avoid waste and duplication of materials purchased and stored;
- to ensure that the Production Department has a constant and reliable supply of materials.

Using a centralised purchasing department brings certain advantages.

- Individual buyers can specialise in a limited range of materials.
- Centralised records make control easier.
- Lower prices can be agreed with suppliers due to larger quantities being purchased.
- It is easier to achieve standardisation of materials purchased.

The Sales Department

This department is often part of the Marketing Department and its activities are usually directed towards achieving the targets set by the board as advised by the Marketing Department. Much valuable information on customer opinions and demands can be collected by a good sales force. The sales personnel in the firm are the main link with the firm's market, and managers in the UK should take more notice of the information that is available to the sales force.

The organisation of the Sales Department will depend on the markets in which it operates. Is the firm a retail organisation that sells directly to the public and requires a large investment in buildings and in the number of sales personnel? Does the firm sell to just a few business customers and therefore requires a much smaller sales force? Are the operations of the firm local or national or does the firm export to a number of foreign countries? All of these questions will have an effect on the number of employees in the department, their location and duties. Many firms that sell to industrial and commercial customers use sales representatives who visit customers and offer advice on the technical specification of the firm's products.

The Marketing Department

As indicated above this department quite often controls the activities of the Sales Department. In recent years the influence of the Marketing Department has increased to the point where it almost controls the business strategy of the firm. The modern concept of marketing is that a firm should identify customer needs, develop appropriate products at the right price and promote and distribute them. All business activity should now be viewed as a customer-satisfying process and it is the marketing department's function to determine these needs. It is the Production Department's function to produce the goods or services that will satisfy these customer needs. The organisation of the Marketing Department will depend entirely on the size of the firm and the markets in which it operates.

In order to prosper, the department will collect and analyse data that relates to the firm's products and services in relation to those offered by the firm's competitors. Firms will seek a competitive advantage that will make its products stand out against those of its competitors. They will consider two major areas: the product and its competition. The *product* will be analysed as to its *price, promotion* and *place* (i.e. where it is sold). These are the four Ps of the marketing mix that you will become familiar with in Unit 3. The firm's competitors' products will also be analysed as will the competitors' apparent marketing strategy. This information should help the firm's managers develop a corporate strategy that will enable it to satisfy its existing customers and generate new customers.

The Accounts Department

All firms must keep accounts and the better firms will develop an accounting system to give its managers the management information that they need to enable them to make better decisions. Accountants are expensive to employ, however, and smaller firms cannot often appoint qualified staff to produce good quality information and advice. Indeed many managers do not understand accounting information and make decisions that are not based upon facts but upon poorly conceived opinions. In a well run organisation all managers will receive the information that they need in a format that they can understand and in a time scale that will allow corrective action to be taken when required.

Almost all accounting systems are run on computers and in many small and medium-sized firms the computer is under the control of the Accountant. When the firm grows or when its staff's ability to use the computer systems increases, the other departments will demand more control over the computer. This is usually the point at which an independent computer department is formed.

The Accounts Department keeps the double-entry bookkeeping system which includes the creditor payments system, the sales ledger and credit control system, the payroll system and the stores ledger. In addition it controls the cost accounts, the budget and the budgetary control systems and keeps management informed of the financial consequences of the firm's actions.

Budgets are financial forecasts that are used to allocate resources to departments and activities. Budgetary control is where the actual results shown in the accounts are measured against the budget. Any significant differences will be investigated and reported to management so that action can be taken to rectify the situation. In Units 6 and 7 you will see how a firm's costing systems, its budgets and budgetary control systems can be integrated in its normal financial accounting system.

ACTIVITY 2.2.2

Write a brief description of the administration and activities of the major departments of the organisation outlined in your answer to Activity 2.2.1.

Element 2.2 Investigate administration systems

THE EFFECT OF INFORMATION TECHNOLOGY ON ADMINISTRATION SYSTEMS

A business needs information so that its managers can make decisions on the present and future operations of the business. The quality of these decisions is dependent not only upon the manager's ability but also upon the quality of the information that is available to the manager and the speed with which the manager is given that information. The information itself must be concise, understandable and relevant to the business problems faced by the manager. Much of the administrative effort of a business is concerned with data processing and the management information system that aims to provide managers with the information that they need.

Organisations can use clerical staff to collect data, summarise and analyse it and then communicate the resultant information to others in the form of memorandums, letters or reports which can be filed away for future reference when they have been used and acted upon.

Today the employment of clerks to process information manually is diminishing, and they are being replaced by sophisticated systems of electronic data capture, analysis and information reporting, filing and retrieval methods.

- The high street banks are closing branches and using more 'hole-in-the-wall' card cash machines.
- Insurance is increasingly sold through 'direct line' companies whereby a single clerk takes the enquiry, opens a computer account, makes a quotation and sells the policy that is processed by the computer instantaneously.
- The use of 'bar codes' and their readers has transformed not only the checkout sales points at retail outlets but also allows the introduction of 'just-in-time' computerised stockkeeping systems that remove the need for shops and factories to hold large volumes of stock on their premises. Their computerised stock systems are updated on every sale that is made and, when the stock reorder level is reached, the computer automatically reorders the stock from the relevant supplier. These orders themselves can be made via computers that are linked together by modems.

All of these information processing systems and many like them were once carried out by clerks who are now becoming redundant following the introduction of new computer-based technology This technology has been found to be a much more effective means of processing data and providing the required management information. The main problem faced today is not the availability of information but the provision of too much information to managers. The challenge to the administrators of modern business systems is to give their managers only the information that supports their job, so that they do not become tied down to sifting through masses of information that may be of use to someone in the organisation but not to them. At the same time managers must know whom to contact and where to find information if it is not supplied to them on a routine basis.

ACTIVITY 2.2.3

PC 2.2.3

Write about 300 words to describe a clerical business system that has changed as a result of the introduction of new technology. Use the above examples as a guide to the type of system that has changed.

EVALUATION OF ADMINISTRATION SYSTEMS AND PLANNING FOR CHANGE

Job evaluation

This is one of the most difficult areas of business administration to assess. All business activity needs administrative support to some extent but the level of that support needs careful monitoring and control. Clerical staff can be expensive to employ and, if their contribution to the organisation is less than their cost of employment, their managers must conduct an investigation of the firm's administrative requirements. *Manpower planning* involves trying to ensure that there is a balance between the organisation's demand for appropriately trained labour and its supply. Where there is a mismatch of supply and demand, either staff will have to be retrained or they will have to be made redundant if their skills are no longer required. If there is a shortfall in staffing levels, new staff will have to be appointed and trained to the appropriate level.

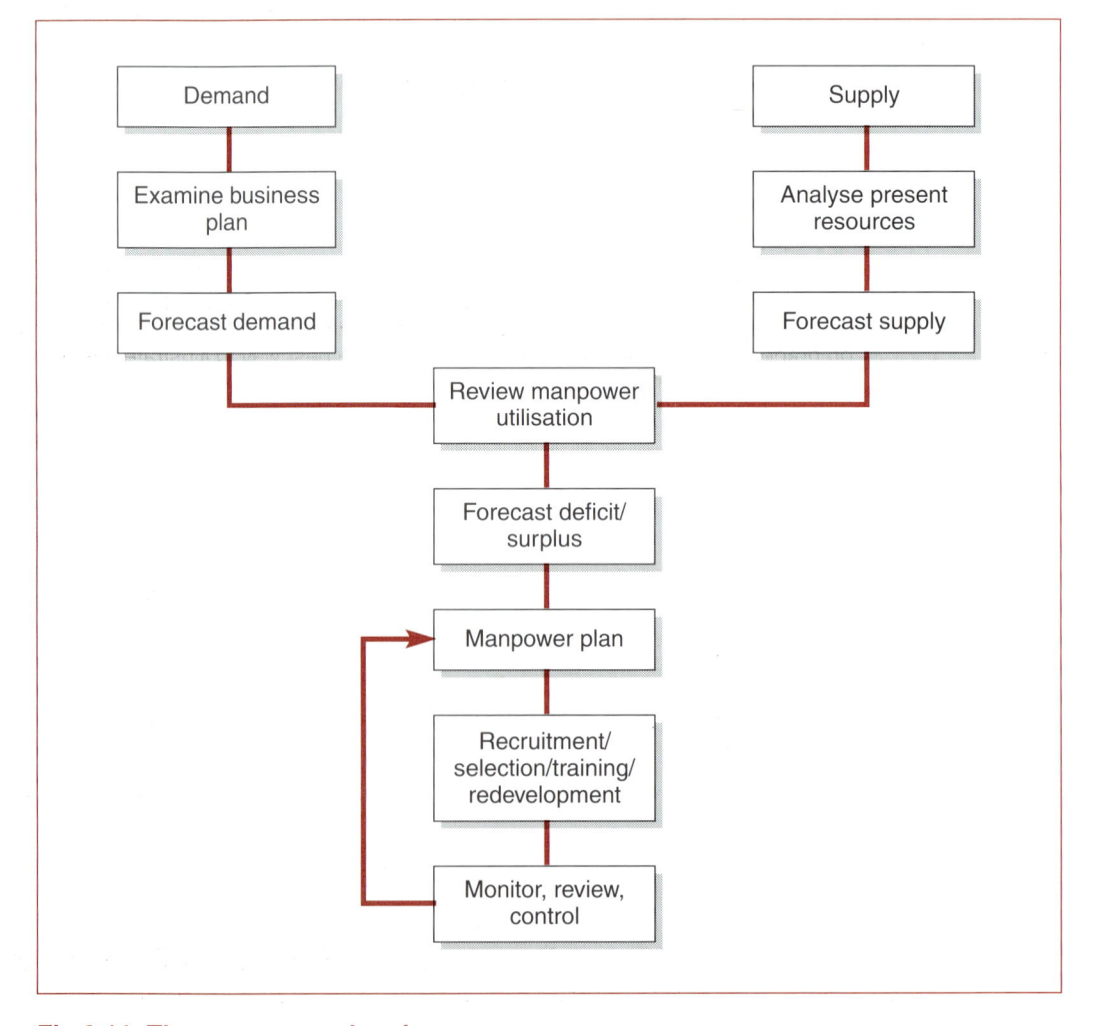

Fig 2.11 The manpower planning process

Element 2.2　Investigate administration systems

Attempts have been made to produce a system that evaluates the worth of a particular job in comparison with others in an organisation. The *ranking method* determines which job in the organisation is most important and then ranks all other jobs in order below it. Such a method is not easy to operate as it requires a comparison between different types of job. The *points rating system* allocates points to various aspects of a job, such as the responsibility for people, finance, skill, education and qualifications. *Pay band*s are used by local and central government and by most large companies. The first step is a job evaluation exercise which is then followed by the establishment of salary scales. This evaluation may use the techniques of points rating and, when the points allocated to a particular job achieve a final total that job is matched to its corresponding grade. This does mean that if the tasks allocated to a particular job are changed the grade of that job may also have to change as its new points score may have changed. The salary grades that are produced will be used in the production of an *establishment* that allocates so many jobs at a certain grade to a department (*see* Fig. 2.12).

The problem with the establishment of posts for departments is that, although it provides a greater amount of control over the organisation's employment costs, it slows down the organisation's ability to react to changing circumstances. New posts are difficult to create and old obsolete posts are seldom deleted. Furthermore, the effectiveness of individuals on the same grade may be vastly different – one being good, the other being poor. Systems of *merit payments* have arisen in order to recognise the claims of the better employee. Over a period of time, however, most employees are paid merit payments and this reduces their effectiveness. In addition to this, the amount of the payments is too low in most schemes to be effective.

The Establishment
A list of all the 'established grades' (i.e. jobs) within an organisation is called its establishment. Thus it can be said that the establishment of a particular department consists of a Head of Department, two principal officers, six senior officers, ten staff on grade 5, six on grade 3 and 14 on grade 1. The best way to illustrate this is to draw up an organisation chart:

```
                              Head of Department
                    ┌──────────────┴──────────────┐
            Principal Officer              Principal Officer
         ┌────────┼────────┐           ┌────────┼────────┐
   Senior    Senior    Senior     Senior    Senior    Senior
   Officer   Officer   Officer    Officer   Officer   Officer
      │         │         │          │         │         │
  3x Grade 5  2x Grade 5 2x Grade 5  1 Grade 5  1 Grade 5  1 Grade 5
      │         │         │          │         │         │
  1 Grade 3  1 Grade 3  1 Grade 3   1 Grade 3  1 Grade 3  1 Grade 3
      │         │         │          │         │         │
  3x Grade 1  3x Grade 1 3x Grade 1  2x Grade 2 2x Grade 2 2x Grade 1
```

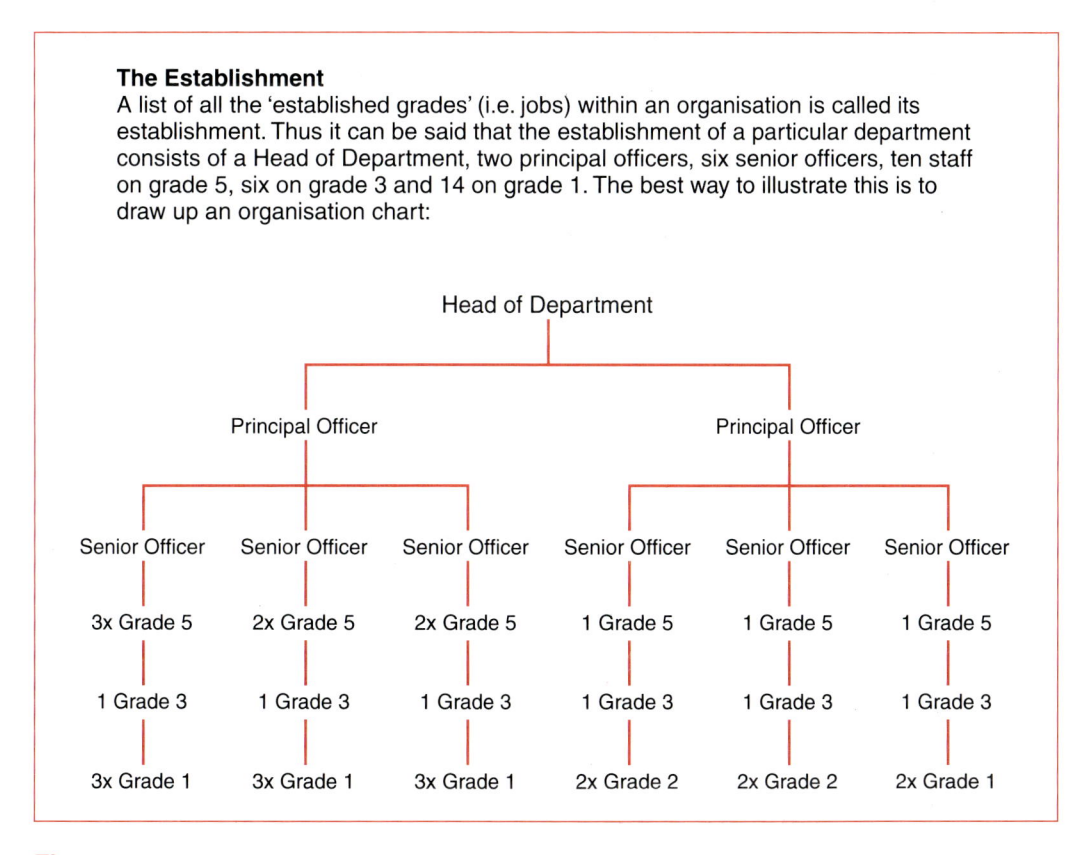

Fig 2.12

In most cases employers are forced to pay the *going rate* for the job. This is the effect of market forces, whereby if the pay rates are too low the firm's employees leave; if they are high the firm is wasting money by paying too much but, on the other hand, it will have lots of good applicants for any job that it wants to fill.

Established posts usually have job descriptions and personnel specifications that state what the person in the job is supposed to do and the type of person that the organisation wants to employ. Again this system provides better control over the employees but it can also lead to a greater degree of inflexibility in employment practices and make it more difficult for the employer to alter employment patterns within the organisation. This can be important when new technology and/or new systems are introduced, leading to a change in employees' work patterns and skills.

ACTIVITY 2.2.4

Explain in your own words how an organisation's supply and demand for labour can get out of balance, particularly when new systems are introduced.

Systems evaluation and improvements in effectiveness and productivity

Different types of organisations have evolved various methods to evaluate and improve their business systems. Some use *work study*, some *organisation and methods*, some *systems analysis* and others *internal audit*. Whatever methods are used, they all have the same objectives and use similar techniques to establish what the current systems are and how they can be improved in order to achieve greater efficiency and effectiveness.

Although some or all of the following activities may exist in large organisations, the functions that they carry out should be done by all organisations, large or small. How systems evaluation is organised is up to the management of each firm. Many managers of smaller firms undertake such activities themselves.

Work study

Work study is defined in the British Standard 3138 (1969) as:

> **a management service based on those techniques which are used in the examination of human work in all its contexts, and which lead to the systematic investigation of all the resources and factors which affect the efficiency and economy of the situation being reviewed, in order to effect improvement.**

Work study can improve the performance of many employees especially if they are involved in repetitive work. Work study engineers can advise on the use of new machinery and the physical layout of equipment within the work-place.

A business system needs to be reviewed in the following circumstances:

- if it fails to operate properly;
- if there is a change in requirements;

- in preparation for major equipment changes;
- in connection with changes in other procedures;
- at intervals of between one and five years to ensure that the systems used are still relevant.

Method study

The methods used to achieve the firm's objectives are investigated and recorded by the work study officer. This involves several stages and a number of interviews with the organisation's personnel to find out each person's view of:

- what is being done?
- how it is being done?
- why it is being done this way?
- when it is being done?
- who does it?
- what skills are required?
- who is responsible?

In many cases these investigations reveal considerable differences between the systems that the managers think are operating and the way in which the employees operate them.

Internal audit

Internal auditors are employed by organisations to establish good financial systems that will provide the management with reliable management information and ensure that, if mistakes are made or frauds committed, the systems will identify them before too much damage is done. It is the internal auditor's job to design new systems, advise on alterations to existing systems and, in particular, to review and evaluate the operation of existing systems. Although primarily done for financial control purposes, all audit investigations should involve a review of the three Es of an organisation's systems: economy, efficiency and effectiveness.

Organisation and Methods (O&M)

This is effectively the application of work study techniques to clerical work. It originated in the Civil Service in the 1940s and its use has spread to many large bureaucratic organisations. In some organisations this type of work is done by the internal audit section, or more recently the systems analysis section of the computer department.

Systems analysis

Often the main impetus behind systems evaluation is the need to change work practices following the introduction of new technology, particularly computers. This will involve the employment of a systems analyst. The job of the systems analyst is to design a system that will operate effectively. This will involve investigating the existing systems, obtaining objectives for the new system from the management, designing the new system, designing all documentation to be used, documenting the new system, liaising with the computer programmers who will put the system on to the computer and eventually testing and implementing the final system.

Unit 2   Business organisations and systems

PC 2.2.4 2.2.5

ACTIVITY 2.2.5

You have been asked by your manager to draft a response to the following statement made by a senior member of your firm at the last staff meeting.

'I can see no point in looking back at past actions and wasting a lot of time on reviewing and evaluating systems that are working well enough at the moment. My staff are working hard enough without all of this additional pressure.'

SYSTEMS DESCRIPTION AND DOCUMENTATION

A large organisation will have countless administrative systems in operation at any one time. Many of the systems will be tailor-made to the particular needs of that organisation. Even systems common to most organisations, two of which are illustrated below, will vary when it comes down to the fine detail of their application.

The following notes and diagrams, based on a fictitious company, VQ Ltd, illustrate two typical procedures that have to be carried out by almost all organisations and the accompanying documentation. They relate to the purchase of goods and the payment of wages.

VQ Ltd
North-Western Trading Estate, Glasgow

Date	Required by	When required	No.
15/	MDJ	1 March	MDJ010

Quantity	Description	Order No.
1	United Machine Tools Ltd Lathe, Model UM 876	6414

Purchase Requisition

Fig 2.13 Purchase requisition

112

Element 2.2 Investigate administration systems

A purchasing system

VQ Ltd has three departments that are involved with the purchase of goods: the Stores Department, the Buying Department and the Accounts Department which will record the activities and eventually pay the resulting supplier's invoice.

1 When the reorder level for an item of stock has been reached the storeman/woman sends a pre-numbered *purchase requisition* (see Fig. 2.13) to the Buying Department and keeps a duplicate copy in a file in the store.

2 The buyer checks that the materials ordered conform to the agreed specification and signs the requisition to authorise the purchase. A four-part pre-numbered *purchase order* (see Fig. 2.14) is produced and sent to the following:

- the supplier
- the Accounts Department
- the stores
- the buyers file.

\multicolumn{5}{c}{**VQ Ltd**}
\multicolumn{3}{l}{**North-Western Trading Estate, Glasgow**}	\multicolumn{2}{r}{Phone GLA8 12024}
Date United Machine Tools Ltd.		Order Date 3/2/95	Order Number 6414	
^		Deliver To Above When required 1/April		
Requisition No.	Quantity	Description	\multicolumn{2}{c}{Price}
^	^	^	£	p
MDJ 010	1	Lathe model UM 876	4,810	—
			Total	4,810	—
Goods Received Note Number	Goods Received Note Date	Invoice Date	Invoice Number	Approved By
0070027	3/April	1 April	678516	ARH
\multicolumn{5}{c}{**Purchase Order**}

Fig 2.14 **Purchase order**

Unit 2 Business organisations and systems

Supplier	Part No.	Quantity	Description
United Machine Tools Ltd		1	Lathe, model UM 876
GRN No. 0070027			
Order No. 6414			
Date of receipt 3 April		Inspection	
Stock posting	Date	Passed	Reject Note No.

VQ Ltd
North-Western Trading Estate, Glasgow

Goods Recieved Note

Fig 2.15 Goods received note

UNITED MACHINE TOOLS LIMITED
Coventry

To: National Pumps Ltd.,
    North-Western Trading Estate,
    Glasgow.

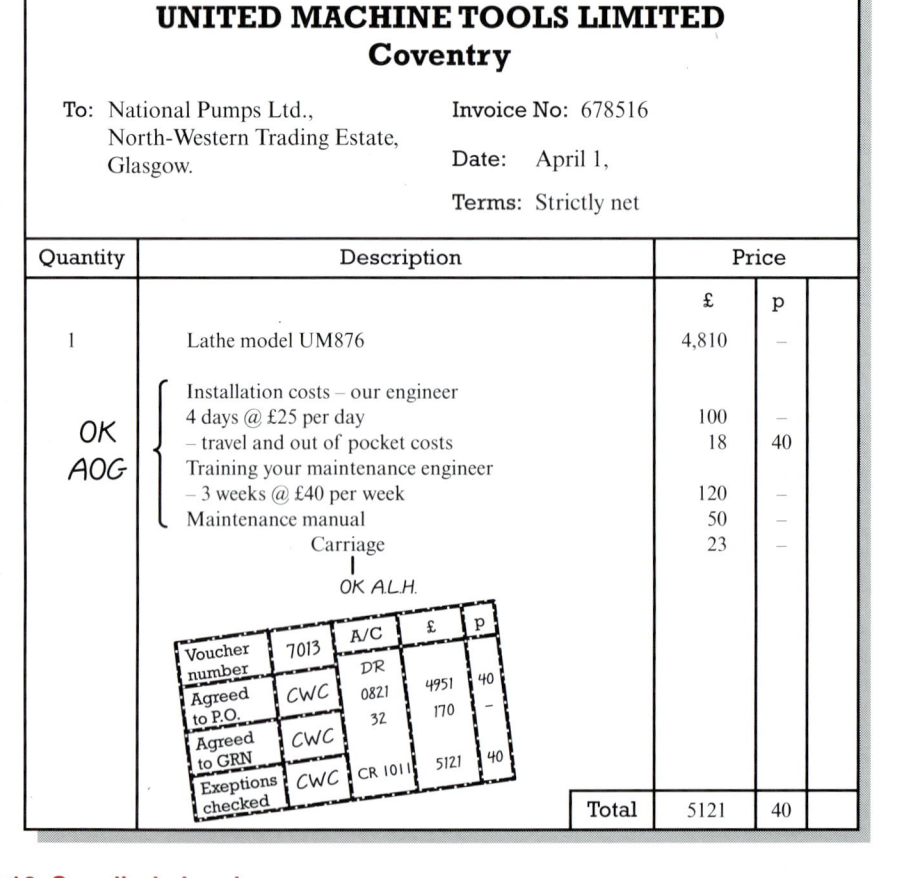

Invoice No: 678516
Date: April 1,
Terms: Strictly net

Quantity	Description	Price £	p
1	Lathe model UM876	4,810	–
OK AOG	Installation costs – our engineer		
	4 days @ £25 per day	100	–
	– travel and out of pocket costs	18	40
	Training your maintenance engineer		
	– 3 weeks @ £40 per week	120	–
	Maintenance manual	50	–
	Carriage	23	–
	OK A.L.H.		
		Total 5121	40

Voucher number	7013	A/C	£	p
Agreed to P.O.	CWC	DR 0821 32	4951 170	40 –
Agreed to GRN	CWC		5121	40
Exeptions checked	CWC	CR 1011		

Fig 2.16 Supplier's invoice

3 When the goods are received in the store they are checked and agreed with the stores copy of the purchase order and requisition. A two-part pre-numbered *goods received note* (*see* Fig. 2.15) is then produced, one copy being sent to the Accounts Department and the other copy being kept in the Stores Department's file.

4 When the *supplier's invoice* (*see* Fig. 2.16) is received in the Accounts Department it is checked against the copy purchase order and goods received note and if all agree and have been correctly authorised the accounts clerk will add the financial/cost accounting code to the invoice and sign it as authorisation for payment. The invoice is then passed to the Computer Department where a cheque is produced for payment.

A flow chart describing this system is shown in Fig. 2.18.

ACTIVITY 2.2.6

Evaluate and suggest any improvements that can be made to the above administrative system.

PC 2.2.5

A wages system

VQ Ltd involves the Personnel Department, the Production Department and the Wages Department in the payment of wages. In order to keep firm financial control over the system, the power to engage, dismiss and promote employees is separated from the tasks of payroll preparation, as is the task of paying the wages. Within the Personnel Department records are kept for each employee containing the employee's signed authorisation for making deductions from pay other than income tax and national insurance. Also contained within this file is the employee's job description, the post's personnel specification, the current wage rate plus any addition to the standard rate of pay. Any changes to the rates of pay, additions or deductions, should only be made after authorisation from the manager responsible.

The payroll should be prepared by clerks who do not have the power to authorise any changes to an employee's pay. When the payroll has been completed, it should be scrutinised by a senior clerk prior to the collection of cash from the bank, or its delivery by a security firm. The cash should be sent straight to the clerks who make up the pay packets. These clerks should have no other payroll duties and the pay packets should only be sealed when all of the cash has been inserted into the packets and no surplus or deficit remains.

When the pay packets are delivered to the employees, the employees should be identified at the pay-out and they should sign for their wage as they receive it. Any queries should be made prior to the employees opening their packet and any unclaimed wages should be returned to the cashiers and entered into an unclaimed wages book for collection by the employee at a later date.

A flow chart showing these procedures appears in Fig. 2.19.

Unit 2　Business organisations and systems

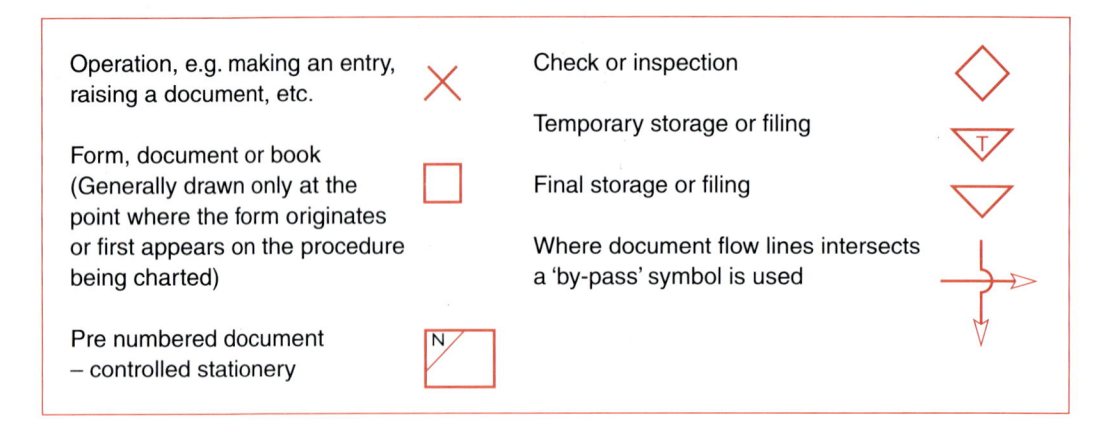

Symbol description	Symbol
Operation, e.g. making an entry, raising a document, etc.	×
Form, document or book (Generally drawn only at the point where the form originates or first appears on the procedure being charted)	□
Pre numbered document – controlled stationery	N (square with diagonal)
Check or inspection	◇
Temporary storage or filing	▽ with T
Final storage or filing	▽
Where document flow lines intersects a 'by-pass' symbol is used	(by-pass symbol)

Fig 2.17　Standard symbols for use in flow charts

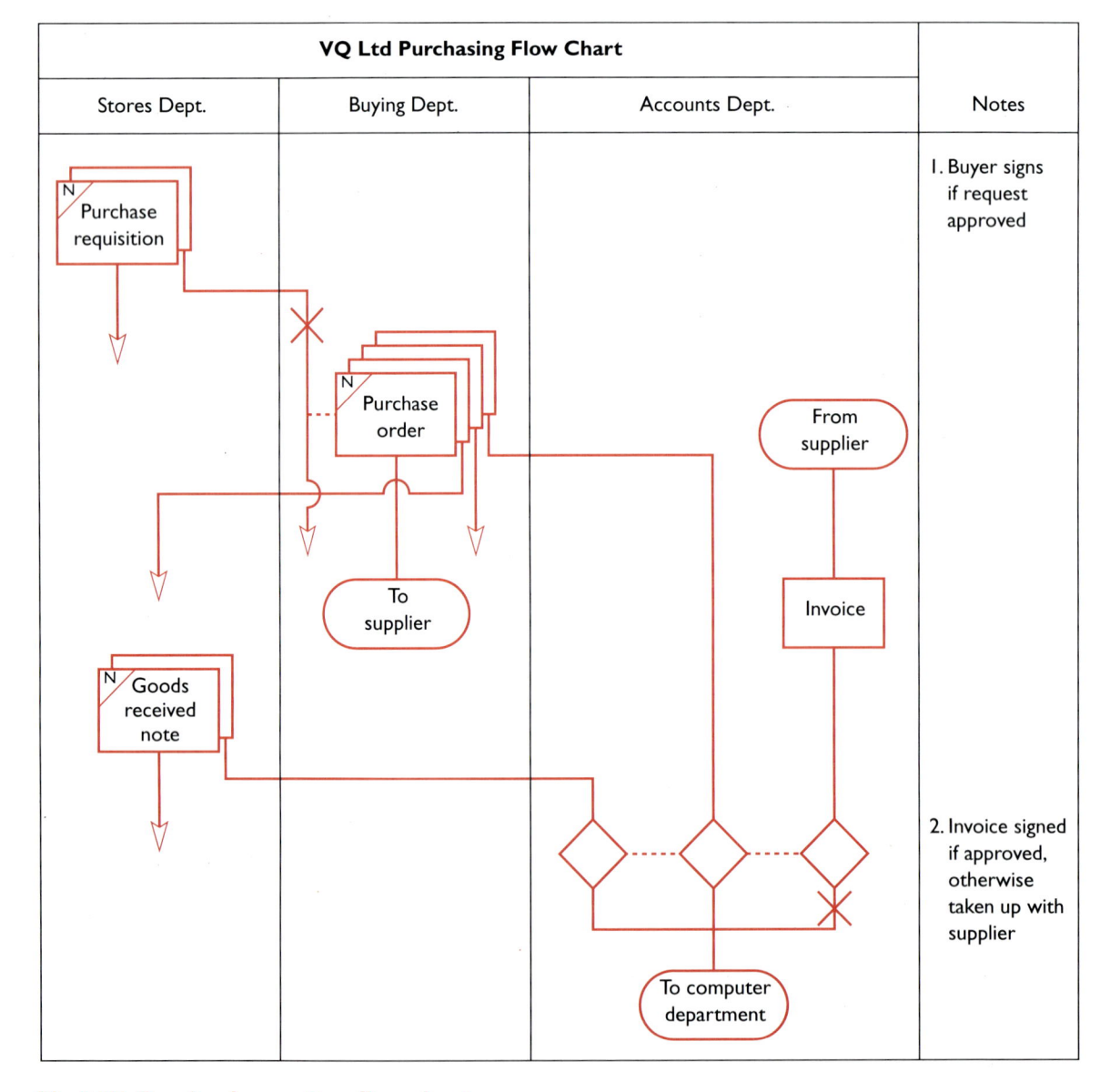

VQ Ltd Purchasing Flow Chart

Stores Dept.	Buying Dept.	Accounts Dept.	Notes
Purchase requisition	Purchase order	From supplier → Invoice	1. Buyer signs if request approved
Goods received note	To supplier	To computer department	2. Invoice signed if approved, otherwise taken up with supplier

Fig 2.18　Purchasing system flow chart

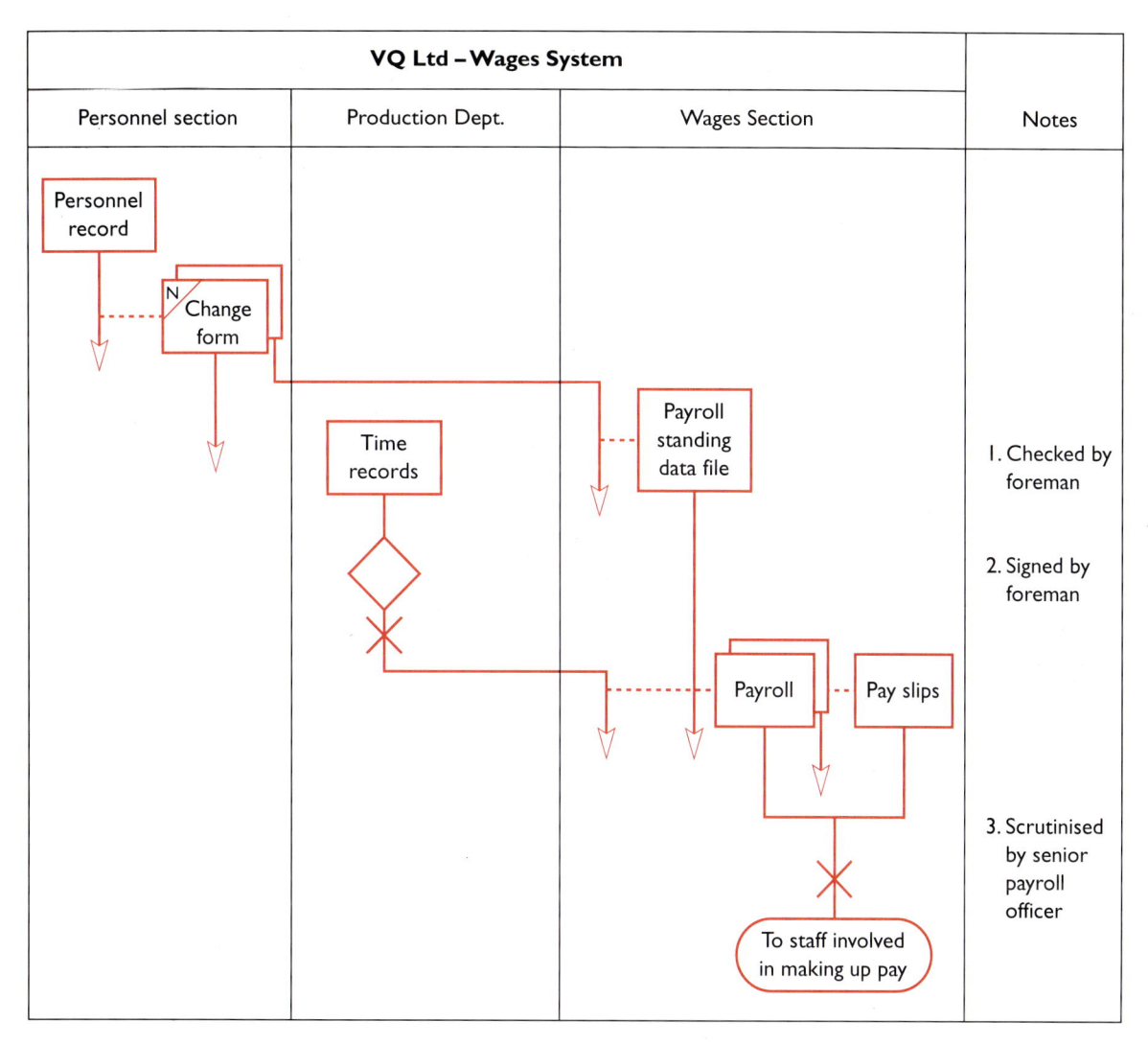

Element 2.2 Investigate administration systems

Fig 2.19

VQ Ltd – Wages System			Notes
Personnel section	Production Dept.	Wages Section	

(Flowchart showing: Personnel record → Change form (Personnel section) → flows to Production Dept. and Wages Section; Time records (Production Dept.); Payroll standing data file → Payroll → Pay slips (Wages Section) → To staff involved in making up pay)

Notes:
1. Checked by foreman
2. Signed by foreman
3. Scrutinised by senior payroll officer

HEALTH AND SAFETY

The Health and Safety at Work Act 1974 imposes criminal liability on all employers and responsible officials for the health and safety of their employees. Non-compliance with the requirements of the Act can result in the closure of the firm's premises.

The employer's duties under the act are:

- to provide and maintain safe plant and work systems;
- to ensure safe use, handling, storing and transport of articles and substances;
- to provide information, instruction, training and supervision;
- to provide a safe working environment without health risk;

- to provide adequate welfare facilities;
- to ensure that the public are not exposed to risk as a result of the employer's enterprise;
- to make no charge for the employees' safety which is required by a specific law (e.g. safety goggles);
- to provide a safety policy and bring it to the notice of employees;
- to consult safety representatives and establish safety committees;
- to prevent noxious or offensive fumes entering the atmosphere;
- to give information in the shareholders' report.

The employees' duties under the Act are:

- to take reasonable care for themselves and others;
- to co-operate with the employer so far as it is necessary for the execution of the employer's duties;
- to refrain from intentionally or recklessly interfering with anything provided for their health, safety or welfare.

The functions of the Health and Safety Commission are:

- to take action appropriate to furthering the purposes of the Act;
- to promote research and training;
- to provide information and advice;
- to carry out via the Health and Safety Executive major investigations or enquiries;
- to establish advisory committees;
- to establish an executive to enforce the law and give advice on the means of complying with it.

The functions of the inspectors are:

- to enter premises to make investigations;
- to serve improvement notices to employers;
- to serve prohibition notices where there is a risk of personal injury (these have immediate effect);
- to seize and destroy dangerous articles and substances;
- to give information to the representatives of employees including copies of improvement and prohibition notices;
- to prosecute employers if necessary.

ACTIVITY 2.2.7

Make a list of any potential hazards that could occur in your college, school or workplace. If you conclude that any of these potential hazards are likely to lead to an accident, what is your duty under the Health and Safety at Work Act as an employee?

Element 2.2 Investigate administration systems

Self assessment questions

1 Which of the following sets of data is of most use to a personnel officer?
   a pay slips
   b labour cost details
   c purchase orders
   d remittance advice

2 Some administrative systems produce both routine and non-routine outputs. Are the following statements True (T) or False (F)?
   (i) The finance clerk entering data on customer payments is a routine function.
   (ii) The sales manager investigating low product sales for a particular sales area is a non-routine function.

Questions 3 to 5 relate to the following information.
Some of the information produced by a management information system is intended to help managers control various aspects of the firm's business. Examples of such information include:
- monitoring production costs;
- identifying slow moving stock items;
- monitoring trends in employee attendance;
- totalling the value of sales.

3 Which of the above is achieved by recording employees' times of attendance on the time clocks?

4 Which of the above is achieved by calculating the cost of raw materials?

5 Which of the above is achieved by recording stores issues and receipts?

6 Which of the following departments deals with PAYE income tax and National Insurance contributions?
   a personnel
   b payroll
   c accountancy
   d administration

7 A successful customer-care system must include all of the following attributes, but which is the most important?
   a pleasant sales personnel
   b motivated employees
   c effective publicity
   d provision for customer feedback

Assignment

Using the example of a wages system given in the text, write a report to the Company Secretary of your evaluation of the current system and any improvements that could be made to it, particularly with regard to the use of new technology and its effect on productivity and quality.

PC
2.2.3
2.2.4
2.2.5

Element 2.3
ANALYSE COMMUNICATION IN A BUSINESS ORGANISATION

Performance criteria

1 **Identify communication in business organisations.**

2 **Identify and explain the objectives of internal and external communication.**

3 **Analyse the effectiveness of communication in a business organisation.**

4 **Explain possible positive and negative effects of changes to communications.**

5 **Suggest changes to communications in a business organisation.**

Introduction

In order for a business to operate, information must be exchanged and communication must take place, both internally within the organisation and externally between members of the organisation and other people in other organisations. All organisations need to collect data, analyse it, produce useful information from it and communicate the information to the people in the organisation that need it. Complex management information and accounting systems have been developed to assist in the communication of information.

All businesses exist to provide either services or products. As you know from Element 2.1, these organisations can exist in either the public or the private sectors of the economy. Not only do organisations in each sector communicate with each other, but there is also considerable cross-sector communication. A local authority will provide services to private firms within its area and will purchase goods and services from such firms. Any sale or purchase will involve the communication of data about products or services, followed by an order, a delivery note, an invoice, a statement and a cheque for payment. This is external communication.

Element 2.3 Analyse communication in a business organisation

Information can be communicated in many forms. It can be text, data, speech or an image such as diagrams, pictures or television and video. We are currently in what has been called the information revolution, in that modern technology enables us to collect more data and analyse and communicate it on a scale that would not have been thought possible a few years ago. The key to a good business information system is to edit out from all communications the information which is not relevant to the person receiving it. Today many managers are faced with too much information – they only need to know the information that affects their ability to make good decisions. It is the purpose of a good business communication system to enable business managers to get the right information to the right people at the right time.

COMMUNICATION CHANNELS

Vertical

A vertical channel of communication relates to information which is both passed down from senior management through to middle management and passed down finally to the workers on the shop floor. Similarly, the flow of information is also passed vertically upwards from the shop floor to management as shown in Fig 2.20.

Lateral

Lateral channels of communication relate to information/instructions which are passed from department to department, or between staff on the same level in the organisation (*see* Fig. 2.21).

ACTIVITY 2.3.1

PC 2.3.1

Write a short description giving examples of both vertical and horizontal channels of communication within your school, college or place of work.

Unit 2 Business organisations and systems

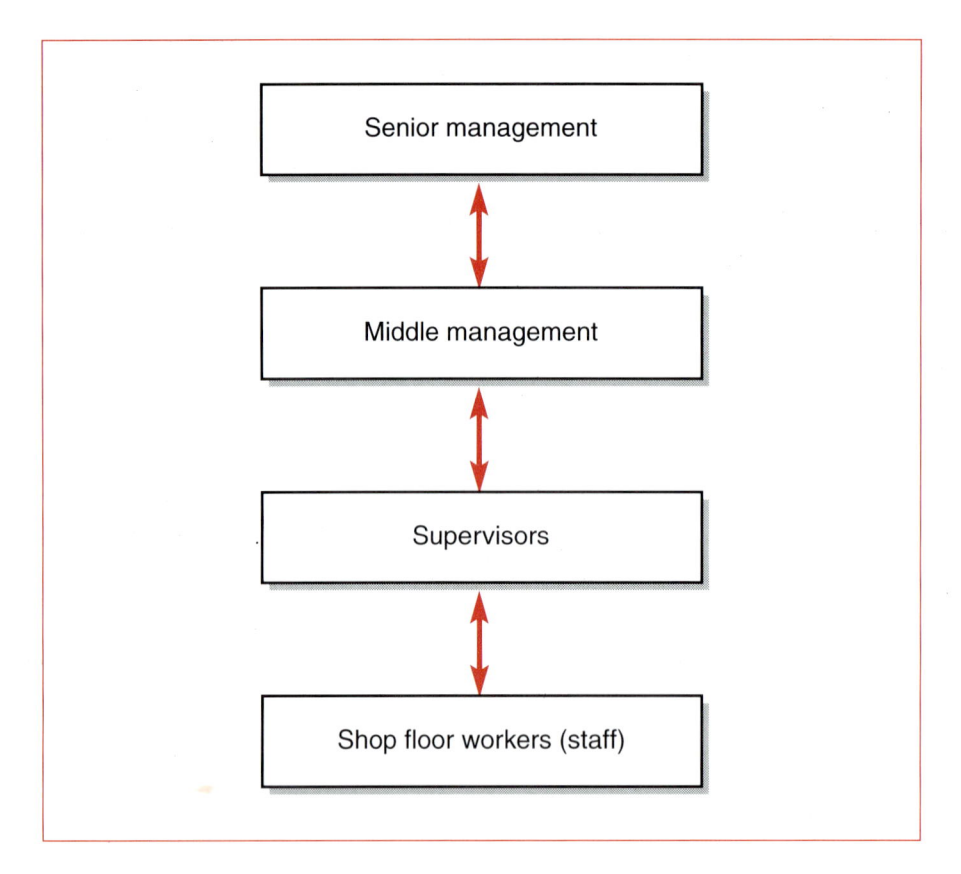

Fig 2.20 Upward and downward flow of information

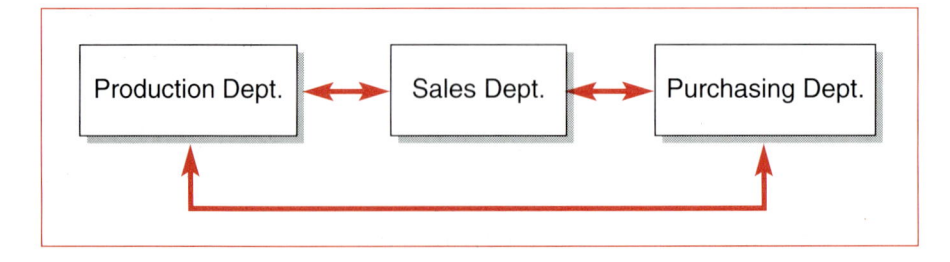

Fig 2.21 Lateral channels of communication

Element 2.3   Analyse communication in a business organisation

TYPES OF COMMUNICATION

Figure 2.22 shows the three types of communication – verbal, written and visual – and list some examples of each.

Verbal communication

We all talk to each other and this mode of communication is often used, on an informal basis, to pass information from one person or department to another. We are at our most effective when we speak face-to-face, and are less effective when using the telephone. Information passed verbally can sometimes be misunderstood, although this can be a quick way of finding out what is happening in the organisation prior to it being announced officially. The problem with the 'grapevine', as it is called, is the information can become inaccurate as it travels down the grapevine, translation eventually being totally lost and resulting in the original information being transformed beyond all recognition (as in the form of Chinese whispers!).

Verbal
Telephone
P.A. System
Two-way radio
Audio Cassette
Committee meetings
Speakers
Satellite video
Interviews
Meetings
Seminars

Written
Letters
Memos
Invoices
Statements
Reports
Note taking
Newspaper articles
Advertisements
Telephone messages
Notices
Agendas
Minutes
Catalogues
Price lists
Fax

Visual
Television
Ceefax, Oracle, Prestel
Video link-up
Sign language
Body language
Confravision
Video-conferencing

Fig 2.22 Types of communication

Fig 2.23 Information can become inaccurate as it travels down the grapevine

Formal verbal communication relates to the way meetings and seminars are conducted.

Working in groups

For a number of people to work together effectively as a group, they need to develop what is known as group awareness – a sensitivity in each member to each of the other members of the group. When you join a group you usually do so for a purpose and, if you and the others in the group are well intentioned, the group will function effectively. It is important to look for signs of unwillingness in the words, behaviour and posture of others, and to try to neutralise the bad effects of such attitudes.

Fig 2.24 Working in groups

The following recommendations to those working in groups will aid communication and make group work more effective. Be confident and believe that your opinion matters and that there will be no bad responses if you are wrong or if the other group members do not share your views.

- Do not over-react to alternative opinions put forward by others and do not hesitate to ask questions if you are uncertain on a particular point. You are probably not the only one. Exchanges with others will clarify your own thinking.
- When you speak in a group, make sure all the members can see you as well as hear you and that they understand what you say. Ask questions to gain feedback on their understanding.
- Be aware of non-verbal signals in others – if they look interested they probably are; if not, you will have to react to their signals by a change in your presentation.
- Use eye contact as a means of control over the group.
- A few moments of relaxation, a brief joke or compliment may make progress easier.

Meetings

A meeting is a gathering together of a number of people to discuss a topic of common interest. By holding meetings members can discuss topics, make decisions and plan a strategy for action.

A meeting can be either formal or informal. It can be held in a conference room (e.g. when inviting shareholders to attend), the board room of the company, or, if informal, then it can be held in someone's office.

Fig 2.25 Meeting of a formal council

A formal meeting has the following requirements.

- Notices must be sent out advising people of the date, time and place of the meeting (*see* Fig. 2.26). Notices must be sent to all interested parties, and not just those who are likely to support the decisions made. If insufficient notice is given, then the meeting is deemed to be invalid.
- An agenda must be compiled setting out the subjects to be discussed at the meeting (*see* Fig. 2.26).

VQ Ltd

A meeting of the Company's Board of Directors will be held in the Board Room, West Brook House, Great Horton Road, Bradford on Monday 14 March 1994 at 10.00 am

AGENDA

1. Apologies for absence
2. Minutes of last meeting
3. Matters arising
4. Launch of new fashion accessory
5. Sales Director's Report
4. Buyer's Report on the Paris Trade Fair
6. Any other business
7. Date and time of next meeting

Signed by the Chairman

Dated

Fig 2.26 A formal notice advising people of the date, time and place of meeting

- Minutes are taken as a complete record of what has been discussed and what action has taken place (*see* Fig. 2.27).
- There must be a quorum – the minimum number of committee members required to be present at a meeting. If the number attending falls below that number, the meeting is not recognised as an official meeting and its members cannot exercise the powers granted to it. The number of members that form a quorum is laid down in the Constitution of the organisation. This is usually one third of the total number of the committee. In a limited company all of the rules governing the company's meetings are laid out in its Memorandum and Articles of Association.

A meeting normally observes the following procedure.

1. At formal meetings there must be a Chairperson who presides over the events. In the absence of the Chairperson, the next senior member must preside over the meeting.

MINUTES OF MEETING

A meeting of the Company's Board of Directors was held in the Board Room of West Brook House, Great Horton Road, Bradford on Monday 14 March 1994 at 10.00 am

PRESENT
Mr Stephen Milton (Chairman)
Mr Derek Benton
Mrs Anne Eastwood
Mr Paul Reems
Miss Ellen Rigby (Secretary)

1 APOLOGIES FOR ABSENCE
The Secretary reported that Ms Jane Myers was unable to attend as she was away on business.

2 MINUTES FROM LAST MEETING
The Minutes of the last meeting held on 13 February 1994 were read, approved and signed by the Chairman.

3 MATTERS ARISING FROM THE MINUTES
There were no matters arising from the previous Minutes.

4 LAUNCH OF NEW FASHION ACCESSORY
The summer launch of the new accessory was discussed and the date agreed was for 1 August 1994. All arrangements to meet this deadline were under way.

5 BUYER'S REPORT ON PARIS TRADE FAIR
The Company Buyer delivered his report on the Paris Trade Fair. He was optimistic that our stand at the Trade Fair was in a better position than last year and this reflects the interest shown in our goods.

6 ANY OTHER BUSINESS
There was no other business.

7 DATE OF NEXT MEETING
The date of the next meeting was fixed for 24 April 1994.
The Chairman declared the meeting closed at 1.15 pm.

(Space for signature)

S Milton
CHAIRMAN

Fig 2.27 Minutes of a meeting

2 At formal meetings only one person may speak at any time.

3 Remarks must be addressed through the Chair (i.e. addressed to the Chairperson).

4 Subjects on the agenda must be discussed succinctly and not deviated from.

5 Members of the meeting must not allow their personal conduct or any offensive behaviour to keep the meeting from achieving its objectives.

6 The Chairperson must take the agenda items in order.

An informal meeting requires:

- only short notice of a meeting;
- very often no formal agenda;
- in may cases, no minutes to be taken, i.e. no record is kept;

Informal meetings are usually impromptu affairs which require decisions to be taken swiftly.

PC
2.3.1
2.3.2

ACTIVITY 2.3.2

Your group should hold a course committee meeting to discuss the progress of the course to date. Prior to this, you have to form into groups of three. Each group must draft an agenda, make notes during the meeting and write up the minutes after the meeting. (Note: the minutes should be written in the past tense.)

Using the telephone

Towards the end of this element we discuss the equipment that has revolutionised the use of the telephone networks in recent years. Staff using the telephone for business

Fig 2.28 Effective use of the telephone can save time and money

purposes, as a means of both external and internal verbal communication, should note the following recommendations. These points will make calls more effective and will save time and money. Always remain polite and friendly even when provoked by people who are not. Keep your conversations concise and to the point.

- Before making the call, check that you have the correct number and the name of the person you need to talk to and that you know exactly what information you require.
- Always ask for the name of the person to whom you are talking.
- Never use slang expressions and do not keep the caller waiting.
- Ask the caller to repeat unfamiliar names and numbers. If you are unsure of the names or words used, ask for them to be spelled out.
- Keep a pad and a pen next to the telephone to take messages or make notes. Write down the name of the caller, the time he or she phoned, the reason for calling and a telephone number if he or she wishes to be contacted. The message should also be signed and dated by the person taking the call.

The local telephone directory

There are over seventy directories covering the whole of the United Kingdom. As well as listing in alphabetical order all of the telephone subscribers in the locality, the telephone directory provides:

- contact point, map, area boundaries;
- contact points for help/services;
- useful numbers: local authorities, hospitals, transport;
- local information: places of interest, etc.;
- postal addresses for local customer services area;
- dialling information/charges: rates, etc;
- local dialling codes;
- Irish Republic: dialling information charges;
- international dialling information/charges;
- international dialling codes;
- names and numbers and how to find them;
- advertisements for British Telecom microfiche and computer directories: whole country on one small slide or disk;
- about British Telecom;
- phone books/directories list: order forms;
- map of Great Britain and the Republic of Ireland.

Procedure when making an overseas telephone call

The prospect of making an important and expensive telephone call to a foreign country can be daunting. This is the procedure to follow.

- Dial the international dialling code.
- Dial the code for the country you require.
- Dial the area code.
- Dial the person's number.

You must bear in mind that to telephone overseas is expensive and in some cases a letter or a fax would be more appropriate and cost saving. Note also that the tones for the telephones vary in different countries. The types of telephone equipment in use in many of today's offices are covered later in this Element.

Advantages and disadvantages of telephones

Advantages	Disadvantages
■ Quick means of communication.	■ There are no written records of telephone calls. Telephones are not always a reliable medium of communication as there is no record made of the conversations or agreements made.
■ Cheaper than travelling.	
■ Ideal for quicker, 'yes' or 'no' answers.	
■ Personal word best for calming a situation (e.g. angry customer).	
■ Automatic answering devices may be employed to record and give messages when personnel have left the office.	■ Telephones may be used by personnel in making expensive private calls.
■ It is personal and offers a link between business people.	■ Time and money are often wasted by personnel in unnecessary long conversations.

ACTIVITY 2.3.3

Write not more than 500 words for inclusion in a training manual for new recruits on how best to use the telephone.

Written communications

Note taking

Taking or making notes at a meeting or during a discussion with others avoids the risk of promising to do something and forgetting, agreeing some point and forgetting what was agreed, making a report and missing out some important parts, or being unable to prove what had been discussed and what the outcome was. The following points are worth keeping in mind when taking notes.

- Note the background detail (subject, date and time, the place and the people involved).
- Record only the key points.
- Note any decisions and any action to be taken.
- Agree your notes with those people with whom you have been talking.
- If you cannot make detailed notes during a meeting, then record the key words as a memory aid and write up the notes as soon as possible after the meeting.

- Use paragraphs, numbers and headings to break up the notes.
- Highlight any key words.
- Leave plenty of space between the notes so that you can add details later.
- Number the pages used in case the notes get mixed up or a page gets lost.

The memorandum

The memo transmits information inside an organisation. Its layout is very simple and quite often appears on a preprinted form in order to increase the speed of its production and keep costs down. A typical layout of a memo is given in Fig. 2.29.

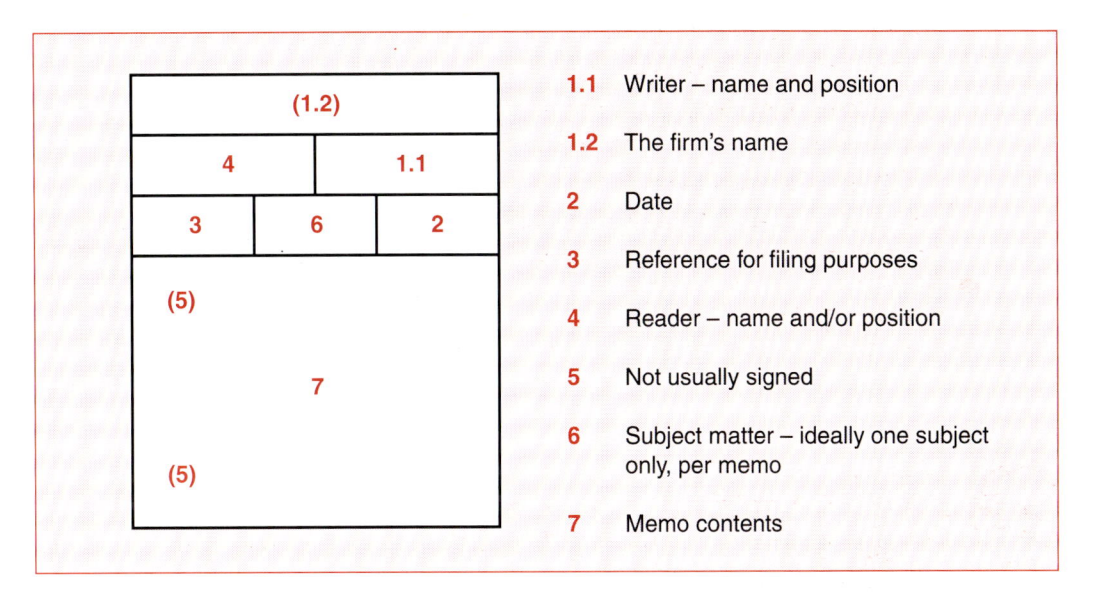

1.1	Writer – name and position
1.2	The firm's name
2	Date
3	Reference for filing purposes
4	Reader – name and/or position
5	Not usually signed
6	Subject matter – ideally one subject only, per memo
7	Memo contents

Fig 2.29 A typical memo layout

The letter

Practically all business letters are now either typed or word processed. Many are still produced by secretarial staff for other members of the organisation, although with the wide spread adoption of lap-top and desk-top computers with easy-to-use software, many people are producing their own letters and reports. The responsibility for the accuracy and content of the letter always lies with the person that originated it.

A standard layout for a letter is given in Fig. 2.30. Most organisations use preprinted letterheads to give the standard information about their name, address, telephone number, etc.

The letter content should contain three kinds of information, in the following order:

- the reason for writing as outlined in the background and introduction;
- the body of the letter giving full details and referring to the specific reason for the letter;
- the outcome expected from the letter.

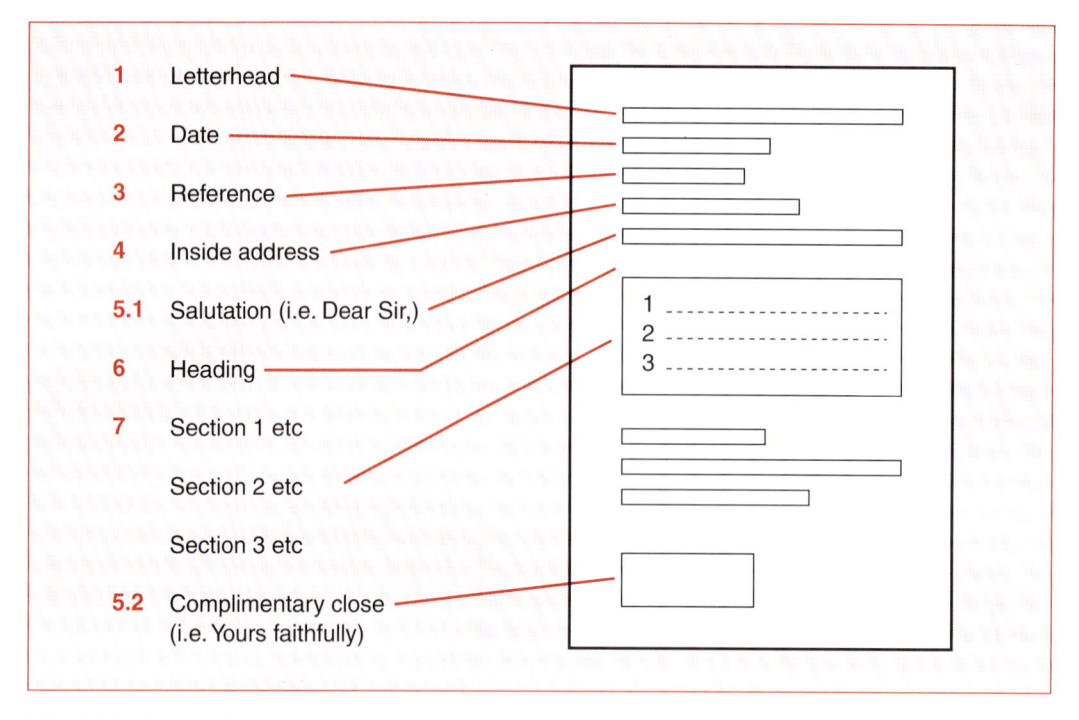

Fig 2.30 A standard layout for a letter

1. Letterhead
2. Date
3. Reference
4. Inside address
5.1 Salutation (i.e. Dear Sir,)
6. Heading
7. Section 1 etc
   Section 2 etc
   Section 3 etc
5.2 Complimentary close (i.e. Yours faithfully)

ACTIVITY 2.3.4

Task 1. You have been asked by the Managing Director of your firm to draft, on his behalf, a letter of complaint to your local council about the poor state of road maintenance in your firm's area and the inadequacy of the street lighting.

Task 2. Having drafted the above letter, enclose it with a memo to Mr Patel, the Managing Director, asking for his comments or amendments prior to sending it to the Town Hall.

The report

There can be many different types of report, each one appropriate to a particular purpose and set of circumstances. The layout and structure of the reports mentioned here refer to general business reports and can be adapted to suit the particular needs of an individual business. The function of the report determines the detail of preparation but the principle remains the same: to transmit information and judgement as economically as possible.

The qualities required of a report writer include a sound knowledge of the subject, unbiased judgement, powers of observation and analysis, accuracy of expression and brevity. The report itself should be addressed to a reader or a body of readers and the writer or writers should be identified. The report should have a short and clear title. Should any explanation of the title be needed, then an explanatory subtitle section should be used. The terms of reference for the report should be given, outlining the scope of the enquiry, who commissioned the report and its purpose. The report should be arranged in a logical sequence with headed paragraphs and, if necessary, numbered paragraphs. Its

Element 2.3 Analyse communication in a business organisation

conclusions or recommendations should be clearly identified and either included at the relevant part of the report or in a separate section at its end. If the report is a very long one, it may be best to include a summary of the recommendations at the start of the report. The document should be dated and signed.

Remember the letters TPFCR when writing a business report:

- **T**erms of reference
- **P**rocedure
- **F**indings
- **C**onclusions
- **R**ecommendations.

Every report must be party objective, that is factual and the outcome of observation, experiment, inspection and/or research. Where it needs to be subjective, i.e. expressing ideas and opinions, the difference between the objective sections and the subjective sections should be clear. The style of the report should suit its readership. If the report is addressed to laymen, it should not use technical language. Where this is unavoidable, the

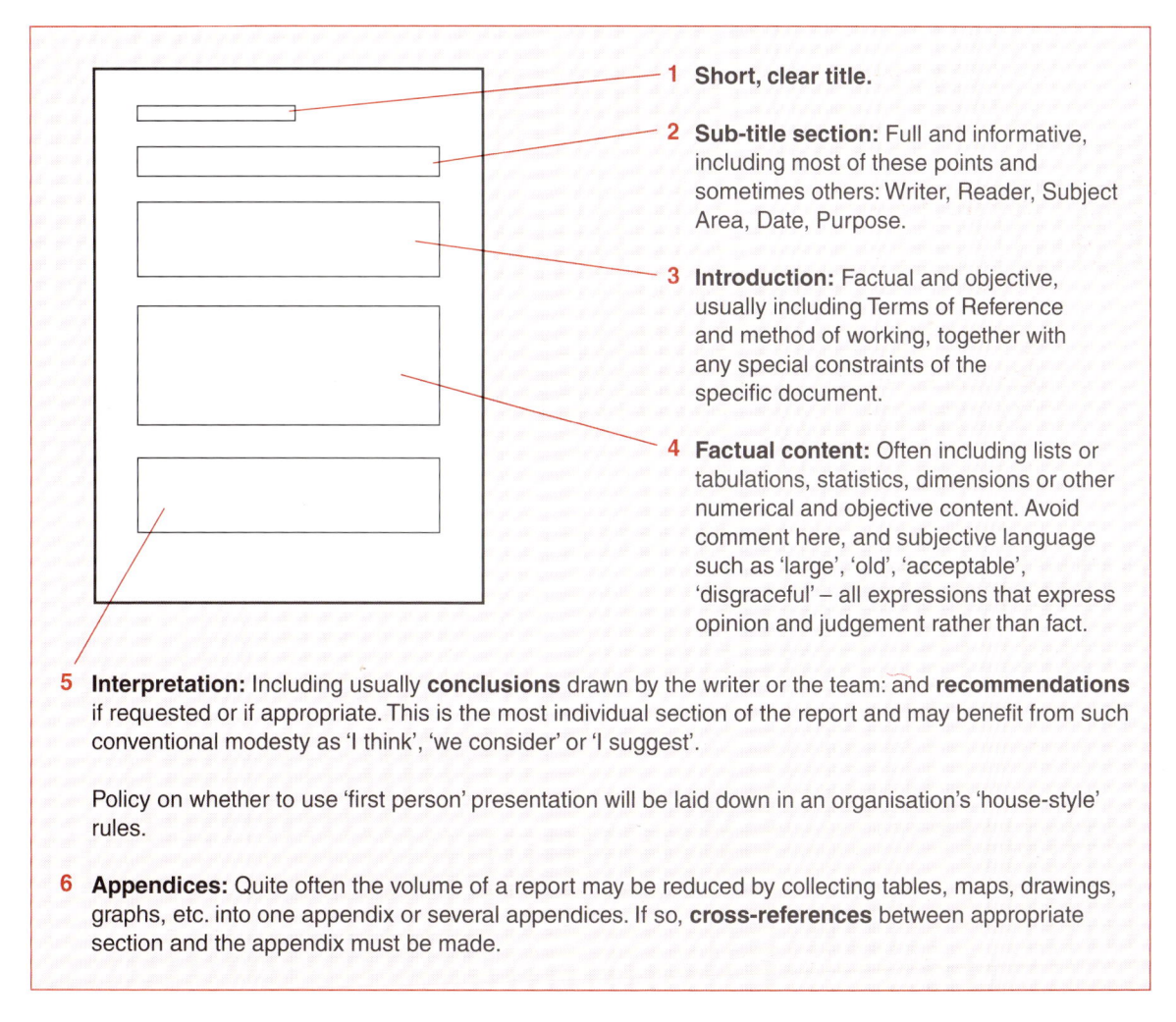

1. **Short, clear title.**

2. **Sub-title section:** Full and informative, including most of these points and sometimes others: Writer, Reader, Subject Area, Date, Purpose.

3. **Introduction:** Factual and objective, usually including Terms of Reference and method of working, together with any special constraints of the specific document.

4. **Factual content:** Often including lists or tabulations, statistics, dimensions or other numerical and objective content. Avoid comment here, and subjective language such as 'large', 'old', 'acceptable', 'disgraceful' – all expressions that express opinion and judgement rather than fact.

5. **Interpretation:** Including usually **conclusions** drawn by the writer or the team; and **recommendations** if requested or if appropriate. This is the most individual section of the report and may benefit from such conventional modesty as 'I think', 'we consider' or 'I suggest'.

Policy on whether to use 'first person' presentation will be laid down in an organisation's 'house-style' rules.

6. **Appendices:** Quite often the volume of a report may be reduced by collecting tables, maps, drawings, graphs, etc. into one appendix or several appendices. If so, **cross-references** between appropriate section and the appendix must be made.

Fig 2.31 A typical report

133

terminology should be explained, either in the body of the report or in a glossary. Tables, charts and graphs accompanying the report should always be titled, explained and cross-referred to the text. The source and date of any statistics quoted or used in the report must be stated. A typical report is shown in Fig. 2.31.

PC
2.3.1
2.3.2

ACTIVITY 2.3.5

Write a report to Mrs A Jones, Head of Department of Business Studies, on the number and type of computers available to the GNVQ Advanced students and the adequacy of the software available.

COMMUNICATION EQUIPMENT

The following section includes a brief description of the communication equipment that is currently in use in many business areas.

Switchboards

- The two types of switchboard are still found in organisations in the UK. *The private manual branch exchange (PMBX)*, now obsolete and very rare, this requires a telephone operator to connect all calls incoming, outgoing and between extensions.
- *Private automatic branch exchange (PABX).* This provides automatic transfer of internal calls and the facility to call an outside line by dialling 9. The same telephone is used to contact another internal office extension by dialling its internal number.

British Telecom (BT) and other telecom firms have been installing over the last few years a range of digital computer-based PBX exchange systems that allow much greater speed and flexibility to their users. The type and names of systems are dependent upon the suppliers, the number of outside lines required and the number of internal extensions. All can give the following services.

- *Automatic phone relocation.* If you leave your desk you can take your telephone with you and plug it into the nearest phone point.
- *Call divert.* Calls can be automatically diverted to another extension.
- *Conference calls.* You can link up an outside caller and internal extensions on one line.
- *Messaging.* The LCD on your phone can alert you to contact the switchboard or can give you the names of colleagues who made internal calls to your extension.
- *Paging.* You can use the phone system like a public address system, your messages are broadcast through the phones' loudspeakers, if they have them.
- *Pick-up groups.* If someone else's extension rings and you want to answer it in his or her absence you can do so by keying a simple code into your extension.

- *Call management systems.* These monitor all outgoing and incoming calls and provide easy-to-understand printouts on how the firm's phones are being used by recording the cost, the time of day, the type of call, the number dialled and call duration for every call made.
- *Cordless handsets.* These are now in wide use in both business and domestic locations and allow you to take the extension with you when moving from room to room.
- *Call waiting.* You can deal with two calls at once and new callers can get through to you even when you are already on the phone.
- *Call diversion service.* You can divert your calls to another number anywhere in the country.
- *Loud speaking telephone.* You do not have to hold the handset, leaving both hands free for taking notes searching through files, etc. Useful for small conferences as the people sitting round the desk can all hear or answer the caller.

Answering machines

A telephone answering machine will 'answer the phone' outside office hours by playing a recorded message and inviting the caller to leave details of his or her requirements and a contact number which is recorded on tape. You do not even have to return to the answerphone to find out who has called; you can use a remote controller or the keyboard of a tone-dialling phone to allow you to listen to your messages.

Pagers

Radiopaging is one of the most efficient and inexpensive means of sending and receiving information, either from one person to another or to a group of people. Radiopagers are a familiar sight in hospitals, and many professional and sales personnel use them when they are absent from their offices. When you need to contact someone, a signal can be sent directly to their pager and a message requesting the user to telephone the sender can be stored on the pager or a variety of other short messages can be recorded on the screen of the pager. BT's system of paging now covers over 98 per cent of the UK.

Cellular mobile telephones

Although car phones have been available for a number of years their technology prevented their widespread usage, limiting the number of subscribers. Cellular radio technology allows thousands of users access to the system within the same region. In terms of operation, the area served by the system is divided up into many small geographical grid units or cells, each with a radius of about eight miles. Within each cell a low powered radio transmitter–receiver carries the calls over an antennae system for as many as 72 radio channels and a computer-controlled call-switching system controls the calls. If the mobile phone is in a car or train and is travelling from one area to another, the system transfers the call to another cell. There are a number of different mobile phone systems available in the UK and each has a large number of different charging methods, some of which can be very expensive. The cost of the phones themselves has fallen sharply as more manufacturers have entered the market with new products, but their purchase is a small consideration in comparison to their running costs. A cellular telephone system is illustrated in Fig. 2.32.

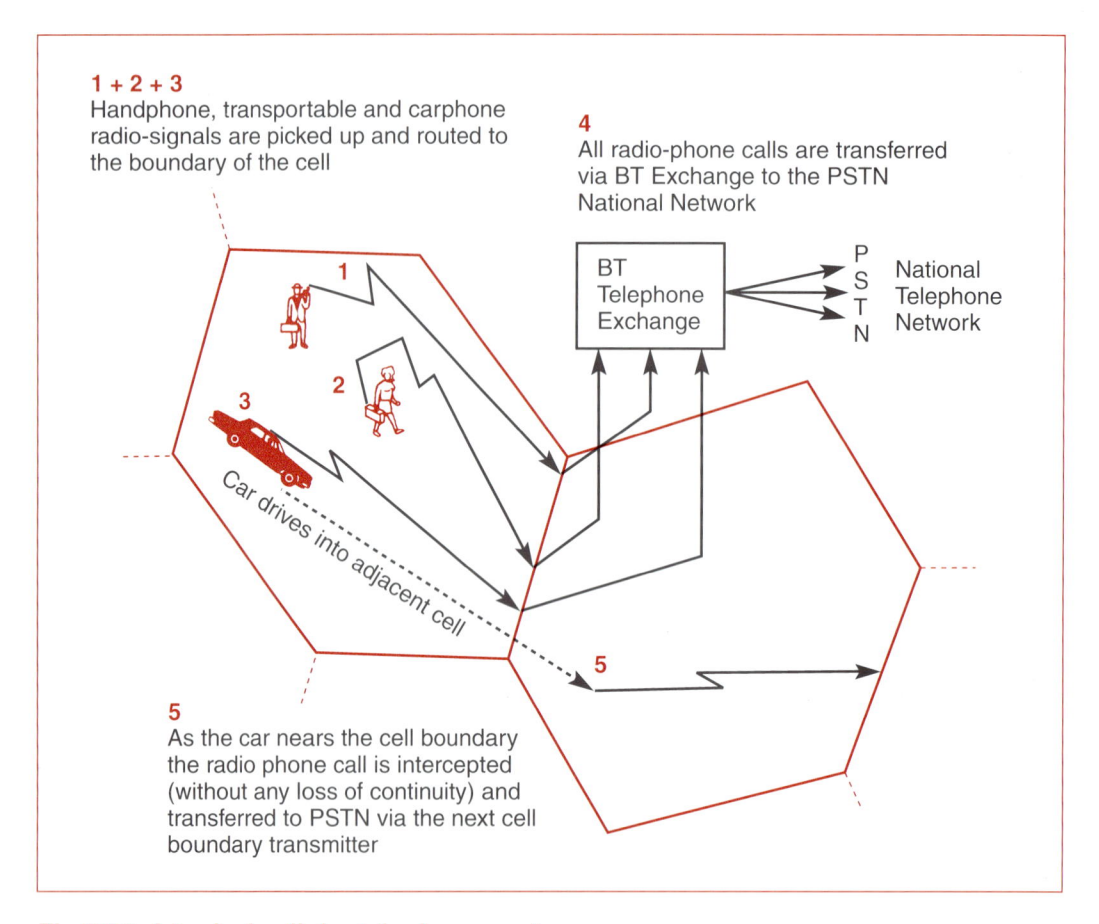

1 + 2 + 3
Handphone, transportable and carphone radio-signals are picked up and routed to the boundary of the cell

4
All radio-phone calls are transferred via BT Exchange to the PSTN National Network

5
As the car nears the cell boundary the radio phone call is intercepted (without any loss of continuity) and transferred to PSTN via the next cell boundary transmitter

Fig 2.32 A typical cellular telephone system

Confertel

This BT conference-by-phone service is available throughout the UK and can be linked with similar systems abroad. It can link up to 20 people. Conference has to be booked by telephoning BT Audioconferencing giving the date, time and duration of the conference, and the callers' names.

Datel

This is a service provided by BT for sending data between computers. It has many applications in everyday life, e.g. the cash point machine which automatically checks your bank balance at a central data store before issuing your cash.

Phonecard

Phonecards can be bought at the post office or other retail outlets in advance, reducing the need to carry cash. Many new call boxes only accept phonecards due to the telephone companies' desire to reduce theft and vandalism in their call boxes.

Credit cards

This allows the user to telephone from a public payphone, give his or her card number, and have the call charged to the card holder's account. Many of the Mercury call boxes allow the automatic use of a full range of credit cards. Mercury may withdraw from this market in the near future, however.

A facsimile machine

Often referred to as a fax, this machine enables an exact image (or facsimile) to be transmitted over the telephone line by combining a photocopier with the telephone network. It is a quick and easy-to-use system and saves time and postage by transmitting exact copies of documents to anyone who has a facsimile machine to receive them.

Ships radiotelephone services

This service is only available via the local exchange operator. The call is made via the telephone of the coast station. When connected to the coast station operator, the caller asks for 'ships radiotelephone call' giving the name, and if known, the position of the ship and the name and designation of the person required.

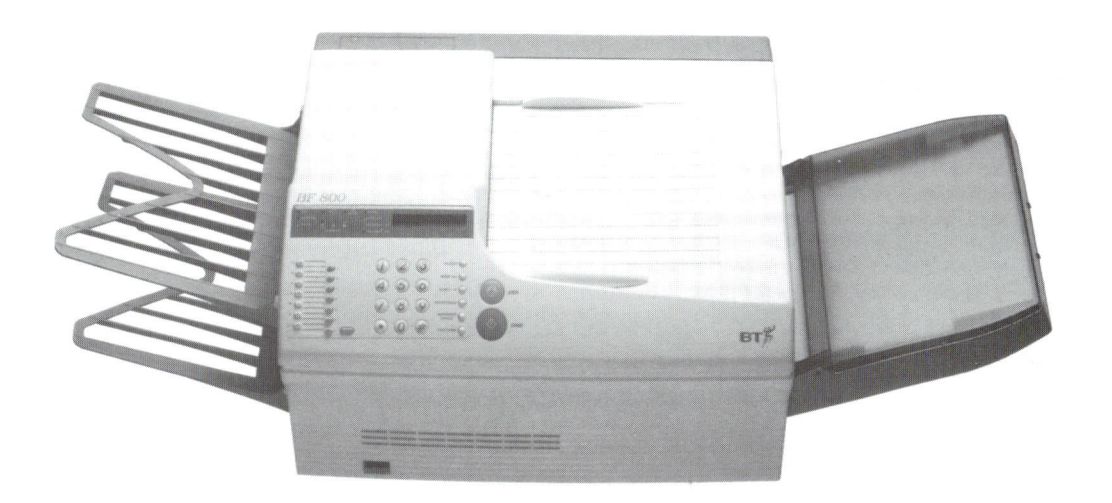

Fig 2.33 Fax machine

Unit 2　Business organisations and systems

Teleprinters and video printers

With teleprinters and video printers text is transmitted via the telephone system from one screen or printer to another. Most people will have seen the one used on the Sports Desk on television. Telex is the main teleprinter communication service in Britain. It provides a quick means of communication in printed form combining the speed of the telephone with the authority of the printed word. Charges for calls are based on the distance between Telex subscribers and the length of time it takes to transmit the message. Telex has its own lines, while a fax uses the standard telephone line system.

Telex messages can be stored and sent automatically at high speeds when required. If the number is engaged the teleprinter will make further attempts; the same message can be sent to more than one destination.

Teletex transmits text or data directly from a word processor or computer, providing a system for electronic mail. Teletex is 50 times faster than Telex. Teletex can also be linked with Telex so that the user can communicate with every terminal on the international network.

Viewdata permits a limited number of pages of text to be transmitted by TV broadcasting stations together with their programme emissions. These special signals are transmitted using lines which are not being used for the ordinary video signal. Teletext services are provided in Britain by both the BBC and ITV and are known as Ceefax and Oracle.

Prestel is similar in appearance on screen but is an *interactive* service that has been operational since 1979 and allows the users to call up parts of the central database and order goods or services. An example of this service is the ability to book hotel rooms via the Prestel system. (*See* Fig. 2.34.)

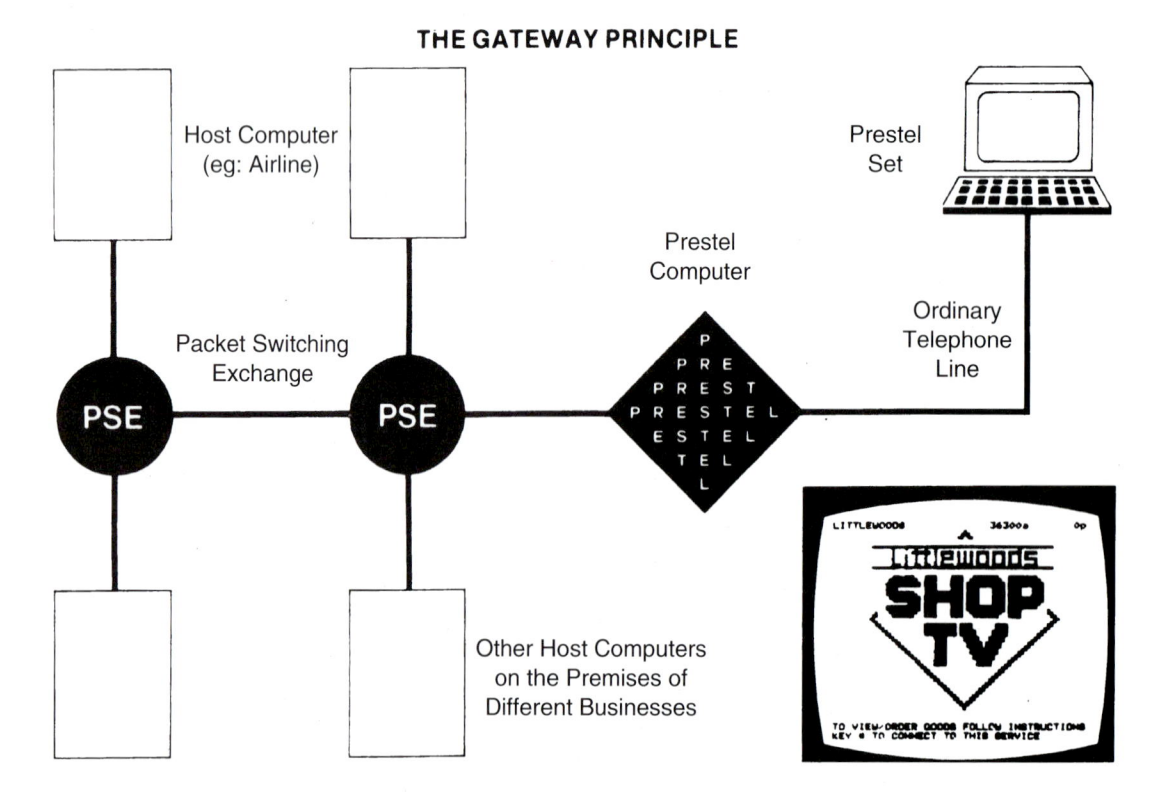

THE GATEWAY PRINCIPLE

Fig 2.34 Prestel system

Videophones and video conferencing

Video conferencing allows two or more people at various separate locations throughout the world to take part in meetings or conferences. Although initially expensive, many thousands of pounds can be saved in travel costs and time. Meetings are conducted as if all of the people were in the same room. Slides, videos, display charts and close-ups of documents and drawings can be transmitted.

Fig 2.35 Video conferencing

THE EFFECT OF CHANGES TO COMMUNICATION EQUIPMENT

In Western Europe and the United States there are now more white collar workers than production workers. Indeed the last 60 years have seen an accelerating decline in the employment of factory and agricultural workers that has been almost matched by a similar increase in the employment of office workers.

This change has been attributed to increasing automation, new technology and changes in work practices. In the last ten years, however, the impact of new technology has hit clerical work and the need for staff in areas such as financial services has drastically fallen. An example of this is the fall in employment in banking, due in part to the increasing use of 'hole-in-the-wall' machines for cash dispensing and the use of credit cards and switch cards for the payment of bills. In spite of employing fewer people, the banks are processing substantially more transactions at greater speed and are giving their clients a better service with more information available to them than ever before.

Although the use of new, smaller and more powerful computers has had a dramatic effect on all our lives, both at home and at work, it is perhaps the application of digital computer systems to communication equipment that is now having the most impact. When this equipment is linked to transmission systems such as satellite and optical fibre cables we see a huge increase in the volume and speed of communications that are balanced with a decrease in the cost of their use. The use of mobile telephones, fax machines and modems that link computers together can even solve our rush-hour traffic problems – many of use can work from home!

At home we are now offered a much wider choice of television viewing, first with the introduction of satellite TV and then the rapid expansion of the new cable TV companies. Indeed most of our cities are currently being dug up in order to lay the new fibre optic cables. The introduction of these new cable companies is not just a worry for the established television companies such as the BBC and ITV but it is potentially a much greater threat to the monopoly position of British Telecom as the user's telephone can be linked to the cable system at a lower cost to the user than to BT's.

With the increasing use of new technology the effectiveness of both internal and external communications has increased way beyond our former expectations. The positive effects of these changes are the increases in efficiency that result from better communications, particularly as most of the new equipment is relatively inexpensive and easy to use. The fall in prices and widespread adoption of mobile telephones is a good example, as is the increasing use of fax machines. Prices of such equipment have fallen quickly due to the very competitive market conditions for their sale. Eventually, the strongest firms in the market will win and impose worldwide standards on the use of equipment. This could have the effect of making the use of non-standard equipment obsolete. An example of this in the UK was the take-over of the BSB satellite broadcasting firm by its better financed rival, Sky. Users of the old system had to change their receiving dishes to the Sky system as their old receiving dishes became obsolete.

Self assessment questions

Questions 1 to 3 use the following information.

ML & Co is a firm of accountants that wants to update its communications systems. The senior partner has identified four areas of concern.
- urgent communication of financial reports
- confidential discussion
- routine non-urgent correspondence
- inter-departmental communication.

1 For which of the above functions should *electronic mail* be used?

2 For which of the above functions should *fax* be used?

3 For which of the above functions should a *word processing package* be used?

Element 2.3 Analyse communication in a business organisation

Questions 4, 5 and 6 use the following information.

When a new electronic communications system is installed problems may arise because:
- procedures are difficult to understand
- data security is a problem
- users have problems that remain unresolved
- there is no one on hand to solve users' problems

4 Which problem is best remedied by monitoring and analysing user complaints?

5 Which problem is best remedied by employing more staff to help and advise users?

6 Which problem is best remedied by using passwords for certain files?

7 Consider the following statements.
   (i) Video conferencing allows users to keep in touch at all times.
   (ii) Video conferencing allows face-to-face conferences at two or more different locations.

Which option best describes the two statements?
a (i) True,   (ii) True
b (i) True,   (ii) False
c (i) False, (ii) True
d (i) False, (ii) False

8 Consider the following statements.
   (i) Modern communications technology allows more people to work at home.
   (ii) Modern communications technology will make all office staff redundant.

Which option best describes the two statements?
a (i) True,   (ii) True
b (i) True,   (ii) False
c (i) False, (ii) True
d (i) False, (ii) False

Assignment

PC
2.3.1
2.3.2
2.3.3
2.3.4
2.3.5

Write a report to your tutor on the facilities offered for both internal and external communications systems for the operation of a small accountancy business. The business has three partners and eight clerical and administrative staff. You must recommend a telephone system and any other communication equipment that you think is necessary and state the purposes for which the firm will use this equipment.

(Note: prior to writing this report, you must prepare notes in order to participate in a group discussion on the positive and negative aspects of changing the accounting firm's communication systems.)

Element 2.4
ANALYSE INFORMATION PROCESSING IN A BUSINESS ORGANISATION

Performance criteria

1. **Explain the purposes of information processing.**
2. **Describe information processing in one business organisation.**
3. **Analyse the effectiveness of information processing in one business organisation.**
4. **Explain the effects of the Data Protection Act on individuals and businesses.**
5. **Explain the positive and negative effects of changes to information processing for individuals and business.**
6. **Propose changes to information processing in a business organisation.**

Element 2.4 Analyse information processing in a business organisation

THE PURPOSES OF INFORMATION PROCESSING

An information processing system takes data and rearranges it into a form that tells us what we want to know, that is information. An accounting system, for instance, takes raw bookkeeping data and changes it into management and accounting information that is useful to both the organisation's operational managers and its accountants.

In order to obtain useful information, an organisation has to perform two basic functions with the data that it collects. It must first sort it into some order and it must then summarise or analyse it into categories which are meaningful, such as sales by area or by each individual salesperson.

Once an organisation has decided on the information that it needs, its managers must organise the information in a way that is most meaningful to them. Some information is required by law, such as the financial accounts, but most of the information requirements of the organisation are stated by the managers themselves. They must arrange for the design and implementation of systems that will capture the raw data, sort it, summarise it and analyse it into a format that is usable. In the design of the systems they must specify both the inputs of data and the outputs of information that they require. Controls must be installed to ensure that the system works as intended.

The transmission and receipt of information was covered in Element 2.3. Information that has been received must be stored until the user requires it. All information processing systems, whether manual or computer-generated are expensive to operate and so it is essential that managers use the information that is produced, otherwise its collection and analysis will have been an expensive waste of time and resources.

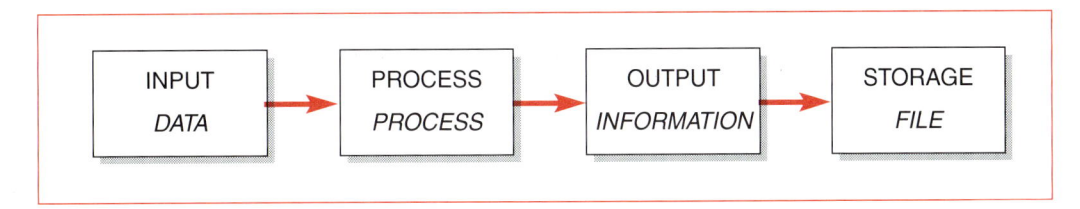

INPUT *DATA* → PROCESS *PROCESS* → OUTPUT *INFORMATION* → STORAGE *FILE*

Fig 2.36 Information processing

ACTIVITY 2.4.1

PC 2.4.1

Task 1. In groups of three, prepare a poster that will illustrate the definitions of both *data* and *information*. You should only spend about 20 minutes on this task and when it is complete all of the efforts of the different groups in your class should be compared and the best should be put on the wall of your room to illustrate to others the two definitions.

Task 2. Prepare a second poster that explains the purpose of information processing. Again discuss each group's effort and leave the best poster on the wall.

COMPUTERS

Computer hardware

The physical parts of a computer are known as its hardware. These include the computer processor with its disk drives and storage devices, its screen and keyboard and whatever input and output devices are linked to it, such as printers. These are explained in more detail later in this element.

For the purposes of this element we shall regard a computer as a digital electronic data processing machine that can process business data at great speed. It has a memory where many thousands of bits of information can be stored and used. As with manual data processing methods, operations can be broken down into four components: data input, process, output and storage. There are many other types of computer, both digital and analogue, that are used for other purposes; we are only interested in those used for processing business data.

Computers come in different sizes. Large, so called *mainframe* computers are used by large companies and public bodies such as local and central government agencies. They are used to process vast amounts of data and can support the use of hundreds of terminals that allow many users access to the systems at the same time. The best example of such a system is the DVLC at Swansea that holds all UK motor vehicle and drivers' records.

Mini computer systems are really small mainframe computers that are usually dedicated to operating a small number of business systems, such as running the accounting system for a large firm. *Personal computers* or *PCs* are small desk-top machines that can run a variety of systems. Initially of a low capacity, these machines are now becoming so powerful that they have replaced most mini computer systems. These machines can run almost all business applications and most of the information in this element relates to them.

All computers can be linked together through either local area networks (LANs) or wide area networks (WANs). These systems allow the files in one computer to be accessed by others in the same network, and data and information can be transferred from one machine to another. This allows one personal computer to act as an intelligent terminal to another, enabling it to pass processed data from one computer to another at any location via the LANs or WANs.

Data input

All data processing systems require data input. When a large computer system uses the *batch processing method* of data input, the objective is to collect a large volume of data and convert that data into a computerised form as quickly and as accurately as possible. In such a system there are five main data input tasks that have been identified.

1 Data is supplied by the data provider, e.g. the completion of a form or a purchase order.

2 The data is transferred to the place of processing. In a manual system this would mean sending the forms to the relevant clerk. In a computer system using batch processing the forms are sent to the Data Preparation Department.

Element 2.4 Analyse information processing in a business organisation

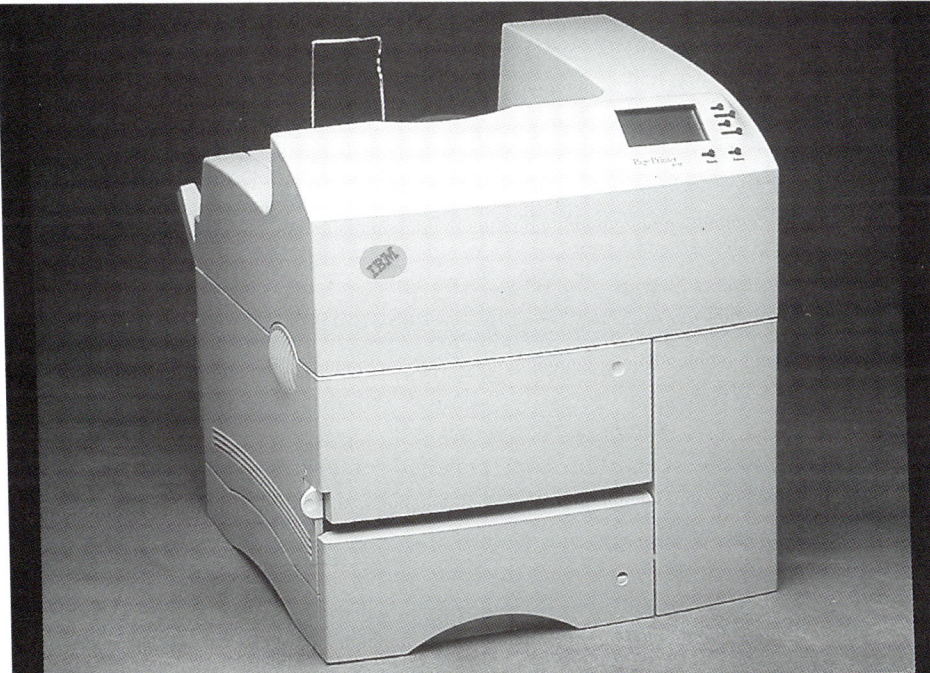

Fig 2.37 A computer and a printer

3 The data is scrutinised for errors or omissions by the data control section.
4 The data is prepared for input to the processor. This step is usually repeated and the two versions are electronically compared to check the accuracy of the input. Any differences are investigated and errors are corrected. This is called *verification*.

5   The data files thus prepared are input into the main computer system. Data validation routines within the computer programs ensure that the data is logical with regard to the file that it is updating. Errors are listed and reported back to the person initiating the input.

Data can be directly input into the system via a computer keyboard. This is the traditional method of data preparation whereby forms are batch processed and are transferred on to a computer acceptable media such as magnetic tapes or disks and the routines outlined above are followed. This system is very labour intensive, slow and costly, and unless the controls over the input are closely followed, errors can occur. Other more direct methods of data capture are now replacing most batch processing systems.

- *Magnetic Ink Character Recognition (MICR)* uses preprinted characters that use magnetic ink in their printing. The system is best illustrated on the bottom line of a cheque (*see* Fig. 2.38). The banks invested heavily in these readers in the past and use them to automatically sort cheques when they are cleared. Although these systems are now quite old, their universal use and high cost of replacement are a barrier to the banks changing their systems – after all they still work!

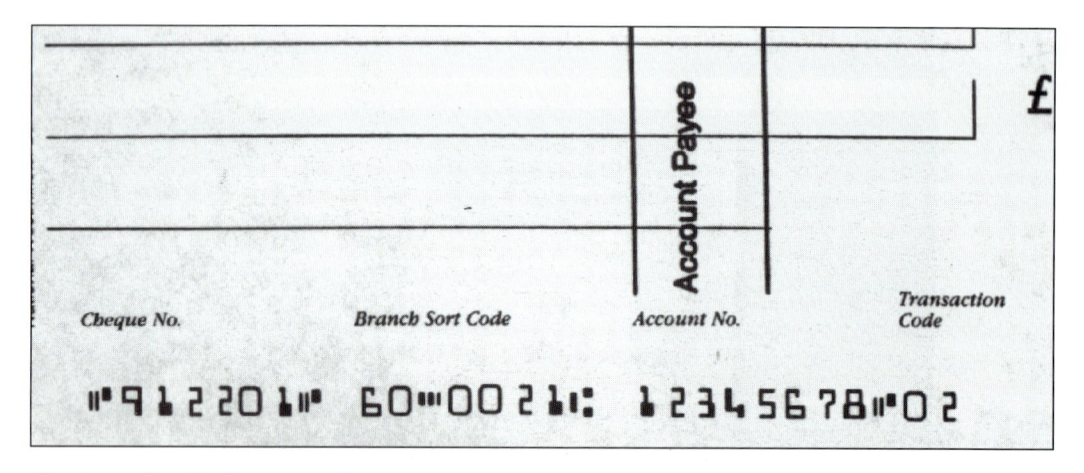

Fig 2.38 On the bottom of cheques characters are preprinted in magnetic ink

- *Optical Character Recognition (OCR)* readers can read handwritten documents and produce computer files. These are best used when inputting data from forms where the respondents' answers to questions can be predicted to some extent and the answers are written in answer boxes on the form so the reader can identify the response.
- *Optical Mark Recognition (OMR)* handles handwritten marks on preprinted forms. Again questions are asked on the form and the respondent makes a mark on the box or circle that contains the correct answer. The best illustration of these forms is the card used for inputting numbers into the UK national lottery. Another example that is related to your course is the external test used by BTEC and the other examination bodies (*see* Fig. 2.39).
- *Bar codes* are now an established method of data entry into a computer system and indeed they are produced by computer printers. An example of a bar code is shown on the back of this book. This allows the organisations in the book trade to input the ISBN code reference for this book into their computers. Almost all retail products sold in the developed world now have bar codes printed upon them. (*See* Fig. 2.40.)

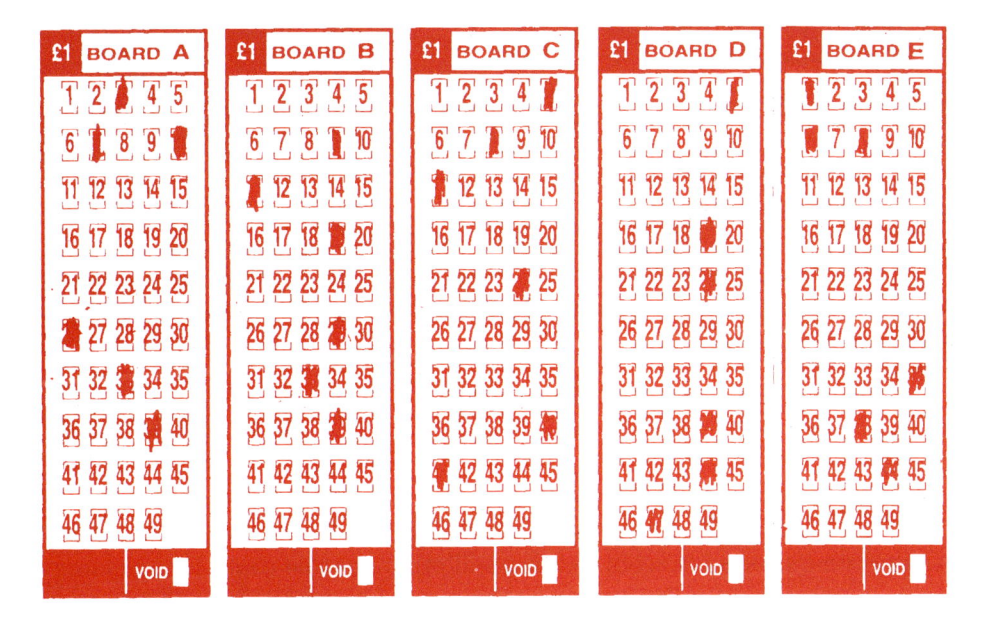

Element 2.4 Analyse information processing in a business organisation

Fig 2.39 The UK national lottery system uses the OMR system

Fig 2.40 Barcoding is now an established method of data maintenance

ACTIVITY 2.4.2

PC 2.4.5

Write a report to the governors of your school or college on the effects on the organisation's management information system of using bar coded identification cards for all students and bar code readers at the building's entrance to record student attendance.

Computer software

There are two basic types of computer programs that are needed to make the computer actually do something. The first type is known as an *operating system*, while the second is known as the *application system*.

Operating systems

For personal computers there are a limited number of operating systems, the most well-known being:

- CP/M
- Unix
- DOS
- Windows.

An operating system is a set of routines and programs that control the running and internal organisation of the computer. This type of program allows the user to run and use the applications that are held on the application system. Operating systems usually deal with the following:

- storage and retrieval of programs and maintenance of program libraries;
- input and output control to manage the movement of data between the backing store, the input and output peripherals and RAM (random access memory);
- storage management to utilise RAM by efficient allocation of space;
- error handling by either taking remedial action or reporting to the user;
- standard operator communications, such as advice on completion of jobs, requests for input, file copies, help messages, etc.

PC 2.4.1

ACTIVITY 2.4.3

Do some research in your local library or use an article from a computer magazine and write a short description of the 'Windows' operating system.

Application packages

Word and text processing

These packages can be split into either word processing or desk-top publishing systems.

Word processing is the electronic preparation and manipulation of text by a computer. Text can be filed on disk and printed in a range of typefaces. It can be updated and checked, its spelling can be checked and most systems have a thesaurus and a dictionary. The final printed copy contains no unsightly alterations and, depending on the ability of the operator, should be perfect. When linked together in a network (LAN or WAN), the word processors can send text to each other through the electronic mail system – E-mail.

The sale of word processing packages is very volatile as new ones appear on the market each year and existing packages are updated. Currently the two most popular systems used by businesses in thc UK are the different versions of Microsoft Word (part of the Microsoft office suite of programs) and Wordperfect (part of the Boreland office suite of programs). The latest applications of all these systems run through the Windows operating system.

Desk-top publishing systems aim to produce top quality print on a personal computer. They can manipulate print sizes, styles and columns and produce high quality graphics to integrate into the text. The input of large volumes of text into these systems is usually done via a standard word processing package. Currently the most popular package on the UK market is Aldus Pagemaker.

Spreadsheets

These packages allow the user to build financial models for analysing rows and columns of figures. These packages are ideal for such jobs as budget preparation as they allow the user to alter any figure and then recalculate all of the totals automatically. Element 7.2 of Unit 7 'Financial Resources' gives more details on spreadsheet systems and shows how a cash budget can be constructed using Microsoft XL.

Databases

These systems are computerised filing systems that enable you to file and retrieve data very quickly. Data can also be sorted and printed out in any order or format. Using a database can be broken down into four operations:

- the creation of a database structure;
- the entry and amendment of data;
- the retrieval and manipulation of data;
- the production of reports.

Accounting systems

There are many accounting systems that will run on personal computers. Most of them are now fully integrated systems that allow for the automatic transfer of data from one part of the system to another – entries into one ledger will insert the corresponding entry into the correct account in another. These systems also produce most of the financial documentation that accompanies the accounts such as sale debtors invoices, pay slips, payrolls and printed cheques and remittance advices.

ACTIVITY 2.4.4

From the above descriptions of computer software, choose one system and give a five-minute presentation to your colleagues on its uses in business.

PC 2.4.1

Computer output

The two most usual forms of output are the visual display unit (VDU) and the various types of printers that can be used. Output can be sent electronically from one computer to another, however, through a network (LAN) or through a modem to another computer in a different location via the telephone system (WAN).

VDUs are the screens used by computers to display text and graphics. The most common types of screen are those that look like televisions. Many lap-top computers use the flat liquid crystal displays (LCD) and as the technology for these advances we may see them increasingly used on other applications (*see* Fig. 2.37 and 2.41).

Fig 2.41 A laptop computer

Computer printers come in many styles, speeds, qualities and prices.

- *Dot matrix printers* are inexpensive printers that are usually used with PCs when the final copy does not have to be of the best quality. Each character is printed separately and is produced by a series of pins which, when the character is formed, strike a printer ribbon as used in an electronic typewriter. As a result of this, dot matrix printers tend to be noisy and relatively slow.
- A *daisy wheel printer* is similar to that used in an electronic typewriter. Each character is held at the end of a spoke which is spun into the correct position for a hammer to strike it on to a printer ribbon. It takes its name from the appearance of the wheel. Although noisy, these printers produce a good standard of print but they are very slow and the printer is restricted to the size and type of character on the daisy wheel. These can be changed but this slows things down even further. They are now only used for dedicated word processors.
- *Ink jet printers* produce an excellent quality print and can print a range of character types and sizes. Many produce good graphics and some can print colours. Although the smaller printers that are used with PCs are relatively inexpensive to purchase, they can be expensive to run as their ink cartridges are small and can be costly to replace. They work by squirting ink directly on to the paper a line at a time. Some of the larger capacity printers of this type are used with large mainframe computer systems.

Element 2.4 Analyse information processing in a business organisation

- *Laser printers* use similar technology to a photocopier. They produce excellent quality prints at a reasonable speed. They can print good graphics and some print colour. Although expensive to purchase, they are inexpensive to run.
- *Line printers* print a full line of text at a time by forming the text on a bar that contains a full character set for each character space. The bar is then struck against a printer ribbon. These types of printers have been in use for a considerable length of time. They are expensive, but are very fast and are usually used with large mainframe computers that require a large volume of print of a low quality.

Organisations that require a considerable amount of output can use Computer Output on to Microfilm (COM) devices which convert the characters small enough for printing on to microfilm rolls or slides which are called microfiches. These can be read through a microfilm viewer, some of which are linked to a photocopier in order to produce a hard copy of the desired information.

ACTIVITY 2.4.5

You have been asked by a group of friends to help them purchase a printer for their new PC. Using a recent copy of a computer magazine, list the types of printer and their prices that you would recommend for purchase.

PC 2.4.1

Computer networks

Initially the use of computers in business involved the installation of a mainframe computer with few input and output devices. Most of the information stored on the computer files was communicated by means of printouts from line printers. To receive the weekly or monthly printout was a significant event that showed the results of the input to date. This in turn produced a flurry of analysis, reports and decisions that then had to be implemented, usually by inputting more instructions into the computer system by means of filling in forms. These forms were batch processed together once per period prior to the next printout. As the advances in the equipment progressed, more terminals could be linked to the mainframe allowing more people access to the computer files and the use of video display units (VDUs) removed the need to print out all of the files each week or month. The communication of the information kept on computer files was still restricted to those people with access to a terminal.

Local area networks

Local area networks (LANs) are a system for moving information between computers on the same premises or geographical area. A local area network consists of the following:

- hardware consisting of a computer work station, either a terminal to a mainframe or a personal computer, plus a network interface expansion card that fits into the computer and the relevant software and operating system;
- a network server, which is usually a computer that carries the software available to the network users;

- cables that link the computers together in the network (radio systems can replace the cables but the costs are much greater).

Computer networks allow the use of *electronic mail* whereby one computer on the network can transfer information to another where it can be stored until the user accesses it. This avoids the use of paper and is an instantaneous and cheap method of communication.

Wide area networks

Wide area networks (WANs) are similar in operation but connect computers together over a wider geographical area, either by radio or through the telephone system allowing electronic mail to be sent from all over the world. These systems are leading towards the concept of the electronic 'super highway' that will give access not only to a wider use of electronic mail but also to centrally held databases of information. An example of this is the ability to access the *Internet* and *Ethernet* networks that are available to users all over the world, allowing them access to a huge number of databases containing vast amounts of information.

PC
2.4.5
2.4.6

ACTIVITY 2.4.6

Your boss, Mrs Jones, the Office Manager, has recently returned from a conference where some of the people were talking about the 'Information Super Highway'. She wants to know what it is and whether it has any uses for a small electronics manufacturing business that makes components for the motor industry. She wants you to write a short report giving your description of the concept and your opinion of its uses, if any, for the business.

DATA PROTECTION

The Data Protection Act 1984

The Data Protection Act 1984 was set up to protect the personal privacy of individuals and tries to enforce good practice when handling confidential information about people.

It was born out of public concern regarding the right of access to information by companies and organisations in the light of the computer technology explosion. Many companies now have a variety of information stored on databases about individuals.

The Act gives individuals the right to see personal data held on computer about themselves and gives them the right to correct that information if it is incorrect. Individuals can also complain if they do not approve of the way in which organisations collect or use information stored about them.

Individuals are entitled to seek compensation through the courts if damage and/or distress has been caused by the loss, unauthorised destruction, or unauthorised disclosure of personal data. The courts can also compensate for damage caused by inaccurate data.

In 1990 the Commission of the European Community published proposals regarding data protection. A draft General Directive was introduced which aimed to bring together the different data protection laws within the Community. The Act also allowed the United Kingdom to ratify the Council of Europe Convention on Data Protection so that data could flow freely between the United Kingdom and other European countries who had similar laws.

A Data Protection Registrar was appointed to administer the Act and report directly to Parliament.

The Act covers the following areas.

- *Data* – information recorded in a form in which it can be processed by equipment operating automatically in response to instructions given for that purpose (section 1.2).
- *Automatically processed information* – information which is put on computer. It does not relate to information which is processed manually (i.e. a paper filing system).
- *Personal Data* – about living individuals (section 1.3).
- *Data users* – companies or organisations who use the information (personal data) for their own use. The term 'data users' applies to both the private and public sector and can be individuals, sole traders, partnerships, PLCs and limited companies.
- A person carries on a *computer bureau* if that person provides others with services in respect of data, either as an agent or as a provider of equipment.
- *Processing* means amending, augmenting, deleting or rearranging the data or extracting the information constituting the data and performing any of those operations by reference to the data subject.
- *Data subjects* – are the people about whom the information is stored.

Registration

With a few exceptions, both data users who hold personal data and computer bureaux which process personal data must register with the Data Protection Registrar.

Data users and computer bureaux who process information about data subjects must also register, otherwise they are committing a criminal offence under the Data Protection Act 1984 and are liable to a fine of up to £5000 in the Magistrates Court or an unlimited fine in a High Court.

Data users must supply information about the personal data held, the purpose for which it is used, where they got the information, who they are disclosing the information to and whether the data is to be sent abroad.

Once registered with the Data Protection Registrar, the data user must comply with the Data Protection Principles of Good Practice. Failure to do so is a criminal offence.

For more in-depth information on the Data Protection Act and its effects on individuals and organisations, contact the Office of the Data Protection Registrar, Wycliffe House, Water Lane, Wilmslow, Cheshire SK9 5AF for a student information pack.

PC 2.4.4

ACTIVITY 2.4.7

Comment in writing on the contention that the Data Protection Act is a waste of time because its provisions cannot protect the individual from the misuse of data kept on files that the individual is not aware of.

Data security and confidentiality

One of the main problems that the widespread use of computer systems has brought is that much of the information kept on computer files is often of a very confidential nature. A company will not want its competitors to know its marketing plans or the details kept in its financial records. Consequently, it will need to keep some of its computer files secure not only from its competitors but also from most of its staff who could either pass on such information or manipulate it for their own profit. Computer fraud is said to cost businesses millions of pounds a year.

Furthermore, the managers should not allow the use of unauthorised disks that may contain computer viruses that could damage the information stored on the machine. Software can be purchased that will check the disks for the existence of viruses.

All computer files should be backed up (i.e. copies kept) and these disks should be stored in fireproof and secure storage. Should the computer be damaged and its files lost the results for the firm will be complete organisational chaos. It is then that the back-up files are essential.

The following safeguards should be adopted.

- All computers and mainframe terminals should be kept in secure accommodation.
- All computer should have locks that can be used to stop unauthorised access.
- All software systems should be protected with a system of passwords that allow the user to have access only to those parts of the system that their job requires.
- All computer disks should be numbered and kept in fire- and theftproof storage.

HEALTH AND SAFETY

Being powered by electricity, computers obviously have to be used with the same degree of caution as any other electrical device. They are no more dangerous, however, than a domestic television or video player. Personal computers use relatively low levels of electrical current (the highest current is needed to power the VDU screen which is similar in its requirements to a television). Unless the user is sufficiently skilled in electronic engineering, any repairs should be left to qualified personnel and in particular the box containing the computer processor should not be opened while the power is switched on. Additionally, it is not recommended that drinks or other liquids are brought near to the computer as a spillage will not only cause damage to the machine but, as it is an electrical device, a spill could also be dangerous to the operator.

In addition to the potential hazards involved with operating any electrical device, there are other potential hazards that are less lethal but more common.

In recent years some employees have claimed damages from their employers for a variety of physical complaints that have been identified as *repetitive strain injury*. This is where a computer operator has suffered pain following the repetitive actions required by the prolonged use of keyboards. Sitting in the same environment doing the same actions 40 hours per week, year after year, has caused damage to the operator's bones and muscles. In some severe cases, this has led to the operator becoming totally unfit for any type of work as well as causing considerable pain.

An additional problem that can arise from using computers relates to the use of VDU screens and their effect on the operator's eyesight. Many large firms now offer free eye tests to their employees as well as restricting their time in front of a VDU, and indeed recent legislation now covers these areas.

One of the European Health and Safety Directives even states the type of chair that a computer operator has to have. Various other claims have been made with regard to the adverse effect on health of the use of computers, but few of these have been substantiated by either the courts or the Health and Safety Executive.

In order to prevent any problems when using computers, the Health and Safety Executive have made the following recommendations.

- If you are working at the VDU for long periods, you need a chair with adjustable height and back support.
- However well designed your chair and desk, sitting in the same position for long periods is undesirable: you should therefore change your posture as often as possible.
- If your system has a detachable keyboard and tilt-swivel facilities on the screen, use them to adjust the system to meet your own needs.
- Some movement is desirable but repeated stretching movements are not. Make sure you have enough work space to take whatever documents you need.
- Do not rest your wrists on the edge of the keyboard or desk or bend your hands up at the wrist. Try to keep a soft touch on the keys and don't overstretch your fingers. Good keyboarding technique is important in prolonged operation.
- Experiment with different layouts of keyboard, screen and document holder to find the best arrangement for you.
- Arrange your desk and screen so that any bright lights are not reflected in the screen. You should not be looking directly at windows or bright lights. Easy-to-operate curtains or blinds should be provided to cut out unwanted light.
- Adjust the screen to give sharp individual characters that can be easily read.
- Do not spend long periods of continuous time at a VDU without sufficient breaks to avoid fatigue. Jobs should be organised to allow a change of activity, but if this is not possible frequent short breaks should be taken.

THE USE OF AN INTEGRATED BUSINESS COMPUTER SYSTEM

A few years ago the use of integrated software packages such as Lotus Works and Microsoft Works was widespread in many business organisations. These software systems allow the transfer of data from one application to another. The applications that are included in the system are word processing, spreadsheet, database, graphics and a facility to link the system to other computers. Today the same benefits are found in the use of the 'Windows' operating system which is easier to use and allows the use of much more powerful applications packages. The use of Windows and similar operating systems allows the user to work on more than one package at a time and to import and export work from one package to another. Almost all applications packages have been developed for use with Windows and the demand from users for hardware that is capable of using all of the facilities of Windows has set the current standard for PCs.

In order to understand the use of information processing systems within a modern business setting the following case study has been prepared.

Margaret Dean is asked to prepare a financial report on the firm's last quarter's performance and a projection of the estimated performance over the next two quarters. The report has to be ready for the Managing Director, Penelope Leake, to take to the board meeting the following day.

Using the spreadsheet on her PC, Margaret retrieves the file that she wants to update. She makes the changes that are required to update the file and the spreadsheet automatically recalculates the totals, and makes new projections based on the formulas that she initially built into the system.

After recalculating the new figures in the spreadsheet, Margaret prepares two charts. The first is a pie chart that compares the relative performance of all of the firm's divisions for this quarter. The second is a line chart that shows the trends of company performance over the last year plus her projections for the next two quarters. In order to obtain the best presentation for her chart, she plays about with various fonts, shading patterns, keys, legends and titles until she achieves the most appropriate. She then saves both charts for later use.

Margaret then writes the report using the word processing package in the system. As she writes, the functions of the package allow her to indent, underline and make bold. She inserts the two charts within the text at the appropriate places, spellchecks it and prints out a draft copy of the report. After proofreading, she decides to delete one part and change the order of the rest of the text using 'cut and paste'. When the report is complete she prints the final copy in the typeface (font) of her choice. She then saves a copy of the report on to a disk for future reference, and gives the report to the Managing Director's secretary.

Later that day the Managing Director thanks her for her efforts and asks her to present it to the board herself as a 'presentation'. She returns to her computer and retrieves the files from the spreadsheet and prepares a graph for each division, prints them in colour on to overhead projector slides and makes her presentation. After the presentation the board ask her to send a copy of the report to each Divisional Manager. This she does using the 'E-mail' facility within the network (WAN).

Element 2.4 Analyse information processing in a business organisation

THE EFFECTS OF COMPUTER TECHNOLOGY

It is almost impossible to overestimate the effects that computers have had on our lives. It is also difficult to predict the future social implications of current and future developments in computer technology. The continued application and development of such technology to both data processing and communications systems will force the current changes in employment patterns to accelerate. Some of the changes that have already taken place have been mentioned earlier in this element and in Element 2.3 of this unit. Can you imagine booking a holiday at a travel agent's without the aid of the computer database? Can you appreciate how difficult it was prior to the current system?

In recent years the sale of PCs for home use has rapidly increased. The latest machines of this type include full multimedia compact disk (CD) and sound facilities that give access to a full range of video games and the use of the vast amount of data that can be stored on a standard compact disk. If you go to your local college or library you will find that most of the information databases, such as newspaper cuttings, Excel and MaCarthy systems are now on compact disk. If you need to find something out about a product or a company you can do so using these CD/ROM systems. The information is now easy to find and can be printed out on the computer's printer. Research is much easier to do using these facilities and this will make assignments and portfolio building activities easier.

It is now possible to buy video disks that are the same size as CDs. These will most probably replace the conventional video tape machines, just as CDs replaced records and tapes for listening to prerecorded music. Full-length feature films can be shown either on the TV or the VDU of a personal computer that contains a CD/ROM drive. Furthermore, the sound output can be fed through a music centre to achieve cinema quality sound to match the high quality vision.

Research has been underway for a number of years to achieve input devices for computers using the sound of the human voice. If these systems can be made to work properly, the major impact will be that you will be able to talk directly to the computer without the need to input text and figures via a keyboard. Typing and word processing will have become a job of the past. You will not even have to be in the same room or indeed the same country, you can talk to your computer on the telephone. Some banks are already using voice recognition to identify customers over the telephone.

The main problem that we face with using new technology in business is the ever-increasing pace of change as new developments and applications come on to the market. Almost every year existing packages are updated and new ones are put on the market. Some need newer more powerful PCs to run them. All will involve a retraining programme for the users. No sooner are the users familiar with a system than it is changed, enhanced, integrated with something else. All change is stressful and unless it is managed well it can have a demoralising effect on staff. In some cases poorly managed changes have almost led to the disintegration of the organisation.

An example is the introduction of a new computer system in a large mail-order firm. Both the hardware and the software were changed, the new systems had faults and staff were inadequately trained to use them. When customers rang up to order goods the computer indicated no stock when in fact there was plenty. The result was a loss of sales, a lot of unsold stock which had to be sold later at below cost price and an appalling cash flow problem as money was paid out to suppliers but no cash was received from customers.

PC
2.4.5
2.4.6

ACTIVITY 2.4.8

Prepare notes for a discussion on the effects that new technology is likely to have on work practices over the next five years. When you are ready, take part in a class discussion on 'How changes in information processing will affect business organisations and systems'.

ACTIVITY 2.4.9

Your firm has just updated one of its data processing systems from a manual system to a computerised system. Write a memorandum to Mrs Jones, the Office Manager, on your opinions of the need to review and evaluate the effectiveness of the new system.

Self assessment questions

1 Many small firms have not changed their data processing systems from manual systems to computer-based systems. The main advantage of continuing to use their present manual system is:
   a The staff are familiar with the present systems and will not require additional training.
   b Computers make too many mistakes.
   c There is nowhere to put the computer.
   d In the long term any change will cost too much money.

   Questions 2, 3 and 4 use the following information.

   Most computers in business use the following applications packages:
   - spreadsheets
   - word processing
   - desk-top publishing
   - databases

2 Which package is associated with the production of forecasts and budgets?

3 Which package is associated with the storage of facts for future retrieval and analysis?

4 Which package is associated with the production of standard memos, letters and reports?

5 Consider the following statements:
   (i) Computer viruses can destroy the information kept on the computer's files.
   (ii) Computer viruses can make the computer unusable.

   Which option best describes the two statements?
   a (i) True,   (ii) True
   b (i) True,   (ii) False
   c (i) False, (ii) True
   d (i) False, (ii) False

6 Computer operators can suffer from physical and mental strain. Which of the following is the best way for an employer to reduce the incidence of such strain?
   a Employ fewer staff.
   b Employ younger staff.
   c Vary the tasks required and allow frequent breaks.
   d Reduce the staff's working hours.

7 Consider the following statements:
   (i) Computers enable more information to be processed more quickly.
   (ii) Input into computer systems can only be made through a keyboard.

   Which option best describes the two statements?
   a (i) True,   (ii) True
   b (i) True,   (ii) False
   c (i) False, (ii) True
   d (i) False, (ii) False

8 The Data Protection Act requires all organisations that keep electronic data files to:
   (i) register each purpose for which it keeps computerised records;
   (ii) be inspected and then register.

   Which option best describes the two statements?
   a (i) True,   (ii) True
   b (i) True,   (ii) False
   c (i) False, (ii) True
   d (i) False, (ii) False

Assignment

PC
2.4.2
2.4.3
2.4.5
2.4.6

This assignment involves research into a business information processing system. The organisation could be your place of work, that of a friend, parent or the school you attend. When you complete your research, write a report to the manager outlining your description of the systems in use, their effectiveness and any changes you consider may be appropriate and their effects on individuals in the organisation.

Answers to self assessment questions

Element 2.1	Element 2.2	Element 2.3	Element 2.4
1. a	1. a	1. d	1. a
2. b	2. a	2. a	2. a
3. d	3. c	3. c	3. d
4. c	4. a	4. c	4. b
5. c	5. b	5. d	5. a
6. a	6. b	6. b	6. c
7. a	7. d	7. c	7. b
		8. b	8. b

UNIT 3

MARKETING

Marketing is the function that integrates all of an organisation's activities and as a result the subject of marketing has its roots in a range of other disciplines, this unit therefore takes in aspects of statistics, economics, sociology and psychology. It sets out the main principles and functions of marketing before discussing the areas of marketing research, marketing communications and sales management in greater detail.

Element 3.1
INVESTIGATE THE PRINCIPLES AND FUNCTIONS OF MARKETING IN ORGANISATIONS

Performance criteria

1 **Discuss marketing principles and marketing functions.**

2 **Explain how the marketing principles underpin the marketing functions.**

3 **Explain an organisation's need to have a customer focus while meeting its own needs.**

4 **Analyse marketing activities in business organisations.**

5 **Explain growth of organisations.**

6 **Identify factors influencing pricing decisions in business organisations.**

Introduction

This element introduces the principles which underpin the marketing functions of an organisation. Marketing activities are analysed and the various approaches to the growth of organisations discussed.

MARKETING PRINCIPLES

The British Chartered Institute of Marketing provides a comprehensive definition of marketing which is a useful introduction to the marketing concept:

> Marketing is the management process responsible for identifying, anticipating and satisfying customer needs profitably.

This definition can be broken down into several parts.

Identifying customer needs

One important aspect of the marketer's job is to be able to identify customer needs and marketing opportunities within the business environment. Marketing research is the process that enables the marketer to identify these opportunities – its function is to provide the organisation with information about its environment.

Anticipating customer needs

By identifying opportunities, the marketer is in a position to anticipate the future needs of the market. This involves a detailed understanding of marketing activities such as market segmentation and consumption patterns (see Element 3.3).

Satisfying customer needs profitably

While it is important that an organisation maintains customer satisfaction, it also needs to achieve this and at the same time earn a profit or some other gain. This implies that an exchange process is taking place. This exchange process is highlighted in another popular marketing definition by the well-known marketing author, Philip Kotler.

> Marketing is human activity directed at satisfying needs and wants through an exchange process.

Exchange processes are the means of effecting both the sale and purchase of products (*see* Fig. 3.1)

During the exchange process something of value is exchanged by both the buyer and the seller. What must be remembered is what is received by each party will be of greater value to that party than what is given. For example, you may have saved up for a new CD player. When you purchase it the value of the product will be judged by the pleasure it gives you, i.e. listening to your favourite music. This pleasure will outweigh any pleasure you may have obtained from just keeping the money in the bank. The added value that the retailer receives is obvious – it is the profit made on the sale.

It is vital for an organisation when setting its objectives to remember that the exchange process should be satisfying to both the buyer and the seller. The seller is responsible for creating and maintaining the exchange relationship. This is achieved by ensuring that the customer is satisfied with the product purchased, because only then can the seller be confident that the customer will return and therefore continue the exchange relationship.

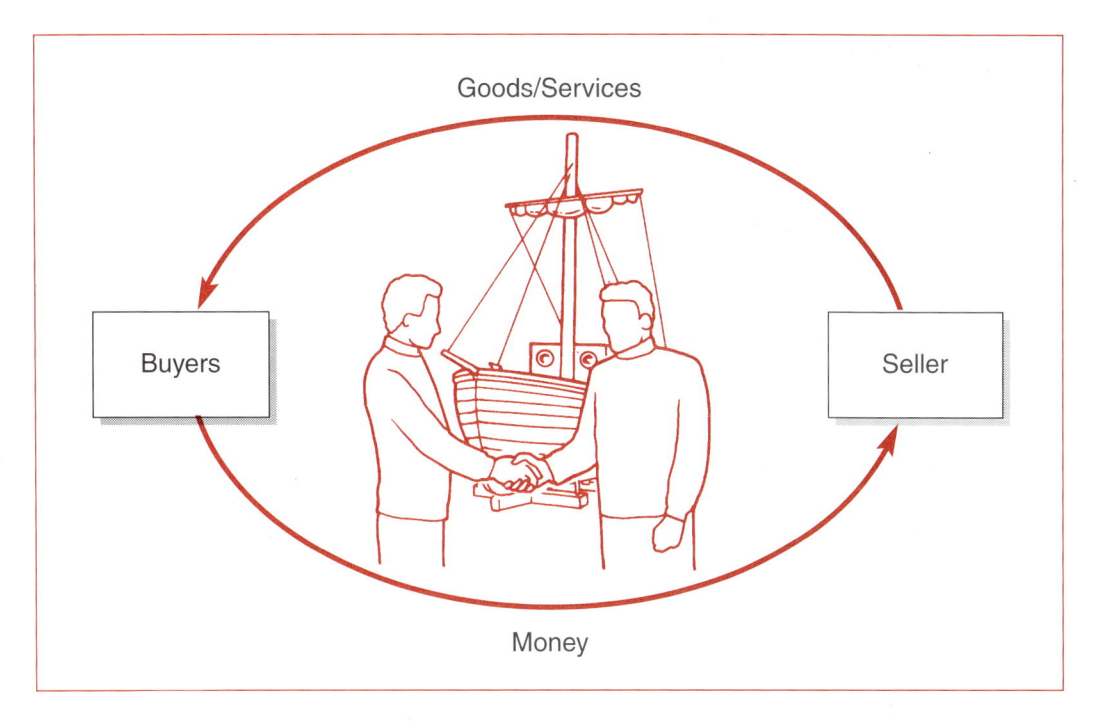

Element 3.1 Investigate the principles and functions of marketing in organisations

Fig 3.1 The exchange process

Marketing activities are performed by organisations in order to assist the exchange relationship, to ensure customer satisfaction and to achieve marketing objectives. For example, the distribution function seeks to ensure that the customer receives his or her goods as quickly and conveniently as possible. The principle aim of any organisation that believes in pursuing the marketing concept should be the creation of customer satisfaction. With this aim in mind specific objectives may then be set without the potential danger of undermining the customer's satisfaction.

MARKETING OBJECTIVES

The objectives that an organisation finds itself setting will depend on numerous factors, e.g. the competitive environment, the size and nature of the market, the state of the economy and even the product itself. It is basically the environment and the nature of the organisation that will shape the objectives set and so influence marketing activities. There are a number of common objectives, however, that are pursued by many organisations.

Increasing sales and profit

To many this seems the most obvious of objectives for an organisation to pursue. The knowledge that demand and therefore sales of an organisation's product are rising reduces the element of uncertainty. If sales are increasing, then there is the likely guarantee that financial resources will be available to consolidate on existing activities or for financing expansion into new business areas. Another benefit often sought is the achievement of economies of scale, i.e. spreading the operating costs over a larger volume of sales and therefore creating the opportunity for larger profit margins or competitive pricing. Many organisations see that by achieving the objective of increased sales volume they are effectively strengthening their position within their market.

It should also be pointed out, however, that the blind pursuit of increasing sales volume can sometimes lead to problems. Diseconomies of scale were discussed in Unit 1. At a certain point costs may actually start to rise as sales volume increases. For example, a company may have to employ more administration staff to cope with the increased bureaucracy resulting from the increase in sales, or an organisation's management team may cease to be effective when turnover reaches a certain size. These situations can be dangerous to companies that have insufficient working capital to cope with rapid growth.

To many organisations the objective of increased sales is an important aspect when establishing marketing activities. It is worth remembering, however, that very clear, attainable targets should be set that are within the resource constraints of the organisation, if that organisation also wishes to increase profits.

One highly visible approach to increasing sales volume can be seen in the fast food industry. Companies such as McDonald's and Burger King ensure that their counter staff are working towards the achievement of this objective. If an order is placed that doesn't include a drink or fries then the staff will always suggest these to the customer. This simple approach maximises the opportunities available for the company to sell its products to the customer.

Increasing market share

Another important objective linked to sales activities is that of increasing market share. This objective usually calls for an increase in the proportion of company sales relative to total market sales. Often an increase in sales volume will result in an increase in overall market share. This is not always the case, however. If a particular market is growing rapidly then an organisation's competitors may be increasing their sales volume at a faster rate. If this is happening then the company will be losing market share. Why then is increasing market share an important marketing objective? Surely, if a company is increasing its sales volume then there should not be any real cause for concern. This may be the case; if the objective of increasing sales volume is being met then the organisation may be content. There are significant advantages, however, for an organisation with a large market share.

Many organisations that are market leaders will actually use this fact in their promotional activities. This is often the case in industrial markets where high value purchases are made. The knowledge that the company you are dealing with is a major supplier within the industry may reassure the customer on such issues as reliability, quality and after-sales service.

Another advantage is that the market leader can be highly influential within the market. It may be able to dictate policy to its smaller suppliers on such issues as price, quality and delivery times. It may also be possible to dominate the channels of distribution, e.g. both Boots and WH Smith hold large shares of their markets and also ensure that they have the best town centre locations. This helps both companies to maintain their positions within their markets. The very large organisations and market leaders may also find it possible to influence political decisions. In the past the large construction companies have banded together in order to lobby the government and influence its decisions on roads policy. This example shows that through the power of large market share some organisations can actually control the demand for their products.

Increasing market share need not depend on growth of sales within a particular industry. If an industry sector is shrinking, it will become a very important objective to maintain or increase market share. This will always be done at the expense of other organisations and marketing activities will be seen to be much more aggressive.

ACTIVITY 3.1.1

For the following product categories select the companies that you believe to be the market leaders:

1 Package holidays
2 Family saloon cars
3 Compact 35mm cameras

Based on research among your friends and family, write down the reasons why people may prefer to purchase the products produced by the market leaders. Identify reasons why people choose *not* to purchase the products of the market leaders.

PC
3.3.1
3.3.2
C
3.2.1

Enhancing product image

There are many organisations that pursue the objective of enhanced product image and their marketing activities reflect this. The reasons for the pursuit of this objective are numerous. The organisation in question may wish to establish a niche in the market; it may be a response to changing demographic trends or it may simply be recognised as a way to increase profit margins.

A recent example is that of Sainsbury's. It sought to enhance the image of some of its own branded products in areas that were traditionally dominated by established proprietary brands. Two of these areas were washing powders/liquids, dominated by Unilever and Procter & Gamble, and cola, dominated by Coca-Cola. The assumption that Sainsbury's made was that if it could improve the image of its own branded products and still maintain the competitive price of an own brand then it would inevitably increase its market share. It successfully achieved this by introducing sub-brands – products that had a unique brand image, through a brand name and logo, while still retaining a connection with the supermarket. The washing powder product was sub-branded Novon and the cola, Classic Cola. This formula has proved successful for Sainsbury's and many competing supermarket companies are following suit. Sainsbury's were almost too successful, however, with the Classic Cola sub-brand as Coca-Cola threatened action over what it considered was a case of brand piracy. This resulted in a quick modification of this sub-brand's label and packaging.

The product's image is a combination of features and benefits that add to the basic core product. This can be seen in Fig. 3.2.

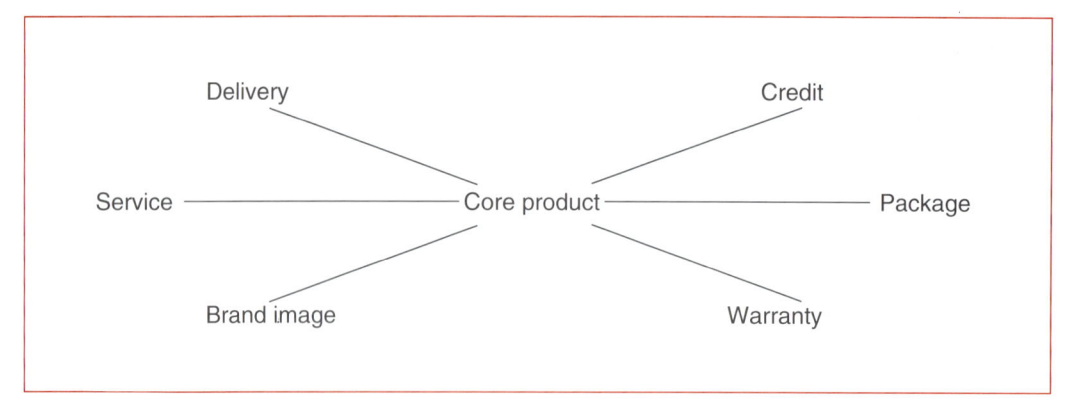

```
                Delivery                              Credit
                        \                            /
                         \                          /
    Service  ——————————— Core product ——————————— Package
                         /                          \
                        /                            \
              Brand image                          Warranty
```

Fig 3.2

In the Sainsbury's example we showed that it was possible to enhance the general image of the product by refining that product's brand image. This approach may not always be possible, especially in industrial markets where branding is not so predominant. Changing any one of the above variables could bring about an enhancement of the product's image, e.g. upgrading the warranty, speeding up delivery or offering a repair service.

Enhancing corporate image

The activities of many business organisations are constantly under the watchful eye of the media and numerous pressure groups. This is particularly true of the large multinational organisations that are seen to have considerable influence on the environment, world resources and even national economies. These organisations appreciate the delicacy of their positions as market leaders and know how damaging bad publicity in any form can be to potential sales.

One current example is that of McDonald's which is presently undertaking legal proceedings to counter recent reports on how its products may be damaging people's health and the environment. McDonald's believes that, if its activities are endorsed by the legal profession, then this will counter the negative comments brought against the company and so improve overall corporate image. McDonald's also uses advertising to enhance corporate image. You will probably have seen these types of adverts yourself. They tend not focus on any particular product but employ an image campaign in order to clarify or improve the public image. McDonald's often uses images of the family or multiracial images with which to promote its own corporate image.

There are four main reasons why an organisation may pursue the objective of corporate image (these are not all directly related to marketing activities):

1 to increase sales;
2 to recruit new employees/raise employee morale;
3 to raise the price of stock;
4 to improve the public's understanding of the company.

When looking at the above, it should be remembered that an increase in sales should be a long-term aim. Activities used to enhance corporate image are costly and should be seen as a long-term investment for future increases in sales.

Element 3.1 Investigate the principles and functions of marketing in organisations

ACTIVITY 3.1.2

Read the article in Fig. 3.3 and then select an organisation that you are familiar with. Identify and describe marketing activities that are undertaken by this organisation, including reasons for selection of the company name if you feel this is appropriate, which aim to enhance the corporate image. Discuss whether or not the organisation that you have selected is applying the principles of the two definitions of marketing described earlier.

PC 3.1.2
C 3.2.1

What's in a name?

Lucy Kellaway asks whether it really matters what a company calls itself

In the aftermath of the first world war there could hardly have been a worse name of a company operating in France than Bosch. The word *boche*, which means rascal, had become a term of abuse for Germans: yet the French bought Robert Bosch engines and pumps regardless.

Equally, Rentokil is about as bad a name as you could think of for a company trying to make it in healthcare and in tropical plants. Yet that name is here to stay. On this page last week chief executive Clive Thompson explained that he had shunned the advice of image consultants to rename his company. Rentokil, he said, has a reputation that transcends any association with hired assassins and is too entrenched now to discard.

So what's in a name? Does it matter what a company calls itself? "If you have a bad name you can still have a successful company," says Wally Olins, who has made a handsome living out of dreaming up new names of companies. "But it is easier for a company if it has a name that helps it."

However good or bad its name, a company needs a powerful reason to change once it has taken root.

According to Adrian Day, a senior consultant at Siegel and Gale, the communications consultancy, companies wanting a new name no longer reach automatically for initials. Not only have most combinations of two or three letters already been taken, but companies are discovering that establishing a new identity around meaningless initials can be expensive. "It takes a lot of time and expenditure to make them mean something," he says.

The most pressing reason for a new name is that the old one has become sullied. Thus Ratners, the UK high-street jeweller, has recently become Signet; Control Securities, the property and leisure company whose former chairman and chief executive has been charged in connection with the BCCI case, has started a new life as Ascot Holdings.

New names come in all shapes and sizes; they also come at all prices. At one extreme British Telecom is estimated to have spent some £50m letting Wolff Olins, the consultancy, transform it into BT. At the other Control Securities and Ratners spent little more than the cost of reprinting their stationery.

The name Signet simply occurred to a Ratners manager one day; he put it to his colleagues, they liked it and that was that. Control Securities' new name was even simpler – Ascot was the name of a shell company it owned.

By contrast, 25 people and a computer working flat out at image consultancy Interbrand for 14 weeks were required to come up with a new name of ICI's pharmaceuticals offshoot. The name Zeneca might seem scant reward for all that effort. Yet Interbrand's Paul Stobart explains that choosing a name is more difficult than it might appear; nearly all the obvious ones have already been taken. Moreover, the more markets a company is in, and the more countries, the more difficult it is to find an available name. A list of 1,000 possibles was checked against six trademark groups in more than 30 countries. Then the foreign language experts had to eliminate anything that was rude or indiscreet in a foreign language.

The next stage was to present the company with a shortlist. "People get very emotional about names. ICI was professional about it, but some companies can be a real nightmare," says Stobart. ICI decided on Zeneca because the Zen part has associations with Zenith. To give the name extra significance, the company explains that a little cross was added to the Z to make it resemble the alchemy symbol meaning to solve.

Such clever twists may be lost on the average consumer of pharmaceutical products, to whom one computer-generated name may be as good as any other. Yet experts can distinguish between names just as winetasters can pick out different vintages. "The way the name appears, the sound and texture of it when spoken, the symmetry of it, are all important. The word needs to have a good look and appeal, with nothing that is ugly or difficult to pronounce," says Stobart.

In choosing a name such as Zeneca, ICI has gone for the industry norm. In pharmaceuticals unusual names, such as Glaxo, are common. In other industries different rules apply. Advertising agencies and most professional firms call themselves after their partners – the more names the better.

Hairdressers cannot resist jokes: Headmasters, Curl up and Dye, Crops and Bobbers and so on. Puns are also acceptable for opticians – For Eyes is a market leader – and bathroom shops; but greengrocers and butchers stick to sensible names like High Class Butchers.

Says Olins: "Most people in any industry do what the peer group dictates." Anyone who breaks out will not be on their own for long. In the computer industry, IBM set the standard, and was followed by lookalike names such as ICL. Then came Apple, which was deliberately daring to be different. It was followed by Apricot and an orchard of computer companies. "Why are fruits like computers?" asks Olins. "Because someone did it once."

Despite all the effort that goes into getting a name right, many of the best names have been created by accident. One of Day's favourites is Virgin Atlantic. The lesson is perhaps that anyone trying to name an airline should think of a good name for an alternative record company, and take it from there.

Fig 3.3 *Source*: The *Financial Times*, October 1993

Quality assurance

The issue of quality is one way in which an organisation may position its products in their target markets. This may be achieved through a number of different marketing activities relating to the product, its price, how it is promoted and where and how in the market it is placed. These four areas, collectively known in marketing as the four Ps – (Product, Price, Promotion and Place (used to indicate distribution) – are important elements of an organisation's marketing mix. These will be discussed in greater detail later, but with regard to quality assurance, we can see how all the elements of the four Ps can be used to achieve this objective. The first area to consider is that of product.

Companies such as Rolls-Royce employ such rigorous quality standards that they have gained an international reputation; their products and name are recognised all over the world. This approach is not just reserved for upmarket products but is also adopted for mass produced goods. For example, the Japanese vehicle manufacturers piloted the concept of total quality management in their factories. This was a cost-effective way of monitoring, maintaining and improving quality and is one of the principle reasons why Japanese products are so competitive in today's world markets.

Quality assurance as an objective may be achieved by improving the physical qualities of a product. A consumer's perception of quality can be influenced by a number of psychological factors, however. Manufacturers and suppliers of so-called luxury products maintain the image of quality by ensuring their products are appropriately priced, promoted and distributed. Companies such as Versace, Valentino and Armani would be undermining their quality/exclusive image if they did not pursue exclusive pricing, promotion and distribution strategies. These are extreme examples of organisations that pursue the objective of quality assurance, but they highlight a practice that is undertaken by many organisations that are household names. If we refer back to the example of Sainsbury's own brands, you will remember that it was pointed out that many proprietary brands were more expensive. Certain proprietary brands are thought by consumers to be of higher quality than competing own brands and this belief is often reinforced by a higher price. An example of how this message is relayed to the consumer can be seen with the Fairy Liquid advertising campaign. This campaign consistently compares the quality differences between Fairy and its competitors.

Assuring the buying public of the quality of its products is a worthy goal for an organisation to pursue. Many consumers will hesitate over a purchase if quality is an unknown factor. Quality can be used to both justify pricing policies and encourage repeat purchases.

Objectives of non-profit organisations

Most of the marketing techniques that we will examine in this Unit apply equally to non-profit making organisations. Generally a non-profit making organisation is one which is concerned with the achievement of some goal other than profit. These types of organisation usually provide services and ideas – for example, education, health, or social services – as an addition to those provided by the state (e.g. Shelter, The Terence Higgins Trust, Children in Need). Your local FE College is a non-profit making business, but will probably use marketing strategy, such as advertising and promotion, to attract your attention to the courses and services that it has to offer.

Element 3.1 Investigate the principles and functions of marketing in organisations

> **ACTIVITY 3.1.3**
>
> Häagen-Dazs is a brand of ice cream that has recently been introduced to the UK market from the USA. It has attracted the attention of the public as a result of its provocative advertising campaign.
>
> *Task 1.* In groups research the product and determine what marketing objective the organisation is seeking to achieve.
>
> *Task 2.* Briefly describe the marketing activities being undertaken. You should look at how the product is promoted, where it is sold, its packaging and its price. Use examples or quote comparisons with other ice cream brands where appropriate.
>
> *Task 3.* Are the present marketing activities consistent with the marketing objective?

PC
3.1.1
3.1.2
3.1.2
C
3.1.2

Non-profit making objectives normally state the reason for the organisation's existence. For example, a college's objective could be 'ensuring high standards in the provision of education and training to all sections of the local community and meeting the needs and expectations of that community'. Alternatively, a charity's objective could be 'to promote a cause and to serve the needs and wants of both clients and donors'. The organisation should ensure that its objective is flexible enough to adapt to the needs and wants of the target public; this will assist in the future development of marketing strategies.

Co-ordinating activities to achieve marketing aims

Marketing is described as a management process. This enhances the status of marketing and suggests that marketing policy is as important as the financial policy of an organisation. Marketing-oriented firms understand the importance of effective marketing planning. Planning and co-ordinating marketing activities is a prime function of marketing management.

Co-ordinating the organisation's marketing activities is really the implementation of the marketing strategy and is an integral part of an organisation's corporate strategy. Therefore, effective co-ordination of the marketing function will contribute towards the achievement of an organisation's aims and objectives.

CUSTOMER FOCUS AND THE MARKETING CONCEPT

We discussed earlier how any business must be viewed as a customer satisfying process. If an organisation is to be successful and make a profit (if that is its aim), the customer must be satisfied. If the customer is not satisfied then the future profits of the organisation are at risk. A successful organisation will pursue the marketing concept: it will find out what people want and will make it available to them.

Companies do not always follow this concept, however, and if market demand exceeds supply, they may not suffer any consequences in the short term. Some organisations pursue the alternative concept – *the product concept*. They believe that success can be achieved by offering products with innovative features that are of high quality or high performance. There are organisations that strive for continuous product improvements. This is all very well but it only focuses on the product and it does not address the customer's need.

One example of this occurred during the early 1980s. The DeLorean motor car (the one used in *Back to the Future* – (*see* Fig. 3.4) was a gull-winged sports car with a brushed stainless steel body; there was no paint work. The car incorporated state-of-the-art technology and had a high performance engine. Everybody agreed – it was a beautifully engineered product. The only problem was that it failed! Commentators at the time blamed it on a number of factors: you couldn't open the doors in a car park; the body work showed up smudges and smears and looked unattractive when dirty; it was too expensive. The basic oversight by the company was that it did not ask itself, What does the customer need and want? The DeLorean Motor Company was product-oriented and not customer-oriented.

Fig 3.4 The DeLorean motor car as seen in the film *Back to the Future*
Credit: Amblin/Universal (Courtesy Kobal)

Customer service is not just about ensuring customer satisfaction with the product but with the complete purchasing process. Customer service should aim to maximise customer satisfaction; it is the final output of all the marketing activities within the marketing mix.

An organisation needs to know if its marketing activities are achieving suitable levels of customer satisfaction and also how it can improve those activities to achieve even greater customer satisfaction. In order to measure customer satisfaction an organisation must apply its research skills to itself. It must analyse its own activities and gather data and customer responses.

Element 3.1 Investigate the principles and functions of marketing in organisations

> One recent example in this area was the Post Office. The Post Office implemented a system that recorded the times of its services from postbox to letterbox. Once information was obtained from this system, resources could be concentrated on reducing the time taken for post to reach its destination. This data is published along with a commitment to strive for further improvements. Subsequent research has shown an increase in the level of customer satisfaction.

The above example shows a commitment to meeting customer requirements and not organisational requirements. There is little point in setting up a complaints department, if no attempt is made to eliminate the source of complaint.

A paradox may arise in the pursuit of customer satisfaction – the cost of providing customer service. Customer satisfaction may be achieved simply by the organisation doing things 'right first time' or through more complex approaches involving customer response surveys. However complex a system is implemented, it must not compromise the objective of customer satisfaction by adding unnecessary costs which may ultimately be passed on to the customer.

ACTIVITY 3.1.4

Your college, as a non-profit organisation, should have a mission statement (a statement of aims and objectives). Find out what it is and describes how it affects you and other students at your college.

Do you think that it fully addresses the issue of customer service? Detail any changes you would make to improve customer service.

MARKETING FUNCTIONS AND ACTIVITIES

In this section we will look at the various marketing functions, focusing initially on the marketing mix, its components and related marketing activities.

The marketing mix

The marketing mix refers to the integration of marketing elements into a programme that will best achieve an organisation's objectives. These marketing elements have been summarised into the four Ps.

- Product
- Price
- Promotion
- Place (Distribution)

Although easy to remember it does omit one very important element of marketing: marketing research (*see* Element 3.2). We will now introduce the four Ps, some of which will be studied in further detail in later elements.

Product

When considering the marketing mix it is always useful to examine the product component first. Decisions about price, distribution and promotion all revolve around the product.

Product definition

Before reading on, stop and think of three products. Quickly write them down. In the majority of cases the products identified will be tangible items or goods, e.g. a biro, a walkman or a can of soft drink. Most people fail to realise that a large proportion of the products that they use are not tangible, but intangible items. This means they are not products that can be picked up or touched. There are three general categories of product:

1 a good
2 a service
3 an idea.

We can all identify products which are *goods*; these are around us and are used every day. The same goes for *services* although these are not as immediately easy to identify, but we do use them with a similar frequency to goods, e.g. the cash point, public transport or a nightclub. The final category – the *idea* – can be difficult to conceptualise. One useful example is that of interest groups. Earthwatch is an organisation that promotes issues relating to the environment. For a fee you can subscribe to this organisation. This may involve you offering your services voluntarily in order to further promote these ideas. All of the above are products and in the following section, when we refer to products, they could be from any of the above categories.

The product mix

Most organisations market more than one product and it is therefore important for an organisation and its marketers to understand the relationships between all these products. The following terms are used by marketers in order to categorise all the products within the product portfolio.

1 A *product item* is a specific version of a product, i.e. it is one product offered by the organisation, e.g. the Ford Fiesta Ghia.

2 A *product line* is a group of closely related products; they may be related due to marketing, design, technical or end-use considerations, e.g. all the Fiestas manufactured by Ford would constitute one of Ford's lines.

3 *Product depth* would measure the number of products in each product line.

4 *Product width* would be the total number of lines offered by the organisation.

5 Figure 3.5 shows a simplified version of Ford's *product mix*, the mix being the actual total of the group of products available from the company.

Element 3.1 Investigate the principles and functions of marketing in organisations

Product width

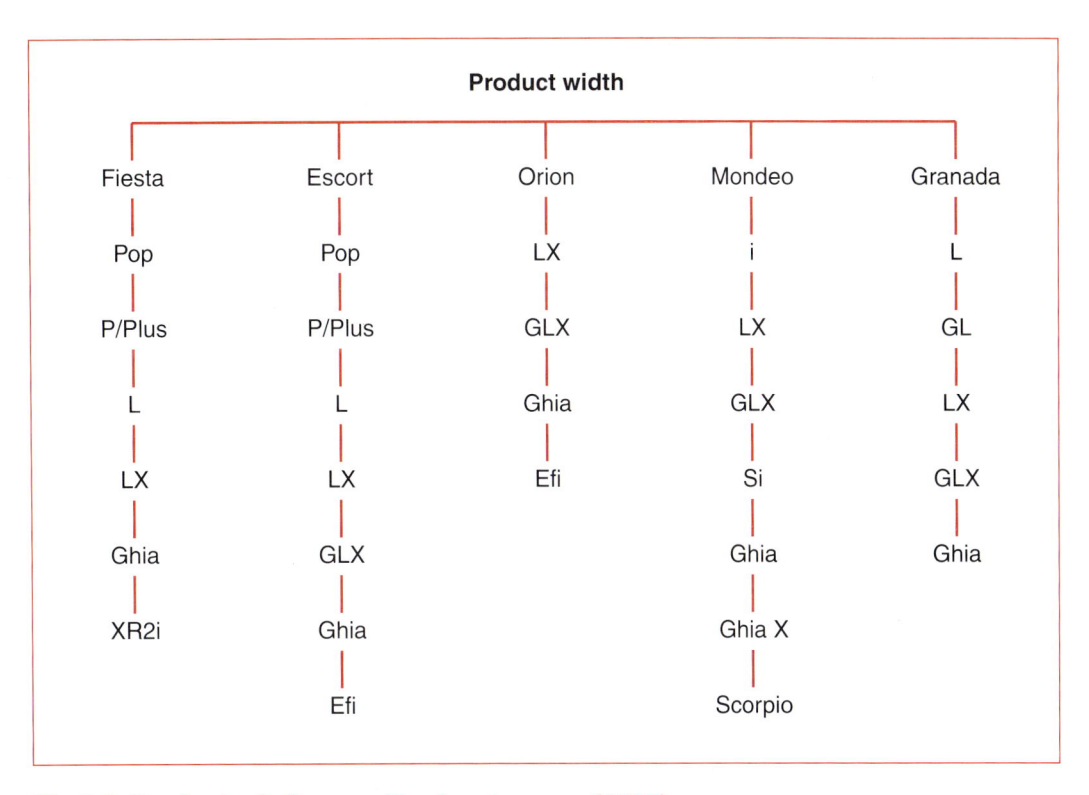

Fiesta	Escort	Orion	Mondeo	Granada
Pop	Pop	LX	i	L
P/Plus	P/Plus	GLX	LX	GL
L	L	Ghia	GLX	LX
LX	LX	Efi	Si	GLX
Ghia	GLX		Ghia	Ghia
XR2i	Ghia		Ghia X	
	Efi		Scorpio	

Fig 3.5 Product mix for new Ford motor cars (1995)

Fig 3.6 Ford Escort, Mondeo, and Granada

175

The product mix in Fig. 3.5 is a summarised version. It does not take into account varying product items by engine size and estate, hatchback, diesel or cabriolet versions. If these variables were to be included, they would simply deepen each product line.

The product mix is not a static formula for an organisation. Some readers will no doubt remember when the above mix included such names as Sierra, Capri, Cortina and even Anglia! Old products are constantly dropped from the product mix to be replaced by new ones.

Fig 3.7 Ford Anglia

This is a dynamic process that is essential if an organisation wishes to maintain a balanced and competitive product portfolio. To understand this concept more fully let us now look at the next key area – the product life cycle.

The product life cycle

Figure 3.5 listed all the 1995 models of Ford motor cars marketed in the UK. It is important to stress the year of the model range. After a few years a model may be dropped from the range and be replaced by a new one.

The conclusion we can make from this observation is that products, like humans, have a life cycle – that is, they are born, they mature, grow old, and die. This phenomenon is called the product life cycle. See Figure 3.8. It can be measured in four basic stages:

1 introduction
2 growth
3 maturity
4 decline.

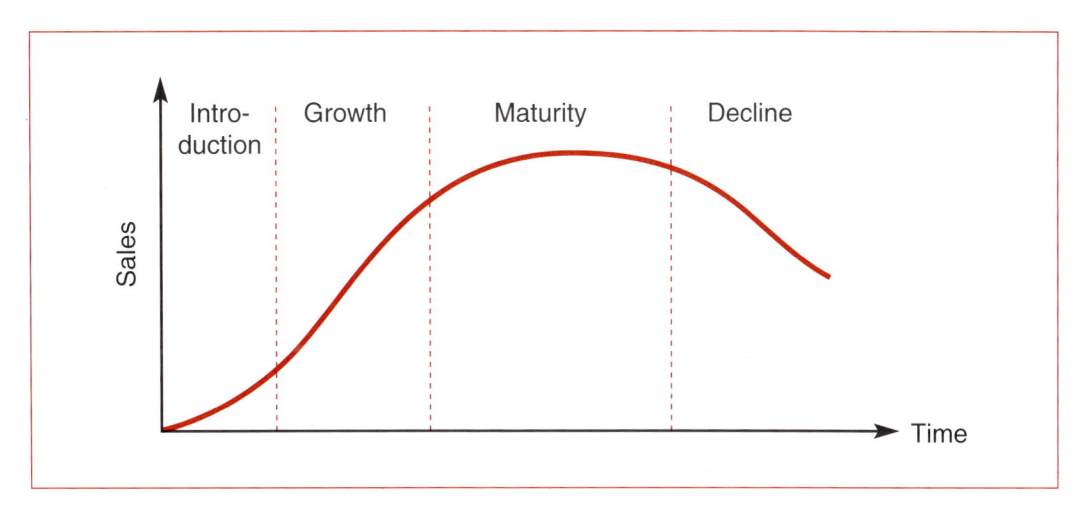

Fig 3.8 Basic product life cycles

Unlike the human life cycle product life cycles vary greatly. Take, for example, the difference between the life cycle of a hit single and that of a product such as Marmite or Bisto. The majority of products pass through the above stages and, as they do, strategies relating to competition, promotion, distribution, pricing and market information must be periodically evaluated and possibly changed. Marketing activities will also vary depending on the average span of time that the life cycle covers for different categories of activity. We will look at the stages in more detail in Element 3.3.

Branding

A brand is the identity given to a product. It can be a name, a design or a symbol and its chief purpose is to make a product distinct from those of other sellers. Brands are an aid to the purchasing process; they help buyers to identify specific products and also give the buyer an indication of quality and the product's characteristics.

Imagine you are abroad on holiday in a country you are visiting for the first time which has a language you do not speak. You are thirsty and would like a soft drink. In the shop there are no brands you recognise, but you do see a bottle which has a picture of an orange and the brand name Fizz. You make the purchase confident that what you are buying is a fizzy orange drink and not a bottle of washing-up liquid. In reality it would be very unusual if you did not see a brand which was instantly recognisable such as Coca-Cola, 7-Up or Sprite.

In the example above we see the brand performing two functions. In the first situation, it is trying to inform the buyer, as quickly as possible, of the nature of the product. In the second situation, it is offering instant recognition and reassurance to the buyer coupled with a guarantee of quality and consistency. It is therefore important that a brand establishes recognition. For many products the brand name is often the only real distinguishing feature; if you consider the competing brands of baked beans, for example, there is little difference between the actual products inside the can. The difference is established with the support of strong brand names and brand images such as Heinz and HP. If this difference did not exist, then the only other effective way of competing would be on price.

The way companies like Heinz ensure that they compete on brand image and not price is by encouraging brand loyalty. When a firm establishes a degree of customer loyalty to a brand, it can then charge a premium price for the product. Heinz managed to establish brand loyalty for its products through popular advertising campaigns and catchy slogans such as 'Beanz meanz Heinz' and 'Heinz buildz Britz'. Brand loyalty does appear to be declining as more and more competitors enter today's markets and the consumer is presented with more and more choice.

> **ACTIVITY 3.1.5**
>
> *Task 1.* Read the article from the *Financial Times*, of 28 October 1993 in Fig. 3.9 and explain how branding can be used to attract new market segments.
>
> *Task 2.* Visit your local superstore and note down all the products and their prices in either the Andrex product line or one of the other products quoted above. Place each one in a diagram representing the product mix and describe the mix in terms of breadth and depth.

Golden touch on brands

After Gold Blend, the American Express gold card, St. Ivel Gold and Capital Gold, comes Andrex Gold. The toilet, too, can now become the repository of a superior premium product.

Scott, the US-owned company which was an early pioneer of a comfortable alternative to scratchy loo paper in the 1940s, is launching in the UK the "softer, thicker, more absorbent tissue" manufactured using new "air-dry technology".

While some manufacturers of branded goods are responding to pressure from supermarkets' own-label products by cutting prices, Scott is doing the opposite. Its Andrex Gold will cost about 7 per cent more than ordinary Andrex – already sold at a premium of up to 40 per cent on own-brands.

So who is going to buy it? Scott believes purchasers will be "more downmarket than up, older rather than younger, and more likely to live in the Midlands or the north". The typical purchaser "needs reassurance" that she is providing the very best for her family.

In spite of a search for alternatives, Scott has fallen back on gold as the most clearly identifiable symbol of superiority.

The new sub-brand will be supported by a £2m advertising and promotional campaign over the next six months. The shock news is that advertisements for Andrex Gold, created by J Walter Thompson, will not feature the puppy. The puppy stands for "functional, family values" and will be reserved for the standard tissue; the Gold campaign will emphasise "indulgent, luxurious, stylish" qualities of the new product.

Diane Summers

Fig 3.9 Source: The *Financial Times*, Oct 1993

Packaging

Packaging and branding are closely connected. It is usually the packaging that carries the brand name or image and the two can sometimes become interchangeable, e.g. the Coca-Cola bottle. However, packaging has another important role to play as it can influence a customer's attitude towards a product and so affect purchasing decisions. In a homogeneous market, it may be the packaging that gives a product its competitive edge. For example, the soft drinks companies found that they could use Tetra packaging to offer convenient, robust, disposable and competitive products to the consumer. One recent development in packaging has been the move towards environmentally friendly approaches, e.g. reusable and recyclable packaging.

There are a number of considerations that should be taken into account when marketers seek to develop product packaging, and these can be put into one of two general categories: projection and protection.

1 *Cost.* If you can reduce packaging costs then you should be able to increase profits or reduce your prices. New technology in the plastics field has enabled many companies to make significant savings on packaging costs. Blow moulding techniques have resulted in much stronger and lighter bottles for the drinks industry with raw material costs, transport costs and wastage being greatly reduced.

2 *Safety.* Ensuring customer safety is another important role that packaging has to play. Many products such as jams and sauces have now been developed with tamper-proof packaging. This encourages consumer confidence and improves company image.

3 *Size.* Package size and multipack presentation may also be a consideration. The marketer needs to know if the consumer uses the product frequently or infrequently. If there is frequent use, then multiple packaging may be an option and this could lead to economies of scale and further benefits to pass on to the customer.

4 *Consistency.* If the product is part of a product line it may be necessary to ensure consistency of packaging within the line. This can be an important measure in reinforcing the brand image and further developing brand loyalty. If the customer is familiar with the packaging, then he or she may be more willing to sample a new product in that product line. For example, the Campbell's label is recognised worldwide and a new soup item may be readily adopted if sold under this label.

5 *Design.* Package designs must be constantly evaluated and changed to keep them looking stylish and up-to-date. Marketers can gain a competitive edge through effective packaging and they employ skilled artists and designers with experience in marketing research to see what sells well. As the typical superstore stocks thousands of items, packaging can be a great help in making products stand out so that they are more likely to be bought.

Pricing

The theory of price determination was covered in Unit 1 and the reader should look over that section again before we examine pricing activities.

From the point of view of the consumer, price is that which is exchanged for a product's benefits and value. The marketer's perception of price is somewhat more complex, however. The marketer must first consider *the economic price* of the product: this is the lowest possible price that can be charged if the organisation wishes to cover both fixed and variable costs and also gain the desired percentage of profit. The marketer's second consideration is *market price*: the price the market is prepared to pay for the product. Ideally, the marketer would like the market price to be as high as possible to enable the organisation to maximise its profits. If the market price is below the economic price, the organisation will be forced to accept lower than desired profits or will be forced to leave the market altogether. It is the consumer's perception of the product within the market environment that will determine the market price of a product.

Factors influencing pricing decisions

Determining at what market price to enter, or exit, a market is an important pricing activity. There are a number of factors that affect the market price of a product. For example, if an economy is entering a recession and supply exceeds demand then the market price of some products is likely to fall. Figure 3.10 shows the factors that most influence pricing decisions. These factors face implications for marketing decisions and it is up to the marketer to determined the strategy to be adopted by examining them.

Marketing objectives

The organisation's marketing objective may be to sustain or enhance product image. The manufacturers of Häagen Dazs ice cream reinforce their product's quality image by attaching a premium price to it. If they attempted to compete with other leading ice cream brands on price then they would be undermining their marketing objective.

Costs

Costs are an obvious issue when establishing price. An organisation may initially sell products below cost in order to generate cash flow, to match competition or as a loss leader.

An example of a loss leader can be seen in the restaurant business when 'eat as much as you can' specials are offered at certain times of the week. In these situations the restaurant hopes to recoup the lost profit in the orders it takes for drinks, starters or desserts. This particular practice also enables the restaurant to increase its turnover in what might normally be quiet times of the week and so generate cash flow.

Other marketing mix variables

The variables of the marketing mix are all interrelated. For example, consumers will associate better product quality with a high price, e.g. the recent Stella Artois advertising campaign offset the high price of the product against its reputation of quality by

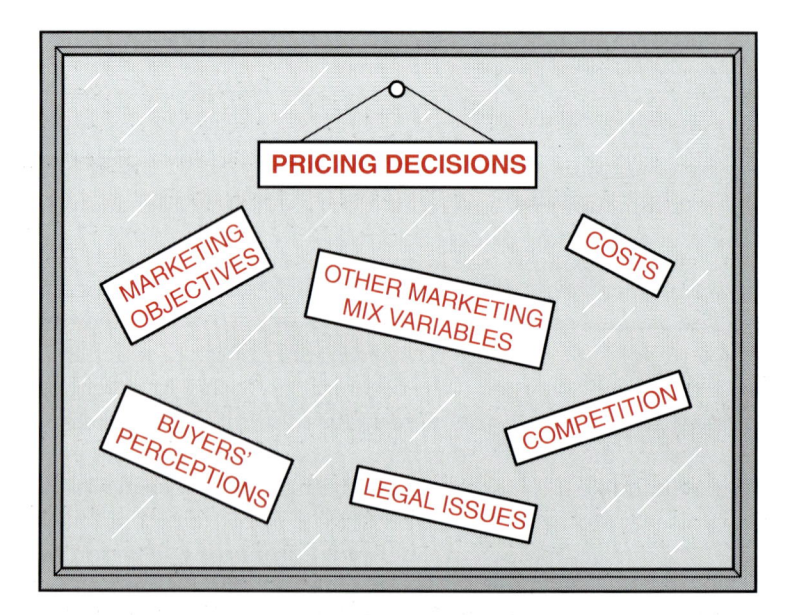

Fig 3.10 Factors influencing pricing decisions

implying it could only be compared with priceless paintings. Price may also determine the degree of status associated with a product and this in turn could influence promotional activities. The outlets through which the product is distributed will also influence price: shoppers at Kwiksave, Aldi and Netto are price sensitive, so manufacturers may supply these outlets with discount brands.

Buyers' perceptions

The marketer needs to understand the importance of price to people in the target market. This will vary from market segment to market segment and also from product to product. Students are highly sensitive to price, for example, and would probably not be prepared to pay a high premium for designer labels. People on high incomes, on the other hand, could actually seek out these types of products as they are prepared to pay a higher price for the value attached to the label. Conversely, these same high earners may shop around for the cheapest petrol as little value is attached to driving around with expensive petrol in your tank.

Competition

Some markets are primarily competitive on price. This is true of the package holiday industry where matching competitors' prices is an important strategy for survival. A marketer needs to know competitors' prices so that the company can adjust its own prices accordingly. If a company does adjust its price, it should also monitor the response of its competitors. These points will all be affected by the market concentration (*see* Unit 1).

Legal issues

Government intervention can also affect pricing activities. When the public utilities were privatised regulatory bodies were set up, e.g. OFGAS, to ensure that customers were not overcharged. The powers of the Monopolies and Mergers Commission were discussed in Unit 1.

Pricing activities

Price skimming

When price skimming, the initial price is set high for one of two reasons. The first is to recover initial development costs. For example, the price of a basic video recorder in 1982 was approximately £450, a skimming strategy that would not be appropriate in today's market. The second reason for setting an initial high price is to cream off the market which will buy the product because it is new or has novelty value. The success of this strategy depends on maintaining low costs at low volume, on a high quality image with few or no competitors.

Penetration pricing

This is considered to be the reverse of price skimming and could represent a price where the profit is below the desired level. The intention may be to secure market share at the initial expense of profit margins. The success of this strategy depends on a lower price encouraging greater demand, lower costs resulting from higher volume and a low price discouraging competition. An example of this strategy was seen with Japanese car manufacturers entering the UK car market. Initially prices were low while maintaining a high quality image. Once market share had been gained and consumers were locked in, prices were increased.

Promotion

The role of promotion is to communicate with potential customers such as individuals and organisations. The intention should be to assist the exchange process by informing the audience of the products and persuading them to accept them. To gain maximum benefit from promotion, marketers must plan and co-ordinate the promotional variables based on information from the market environment. For example, advertising is one of the promotional variables but it would be pointless advertising a product through a medium that the target audience does not watch, listen to or read. It is equally pointless using imagery or style that does not appeal to the target audience.

Many products that appeal to target audiences in their late teens and early twenties, e.g. jeans, CDs and fast food, are advertised on late night slots to coincide with youth magazine and music programmes. The adverts will often use role models, bright colours, fast moving images or the humour of alternative comedians. The advertisers hope that by adopting such techniques they are reaching the widest possible number of people in the target market with a message that will appeal to them and that they can relate to.

Promotional activities can be classified under the four headings of the promotional mix:

1 Advertising
2 Sales promotion
3 Personal selling
4 Publicity and public relations.

Some organisations will use all four classifications; others will use two or three. Fast moving consumer goods will rely on advertising and sales promotion with personal selling being totally inappropriate.

Companies that sell large capital items, on the other hand, do not need to reach a wide audience and would rely heavily on well trained technical sales staff.

These promotional activities will be looked at in detail in Elements 3.3 and 3.4 when we cover marketing communications and customer service.

Place (or distribution)

Distribution is the activity that makes the product available to the customer for purchase. Good distribution is vital to the successful marketing of products. If consumers cannot get the products as conveniently as possible in the size and condition they require, then they will purchase their goods elsewhere. There are two aspects to the distribution function: *the channels of distribution* and *physical distribution management*.

Marketing channels are the 'routes' that products take through various intermediaries in order to reach the consumer. These will be discussed in greater detail in Element 3.4.

It is also important to manage the physical activities of the distribution function. What kind of boxes should the products be packed and transported in? Where should the products be stored? Do they need special storage facilities like refrigeration? How should products be transported to intermediaries/customers/consumers? These are some of the questions that will be considered by personnel involved in physical distribution management.

Physical distribution deals with physical movement and inventory holding among the marketing channel members. Its main activities are:

1 *Order processing.* This is the receipt and transmission of sales order information. Many order processing activities are now computerised and efficient order processing contributes to customer satisfaction and repeat orders.

2 *Materials handling.* This is the careful monitoring of the handling of goods in order to minimise the number of times a good is handled, increase warehouse space and reduce packaging costs.

3 *Warehousing.* This is necessary as it is not always possible to match production to consumption, and so buffer stocks will need to be stored.

4 *Inventory management.* This is an activity that involves the monitoring of stock levels, decisions on safety stocks and judging reorder quantities. If an organisation carries a large inventory, then inventory management will be a complicated process. This is because different items sell at different speeds. Expensive champagnes will not sell as quickly as loaves of bread, so safety stocks and reorder levels will be low for champagne. Bread has a limited shelf life, however, which again will affect safety stocks and reorder frequencies.

5 *Transport.* This is the method used for moving the goods from where they are purchased to where they are used. A good transport system will help build customer satisfaction; a bad one can ultimately restrict the growth of an organisation. There are six main transport modes and each one offers unique advantages; motor vehicles, inland waterways, railways, airways, shipping and pipeline.

ACTIVITY 3.1.6

Task 1. Read the article from the *Financial Times* of 22 October 1992 in Fig. 3.11 and summarise the marketing mix for Gillete and Avon.

Task 2. Both companies are using established brand names to promote their products. Of the two, which do you think will be the most successful and why?

PC
3.1.4
3.1.5
C
3.2.1

MANAGING CHANGE

No organisation exists in a purely static environment; there will always be some feature of the organisation's environment that will be changing. This can be as straightforward as the coming and going of employees or as complex as fluctuating exchange rates in the currency markets. Each one of these examples could have an effect on marketing within the organisation. For example, a sales person may leave the company and take his or her personal contacts in the industry to a competitor, or the value of sterling could rise and subsequently affect the price of the company's exported products.

When considering the changing environment, the marketer should first divide it into two distinct categories: the micro-environment and the macro-environment.

Gillette and Avon are launching multi-million pound promotional campaigns to re-establish their brand names. **Gary Mead** reports

Sharpening the image

Tinkering with a brand image is a dangerous game. But when competitive pressure reaches critical mass, there is little choice.

Two of the oldest brand names in mass-market personal care products have decided that now is the time for a rethink. The experience of both Avon (founded in 1886) and Gillette (1903) shows that even leading brands can be vulnerable.

Both companies lost sight of their core strategies in the late 1970s and early 1980s, diversifying and thereby losing ground to competitors. Gillette followed the pack into disposable razors; Avon took its eye off its main market, cosmetics.

Companies with successful brand name longevity appear to concentrate on doing one thing supremely well and keeping a single brand name firmly at the forefront of consumer awareness.

Thus Gillette has now decided that the future for its personal care division – one of three divisions – is to attempt to replicate the success of its non-disposable razor, Sensor, which is heavily branded with the Gillette name. Gillette's new male toiletries range – launched in London recently with more dry ice and flashing lights than a Christmas panto – is called Gillette Series. The 13-product range results from $75m (£43.6m) spent on research and development.

The new line is backed by a $75m marketing budget in its first year in three launch markets. The US, Canada and the UK. The company's UK marketing budget of £15m for Gillette Series is 12 per cent of its turnover in the British shaving business.

Bruce Cleverly, Gillette's general manager for northern Europe, says the company is trying to develop a "mega-brand strategy. In 1988 we said we really needed to do something about the Gillette business, it's becoming a commodity market, we have a lot of well-known sub-brands but our biggest strength is the name Gillette and we really haven't treated that brand name with the importance it deserves."

Thus when Sensor was launched in 1990, it was accompanied by a global advertising campaign which hinged on emphasising the Gillette brand name, with the slogan "Gillette, the best a man can get."

Sensor revived the company's fortunes which had been flagging under pressure from the plastic disposable razor, bought on price, not brand name. But the premium-priced Sensor launch was not just about new product development. It coincided with restored marketing budgets, which (measured in 1987 terms) had in the US fallen from $61m in 1975 to £15m in 1987.

Gillette is minimising risk of failure for its new range by taking a leaf out of the successful Sensor campaign and piggy-backing on a reinvigorated brand name.

Avon, the US cosmetics company, had a different set of problems which largely flowed from the changing nature of industrialised society. For a company which depended on direct selling, one big social change – women increasingly leaving the home in the 1970s and 1980s to go to work – was a serious problem.

Avon's US sales rep force fell by 10 per cent between 1980-84, to 400,000. Americans are annually working an average 158 hours more than 20 years ago; fewer people are interested in part-time selling and there are fewer at home to buy.

Avon diversified into speciality chemicals and healthcare, moving from being in 1982 almost debt-free to having debts of $1.13bn in 1989. That, in turn, attracted four unwelcome takeover bids in three years.

Jim Preston, the current chief executive, took over in mid-1988 with a brief to return the company to its core cosmetic business and reverse the tide. He sold off peripheral companies. Sales increased from $3bn in 1988 to $3.6bn in 1991; debt has been reduced to $352m at the end of 1991.

In the process, Preston has carved Avon's glove in two, with different marketing strategies for industrial and emerging economies. With the latter, he anticipates sales growth of 10-12 per cent annually, largely using the tested method of direct sale reps.

But it is in already highly developed markets where Avon faces stiffest competition, and where Preston hopes the company's revamped image will make the most difference: "Our key challenges in these developed markets are image and access."

Preston acknowledges that Avon has had a very dowdy image. To counter that, Avon is quadrupling its advertising budgets, taking it to 2-3 per cent of sales over the next two years, and turning towards images more in tune with contemporary women.

The new advertising campaigns hope to make a virtue out of the declining numbers of house-bound women in developed economies, by making it possible to purchase Avon products via fax, telephone and mail, as well as the traditional sale rep.

Now using the generic slogan "It's never been so simple to look so great", Avon's new global advertising campaigns try to combine its old strength – ease of purchase – with a new appeal to sophisticated lifestyle. But Avon faces serious competition in the estimated $45bn global personal products market. The market is relatively fragmented with 70 per cent in the hands of some 15 companies.

However, four of the big five – Procter & Gamble (US), L'Oreal (France), Unilever (Anglo-Dutch) and Shiseido (Japan) – spent the late 1980s making acquisitions which, unlike Avon's, meshed into their existing core businesses. Avon's recent expansions into China, east Europe and other emerging economies make sense; but closer to home its greatest need is for its own current facelift.

DURABLE BRAND NAMES

Category	Leading brand in 1923	Current rank
Cameras	KODAK	No. 1
Canned fruit	DEL MONTE	No. 1
Chewing gum	WRIGLEY'S	No. 1
Crackers	NABISCO	No. 1
Razors	GILLETTE	No. 1
Soft drinks	COCA-COLA	No. 1
Soap	IVORY	No. 1
Soup	CAMPBELL	No. 1
Toothpaste	COLGATE	No. 2

Sources: Business Week/Boston Consulting Group, July 1991.

Fig 3.11 *Source: The Financial Times,* Oct 1993

The micro-environment

The micro-environment is the environment within the organisation and its particular industry sector. The components of this environment could be summarised as:

- The company (by department and management structure)
- Competitors
- Intermediaries (middlemen, retailers, etc.)
- Suppliers
- Customers
- Publics (interest groups, e.g. banks, workers, local government).

The marketer needs to monitor all of the above areas so that marketing activities can be adapted to suit any changes that may occur in these areas. For example, suppliers may increase their prices or customers may change their preferences. Many of these areas will be discussed later in this Unit, but one area of obvious interest to the marketer is the changing status of the organisation's competitors.

Competitor analysis

The only way to achieve a competitive advantage is for an organisation to know about its competitors and then do something different or better than them. The following is a list of useful sources of competitor information.

- buyers guides
- advertisements
- dealers
- published accounts
- trade press
- sales representatives
- newspapers
- trade associations
- products
- company literature
- *Yellow Pages*
- statistical sources (Mintel)
- government reports

The Marketing Department would be keen to obtain the following classes of information on competitors:

- Competitive position – strengths, weaknesses;
- Marketing strategy – objectives, prices, promotional campaigns;
- Research & Development – products in development;
- Production capabilities – capacity, costs, suppliers;
- Financial status – sales, profits, liquidity.

Only with this type of information is it then possible to develop an effective competitive strategy.

Unit 3 Marketing

The macro-environment

The macro-environment is the larger environment of forces that shape opportunities and pose threats to the success of an organisation. One method for remembering these forces is through the acronym PEST. This summarises the major forces that are likely to affect an organisation:

> **P**olitical (this also includes legal)
> **E**conomic
> **S**ocial (this also includes demographic and cultural)
> **T**echnological

The macro-environment can be extremely complex. It is not always possible to monitor all variables. Marketers need to determine which variables are most important for their organisation to monitor.

Political change

The political and legal environment in the UK is relatively stable with most recent changes resulting from new legislation due to closer European integration. We shall therefore concentrate in this section on the economic, societal and technological factors which are more dynamic and the source of more serious problems for marketers.

Economic change

Let us consider the types of economic information which can be analysed by marketers.

Income

We generally regard income as the wages we receive in exchange for our efforts at work. This is too simple a definition, however. For example, people who no longer work and are retired still receive an income in the form of their pension. It is important to understand the full definition of income so that important market segments are not overlooked when we study consumer trends that are influenced by income.

Income is the amount of money received through wages, pensions, investments, rents and welfare or subsidy payments over a period of time (weekly/monthly/annually). As you can see this definition covers more than the employed within our economy. Income has already been identified as a consumer variable and you should be familiar with the different purchasing habits of the different income brackets. It is important for marketers to be aware of the economic conditions that can affect an individual's, a segment's or an entire market's income levels.

Inflation

The causes of inflation were discussed in Unit 1. Buying power is linked to the size of income, but buying power is also affected by the relationship of incomes to the general price of goods. During inflationary periods, prices rise. This means that more money is needed to make the same purchases that consumers normally make. If price inflation exceeds wage inflation, i.e. prices rise faster than wages, then more of the consumer's income will be used for purchases. This is a very important consideration for the majority of people because inflation may influence purchasing patterns in terms of basic necessities and luxury items.

Taxation

A person's income is normally allocated to the following three areas: taxation, spending on goods and services and savings. After tax the remaining income is known as *disposable income* and is used for spending or saving. It is therefore apparent that the amount of taxes paid will directly affect the level of disposable income. Fiscal policy and the relationship between taxation and government spending were discussed in Unit 1.

The implication for marketers of the government's fiscal policy is significant. If the Public Sector Borrowing Requirement (PSBR) is growing, then the government is spending more than it is earning in tax revenue. The implications for the market are obvious – if government spending cannot be reduced, then the level of taxation must go up (disregarding receipts from privatisation). Income tax, national insurance contributions or council tax may be increased; alternatively levels of tax relief may be reduced. If this is the case, then the disposable income of consumers will fall. Marketers need to be aware of whether or not the Chancellor needs to raise taxes. If taxes are increased then there will be less money available in the economy for spending on goods and services.

The UK economy has recently seen this happen. During the last recession the government ran up a large PSBR. In 1993, in two separate budgets forthcoming tax increases for 1994 and 1995 were announced. This resulted in concern being expressed by the business community over the fragility of the recovery. If disposable incomes are reduced, then consumers stop spending and may plunge the economy back into recession.

The opposite of this effect must also be considered. By deciding to give tax cuts, the government will effectively increase the disposable income of consumers. Again marketers must be aware of this eventuality if they hope to maximise the benefits of such a policy.

The level of disposable income will therefore determine the type of strategies that organisations adopt. For example, when disposable income is falling, marketers may adopt pricing and brand strategies that ensure that all market segments are catered for. This approach has been used by the major supermarket chains as they have implemented aggressive strategies such as discount pricing (Tesco's Super Value) and own branding (Sainsbury's cola) in an attempt to retain or increase their market share.

Discretionary income

A consumer's disposable income can also be further broken down. The majority of us have to spend some of our income on basic necessities such as food, clothing, housing and heating. The money that is left to us to either spend or save is called *discretionary income*. This is a better indicator of buying power than disposable income. The products or services that are purchased with discretionary income include entertainment, holidays, furniture, cars and so on. Levels of discretionary income can be altered in much the same way as disposable income.

One recent change for many people occurred as a result of the 1993 double budget. VAT was for the first time levied on domestic heating. We all pay for domestic heating out of our disposable income; unfortunately due to our climate heating is a necessity. With an increase in the cost of domestic heating, people automatically experience a fall in discretionary income. This means there is less money to spend on those items such as holidays and cars and is of obvious importance to marketers within these particular sectors.

Distribution of income

The distribution of income is another important economic indicator that is useful to marketers. As mentioned earlier, income can be broken down into three levels: low, medium and high. What constitutes membership of these levels is not of concern here, but rather what percentage of the population is included in each level. Look at Figure 3.12. Which graph do you feel represents the country with the most uneven distribution of income?

This is useful for marketers, particularly when studying international marketing potential. A country with a low national income may have a relatively high proportion of wealthy people. This would be a potentially good market for luxury items, e.g. Rolex, Mercedes, BMW. Alternatively, a country with a high national income may have very few rich or poor but a high percentage of people in the middle income bracket. This second scenario would present more market opportunities for normal and basic goods, e.g. Levi, Hitachi, Nissan and Ford.

Gross Domestic Product

As discussed in Unit 1, Gross Domestic Product is a measurement of the level of demand in an economy. It can also be used to compare average incomes between different countries. A number of measurements can be used – collectively referred to as measurements of national income – and are known individually as Gross Domestic Product (GDP), Gross National Product (GNP) and net national income. There are only minor differences between these measurements, but when using them to compare levels of national income it is important to ensure consistency, i.e. only compare GDP with GDP.

An effective way to compare different levels of national income is to take one of the above measurements of national income (e.g. GDP) and divide it by the population of the country under consideration (GDP per capita). Often, to make interpretation and comparison easier, the GDP per capita will be converted to US dollars. This figure is a measurement of how much every man, woman and child would receive if the total year's income for an economy was divided out among the population.

These measurements are very useful to marketers who may wish to assess average income levels or may wish to study long-term trends of increasing or declining wealth.

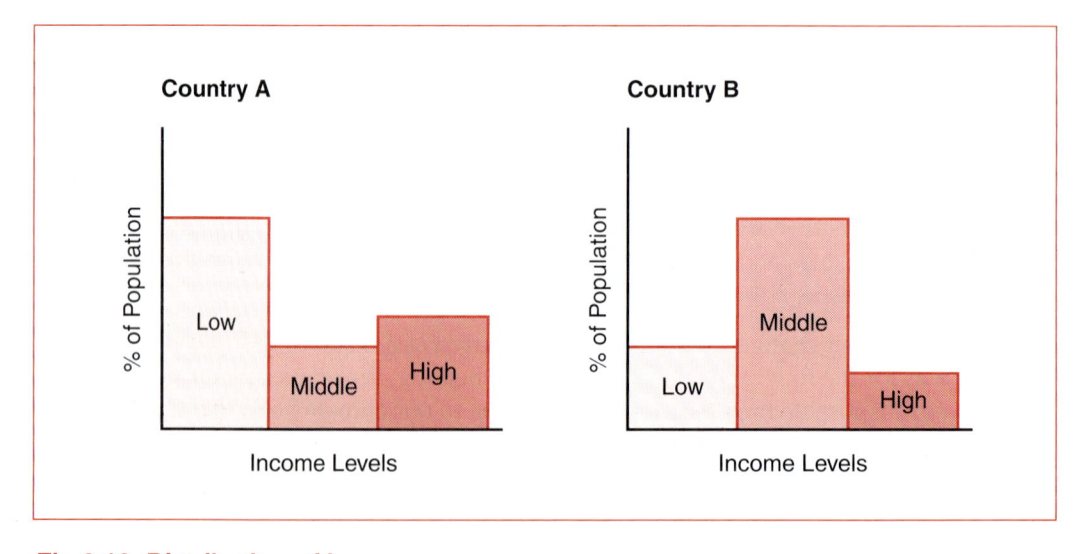

Fig 3.12 Distribution of income

Element 3.1 Investigate the principles and functions of marketing in organisations

The Tiger economies of South-East Asia have all experienced remarkable rates of growth over the past decade with a subsequent increase in the standard of living of its populations. The leading multinationals have all closely monitored this growth and been ready to take advantages of the increased opportunities within these markets.

Spending patterns

Consumer spending patterns indicate the relative proportions of family expenditure that are spent on different kinds of goods and services. This information can be obtained in the UK from the *Family Expenditure Survey* and is produced by the Central Statistical Office.

ACTIVITY 3.1.7

Refer to a copy of the *Family Expenditure Survey* in your library and identify the differences in average weekly household expenditure between households of different incomes. Present your findings to your tutor.

PC
3.1.5
3.1.6
C
3.2.1

Employment statistics

Until the mid-1970s the unemployment rate was relatively low in the UK. From a marketing perspective, the primary concern is the effect unemployment, or the threat of unemployment, has on spending patterns.

As unemployment declines, consumer confidence increases. If people are not concerned regarding the prospect of losing their jobs, or they are confident of quickly finding

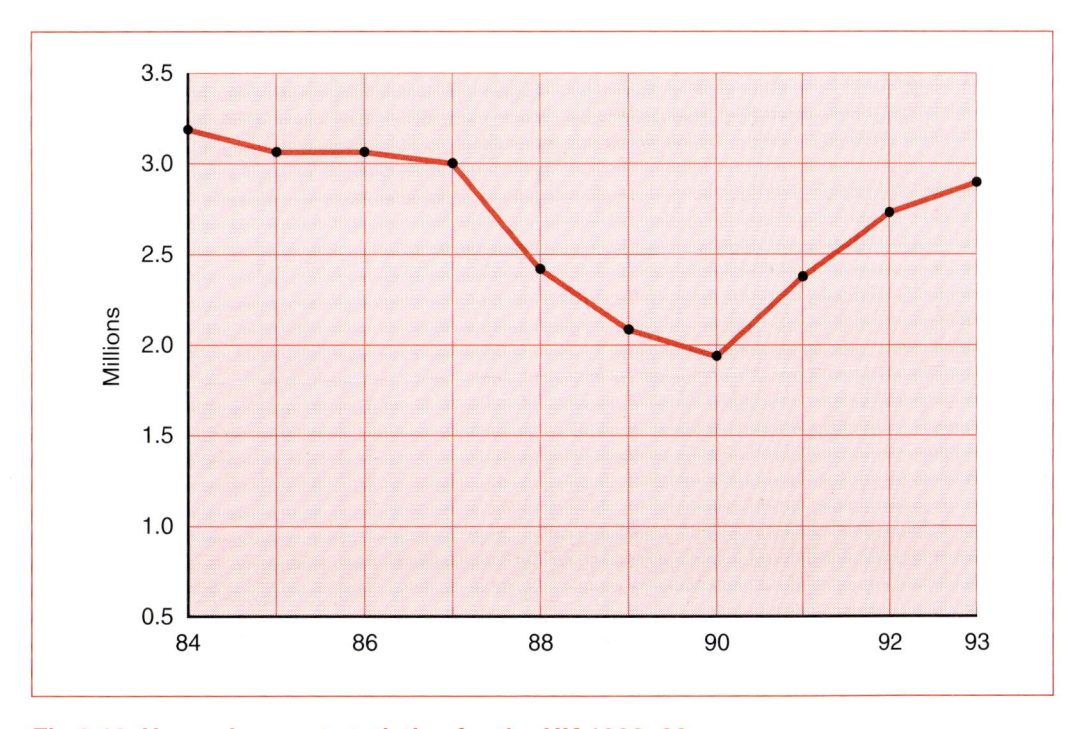

Fig 3.13 Unemployment statistics for the UK 1983–93

another job, then they will be less hesitant about spending their discretionary income on goods or services such as holidays and cars.

Employment statistics are a real concern to marketers. They are frequently published and make headlines in the media if there are sharp increases or falls. The majority of consumers are therefore aware of employment levels and any subsequent movement in them. Marketers must also monitor them closely in their efforts to anticipate future demand in their markets.

ACTIVITY 3.1.8

The article from the *Independent on Sunday* of 29 May 1994 in Fig. 3.14 is aimed at students in higher education. It is mentioned that a product group frequently purchased by this segment is convenience food. Analyse the marketing activities of businesses in the convenience food market. Highlight those activities that you feel are specifically aimed at the student market.

Marketing: companies are recognising that student consumers may stay brand-loyal in later life

Chasing future big spenders

By Helen Jones

THERE are a million students in the UK, but as a consumer group they are notoriously difficult to target.

The main problems are that students are fickle, influenced by rapidly changing fashions, and lead a relatively insular life, which revolves around work, dating and drink – although not necessarily in that order.

However, as students have an estimated spending power of £4bn a year, a growing number of companies are attempting to target effectively these consumers of tomorrow while they are in higher education.

One such company is Beatwax. It was set up Chris Ward, who used to manage bands and organise tours to universities and colleges.

Beatwax began by organising university promotions for record companies, and this quickly expanded into video and film promotion. In the past two years, as companies have become aware of the value of the student market, the client range has broadened to include Bass, Cadbury and Virgin.

Mr Ward says that students are an ever-growing market. Universities and colleges of higher education are better attended than at any time in their history.

There has been a 20 per cent rise in enrolment in the past three years due to demographic changes and the trend for young people to opt for further study if they cannot find employment.

He is also keep to dispel the perception that students do not have any money. "With student loans, they have as much money to spend as they ever did. They are just further in debt when they leave higher education. But it doesn't stop them spending money on the clichéd things that students have always spent money on – drink, music, cigarettes and convenience foods."

Despite students' spending power, Mr Ward concedes that perhaps the easiest way to attract them is through free products or discounts. One of Beatwax's most recent campaigns has been for tea producer, Twinings. It has distributed 20,000 herbal tea sachets around universities and colleges in the expectation that if students try the product and like it, they will buy it on a regular basis and continue to do so after graduation.

Golden Wonder has also run a promotional campaign for its "Pots of the World" brand – which is a more exotic version of that staple student fare, "Pot Noodles".

Beatwax targets advertising and promotions at students on their home territory. Mr Ward says: "They don't all watch the same television programmes or read the same newspaper – many of them don't read newspapers at all."

However, 86 per cent of all students read their university or college publications. Beatwax runs ad campaigns in these and has access to other on-site media such as campus radio stations and poster sites.

There are also growing opportunities to use video. As many as 85 colleges have mass-access video facilities – large multi-screen arrangements in bars, unions, refectories and discos.

Nearly all colleges also have their own on-site shop, which is often the only retail outlet nearby – particularly on campus sites. Beatwax organises in-store promotions, point-of-sale material and marketing campaigns for clients to increase sales of its stocked products.

Much of the marketing activity that Beatwax produces is particular to the student body and other consumers never see it. Mr Ward points out: "Companies can be more daring in the campaigns that they direct at students and often use more outrageous humour."

"It is not something you could do generally, but you can be more controversial when marketing to students," Mr Ward says.

Mr Ward says "smart companies are realising the value of getting them young" and retaining vital customer loyalty into salaried life.

Fig 3.14 *Source*: The *Independent on Sunday,* May 1994

Societal change

The standard of living in the UK has changed dramatically over the last 50 years. The basics that most people require are food and water, shelter, a loving partner/family, the respect of friends and a rewarding role in society (*see* Maslow's hierarchy of needs in Unit 4). Marketers are always devising new ways for the consumer to satisfy these needs, or to believe they are satisfying these needs. This has resulted in the proliferation of consumer goods and services that dominate our markets today. This increase in consumer demand for goods and services has not taken place at a steady pace but at an exponential rate, i.e. it has been accelerating.

Consumer demand is not a new phenomenon: traditionally, most people have wanted more than the bare necessities. We want to achieve the highest living standards possible, that is, we have consumer wants other than just basic needs. In the modern market we have a multitude of goods and services to satisfy our needs and wants. This can be attributed to social change, innovation and technological change. We can therefore conclude that as a direct result of these changes our lifestyles and consumption patterns have altered significantly.

Consumers in today's modern markets want different products to those that existed a generation ago. Consumers want up-to-date, around-the-clock information, e.g. cable and satellite networks; they want homes that provide comfort and luxury, e.g. spa baths and central heating; they want food that is easily prepared, readily available and varied, e.g. microwave ovens, a choice of fast foods; they want travel that is safe, fast and efficient, e.g. APEX fares, motorway networks.

The examples above all highlight the changes that have taken place in our material standards of living. In a modern society this is not enough; we also desire a high quality of life. The majority of people do not want to spend all their waking hours working, as many of our ancestors did. One major change in our society has been the increase in leisure time for a large proportion of the working population. This has led to an increase in the demand for related products – hobbies, recreation and relaxation.

Other phenomena of recent times that have had a direct impact on consumption patterns are changes in the domestic arrangements of the population. The majority of people still live in a family context and the family life cycle is still a valid consumer variable. The liberalisation of attitudes towards divorce and birth outside of marriage, however, has resulted in an increase in the number of family units with the number of households increasing in inverse proportion to their average size. This change means that the purchase and consumption of some goods and services will have increased at a disproportionately greater rate than that of other goods and services. For example, the requirement for household content insurance will have increased at roughly the same rate as the number of households; total food product purchases will have remained constant with the drop in average household size cancelling out the effect of the increased number of households.

Another major change in the family unit has been that of the role of the breadwinner. The number of women in paid employment has been continually increasing since the 1960s. Although it is generally recognised that there are still large imbalances relating to female and male pay, the contribution to the family budget by women should not be ignored. Women can either be joint or sole contributors to the family budget. In either case women now experience much higher levels of autonomy or control over their expenditure and consumption than they have in the past. A result of this is that advertising is now often targeted at working women, whereas in the past it tended to be aimed at housewives. Birdseye Menumasters target their adverts at working women who do not have the time to prepare meals after a full working day. A recent advert for the Ford Fiesta shows two working women, a manager and her assistant, involved in a scramble from London to Paris in order to meet a conference deadline. The Ford advert could quite easily have reverted to stereotypes and shown the happy housewife conveniently parking the car and putting the shopping in the boot.

One final word on societal forces. As well as enjoying the material and leisure benefits of a modern society, consumers are becoming increasingly concerned about the quality of the environment in which they can enjoy their modern lifestyles. We have already discussed the importance of conscience spending. It should be regarded as a major recent change to consumption patterns as consumers now use their purchasing power to influence the activities of businesses and to reflect their concern for the millions in the third world omitted from, or exploited for, our modern market.

Technological change

Technological advances have had a substantial effect on the variety of goods and services available to consumers. Technology often produces new products, but it can also lead to the death of old ones. For example, the photocopier has had a significant effect on the sale of carbon paper.

Organisations need to monitor those technologies that are most likely to affect them – not just to prepare against future threats, but also to identify any potential opportunities. The technologies that currently have the most impact on our lives and on the environment of organisations are microelectronics, telecommunications and genetic engineering.

Monitoring and managing for change in the environment is not limited to those factors mentioned here. Each organisation needs to identify those factors that pose significant threats, or offer opportunities, that are most likely to affect them.

GROWTH OF ORGANISATIONS

Having examined marketing activities let us now consider the future directions that an organisation may wish to pursue. An organisation will need to develop a competitive strategy and, if possible, one that will achieve growth. There are a number of growth strategies – we shall discuss two of them: *new product development* and *market development*.

New product development

As a product approaches the end of its life cycle, it enters into a declining stage and, even before this, a product's profit margin is likely to be eroded by increasing competition. The only apparent answer for a company wishing to maintain healthy profit margins and ensure continued growth is to introduce new products. It is important, therefore, that marketers understand the process of new product development.

We have already mentioned that a high proportion of new products fail at the introductory stage. To overcome this, marketers use a systematic, six-stage process for new product development (*see* Fig. 3.15).

Idea generation

Idea generation is a difficult task – the marketer must foster a creative environment and this is done in a number of ways. Some organisations encourage all employees to contribute, from the Managing Director down. One recent example of success is the 3M Post-It pad. This was thought up by an employee who thought that a small adhesive-backed notepad would be useful for marking pages in books. Another approach is to get key personnel involved in brainstorming sessions to see if they can 'feed off' each other generating ideas. New ideas can sometimes come from outside the firm. The Black and Decker Workmate was an idea put forward by a customer who happened to be a keen handyman – it has since proved to be enormously successful.

Screening

Screening is the next stage. The new product ideas are analysed to see whether they match the organisation's objectives and resources. It is also important to evaluate potential changes within the market and the wider environment. It may be prudent, for example, for an organisation to shelve the idea of a new luxury saloon car when the economy is in the grip of a recession.

Business analysis

Business analysis looks at how the product might fit into the existing product mix. It also looks at how the product is likely to be made and calculates figures on expected sales, costs and profits. This stage involves detailed research and uses data from both primary and secondary research to establish the above information.

Product development

It is at this stage that the idea is transformed from a concept into a *prototype*. Once a working model is constructed, it is possible to evaluate all the attributes of the product. These attributes may or may not have been anticipated, so extensive testing is important at this stage to establish whether the product has any specific features that appeal to the

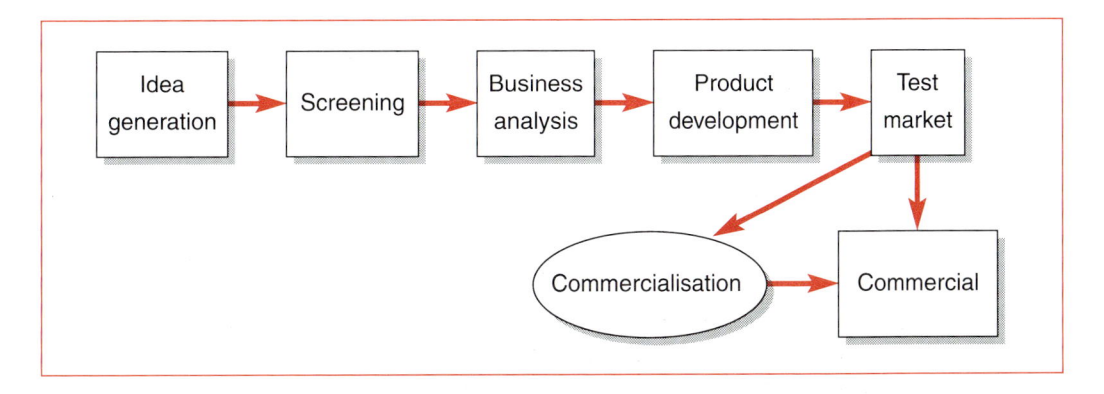

Fig 3.15 The six stage process for new product development

consumer that may have been overlooked. The opposite is also true in that the product may have features that do not appeal to the consumer. Clive Sinclair found this out to his cost when potential consumers spurned his C5 electric car because it was too close to the ground and felt 'unsafe'.

Producing a working prototype can be expensive and time consuming and for this reason only a small number of product ideas make it to the product development stage.

Test marketing

When a new product is test marketed, usually a representative geographic area is chosen. The aim is to gauge the reactions of the buyers in the test area to the new product. This is a valuable exercise as it does not commit the organisation to the entire market and allows any teething problems to be ironed out or the product to be withdrawn entirely without suffering any harmful publicity.

Fig 3.16

Test marketing was undertaken by Cadbury's when it first developed the Wispa bar. The initial idea came about as a response to competition from Rowntree's Aero bar. The new product took a development team five years to perfect and it was decided to test market the product in the Tyne Tees region. The product proved so popular that supplies ran out after eight weeks. These results encouraged Cadbury's to invest in a new £11 million plant so that the product could be marketed across the UK. That the product has proved to be highly successful is a clear endorsement of investment in new product development.

Element 3.1 Investigate the principles and functions of marketing in organisations

Commercialisation

As seen in the Cadbury's Wispa example, once the product has been proven in the test marketing stage then there is still much planning and preparation needed for the actual product launch. Extra production capacity to match expected demand must be planned for and an initial marketing campaign has also to be thought out.

The Wispa's launch was accompanied by a large promotional campaign. There were special promotional offers of Wispa mugs, pens, rulers, etc. plus coupons on the wrappers offering five free bars for every 25 wrappers. All this was done in conjunction with a major advertising and public relations campaign. The response to the free offer campaign alone was a remarkable one and had a half million applications!

Commercialisation is an expensive process. It is made easier when the return on the investment is quick. This can only be achieved if customers accept the new product rapidly. The best chance of this occurring is if marketers can make potential customers aware of a new product's benefits.

The above examples show how innovation and new product development are important to assure organisational growth and survival. Let us now look at how new product development may be used in conjunction with the evaluation of markets, to achieve growth.

Market development

Market development is a direct alternative to new product development. It is a strategy which takes existing products and attempts to increase sales by entering new markets. This is most often achieved by entering a new geographic location, e.g. McDonald's has ensured growth by entering the new markets in Eastern Europe as the old communist regimes have fallen. A new market could also exist in the same location but simply be a new application for an existing product. There are several good examples of this: chewing gum as a dental aid, baby soaps and lotions as beauty products.

The product–market matrix

To summarise this section on growth, we can look at the options open to an organisation, if it wishes to achieve growth.

1 *Market penetration* – Continue with existing products in existing markets.

2 *Product development* – Develop new products for existing markets.

3 *Market development* – Market existing products in new markets.

4 *Diversification* – Develop new products for new markets.

This is clearly shown in Ansoff's product–market matrix shown in Fig. 3.17.

	Product Present	Product New
Market New	Market development	Diversification
Market Present	Market penetration	Product development

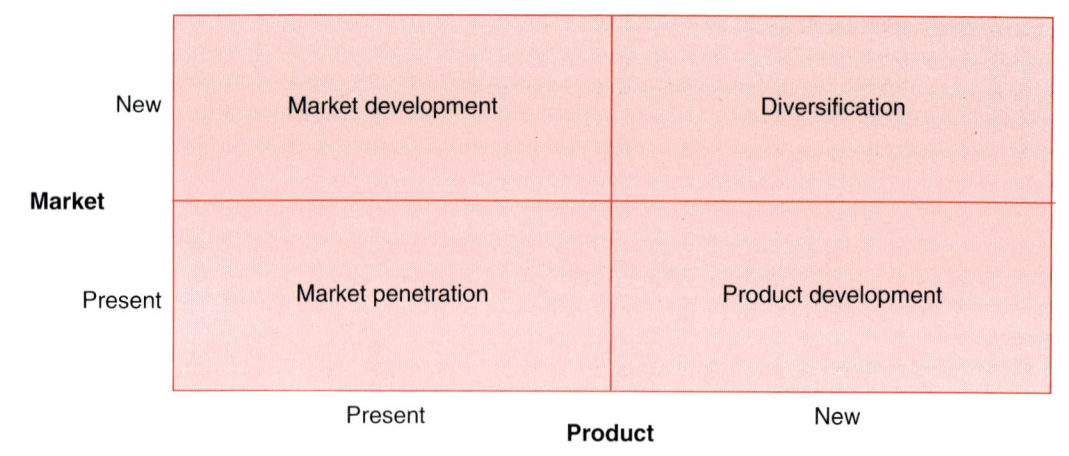

Fig 3.17 Ansoff's product–market matrix

ACTIVITY 3.1.9

Consider the following products/services.

- Pop Tarts
- Virgin Atlantic
- Cadbury's Dairy Milk
- Kellogg's Cornflakes

Each one of the organisations responsible for the above products/services has ensured growth through the pursuit of one of the four strategy options indicated in Ansoff's matrix in Fig. 3.17. Match them to the strategy that you think has been pursued, using examples where possible, and detail your reasons.

Self assessment questions

1 Pursuing an increase in market share would be
  a a marketing objective
  b a marketing plan
  c a marketing mix
  d a marketing activity?

2 The World Wildlife Foundation is an organisation that primarily markets
  a services
  b goods
  c ideas
  d tangible products?

3 A product mix is best described as
  a product, price, promotion and place

b all products of a particular type
   c all products offered by a firm
   d many products offered by one firm?

4 The marketing concept requires that an exchange process, in order to be successful,
   a must hold something of value to both parties
   b should provide the business with profits
   c takes place between two parties
   d does not involve money?

5 Which of the following is an activity of physical distribution management?
   a Establishing marketing channels
   b Prospecting
   c Following up
   d Materials handling

6 A group of people who, as individuals, have needs for products and are willing and able to purchase such products is called
   a a social group
   b a collection
   c a market
   d an aggregation?

7 Ideally, test marketing should follow which stages in the new product development process?
   a Product development
   b Screening
   c Idea generation
   d Commercialisation

8 Which of the following is not a factor influencing price?
   a Competition
   b Diversification
   c Perceptions of buyers
   d Marketing objectives

9 The cost of customer service
   a limits the level of service that an organisation can offer
   b is a consideration for the service sector only
   c makes customer service prohibitively expensive
   d should not compromise customer satisfaction by adding unnecessary costs?

10 Which of the following represents a diversification strategy?
   a A new product in an existing market
   b An existing product in a new market
   c A new product line
   d A new product in a new market

Unit 3   Marketing

Assignment

Fiat has recently introduced a new 'baby' mini to the UK market; it is called the Cinquecento. It was officially launched in the UK in June 1993 and was introduced to replace the ageing 126. Production of the 126 has not ceased, however, as the car will still be manufactured and sold in Eastern European markets.

FIAT

Fig 3.18

Task 1. Plot the product life cycle of the Fiat 126, for the UK market only, from its original introduction to its final withdrawal. Annual registrations for the car are listed in Table 3.1.

Table 3.1 Registrations of Fiat 126 range

Year	Units
1973	5 530
1974	10 293
1975	6 621
1976	8 626
1977	7 408
1978	6 105
1979	9 627
1980	5 069
1981	3 466
1982	1 516
1983	1 595
1984	1 325
1985	1 260
1986	2 013
1987	1 996
1988	2 217
1989	2 549
1990	2 244
1991	1 381
1992	27

Give reasons for the increased sales experienced in 1979 and 1986. Your reasons should be supported with evidence of appropriate research.

Task 2. What product features of the 126 have Fiat retained in the new Cinquecento? What new features does the Cinquecento incorporate? Identify the environmental factors that influenced the introduction of the Cinquecento's features.

PC
3.1.1
3.1.2
3.1.3
3.1.4
3.1.5
C
3.1.1
3.1.2
3.1.3
3.1.4
3.1.5

Task 3. Identify the products that compete directly with the Cinquecento in the UK market. How do these products differentiate themselves in terms of their features? Of those mentioned earlier, what marketing objective do you think these companies are pursuing?

Task 4. Identify and summarise the differences in the marketing mixes of the Cinquecento and one other competing product.

Task 5. The Renault Twingo is a competitor of the Cinquecento, but it was not launched in the UK due to cost implications. Research this and explain why the Cinquecento was launched and the Twingo was not.

Element 3.2
PROPOSE AND PRESENT PRODUCT DEVELOPMENTS BASED ON ANALYSIS OF MARKET RESEARCH INFORMATION

Performance criteria

1 **Identify marketing research methods and explain their suitability for selected products.**

2 **Analyse marketing research information from different sources for its contribution to marketing decisions for selected products.**

3 **Propose and justify product development with reference to marketing research information.**

4 **Present proposals for product development.**

Introduction

All organisations operating in the business environment need appropriate information to enable managers to reach decisions that will improve their organisation's competitiveness. This information can be obtained from a number of sources, both internal and external to a company. Appropriate information may not always be available, however and information may have to be interpreted from data – the raw material of information.

- Data. These are the facts and figures as they are collected, (e.g. in 1986 25 per cent of petrol purchases were for unleaded; in 1991 75 per cent of petrol purchases were for unleaded.
- Information. This is the story that interpreted data tells, (e.g. over the five years from 1986 to 1991 sales of leaded petrol have fallen significantly as a proportion of overall petrol sales).

It is necessary, therefore, that marketing personnel are skilled in producing useful information from raw data. This process of data and information gathering and examination is generally known as *marketing research*. The first step for the marketing researcher is to define why the research is needed. The next step is to realise what types of research data are available (secondary data) and then determine how to acquire any additional data (primary data).

Element 3.2 Propose and present product developments based on analysis of market research information

SECONDARY DATA

Of prime importance to the marketing researcher are the sources of information and data that are already available.

Data that already exists is commonly referred to as *secondary data*. Secondary data will have been compiled for some purpose other than the current investigation, and because of this there are a number of drawbacks associated with using secondary data.

- The quality or reliability of the data may be in question.
- The data may not be precise or specific enough for the current investigation.
- The data may be in the wrong format (for example, miles per gallon or kilometres per litre).
- The data may be out of date.
- The conditions under which data was collected may not be known (for example, during recession or during economic growth).

We will now consider various sources of secondary data.

Internal sources

The first stage in a marketing research process will often be the gathering of data from within the company. Internal sources of data can contribute significantly to research. Much useful data can be extracted from the company's accounting system. All large companies and many smaller ones now have computerised accounting systems that not only record the simple debits and credits of transactions but also contain a considerable degree of management information. This source will contain detailed information about costs, sales, customer accounts and profits by product category.

Another important source of internal data is the company's own marketing databank. This may contain information about past marketing activities, such as sales records and previous marketing research reports. These can be very useful as they may help identify any problems encountered in the past.

External sources

Government publications

The government, through its various departments and agencies, collects, analyses and publishes statistics on practically everything. This leaves the researcher with a bewildering range of statistics to choose from. A number of indexes and guides are available, such as the government's weekly *British Business* or the free guide from the CSO (Central Statistical Office) entitled *Government Statistics: A Brief Guide to Sources*. The following publications are of particular relevance:

- *Annual Abstract of Statistics*
- *Social Trends*
- *Family Expenditure Survey*
- *Business Monitors*
- *Regional Trends*

Obviously it is important to know from the outset what information is being sought. This avoids time and money being squandered by wading through irrelevant statistical data.

Periodicals and journals

Almost every industry or type of business has a trade journal. A trade journal is useful to the marketing researcher as it provides a feel for the industry in question. For example, it will give indications of size, degree of competition, range of companies involved, and industry specific problems. If a particular industry is of interest, there is a reference book that lists periodicals by subject: this is known as *The Source Book*. If the required information is more specific, however, publications such as *ABI Inform* and *The British Humanities Index* catalogue every article published in the major periodicals. There are also computerised literature-retrieval databases available – a rather grand title for what are basically periodicals stored on computer, usually in CD-ROM format. You should have access to one of these in your college or local library. Each CD stores articles going back over several years from a number of broadsheet newspapers. Key words such as the name of a subject are used to search a database and generate references. One popular commercial computerised database is McCarthy's. This database is updated on a regular basis and contains articles from the broadsheet newspapers that are catalogued quarterly.

Commercial data

Virtually every industry, product category and profession has its own association. Depending on the strength of the individual groups, they may conduct their own research, run training sessions, and hold conferences and exhibitions. Contacting these associations, either by telephone or letter, may yield information suitable to your specific research that is not available in published sources. Examples of these associations include the SMMT (Society of Motor Manufacturers and Traders) and the ACT (Association of Chemical Traders).

Internet

The Internet is a vast, co-operative network of computers. It currently consists of more than three million computers and more than 32 million users in 81 countries. The Internet began as a network to connect government research labs and universities within the United States, but now more than 60 per cent of its members are commercial

ACTIVITY 3.2.1

During the last five years the UK economy has been through a severe recession. Individuals changed their purchasing habits as more and more people began to be worried about the security of their jobs. Due to this phenomenon many businesses that grew during the 1980s' boom either retrenched or closed down.

Visit your local/college library and, using one of the sources of information identified under government publications, analyse the historical sales trends for two consumer durables (products with a useful life of more than 12 months): one which declined in the UK market and one which grew in the UK market (you will need to look back five years). From the sources listed above, identify reasons for this trend.

organisations based all over the world. This means that the Internet is a truly global database and a valuable medium for information gathering.

One very useful service provided through the Internet is WAIS (Wide Area Information Service) and is a system for searching the network for information. The user provides a set of key words and the system will fetch documents matching those key words. This system is a very effective general research tool for gathering secondary data.

PRIMARY DATA

It is often not possible for the researcher to obtain the necessary information from secondary sources. This may be due to the problems highlighted earlier or because there are simply no secondary sources available. This lack of secondary information is sometimes referred to as an information gap and necessitates the generation of data and information specifically for the current research investigations. The data generated under these circumstances is known as *primary data*. The collection of primary data is a more lengthy and complex process than the collection of secondary data. As a result primary data is expensive to acquire – it is essential, however, in preparing a new product or service for the market. For example, if an ice cream manufacturer wished to introduce a new tropical fruit flavoured ice cream, primary data on people's reactions to the product would be necessary before the final product was agreed upon and launched.

The different processes used for collecting primary data are discussed in the next section. Selecting the appropriate research methods is vital to the success of ongoing marketing research. As will be seen, different research methods will suit different desired outcomes.

Experimentation

The best way to describe this particular method is to first think of all the activities that a company undertakes in getting its product or service to the customer. All of these activities – advertising, pricing, packaging, type of outlet, etc. – are variable, that is they can be changed and can be changed independently of one another. A company may wish to see what would happen to the sales of its product or service if it were to change one of those variables. This is known as *experimentation*. It is vital that only one variable at a time be changed. If more than one variable is changed, it will be impossible to know which of the changes has affected sales. As the company's activities are known as *independent variables*, so the resulting sales figure is known as the *dependent variable*, i.e. sales are dependent on the activities of the company.

A company may wish to see how its customers will react to a change in product packaging. A new design is introduced and results in an increase in sales. The company now knows that new packaging has increased sales and may now wish to extend the new design features to other products in the product range. The company may also be interested in changing its type of retail outlet for the product, e.g. from high street to superstore, but if it had done this at the same time as changing the packaging then the company would not have known what was responsible for the increase in sales.

When designing experiments the techniques that are used should be reliable and valid. Reliability would ensure that successive repeated trials produced almost identical results. Validity would ensure that what is supposed to be measured is in fact being measured. In our above example, the increased sales may have been partly due to decreased competitive activity. Experimentation over an acceptable time span should counter the effects of unknown phenomena and guarantee reliability and validity.

Observation

Answers to some marketing research questions can often be found through observing the particular marketing process at work. When using this method, researchers will record the respondent's behaviour in a given situation. For example, the researcher may wish to study customer movements and customer responses to sales techniques.

In the supermarket industry details of customer movement are useful for designing store layout. Recent research has shown that supermarket customers prefer to travel around the edges of the store and dip into aisles. This has resulted in radical new layouts in some of the most modern superstores.

The main advantage of observation is that it leads to a more objective picture of overt behaviour. Personal accounts from people on how they behave tend to be subjective, thus encouraging bias. There are disadvantages, however. Plain observation does not yield conclusive proof of cause-and-effect (causal) relationships. It gives no insight into buying motives and uncertain data on the income level or educational background of the respondents. The information produced is limited and the process usually expensive in terms of time taken by observers. Always bear in mind that observation is really only a descriptive research method.

Sampling

A sample is a limited number taken from a large group for testing and analysis. We must assume that the sample we have selected is representative of the whole group (the group is known as the population). Samples are used to make an estimate of the attributes of the population, e.g. what it likes, what it thinks, what it does. In practice it would be difficult to question all members of the population of interest; it would also be expensive. The smaller the number of people from whom data is to be collected, the cheaper and quicker the analysis of data will be. For a small sample size, however, accuracy may be sacrificed.

There are several different methods used for selecting samples. We shall consider random sampling, cluster sampling, stratified sampling and quota sampling.

Random sampling

This is sometimes referred to as basic probability sampling. A random sample is one in which every member of the population has an equal chance of appearing in the sample. The events that may occur have an equal or known chance of taking place. For example, if there are 20 students in your class and you all put your names into a hat to see which one of you will stand up and give a presentation on a given topic, then there is a 1 in 20 probability that it will be you (thus the term *probability sampling*). The methods actually used in selecting a random sample are a little more sophisticated than drawing names from a hat. A list of all the members of the population in question must first be drawn up. This is known as the *sampling frame*. (Many sampling frames already exist, e.g. electoral registers, directories, trade directories.)

The most commonly used method of selecting the sample is to assign a number to every item on the frame and then select the required number at random by using random number tables (published lists of random numbers). Another method used is to select every nth number from the frame. The number, n, is determined by dividing the number of items on the list by the number required in the eventual sample. This is known as *systematic random sampling*.

It is important that all of the individuals selected in the samples are interviewed. If initial contact is not made, then the interviewer must call back. It is this need for callbacks which makes random sampling one of the most expensive systems to use.

Cluster sampling

This is another commonly used method for obtaining a random sample. The researcher selects one or more representative areas and a random sample is then drawn from these tightly defined locations (these are known as *clusters*).

This method is easy to administer and carry out and so reduces the cost of the marketing research. The results can lack precision and could be biased if the cluster is unrepresentative of the population. For example, if the cluster was obtained from a coastal area, then the sample may be distorted by an unusually high proportion of retired people or seasonal workers.

Stratified sampling

When stratified sampling is used the population of interest is divided into groups which are each based on a common characteristic or attribute – for example, age, sex, income, or occupation. These characteristics are classified as strata within the population. A stratified sample is one where the respondents or items are specifically chosen from each stratum to represent the population. Random sampling is then used to select respondents from each stratum. This process is more complex than simple random sampling and although it is generally more accurate, without a computerised database it can be time consuming and expensive. Stratified samples are usually applied when researchers believe that there may be variations among different types of respondents.

A good example of this are the political opinion polls. These surveys are stratified by sex, race and age as there are often wide variations of opinion within these different strata.

When establishing a stratum the researcher must ensure that there is a degree of homogeneity within that stratum; otherwise accuracy will be affected.

Quota sampling

In many ways quota sampling is similar to stratified sampling in that the known characteristics of the population are represented in the correct proportions within the sample (the sample is stratified). The difference between the two forms of sampling is seen in the next stage, however. The quota sampling method does not select the respondents randomly; the selection of the respondents is left to the judgement of the interviewer. The interviewer is presented with a set of target interviews to complete (a quota), and the interviewees are described in terms of the characteristics of the respondents required.

It is up to the interviewer to locate the appropriate number and type of people within a given working area in the required time. The interviewers apply local knowledge to complete their set quotas as quickly and efficiently as possible.

Named individuals do not have to be found, as they do for random sampling, therefore significant cost savings over random sampling methods can be achieved. Although the potential for bias is increased, studies have suggested that as long as adequate controls are exercised quota sampling is perfectly acceptable for the majority of commercial purposes. The cost benefits of this method outweigh the disadvantages and it is now the major method used by most research projects.

Survey methods

After establishing a sample, the researcher must then decide upon the method of contact. Gathering the information for marketing research is becoming more and more difficult. Respondent rates are declining and some of the problems stem from a number of factors.

- *Sugging* (*a false market survey*). This is a sales technique disguised as a market survey. Frugging is a similar practice used to raise funds in the guise of marketing research. The result of these practices is that respondents are more wary when approached by interviewers and either refuse to answer questions or restrict their replies.
- *Fear of crime*. Due to an increase in daylight muggings and con tricks, respondents are less willing to trust interviewers.
- *Quality problems*. These have arisen due to problems associated with hiring qualified interviewers and the design of suitable questionnaires.

ACTIVITY 3.2.2

A marketing research agency is an organisation that offers its research services to other organisations throughout industry. There are agencies that specialise in industrial marketing research and agencies that specialise in consumer research. Market sectors within both industrial and consumer markets vary greatly in composition and size, however, and different sectors require different research techniques. Marketing research organisations are highly experienced, therefore, in selecting the appropriate methods. The following list details the different ways populations may be surveyed.

1 One person in 30 000 is interviewed.
2 A postal questionnaire is sent to every *n*th household in a town.
3 A predetermined group of people is selected based on age, income, and social class.

Identify the sampling method that will have been used by the researcher in each case and highlight the advantages and disadvantages of each sampling method identified.

Element 3.2 Propose and present product developments based on analysis of market research information

The selection of the correct survey method is important. There are a number of points that should be considered before a decision is made on the survey method:

1 the nature of the problem;

2 the data needed;

3 the resources available, e.g. funding, personnel.

Only after the above have been considered can a suitable survey method be chosen. The three most common choices are postal, telephone, and personal interview.

Postal surveys

With a postal survey, a questionnaire is usually mailed to the respondents. These types of survey are used most often when the respondents are located over a wide geographical area – for example, the sample may be two car families in the UK and the most effective way to reach the respondents would be by post.

Traditionally, the response rates for this type of survey have been low. Researchers adopt a number of methods to encourage response. First, questionnaires should be well constructed and easy to fill in – a confusing questionnaire will immediately discourage the respondent. Next, an incentive may be offered by the researcher; this may be in the form of free gifts, discounts, vouchers, coupons or simply a prepaid reply envelope. Some researchers attempt to personalise the questionnaire pack, and follow-up questionnaires are often sent to respondents who fail to complete the initial questionnaire.

Although response rates are low, the system is widely used for the following reasons. Its cost is relatively low; it can reach all geographic locations; and it does not require skilled personnel for personal interviews. Due to these factors the system is often used in industrial research when a supplier wants to identify customer needs and requirements in order to improve service and products. As the customer can readily see the benefits to be gained from completing the questionnaire, the response rate is high in this particular application of the postal survey.

Mail panels have evolved from postal surveys. They are made up of respondents who regularly reply to surveys and are especially useful for evaluating new products, providing general information about consumers, and providing records of consumers' purchases. For certain types of mail panel to work effectively, respondents are sometimes asked to keep a consumer purchase diary and are either paid or offered other forms of incentives, e.g. coupons, for their co-operation.

An interesting example of the postal survey technique is that applied by Procter & Gamble. This multinational organisation owns a large number of leading consumer brands from washing powder/liquids and household cleaners to baby care products such as disposable nappies and baby wipes. They apply a successful survey method which targets new mothers who have applied for free samples of their baby care products. The questionnaire, however, is not just limited to baby care products but includes questions on usage of a whole range of washing and cleaning items. Procter & Gamble have been very effective in targeting respondents for their postal survey. The respondents in question will be using baby care products but are also likely to be regular users of the other product categories.

Telephone surveys

In a telephone survey, the respondents' answers to the questionnaire are recorded by interviewers on the phone. The main advantage of this technique is that response rates are high. There is much less effort involved in answering questions over the telephone than there is in filling in a questionnaire. Another advantage is that travel expenses for interviewers are eliminated, so making telephone surveys a more economical method than personal interviewing.

Telephone surveys can now be linked to computerised questionnaires. The system is known as CATI (computer-assisted telephone interviewing) and combines the benefits of the telephone interview (quick response, low cost) with the control of a computerised collection and analysis system. Answers are keyed in directly to a computer terminal by the interviewer, while the next question is displayed on the screen.

This method does have its drawbacks. As it is based on oral communication, visual aids or observation cannot be included. Results may be affected if respondents within the sample do not have telephones. As a result of this last point, telephone surveys are sometimes used to develop panels of respondents.

Personal interview surveys

This is the traditional method favoured by marketing researchers. It offers the researcher a great deal of flexibility: for example, visual aids can be incorporated into the interview; rapport may be established leading to more in-depth questioning; confusion over questions can be identified from the respondent's expressions.

In addition to greater flexibility, another significant benefit of this method is that the interview can be longer and probing questions can be utilised in order to extract more information from respondents. Furthermore, reasons for non-response to questions can be examined in the field by the interviewer.

There are three common types of personal interview.

Fig 3.19

In-home interviews

The real advantage of using the in-home method is the flexibility it provides in terms of the length of the interview. The respondent will be willing to spend more time with the interviewer. Another advantage is one of security, the respondent is in a familiar environment and is therefore more likely to disclose real motivations, feelings and behaviour. These factors enable researchers to conduct in-depth surveys.

Shopping centre intercept interviews

These are a common way of conducting surveys and are often used in conjunction with quota sampling methods. They offer a good response rate for a lower cost than the in-home method. The same depth of questioning is difficult to achieve, but research has shown that shopping centre surveys provide similar response rates to telephone surveys with the added benefits of face-to-face contact, product testing and the use of visual aids.

Focus group interviews

The most creative interviewing technique is the focus group interview. Usually conducted in an informal setting where a group of respondents are exposed to an idea. They are allowed to interact and discuss the idea with other group members. This gives the interviewer the opportunity to identify attitudes and behaviour to the idea. As it doesn't use a structured questionnaire, this method is probably the most creative interview technique. The resulting qualitative data can be difficult to analyse, however, and is open to interpretation by the interviewer leading to the possibility of bias.

Survey types

In the above section we concentrated on survey methods. It would now be appropriate to consider some of the different types of survey that are adopted by researchers.

Product test surveys

Samples of a product are normally left with the respondent to give adequate time for testing and reflection. The respondent is then interviewed at a later date.

Usage/Habit/Attitude surveys

These surveys attempt to discover the behaviour of respondents and also their likes and dislikes. The researcher may wish to find out about attitudes to products, shopping habits or how products are actually used by consumers.

Advertisement test surveys

The objective of this type of survey is to measure and evaluate the effectiveness of advertising. Advertising is expensive and it is important to know whether or not it is or will be effective in introducing or reinforcing the product image and generating sales.

Retailer surveys

Retailer surveys are carried out by manufacturers into their retailers or intermediaries. Retailers are the intermediaries that deal with the consumers of products and services –

for example, Comet or Swinton Insurance. This means that manufacturers do not have direct contact with consumers. (Consumers and customers can be the same, but consumers actually consume or use the product, customers may not – they may be intermediaries.) It is therefore important that manufacturers receive regular information about consumers from their intermediaries.

Shop audits

The introduction of new technology has made this a regular practice. Computerised stock control procedures make it possible for an organisation to monitor the movement of their products, from individual products, product lines and whole product ranges. It can also be possible for some companies to monitor the movement of their competitors' products.

EPOS (electronic point of sale), the bar coding and scanning system that most supermarkets use, can now be combined with the Catalina system. This system not only tells the supermarket what products have been sold at any one moment in time but also provides the supermarket with the opportunity to target individual customers with promotional offers if they are buying competitors' brands. Instantaneous response to a marketing research method!

Omnibus surveys

Due to the high costs of certain survey methods, e.g. personal interviewing, a number of companies will co-operate and use a single questionnaire to obtain data from respondents. Some of the questions may be specific to their products, but much of the general information can also be shared, i.e. social grouping, income, age, sex, etc. This approach gives the companies involved considerable cost savings on their research activities.

Continuous surveys

These are surveys that are carried out over an extended time scale, usually a year. In order to maintain respondent motivation and interest, gifts are given and competitions run. These surveys are costly but they provide detailed data on the respondents.

ACTIVITY 3.2.3

Some of the survey types discussed above can utilise all three of the survey methods previously mentioned; some can not. In groups, choose the most appropriate survey methods (post, phone, interview) for the survey types above. Justify your choices.

ACTIVITY 3.2.4

Working in groups, consider the points discussed in the section on surveys. Each group should attempt to construct a chart detailing in point form the respective attributes or problems associated with each type of survey (divide this into the three categories of postal, telephone, and personal). You should look at the attributes/problems under the following categories: economy; flexibility; interviewer bias; respondents' co-operation. Feed back your findings to the rest of the class.

Element 3.2 Propose and present product developments based on analysis of market research information

ENSURING SUITABILITY OF INFORMATION

Questionnaire design and construction

The questionnaire is the instrument used to collect data. It has four main purposes in the data collection process:

- to collect relevant data;
- to make data comparable;
- to minimise bias;
- to motivate the respondent.

The quality and suitability of the data gathered are highly dependent on the design of the questionnaire and the questions it contains. A poorly designed questionnaire will collect inappropriate or inaccurate data. Poor design is usually the result of ambiguous or misleading questions or questions that influence the response of respondents. To ensure satisfactory design a pilot study is normally carried out. This satisfies two requirements: the first is an indication that research objectives will be met; the second is that poor questions can be identified and removed before research is carried out on a larger scale.

A well designed questionnaire will take the respondent through three sections. The purpose is to distinguish between three different types of data: identification data, classification data, and subject data.

1 *Identification data.* To generate identification data, questions are asked which identify each particular interview – for example, name and address, time and place of interview. These are asked at the end of an interview after sufficient rapport has been established between interviewer and respondent. Assurances of confidentiality should also be given at this stage.

2 *Classification data.* Each respondent must be classified. This is done by obtaining data on age, sex, occupation, social and income groups, etc. of respondents. This data helps to define the individual for the purpose of analysing responses. For example, the responses of a single employed male in his twenties are likely to be different to those of a retired female on a state pension. Knowing this information helps the researcher understand to some extent why the responses are different.

3 *Subject data.* Subject data refers to the information being gathered to meet the survey objectives; it forms the major part of the questionnaire. The following points should be considered when designing this section.

- Ensure a logical sequence of questions.
- Make sure that early questions generate interest.
- Make sure the questions are easy to answer.

There are four main question types: dichotomous, multiple-choice, rating-scale and open-ended questions. Dichotomous, multiple-choice and rating-scale questions are all closed-ended question types.

Dichotomous questions

These are questions with only two possible answers. For these to be valid, their answer must fall unambiguously into one of the two categories offered, e.g. do you subscribe to a daily newspaper? In some cases the respondent may not have an opinion on the question being asked and a third response may be added 'Don't know' – for example, with a question like, Do you think that Vauxhall make the best cars? The three possible responses (yes/no/don't know) can be assigned code numbers which are printed on the questionnaire. The interviewer just rings the response given. This saves time when the responses are processed for computer analysis. Examples of dichotomous questions can be seen in Fig. 3.20.

A question offering two answer choices

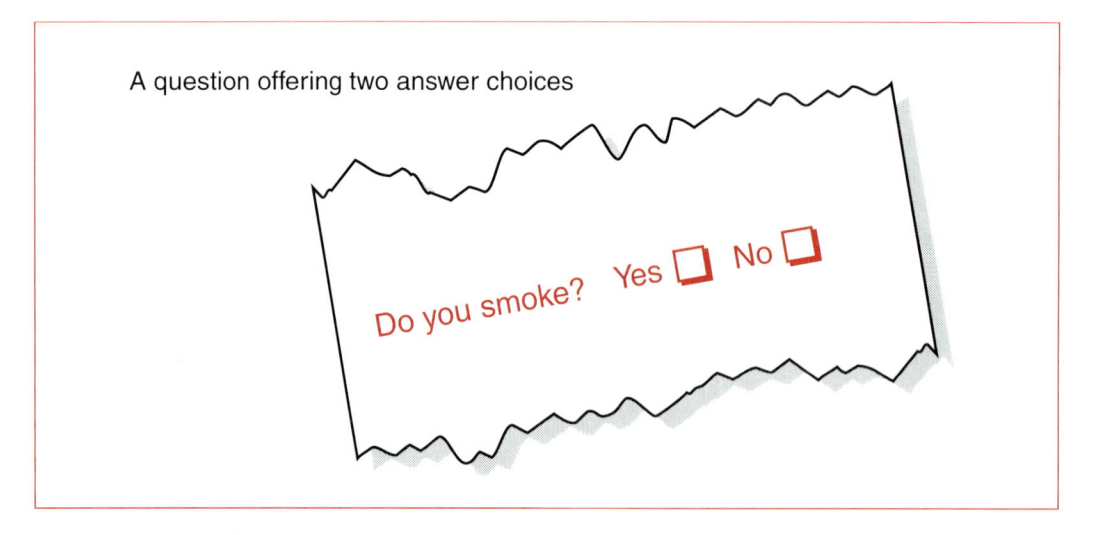

Do you smoke?   Yes ☐   No ☐

Fig 3.20 Examples of dichotomous questions

Multiple-choice questions

These are another form of closed question, but in this case the respondent usually has several answers to choose from. The questions are relatively easy to answer, but they are very difficult to design. If you ask a question, then you must be aware of all the possible answers. The range of answers provided must be both comprehensive and mutually exclusive; for example, the respondent should not feel the need to offer an answer that has not been provided, nor should he or she feel compelled to give more than one answer to each question.

Multiple-choice questions are easy to analyse and not open to interviewer bias. As precoding can also be applied to this type of question, response processing is also easy. Examples of multiple-choice questions can be seen in Fig. 3.21.

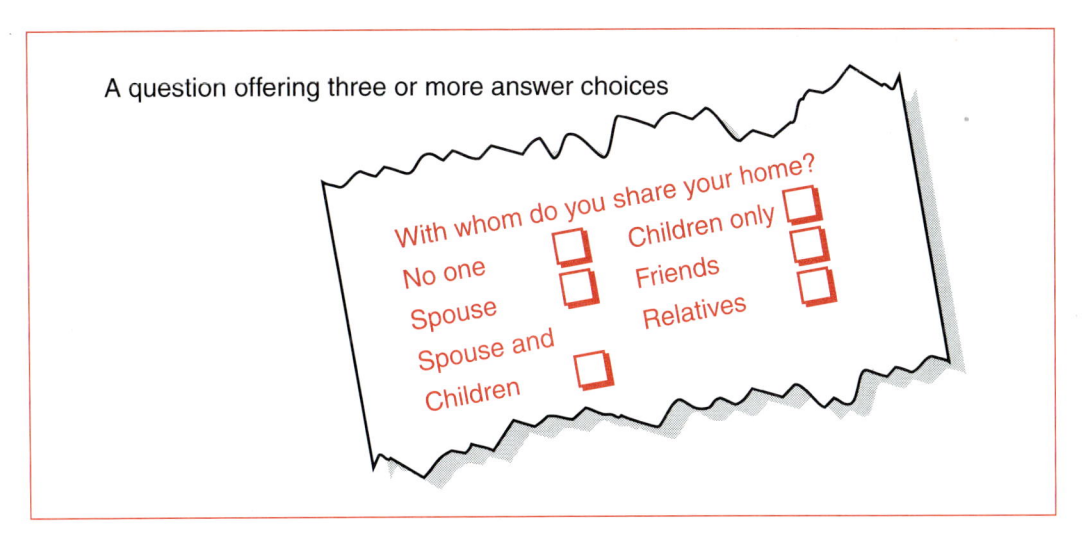

Element 3.2 Propose and present product developments based on analysis of market research information

A question offering three or more answer choices

With whom do you share your home?
No one ☐
Spouse ☐
Spouse and Children ☐
Children only ☐
Friends ☐
Relatives ☐

Fig 3.21 Examples of multiple-choice questions

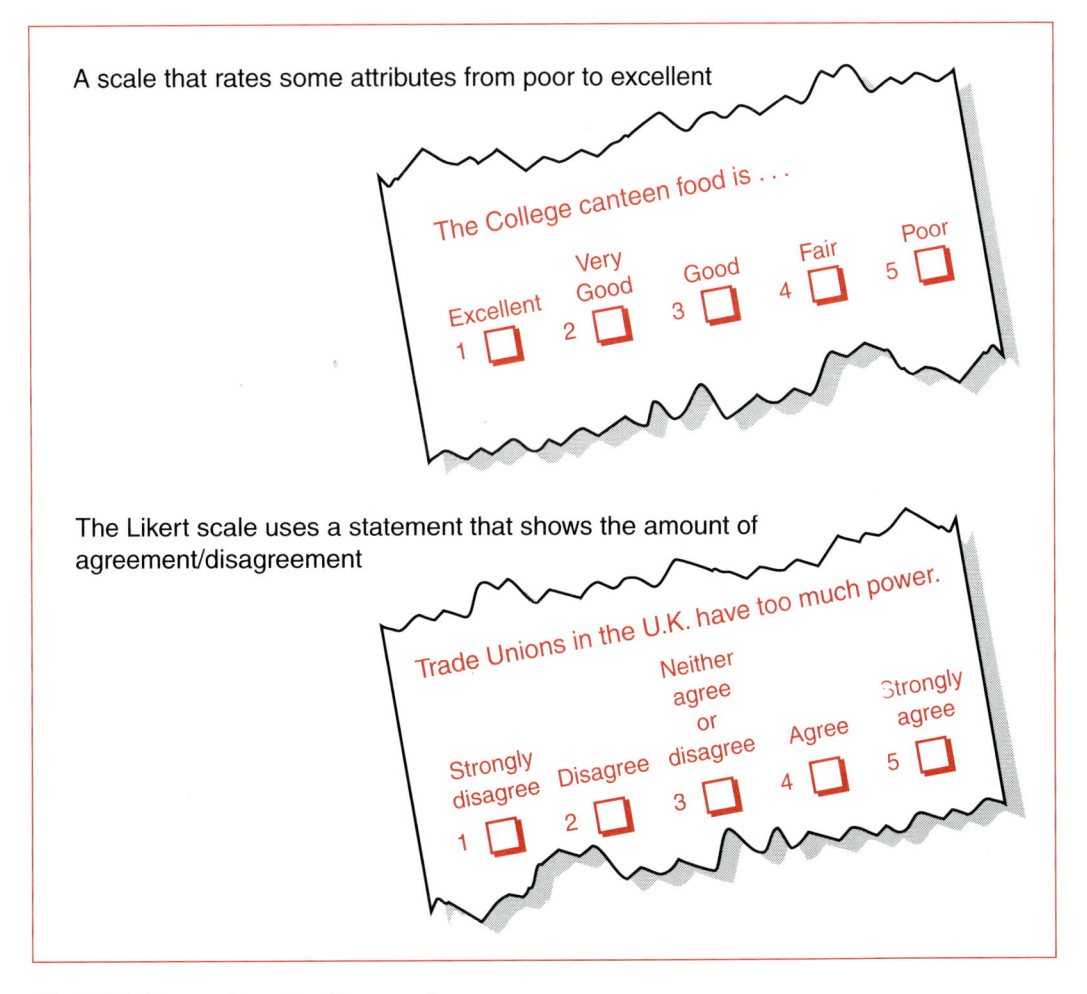

A scale that rates some attributes from poor to excellent

The College canteen food is . . .
Excellent 1 ☐ Very Good 2 ☐ Good 3 ☐ Fair 4 ☐ Poor 5 ☐

The Likert scale uses a statement that shows the amount of agreement/disagreement

Trade Unions in the U.K. have too much power.
Strongly disagree 1 ☐ Disagree 2 ☐ Neither agree or disagree 3 ☐ Agree 4 ☐ Strongly agree 5 ☐

Fig 3.22 Examples of rating scales

Rating scales

This type of question allows the respondent a choice from a spectrum of statements: for example, Did you think the service at the hotel was excellent, good, satisfactory, or poor? This technique is a simple way of collecting data, and precoding is also possible, facilitating data processing.

There are a number of different types of rating scale – one of the most common is the Likert, scale (named after Rensis Likert, an organisations theorist). This uses a range of statements from strongly agree to strongly disagree. Some further examples are shown in Fig. 3.22 on page 213.

Open-ended questions

These types of question encourage the respondent to suggest their own answers. The interviewers must record all that the respondent says; if not, then problems may arise usually in the form of biased data. When the completed questionnaires are returned, the responses require manual analysis which is time and labour consuming and therefore expensive. These factors tend to limit the number of open-ended questions on a questionnaire. Examples of open-ended questions can be seen in Fig. 3.23.

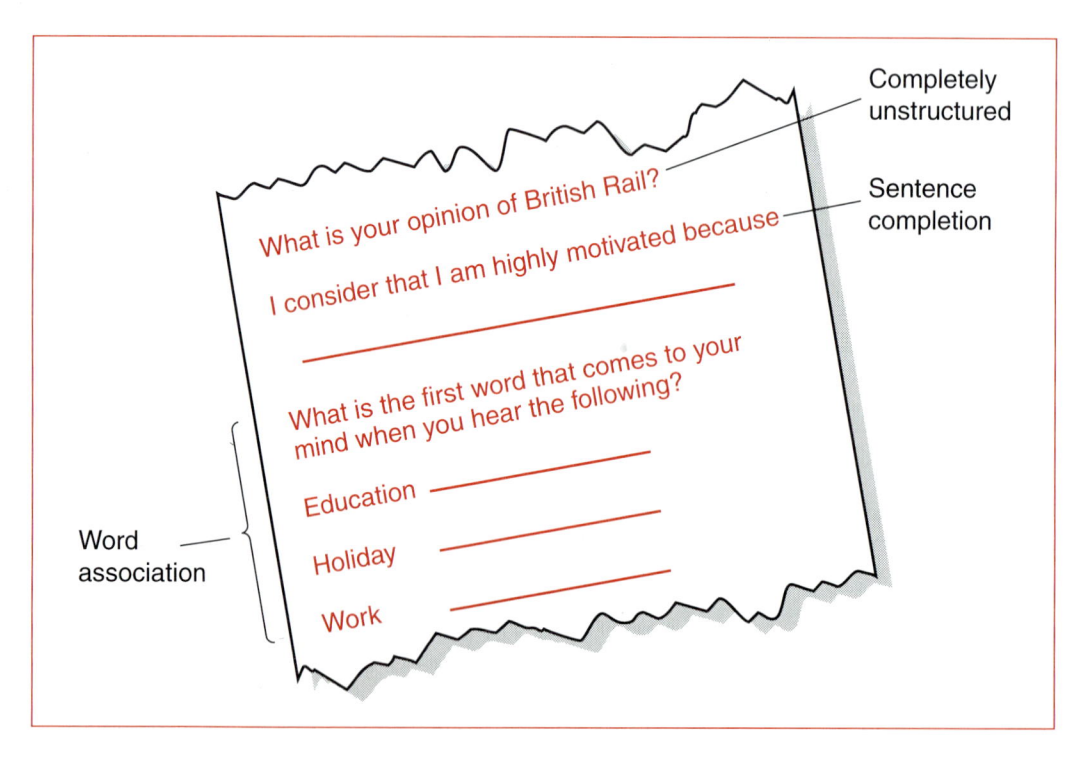

Completely unstructured: What is your opinion of British Rail?

Sentence completion: I consider that I am highly motivated because _____

Word association: What is the first word that comes to your mind when you hear the following?
- Education _____
- Holiday _____
- Work _____

Fig 3.23 Examples of open-ended questions

Element 3.2 Propose and present product developments based on analysis of market research information

Practical advice

The following lists may be useful when preparing for a market survey.

Order of questions

1. Set one or two bland questions to relax the respondent, e.g. Is this your first visit to ...?
2. Follow up with direct closed or multiple-choice questions.
3. Expand on the above answers with probing questions.
4. If relevant, introduce a ratings scale or attitude measurement.
5. Finish the questionnaire with open-ended questions.

Useful tips for field work

1. Give interviewers some form of identification.
2. Provide interviewers with visual aids, e.g. prompt cards.
3. Avoid imprecise terms, slang or jargon words, as you would in the questionnaire design.
4. Use routing statements; they can save time, e.g. If 'No', then go to question 5.
5. Do not suggest answers; this may introduce bias.
6. Do not ask questions people cannot or will not answer.
7. At the end of an interview a 'Thank you' leaflet is good practice. It should show the reasons and objectives of the survey and assure the respondent of confidentiality.

Research stages

Stage 1: discussions between client to research executive

The client is the organisation who pays for the work to be done, e.g. industrial firms, FMCG (fast moving consumer goods) companies, government departments, political parties, charities.

The research executive is the person with the knowledge of marketing research and how it can be applied to a particular problem.

The proposal is formulated from discussions between the above two parties. It will describe practical details, e.g. survey type, sample size and method, a draft questionnaire. The proposal should also highlight the kind of information the research will provide as well as time scales and costs.

Many large organisations have the resources available to conduct their own marketing research and may not need to conduct research through a marketing research agency.

Stage 2: pilot study

This is a limited survey and ensures that the questions selected are the right ones and that they are being asked correctly. It also highlights whether or not the right people are being interviewed and will lead to revised time scales and costs for the marketing research project.

Stage 3: field work

After the discussions and the pilot study it is now the time for interviewers to be recruited in order to target respondents in the approved sample. Interviewers must be given detailed information on the respondents they need to interview.

Stages 4 and 5: data processing and the final report

These stages will be discussed in the next section.

ANALYSING MARKETING RESEARCH INFORMATION

The data that primary research produces can be in two formats: quantitative or qualitative. The type of data produced will affect the methods by which it is analysed.

Quantitative data

This type of data is statistically definitive or precise. In more simple terms, the findings can be displayed numerically. For example, the ages of everyone in your class would be quantitative data. A quantitative approach can also be applied to a person's behaviour, e.g. how many times a day a person brushes his or her teeth, how many times a week a person uses a cash dispenser? It is a relatively straightforward process to retrieve, collate, analyse, and present quantitative data.

Qualitative data

In contrast to the above, qualitative data is not based on precise information. This type of data only conveys opinions and is the result of studies into people's perceptions, motivations and attitudes. For example, a person's opinion of a particular advertisement would not have a precise statistical value; a typical response might be that he or she found it 'quite funny', or 'not very informative'. This is useful information to the researcher, but not easy to use when the researcher wants to compare it to other responses. This is where attitude scales are most effective; by creating a graded spectrum, the researcher now has the opportunity to attach statistical values to your opinions (*see* the earlier examples of ratings scales).

Preparing data

The data must first be prepared before it can be analysed. The preparation of data is normally conducted in four stages:

1 editing;

2 coding;

3 tabulation;

4 summarisation.

Editing

A checklist should be referred to which will enable the researcher to separate out useless responses. This is based on the following questions.

- *Are the responses legible?* If not, then the researcher can either go back to the respondent, infer the meaning from other responses, or discard the response.
- *Are the responses consistent?* An example of inconsistency would be if the respondent has indicated that he or she is in the age bracket 16–19, but then declares his or her occupation as dental surgeon. These types of inconsistency are usually the result of the respondent failing to understand the question. It is best to discard all inconsistent responses.
- *Are the responses complete?* This can be avoided if the interviewer is present. Whether or not the response was discarded would depend on the number and type of questions not completed.
- *Is the respondent a comedian?* These are easy to identify – for example, 'occupation: astronaut'. The offending response can be safely thrown out.

Coding

Once the initial screening process is complete, the remaining responses should then be collated into specific response categories. This process is known as coding.

Coding ensures that response categories are established and allocated a number. There are two approaches to coding: precoding and postcoding.

Precoding is appropriate to closed-type questions. The researcher knows that there is only a limited number of responses and these can be given numerical codes in advance.

Postcoding is appropriate to open-ended type questions where it would be impossible to allocate codes in advance before answers had even been formulated. It is safe to assume that only a certain number of responses of a certain type will be generated, however. For example, 'I drive a Mini because ...' (a) 'it is fun to drive'; (b) 'it is good on fuel'. The different responses can be classified during the editing stage and then numerically coded.

Tabulation

Once responses have been assigned to categories, the number in each category can be counted. This is known as *tabulation*. Tabulation can take two forms:

1 Simple tabulation

This will give us a frequency distribution for each category. For example, Table 3.2 tabulates the ages of a sample of account holders for a national bank.

Table 3.2

	Under 16	16–20	21–30	31–40	41–50	51–60	Over 60
No. of accounts	210	451	842	913	902	864	741

Age of account holder

2 Cross tabulation

Quite often the more useful results of marketing research are those that show important relationships between variables. For this a cross tabulation (or matrix) is used. For example, we may wish to represent two variables: the age of the customers and the type of account held. These variables will become the headings on a two-way table so that relationships between the variables can be studied. (*See* Table 3.3.)

Table 3.3

	\multicolumn{7}{c}{Age of account holder}
Type of account	Under 16	16–20	21–30	31–40	41–50	51–60	Over 60
Cheque	0	120	657	705	758	720	431
Deposit	210	331	185	208	144	144	310

Cross tabulation is one of the most popular ways of summarising marketing research data. It allows the analyst to identify relationships between variables while also presenting a logical display of data that is easy for both researcher and non-researcher to examine.

ACTIVITY 3.2.5

Look at the findings in Table 3.3 and identify any relationship between age and type of account.

Summarisation

There are three common measures of summarising data statistically: centrality, dispersion and percentage. Do not be put off by the terminology; you are probably already aware of some of these measures under different names.

Centrality

The measures of centrality are most commonly known as the mode, the median and the mean. These three measures are simply different types of average. The best way to illustrate them is by using an example. Let us assume that a manufacturer of brake pads has done a study to determine how many miles the product lasts. The results in Table 3.4 are from a sample of nine motorists.

The *mode* is the value that occurs most frequently. You could also describe it as the most typical response. In our example for working out the mileage per set of brake pads, we might arrange the data as it is in Table 3.5 in order to obtain the mode.

Element 3.2   Propose and present product developments based on analysis of market research information

Table 3.4

Motorist number	Number of miles
1	27 000
2	28 000
3	24 000
4	29 000
5	29 000
6	27 000
7	34 000
8	27 000
9	35 000

Table 3.5

Number of miles	Number of motorists obtaining these miles
24 000	1
27 000	3
28 000	1
29 000	2
34 000	1
35 000	1

In our example the mode is 27 000 miles, as this result was obtained by a greater number of motorists than any other. This information could then be used by the company to state that in a consumer test the brake pads typically provided 27 000 miles' worth of motoring. That may be, but in our example the company would not be doing itself justice as the majority of the respondents got more than 27 000 miles' worth of motoring per set of brake pads. Let us consider another method of centrality.

The *median* value in a set of data is worked out by first placing the responses in rank order and then finding the value which has the same number of values above it as it has below it. In our example it would appear in the following way.

35 000, 34 000, 29 000, 29 000, 28 000, 27 000, 27 000, 27 000, 24 000

28 000 is median of the mileages obtained by the sample of nine motorists. Four people got more than 28 000 and four people got less. If there had been an even number of responses, then there would have been two numbers in the middle. To find the median in this situation we would add the two together, divide by two, and find the average. The median tends to be more representative than the mode; it is also less affected than the mean by extremely high or low scores.

The *mean* is the most commonly used measure of centrality and you probably already know it as the average. Its statistical definition is the sum of the data divided by the number of data points. In our example it would be obtained by adding up all the individual responses and dividing by nine.

$$\text{mean} = x = \frac{(24 + 27 + 27 + 27 + 28 + 29 + 29 + 34 + 35)}{9}$$

$$= 28.9 \text{ thousand miles}$$

There are advantages to using the mean. First, it can be calculated without having to arrange the data into a frequency distribution or rank order. Second, it can be used to make generalisations from the sample mean and apply them to the population.

Dispersion

In addition to describing the centrality of a set of data, it is also useful to calculate the amount of dispersion, or spread, that exists among a set of measurements. There are three measurements for determining dispersion: the range, the standard deviation and the variance. In this unit we consider the most simple of the three – the range.

Unit 3   Marketing

ACTIVITY 3.2.6

As mentioned above, the key weakness of using the mean is its susceptibility to extreme values. Imagine if, in our example, we had had a tenth respondent. What would the mean have been if that respondent had recorded 50 000 miles? How would that have compared with the other measures of centrality?

The range is simply the distance between the two most extreme values. Let us consider the following example.

A customer for stainless steel pipe is researching different manufacturers of the product and is principally concerned with quality. The customer identifies two manufacturers who both manufacture stainless steel pipe. Both factories produce 5 cm diameter pipe which the customer is most interested in. The customer obtains two sample batches of the 5 cm pipe to check how accurate the diameter is. The findings are presented on the frequency distribution graph in Fig. 3.24. You will see that the results for both pipes are spread evenly about the point representing 5 cm. If we were to calculate the mean, median, and mode then both factories would score 5 cm. Factory A obviously produces more accurate pipes than Factory B, however. The way we would distinguish between the two factories would be by identifying their respective ranges. Factory A's range would be from 4.99 cm to 5.01 cm, or a range of 0.02 cm, whereas Factory B's range would be from 4.97 cm to 5.03 cm, or a range of 0.06 cm.

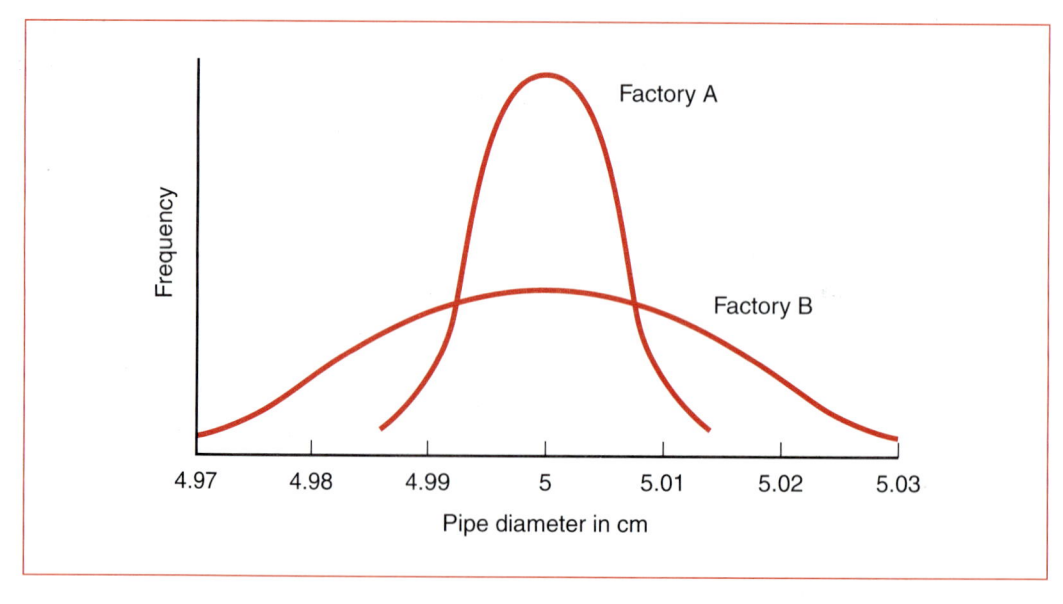

Fig 3.24 Frequency distribution – factories A and B

This method gives the researcher additional insight when analysing data. The main advantages of the range are that it is easy to calculate and easy to understand. There are disadvantages, however, the main one being that extreme values can make it misleading.

Element 3.2 Propose and present product developments based on analysis of market research information

ACTIVITY 3.2.7

A company has just developed a new type of soap powder and wants to know how many washes per standard pack it is likely to get. The tests are undertaken by twelve respondents and the findings are shown in Table 3.6.

Table 3.6

Number of respondent	Number of washes per pack
1	40
2	35
3	37
4	31
5	35
6	33
7	36
8	38
9	33
10	35
11	39
12	36

Find the centrality of the above data by using all three methods of measurement (i.e. mode, median and mean). Identify which measurement the company would be best publishing. Add a 13th respondent whose number of washes totalled 21. How has this affected the three measurements. Plot the data on a frequency distribution graph for the first twelve respondents and then with thirteen. Calculate the range for both distributions.

Percentages

Another approach to summarising data is through the use of percentages. These can be used to represent the proportion of sample items that fall into different categories. For example, if 100 people were interviewed then the data could be summarised by saying that 48 per cent were male and 52 per cent were female, or that 25 per cent were in the age group 16 to 30, 32 per cent 31 to 45, and 43 per cent 46+. The percentage is easily calculated and simple to understand.

Trend analysis

When the researcher has summarised the data generated by the marketing research project, it may be possible to identify any apparent trends highlighted by that data. For example, if a continuous survey were carried out, it might show the increasing trend of a particular age group's preference for a certain product. The recent rise in popularity among teenagers and young adults for Doc Marten's footwear comes to mind. Once a trend has been identified, the researcher will then try to determine whether or not that trend is likely to continue.

Unit 3   Marketing

The method adopted for analysing future trends is generically known as forecasting. There are many approaches that can be taken in forecasting, some of which require an in-depth knowledge of mathematics. We will consider the more common, basic methods. There is also a wide variety of variables that can be the object of a forecast, including sales, market share, participation rates, and technological developments. We will concentrate primarily on sales as the object of our forecast.

Time-series based forecasting (analytical methods)

Past sales and time are the key variables from which we try to make our predictions. The two most common methods are the *naive method* and *trend extrapolation*. Let us consider both these methods in terms of an example.

Research has shown that sales of packs of Aunty Beryl's frozen Yorkshire Puddings have increased rapidly since their launch two years ago. The quarterly sales figures are shown in Table 3.7.

Table 3.7

Quarter	Aunty Beryl's sales
1st	55
2nd	80
3rd	120
4th	150
5th	195
6th	240
7th	285
8th	330

To help with production Aunty Beryl may want an idea of the next quarter's possible sales. She knows that the trend is increasing, so she applies an arbitrary growth factor of 1.1 to the eighth quarterly figure, i.e. 1.1 × 330, or 363 packs. This approach is known as the *naive method* and may be suitable under basic conditions.

The second method is more scientific and is known as *trend extrapolation*. This simply involves projecting or extrapolating past sales data into the future. It usually involves a graphical picture of past sales as shown in Fig. 3.25.

The extrapolation can be done visually or mathematically. If the nearest line of fit is plotted through the coordinates, then by using the visual method the sales forecasted for the ninth quarter can be estimated at 400.

To extrapolate the trend for the ninth quarter mathematically, we use the linear regression equation:

$y = a + bx$

where y = sales for the ninth quarter
$x = 9$
a = the intercept on the y axis
b = the gradient of the line

Element 3.2 Propose and present product developments based on analysis of market research information

[Graph showing sales of packs of frozen Yorkshire Puddings vs Quarter, with past sales data points from quarters 1-8 and extrapolated future sales as a dashed line]

9th quarter forecast = 355 packs
10th quarter forecast = 395 packs

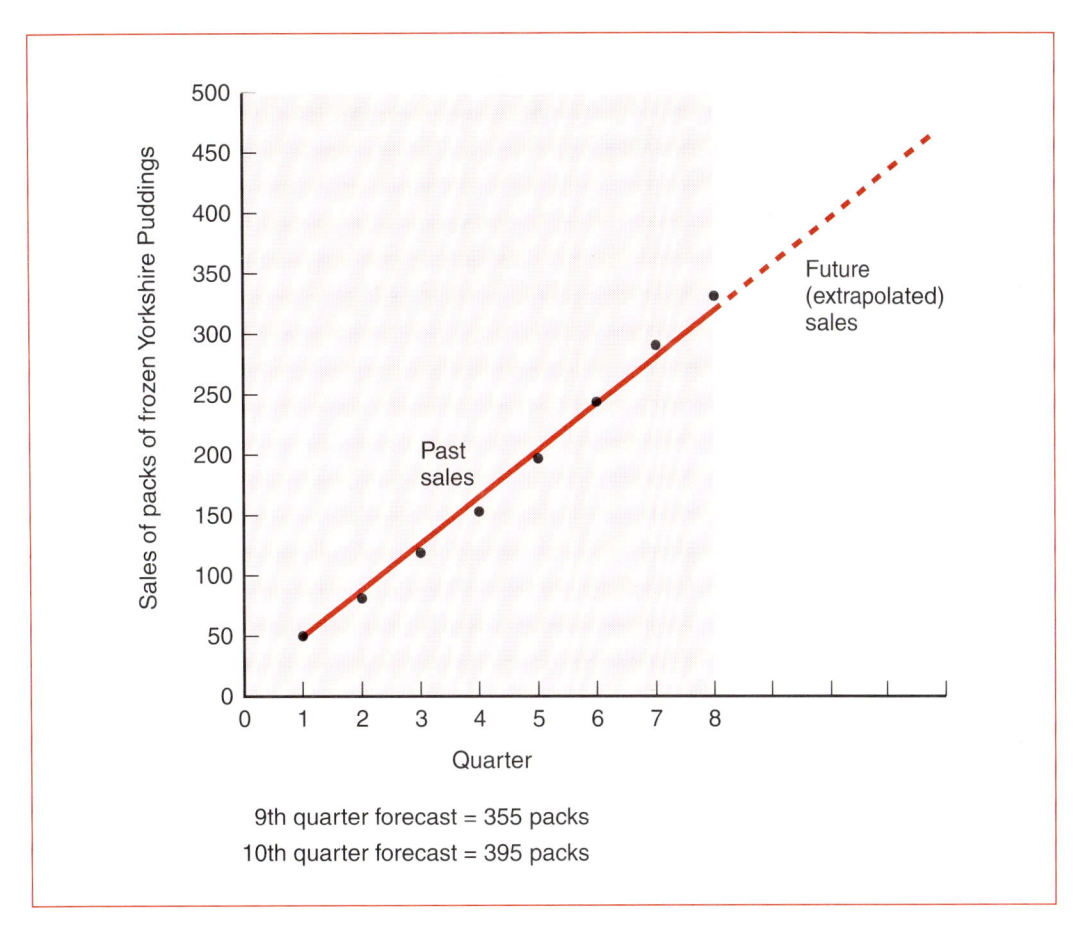

Fig 3.25 Trend extrapolation

Subjective forecasting (synthetic methods)

Subjective forecasting is based mainly on judgement. There are a number of approaches and we will consider two of the most common: juries of executive opinion and surveys of buying intentions.

Juries of executive opinion get sales forecasts from each company executive and combine them to form a single sales forecast. The 'combining' process usually involves discussions and adjustments in order to arrive at a consensus.

A survey of buying intentions may use the survey methods mentioned earlier in this element, i.e. post, phone, or interview, to find out the anticipated needs of customers for the period ahead.

Presenting and reporting research findings

The results of marketing research are usually presented in the form of a formal written report. To keep the reader interested and help ensure understanding, tables, graphs and charts should be used throughout the report. These are an effective way to summarise data further and many people find it much easier to assimilate information when it is presented in these formats. For example, percentages can be highly effective when shown as a pie chart and bar charts are very good for comparing different values.

Unit 3 Marketing

Before preparing the report the researcher must take an objective look at the findings to see how well the gathered facts answer the research question. It will be unlikely that the research can provide everything needed to answer the research question. It is important, therefore, that the researcher points out any deficiencies, and reasons for them, at the beginning of the report.

MARKETING RESEARCH AND ITS CONTRIBUTION TO MARKETING DECISIONS

The business environment is constantly and rapidly changing, and for this reason marketing research should not be a one off activity, but should be built into the business as a continuing operation to provide the marketer with a steady flow of facts.

All firms need facts to assist the decision-making process. Gathering these facts is what marketing research is all about: it offers a firm basis for a clear appreciation of the present situation. It can also provide a base for which current trends may be extrapolated and future forecasts made.

Marketing research increases the probability of successful marketing; it is essential in the planning and development of marketing strategies.

Self assessment questions

1 Which of the following is *not* a limitation of using secondary data to solve marketing problems?
   a Its cost
   b Its accuracy
   c Its format
   d Its published date

2 From which of the following can secondary data *not* be obtained?
   a Trade journals
   b Surveys
   c Internal sources of information
   d Computerised databases

3 Primary data is best described as
   a the data necessary for a correct decision
   b an information gap
   c the data generated specifically for the current research investigations
   d the data collected for some purpose other than the current research investigations?

4 If Cadbury's tests the effect of new packaging on chocolate purchases in an environment where advertising, promotion, distribution and pricing are controlled, Cadbury's is using

Element 3.2 Propose and present product developments based on analysis of market research information

  a observation
  b sampling
  c random sampling
  d experimentation?

5 Which sampling method divides the population of interest into groups based on common characteristics?
  a Random sampling
  b Cluster sampling
  c Stratified sampling
  d Total population sampling

6 Which sampling method gives every member of the population an equal chance of appearing in the sample?
  a Random sampling
  b Cluster sampling
  c Quota sampling
  d Stratified sampling

7 A continuous survey is one which
  a is carried out over an extended time scale
  b uses a variety of survey methods
  c uses a panel of respondents
  d has no conclusion?

8 Which one of the following questions is dichotomous?
  a How often do you drive?
  b What is your opinion of the Ford Probe?
  c Do you own a car? Yes__ No__
  d Rate the new Ford Probe on a scale of 1 to 5 (1 dislikes to 5 likes).

9 Attitude scales are most effective in measuring
  a quantitative responses
  b qualitative responses
  c negative responses
  d positive responses?

10 Which is the correct order of stages for the preparation of marketing data?
  a Coding, editing, tabulation, summarisation
  b Coding, tabulation, editing, summarisation
  c Coding, tabulation, summarisation, editing
  d Editing, coding, tabulation, summarisation.

Unit 3   Marketing

PC
3.2.1
3.2.2
3.2.3
3.2.4

Assignment

Select a service provided by your college (for example, the refectory, library, or computer workshop). Your brief is to find out what fellow students want from the service you have selected. Once this is achieved you should establish whether or not the needs of the students are being met by the existing provision of service.

The following stages are for your guidance.

1. Identify any previous data collected.
2. Assess the suitability of available secondary data.
3. Select an appropriate method by which to update any secondary data.
4. If no secondary data is available then select methods for collection of primary data.
5. Edit, code and summarise the data you have gathered from your research.
6. Analyse and then present your findings in report format to your tutor. Use your report to highlight any specific changes needed that you feel your research has uncovered.
7. Detail your proposals for modification of the service.

Element 3.3
EVALUATE MARKET COMMUNICATIONS DESIGNED TO INFLUENCE A TARGET AUDIENCE

Performance criteria

1. Explain the suitability of advertising and publicity for promoting goods and services and organisational image.

2. Identify and give examples of public relations to promote goods, services and organisations.

3. Evaluate sales promotion methods for their effectiveness in reaching a target audience.

4. Evaluate the effect of marketing communications on product performance.

5. Explain growth in direct marketing methods in terms of customer needs and new technology.

6. Compare marketing communications within two organisations.

7. Explain guidelines and controls relating to marketing communications.

ADVERTISING

Advertising is a form of non-personal communication which promotes an organisation and its products and is directed at a target audience through a paid medium. There are a number of different media available:

- television
- radio
- newspapers
- magazines
- direct mail
- public transport
- outdoor displays
- cinemas.

Advertising is highly flexible and provides the opportunity of reaching a wide target audience. Advertising is an expensive form of promotion and the selection of appropriate media is critical.

A company that manufactures climbing equipment such as climbing boots and harnesses may wish to advertise its products. If it were to advertise on TV, it may well reach a large proportion of its target market but there would also be a lot of wastage as its message would also be received by people not interested in climbing.

This company would find advertising in a specialist climbing magazine far more cost effective as the message would be aimed only at the climbing fraternity.

We mentioned above that advertising is an expensive process, but how can the costs of using the different types of media be compared? Advertising costs are normally worked out on a cost per thousand basis (per viewer or reader). For example, for an organisation that manufactures biscuits the target audience will be large and varied, as most people eat biscuits. It would therefore make sense to advertise during the most popular TV viewing times. It can cost tens of thousands of pounds for a 30 second slot during peak viewing times. For the biscuit company it may cost £50 000 for one advert to reach approximately 5 million viewers. The cost per viewer would be 1p and the cost per thousand viewers £10. This sum can be used as a measure of effectiveness against other forms of media.

Advertising can have its drawbacks. Initial outlay can be very high, as in the example above, and its effectiveness can be difficult to monitor – has the advertising had a positive effect on sales?

Element 3.3 Evaluate marketing communications designed to influence a target audience

PUBLIC RELATIONS

Public relations (or PR) is responsible for creating a positive corporate image within the company's external environment. If we refer back to Element 3.1, we can see how important this function is and that it relates directly to the common marketing objective of enhanced corporate image.

Public relations can be difficult to control and bad publicity resulting from weak PR can be extremely damaging.

Recently, the Swiss firm Nestlé received bad publicity over the promotion techniques it used for its baby milk formula in third world countries. Mothers were encouraged to abandon breast-feeding in favour of the product, contrary to current medical advice.

It is important to remember that public relations is not a free form of communication and costs are incurred with the preparation of news releases and encouraging media personnel to broadcast or print them.

Public relations is the function that monitors and controls publicity. Quite often this function is contracted out of the organisation to public relations or advertising agents.

SALES PROMOTION

Sales promotion is a distinct function within the promotional mix. Care must be taken not to assume that sales promotion activities are the only part of the promotional function. Sales promotion is primarily used to support other promotional mix ingredients with the offer of a direct inducement, added value or an incentive. Sales promotions can be targeted at either the consumer or the retailer and we will look at examples used for both groups.

Sales promotion methods

1. *Coupons* – e.g. 50p off, often used in conjunction with print advertisements.
2. *Frequent-user incentives* – e.g. trading stamps at petrol stations.
3. *Point-of-sale displays* – e.g. display racks, signs, counter pieces.
4. *Free samples*.
5. *Money refunds* – usually linked to multiple purchases.
6. *Twofers* – two for the price of one.
7. *Percentage extra free* – e.g. $12\frac{1}{2}$ per cent extra on cans of soft drink.
8. *Premiums* – bonus items offered free on-pack, e.g. Taboo and Mirage were offered as sample miniatures with the purchase of either product.
9. *Competitions and contests*.

All of the above sales promotion activities are targeted at the consumer. The following are offered by the manufacturer to the retailer to encourage the retailer to concentrate sales efforts on the manufacturer's products.

1. *Buying allowances* – a temporary price reduction to the retailer if a specified quantity is bought.

2. *Co-operative advertising* – the retailer advertises the manufacturer's products and the costs are shared.

3. *Dealer listings* – an advertisement by the manufacturer that identifies participating retailers.

4. *Sales contests* – used to motivate retail staff, e.g. travel agent staff may be encouraged to sell the products of one travel company with the incentive of a free holiday for achieving the highest sales.

The above list are not exhaustive and there are also a great number of variations on the above themes.

ACTIVITY 3.3.1

Consider the article from the *Financial Times* of 24 June 1993 in Fig. 3.26.

Task 1. What marketing objectives has Holsten set in the UK market?

Task 2. What communication strategy has it used in its home market?

Task 3. How does it adapt its marketing communications mix for international markets?

ACTIVITY 3.3.2

Establish a profile of the promotional mix of three different products, one from each of the following product categories:

- Consumer durable
- Consumer non-durable
- Service

You should try and gather as much evidence as you can on the different promotional activities for your chosen products. Once you have gathered this evidence, break down each promotional mix into its components and explain why these activities have been adopted for these products.

Element 3.3 Evaluate marketing communications designed to influence a target audience

Raising its glass to a new niche

Holsten has spent three years on a new beer, says **Philip Rawstorne**

Holsten, the German brewer, has launched its first new beer for 40 years in the UK premium-packaged lager market – a market it helped to create and now leads.

The Hamburg-based brewer, with UK sales of 160m bottles and cans of Holsten Pils a year, aims to consolidate a position it has been building since the 1950s when its beer was marketed as a drink suitable for diabetics.

Competition has been growing rapidly. Imported lager brands were entering the market at a rate of one every 19 days during the peak period 18 months ago, and consumers have about 400 to choose from, says Carol Fisher, UK marketing director.

Consumer familiarity with Holsten's established product made it vulnerable to newcomers in the more fashionable bars and restaurants. Holsten Bier, the new brand, is brewed in Germany and is targeted at this niche in the market. Three years of research have gone into preparing the product, from its taste to the acid-etched logo on the bottle.

Holsten's move reflects an immediate concern to secure its place in a market to secure its place in a market that offers profit margins five times greater than those available in Germany.

It also marks another tactical advance in a long-running export drive that has enabled the brewer to double sales to 7.85m hectolitres (172.68m gallons) and turnover to DM989m (£394m) in the past five years.

The German beer market is a difficult place in which to grow. Its consumers have the biggest thirst in Europe, but over the past few years they have reached their limit at a yearly 144 litres a head. That demand is being met by 1,300 brewers catering for mainly localised tastes with more than 5,000 brands.

Holsten's response has been to mount a three-pronged attack on its domestic market. It is promoting its pilsener as a national brand, supporting it with television advertising, and sponsorship of soccer teams, tennis tournaments, horse-racing, cultural events and environmental projects.

The Holsten brand has been extended to alcohol-free and light beers; and the national portfolio has also been enlarged to include Foster's lager, brewed under licence, and specialities such as Duckstein ale and Franziskaner white beer, which is distributed for a Munich brewer.

At the same time, the company is strengthening its base in northern Germany and pushing out the market boundaries of its regional brands. This process was given a fillip by the razing of the Berlin Wall and reunification.

In 1991 Holsten bought the Lubz brewery in Mecklenburg, and with it a brand of pils that dominates a sales territory stretching from the Baltic to Berlin. Last year, Holsten acquired a brewery in Dresden that, like the company's plant in Brunswick, produced a brand named Feldschlossen. Brewed to one recipe, the brand is now one of the country's largest with sales of 1.1m hectolitres across Saxony.

But until these successes took Holsten's share of the German market to about 5 per cent, expansion at home was difficult and slow. Paul von Ostman, Holsten's international director, says the brewer's early decision to seek growth in overseas markets – it shipped its first beer to the UK from Hamburg in the late 1890s – was one of its shrewdest moves.

Of Holsten's total German production of 7m hectolitres last year, 18 per cent was exported – roughly 3½ times the percentage for the industry as a whole – to more than 70 countries.

Another 900,000 hectolitres are brewed under licence in the UK, Hungary, Nigeria, Namibia and China, which supplies the Hong Kong market. That means that 25 per cent of the company's beer – and 40 per cent of the Holsten brand – is sold outside Germany.

The company continues to push strongly for further international growth. In Europe, Italy was targeted last year, and production will be licensed in Poland this year. A barter agreement has even gained entry to Vietnam. The importer is paying for the beer with sisal matting.

Fig 3.3 Source: The *Financial Times*, June 1993

SEGMENTATION AND TARGETING

Defining markets

The marketing function of organisations is principally interested in the activities of the demand element of the market. For our purposes a market can be identified as a group of people who are willing and able to purchase a certain product category in order to satisfy a particular need.

This explanation enables us to consider markets from as wide or as narrow a perspective as we wish. For example, the major supermarket chains may wish to consider the mass market (the total population). It is very rare these days to find people who do not use supermarkets, and it may be useful for the supermarket companies to know about conditions affecting the general buying public. It soon becomes apparent to companies who study their markets, however, that there are markets within markets. If we continue with the example of supermarkets, we can see that within the mass market there are different groups of people with different buying habits. This is illustrated by the proliferation of own branding among the supermarket chains with the supermarkets attempting to satisfy the needs of their different markets (see Table 3.8).

Table 3.8 Markets within markets for supermarket chain

Market	Product	Market description
1	Low price brands 'discount'	Low income families
2	Premium own brands	Middle income/High store loyalty
3	Proprietary brands	Middle income/Low store but high manufacturer loyalty

The examples in Table 3.8 are in no way specific but serve to illustrate the point of markets within markets. All three markets are involved in the purchase of different product categories. Market 1 may be interested in buying proprietary brands but may not be able to afford them. Markets 2 and 3 may be able to afford discount own brands but may not be willing to purchase them because of perceived quality. Market 3 may be unwilling to purchase premium own brands due to a lack of product knowledge.

We may also wish to define markets in terms of product categories. This is done in the broadest sense by distinguishing between goods and services. A good is a product of a tangible nature; that is it can be touched or picked up. A service is a product of an intangible nature; it is not something that has a physical presence but it does satisfy certain needs (for example, the need for security and safety may be satisfied by insurance policies).

ACTIVITY 3.3.3

Visit your local superstore and identify the different types of brands (high value, low value, own brand, premium own brand). Identify the groups that may purchase the different varieties of these products. (To help you identify these groups, you may wish to use your library's CD ROM to find out if any newspaper articles exist which relate to this area. This could be done by conducting a key word search based around the word 'brand' or on the generic product areas.)

Markets are usually classified into the two categories: consumer goods/services markets and industrial goods/services markets.

Consumer markets

Consumer markets are markets where the goods and services are purchased for end use or consumption. We are all members of numerous consumer markets, e.g. entertainment, clothing, vehicles, insurance, recreation and food. Consumers do not always buy products direct from the manufacturer; this leads us into another market category, the industrial or organisational market.

Industrial/organisational markets

These markets consist of organisations that purchase specific products with the ultimate aim of making another product or selling on to another purchaser. There are three possible reasons for purchase:

1. direct use in producing other products, e.g. purchase of raw materials;
2. use in general daily operations, e.g. forklift trucks, tools;
3. purchases for resale, e.g. wholesalers, retailers.

The type of market being targeted will affect the marketing communications mix. For example, a company like McDonald's which aims its products solely at consumer markets will use a combination of TV advertising and sales promotion. An electronic component company such as Texas Instruments will use sales literature and personal selling along with advertising in trade journals.

Segmenting the market

We have already identified a number of smaller markets within the mass market. These smaller markets are known as *market segments*. By segmenting the market, the marketer hopes to turn a heterogeneous (diverse), large market into a number of smaller, homogeneous markets.

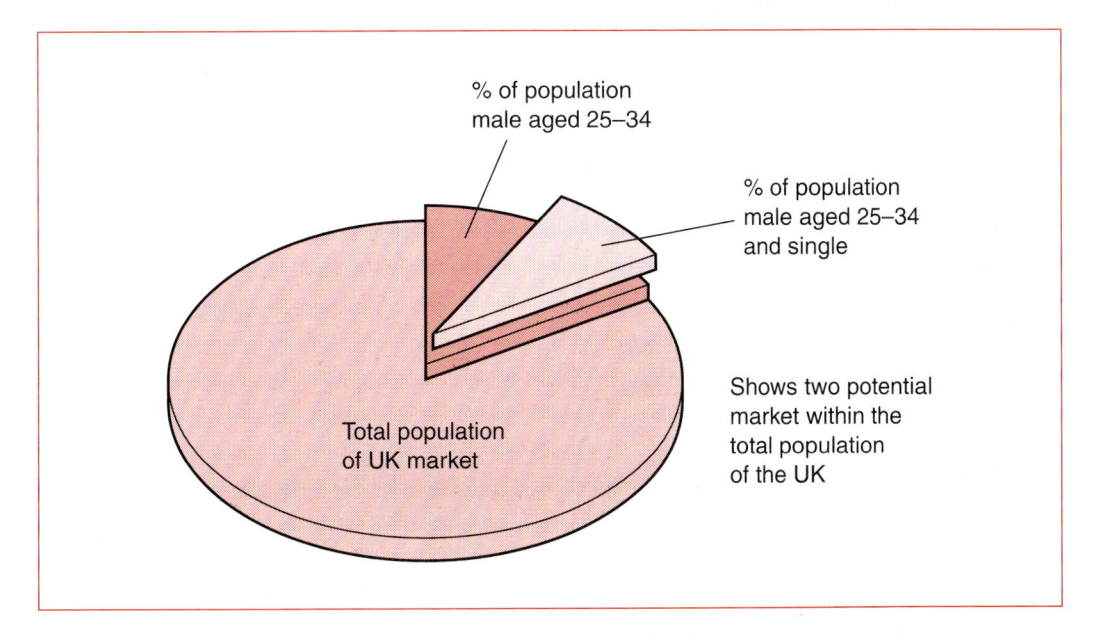

Fig 3.27 Market segmentation

Homogeneity is a very important concept in marketing. It is derived from the two Greek words 'homos' (meaning one, or the same) and 'genos' (meaning kind). So if we have a homogeneous market, it means that the members of that market are all similar, or of the same kind. This is very useful when marketing personnel are trying to get a message across to the market, for example through advertising. If the marketer can break the mass market down into a number of similar (homogeneous) markets, then the advertising can be more specific, or relevant to each market segment. This process of splitting the market is known as *market segmentation*.

Careful segmentation can provide companies with the information needed to identify marketing opportunities. The areas of activity that should be studied are:

1. customer activity
2. competitor activity
3. resource allocation
4. planning.

Customer activity

By analysing their customers within segments, marketers are able to establish buying behaviour characteristics for each segment. The questions of how, why, when, where and what customers buy can be addressed.

People who purchase petrol could fit into a number of segments. Consider a middle-aged business person. He or she may purchase by credit card (how), weekly (when), at leading brand stations (where), for tokens/vouchers (why), super unleaded (what). Compare this example with the purchase activity of a student. He or she may purchase with cash (how), fortnightly (when), in the local superstore (where), at the lowest price (why) four star (pre-1986 car) (what).

If marketers are well informed regarding segments, they can be more responsive to any changes in customers' needs. They can tailor their marketing communication strategies to the needs of specific market segments. This leads to more effective communication both in terms of consumer response and resource allocation.

Competitor activity

Many markets are highly competitive. Marketing concerns itself with making the most of situations and resources in order to gain a competitive advantage. Marketers may wish to categorise market segments by the degree of competitive activity taking place within them. For example, in the fast food market many of the leading companies compete on promotional issues; it would be unwise for a small company competing against much larger organisations to try to increase its market share of the target audience by matching leading promotional campaigns.

Resource allocation

Targeting the whole market can often be unrealistic as all companies are subject to limited resources. For example, a small bicycle manufacturer with a good design team would be unwise to attempt penetration of the whole market. That should be left to the largest manufacturers like Raleigh. Instead the company would be better off concentrating the effectiveness of its limited resources (human and financial) on certain target segments – that is, establishing a niche. In this example the niche could be in state-of-the-art mountain bikes or racing bikes within the market-place. This enables companies to build up competence and expertise within their own niche segment – a strong form of defence against any future competitive activity. This could be reflected in any promotional campaign.

Planning

If a company is operating in a number of different segments, it is likely that each segment, will need its own special communications plan to suit the particular needs and requirements of its customers.

Consumer characteristics

All consumers are engendered with their own individual sets of characteristics. Many consumers also share similar characteristics which is very useful when companies attempt to segment their markets. These characteristics are sometimes referred to as *user*, *consumer* or *segmentation variables*. The variables which a company chooses will depend on that organisation's product range.

Video equipment manufacturers might segment the VCR market on the basis of income and age; while the suppliers of prerecorded video films may include an additional variable – that of ethnic background. The equipment needs may not differ much between different cultures, but there would be some differences in viewing preferences and hence the need for the additional variable.

The following list highlights the common variable categories:

1 demographics variables;
2 socio-economic variables;
3 geographic variables;
4 motives and lifestyle variables;
5 buying behaviour.

This list of variables is by no means exhaustive, but does cover the most common variables encountered. Each category of variables will now be considered in greater detail.

Demographic variables

These variables are in widespread use in segmenting markets due to the fact that they are easy to collect. The most common characteristics used are those of age, sex, family, race and religion. To explain how demographics help segmentation, we shall considering examples for each of the above characteristics.

Age

For age, let us consider the confectionery market. Cadbury's targets children with fun products designed to appeal to younger tastes, e.g. Cadbury's White Chocolate Buttons. At the same time the more mature tastes of adults are catered for with sophisticated

Unit 3   Marketing

products such as Jamaican Rum and Raisin or Bourneville. It is important that marketers understand which segments are declining and which are growing in order to meet demand effectively. This can be done by closely monitoring population statistics. By studying the graph in Fig. 3.28 it is possible to see the projected change in age structure for the UK up to the year 2021.

This information is very useful for marketers when planning their marketing effort. As you can see, the baby boom years of the 1950s and 1960s mean that the 40–64 age bracket will gradually increase in size in the coming years as those people born in the '50s and '60s move into this bracket.

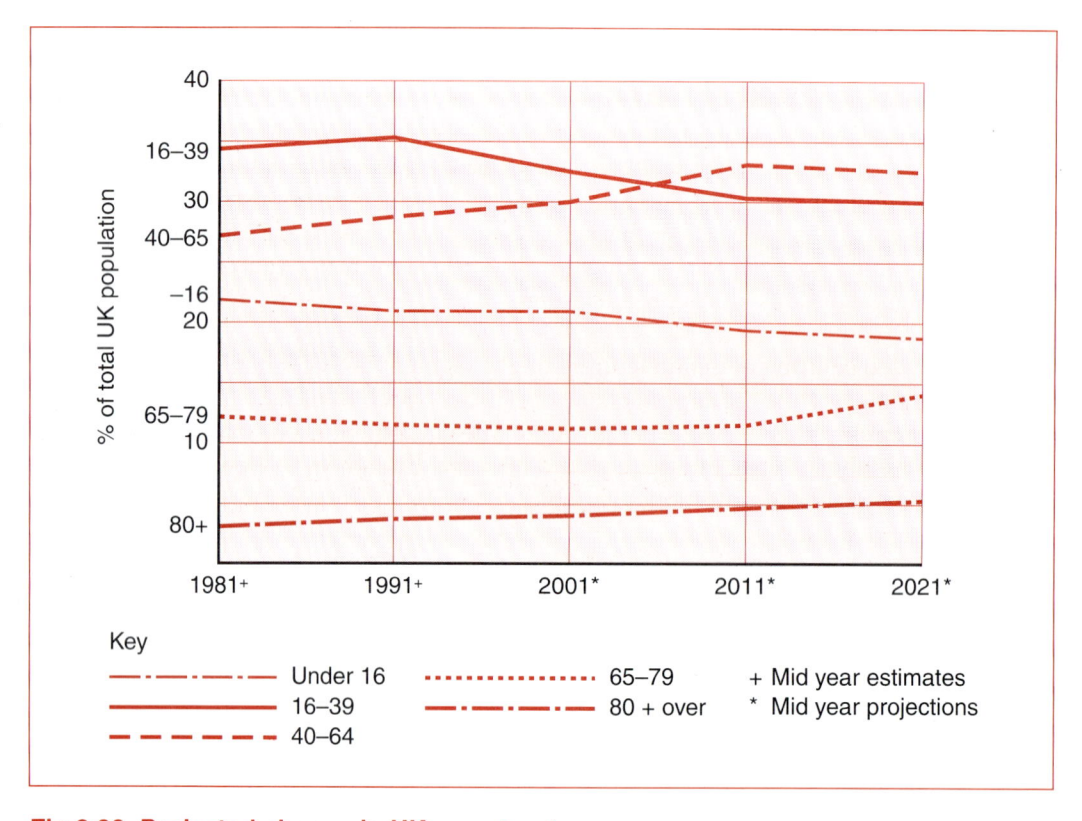

Fig 3.28 Projected change in UK age structure

ACTIVITY 3.3.4

Study the article from the *Financial Times* (28/10/93) in Fig. 3.29, and note how Safeway's has responded to the needs of its elderly customers. Choose an organisation, whose target audience is the elderly, and evaluate the effectiveness of its promotional strategy.

Gender

Gender is a key demographic variable for many markets. There are some very obvious ones such as clothes, magazines and cosmetics, and some which are not so obvious such

Element 3.3   Evaluate marketing communications designed to influence a target audience

Hugh Aldersey-Williams looks at design for an ageing population

New dawn for fiftysomethings

Forget the youth market. The only growing sector of the UK population is the over 50s, according to Danielle Barr of the 3rd Age marketing consultancy. National census figures indicate the population aged 50–54 will rise by 290 per cent between 1991 and 2001. The same group, by then aged 60–64, will increase 32 per cent over the next decade.

Marketers and manufacturers have arguably been slow to awaken to this grey dawn. But at a conference at London's Royal College of Art next month, designers and advertising people will attempt to show that design for this age group can bring a wide range of benefits.

In the past, design for the elderly demanded the creation of products to satisfy "special needs" associated with various degrees of disability. Innovation is still vitally necessary here, but there is a new agenda, too. Increasingly, people entering what has been called their "third age" from 50 to 75 are able-bodied, mobile and affluent.

The problem is that there are not yet the products aimed to please these people. "What I don't see enough of are things I can't wait to own," says Roger Coleman, director of the Design Age programme at the RCA who turned 50 this year. Services such as holidays and financial services can be safely targeted at this group, but it seems products cannot afford to be explicit about their suitability for older people for fear of deterring other buyers. Yet, as Coleman points out, "these are the people who were led to believe in their youth that their wish was the manufacturer's command. Should we expect them, for example, now to wear dowdy clothes?"

A few manufacturers recognise the 50-plus generation is the one that grew up with rock and roll. Levi's range of jeans using the euphemism "loose fit" could be seen as hinting that they suit the broader beam of older people. Some car manufacturers have not taken on board – either in their designs or in their advertising – the fact that more than 40 per cent of small to medium-sized cars are bought by people aged 45 or more.

The supermarket chain, Safeway, was sceptical, too. It became a sponsor of the Design Age programme because it thought it might gain publicity, rather than because it thought it might learn something.

However, in projects with Royal College of Art students aimed at finding ways of making shopping easier for the elderly, Richard Scott, director of construction at Safeway Stores, discovered that many ideas benefit all customers and some bring immediate advantage to the retailer as well.

One idea was to lower the height of the top shelves in Safeway stores, helping the young and the old and easing shelf-loading.

Another project was to create a basket carrier for elderly customers with relatively small amounts of shopping, so they would not be encumbered by a heavy basket on one arm. The right carrier design should bring additional benefits. By pushing their baskets in front of them, customers would carve a narrower path, allowing more comfortable shopping.

"The most extraordinary thing is how quickly people understand the principle of universality in design," says Scott. Design for the elderly can lead to better design for all.

Fig 3.29   *Source:* The *Financial Times*, Oct 1993

as cigarettes, slimmers' meals and alcoholic drinks. Segmentation by gender is just one opportunity for marketers to be able to differentiate their products and so gain competitive advantage. You can probably expect to see many more products which have not previously been segmented by gender being segmented this way.

ACTIVITY 3.3.5

Consider the following products/services:

- package holidays
- confectionery
- soft drinks.

In groups, choose one of the above and develop promotional strategies that would appeal exclusively to either males or females.

PC
3.3.1
3.3.2
3.3.3
C
3.1.1
3.1.2
3.1.3
3.1.4
3.2.1
3.2.2
3.3.3
3.4.1
3.4.2

237

Family

Marital status and number of children will also affect purchasing habits and are therefore useful segmentation variables. For example, extravagant long-haul holidays in exotic locations may be affordable to a married couple without children who are both working (Dinks – Double Income, No Kids). This may soon change when a child comes along and one income is temporarily lost! This can be clearly illustrated by considering the stages that families go through (*see* Fig 3.30). The types of products that will be bought by each of the categories in Fig. 3.30 will vary. Older married couples whose children have left home will have more disposable income than married couples with young, or very young, children.

Ethnicity

When considering the different segments characterised by race and religion, the immediate focus is on the different cultures to be found in different countries around the world. This is very important for international marketing activities as it is possible to segment large areas of the world by their similarity of culture (for example, the Middle East, Western Europe and South Western Europe are groupings based partly on culture). It is also important to remember that cultural variations can occur on a regional basis. This is clearly seen in England with the concept of the North/South Divide, not to

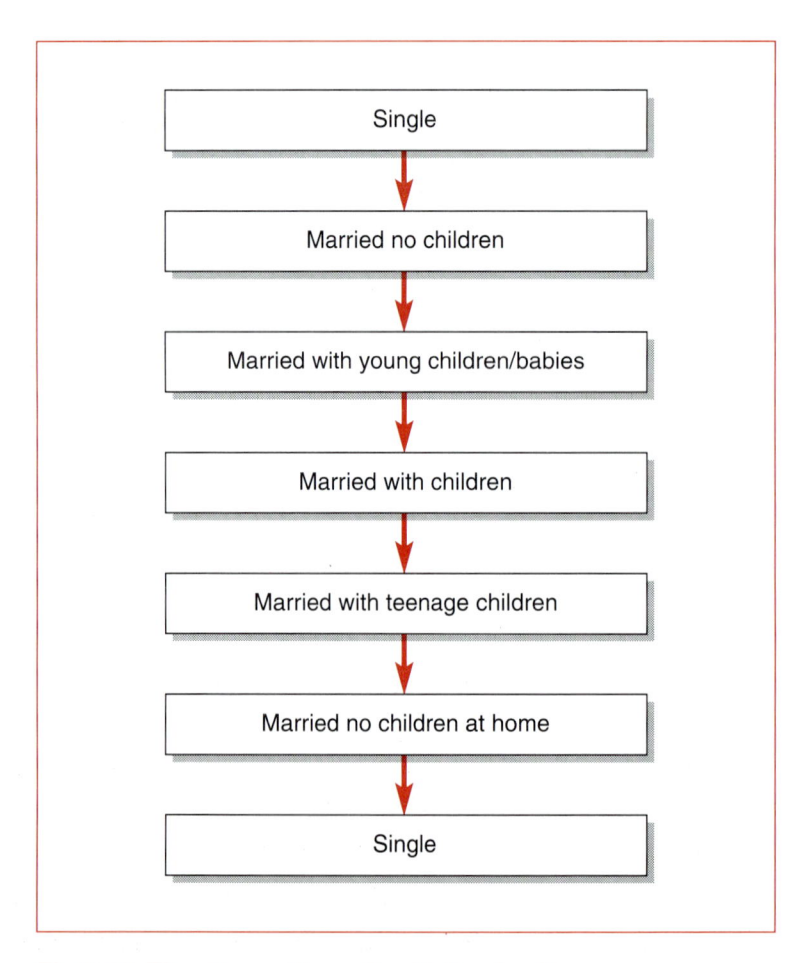

```
Single
  ↓
Married no children
  ↓
Married with young children/babies
  ↓
Married with children
  ↓
Married with teenage children
  ↓
Married no children at home
  ↓
Single
```

Fig 3.30 The stages through which a family goes

Element 3.3 Evaluate marketing communications designed to influence a target audience

mention the cultural differences that exist between England, Scotland, Wales and Northern Ireland.

Socio-economic variables

Variables in this category look at the combination of social and economic factors (for example, relationships between income, occupation, social class and education).

Income

There is a clear connection between income and the ability to satisfy needs and wants. Element 1.1 covered the concept of normal, inferior and luxury goods. Let us consider the following example in order to recap on this area.

Three separate families – one low income one middle income and one high income – all purchase groceries weekly. The low-income family is highly cost conscious and will purchase food that provides maximum energy for the lowest price (for example, sausages, tinned beans, sliced white bread, eggs (normal and inferior goods)). The middle-income family substitutes more expensive items for some of these products e.g. granary bread for sliced white bread, or steak for sausages (replacing inferior goods with luxury goods). The high-income family purchases very few inferior goods and in fact consumption of the luxury goods may fall as this family replaces luxury groceries with eating out.

Income variables have been utilised effectively by the supermarket companies in the way that they target different market segments. For example, Netto (the Danish chain based in the North of England) and Kwiksave compete for the low-/middle-income custom with a 'pile it high, sell it cheap' message. Sainsbury's and Marks & Spencer's target the middle-high-income bracket by offering choice and premium brands.

Social class and occupation

Probably the most widely used method of segmentation in consumer marketing is socio-economic grouping (SEG). The *National Readership Survey* grades these variables by status and occupation (*see* Table 3.9).

Table 3.9 Socio-economic groupings

Social grade	Social status	Occupation
A	Upper middle	Higher managerial, professional, e.g. barrister, managing director
B	Middle	Middle management, professional, e.g. solicitor, marketing manager
C1	Lower middle	Supervisory, junior managerial, e.g. office manager, foreman
C2	Skilled	Skilled manual workers
D	Working class	Semi-skilled and unskilled manual workers
E	Lowest level	Pensioners, unemployed, casual workers

Education

Education may be closely linked to those socio-economic variables already mentioned as level of education, e.g. secondary, technician, degree, post-graduate, will have a direct effect on employment prospects and ultimately social grouping.

Geographic variables

The geographic location of a market may also have some effect on the buying habits of consumers. One obvious condition is climate and the effect that this has on the buying process is significant. For example, in some hot countries there is heavy competition between the ice cream and soft drinks manufacturers – an obvious effect of climatic differences on a market. There are more subtle differences, however. People in hot countries tend to shop at the coolest times of the day. This can be seen in Mediterranean countries where the shops all shut for several hours from midday for the daily 'siesta'.

In the UK, purchasing habits have evolved from the differences best described by the North/South Divide. Western economies have experienced a general shift away from manufacturing activities towards service based activities. As the 'North' was more reliant than the 'South' on manufacturing, due to the location of major coalfields, this decline has resulted in lower general standards of living in Northern England. The North has seen consumers dependent on discount and budget shops for their regular purchases and this has resulted in a profusion of these types of outlets.

Differences in terrain will cause consumers to differ from one region to another. If you look at a map of Europe you will see that national borders will often match natural barriers (for example, the Alps, the Pyrenees and the English Channel). These barriers often mark a change in language and cultures. This can even occur within a single country, e.g. the Basque country in comparison with Majorca in Spain. This has implications for suppliers in terms of languages and labelling of goods.

Geo-demographic variables

It is also possible to consider geographic, socio-economic and cultural factors under one heading. These are known as geo-demographic factors. ACORN (A Classification Of Residential Neighbourhoods) is a classification tool that takes geographic location one step further by combining these three factors in order to establish profiles for particular neighbourhoods. The reasoning behind this is that customers' buying habits may be identified from the type of neighbourhood and house that they live in. ACORN categories are often established by postcode area and are particularly useful when undertaking direct mail campaigns.

Motives and lifestyle variables

Benefit segmentation

The motivation behind the purchase of a product can often be linked to the perceived benefits to the consumer. This is often referred to as *benefit segmentation*. A consumer's motives for purchasing a product can be viewed from two different perspectives:

- intrinsic to the product
- extrinsic of the product.

The first perspective really concerns the features of the product (for example, quality, design, price). These features, and many others, can motivate us to buy certain products. Alternatively, the motivating factors may not come from the actual product but are extrinsic to it. These come from features of the product's environment, e.g. availability, peer group pressure, fashion trends. The recent rise in the popularity of Doc Marten's was in part due to the product's intrinsic features, such as style and comfort, but also to the product's extrinsic features, such as status and self-image. It can be difficult to differentiate between intrinsic and extrinsic features, but in the above example we can separate the two by acknowledging that the intrinsic features existed before the recent revival in popularity of Doc Marten's.

Lifestyle segmentation

Lifestyle segmentation may group individuals according to surroundings and trappings (e.g. Yuppies) or beliefs about broad issues. One important issue where there is a growing body of opinion is the environment. Many consumers' buying motives are now influenced by the environmental debate.

As more consumers consider the ethical implications of their buying habits, more organisations will attempt to satisfy this need. Social responsibility is where an organisation will attempt to maximise the positive impact that it has on society. Organisations successful in this area are considered to be good corporate citizens and many recent 'green strategies' illustrate the extent of that success. For example, many companies now package their products in recycled paper and cardboard – a feature that some consumers actively seek out when they purchase a product. This is just one of many examples of how organisations are trying to minimise the negative effects that their products have on the environment.

ACTIVITY 3.3.6

Visit your local superstore and identify as many products as possible that attempt to differentiate themselves from their competitors by highlighting a positive environmental feature. Categorise your findings (for example, natural ingredients, the recycled logo, etc.). How are these environmental features used in the companies' public relations activities?

ACTIVITY 3.3.7

Read the article from the *Financial Times* of 24 June 1993 in Fig. 3.31 and discuss the problems that can occur for the communications strategy when only a limited number of segmentation variables are used in researching markets.

Specific definitions of the consumer psyche are replacing the old market research groupings, says **Gary Mead**

More than just ABC

Are you an Age Acceptor or an Age Modifier? Perhaps you are a Successful Idealist, an Affluent Materialist or a paid-up member of the Resigned Poor. Do you live in an Along-with-the-Drift or a Boom-then-Decline neighbourhood?

One thing's for sure – you are no longer just a dull old A, B, C1/C2, D or E.

It used to be said that A/Bs had money and taste; C1s taste but no money; C2s money but no taste; and D/Es no taste and no money.

But today there are many ways of slicing the population cake other than by simply cutting such crude wedges. The old socio-economic categories – on which so many vital marketing and advertising decisions have depended – are increasingly being displaced by other, more sophisticated segmenting techniques that try to probe consumer psyche, not just allot social class.

"We may think we know A/Bs are different from D/Es," says Peter Sampson, development director with the market research company Infratest Burke. "But consumers today are adopting contradictory buying modes. How can socio-economic categories tell us why someone driving a £300,000 car also wears a £10 wristwatch? Or why another person buys premium price Haagen-Dazs ice cream yet also buys the cheapest own-label toilet paper? There's no predicting an overall consumer type anymore."

Successfully identifying these new distinctions increasingly looks like the key to finding customers, retaining their loyalty and targeting money spent on advertising. The fragmenting of consumer types also bode well for the market research industry, whose turnover as measured by the 26-member Association of Market Survey Organisations increased by 8.7 per cent in real terms last year.

Given Europe's shifting social and demographic patterns – the current breakdown on the two-partner family, the forecast reduction in 15–25 year-olds and the growth of the 45–54 age group – there is every reason why this trend will continue.

To combat the risk of making wrong assumptions, though, companies themselves are also branching out into consumer research.

The UK branch of Nestlé, for instance, is pilot-testing a scheme that is being closely watched by its French and German counterparts.

Nestlé UK is collating a list of 100,000 customers who have demonstrated their attachment to its Buitoni brand Italian food range.

David Hudson, the company's director of strategic marketing, says that the database will be turned "into a club of people who all share a love of Italian food".

Hudson compares the old socio-economic categories to a map that tells travellers nothing more than which continent they are on.

"I need usage and attitude-related data which actually tell me what the consumer is thinking about our products. Our Casa Buitoni club will have a newsletter about Italian food. It won't just be a means of dishing out money-off coupons. It will allow us to know where our customers live, who they are, what they like doing, which of our competitors' products they use and why."

Martin Glenn, new product development director of Pepsi Foods International in the UK, shares Hudson's sceptical view of the old ways of analysing customer types. "Socio-economic classifications are no longer useful for products which are closely substitutable, such as snack foods or cars. They do not segment most mass markets; all A/B/C1/C2/D/E types buy Walkers crisps or Ford cars. You need to understand your own market on a specific level, to look at usage and attitudes within a market."

Glenn, formerly with Mars' European Petcare division in German, has spent the past decade bringing new consumer products to market. "Ten years ago every good brand manager would have his target group of consumers, skewed towards A/B/C1s or C2/Ds or whatever. But marketing understanding has greatly improved. These definitions now don't discriminate with sufficient accuracy. The A/B/C/D/E categories don't discriminate even by income – E is meant to be pensioners but you can have some very wealthy pensioners."

While socio-economic segmenting can still give a broad-brush picture of the market place, researchers and advertising agencies now deploy hundreds of different lifestyle categorisations such as the ones used at the beginning of this article.

Take Young & Rubicam's model, which is called The 4 Cs. Paul Edwards, head of planning in the UK, says it stands for cross-cultural consumer classification.

"It's a socio-psychological way of measuring people, dividing them into seven value groups. Two people can have the same behaviour but different values behind that behaviour. This system allows us to segment for any product across different cultures, where we couldn't possibly use the old socio-economic categories."

There are also geo-demographic analyses, most of them variations on the theme of postcode exploitation. The theory is that housing types are more subtle guides to purchasing habits – consumers tend to buy the same sort of goods and services as their neighbours.

In the late 1980s, CACI Information Services developed Acorn, the world's first geo-demographic classification system. Acorn has since come up with dozens of classifications, based on UK government population census information.

The old socio-economic distinctions seem even more outdated now that companies are calling for pan-European market research in order to help them market their products on a pan-European basis. If socio-demographics are inadequate on a single-country basis, they seem even more so when crossing borders.

Sampson of Infratest Burke was also a member of a working roup of the Amsterdam-based European Society for Opinion and Marketing Research. In the late 1980s the group investigated the possibility of harmonising socio-economic definitions.

The task proved impossible as Esomar discovered that such harmonisation was not only difficult but misleading. Socio-economic analysis of European consumers could not be satisfactorily harmonised because class-plus-income patterns were so different in each country. Instead, Esomar now uses a system of research based on ownership of consumer durables.

Fig 3.31 *Source: The Financial Times, June 1993*

Targeting

Once an organisation has identified different market segments, how does it then decide which markets present the best opportunities for its products? This question is tackled by the adoption of a suitable targeting strategy, that is, deciding on the markets to aim for. The procedure for developing a strategy is not as straightforward as it might first appear and requires careful planning. For example, does your organisation target a wide range of segments? If so, is management confident that the product has the necessary features for general appeal?

The targeting strategy that an organisation adopts depends on both internal and external factors. These factors can be identified from the results of a SWOT analysis:

- *Strengths & Weaknesses* (internal factors)
  and
- *Opportunities & Threats* (external factors)

A *SWOT analysis* is a business tool that assists the decision-making process by looking at the internal and external factors. Strengths could include human resources, manufacturing capability, design capabilities and financial position. Alternatively, some of these factors could be weaknesses within the organisation. The benefit of the SWOT analysis is that it enables managers to consider these strengths and weaknesses in conjunction with market opportunities and threats. Opportunities and threats could include competitive position, government intervention, consumer demand and new technology. Which of these would be an opportunity and which a threat would depend on the strengths and weaknesses of the organisation. The results of a SWOT analysis should help the organisation understand its resources and capabilities, the competitive environment and the characteristics of the market segments under consideration.

Once an organisation has established an understanding of the position it holds within its market, it is possible for it to select an appropriate targeting strategy. There are three conditions which form the basis of a targeting strategy:

1. the experience effect;
2. specialisation;
3. differentiation.

Experience effect

The experience effect can best be illustrated by considering the fall in long-run average costs known as economies of scale. If an organisation is confident that its products appeal to a wide cross-section of market segments (e.g. tomato ketchup) it will be operating on a large scale, therefore achieving economies of scale. The organisation will spread its operating costs over a high volume of output; this means that the cost for each product unit produced will fall as the organisation increases its output. Another aspect of the experience effect is that by increasing output the organisation may discover newer, lower cost approaches to producing its product. The organisation can take advantage of the experience effect to become a low-cost producer within a competitive environment. The type of communication strategy would therefore have to reflect the desire to reach a wide target audience.

This means that the organisation will be able to target a mass market through the adoption of mass production, competitive prices and mass media advertising.

Specialisation

If an organisation feels that it does not have the resources to be able to target across market segments, it may choose to concentrate its capabilities on one market segment. This means that an organisation has the opportunity to concentrate its resources and efforts in developing a marketing mix to suit a specific and narrow customer target. The risks associated with this can be high – for example, a company that specialised in manufacturing high quality turntables for the hi-fi market would have been severely affected by the introduction of CDs. Radical innovations such as this can sometimes wipe out a narrow market segment. This approach may also have significant benefits, however. In industrial markets there are many small companies who concentrate their efforts in highly specialised areas – for example, in the aerospace industry there are companies who specialise in polishing components that go into jet engines for aircraft (an application where expertise and experience are vital). This degree of specialisation can offer a small company some protection as it makes it difficult for other companies to enter the market and target existing customers. It is an effective barrier to entry (*see* Unit 1). These types of organisations rely heavily on word-of-mouth to promote their products and services.

Differentiation

With differentiation, an organisation will attempt to create a unique aspect to its product or service. This is usually linked to the perceived quality of the product and can be associated with benefit segmentation. For example, Persil's accelerator formula gives the consumer a better quality wash. If this is the benefit that the consumer is looking for, Persil could justify a higher than average price.

Differentiation may also help an organisation to focus on specific market segments. For example, the leading package holiday companies have developed different products to appeal to different segments. These are mainly based on demographic and socio-economic variables such as age, family, income, etc. and have resulted in such products as Club 18–30.

PRODUCT PERFORMANCE

Brand loyalty

One way in which organisations can assess a product's performance and the success of a communication strategy is by judging the degree of brand loyalty that exists.

Brand loyalty is seen to work on two levels: the behavioural and the emotional.

Behavioural brand loyalty is quite literally the automatic purchasing of a familiar product – you've always bought that brand so why change! Marketing communications can reinforce this type of loyalty through regular messages to the target audience which are designed to reassure or congratulate the consumer on his or her choice of brand. Cigarette advertising has utilised this phenomenon for many years with its use of powerful role models, e.g. the Marlboro Man.

Emotional brand loyalty occurs where there is a strong attachment to the actual product. Nostalgia plays a significant role in establishing emotional brand loyalty. For example, when Coca-Cola launched its new taste Coke the company came under intense pressure from loyal Coke drinkers. They apparently associated the taste of the original Coke with teenage memories – something that the new brand could not provide. The original brand was reintroduced alongside the new one.

Varying degrees of brand loyalty exist between product groups. There are high-loyalty products, such as beer and toothpaste, and low-loyalty products, like binliners and paper towels. An awareness of the level of brand loyalty for generic products is important when developing the marketing communications strategy. A message which attempts to generate brand loyalty for typically low-loyalty products may not be the best use of marketing resources. Some companies have actually seen this as an opportunity to establish brand loyalty in a traditionally low loyalty area, however. Kimberly-Clark has done this for its paper towel products.

Product life cycle

The concept of the product life cycle was introduced in Element 3.1; we shall now look at each stage in more detail and assess how the product life cycle can influence the performance of individual products.

Introduction

The introduction stage is when a product first appears in the market-place. Sales will be zero and profits will actually be negative. The reason for negative profits is that money will have been spent on promotion and distribution before the new product has had a chance to earn revenue for the organisation.

This can be seen in the music industry where recording companies are often accused of tying artists to restrictive contracts. This can be very frustrating for the artist but what the recording company is trying to guarantee is a profitable return on its initial investment in the promotion of the artist. This is most likely to happen in the case of a new artist where the risk of failure is higher.

The failure rate of new products is very high – for example, in the food and drinks industry some estimates show that 80 per cent of new products fail (that is, they do not survive beyond the introductory stage). Due to the high risk and high investment costs of introducing new products, most introductions are for new packaging, upgraded models or slightly different styles rather than genuine innovations.

Growth

During the growth stage, sales rise rapidly. Profits also rise but the upward trend will level out and then begin to fall. This is due to the response of the products competitors who will have been watching the progress of the product. When its success is confirmed, competitors will move in with their own variants. The original seller must then use revenue from the product to compete most typically through pricing and promotional campaigns.

A recent example of this is Boddington's success with the Draughtflow widget. Once that success was established, the other major brewers moved into the market with their own versions – John Smith's, Tetley and Bass to mention a few. The result has been an aggressive promotional and pricing campaign with heavy TV advertising and significant price reductions.

Maturity

It is during the maturity stage that competition reaches a peak. It is at this stage that competitors' products become established and the consumer becomes familiar with the differences between competing products. Sales will now start to level out and either remain constant or fall depending on the strategies adopted by the company. The marketing manager may feel that it is worthwhile to continue investing in the product to maintain turnover or that resources would be better diverted to the introduction of another product. There are many organisations that continue to maintain mature products over many years often competing with competitors over market leadership.

Bisto and Oxo have both established strong advertising campaigns to maintain their traditional products, although each has also introduced new products in the form of instant gravy granules.

Decline

The decline stage sees sales falling rapidly. This is usually the result of high levels of competition or the introduction of new technology. Over the last few decades, as technological progress has accelerated, we have seen many examples of products declining and dying.

There has been a revolution in personal computer technology through further miniaturisation, with 286s first being replaced by 386s, then by 486s and now with the 586s, or Pentiums, appearing in the market. The record industry has experienced major changes with the decline in vinyl records and record players and their replacement first by magnetic tapes and then CDs.

ACTIVITY 3.3.8

In groups select one of the following three generic products:

1 the television;
2 the camera;
3 the record player.

Task 1. Research your chosen product and identify significant innovations and changes to that product. Also identify any new benefits these changes have brought for the end user.

Task 2. Chart your findings on changes and benefits over the product's life cycle and present this to the rest of the class.

Task 3. What are the implications for the marketing communication strategy of these changes?

This acceleration of technology is resulting in much shorter life cycles as many organisations constantly seek to gain a competitive edge through the application of new technologies. We can confirm this by referring back to our example of a product mix in Element 3.1 and seeing how Ford has used technology (e.g. air bags, catalytic converters, anti-lock brakes) to maintain a competitive product portfolio.

DIRECT MARKETING

Direct marketing entails those marketing communication activities which use personal contact with the prospective customer and the opportunity for a direct response. The two main forms of direct marketing are *telemarketing* and *direct mail*.

Telemarketing

Telemarketing uses the telephone to communicate directly with individuals in the market. There are two main methods of telemarketing:

1 In-bound telemarketing

Consumers contact the company, or an agent handling the promotion, by telephone in response to an advertisement or other promotional activity. For example, new car dealers often place adverts in local press inviting consumers to telephone to arrange a test drive of a new model.

2 Out-bound telemarketing

The company uses a database of potential customers and telephones them in order to deliver a promotional message and receive an immediate response. For example, this method is often used to arrange appointments for sales personnel and to gauge initial interest. The type of companies using this method include those offering home improvements (e.g. replacement windows, fitted kitchens) and those offering financial services (e.g. personal pensions, home insurance).

Direct mail

As with out-bound telemarketing, with direct mail a database is used to target specific market segments. The chosen households, individuals or companies are then sent promotional material through the post. This material usually invites a direct response by using order forms, prepaid response envelopes or cards, freephone numbers, etc. A wide variety of companies use direct mail. Some common examples are mail-order catalogues, book clubs and charities.

Unit 3   Marketing

The growth of direct marketing

Advances in telecommunications and information technology have lead to a sharp increase in the use of direct marketing. The value of the industry was estimated at (2.43 bn in 1990 which showed a 43 per cent increase since 1986. This technological change has meant that computerised databases are widely available and can be linked directly to phone systems for automated dialling and used to produce personalised direct mail.

This computerisation has meant that databases can be customised to provide target information for a variety of companies and are cheaper to purchase and utilise. What was once a highly labour-intensive business is now fully automated.

A whole new industry sector has grown up around direct marketing providing a variety of support services. These range from telephone answering services to full design and handling of the promotional campaign.

Advantages and disadvantages of direct marketing

Advantages	Disadvantages
■ Precise targeting of prospective customers.	■ Can be seen as intrusive, unsolicited, an invasion of privacy.
■ Efficient use of promotions budget.	■ A growing number of environmentally conscious consumers perceive direct mail as a waste of resources.
■ High impact of the message due to personal contact.	
■ High response rate achieved.	■ Overuse leads to the 'junkmail' response where posted information is discarded unread and telephones are hung up.
■ Easily measured results.	
	■ The ethics of the use and sale of databased personal information is questionable and is now subject to new European Union legislation.

PC
3.3.3
3.3.4
3.3.5
C
3.1.1
3.1.2
3.1.3
3.2.1
3.2.2
3.2.3
3.2.4
3.4.1
3.4.2
3.4.3
3.4.4

ACTIVITY 3.3.9

Collect three different samples of direct mail promotional material recently received at your house and for each one consider:

1 the promotional message being communicated;

2 the methods used to encourage a response;

3 the reasons why your household was targeted;

4 why these companies have chosen to use direct mail.

Element 3.3 Evaluate marketing communications designed to influence a target audience

GUIDELINES AND CONTROLS

Ethics

Ethics define what is right or wrong behaviour. This can also be applied to the field of marketing. Laws and regulations set a minimum standard that all organisations should adhere to, but marketing ethics go beyond legal issues. The difficulty arises in deciding what is ethical and what is unethical. The Benetton campaigns of the early 1990s were appalling to some members of the public but considered artistic by others. In this situation it is difficult to draw a line or make a decision to ban such advertising. Many of those who did find the approach of Benetton distasteful would still like the opportunity to see the evidence and judge it for themselves.

The Benetton campaign is an example of the grey area in determining ethical procedures in marketing. There are a number of practices which are considered universally unacceptable and that consumers generally regard as unethical.

1 *Deceptive advertising* – e.g. unsubstantiated claims on product performance.

2 *Misleading selling tactics* – e.g. obtaining appointments under false pretences.

3 *Price fixing* – e.g. in oligopolistic markets.

4 *Deliberate marketing of harmful products* – e.g. the tobacco companies' promotional activities in the third world.

The above practices are unacceptable to consumers and they will often refuse to do business with marketers that engage in them. If marketers attempt to further their own interests at the expense of others, therefore, they jeopardise future sales for the organisation.

Legislation and authorities

There are a number of laws that have been introduced over the years to protect the consumer from unscrupulous business activities. These laws affect marketing activities by ensuring that the customer's interests are protected with regard to the description and performance of goods and services. The main areas of legislation that affect marketing activities are:

1 The Misrepresentations Act 1967

2 The Trade Descriptions Act 1968

3 The Prices Act 1974

4 The Unfair Contract Terms Act 1977

5 The Sale of Goods Act 1979

6 The Supply of Goods and Services Act 1982

7 The Weights and Measures Act 1985

8 The Consumer Protection Act 1987.

Unit 3 Marketing

PC
3.3.7

ACTIVITY 3.3.10

In groups, select two of the above consumer protection laws. Summarise the main areas of each law into simple, easy-to-understand point form. Create a factsheet detailing how marketing activities must operate within the limits of the law; use examples to illustrate activities outside of the law. Circulate your factsheets to the rest of the class.

In addition to the above legislation, consumer advice and information are provided to the public by the Citizens' Advice Bureaux and the Trading Standards Departments of local authorities. These authorities monitor the activities of trading organisations to ensure that laws are not being broken. One other piece of legislation – The Fair Trading Act 1973 – was introduced to enable the Director General of Fair Trading continuously to review consumer affairs. This involves action on practices which unfairly affect consumers' interests, action against persistent offenders within the law and the negotiation of self-regulating codes of practices for industries' representative bodies.

Many businesses attempt to regulate themselves. Trade associations establish codes of ethics by which their members must abide or risk exclusion. For example, ABTA (the Association of British Travel Agents) has strict guidelines which lay out customs and practices for its members. If a customer feels that any member is in breach of these customs, he or she can refer the issue to ABTA without reverting to legal action. Any business expelled from ABTA would find it very difficult to gain sufficient consumer confidence for future trade.

The IBA (Independent Broadcasting Authority) and the Advertising Standards Authority regulate the practices and customs for the entire advertising industry. The aim of the two authorities is to ensure that all advertising is 'legal, decent and honest'.

Self assessment questions

1 Which advertising medium would you use to promote sailing equipment?
   a Television
   b A specialist magazine
   c Cinema
   d Transport

2 In which stage of the product life cycle do profits peak?
   a Introduction
   b Growth
   c Maturity
   d Decline

3 Which of the following is a consumer segmentation variable?
   a Motives and lifestyle
   b Consumer activity
   c Competitor activity
   d Resource allocation

Element 3.3 Evaluate marketing communications designed to influence a target audience

4 Which of the following is not a demographic segmentation variable?
   a Gender
   b Ethnicity
   c Age
   d Climate

5 For which of the following products would an organisation be likely to develop brand loyalty?
   a Bin liners
   b Cornflakes
   c Sand paper
   d Paper clips

6 Which of the following factors have encouraged the growth of direct marketing?
   a Information technology
   b Cultural factors
   c Rising incomes
   d Demographic change

7 Cost per thousand is an indicator of
   a production costs
   b distribution costs
   c the effectiveness of advertising
   d the cost of free samples?

8 The mature stage of the product life cycle may be extended by
   a launching a new product
   b doing nothing
   c reducing production costs
   d an advertising campaign?

9 Which one of the following monitors, rather than regulates, business ethics?
   a Trade associations
   b Independent Broadcasting Authority
   c Central government
   d Citizens Advice Bureaux

10 Which of the following statements is false?
   a Advertising is controlled by legislation.
   b Advertising is controlled by the advertising industry.
   c Advertising is the only marketing communications activity controlled by legislation.
   d The Trade Descriptions Act controls advertising.

Unit 3   Marketing

PC
3.3.3
3.3.4
3.3.5
3.3.6
C
3.2.1
3.2.2
3.2.3
3.4.1
3.4.2
3.4.3
3.4.4

Assignment

Action against Hoover ruled out

By Guy de Jonquières, Consumer Industries Editor

TRADING standards officials yesterday ruled out criminal action against Hoover over its disastrous free-flights offer, but criticised the company for failing to foresee that the scheme would go so badly wrong.

Mid-Glamorgan trading standards department, which has received almost 2,000 complaints from Hoover customers, said it had received legal advice that there were no grounds for prosecuting the company under the Trade Descriptions Act.

The department, which has spent six months investigating the offer, said criminal action could be brought only if Hoover could be shown to have known in advance that its statements about the free flights were false and if it was criminally careless.

It said that while Hoover might be accused of "extreme gullibility" for miscalculating the likely take-up of its offer, there was no evidence that the company had set out to deceive or defraud customers.

The department said it was calling on the Department of Trade and Industry to review the Trade Descriptions Act, which had not kept up with advances in technology and marketing techniques.

The department, which conducted its investigation on behalf of trading standards authorities through-out the country, said Hoover customers who had not received free flights to which they believed they were entitled could still take civil action.

The Hoover Holiday Pressure Group, which claims to represent 1,600 dissatisfied customers, said yesterday that about 40 actions were pending in small claims courts.

Hoover said it was pleased by the department's decisions. It said 103,000 people had so far flown under the free-flights scheme and that about 12,500 tickets were being issued every month. It would not say how many applications remained to be dealt with.

Fig 3.32   *Source:* The *Financial Times*, Sept 1993

Task 1. Read the article from the *Financial Times* of 30 September 1993 in Fig. 3.32 and gather as much information as you can on the Hoover 'free flights' promotional campaign. Explain the suitability of this campaign.

Task 2. Evaluate the effectiveness of the Hoover promotion in reaching Hoover's target audience.

Task 3. What communication strategy would you recommend Hoover now adopts in order to improve its public image?

Task 4. Look at one of Hoover's competitors and compare its existing marketing communications.

Task 5. Do you agree that the Trades Description Act should be reviewed in the light of this case?

Task 6. Comment on the long-term effect of the 'free flights' campaign on Hoover's products.

Element 3.4
EVALUATE SALES METHODS AND CUSTOMER SERVICE TO ACHIEVE CUSTOMER SATISFACTION

Performance criteria

1. Compare sales distribution channels and direct and indirect sales methods for their suitability to meet the needs of customers and organisations.

2. Explain and give examples of the duties and responsibilities of salespersons.

3. Describe sales communication methods.

4. Explain the importance of effective sales administration to a business and its customers.

5. Evaluate customer service and propose improvements to customer services.

SALES DISTRIBUTION CHANNELS

A sales distribution channel is sometimes referred to as a marketing channel and is simply the flow of products from the producer to the consumer. Good channels of distribution ensure availability of products at an acceptable price. The length of the channel that a product travels down will be determined by the number of intermediaries involved in moving the product from producer to consumer. Long channels may have several companies acting as intermediaries whereas a short channel may indicate that the product is supplied direct from the producer to the consumer (see Fig. 3.33).

(a) Example of a long channel

Producer → Agents/Brokers → Wholesalers → Retailers → Consumers

(b) Example of a short channel

Producer → Industrial Buyer

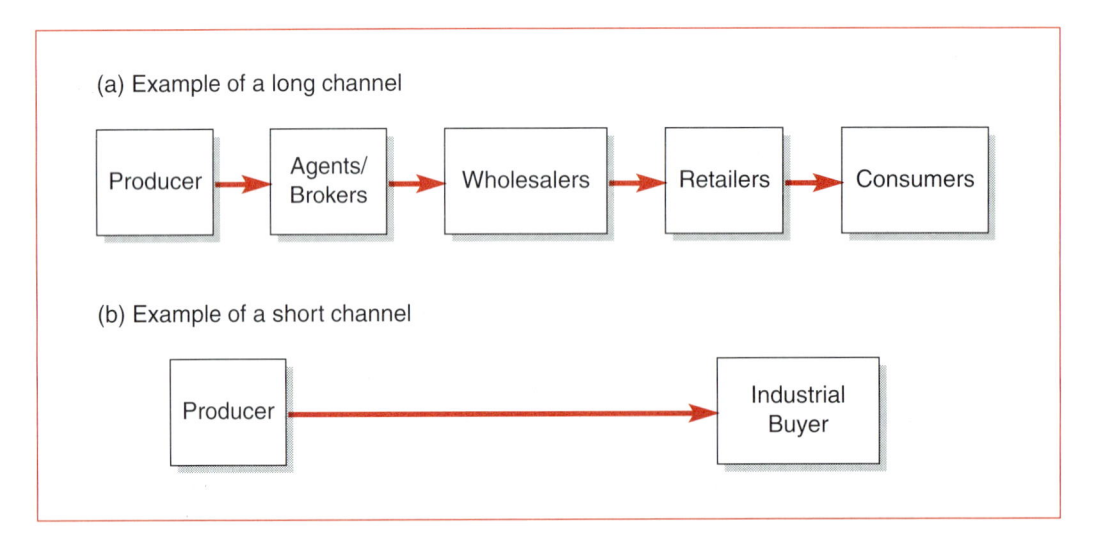

Fig 3.33 Marketing channels

The choice of marketing channel will depend both on the market environment and the product. Industrial channels tend to be shorter as industrial buyers can take advantage of economic order quantities, i.e. buying in bulk, which make it more economical for both the producer and the customer. This opportunity does not exist in consumer markets so intermediaries exist in order to break down bulk and facilitate the purchasing process.

The role of the intermediary

The intermediary plays a vital role in ensuring the smooth operation of the movement of goods from producer to consumer. The problem that the intermediary has to overcome is that the producer will always seek to achieve economies of scale through mass production. At the same time it is rare to find a consumer that is prepared to purchase in mass quantity. This is where the intermediary provides an important function; it can purchase in bulk from the producer and then distribute this bulk to a wide range of consumers with maximum convenience (see Fig. 3.34).

Element 3.4 Evaluate sales methods and customer service to achieve customer satisfaction

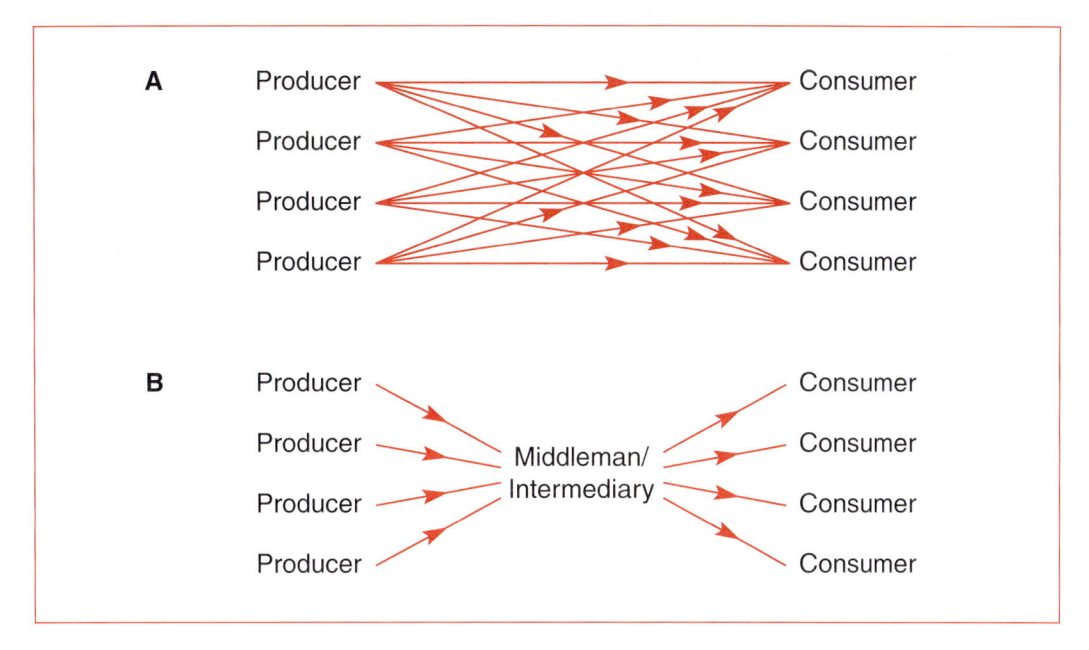

Fig 3.34 The intermediary ensures the smooth movement of goods from producer to consumer

Figure 3.34 shows how complex distribution would be if we did not have intermediaries. Intermediaries specialise in their particular functions and this means that distribution activities can be run efficiently. For their efforts intermediaries purchase products at trade prices. This does not mean that we all pay inflated prices to pay for intermediaries. If intermediaries did not perform this function, producers' costs would soar as they tried to manage the complete distribution function, so resulting in higher factory gate prices.

The following are common types of intermediary operating in both industrial and consumer markets.

1 *Brokers/Agents.* These act on behalf of either the buyer or the seller. Their main function is to bring buyer and seller together. For this they normally receive a commission. Most commonly found in industrial markets.

2 *Wholesaler.* These normally take title to the products of the producer (i.e. buy them). Their intention is to use the product for resale to a retailer (or any other customer other than the end user). The benefits to the producer are that wholesalers hold inventory, assist with transport costs and provide feedback on market opinion. Some examples include builders' merchants, cash and carry warehouses, industrial suppliers.

3 *Retailer.* These are organisations that purchase products for the purpose of reselling to the end user (consumer). The retailer provides the consumer with an assortment of goods at a location and a time that suits the consumer. Location is an important factor in retailing; retailers and consumers can now choose between the high street, mail order, edge of town and retail parks. Some examples that you will be familiar with are multiple chains (Next, Boots), superstores (Tesco, Asda) and convenience stores (Spar).

4 *Distributor.* These operate mainly in industrial markets. The distributor takes title to the goods and sells on to the industrial end user.

5 *Franchising.* This is where someone can buy into the marketing success of another organisation. For an initial fee and payment of an annual commission, the franchisee receives help in terms of furnishings, equipment, management know-how, marketing assistance and brand image. The benefits to the franchisers are that they get to keep their operating costs to a minimum while increasing outlets and sales. Many high street names operate on a franchise basis, e.g. Body Shop, Benetton, Kentucky Fried Chicken.

Direct sales methods

Traditionally direct selling has been most common in industrial markets. More than half of all industrial products are sold through direct channels. Industrial buyers like to communicate directly with producers, particularly for expensive or technical products. Consumers have also experienced forms of direct selling, such as door-to-door sales people for double glazing, encyclopedias and insurance, but this has formed only a very small percentage of consumer purchases. Direct selling methods aimed at the consumer market are becoming increasingly popular for a number of reasons, however. As already mentioned innovations in technology have lead to the use of new media forms for direct selling. For example, satellite and cable TV now make it possible for viewers to tune into programmes only transmitted for the purpose of generating sales. This is made possible through the combination of effective telecommunications and the widespread use of credit cards. The availability of huge consumer databases, which classify consumer information by using segmentation variables, has made it easier for organisations to screen and select appropriate prospects for canvassing by phone – a method frequently used by charities.

One recent development in direct selling is *network marketing* – an approach that offers incentives and bonuses to sales staff that recruit more sales staff to sell the company's products (so increasing the organisation's network). One hugely successful company that has pioneered this approach is Amway.

The adoption of these direct approaches are justified on the following basis.

1 Intermediaries are cut out so enabling the supplying organisation to reduce costs, and this saving can then be passed on to the consumer.

2 As the distribution channels are shortened, responsiveness to consumer needs can be improved.

3 The consumer enjoys the convenience of shopping from home.

The increase in direct selling methods has not been without problems, however. For example, some people are concerned that complete strangers seem to have access to personal information regarding buying habits, profession, home address and telephone number. Also high pressure techniques may be employed in order to close a sale or to sign up a network distributor as in the case of network marketing. This last point is always a danger where sales rewards are solely based on actual sales generated.

Direct selling is open to abuse to a far greater degree than any other method of marketing communication. This is mainly due to the fact that direct selling involves one-to-one communication and controlling that communication is much more difficult than controlling a single advertising message that is targeted at thousands of people. It is the responsibility of the organisation that employs such techniques to monitor its employees closely to ensure that customer satisfaction, and therefore future profits, are maintained.

DUTIES AND RESPONSIBILITIES OF SALES STAFF

Personal selling is a much more specific form of communication than advertising and it is generally aimed at one or a few people at a time. The cost of personal selling can be high, but, as a form of communication, it has greater impact on the customer. It also provides immediate feedback so that the message can be tailored to suit individual customers and it also helps marketers to determine and respond to customers' needs for information.

There are three basic elements to personal selling:

1. prospecting;
2. selling;
3. following up.

Some large organisations divide the three activities up between different types of personnel. This means that the organisation can achieve economies of scale by allowing the sales staff to perfect their different skills.

Prospecting

Prospecting is the act of looking for potential customers. Prospects can be obtained from advertisement responses and a number of databases exist ranging from telemarketing lists to telephone and trade directories. After choosing suitable prospects, the salesperson may make an initial contact by phone to see whether the prospect would be interested in a visit from a salesperson.

Selling

The first stage of the selling process is *the approach*. This is very important as it creates the customer's first impression. Most often the first visit is used as an opportunity to develop the relationship and the salesperson may have to call on the prospect several times before the product is considered.

The next stage is the *sales presentation*. The salesperson, through careful questioning of the prospect, will take great care to present those features of the product that he or she feels will give the prospect maximum benefit. For example, if the salesperson is selling someone a car who has stated that safety is an important feature, then he or she will concentrate the presentation on the anti-lock brakes, side impact bars and air bag, not the fact that the car can go from nought to 60 miles per hour in 8.2 seconds!

The salesperson will have to handle *objections* raised by the prospect. Responses to many objections can be thought out in advance and, if possible, these responses should relate back to the benefits of the product features. It may be possible to obtain a guarantee from the prospect if you can satisfactorily answer the objection.

The sale is *closed*, when the salesperson asks the prospect to buy the product. A salesperson will often gauge how near to closing he or she is by asking questions that assume the prospect will buy, e.g. delivery arrangements, order quantity.

Following up

After a successful close, it is essential that the sale is followed up. This generates important feedback on issues such as delivery and installation. It also helps to reassure the customer and is the first stage in obtaining a repeat order.

PC
3.4.1
3.4.2
C
3.1.1
3.1.2
3.2.1
3.2.2
3.4.1
3.4.2

ACTIVITY 3.4.1

Consider how the role of the salesperson varies and why it varies in the following situations.

1 *The retail trade* – selling to newsagents, grocers.
2 *Consumer durable stockists* – electrical shops, furniture shops.
3 *Products and services for industry* – pumps, components, waste handling.
4 *Specialist products and services for industry* – plant, CNC machines.
5 *Direct to the public* – double glazing.

CUSTOMER SERVICE AND THE SALES STAFF'S ROLE

Sales staff normally have two distinct roles to fulfil: servicing the requirements of existing customers and seeking potential sales from new customers. This second duty is the way an organisation will attempt to guarantee future growth, but growth will only occur as long as existing customers are fully satisfied with the sales service. It must be stressed that making the sale is not the final outcome of the marketing process! Ensuring maximum customer satisfaction should be the final outcome.

From this we can conclude that the best way to retain and build on an existing customer base is to provide the highest level of service in all aspects of the salesperson's role. The following points are important guidelines for the salesperson in ensuring customer service.

1 Deal with enquiries as efficiently and professionally as possible.
2 Provide the customer with clear, unambiguous information for any query.
3 Solve problems for the customer's benefit and not for the organisation.
4 Process internal information on behalf of the customer, e.g. order status.
5 Handle complaints.

Let us now look at this last point in more detail.

Element 3.4 Evaluate sales methods and customer service to achieve customer satisfaction

Handling complaints

Complaints should be looked at as a useful input in the process of monitoring customer service. Sales staff should take the following steps to ensure a complaint is handled properly.

1. Listen and understand the complaint.
2. Thank the customer for pointing it out and apologise for any inconvenience.
3. Let the customer know what you intend to do and how long it will take.
4. Give an idea of the outcome, if possible.
5. Do what is necessary to deal with the complaint.
6. Get back to the customer and let him or her know the outcome.
7. Keep a record of the complaint, including details, action taken and customer's response.

SALES COMMUNICATION METHODS

Most sales staff are required to compile regular reports on both a daily and weekly basis (*see* Fig. 3.35).

These are a vital input for the organisation. They not only provide the Sales Manager with essential information for co-ordinating sales efforts, but are also a valuable source of market intelligence for the organisation. Communication between the salesperson and the organisation should be a two-way flow, however. One reason for this is that field sales can be a very lonely occupation and it is important for the salesperson to feel that he or she is part of a team. This can be achieved with regular contact from head office.

Other common types of information needed by sales staff are:

1. information on the state of the market;
2. information on recent competitor activity;
3. the company's forward plans;
4. advertising activities;
5. updates on product information.

One useful way of passing on this information is via the sales conference. These should be held on a regular basis, e.g. twice yearly, and help to foster a sense of team spirit and company loyalty. Conferences should also be complemented by regular sales meetings, which, depending on the size of the organisation, can be held on a regional basis. It is a useful and common method of ensuring regular face-to-face contact between sales personnel, both internal and external, and their immediate superiors, e.g. regional and area managers.

Unit 3 Marketing

GW Ltd Field Sales Report

Tel/Fax No: 42871/42873

Customer: Bay Hall Ltd
Contact Name: C McPhee
Salesperson: Z Hoffman
Date of Visit: 7/8/95

(Customer details)

Multiple copies to:
1. Sales Admin.
2. Sales Manager
3. Sales Rep.

Report

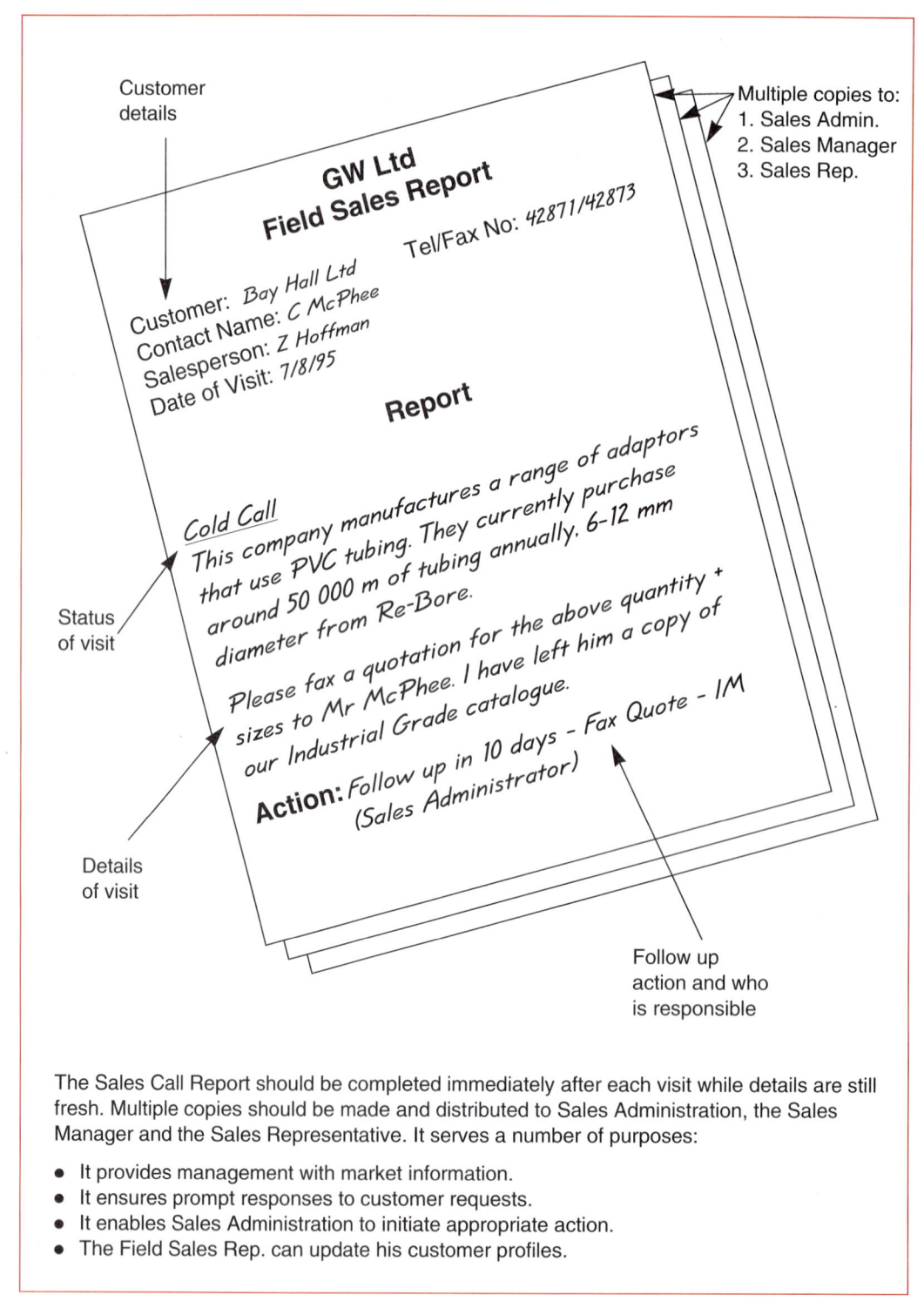

Cold Call
This company manufactures a range of adaptors that use PVC tubing. They currently purchase around 50 000 m of tubing annually, 6–12 mm diameter from Re-Bore.

Please fax a quotation for the above quantity + sizes to Mr McPhee. I have left him a copy of our Industrial Grade catalogue.

Action: Follow up in 10 days – Fax Quote – 1M (Sales Administrator)

(Status of visit)
(Details of visit)
(Follow up action and who is responsible)

The Sales Call Report should be completed immediately after each visit while details are still fresh. Multiple copies should be made and distributed to Sales Administration, the Sales Manager and the Sales Representative. It serves a number of purposes:

- It provides management with market information.
- It ensures prompt responses to customer requests.
- It enables Sales Administration to initiate appropriate action.
- The Field Sales Rep. can update his customer profiles.

Fig 3.35 The Sales Call Report

Written communication with customers is another important feature of the salesperson's role. Several examples of different letter styles addressed to customers are featured in Fig. 3.36, 3.37 and 3.38.

Element 3.4 Evaluate sales methods and customer service to achieve customer satisfaction

Dear Mr Fratelli

Thank you for the interest shown in our products in your letter of 22 August.

A copy of our illustrated catalogue is enclosed, together with samples of some of the skills we regularly use in our manufactures. Unfortunately, we cannot send you immediately a full range of samples, but you may rest assured that such leathers as chamois and doeskin, not represented in the parcel, are of the same high quality.

Mr Frank North, our Overseas Director, will be visiting Rome early next month. He will be pleased to visit you and bring with him a wide range of our goods. When you see them we think you will agree that the quality of materials used and the high standard of the craftsmanship will appeal to the most selective buyer.

We also manufacture a wide range of handmade leather handbags in which you may be interested. They are fully illustrated in the catalogue and are of the same high quality as our gloves. Mr North will be able to show you samples when he calls.

We look forward to the pleasure of receiving an order from you soon.

Yours sincerely

Fig 3.36 Introductory sales letter

Dear Mrs Larkin

As we have not heard from you since we sent you our catalogue of filing systems, we wonder whether you require further information before deciding to place an order.

The modern system of lateral filing has important space-saving advantages wherever economy of space is important. However, if space is not one of your problems, our flat-top suspended system may suit you better. The neat and tidy appearance it gives to the filing drawers and the ease and speed with which wanted files are located are only two of its features which many users find attractive.

Would you like us to send our Mr Robinson to call and discuss you needs with you? He has advised on equipment for many large, modern offices and would be able to recommend the system most suited to your own requirements. There would, of course, be no obligation of any kind. Alternatively, perhaps you would prefer to pay a visit to our showroom and see for yourself how the different systems work.

You may be sure that whichever of these opportunities you decide to accept, you would receive personal attention and the best possible advice.

Yours sincerely

Fig 3.37 Follow-up letter from a supplier

ELECTRICAL SUPPLIES LTD
29–31 Broad Street, Birmingham B1 2HE
Tel: 0121-542 6614

HT/JH

17 November 19--

Mr G Wood
Messrs G Wood & Sons
36 Castle Street
Bristol
BS1 2BQ

Dear Mr Wood

QUOTATION NUMBER E542

We welcome your enquiry of 15 November and are pleased to quote as follows:

	£
Swanson Electric Kettle, 2 litre	25.00 each
Cosiwarm Electric Blankets, single-bed size	24.50 each
Regency Electric Toasters	25.50 each
Marlborough Kitchen Wall Clocks	27.50 each

The above are current catalogue prices from which we would allow you a trade discount of $33\frac{1}{3}\%$. Prices include packing and delivery to your premises. All these items are available in stock for immediate delivery.

I hope these prices and terms are satisfactory. We look forward to receiving your order.

Yours faithfully

Harry Watts
Manager

Fig 3.38 Quotation from a supplier

Element 3.4 Evaluate sales methods and customer service to achieve customer satisfaction

SALES ADMINISTRATION

An external salesforce needs the back-up of an effective sales administration department. Sales administration is the interface between the salesperson and the organisation. It is responsible for processing the orders that the salesperson has generated, while also providing the salesforce with information such as customer credit status, delivery schedules and the state of customer accounts. It is a vital ingredient in ensuring an effective sales function and providing appropriate levels of customer service.

Self assessment questions

1. Of the following intermediaries, who does not take title to the goods?
   a The retailer
   b The wholesaler
   c The agent
   d The distributor

2. Which of the following is a stage in the personal selling process?
   a Breaking bulk
   b Prospecting
   c Processing orders
   d Communicating with line managers

3. Personal selling is most common in
   a consumer markets
   b supermarkets
   c industrial markets
   d second-hand markets?

4. Network marketing is a form of
   a sales promotion
   b advertising
   c indirect sales
   d direct sales?

5. Which of the following is false?
   a An intermediary sells to the customer.
   b An intermediary sells to the retailer.
   c An intermediary produces the product.
   d Intermediaries can deal in services as well as products.

6 What is the final stage when handling a customer's complaint?
  a Listen and understand the complaint.
  b Thank the customer and let him know what you intend to do.
  c Record the complaint giving customer details and action taken.
  d Pass it on to someone else to deal with.

7 Of the following sales communication methods, which would take place most frequently?
  a Customer visit report writing
  b Sales meetings
  c Sales conferences
  d The weekly sales report

8 Who would most likely attend an annual sales conference?
  a Regional and area sales managers
  b Sales directors and sales managers
  c All external and internal sales staff and middle and senior sales and marketing management
  d The external salesforce

9 Which of the following information does the salesforce need?
  a Information on the state of the market
  b Information on recent competitor activity
  c Advertising activities
  d All of the above

10 Which of the following is not an intermediary in a sales distribution channel?
  a Broker
  b Agent
  c Franchisee
  d Franchisor

Assignment

Task 1. Describe two sales distribution channels available for purchasing a return flight ticket to Paris.

Task 2. For each sales distribution channel, list the benefits to the customer, and the benefits to the airline company.

Task 3. Compare the role of the salesperson in each situation. What information is available to support the salesperson in his or her role?

Task 4. What are the sales administration procedures for each channel and why are these procedures so important?

Task 5. As a customer of the airline what do you expect in terms of customer service?

Element 3.4 Evaluate sales methods and customer service to achieve customer satisfaction

Answers to self-assessment questions

Element 3.1	Element 3.2	Element 3.3	Element 3.4
1. a	1. a	1. b	1. c
2. c	2. b	2. c	2. b
3. c	3. c	3. a	3. c
4. a	4. d	4. d	4. d
5. d	5. b	5. b	5. c
6. c	6. a	6. a	6. c
7. a	7. a	7. c	7. a
8. b	8. c	8. d	8. c
9. d	9. b	9. d	9. d
10. d	10. a	10. c	10. d

UNIT 4

HUMAN RESOURCES

This unit investigates how organisations succeed in managing their most valuable resource – their personnel or human resources. Although the Human Resources unit is an entirely separate mandatory GNVQ unit, some of the areas covered are similar to those looked at in Unit 5, Production and Employment in the Economy.

Element 4.1
INVESTIGATE HUMAN RESOURCING

Performance criteria

1 **Analyse the rights of employers and employees.**

2 **Explain employer and employee responsibilities in human resourcing.**

3 **Describe procedures available to employers and employees when rights are not upheld.**

4 **Explain the roles of trade unions and staff associations.**

5 **Explain employers' methods of gaining employee co-operation.**

Introduction

The success of any organisation depends upon the efficient use of its resources. Organisations primarily depend on people, among other resources, to be able to function effectively. The people needed to make this happen, or human resources, have to be managed carefully in order to obtain the best performance from them. The objective of this element is to investigate how organisations go about managing their human resources.

In the first element of this unit we begin by identifying exactly what the role of human resourcing is in an organisation by outlining some of the responsibilites it involves. This is followed by an explanation of the legal framework known as 'industrial relations' which underpins the employer–employee relationship.

THE RESPONSIBILITIES OF HUMAN RESOURCING

All managers are responsible for managing people to some extent. The function of the human resource manager is different in that it specialises in planning, developing and controlling the personnel who help to make up the organisation. Human resource managers more commonly have the job role title of Personnel Manager. Similarly, the department or function of an organisation where staff dealing with human resource management are located is more frequently called the Personnel Department than it is the more cumbersome title of Human Resource Management Department. For the purposes of this unit, we speak throughout in terms of a personnel department; that is, we make the assumption that such a separate department or function exists to carry out the activities outlined in this section. Some organisations may be too small for a separate, specialised personnel department, however – for example, a partnership consisting of a dozen or so full-time employees. In such cases managers often have more than one specialised job role and the responsibility for the personnel or human resource management function is likely to be shared by managers who have additional responsibilities or other functions within the organisation.

Defining the human resource management/personnel function

One way of understanding the function of the personnel department is to look at the career path of an individual employee through an organisation. Figure 4.1 illustrates this path.

Employees have varying needs from their point of entry into the organisation, during employment, right through to the point of exit from the organisation. At each of these three stages above the personnel function has key responsibilities.

Employee's career path	Entry →	In employment →	Exit
Functions of personnel department	• Recruitment • Selection • Induction	• Training and development • Retention • Transfer	• Termination • Redundancy

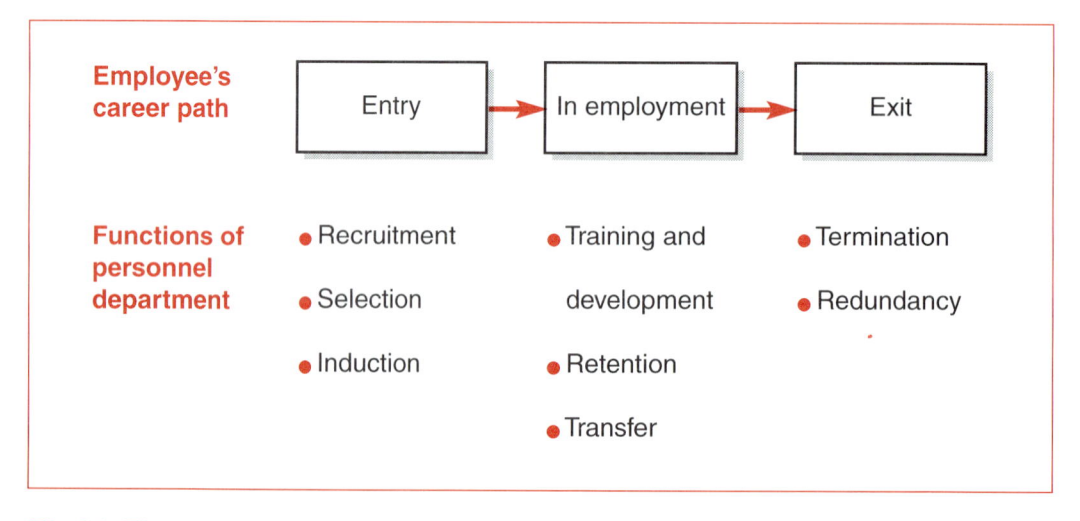

Fig 4.1 The career path of an employee through an organisation

Entry

At the point of entry the personnel department will be responsible for finding and selecting new recruits to the organisation. New employees will then need to be helped to adapt to their new job situation during a period of induction.

In employment

While in employment staff will require training in order to update their skills and develop their full potential. Well trained employees, who perform their tasks efficiently, are an asset to the organisation. Good human resource practice ensures that this type of employee is 'retained' (that is, these employees remain with the organisation for as long as the organisation needs them) and they feel useful to it. While in employment the need may also arise for an employee to transfer to another department or job.

Exit

At the point of exit when the employee comes to leave (termination) or is made redundant from the organisation, the personnel department has the task of ensuring that this process is carried out in a satisfactory manner and in accordance with the law.

Other examples of the responsibilities of the personnel department include:

- *Employee representation and consultation* – ensuring the collective views of employees are represented and acknowledged by their management.
- *Analysing training needs* – establishing the training and development requirements of personnel.
- *Staff appraisal and performance review* – implementing and maintaining systems that monitor and encourage good performance from employees.
- *Employee welfare* – maintaining the general well-being of employees.
- *Discipline and grievance procedures* – dealing formally with employees who do not keep to the rules and regulations of the organisation as well as dealing with any serious complaints employees may have.
- *Implementation and maintenance of payment and reward systems* – ensuring employees are paid and rewarded for their efforts promptly and regularly.
- *Compliance with employment legislation* – ensuring that the organisation remains within the law in matters relating to employment.
- *Equal opportunities* – ensuring equal treatment of all existing or prospective employees in matters of employment on grounds of race, ethnic or national origins, sex, or marital status.
- *Health and safety* – making employees aware of safety rules and ensuring that work is conducted in a safe and healthy environment.

THE RIGHTS OF EMPLOYERS AND EMPLOYEES

Most organisations have the goal of a good working relationship between managers and workforce. In order for this to come about, the legal obligations of employment need to be carefully observed. This makes good business sense, as legal disputes can be expensive, damaging and time consuming for all those involved. The amount and complexity of law relating to employment in organisations in the UK have been growing over the past two decades. With the increasing influence of the European Union this trend is likely to continue.

The contract of employment

The conditions under which employees are employed by an organisation are set out in their employment contracts. A contract is basically an agreement set out in a legally binding document. A contract does not have to be in writing, however, and can still be binding in a verbal form, but it is easier to prove that an agreement exists if it is in writing. The employment contract, or contract of service, contains the main details about the terms and conditions of employment. Both employers and employees are legally bound to comply with the terms of the contract. There are three ways in which the contract can be established:

1 *Through collective bargaining*, whereby the contract is established through negotiation between the employers and representatives of the employees (for example, a trade union).

2 *Through one-way presentation*, where the employer presents the employee with the contract on a 'take-it-or-leave-it' basis.

3 *Through individual bargaining*, where the individual employee negotiates his or her own contract.

In most cases in the UK the contract will be established in the manner described in 1 or 2. Employees bringing particularly highly valued skills or resources to the company are more likely to be able to negotiate their contract on an individual basis. For example, an experienced salesperson bringing skills and potential customer contacts would be in a strong position to negotiate his or her own contract because of the obvious potential benefits on offer to the organisation.

Who is entitled to a written contract?

Under the Employment Protection (Consolidation) Act 1978, most workers have a right to a 'written statement of their terms and conditions of employment'. There are some qualifications to this statement, however, that relate to the number of hours worked per week.

- Those employed for 16 hours or more a week must be supplied with a written (expressed) statement within 13 weeks of commencing employment.
- Those employed for less than 16 hours but more than 8 hours per week have the right to a written statement after five years' continuous service with their employer.
- Those employed for less than 8 hours a week have no right to a written statement.

The formal letter of acceptance

All new employees have the right to a formal written letter of acceptance from their new employer giving confirmation of acceptance for the post. This formal letter should contain such details as a definite offer of work, start and finish times, hours of work and who the employee should report to in the first instance.

The expressed terms of the contract of employment

A written (expressed) contract of employment can include an enormous amount of detail but must, as a minimum, contain the following:

- the names of both the employer and the employee;
- the job title;
- the start date of employment and whether any previous employment is to count as continuous service;
- details of wages or salary payments;
- hours of work and normal working hours expected;
- holiday entitlement, pay and public holidays;
- information relating to pensions;
- details relating to sickness, injury and sick pay;
- length of notice period the employee is required to give and is entitled to receive from the employer;
- details of grievance and disciplinary procedures.

Individual rights of employees

When an individual becomes an employee he or she automatically becomes eligible to certain rights under statute (the law). These include:

- the right to equal pay for work of equal value (*see* Equal pay below);
- the right to belong to a trade union and to take part in union activities;
- the right not to be discriminated against on the grounds of race, ethnic origin or nationality, sex or marital status (*see* Equal opportunities below);
- the right to continue to keep a job on the same terms and conditions in the event of a transference of undertakings (for example, if the organisation is taken over or merged);
- the right to work in safe working conditions that comply to at least minimum national standards (see Health and safety below).

Employees who have worked on a continuous basis for the same employer for a minimum of two years qualify for some additional rights under statute:

- the right to a certain period of notice for termination of contract;
- the right not to be unfairly dismissed;
- the right to redundancy pay;
- the right to written reasons for dismissal;
- the right to an itemised payslip and full payment as agreed;
- the right to guaranteed payments;

- the right to statutory sick pay;
- the right to return to work following illness;
- in the case of women, the right not to be dismissed in the event of pregnancy, to statutory maternity pay, to return to work, and to time off for antenatal care.

Equal opportunities

It is recognised under law in our society that it is unfair to discriminate against people on grounds of race, ethnic origin, nationality, sex, or marital status. During the past two decades equal opportunities at work have become an increasingly important employment issue. Equality laws exist to protect people against discrimination at work and promote equal opportunities.

The laws on equal opportunities

The Sex Discrimination Act 1975 and the Race Relations Act 1976 state that an employer must not discriminate against anyone on the grounds of sex or race by treating him or her less favourably in all aspects of employment. If an employer discriminates against employees in areas such as recruitment, training or promotion then this is deemed as *direct discrimination* – for example, advertising a vacancy and requesting that applicants of only one sex, race or marital status need apply.

Discrimination may also take a more subtle form known as *indirect discrimination*. This occurs when a condition or requirement is imposed on everyone in the workforce but the

ACTIVITY 4.1.1

Consider the examples of discrimination in employment given below. Some are cases of direct and some of indirect discrimination. Identify which are examples of direct discrimination and which indirect.

1. A woman is sacked when she informs her employer that she is pregnant.
2. A man and a woman both go for a job as a bricklayer and the man gets the job on the grounds that it is 'men's work'.
3. An Asian woman is refused a job as a nurse because she wants to wear trousers but the nurse's uniform requires a skirt to be worn.
4. Men are encouraged to go on training courses in a bank but women are never asked.
5. A man with a 'dreadlock' hairstyle is asked whether he would be prepared to get his hair cut before starting work and is rejected for the post when he refuses.
6. A man and a woman go for a job interview and the man is selected because the woman states she plans to have a family eventually.
7. An organisation employing a wide cross-section of ethnic minorities states that everybody must take their religious holidays at the same time.

nature of the condition or requirement gives a larger proportion of one race, sex or marital status a greater chance of being able to comply than another – for example, requesting that applicants for a job be over a certain height would almost certainly deter more women from applying for the job than men.

Equal opportunities policies

Organisations wishing to take advantage of the widest possible available pool of human resources offer equal opportunities policies which go beyond the basic minimum requirements of the law. For example, some organisations explicitly include positive discrimination for the disabled in their equal opportunities policy. An organisation adopting such a policy is doing more than just expressing good intentions. It is a useful mechanism for avoiding unfair management decisions and offering all employees the chance to realise their full potential within the organisation. In addition it helps to bring diversity to the organisation which may be a positive end in itself. A typical equal opportunities policy might include the following:

- a statement of intent to avoid and challenge cases of direct and indirect discrimination;
- a statement of how the policy will operate in terms of recruitment, selection, training and promotion;
- a statement of who will be responsible and accountable for the policy and how it will be monitored.

Implementation of an equal opportunities policy should be accompanied by staff training where the advantages to the entire workforce of its adoption are emphasised.

Equal pay

The *New Earnings Survey*, published annually by the UK government, found that in 1994 women's average weekly earnings were equivalent to just over 72 per cent of those of men. Men and women can sometimes be discriminated against in terms of pay and other terms of their contracts of employment (for example, payment for overtime or holiday entitlements). The Equal Pay Act 1970 was introduced to abolish discrimination of this kind. In 1983 it was amended to give workers the right to equal pay for work of equal value. This means where two jobs are equal in terms of the amount of effort, skill and decision making required to do them, the pay should also be equal.

Health and safety at work

Four hundred and thirty people in the UK were killed at work in 1992–3. The Health and Safety at Work Act 1974 imposes a duty on all employers to ensure, as far as is 'reasonably practical', the health and safety of all their employees or others who use their premises. Organisations are encouraged, and it is in their interests, to provide a safety representative at the work-place. A government body, the Health and Safety Executive, has the responsibility for enforcing safety laws, encouraging training about safety and publishing information including codes of conduct. Employers have additional obligations to provide a safe working environment for their employees under civil and common law (*see* 'Civil legal action' below).

GRIEVANCE PROCEDURES

The contract of employment should make reference to what individual employees can do if they feel their rights have not been observed by their employer. Grievances can also be presented collectively – for example, a trade union may bring a collective grievance on behalf of a group of employees who wish to settle a common complaint.

The first step towards resolving a grievance is usually to talk with the employee's immediate supervisor or line manager to see if the difficulty can be settled. It may be the case that a settlement cannot be made here – for example, it may be the actual relationship with the supervisor that is the problem! In this situation the employee is either directed to the supervisor's manager or the person or department responsible for employee welfare (the personnel department). At this stage the employee may also wish to discuss the matter with a trade union or staff association representative. If, at this second stage, the matter still remains unsettled then the employee may wish to have his or her complaint formally entered into the grievance procedure.

The stages of the grievance procedure

Most grievance procedures consist of three stages: beginning within the department, moving outside the department but still within the organisation and in some cases a final stage that involves a third party outside of the organisation. See Figure 4.2.

1 *The departmental stage*. Here the departmental manager checks all the facts involved in the grievance. If necessary, any decisions taken earlier by the employee's supervisor may be altered or even reversed. If this occurs, the grievance ends at this point in the procedure. If not, the grievance proceeds to the next stage.

2 *The organisational stage*. The grievance is taken to the next layer of management above the departmental level. Once again, the facts are checked and evidence considered before reaching a decision. At this stage a joint committee consisting of staff and management representatives may become involved.

3 *The third party stage*. Some organisations allow a third party organisation or entity to act as mediator when grievances appear to be reaching no conclusion within the organisation. The 'third party' acts as a neutral judge of the fairness of the issue at stake. The Advisory Conciliation and Arbitration Service (ACAS) is an example of an organisation often called upon to intervene at this stage.

Civil legal action

Employees who suffer injury from accidents in the course of their work or who contract classified industrial diseases are entitled to compensation from the government. If the injury was caused through the fault of the employer or a fellow employee, however, the injured person is entitled to bring a civil action to claim for damages against the employer through the courts.

Element 4.1 Investigate human resourcing

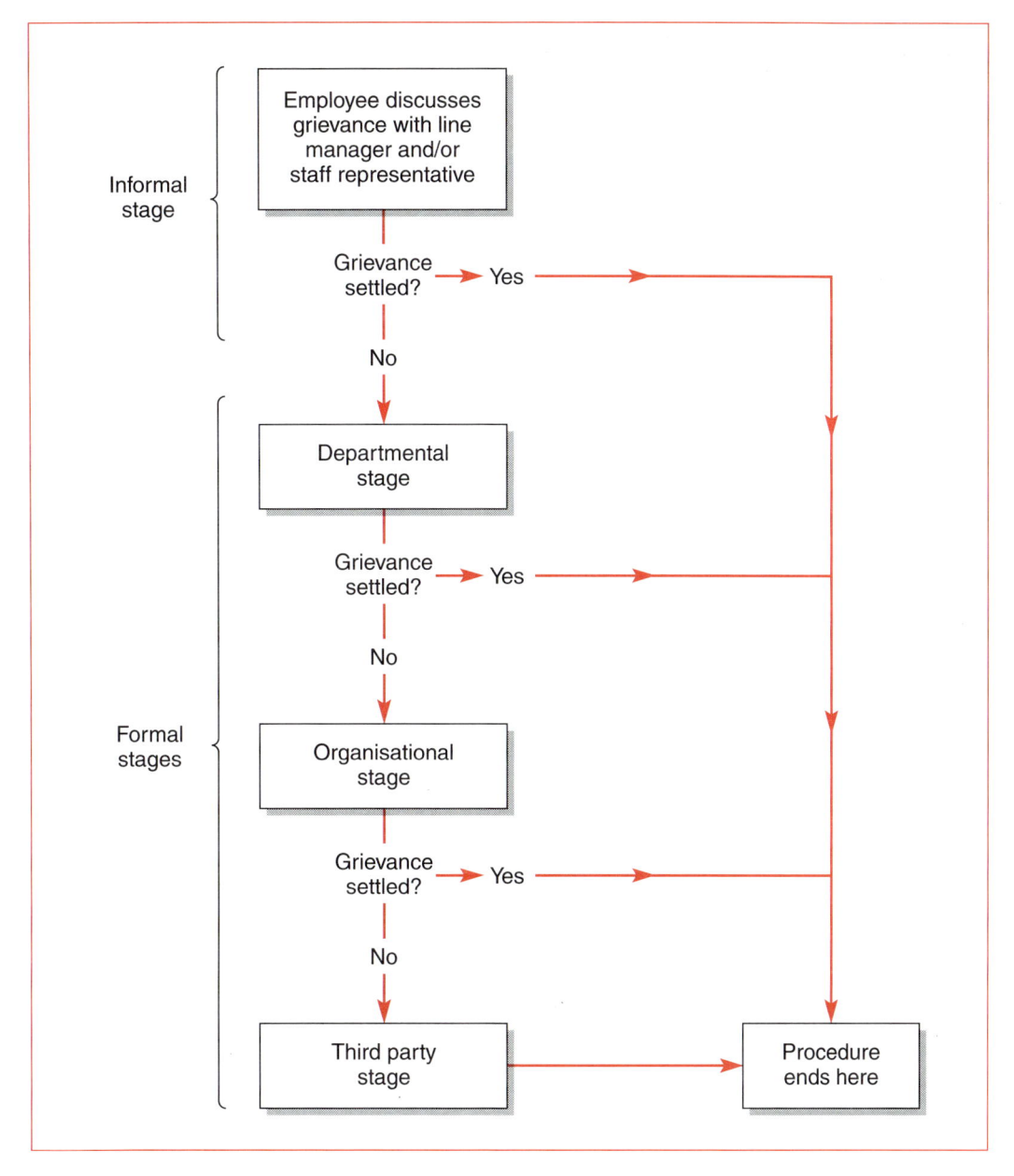

Fig 4.2 The grievance procedure

Alternatively, employees who suffer harm due to the fault of their employer or fellow employee can sue under common law. Under common law, employers owe a legal duty to take care with regard to the safety of their employees by providing a safe system of work. If the employer has not taken reasonable care under his or her common law duty and an injury is caused to the employee as a result, then the employee can make a claim based on common law negligence.

DISCIPLINARY PROCEDURES

Employers have a right to expect employees to keep to the terms and conditions of their contract of employment and also to behave reasonably. Employers are entitled to take disciplinary action against employees who do not do so. Disciplinary problems have to be dealt with in a uniform manner across the organisation to ensure fairness and equality of treatment. To this end most organisations publish guidelines on dealing with disciplinary matters in a disciplinary policy statement (*see* Fig. 4.3).

COMPANY DISCIPLINARY POLICY

1. It is the employee's responsibility to follow all company rules and working procedures.

2. If an employee is performing or behaving badly, the first step management will take will be informal counselling.

3. Formal disciplinary procedures will be entered into only when informal counselling has been unsuccessful or where the actions of the employee show that informal counselling is inappropriate.

4. No employee will be formally disciplined without a fair hearing and an opportunity to put his or her case.

5. Management will seek to act fairly and consistently when carrying out any disciplinary action.

Fig 4.3 A disciplinary policy statement

The formal disciplinary procedure

The example of a company disciplinary policy in Fig. 4.3 refers to a 'disciplinary procedure'. Details of this procedure should be made available to all employees. The form the disciplinary procedure takes is up to the organisation concerned but many choose to follow the guidelines recommended by the Advisory Conciliation and Arbitration Service (ACAS) Code of Practice. This publication recommends that formal disciplinary procedures should:

- be formal and written;
- state to whom it applies;
- state what disciplinary action may be taken and which level of management has the authority to take such action.

When a complaint is made against an employee the person concerned is notified and then given the opportunity to state his or her case. The employee is normally allowed to be accompanied and supported by a trade union representative or fellow employee when he or she does so.

ACAS ADVISORY CONCILIATION AND ARBITRATION SERVICE

Fig 4.4

The stages in the disciplinary procedure

Disciplinary action against an employee normally has four main stages:

1. a formal oral warning;
2. a first written warning;
3. a final written warning;
4. dismissal.

Most employers give employees at least one informal oral warning before the formal oral warning which begins the formal disciplinary procedure. The employee should be provided with a right of appeal against disciplinary action for situations where the employee feels he or she has been treated unfairly. At all stages of the procedure the employee needs to be informed of any previous warnings given and made aware of the next stage in the disciplinary procedure. It is good practice for the employer to keep careful written records at all formal stages of the procedure and get employees to sign a statement that states that they have received and understood their warnings.

Gross misconduct

Sometimes the employee's conduct leads to instant dismissal – that is, dismissal after an incident without notice or further discussion. This could happen if the employee commits a single offence serious enough to be deemed gross misconduct, such as theft, fraud, vandalism or violence. Whatever the regulations, the employees should be aware of which offences will result in disciplinary action and which offences would be considered as gross misconduct.

Unfair dismissal

When an employee terminates his or her employment with an organisation in most cases it will be because alternative employment has been found elsewhere. In a minority of cases, however, the employee may feel that he or she has not been fairly treated and may resort to the law to gain redress (compensation). Some categories of employee have the right not to be unfairly dismissed, and those who think they have may seek redress by making a complaint to an Industrial Tribunal. Cases of unfair dismissal, when they occur, can cause enormous problems and be very costly to the organisation concerned.

For these reasons it is very much in the interest of managers to follow good disciplinary practice and procedure so that they are able to deal with disciplinary matters fairly. The human resources department either assumes responsibility for dismissal or provides detailed guidance for line managers. The independent body ACAS publishes a code of practice giving practical advice to employers on dealing with disciplinary matters.

Employee protection from unfair dismissal

Two pieces of legislation protect certain employees from unfair dismissal: the Employment Protection (Consolidation) Act 1978 and, more recently, the Employment Act 1989. Not everyone is able to claim unfair dismissal. The groups of employees excluded are:

- those with less than two years' continuous service with the organisation; and
- those past normal retirement age for their employment, or, where there is none, those who have reached age 65.

Employees can complain to an Industrial Tribunal in unfair dismissal cases relating to trade union activities or membership regardless of age or hours per week worked.

What constitutes unfair dismissal?

This is not an easy question to answer as most people's interpretation of fair and unfair is quite subjective. In most cases common sense dictates how employees should behave in the work-place and how managers should treat employees. If a dismissal takes place the manager must be sure that the reason for dismissal is fair and it fits into one of three statutory categories:

- employee misconduct;
- a lack of capability to do the job as it should be done;
- redundancy.

Most dismissals will fall into one of these three categories. This being the case, the manager has a further duty to ensure that the individual's circumstances have been taken into consideration – for example, the employee may have been having personal problems not related to his or her job but having an adverse effect upon it.

Constructive dismissal

In some circumstances an employee may not have actually been dismissed, but instead may have been put in such a position, that he or she had no alternative but to resign – for example, where an employee resigns after repeatedly being physically threatened or harassed by a manager. Even though the employee has given up his or her job in a voluntary sense, the employee is still able to claim wrongful dismissal as he or she was forced into the decision to leave the employment.

Remedies for unfair dismissal

Those employees with the right not to be unfairly dismissed can seek redress by making a complaint to an Industrial Tribunal. The complaint needs to be made to the tribunal within three months of the date of the termination of employment. The onus is on the employee to prove that he or she was dismissed actually or constructively; the employer will then be required to show the statutory reason. In the event of the tribunal finding for the employee that the dismissal was unfair, there are three remedies it can propose:

- *Reinstatement* – the employee gets the job back.
- *Re-engagement* – the employee is offered an alternative job, not necessarily on the same terms and conditions as the previous job.
- *compensation* – consisting of a basic award plus an award based on loss of earnings.

Industrial tribunal settlements

The 1992 survey of industrial tribunal applications by the Employment Department found that around two thirds of applications by employees never actually reach the tribunal stage. The employees surveyed either reached a settlement with the employer beforehand or withdrew their application. Of the third of cases actually going to a tribunal, 45 per cent found in favour of the applicant and 55 per cent against. The highest average compensation awarded was £2000 in cases of unfair dismissal (source: *Employment Gazette*, Jan 1994).

REDUNDANCY

Employees are said to be redundant when they are dismissed because the employer no longer carries on the business for which they were employed. For example, an organisation may be affected by a significant fall in demand for its main product and may have to cut back on part of its workforce as a result. An employee who is made redundant in such circumstances cannot claim unfair dismissal, but may be entitled to a tax-free lump sum set as a minimum by the government State Redundancy Payments Scheme. In practice, the redundancy terms on offer to employees are often more generous than the government minimum but this arrangement is entirely at the discretion of the organisation concerned.

Rights of employees made redundant

The Employment Protection (Consolidation) Act 1978 states that provided employees meet with certain conditions they are able to claim redundancy payment and the right to reasonable time off to look for other work. The conditions depend on the employee's age, hours worked per week and how long he or she has worked with the company (length of service). In addition, the size of the redundancy payment will be affected by the size of the weekly salary. The conditions are described in more detail below.

Age

Employees aged less than 18 or over 65 are not entitled to redundancy payments.

Hours of work

- Employees who work less than 8 hours per week have no rights to redundancy payment.
- Employees who work more than 8 but less than 16 hours a week have no rights to a redundancy payment until they have worked for five years.
- Employees who work 16 hours or more a week have rights to redundancy payment after they have worked for the same employer for two years.

Length of service

Redundancy payments are calculated on the number of years' continuous service an employee has had with the same employer from age 18 until the date of the redundancy notice. The maximum number or years' service which can count towards redundancy payment is 20.

The right to time off to look for other work

Employees with a minimum of two years' service have the right to paid time off to look for another job. Employees selected for redundancy without two years of service should still be allowed time off to search for other work.

INDUSTRIAL RELATIONS

Industrial relations consists of those aspects of human resource management where employees are dealt with collectively. It is concerned with communication between the representatives of the employer (the management) and representatives of employees (the trade union or staff representative).

The importance of the quality of employer–employee relations cannot be understated. An organisation is most likely to perform effectively when the workforce and management are in a constructive partnership rather than a conflicting one. It is generally accepted that employee relations is a managerial responsibility and that good employee relations practice is a task for management. For example, line managers are personally involved due to their responsibility for employees within their particular work area. Maintaining good employee relations is made difficult, however, by the constant change in the work environment due to changing technology, work-place reorganisation, and the changing economic and social climate. Increased legislation affecting employment such as contract of employment, training, equal opportunities, health and safety, and redundancy creates a need for a greater awareness among managers of their responsibilities towards employees. It is the responsibility of the human resource department to ensure that this awareness exists, is maintained and is updated when necessary.

Representation

Many UK employees have their terms and conditions of employment and the rewards they receive determined by individual negotiation between themselves and their employer. The majority of employees in the UK and in Europe, however, have their terms, conditions and pay determined by direct negotiation with someone who represents them and negotiates on their behalf. This representative is usually a member of a trade union or staff association/organisation to which the employees belong. Other employees will have their terms and conditions determined indirectly as a result of such negotiations. All aspects of employment relating to rewards received for work carried out tend to be negotiated collectively (as a group) with employees.

Apart from negotiation relating to rewards, employers are involved in consultation and other forms of communication with employees collectively on a wide range of issues. The relationship which develops between management and workforce is determined to a great extent by the prevailing attitude of both parties. The personnel function is involved in fostering a constructive attitude towards industrial relations in both management and in workforce representation in order to discourage the occurrence of situations of conflict.

Employee representation by trade unions

Over 40 per cent of the UK workforce is represented by a trade union (approximately 9 million employees). A trade union is an association of workers formed collectively to protect their interests in employment situations. Trade unions have many goals concerned with improving and protecting the rights of employees. They can be seen as having the following specific objectives:

- obtaining better wages and working conditions for employees;
- obtaining greater job security;
- obtaining improved welfare benefits in employment.

Unions may wish to negotiate on many issues and often have wider social aims, such as wider employee participation in management decisions (employee involvement) and higher levels of social security for the unemployed.

Types of trade unions

Craft unions

Originally, trade unions were formed to protect the interests of manual workers. Clearly if the worker had valuable skills then it was easier to bargain with employers. This is why the earliest unions tended to be 'Craft' unions – that is, they represented skilled workers such as printers, fitters, boilermakers, etc. As such they saw themselves as an elite group. The possession of high levels of skill acquired through long apprenticeships, often seven or more years, both improved bargaining power and helped to strengthen collective identity. Most often these unions were concerned to protect the privileges and relative standing of their members – especially their pay differentials. An important way of achieving this was through the exclusion of non-members from their occupational areas. This was known as the 'closed shop'. In the 1960s this led to disputes over demarcation – that is, who should be doing what particular job within an organisation. In the 1980s the closed shop led to new technology disputes for example in the newspaper printing industry.

The key feature of the last 30 years has been the decline of craft unions. The decline in membership has lead to union mergers, initially with other craft unions but since the 1970s also with other general unions. For example:

- Engineers, electricians and plumbers were formed by merger between the AEU and the EEPTU.
- In the case of printworkers, SOGAT was formed by mergers between compositors and distributive workers.
- The National Union of Dyers and Bleachers is now part of the Transport and General Workers Union.

General unions

General unions attempted to organise on the basis of industry rather than skill. Examples are the TGWU and the GMBATU. The GMBATU represented manual workers in local authorities and the TGWU represented workers such as transport workers, but with rapid decline in membership throughout the 1980s even the large general unions found it necessary to merge to gain economies of scale. Since 1979 trade union membership is estimated to have fallen from 13 million to approximately 8 million.

'White collar' unions

A key change since the end of the Second World War has been the rise of 'white collar' or service sector unions. Examples are BIFU for banking and insurance workers and MSF for technical managerial and scientific staff.

Employers in the service sector, which tends to have smaller offices and fewer branches, have not needed trade unions to negotiate with. The level of union recognition and membership is consequently lower in the service sector than in manufacturing. As clerical and managerial occupations become more increasingly de-skilled (a lower level of skill is required) with the advent of information technology, however, and the degree of control over individuals increases, it has been predicted that employees in this sector will turn more to union membership. Recent developments in the European Union – the Maastricht Treaty, Social Chapter – which guarantee consultation and negotiating rights may further encourage this development.

Women and trade unions

Given that trade unions tended in the past to exist in the manufacturing sector and particularly in the manual sub sectors, it is not surprising that until the rise of white collar unions women tended to have both lower levels of membership and active participation in trade unions. In part this was previously attributable to the prevalence of women in part-time occupations, which have always been more difficult recruiting grounds for trade unions. Women are now becoming more prominent. For example, Brenda Dean was, until recently, the President of the printworkers' union, SOGAT.

Single union deals

Unions have traditionally represented a particular type of worker in a certain group of occupations – for example, maintenance staff are represented by one union in an organisation but office administrative staff by another. As organisations are made up of many different types of workers, it is quite common for several unions to represent workers in an organisation. This will also be the case when workers of the same type, in the same occupation, have a choice of unions – for representation. For example, teachers can be in one of five separate unions.

In either of the above cases, the management often finds itself negotiating with more than one group of representatives of the workforce. Recognising the difficulties this can cause for both management and unions, some unions have recently struck deals with new employers whereby they agree to be the sole union representing the workforce. These arrangements are known as *single union deals*. Whether single union or multi-union, all organisations dealing with unions do so on the basis of collective bargaining.

Collective bargaining

When negotiation takes place in which employees do not negotiate individually, but do so collectively through representation, then collective bargaining takes place. This is joint negotiation in which decisions are made on matters of interest to both employers and employees. In the UK collective bargaining is generally carried out at two levels: national or work-place (local) level. In most cases the employers will be bargaining with trade unions but staff associations/organisations may bargain collectively also.

The agreements reached may be 'substantive' in nature, that is, covering pay, hours of work, etc. (or 'procedural'), relating to methods applied to resolving disputes and conflicts, for example, an agreement on a grievance procedure. It can be argued that collective bargaining helps to make the management more democratic, because it involves workers in vital decisions affecting their circumstances of employment. Collective bargaining does tend to make demands on both managerial time and skills.

Advantages and disadvantages to employers of negotiating with trades unions

Advantages	Disadvantages
■ Ease of salary and conditions negotiations.	■ Improves employees' relative bargaining power. This is only significant, however, if the employer is making excess profits or can pass on cost increases to customers without losing sales.
■ Simpler to meet the needs of Health and Safety legislation.	
■ Provides a standard method for conflict resolution.	
■ Encourages employee participation and improves morale (may lead to improved productivity).	■ May encourage demarcation disputes.
	■ Consultation and agreement slows down management decision making.
■ Prevents managers from breaking employment law and thus avoids unfair dismissal cases.	■ May provide focus for opposition to new technology or working practices.

Clearly the issue of whether trade union representation is beneficial or harmful to an organisation will depend on its initial conditions. In some small firms there is less need for trades unions. It is true, however, that small firms are more likely to face wrongful dismissal or discrimination cases than larger ones.

Consultation

There are many management decisions on fundamentally important matters that do not lend themselves to formal negotiation – for example, planning the long-term strategy for the organisation. Consultative arrangements provide other ways in which the workforce can present its views and play a part in the day-to-day management of the business. Matters for consultation (sometimes known as joint consultation) usually exclude pay and terms and conditions of employment, but include such matters as company policy, trade results, health and safety and training.

Consultation is purely advisory in nature with management reserving the right to make the final decisions.

Staff associations/organisations

Some management prefer to have employees represented by staff associations/organisations rather than trade unions. Staff associations are formed by the employers themselves to represent the staff collectively. This type of representation has become more popular in recent years and the number of staff associations has grown.

ACTIVITY 4.1.2

Read the article from the *Financial Times* of 13 October 1993 in Fig. 4.5 and then answer the questions.

1 Which unions represent workers at Ford?

2 How will the introduction of multiskilling help Ford?

3 What does the union mean when it asks for 'job security'?

4 How has Ford managed to cut its workforce so far?

5 What does Mr Woodley argue about other UK car plants in relation to Ford?

6 Summarise the union argument. Is it a strong one?

Unions at Ford to demand jobs for life

A demand for 'jobs for life' will be made today when unions representing Ford's 20,000 manual workers present their annual claim. Mr Tony Woodley, TGWU general union negotiator for the car industry, hinted yesterday that the unions are prepared to negotiate on the introduction of multi-skilling for Ford workers in return for a guarantee of employment security.

But it was unclear last night whether the other unions at Ford, notably the AEEU engineering and electricians' union, will support this position. In spite of the recession Ford has managed to avoid any compulsory redundancies and has cut its workforce through natural wastage and voluntary severance. But union leaders are concerned that the company may not be able to continue with this policy.

'Our top priority in these negotiations will be job security,' said Mr Woodley. He added that the unions at Ford wanted only what been achieved at other UK-based car plants such as Rover, Nissan, Honda and Toyota. The unions will also be seeking a 'substantial' increase in basic wage rates for manual workers.

'Ford UK has a world-class workforce with the lowest labour costs in Europe,' said Mr Woodley. 'We want to see them have the same wages and job protection that the best has to offer.' He added that only Peugeot Talbot paid lower basic wage rates than Ford among car companies in the UK. The unions want Ford to drop what they see as its piecemeal approach to work-place change and take a more comprehensive view of what needs to be done.'If they want to compete with the best, the company must provide job protection to its employees so they can deliver the goods,' said Mr Woodley.

Fig 4.5 *Source:* The *Financial Times*, Oct 93

Element 4.1 Investigate human resourcing

METHODS OF GAINING EMPLOYEE CO-OPERATION

Any organisation depends on the effectiveness of its employees for success. In an increasingly competitive environment organisations are depending more and more on the performance of their employees to give them a competitive edge. Organisations that flourish tend to have an effective and motivated workforce. This does not happen by accident, however; it is the result of well thought out human resource management policies and practices.

A co-operative and well trained workforce is likely to bring the following benefits for an organisation:

- achievement of increases in levels of productivity;
- low levels of absenteeism;
- a high staff retention rate avoiding the need to be recruiting new employees frequently;
- the provision of good quality service and the promotion of good company image;
- motivated staff and increased morale;
- better co-operation between staff; and as a result of all the above
- increased levels of profit.

Motivating employees

Motivation is about what causes people to act or behave in one way rather than another. Motivation comes in two basic forms:

1 *Extrinsic motivation* influences that come to people from outside of them, that then motivate them.

2 *Intrinsic motivation* influences that people have themselves that motivate them.

In practice the two forms are closely linked. What is done for (or to) people will affect their inner motivation and people already motivated by themselves may get less, or more, encouragement from outside as a result of being so.

Researchers have attempted to explain what it is that motivates people.

Maslow's hierarchy of needs

Abraham Maslow, an American psychologist in the early 1950s, formulated a hierarchy of human needs, as illustrated in Fig. 4.6. The needs are arranged in ascending order of precedence.

Physiological needs

The most basic need is physiological, that is the need to eat, drink and have clothes. Unless this need is met, nothing else is of importance. In Sarajevo, the Bosnians risk death from snipers and landmines to get food. In the face of hunger and thirst, we risk our

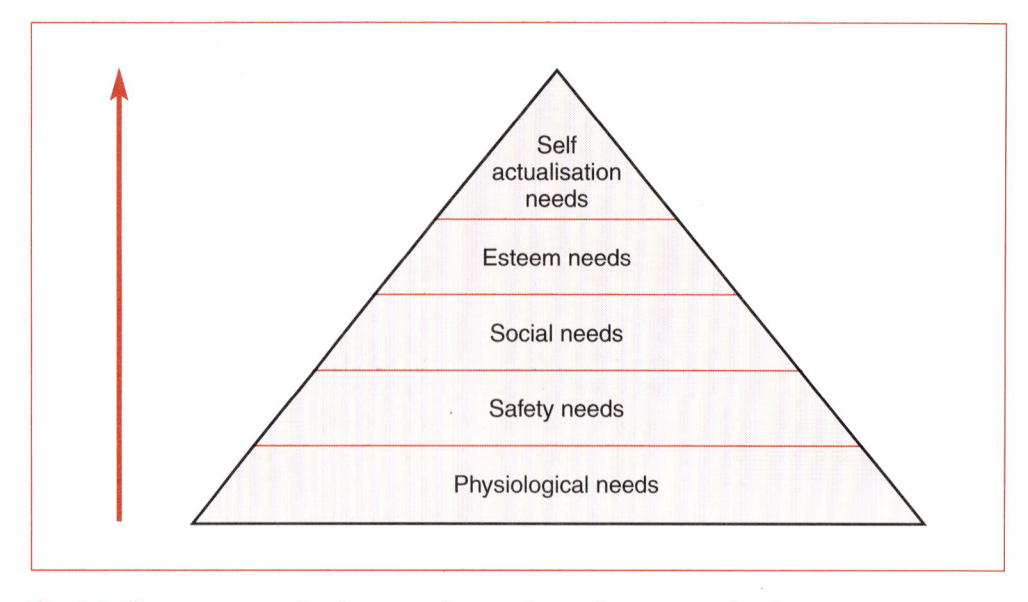

Fig 4.6 The career path of an employee through an organisation

lives, let alone our reputations. Of course the presence of life-threatening hunger is not common in most work-places. The approach of mealtimes does lead to marked decline in activity, however.

Safety needs

Once we are not hungry, thirsty or cold, we worry about our safety and security – expressed in general terms as shelter, warmth and the ability to defend ourselves. In the working environment this need manifests itself as the need for job security and a safe working environment. A threatening or unsafe environment commands our attention and avoiding physical and psychological harm becomes our most important goal.

At work the main threat is that of losing our jobs and all the accompanying benefits. Under such circumstances a degree of stress leads to a decline in performance. Often the threat of redundancy is communicated by rumour or gossip, making it difficult to gauge the size of the threat, and in turn making the threat much worse. Knowing that we are to be made redundant, under what conditions and when, is actually easier to deal with than guessing. Of course, if the loss of job appears to threaten physiological survival then the reaction can be extreme.

Social needs

Social needs reflect the desire to belong, to have friends, to be respected and, not least, to be loved. In work teams, we want to get on with our colleagues and workmates. The crucial feature is the state of internal working relationships. Managers, employees and children can all be equally bullying and vicious to one another. There is a growing awareness of the extent and seriousness of bullying at work. This reveals itself in higher absenteeism and poor output performance.

Esteem needs

Next we come to esteem, or ego, needs. These reflect our desire to be recognised, to be valued, to be trusted. We need external confirmation of our abilities – the word of thanks, the praise for a task well done. We like to believe that we are self-sufficient, that what other people think does not matter, but all the research proves otherwise. We value praise from perceived superiors or peers more highly that praise from inferiors, but being praised is always preferred to being ignored. At work the needs are met by conduct such as congratulations from supervisors, being delegated important tasks and having the opportunity of promotion.

Self-actualisation needs

Under Maslow's hierarchy the highest level of need is that of self-actualisation. We need to be able to express ourselves – to be the secret person we know ourselves to be. We all have hidden talents and desires. If Maslow is correct, we are all creative, competent and unique persons; what we crave is the chance to prove it. Given the chance to use our abilities to the full, we do not need to be supervised, or controlled, as long as the task is important to us.

Sir Clive Sinclair's main motivation appears to have been the need to create new products, that had not been previously conceived, let alone, completed. In interviews he often talked of the challenge and the thrill of creating his pocket TV and the ZX80. Having created these, he then wanted to create something new. The reports of Bill Gates, head of Microsoft, are very similar. Monetary reward hardly receives a mention.

Herzberg's hygiene factors

Frederick Herzberg accepted Maslow's basic approach but found that it was difficult for managers to implement. He therefore reclassified the needs into terms that were directly meaningful to managers. He invented the expression 'motivators'. Motivators include:

- recognition;
- promotion chances;
- sense of achievement;
- being allowed responsiblity;
- interesting and challenging jobs.

Motivators by themselves do not generate high levels of output, however. People also need certain enabling conditions before they can give of their best. Hertzberg called these conditions *hygiene factors*. Their presence does not guarantee high motivation but their absence can cause job dissatisfaction. Hygiene factors include:

- personal relationships within an organisation;
- social facilities and fringe benefits;
- pay;
- pleasant physical environment;
- effective management style;
- status.

An effective management is one that can maintain all the above features even in a changing environment. Underlying the management style and personal relationship elements is the need for equity, or fairness. If a manager or organisation is felt to be unfair – that is rewarding or punishing people unjustifiably – then two key hygiene features are absent. Curiously the same effect on motivation is seen in schools and colleges if high marks are felt to be awarded on the basis of favouritism.

McGregor's Theory X and Theory Y

In 1960 McGregor suggested that managers operated under one of two distinctive sets of beliefs. He termed these Theory X and Theory Y (*see* Table 4.1).

Table 4.1 McGregor's theories

Theory X	Theory Y
• People dislike work and will avoid it unless watched. • People must be forced to work. • Typically people prefer to be told what to do.	• Work is as enjoyable as play. • People can organise themselves. • People actively seek responsibility. • The potential of workers is not fully realised by managers.

Theory X is called work-, or task-centred management and Theory Y people-centred management. McGregor believed that Theory Y managers were more successful in achieving organisational objectives.

Motivated staff work well and do not need to be closely supervised in their job role. Leaders can increase motivation or in some cases can do the opposite and demotivate or discourage staff. The management of the organisation needs to provide the type of work environment where employees feel motivated rather than demotivated. This is sometimes a difficult task as the 'culture' of an organisation can sometimes work against the manager. For example, employees may expect to be given orders at all times, or to be constantly reprimanded. There is no secret formula for successfully increasing motivation in employees or changing demotivated employees into motivated ones. It is possible to identify a number of factors, however, which serve as motivators for people in employment:

- the nature of the work itself;
- a sense of achievement;
- recognition of achievement;
- status;
- financial rewards;
- career prospects;
- long tenure of employment (job security);
- responsibility.

Employee involvement

Employees are more likely to feel they are participating in the organisation as a whole if they have some way of being involved in its wider functioning. Examples of arrangements which increase employee involvement are explained below.

Job extension

The nature of the work or job itself is generally agreed to be a major factor in influencing the level of employee motivation. For example, employees cannot be expected to be enthusiastic about repeating the same monotonous tasks day after day. Job extension is a way of making work more satisfying to employees. Two examples of job extension are job enrichment and job enlargement.

Job enrichment

A job can be enriched by giving an employee greater responsibility and scope for decision making. This can be done, for example, by increasing the employee's area of supervision. It can also mean acquiring new skills to meet the new demands of the job. A job extended in this way is said to have been extended *vertically* or vertically extended. The desired effect is to give the employee greater job satisfaction, mainly through a greater sense of achievement, importance and recognition. Not all jobs can be enriched, however, and not all employees are happy to move to positions of more responsibility.

Job enlargement

A job can be enlarged by giving the employee a wider range of tasks but at roughly the same level of difficulty as those worked on before. Rather than being a specialist in one area, the employee becomes specialised in several. The job is said to have been extended *horizontally* or horizontally extended. The desired effect here is to increase the challenge and variety of tasks the employee is involved in, giving a greater sense of achievement and job satisfaction. The employee may also gain a greater understanding of how his or her work fits into the business of the whole organisation.

Job rotation

Where the scope for job enrichment or job enlargement does not exist, job rotation may be applicable. Here employees are trained in several skills at the same level and then exchange jobs with one another at regular time intervals. Through experiencing several jobs, the employee gains a greater understanding of the production process and has less chance of finding tasks monotonous. Job rotated employees also become more flexible between jobs.

Quality circles

As well as attempting to motivate employees individually, organisations may motivate employees by means of groups or teams.

Quality circles are a recent UK development where small groups (typically between five and eight people) voluntarily meet at intervals to discuss matters relating to quality or other work-related issues. Members of quality circles are normally involved in the same work areas. Quality circles have been particularly effective in Japanese manufacturing industries where they have had the following effect of:

- increased co-operation and teamwork;
- increased employee participation and involvement;
- increased job satisfaction and commitment;
- increased quality of product;
- increased speed at which work-related problems are resolved.

Financial participation

The following schemes encourage participation by enabling the employee to share in the financial success of the company. These can be valuable in improving the climate within an organisation so long as the expectation of the benefits accruing from them are realistic.

Profit-sharing schemes

Profit-sharing schemes allow for the employer to pay certain sums to workers in the form of cash or shares, the amount of which is related to the overall profits of the business.

Employee shareholding

Shares can be issued to employees directly or as part of a profit-sharing scheme. Employees holding shares rather than cash are more likely to take a more long-term view of the operations of the company that employs them.

Share-option and share-saving schemes

Employees are granted an option (share option), usually without payment, to purchase shares in the company at present market value. The option may be extended for a certain time period, after which the employee may exercise the option when the shares stand (hopefully) at a higher value. In the UK employees can sometimes be entitled to take part in save-as-you-earn schemes related to eventual share option purchase.

> **ACTIVITY 4.1.3**
>
> Explain why an employee on a profit-sharing scheme might be inclined to work harder than an employee who is not on such a scheme.

Communications

Communication systems can be put in place within organisations with the primary objective of improving efficiency. The systems which form a basis for two-way communication between workers and management will increase the level of employee participation in the management decision process.

Team briefings

Team briefings are a means of communicating with the workforce in a structured manner. Employees are briefed by line managers in small teams on a frequent basis. The objective is to ensure that they are kept fully up to date about the policy of the organisation and how it affects their work. The briefings are usually kept fairly short and should concentrate on the issues management wishes to address rather than be general discussions. It is vital that management maintains control of briefings and for this reason

Element 4.1 Investigate human resourcing

the line manager needs strong leadership skills for briefings to be effective. Timing is also important as information given at briefings has less value if it is not fresh or current.

Joint consultation

Consultative arrangements provide ways in which the workforce can represent its views directly to managers and play a part in the day-to-day running of the organisation. A joint consultative committee is the usual form joint consultation takes in an organisation.

Joint consultative committees exist to provide a two-way communication channel for workers and managers. They usually consist of representatives from management and employees who meet formally at regular intervals. As already mentioned matters for joint consultation usually exclude pay and terms and conditions of employment, but include such matters as, for example, company policy, trade results, health and safety and training. Consultation is purely *advisory* in nature with management reserving the right to make the final decisions. Information resulting from the meetings of the joint consultative committee has to be made easily accessible to the rest of the work-force in the organisation. The goal of consultation is participative management, where employees have some influence over the eventual form management decisions affecting them take. The results of consultation should be a better understanding and improved communication between management and employees which in turn should lead to improved employee relations.

Involving employees via collective representation

In some organisations arrangements exist whereby managers and workers are able to arrive at important decisions *jointly* after bargaining and negotiation. This process is normally carried out on a collective rather than individual basis – that is, employees do not bargain and negotiate separately but rather as a represented group. The name given to this kind of decision making is *collective bargaining*.

ACTIVITY 4.1.4

State the two major differences between joint consultation and collective bargaining in terms of industrial democracy.

PC 4.1.5

Working representation on final decision-taking bodies

In a small number of organisations employees are represented on the bodies that make the highest level decisions.

A worker director is a representative of the employees who sits on the supervisory board of directors of the organisation. The objective is for the worker director to represent the interests of the employees at the top level. Worker directors are a high-level form of worker participation and their presence is generally seen as a great extension of industrial democracy. Examples of worker directors exist in countries such as Germany and Spain, but in the UK worker directors on boards of directors are rarely seen.

Absenteeism and staff turnover

High levels of absenteeism and staff turnover are signs that staff co-operation and motivation are not as high as they should be.

Absenteeism

Absenteeism is deliberate non-attendance at the workplace by employees. It can be measured as a rate (that is, as a percentage of total working time in a year a person (or workforce) is absent), or simply in days absent per year. High levels of absenteeism are a major source of cost and disruption and can damage the performance of an organisation. Employees in the UK are estimated on average to have an absence rate of 4 to 5 per cent – more time off than their leading competitors abroad.

High levels of absenteeism can result in the following problems:

- low production levels;
- missed production targets and deadlines;
- high sick pay costs;
- higher administration costs;
- additional costs to pay for cover of absent employees;
- projects needing to be put back or rescheduled.

A combination of the above difficultuties occurring at the same time can seriously damage the ability of the organisation to perform effectively. Absenteeism, therefore, needs to be kept to an absolute minimum.

There are many possible causes of non-attendance. The factors below may contribute to the likelihood of an individual employee not attending his or her place of work.

Relating to the individual employees:

- state of health;
- inclination towards work – conscientious or 'work-shy'?;
- age – older employees tend to take less time off;
- length of service – employees with longer periods of service tend to take less time off;
- travel considerations;
- family commitments.

Relating to the nature of employment:

- the physical working conditions;
- monotonous work;
- bad management or supervision;
- high levels of stress;
- poor interpersonal relations;
- inconvenient hours of work.

The following factors would be further influences on an employee's attitude to non-attendance:

- financial incentives to attend (for example, an attendance bonus);
- availability of sick pay;
- existence of pay by results or performance-related pay schemes;
- disciplinary policy on non-attendance;
- effectiveness of management in persuading employees to attend regularly.

Controlling absenteeism

An effective set of measures for controlling absenteeism could include the following:

- careful job design to make work more satsifying;
- job rotation to make work more interesting;
- provision of no-smoking areas;
- increased employee participation in decision making;
- smaller working groups;
- allowing employees to work flexitime;
- allowing job sharing;
- accurate recording of rates of absenteeism and communication of records to departments/individuals;
- employee counselling arrangements for persistent non-attenders.

ACTIVITY 4.1.5

PC
4.1.5
4.1.2

Task 1. Consider the following case study based on an article from the *Financial Times*, 28 March 1994.

A CBI report carried out with Percom, a UK consultancy, suggested that absenteeism was one of the biggest blights on UK business, costing employers £13bn pounds a year. Absence rates on average are running at about 4 to 5 per cent.

Nissan Motor Manufacturing (UK), the Sunderland-based car manufacturer, records absence figures of around 1.5 per cent to 2 per cent, less than five days per employee per year, in an industry that has been notorious for absenteeism. Peter Wickens, Nissan's Personnel Director, says: 'I always regard absence as having very little to do with sickness and a lot to do with lack of motivation. Nissan pays everyone from day one of sickness. I think that people who are paid when off sick are less likely to be sick,' says Wickens, who argues that a system where people are not paid when they are off encourages employees to believe that no one loses when they are away. The company's sick pay agreement includes a penalty: if people abuse the system, they are liable to be disqualified from sickness benefit or face disciplinary action. Workers are expected to telephone when they are sick and are asked about their sickness when they return.

Task 2. List the steps Nissan takes to help to encourage attendance and discourage absenteeism.

Task 3. If it were your responsibility as a personnel manager to reduce the level of absenteeism, how would you go about it?

JOBS: The business case for paying close attention to employee issues

Happy workers can generate high profits

Are unions good for business? A question such as this would probably have been laughed off the page 10 years ago, dismissed as absurd in its very naivety.

Yet, according to an academic who has been no stranger to this column over the years, even the most anti-union companies in the US are no longer able to ignore the successes of competitors which have chosen to accept, and even encourage, collective organisation among their employees.

In his latest book, Competitive Advantage Through People, Jeffrey Pfeffer, professor of organisational behaviour at Stanford Graduate School of Business, points to the five top performing US companies between 1972 and 1992 in terms of percentage returns on their shares: Southwest Airlines, Wal-Mart, Tyson Foods, Circuit City and Plenum Publishing. All, he writes, have one thing in common: not a reliance on technology, patents, or strategic position, but in the approach they use to managing their workforces.

Pfeffer was speaking to former students in London last week about potential solutions to the employee malaise that is sweeping the US and manifesting itself in parts of the UK workforce. That there is a deep employee disenchantment in what prides itself as one of the world's most deregulated labour markets was confirmed in a recent survey carried out for President Bill Clinton's commission investigating employer-labour relations. It found widespread dissatisfaction with jobs and mistrust of managements.

Pfeffer was urging managers to consider employment practices which many companies appear to have ignored in the clear-outs of the last few years. Security of employment, union membership, high wages, full-time employees and greater employee share ownership, said Pfeffer, should not be regarded as millstones to competitiveness, but as features that can help define successful companies.

He left some members of the audience wondering if he was preaching a form of corporate socialism. Many of his ideas seemed to conflict with the political dogma supported by most employers' bodies in the US and the UK, Pfeffer however, was advancing a business argument.

In addition to his five top performers, he threw into the pot a few more companies such as Nordstrom, Lincoln Electric and the New United Motor plant of the Toyota-GM joint venture at Fremont, stressing that all had achieved exceptional economic returns in highly competitive and often mundane industries.

Their secret was to pay close attention to the needs of their workforces. A common mistake made by many employers, said Pfeffer, was to confuse labour rates with labour costs. High pay, in both motivating and attracting a more productive workforce, he argued, could be a far more cost effective approach to employment than having a low paid unproductive workforce.

To make his point he offered these 1991 statistics which show that compared to averages for the US airline industry, Southwest Airlines had fewer employees per aircraft (79 against 131) and flew more passengers per employee (2,318 against 848).

Some of the airline's success in the high volume-low cost air travel market involved other factors such as a 5 minute turnaround for aircraft, but even that needed highly motivated and reactive employees to make it possible.

Another important ingredient of the Southwest Airlines formula can be found in its charismatic chief executive, Herb Kelleher, who has a hands-on approach to the business. He is as likely to be found serving in-flight peanuts, chatting to passengers and staff or shifting luggage in the baggage handling bays as in the boardroom.

Kelleher has put a late 20th-century gloss on a discovery of the more enlightened employers of the 1920s and 1930s: that a happy workforce pays productive dividends. As Pfeffer said:

"You can't provide a great customer service if your employees are miserable."

Southwest Airlines, he said, had the lowest staff turnover and best labour relations in the US airline industry and also the most productive people in the industry. Part of this formula is in operating a "fun to be at work policy". This is epitomised in some of its recruitment advertisements. In one Kelleher is dressed as Elvis Presley and the slogan says: "Work in a company where Elvis has been spotted".

Nordstrom, the department store chain, puts a strong emphasis on commissions for staff, but competitors who have introduced similar systems have not enjoyed the same results and some have found that it has led to grievances. The secret seems to be not so much in what is done as how. As Pfeffer observes in his book, the workplace policies of these successful companies have proved difficult to imitate.

Another feature of the company policies he is examining is that many of them are not new. Lincoln Electric's incentive management programme has its roots in a system of elected employee representatives to an advisory board first established in 1914. It also pays well. Some of its most skilled hourly-paid production workers are drawing $100,000 a year.

Many of the companies, including Lincoln Electric, Nordstrom and Wal-Mart, have promotion from within. Many also run their operations with few part-time employees, preferring more committed full-time workers.

Some companies which have embraced union involvement, he writes, have found that union hostility was far less pronounced than might have been expected. When the joint venture between Toyota and General Motors occupied the Fremont plant formerly run by GM, most of its recruits were from the United Auto Workers union, including the union hierarchy that had dominated in the old GM factory. Recruitment was carried out jointly by management and union officials. The selection process included an arbitration procedure to handle disputes over selection.

Employees went through a three-day selection and assessment procedure. All had a four-day orientation programme explaining team working, the production system, quality system, attendance rules, safety policies and labour relations, and job security was formally written into the contract.

All those in production wore the same blue smock and management cafeterias and reserved parking disappeared. Many job classifications were also removed. Instead of inspectors, inspection became everyone's job. The result was that absenteeism fell dramatically.

Another feature, highlighted and supported by Pfeffer is "wage compression", meaning that team leaders earn little more than other team members.

His argument for greater wage compression – creating less of a disparity between the pay of the highest and lowest paid employees – would seem to have lessons in the debate over increasing pay levels for some of the UK's top company chiefs. In his book, Pfeffer argues that where there is no great disparity between lower and higher paid employees, pay is likely to be less emphasised in the reward system and the company culture. In those circumstances, he writes, people are not constantly worrying about whether they are compensated appropriately and attempting to renegotiate their salaries.

Pfeffer quoted a recent survey where employers were asked to list the most important requirements for improving the business. Most place advanced computer technology at the top of their list.

"When everyone has the same computer technology, where is the competitive advantage? We are looking for the technological fix," said Pfeffer, adding: "It's easy to talk about the competitive advantage of people. It's hard to do it."

Richard Donkin

Fig 4.7

Element 4.1 Investigate human resourcing

Staff turnover

Staff turnover is the rate at which employees leave an organisation per year. Another way of looking at staff turnover is to measure the number of employees staying on or being retained (retention rates) rather than leaving the organisation.

A well motivated workforce with a high level of morale should, by itself, reduce staff turnover. Staff who are contented, feel valued and work in a good environment are more likely to be retained.

A certain level of staff turnover is bound to exist but high levels are costly in that recruitment, selection, training and termination have to be carried out more often. It is therefore important that working for an organisation remains an attractive proposition for the employee.

The article from the *Financial Times* of 8 February 1995 in Fig. 4.7 gives an interesting account of the importance of a contented and well motivated workforce to the success of a business.

Self assessment questions

1 Which of these is the responsibility of the HRM department?
   a monitoring an organisation's human resource needs
   b monitoring production levels on the shop floor
   c calculating accurate profit margins
   d maintaining an inventory of physical resources

2 Higher levels of job satisfaction should result in
   a lower levels of absenteeism
   b requests for more pay
   c more people leaving
   d more strike action

3 Which would be the most suitable training course for a departmental manager?
   a full-time Master of Business Administration
   b part-time programme in administration skills
   c short course in reception skills
   d short course in leadership skills

4 Employees can be represented in a variety of ways.
   Decide whether each of these statements is true (T) or false (F)
   (i) trade union officials represent employees
   (ii) employees may elect themselves to represent employees

   a (i) T   (ii) T
   b (i) T   (ii) F
   c (i) F   (ii) T
   d (i) F   (ii) F

5 How might a business improve poor industrial relations?
   a employ all staff on short-term contracts
   b have an employee representative on each decision making team
   c operate a non-trade union policy
   d make sure management make all the important decisions

6 An employee has both a contractual and an ethical duty
   a to be honest
   b to set a good example
   c not to delegate to excess
   d to be nice to colleagues

7 Employees seeking redress for unfair dismissal can take their case against their employer to
   a an industrial tribunal
   b a county court
   c the High Court
   d the Court of Appeal

8 Collective bargaining takes place between
   a trade union representatives and employers
   b an employee and the employer
   c union members and union representatives
   d the government and employers

9 Which of these does not form part of the requirement of a contract of employment?
   a the rate of pay
   b qualifications required for a post
   c the frequency of payment
   d the title of the post

10 Under Health and Safety legislation who is responsible for health and safety in an organisation?
   a employers and employees
   b employers
   c management
   d employees

Element 4.2
INVESTIGATE JOB ROLES AND CHANGING WORKING CONDITIONS

Performance criteria

1. **Identify job roles in business organisations.**
2. **Describe responsibilities for human resources in job roles.**
3. **Explain reasons for changes to working conditions.**
4. **Evaluate change to working conditions.**
5. **Propose a plan for a business implementing change to working conditions.**

Unit 4   Human resources

JOB ROLES WITHIN BUSINESS ORGANISATIONS

Hierarchical roles

Many of the roles in an organisation can be described in terms which relate to the employees' position in the hierarchical structure of the organisation.

Directors

Directors 'direct' the company in the sense that they concentrate on matters pertaining to the long-term direction of the company – for example, planning company strategy, acquisition of major assets, and future manpower requirements. Private companies must have at least one director and public companies a minimum of two. Usually a 'board of directors' is appointed, consisting of a group of directors. Directors occupy the top rung of organisational structures and are directly accountable to company shareholders (the owners of the company). Although not compulsory, directors themselves may often have shareholdings in the companies they direct.

Directors can also be involved in the management of the company on a day-to-day basis. *Executive directors* are directly concerned with the organisation's operations and use of resources and implement decisions relating to them.

Managers

In order for any organisation to operate effectively, a number of key tasks need to be carried out on a day-to-day basis. In a small organisation only a few managers may be employed to carry out the range of tasks involved. This means that each manager will be responsible for a range of jobs and be expected to alternate between them. For example, a manager might be asked to contribute to sales, marketing, purchasing supplies and general administration as and when required. Here the manager's role is a flexible one.

In larger organisations, however, managers tend to be less flexible but more specialised in the type of tasks they perform. A large organisation, depending on its structure, may be split up into many functions. Each function may serve a different purpose (for example, financial control, administration, production, marketing, etc.). Within each of these functions managers will have different roles but they will all be related to the main purpose or activity of that function. For example, sales managers will deal with matters confined to sales, production managers to production matters, and so on.

There will also be several different levels or 'layers' of responsibility within each department. At each layer a different job role exists for the manager. Large organisations usually incorporate the following managerial roles at each layer of responsibility within the organisational structure.

Senior managers

Senior managers, if there are also executive directors, occupy the highest level of an organisational structure. Often as part of a senior management team, they are responsible for setting up policies and procedures. In addition they produce and update the organisation's mission statement, where the main aims and objectives of the organisation

Middle managers

On the level below senior managers, middle managers have the task of implementation of policies and procedures and liaising with supervisory managers. In some cases they may be supported in their role by an assistant or deputy manager.

Supervisory managers

Further down the layers, supervisory managers oversee the day-to-day activities within the work-place and deal directly with workers/operatives. This role is often a demanding balancing act in that they have to implement the directives coming from the managers above them while at the same time maintaining the goodwill of the workers/operatives that they manage.

Workers/operatives

Workers, either individually or organised into teams, are sometimes referred to as operatives, employees, staff, or less commonly, subordinates. Operative job roles will often involve manual work, operating equipment and machinery, or carrying out the more routine tasks and operations in the organisation. Operatives may often be close to the bottom of organisational hierarchies but that does not mean to say that their importance should be underestimated. Directed by management, they are responsible for carrying out the activities that make up the life-blood of the organisation. Although everyone employed by an organisation is technically an employee, the term is often used to refer to those working at an operative level and to distinguish them from those at a management or supervisory level.

Non-hierarchical roles

Other job roles exist within organisations that do not relate directly to a layer within an organisational structure.

Assistants

The role of assistant can be a temporary or permanent one located at any level of the organisational structure. For example, there could be an Assistant Managing Director, Assistant Supervisory Manager or Assistant Operative. An assistant is normally justified when the workload involved in a single job role is, or becomes, too large for one person to achieve effectively alone. The assistant is usually accountable to the person he or she is assisting.

Team roles

All employees, at any level, can be involved in teams. This team role may be permanent, as when it is just another part of the everyday job role, or fixed term, as when it is related to a particular work project. Often a specific goal or objective may need to be achieved, or project undertaken, and a team made up of individuals from across the organisation will be selected to achieve this. For example, a team may be selected from all levels to address the issue of improving quality or updating an existing communications system. The team role in this case will supplement the individual's everyday role rather than replace it, and normally will take second place to his or her main job role.

Representative roles

Staff/trade union representatives are elected by the members of the workforce to represent them and speak on their behalf. They will deal with management directly over issues mainly relating to pay and conditions of service (*see* Element 4.1).

Specialist and professional roles

These staff carry out specialised roles which may go across the structure of the organisation – for example, a health and safety representative or a fire prevention officer. Other specialists may hold professional knowledge or technical skills – for example, accountants and solicitors, or market researchers and systems analysts.

ACTIVITY 4.2.1

Consider the following job roles:

accounts clerk	telephone engineer
computer technician	wages supervisor
machinist	computer analyst
company solicitor	receptionist
marketing manager	market researcher
packer	warehouse operative
director of personnel	assistant finance manager

Decide in which of the following general skills categories each of the above job roles belongs, e.g. a chief executive is managerial.

- Manual/operative
- Administrative
- Service/technical
- Professional/specialist
- Managerial

THE HUMAN RESOURCE RESPONSIBILITIES OF JOB ROLES

Responsibilities for human resources do not end at the door of the personnel department in an organisation. Directors, managers and supervisors all have responsibilities relating to human resource management in their job roles even though their job title may not explicitly state this. In addition to their other responsibilities, in many cases their job descriptions will make direct mention of the human resource responsibilities they have. It is standard for general management development programmes to include elements on managing or motivating human resources.

The extent to which a managerial job role will include human resource responsibilities will vary depending, among other factors, upon the position in the organisational structure the manager holds. The reason for this is that job roles tend to expand and extend as they progress upwards in an organisation. For example, a director's strategic decisions may have human resource implications for the firm's customers, employees, shareholders and suppliers. The decisions a supervisory manager makes may only affect the individual or team that he or she manages. In both cases, however, the responsibility for human resources is an important managerial consideration.

An organisation's managers are concerned with:

- identifying business objectives;
- meeting targets;
- monitoring performance;
- implementing changes in working conditions;
- working with others;
- providing training;
- giving advice;
- disciplining employees;
- handling grievances.

All of the above are parts of the manager's role that involve responsibilities for dealing with human resources. Some of the more important of these responsibilities are described in more detail below.

Identifying business objectives

In some respects the objectives of the business organisation are obvious to all involved with the day-to-day activities of that organisation. Recently many organisations have recognised the usefulness of publishing a comprehensive list of these objectives in a widely available format, however.

Mission statements

All organisations have objectives or goals and strategies for achieving those objectives. Organisations must have a sense of purpose or a 'mission' or they will have a tendency to become directionless. Sometimes the (strategic) objectives are formalised in a written document known as a *mission statement*. The mission statement is defined at the highest level and made available to all employees but in particular managers. Consequently the strategic objectives of the organisation become common knowledge and managers and employees alike know exactly what their collective purpose is.

> **ACTIVITY 4.2.2**
>
> Attempt to obtain a copy of the mission statement of the college/school you attend or the organisation you work for. Evaluate it according to the following criteria:
>
> - how easy it is to understand;
> - how realistic its overall goals and objectives are;
> - how beneficial the statement is to the organisation's public image.

Meeting targets and monitoring performance

Management by objectives (M by O)

The strategic objectives of the organisation are the basis of management by objectives, a technique of managing people first advocated by the 'management guru', Peter Drucker. The basic principle of M by O states that people who know exactly what is expected of them, and agree that it is achievable, are more likely to achieve their objective. The objective set for the individual also needs to be placed in the context of the part it plays in the overall mission of the organisation.

The following illustrates the M by O method. The employee agrees with the manager what his or her performance objectives should be over a set time period. Ideally, these objectives are expressed quantitatively (for example, a percentage increase in sales turnover) and are based on essential tasks involved in the employee's job role. When the set time period expires, the employee and manager meet again to review jointly the resulting success or failure in achieving the objectives.

Advantages and disadvantages of M by O

Advantages	Disadvantages
■ An increase in employee's sense of achievement	■ In practice it may work against some management styles.
■ Targets are set and clarified.	■ New objectives may sometimes be difficult to find.
■ Manager appraises employee on an objective, rather than a subjective basis.	■ Can have the unintended consequence of encouraging selfishness among employees.
■ Makes employees focus on the best way of performing their role.	■ Some objectives are difficult or impossible to quantify.
■ Level of communication is increased between managers and employees and across the organisation in an effort to achieve goals set.	■ Objectives may not match resources required to achieve them, causing difficulties.
■ Raises awareness of training requirements.	■ Short-term goals may become the focus, to the detriment of longer-term objectives.

Performance appraisal

Managers still need to monitor those aspects of an employee's performance that are not easily quantifiable. One method of achieving this is known as the *performance appraisal*. This is basically a formalised judgement on an employee's performance over a period of time. The form the appraisal takes is the same for all employees and is carried out in a systematic manner at a prearranged time. In most cases the appraisal is carried out by the manager that has the most knowledge of the employee's performance, usually his or her line manager. During the 'appraisal interview' the line manager analyses the employee's past performance with the objective of improving future performance. Items on the list for discussion at the interview may include:

- successes and failures;
- achievement and non-achievement;
- strengths and weaknesses;
- rewards and training.

There are usually two areas where an employee has the right of appeal in performance appraisal – regarding who is to actually carry out the interview and, against judgements made on his or her performance during the appraisal interview. A successful appeal usually means a repeat performance appraisal with a different manager, who has the final say on the matter.

Implementing changes in working conditions

Organisations today are often involved in rapidly changing environments which mean that they have to respond by changing themselves. This means that organisations have to be dynamic rather than static, that is, they need to be constantly changing along with the changing circumstances they plan to encounter or experience. This process will almost certainly include changing the working conditions of employees. Human nature dictates that employees do not always welcome changes and in some cases they may resist them. Resistance can take a number of forms ranging from:

- *passive resignation*, which can manifest itself as a loss of interest in the job;
- *passive resistance*, such as a failure to learn, or increased absenteeism;
- to *active resistance* which could involve working to rule, industrial action or even leaving the organisation.

All of the above can damage the effectiveness of the organisation in achieving a successful adaptation to change. As a result the performance of the organisation will not be as good as it might otherwise be. Managers, therefore, have an important role to play in averting resistance to change.

Dealing with change resistance

Overcoming resistance to changes in working conditions can place heavy demands on the human resource skills of managers. Managers are more successful in implementing changes if they ensure the following conditions are met.

- The changes have the complete support of management.
- The change is seen as reducing rather than increasing present workloads.

- The change involves new experience which interests employees.
- Employees do not feel that their security is threatened.
- The change has been agreed on as democratic a basis as is possible.
- Employees have been involved in discussions surrounding the likely problems involved in the change.
- Managers take time to relieve the feelings of fear of those affected by change and attempt to allay them.
- Some provision is made for the fact that many new proposals are misunderstood, such as feedback and discussion points, where clarification can be offered to employees.

Working with others

Two essential elements of every manager's job are working well with others and getting others to work well together. Teamwork has to be actively encouraged as people tend to head off in different directions and go their own way about things. Employees do not necessarily see the advantages of co-operating with one another at first.

There are some factors that will affect how much teamwork goes on. These relate to the structure of the organisation. Getting people to work well together is easier if the structure is an integrated and co-ordinated one, that is:

- the activities are logically grouped together;
- communication lines are short and easily recognisable;
- managers have a workable span of control.

Teambuilding

Assuming a well co-ordinated and integrated structure, managers have an important role to play in building teams. The objective is to build up a united, self-supporting group of people that have a clear idea of where they are going. This type of team may display the following characteristics:

- an informal atmosphere;
- team members listening to each other and feeling free to express their views;
- a fair amount of discussion of tasks involving all team members;
- frank criticism relating to the tasks in hand;
- a leader that does not dominate and is respected on the basis of merit;
- the main objectives and tasks of the team clearly grasped and accepted by members;
- all members feeling involved and demonstrating ongoing commitment on a non-competitive basis.

In the real world a manager would be extremely fortunate to succeed in building a team that displayed all of the above qualities. A great deal will depend on the interpersonal skills of the manager and the availability of good quality staff. Nevertheless, there are measures managers can take to help establish effective teams. A college principal, Howard Green, contends that there are four main strategies that can help to build good teams.

1 *Teams should be properly prepared.* They need clear understanding of the roles and responsibilities of team members, their tasks and targets. In addition they need to know the resources available to them (including training) and how the results of their efforts will be evaluated.

2 *It should be acknowledged that team leadership is a subtle and complex business.* A team's competence to undertake a task may vary widely. The spectrum from low to high competence needs a corresponding range of leadership styles from the directive to the delegating. Most teams will take time to become confident in their tasks. Helpful leaders ensure that enough time is spent on preparation and planning and that the team experiences some early success at the implementation stage. Leaders who either tell the team what to do or undertake most of the work themselves are not helping their team members to gain confidence.

3 *Teamwork will not flourish without an atmosphere of trust.* This applies both within and between teams at all levels. Trust must be generated from the top. It includes a greater openness with information, allowing people more responsibility and taking calculated risks.

4 *It has to be accepted that, in reality, very few teams are perfect for the task.* Strategies are needed to make the best of what is available. The use of a facilitator (a 'fly on the wall' team member) can help to bring both understanding about group dynamics and conflicts that need resolving, and a clearer focus on the task. Although most team members will have strengths to be encouraged, frankness about weaknesses in the team may be necessary. All leaders should have training in interpersonal skills like negotiation and resolving conflict.

Training and development

Training today plays a vital role in the business organisation that demands a flexible, multi-skilled workforce. This kind of workforce can only exist if skills are updated through training. Training should therefore be seen as an ongoing and necessary process rather than a one-off event. Training has a dual role. First, it improves the ability of employees to do the job required of them and enhances their future career development. Second, it benefits employees by increasing their level of job satisfaction. In both these ways better use is made of the organisation's human resources.

When properly implemented and carried out, training can bring the following benefits:

- increased levels of productivity;
- a more flexible workforce;
- good quality output;
- higher levels of morale and greater job satisfaction;
- lower rates of absenteeism and staff turnover;
- fewer accidents.

Types of training

Training can be carried out within the organisation (in house) or outside of it (for example at a college or conference centre). In on-the-job training employees learn, in house, to carry out a specific task or function and are usually closely supervised during the process. In off-the-job training employees attend an agency outside of the organisation to learn or develop skills.

PC 4.2.3

ACTIVITY 4.2.3

For each of the following training opportunities, identify the ways in which this training could be undertaken. In each case prioritise your answer, putting the method you consider the most suitable first and the least suitable last.

- Learning how to use a word processing software package;
- Learning time management skills;
- Studying for a Masters in Business Administration (MBA);
- Learning how to enter data into a database on a computer;
- Learning how to work effectively in a team;
- Learning a European language to use in your work.

PC 4.2.4

ACTIVITY 4.2.4

Some employees are lucky enough to have all their training costs paid for by their employers. Others have to meet all or some of the costs themselves. Why don't all employers pay for training? What are the advantages and disadvantages to employers of doing so? Should employers have to pay anything? Discuss.

Induction training

New recruits to organisations usually undergo a short period of training during which they are introduced to their new environment and familiarised with the workings of the organisation. The aim of induction training is to make the new employee's transition into his or her new job role a smooth one.

PC 4.2.5

ACTIVITY 4.2.5

Imagine you are organising an induction training programme for new recruits to a company. What type of information should the new employees be supplied with at induction training? In what order should it be given to them?

Professional qualifications

Professional qualifications, validated (given status) by professional bodies, are required by those trainees wishing to enter a particular profession. For example, an individual wishing to be a personnel manager would need to train to gain qualifications validated by the Institute of Personnel Development. Employees may wish to study for professional qualifications to improve their position within the organisation. The costs in terms of time and money may be borne entirely by the organisation or the individual may be asked to contribute a proportion of his or her own resources.

Vocational qualifications

National Vocational Qualifications (NVQs) and General National Vocational Qualifications (GNVQs) are qualifications relating to work. Their attainment is based on achieving standards of competence which have been set by industry. NVQs can be gained by an assessment of competence at the work-place and are thus attainable in house. GNVQs combine assessment of competence with exams and aim to be more broad-based than NVQs. Both types of qualification are validated to standards which are common nationally. The qualifications are now well established in a wide range of industries in all sectors. The introduction of NVQs and GNVQs are part of the government reform package for UK training and education.

Fig 4.8

Investors in People

The Investors in People (IIP) award is a government-inspired training award administered and awarded by local Training and Enterprise Councils (TECs) across the country. The award is given to organisations that can demonstrate a continuing commitment to training and developing their workforce. Once an organisation has met the criteria that qualify it for the award it is reassessed annually to ensure it continues to meet the standards required for the IIP award. The case study below illustrates how a small organisation went about becoming eligible for the award.

Giving advice

Managers have an important role to play in giving advice to employees in a number of contexts that can range from methods of dealing with tasks to personal problems. Some managers are born good advisers and others become better with experience. Good advisers need a variety of skills that may require training, including listening and counselling skills. Short courses and a wide variety of literature are available to provide managers with expertise in this area. An example of two areas where good advisory skills are in great demand are the sensitive areas of discipline and grievances.

ACTIVITY 4.2.6

Task 1. Consider the following case study (adapted from *Business* (Oct 1994)).

Fig 4.9

Colin Gregg, administrator of the Yellow Brick Road (YBR), a Newcastle-based children's charity, was asked to consider the Investors in People award by a member of his staff, and on reflection he found two reasons for taking the idea further – the first was the networking with other likeminded businesses that were also putting people first, and the second was that IIP helped identify areas for improvement (although in this case there were few). Tyneside TEC's first visit to assess the charity was in February 1994 and the final one was shortly after in April (which must make it one of the speediest decisions made). It gave a major boost to staff morale when confirmed.

Colin Gregg commented: 'IIP, is what business and the YBR is all about. It is my firm belief that fundraising has got nothing to do with money, but is all to do with people. People give to people.'

The staff at the charity asked Tyneside TEC to help them with their programme when they applied for recognition. The Business Development Team from the TEC, which has responsibility for IIP on Tyneside, saw intensive investment in training at all levels of the charity, whether at the committee stage, the fundraisers, voluntary supporters or permanent and part-time staff. The small team was involved in Open University degrees and public relations and marketing courses. All staff members had been on Total Quality Management courses at Procter & Gamble – another Investors in People organisation – and in-house courses were run for fundraising and training.

The YBR is on target for the £12 million needed to create one of the world's finest children's medical centres, now nearing completion at the Royal Victoria Infirmary in Newcastle.

Task 2. Answer the following questions.
1. For what reasons did Colin Gregg decide the organisation should go for the IIP award?
2. What effect did gaining the award have on staff morale?
3. Why did Tyneside TEC decide to award Investors in People to the charity?
4. List the kinds of training the small team at the charity were involved in? Which of these could be classified as professional qualifications?

Element 4.2 Investigate job roles and changing working conditions

Handling discipline and grievances

Disagreements and difficulties between people always happen and an organisation is no safe haven in this respect. Conflicts can arise for all kinds of reasons – for example, an employee may be asked to do something that he or she feels is outside of his or her contractual obligations or an employee may be absent or late on a regular basis. Grievance procedures enable employees to express their dissatisfaction about work to their managers. On the other hand, disciplinary procedures allow managers to express their dissatisfaction, and to take action, if necessary, against employees behaving in an unsatisfactory manner. Disciplinary and grievance procedures were both explained in more detail in Element 4.1.

CHANGES TO WORKING CONDITIONS

In Element 4.1 we saw that working conditions are included in the employees' contract of employment. The contract of employment, once established, cannot be changed without the consent of the employee. This puts limitations on the possible extent of any changes to existing contracts. Nevertheless, when posts are replaced or new posts created, the opportunity arises for changing the working conditions of the employees. The following list gives examples of some of the areas likely to be affected by changes in working conditions.

- *Permanency of employment*. Contracts can specify that a job is permanent, that is, it is not scheduled to terminate at some date in the future. Currently many organisations are moving away from this contract to *fixed-term contracts* where there is a fixed end date, either in the short or long term when the employment will definitely end.
- *Patterns of employment*. Contracts can feature either full- or part-time conditions on a variety of patterns of employment. For example, a full-time employee may be asked to work a number of *shift patterns*, usually amounting to between 35 and 40 hours per week. More and more employees are offering part-time rather than full-time contracts which normally feature less than 16 hours per week guaranteed work. Shifts can fall at any part of the day or night. A small minority of employers are offering 'zero-hours' contracts where the employee is actually guaranteed no hours at all but is asked to wait to be called in, if and when required.
- *Holiday and sick pay, redundancy terms*. Full-time contracts normally feature holiday pay and sick pay benefits. They may also feature redundancy terms more generous than the government minimum. Most part-time contracts do not feature any of these benefits.

Reasons for changes to working conditions

Business organisations will have many different reasons for wanting or having to make changes to working conditions. Unit 1 analysed the effects of the external environment on businesses. Today's competitive business environment is a global one, forcing many organisations to make radical changes to working conditions in order to remain competitive. Other changes are necessary in order to conform to the requirements of being a member of a trading bloc, such as the European Union.

Unit 2 described the wide variety of business organisations that exist. It is important to bear in mind that although all business organisations may need to change working conditions, the changes they need to make, and the way in which they carry them out, will differ according to the type of business organisation concerned and the structure it has. For example, a small retail outlet run by a sole trader may have far less scope for changing the working conditions of its staff than a multinational company mass producing motor cars. Keeping this point in mind, there are still a few general considerations that can be emphasised with respect to the reasons for changes in working conditions of employees.

Labour mobility

Labour mobility usually relates to the geographical distance workers are willing to travel in order to find employment or to get from home to their daily place of work. Historically, for workers in Britain the distance they have been willing to cover has not been great. Workers in Britain have traditionally been 'immobile' rather than 'mobile'.

During the 1980s, this began to change and research produced evidence of greater worker mobility becoming apparent. There are social and economic reasons for the increase in mobility. The advent of mass ownership of motor cars, concurrent with a massive roadbuilding programme, has undoubtedly been a major contributor to greater worker mobility, even when we consider this against the deterioration in public transport services that occurred at the same time. Another important contributory factor is the mass unemployment that has characterised the British economy since the early 1980s.

Worker mobility during the 1980s and early 1990s has taken two major forms:

Enforced mobility

Some manual, professional and managerial workers expect to have to move to their work, if this is an explicit condition of their employment. For example, site engineers may be employed in North Sea oil rigs or builders on European construction sites. Many workers did not accept such wanderings as part of their career plan, however, but now need to travel widely to find work as there is none close to home. Human resource managers need to be aware that long-distance commuting will be undertaken by some of the professional workforce, at least when faced with local unemployment.

Financially induced mobility

Worker mobility does not have to involve great geographical distance but can also occur between organisations, especially when organisations are competing for a type of worker who has skills and abilities that are in short supply. 'Poaching' occurs when one organisation tempts an employee or employees from another organisation, usually by means of financial inducements. The practice of poaching was widespread between rival firms in the City of London during early 1980s as the financial markets deregulated. Human resources managers needed to consider changes in working conditions in relation to financially induced worker mobility.

Improving productivity

In Unit 5, Production and Employment in the Economy, productivity is discussed. The maintenance of competitive levels of productivity in business organisations is essential to the success and sometimes even the survival of the organisation. Maintaining or raising the productivity of employees is therefore a critical interest of human resource management. Any changes in working conditions that are made need to first take into account the likely effect on worker productivity. Will the planned change result in an increase or decrease in productivity? Obviously, if a decrease is the likely result, then the planned change needs to be either dropped or reconsidered.

Productivity and job design

Some aspects of labour productivity are related to job design. For example, a worker may not be very productive through no fault of his or her own, but simply because the job the employee has been assigned to is structured in such a manner that it is very difficult to improve on the amount he or she is able to produce. It is here that job analysis (*see* Element 4.3) can perform a second useful role in identifying job areas in need of redesign. Poor job design can also be discovered, or indicated by employees themselves, through the system of appraisal by which they are able to review their performance.

Productivity and employee motivation

Labour productivity is inseparably linked to motivation. Demotivated employees are never likely to deliver the competitive levels of productivity required. The effort required to improve levels of production will simply not be forthcoming. All planned changes to working conditions have to make the likely effects on worker motivation a paramount consideration. Changes that might bring about improvements in employee motivation and co-operation are obviously an end in themselves and these were explained in Element 4.1.

Technological change

The effects on organisations and employment of technological change are explained in Unit 5, Production and Employment in the Economy. Technological change is probably the most common single factor causing changes in working conditions in employment today. Positive technological change within organisations cannot take place successfully without the co-operation of employees. We have already seen that in many management roles it is a human resource responsibility to implement changes in working conditions, and encouraging adaptation to new technology is part of that role. Most employees will be less 'technophobic' if they are prepared for the introduction of new technology by the acquisition of new skills through training.

Employing new skills

We have seen above that the introduction of new technology may make it necessary to employ new skills. New skills can be acquired through retraining but in some situations it may be necessary to recruit new staff members ready equipped with the required skills. This can often be the case when the cost of retraining is seen as prohibitive.

PC
4.2.1
4.2.2
C
3.2.1
3.2.2
3.2.3
3.2.4
3.2.5
IT
3.2.1
3.2.2
3.2.3
3.2.4
3.2.5
3.2.6

ACTIVITY 4.2.7

Task 1. Preferably as part of a group, research an organisation and identify five different job roles that exist within that organisation. The organisation can be any size or form but must feature at least five distinct job roles. For each job role describe the responsibilities each has in the following areas:

- identifying and meeting targets;
- working with others;
- training;
- discipline;
- implementing change in working conditions.

Task 2. Preferably individually, explain in general terms why working conditions are subject to change. More specifically, give an example of a change in working conditions that has taken place in the organisation you have researched. Explain in depth at least one reason for the change.

Present this work in a report format, preferably word processed.

PC
4.2.5
C
3.2.1
3.2.2
3.2.3
3.2.4
3.2.5
3.4.1
3.4.2
3.4.3
3.4.4
3.4.5

ACTIVITY 4.2.8

Task 1. Devise a plan to implement change in working conditions in the following organisation.

Putting the bounce back in Sprocket Springs

Sprocket Springs PLC is suffering from a low level of productivity relative to its competitors. Many of its workers are demotivated and see themselves as undervalued by the management. Others are close to retirement and are happy to 'coast' up until that time. This being the case, there is little incentive for the younger employees to work harder and, to compound this, they are actually paid less than the more senior staff members. Most workers are on a full-time permanent contract. The management have stated that the current technology in use in the organisation is out of date and in need or replacement. They plan to introduce newer, far more efficient technology from Sweden. Despite attempts by management to allay their fears, many of the staff fear that redundancies will result from the introduction of the new machinery. The company is in danger of being taken over by a rival organisation, Psycho Springs PLC, if it does not improve performance soon.

Task 2. Outline how you would change working conditions at Sprocket Springs PLC to improve matters. The plan should include the following areas:

- identified goals for the organisation;
- forward planning;
- targets set;
- training required;
- how progress is to be monitored and reviewed.

Element 4.2 Investigate job roles and changing working conditions

Self assessment questions

1 Which of the following would not be appropriate for a team?
   a not to have rules
   b to have a common aim
   c to have a form of communication
   d to be able to identify themselves as belonging

Questions 2–4 relate to the following information:

The following are examples of job roles:
- director
- supervisor
- worker/operative
- manager

Select the job role which you would associate with the following activities.

2 Deciding how an organisation's resources are to be used

3 Making policy and strategic decisions

4 Controlling the resources of an organisation within guidelines

5 Which of these staff has day to day responsibility for running an individual department?

6 The statement that contains the duties and responsibilities of a job is known as a
   a job role
   b job evaluation
   c job analysis
   d job description

7 In a very large organisation who would make major policy decisions?
   a supervisor
   b trade union official
   c team operative
   d board of directors

8 Which one of the following list of jobs can be said to be a specialist role?
   a systems analyst
   b accounts clerk
   c supervisor
   d managing director

9 Which of the following documents will outline the objectives of the organisation?
   a company accounts
   b job specification
   c mission statement
   d press release

10 'Change resistance' is most likely to occur when
   a managers support staff during the changes
   b security is not threatened
   c workers feel they have no control over the situation
   d changes are introduced after consultation

Element 4.3
EVALUATE RECRUITMENT PROCEDURES, JOB APPLICATIONS AND INTERVIEWS

Performance criteria

1. **Evaluate the effectiveness of recruitment procedures in attracting and recruiting applicants.**

2. **Explain how job descriptions and person specifications match applicants with vacancies.**

3. **Produce and evaluate letters of application for clarity and quality of presentation.**

4. **Produce and evaluate curricula vitae for clarity and quality of presentation.**

5. **Practise and appraise interviewer techniques.**

6. **Practise and appraise interviewee techniques.**

7. **Explain and give examples of legal obligations and ethical obligations in recruitment procedures and interviews.**

RECRUITMENT AND SELECTION PROCEDURES

Job applications are made to organisations by individuals hoping to begin employment with, or be 'recruited' to, those organisations. In most cases more than one application for a particular job is received by the organisation concerned and so a process of 'selection' takes place – that is, sorting, narrowing down alternatives and finally choosing the most suitable applicant. This process is often assisted by an interview with the applicant. The selection interview is not the sole method of selection available to personnel managers but remains the most common method in use by organisations today.

The recruitment procedure

Some employees are recruited to new posts that have not existed previously but the majority of employees are employed to replace someone who has terminated his or her employment with the organisation. In both cases the personnel manager has important decisions to make at the start of the recruitment procedure. The following questions need to be carefully considered:

- Who is to be recruited?
- Why?
- What gap will he or she fill and what will his or her role be?
- When and for how long will he or she be required?

When satisfactory answers to the above questions have been arrived at, the personnel manager will be in a position to decide whether recruitment needs to take place at all, and if so, which method of recruitment should be used.

Sources of recruitment

All of the following sources are available to a personnel department:

- internal (within organisation) advertisements;
- external advertisements (including local or national newspapers, trade journals, or minority publications);
- job centres;
- job clubs;
- chance applicants;
- training agencies (for example, Youth Training or Adult Training centres);
- careers service;
- employment agencies;
- management consultants;
- recruitment agencies;
- executive search agencies (sometimes termed 'headhunters');
- contacts with schools, colleges and universities;
- the Higher Education milk round;
- careers conventions.

Element 4.3 Evaluate recruitment procedures, job applications and interviews

> **ACTIVITY 4.3.1**
>
> Imagine you have the following three vacancies to fill:
>
> 1 warehouse assistant;
> 2 credit controller with a background in accountancy;
> 3 trainee accounts clerk.
>
> Using the list above, attempt to identify the best recruitment source for each vacancy. Justify your choices.

PC
4.3.1
C
3.2.1
3.2.2
3.2.3
3.2.4
3.2.5

JOB DESCRIPTIONS

Organisations need specific people to do specific jobs. The purpose of a job description is to help match a suitable applicant to a particular job. The Department of Employment defines a job description as 'a broad statement of the purpose, scope, duties and responsibilities of a particular job'. The description is sent out along with an application form to potential job applicants. However, before a job description can be prepared, the job vacancy itself has to be analysed.

Job analysis

The purpose of job analysis is to help the personnel manager work out what he or she is looking for in a potential employee. Job analysis seeks to establish what the tasks, duties and responsibilities of the job actually are. If this is properly carried out, there is far more chance of eventually matching the right applicant to the vacancy in question. Job analysis involves gathering information. In most cases the information required will be:

- the job title;
- the job's position on an organisation chart showing who supervises, and who is responsible to, the job holder;
- a definition of the purposes and objectives of the post;
- a list of the main tasks, duties and responsibilities that the job holder will carry out;
- details of any special tools or equipment used or required;
- any special circumstances connected with the post (for example, a requirement to travel away from home, keep unsociable hours or unpleasant working conditions);
- information on any special requirement to deal with people outside of the organisation.

The above information can be obtained through an interview with the current job holder or his or her supervisor. This can be assisted by a supporting questionnaire which is talked through with the interviewee. When enough information has been gathered, and its accuracy is established, the next stage is to use it to compile the job description.

Compiling the job description

The content of a job description can be summarised under four headings:

1 *The job title* – put as briefly and plainly as possible.

2 *The person to whom the job holder is responsible and the staff or area for which the job holder is responsible.*

3 *The prime objectives of the job* – in broad terms (for example, one or two concise sentences that explain what the job exists to do).

4 *The main duties, tasks or activities involved in the job* – listed as briefly as possible, and in a single sentence. The aim is to indicate what is to be done rather than how it is to be done. Each of the tasks or activities listed should start with either an active verb or an active verb preceded by 'To' (for example: Plan...; Assist...; Check...; or To plan...; To assist...; To check...).

Job descriptions as outlines

Every description compiled in the above manner will give a broad description or 'outline' of all the duties and responsibilities of the job rather than a detailed list. For this reason most job descriptions used in practice are headed 'outline job description'. A sample of an outline job description for a trainee clerk in a personnel department is shown in Fig. 4.10.

Other uses for job descriptions

The job description is an essential tool of human resource management. As well as providing important information for recruitment purposes, it can also be used in such areas as human resource planning, training, management development, performance reviews and job evaluation relating to salary.

PC
4.3.2
C
3.2.1
3.2.2
3.2.3
3.2.4
3.2.5

ACTIVITY 4.3.2

Compiling a job description requires detailed knowledge of the job under consideration. If you have, or have had, a job yourself, either full-time or part-time, attempt to analyse and then write a job description for that job. If you do not have, or never have had a job, then compile a job description for a student on a full- or part-time business studies course.

PERSON SPECIFICATIONS

After the job vacancy has been analysed and the job description compiled, the next stage is to prepare a person (or personnel) specification form. This is basically a written description of the ideal candidate for a vacant position. The purpose of the person specification is to help the manager decide what type of person would ideally suit the job.

Element 4.3 Evaluate recruitment procedures, job applications and interviews

OUTLINE JOB DESCRIPTION

Post title: Trainee Clerk (Personnel)   **Post ref:** Example 1

Prime objectives of the post
To provide clerical and administrative support to the department as directed by the Administrator of Personnel.

Supervisory/Managerial responsibilities
No supervisory responsibility undertaken.

Supervisory and guidance
Directly responsible to the Administrator of Personnel who will set work priorities, objectives and give guidance on all aspects of the post.

Postholder is expected to exercise some initiative and work to deadlines within established procedures on routine matters.

Responsibilities for assets, materials, etc.
Access to all highly confidential information relating to staff throughout the Directorate, held either manually or on computerised records.

Responsible for maintaining the security of information systems, both manual and computerised.

RANGE OF DUTIES:
To assist the Administrator of Personnel and Clerk in routine clerical duties including:

- sending out of application forms;
- maintaining recruitment files;
- compilation of further information to accompany application forms;
- recording and filing of returned application forms.

To assist in recruitment and monitoring.

To compile and distribute interview/rejection/reference letters, etc.

To complete documentation for new starters, promotions, leavers, etc.

To assist in the administration of the company pension scheme, including the completion of appropriate forms, maintenance of records.

To respond promptly to bank/building society requests for salary/employment details, checking with employees first.

To assist in validating car insurance cover for employees with company cars.

To assist in the maintenance of personnel information systems including the input and extraction of information both on manual and computerised systems.

To undertake general routine payroll work as required.

To promote and implement the company's Equal Opportunities Policy.

To assist in the maintenance of the departmental filing system.

Fig 4.10 Outline job description

The person specification form normally covers six areas of candidate requirements which can be further classified as essential or desirable in a candidate:

1. knowledge and skills;
2. education, qualifications and training;
3. experience;
4. personal attributes;
5. physical attributes;
6. other requirements (for example, age limits, travel, unsocial hours, etc.).

Some person specifications may also feature the terms and conditions of employment for the post. A sample person specification for the post of trainee clerk is reproduced in Fig. 4.11.

PERSON SPECIFICATION

Post title: Trainee Clerk (Personnel) **Post ref:** Example 2

Summary of job: To provide clerical and administrative support to the Personnel Dept.

Attributes	Essential	Desirable
Knowledge and skills	A knowledge of general office work which must include dealing with people on the telephone obtained through work placement or vocational training.	
	Ability to communicate with people in different situations either in person, by telephone or in writing.	Ability to input information and extract details from computer system. Keyboard skills.
Education & qualifications	No specific qualifications but candidates must be able to demonstrate that they are literate and numerate.	Maths and English GCSE at A to C (or equivalent qualification).
Training	Willing to undertake further training as required.	Additional training in interpersonal and office skills.
Personal attributes	Friendly and helpful. Must be reliable, honest and trustworthy. Be prepared to work in a team. Be committed to Equal Opportunities.	
Physical attributes	Only completed when it is necessary for the postholder to undertake strenuous physical tasks or possess specific physical attributes.	
Other requirements	Applicant must be within the age range 16–18.	

Fig 4.11 A sample person specification for post of trainee clerk

Element 4.3 Evaluate recruitment procedures, job applications and interviews

Using the person specification

Person specifications are sent out to potential candidates for jobs, together with job descriptions and application forms. By matching up completed job application forms with both the job description and the person specification, managers can decide on the suitability of candidates for the job. Furthermore managers can determine what potential job holders will be able to contribute. The person specification can also be used to help draw up copy for a job advertisement for the post should it be advertised. Finally, the person specification is a detailed source of information for candidates to the post.

ACTIVITY 4.3.3

Task 1. Drawing up satisfactory person specifications requires some training and a good deal of practice. What are the main skills required for the following list of jobs?

- A word processor operator
- Hairdresser
- Sales representative
- Creche supervisor
- Maintenance engineer

Task 2. Select one of the jobs mentioned above and write out ten points associated with it. Half the points should relate directly to the job itself (which we shall call the job description) and the other half should relate to the skills needed to carry out the duties of the job successfully (which we can call the person specification).

Task 3. Experience is an essential requirement in many jobs and, therefore, important to identify. Suggest how experience can be identified in the job you selected here.

PC
4.3.2
C
3.2.1
3.2.2
3.2.3
3.2.4
3.2.5

LETTERS OF APPLICATION

In most cases, a letter of application is sent by a job applicant in response to a job advertisement. Unsolicited letters of application are often received by organisations, however, from individuals seeking employment 'on spec'. In some cases an organisation may request that a letter of application be returned along with a completed application form and/or a curriculum vitae. In these cases the letter of application is sometimes termed a 'covering letter'. The letter of application contains personal details and other relevant information supporting the job applicant's application for employment. A sample letter of application is given in Fig. 4.13. The job advertisement to which it corresponds is shown in Fig 4.12.

> **GREENACRE COMMUNICATIONS LTD** require a
> **PERSONAL ASSISTANT to the EUROPEAN SALES DIRECTOR**
>
> A knowledge of at least two European languages is essential and knowledge of export sales procedures an advantage. The successful applicant will be self-motivated and be competent in handling telephone and fax messages as well as documentation from French and Spanish agents. Must also be willing to travel to Europe occasionally.
>
> A comprehensive benefits package is on offer to the right individual, including 25 days' paid annual leave. Salary negotiable according to age and experience.
>
> **Apply in writing to:** The Personnel Manager, Greenacre Communications Ltd, 12 Lane Ends Industrial Estate, Bradford BD20 9TL. Closing date for applications 25 February 199–.

Fig 4.12 A sample job advertisement

'Rose Cottage'
Sykes Lane
Bradford BD10 1AY
Tel: 01274 740238
20 February 199-

The Personnel Manager
Greenacre Communications Ltd
12 Lane Ends Industrial Estate
Bradford BD20 9TL

Dear Sir/Madam,

I would like to apply for the post of personal assistant to your European Sales Manager recently advertised in 'The Herald and Tribune'. I enclose my completed application form and a copy of my CV.

The advertised post is particularly attractive to me, since my own career aspirations and education have been specifically directed for the last two years towards an office administration post, particularly in the field of European sales.

In my final year at Sixth Form College I specialised in Advanced level French, Spanish and English. I am now attending a local College of Further Education and have embarked on a bilingual secretarial course leading to a Diploma from the Institute of International Marketing.

The course features intensive study of commercial language (my specialism is French), communication, office administration and international marketing. In addition the Diploma course provides training in shorthand, keyboarding and telecommunications skills. I anticipate achieving good final grades in the June Examinations and have already achieved above average shorthand and keyboarding speeds.

In the course of my full-time education, I have travelled extensively in France and Spain and am familiar with many of the customs of both countries. Work experience placements and assisting a relative in his own small company have given me the opportunity to use my own initiative and develop my business skills, particularly in the areas of sales order processing and customer relations.

If called, I am available for interview at any time convenient to you. My current course programme finishes at the end of June this year and I will be free to take up full-time employment from this time onwards.

Yours faithfully,

Anita Mistry

Fig 4.13 A sample letter of application

Element 4.3 Evaluate recruitment procedures, job applications and interviews

The letter of application in Fig. 4.13 can be broken down into the following components.

- Anita Mistry begins by acknowledging the source of the advertisement, states her interest in applying and refers to other documents enclosed.
- Anita next attempts to establish a close connection between her own career aspirations and vocational education and the nature of the advertised post.
- Anita goes further down this path to draw attention to those particular aspects of her more recent education which she believes have equipped her with a sound grounding for the post.
- In case her prospective employers are unaware of them, Anita outlines the relevant units of the Diploma, highlighting those parts which would be of most interest to her potential employer.
- Anita tries to display self-confidence without over-confidence, and evidence of existing achievement. Since Anita lacks full-time work experience, she points to her travels, and existing knowledge of the countries relating to the advertisement.
- Anita emphasises the practical work experience she has had, and highlights relevant aspects of it which she hopes will support her application.
- Availability for interview is made uncomplicated.
- Demonstrating enthusiasm for the post, Anita points out that she is able to start as soon as her course programme is ended.

ACTIVITY 4.3.4

Study Anita Mistry's letter in Fig. 4.13 from the point of view of Greenacre Communications' Personnel Manager. Decide for yourself whether or not the letter meets with the company's requirements. Give reasons to support your decision.

PC
4.3.3
C
3.2.1
3.2.2
3.2.3
3.2.4
3.2.5

ACTIVITY 4.3.5

Task 1. Making the assumption that you live in the right area and have all the qualifications required for the job, draft a letter of application for the post advertised in Fig. 4.14 on page 326. Use the example given in Fig. 4.13 and accompanying breakdown of the letter for guidance as to the structure and content of your letter.

Task 2. Swap your letter with a partner and evaluate the quality of the letter you have on the following terms: ability to raise interest; structure; tone; style; extent to which it matches the requirements implied in the advertisement. Write down your evaluation, mentioning any items that particularly put you off or attract you to the letter. Try to make any criticisms constructive.

Task 3. Swap back your letters and discuss the two evaluations with each other, other group members, or your tutor. After the discussion, write down any ideas you have as to how your letter of application could have been improved.

PC
4.3.3
C
3.2.1
3.2.2
3.2.3
3.2.4
3.2.5
3.4.1
3.4.2
3.4.3
3.4.4

> **ChildHelp**
>
> A Registered Charity working for a safe future for children
>
> Jansel House
> Ashcroft Road
> Nelson
> Lancashire
>
> **FINANCIAL ASSISTANT**
>
> This nationally known charity requires a Financial Assistant to help our regional groups to put together bids for funding from our central funds. We are looking for someone with relevant qualifications at Level III, possibly with experience of work in the public sector. The successful applicant must be prepared to travel and spend some time away from home. Limited foreign travel may be involved.
>
> We offer a salary commencing at £11 000, and a pleasant working environment, based in our Nelson offices. Application forms can be obtained by writing to us at the address above and further details can be obtained from Bill Green, Personnel Officer.

Fig 4.14 Job advertisement

THE CURRICULUM VITAE

A curriculum vitae (or CV) is a brief biographical sketch of the course of a job applicant's life. A CV can include a wide range of information about a job applicant but generally tends to focus on relevant career information. It is normally up to the individual concerned to prepare and supply his or her own CV. A copy of a job applicant's CV may be requested by an interested organisation in need of an employee or employees. In this case the CV is usually one of the first documents requested. The information contained in the supplied CV is used by the organisation to assist in the selection of suitable candidates for employment. Unsolicited CVs are also sometimes sent out to organisations 'on spec' by individuals in search of employment. In both cases organisations need to be in a position to evaluate the CVs they receive.

ACTIVITY 4.3.6

What is an 'unsolicited CV'? Outline how unsolicited CVs can be: helpful to personnel departments; unhelpful to personnel departments.

Evaluating a CV

In the real world there is no such thing as an 'ideal CV', but the following information describes commonly accepted properties of a satisfactory CV.

Content

When and where appropriate, a CV should always include the contents listed below:

- name;
- address and day and evening telephone numbers;
- education;
- training and qualifications;
- achievements; career history and work experiences;
- any skills the applicant has, e.g. foreign languages.

Presentation

The CV should not be too long – two to three pages of A4 paper at the most. Unless the organisation specifically requests otherwise, the CV should be typed or word processed on one side of the paper only. Good quality paper may impress, although good grammar and spelling are far more important. Folders, binders and title pages for the CV are unnecessary.

Clarity

A clearly laid out CV is obviously easy to read, with each content area (for example, education, or training and qualifications) listed under or next to its own subheading. The information given should be informative and concise and not over detailed. All work experience information should be supplied with dates and preferably listed in reverse chronological order. If exam or degree results are important, then the grades or levels attained for each subject should be included. A short career summary included somewhere in the CV is a helpful addition.

Further tips for evaluating CVs

- The best CVs are those which are specific and give a positive impression about what the job applicant has achieved.
- Be aware of vague words or phrases which everybody applies to themselves, such as 'good communication skills' and the over-use of clichés.
- Look out for unexplained career gaps and other important missing facts. Ask yourself why these omissions exist.

Using the CV

In addition to the evaluation outlined above, the job applicant's CV should be examined alongside the job description and person specification in order to establish the extent to which there is a match between the person applying and the person required for the post. In this way unsuitable candidates are eliminated from the selection process and a 'shortlist' of potentially suitable candidates can be drawn up for further consideration.

Unit 4 Human resources

PC
4.3.4
C
3.2.1
3.2.2
3.2.3
3.2.4
3.2.5

ACTIVITY 4.3.7

Task 1. Draw up your own CV using the information given above as a guide to content, presentation and clarity.

Task 2. When you are happy with your CV, compare it with at least one other person's CV, then pass it over to someone else for an objective opinion.

Task 3. After any changes have been made resulting from Task 2, produce two versions of the CV. The first should be handwritten and the second typed or word processed. In both versions pay attention to quality of paper, presentation and layout.

INTERVIEWS

Interviewing skills are required not only in the recruitment and selection of staff but also in the collection of market research data and appraisal of staff performance. Interviewing in the context of recruitment and selection is an important managerial task because an employer may have to live with his or her decision for a long time afterwards. Reliance on interviews assumes that experienced managers are good judges of an applicant's character and skills, and are able to sum up an individual in an interview that may last only a few minutes. Such a process is fraught with difficulty if the interviewer(s) have never met the candidate before. Prior acquaintance of the candidate, on the other hand, may bias the interviewer either for or against the person concerned. The work of the interviewer is also difficult because no two individuals are alike. For example, some people express themselves far better in writing than in conversation, and factors like this have to be taken into consideration. People whose work requires them to interview candidates for posts should themselves undergo training in interview techniques. For example, effective listening skills and care taken over question choice help to encourage candidates to respond openly.

The informal interview

As part of the recruitment and selection process, both informal and formal interview methods can be used. 'Informal interviews' are occurring far more frequently now in professional practice . They occur prior to the formal job interview and offer the applicant a chance to discuss the job and see the work environment often before making a final decision to apply for the job. Informal interviews also offer the prospective employer (and sometimes prospective colleagues) the opportunity to influence what the applicant thinks of the job and may indirectly shape the shortlist for formal interview by dissuading some candidates from continuing with their application.

Element 4.3 Evaluate recruitment procedures, job applications and interviews

The advantages and disadvantages of an informal interview.

Advantages

- It provides the opportunity to 'sell' the job and the employing organisation by emphasising the advantages of the post.
- It publicises the work of the organisation to a group of potential future employees.
- It can involve a broad range of colleagues in vetting applicants.
- It provides additional information on which to base the shortlist for a formal interview.
- It gives encouraging feedback to good applicants.
- It allows applicants to clarify any misconceptions they may have had about the job and, possibly, de-select themselves.

Disadvantages

- Interviewing can be time consuming.
- It requires careful prior preparation of programme, information hand-outs and appropriate questions.

The formal interview

Formal selection interviews now encompass a range of methods: they can involve one interviewer or several in a panel; they can involve an individual or group of interviewees (those being interviewed); they can entail a number of meetings, sometimes spread over several days; and they can be used together with other selection or assessment techniques, such as psychometric tests.

Preparing to interview formally

Whatever the circumstances, good interviews are well prepared and conducted in a systematic and thorough manner. The decision making and judgement of interview candidates should wait until after all the interviews have taken place. The primary purpose of the interview is to make the best match between the candidates interviewed and the job or jobs on offer. Candidates should be compared with the person specification before they are compared with one another. In most cases the application form or a curriculum vitae for each candidate is available for the interviewer(s) to read well before the interview takes place.

In further preparation the interview organiser should:

- compare the person specification with what is already known about the candidate to establish what needs to be explored more deeply;
- plan questions that probe the candidates' knowledge, ability and attitudes, leaving out questions asking for personal information or views not relevant to the job;
- in the case of more than one interviewer, allocate the questions to each according to subject areas: e.g. job knowledge, training, qualifications, experience;
- be properly organised, making sure enough time is allocated, there are no interruptions and there is someone to greet candidates when they arrive. Unsuccessful interviews are often caused by inadequate preparation.

Fig 4.15 Unsuccessful interviews are often caused by inadequate preparation

Interview technique

An interview should clearly give the candidate the opportunity to do most of the talking. Interviewers should only ask questions, keeping their contribution to a minimum. Obviously the interviewer's first task, given the rather formal setting of an interview, is to encourage the applicant to relax, to speak freely and to perform well.

Here are a number of suggestions which, if practised, will foster good interviewer technique.

- The seating should be arranged so that neither the interviewer nor candidate is at a disadvantage.

Fig 4.16 The seating should be arranged so that neither the interviewer nor the candidate is at a disadvantage

- Start slowly and deliberately, introduce the other interviewers if any are present.
- Make the candidate feel at ease. Aggressive interviewing is not likely to bring out an individual's qualities.
- Give the candidate some background information about the organisation and job involved.
- Start the questioning on areas familiar to the candidate, such as his/her present job. Work backwards to previous experience; then forwards to his/her ideas about the job for which he/she has applied.
- Ask questions which require the candidate to speak freely – those which cannot be answered by 'yes' or 'no'.
- Remember to avoid allowing personal prejudices for or against certain types of person, dress, appearance and so on, to get in the way of sound judgement.
- Keep an eye on the time.
- Take notes discreetly.
- Make sure there is time at the end of the interview for the candidate to ask questions.
- Make sure the candidate is familiar with the more important terms and conditions of employment. Check that these are acceptable.
- Tell the candidate at the end of the interview when to expect to hear the outcome.

Dos and don'ts of interviewing

Do	Don't
■ plan the interview	■ begin unprepared
■ establish an easy, open relationship	■ plunge too quickly into demanding questions
■ encourage the candidate to talk	■ ask leading questions
■ keep to the interview plan	■ come to conclusions too early on
■ probe only where required	■ put too much emphasis on isolated strengths or weaknesses
■ look for strengths and weaknesses	■ allow candidates to gloss over important facts
■ keep control of the timing and direction of the interview.	■ talk more than you need to.

After the interview

Immediately after the interview the interviewer(s) should write up any further notes on impressions gained – in particular, points strongly for or against the candidate. This helps in making the final decision and in the discussions that may take place with others if the decision is to be a joint one. The notes will also help with monitoring the effectiveness and fairness of the procedure.

The selection decision

After any job interview there is always a great deal of information for the interviewer(s) to evaluate. Each candidate has to be compared first with the others, and then on an individual basis to assess his or her suitability for the post on offer. The interview is usually followed by the preparation of a shortlist. For ease of comparison the candidates on the shortlist can then be broken down under the following headings:

Experience

- What experience/openings has the candidate had?
- What are the positions of responsibility he or she has held?
- On what scale has he or she made decisions?
- What achievements have resulted?

Motivation

- What career choices has the candidate made?
- What risks has he or she taken?
- What influenced his or her choices?
- What has the candidate put into his or her career and what has he or she got in return?

Achievements

- What has been a success in his or her career so far?
- What problems has he or she overcome?
- What new ideas has he or she contributed?
- Has he or she tended to be supported or supportive?
- Is there any evidence that the candidate can work on his or her own initiative?

The sources of the above information can include letters of application, application forms, interviews, references from past employers and even selection tests.

By its very nature the interview process must result in more losers than winners. A good interviewer will always select the best person for the job, however. The final decision as to which candidate(s) to select must result in the candidates feeling that they have had fair treatment and the organisation feeling it has secured the best candidate available in the circumstances. Candidates narrowly missing a job who would do well elsewhere in the organisation should have their details kept on file so they can be contacted if the need should arise. Some organisations keep a waiting list of suitable applicants for future jobs. All applicants, whether successful or unsuccessful, should be informed of the outcome of their interview. Through the recruitment process they have had close contact with the organisation and it is in the organisation's interests to ensure that the impression they form is favourable.

INTERVIEWEE TECHNIQUE

There are some people who are naturally very good at interviews, that seem to be able to give a good impression with very little prior preparation or effort. Most people benefit from taking a few measures before their interview, however, to increase their confidence and chances of being selected. The type of measures taken are mainly concerned with *preparation* and *improving interview skills*.

Preparation for the interview

The following measures can be taken to ensure that the applicant is well prepared for the interview.

- *Be aware of information relating to the organisation*. Some helpful information may be supplied to applicants by the organisation itself. Additional background research into what the organisation actually does will also be useful. The information might relate to activities, products or services, size, structure or future plans. Ensure that the information you access is as current as possible.
- *Try to anticipate, and rehearse answers to, likely interview questions*. For example, 'What do you consider to be your main strengths and weaknesses?', or 'Give me two good reasons why I should offer you the job.' The exact anticipated question may not come up in the interview, but there is a reasonable chance that a question of a similar nature could arise.
- *Consider your appearance*. In deciding what to wear, it is a good idea to imagine what the people already doing the job would wear (uniforms aside). To check your decision, ask for an objective opinion from a friend or relative.
- *Be punctual*. This means arriving *on time* rather than too early, or worse, too late. It is a good idea to know exactly where the firm is located, how to get there, and how much time it is going to take. A trial run is a good idea, especially if public transport is being used. On the interview day make sure, before you start out, that you have the telephone number of the organisation with you in case you should be unavoidably delayed.
- *Find out the interviewer's name*. If the information has been supplied at any point before the interview, make sure you are aware of the name(s) of the interviewer(s). Ask the interviewer(s) to repeat the name if you have not heard it before to ensure correct pronunciation.
- *Take your National Record of Achievement (NRA) to the interview* (if you have one). This will be a useful focus for some of the more straightforward initial interview questions. Answering these will help you to relax into the interview.

Being prepared will hopefully increase the level of confidence an interviewee has before the interview. Some knowledge of interview skills may serve the same purpose during the interview.

Unit 4 Human resources

Interview skills

- *Smile* when first introduced to the interviewer and then take the interviewer's lead. For example, shake hands if the interviewer wants to and sit down when asked.
- *Body language* is important. Remain pleasant and try to look interested and enthusiastic. Sit up straight rather than slouch and look at the interviewer rather than the floor.
- *Nervousness* is to be expected at an interview. A trained interviewer should take this into account and attempt to put the interviewee at ease. Look out for signs of this happening. If it does not, then cope as best you can under the circumstances.
- *Listen* to the interview questions carefully. The interviewer may also be assessing your listening skills during the interview.
- *Answer each question as fully as you can*, without being long-winded. Most questions asked will require more than a 'yes' or 'no' answer. Trained interviewers should be able to prompt fuller answers from interviewees. If this does not happen, be prepared to expand an answer of your own accord.
- *If you have no answer to a question then say so*. Do not hesitate or 'invent' an answer.
- The interviewer may ask if you have any questions of your own at the end of the interview. Try to have some in reserve by the end of the interview by logging points you would like to probe further as the interview progresses.
- When the interviewer indicates the interview is at a close, thank him or her and remember to take out anything you brought in with you.
- If you know you want the job, and are offered it there and then, then accept it straight away. You take the risk of it being offered to someone else if you ask for time to think about it. If you are really unsure, then ask for a day to discuss it with your parents or someone else.

PC
4.3.6
C
3.2.1
3.2.2
3.2.3
3.2.4
3.2.5
3.4.1
3.4.2
3.4.3
3.4.4

ACTIVITY 4.3.8

Task 1. How might you go about researching background information on an organisation? Draw up a chart listing sources of information on organisations in one column with corresponding places where this information can be obtained in a second column.

Task 2. Assume you are going to an interview where you anticipate that you might be asked what you consider to be your major strengths and weaknesses. Make some notes on your possible answers. Swap your notes with a partner and assess the notes in front of you according to how well an interviewer would receive these answers. Be constructive in your assessment.

Task 3. A National Record of Achievement is a useful item to take to an interview. Would a completed GNVQ Portfolio of Evidence be useful at an interview? Justify your answer.

Element 4.3 Evaluate recruitment procedures, job applications and interviews

ACTIVITY 4.3.9

Task 1. The following is a group activity. Obtain a local newspaper and select two suitable job advertisements from the recruitment section. Prepare a list of qualities an interviewer would be looking for in candidates for the posts, using the following interviewer checklist to help you:

- Appearance
- Qualifications
- Experience
- General intelligence
- Special skills
- Personality type
- Background

Task 2. Next select two 'applicants' from the group who will need to produce a CV each for the posts and a written letter of application. It will also be helpful if they can be supplied with background information on the organisations concerned.

Task 3. Plan and carry out mock interviews for the posts with group members posing as interviewers and interviewees. The interviewers will need to prepare questions in advance. A panel of interviewers can be used, if required.

Task 4. Ask your tutor to observe and, if possible, record the proceedings on video tape. Then carry out an evaluation of your own performance as interviewer/interviewee, considering the following questions:

a How well prepared were you for your interview?
b How did the interview go?
c What did you think of the interviewer's/interviewee's performance?
d How could things have been improved?

PC
4.3.4
4.3.5
4.3.6
C
3.2.1
3.2.2
3.2.3
3.2.4
3.2.5

LEGAL OBLIGATIONS

The written offer and contract of employment

At the end of an interview an interviewer may offer the job to the candidate there and then. If the offer is accepted, the employer must legally confirm the offer in writing repeating any terms and conditions stated at the interview. This letter must be drawn up carefully as it forms the basis of the contract of employment. The Employment Protection (Consolidation) Act 1978 requires that employees must be given a written statement of their terms and conditions of service within the first 13 weeks of employment. (For details of the minimum contents of the written statement *see* Element 4.1.)

Equal opportunities in recruitment and selection

The laws on equal opportunities and the types of discrimination they protect against are also covered in Element 4.1. Discrimination means the less favourable treatment of a person by reason of sex, marital status, colour, race or ethnic or national origins. In the context of recruitment and selection special attention has to be given to discrimination in the content of job advertisements, job descriptions, person specifications and criteria used to select candidates. They must not discriminate, either directly or indirectly, against candidates.

Lawful discrimination

There are some exceptional cases where the employer may lawfully discriminate on grounds of sex or race. For sex discrimination:

- Where discrimination is unavoidable due to the nature of the job itself, e.g. a female model, a male actor or a male lavatory attendant.
- Jobs in single-sex establishments, e.g. a women's prison officer.
- Jobs where employing more than one sex is prohibited by law.
- Jobs where people are provided with personal education or welfare services that are most effectively provided by a person of a particular sex, e.g. an adviser to battered wives.
- Employment carried out mainly or completely outside of the UK.
- Jobs in private households where the degree of contact with the occupants might reasonably cause objection to the employment of a person of a particular sex.

The exceptions for racial discrimination are:

- Where discrimination is unavoidable due to reasons of physiology, e.g. Indian model, authenticity, e.g. French actress, or to help contribute to a special ambience in an ethnic restaurant, e.g. Chinese waiter.
- Jobs where special personal welfare services are provided for a racial group and these can be delivered most effectively by someone from that racial group.
- Employment carried out mainly or completely outside of the UK.

ETHICAL OBLIGATIONS

Ethics in organisations relate to knowing the difference between what is right and what is wrong and actively pursuing policies which encourage correct practice. This means doing what's right, not simply due to legal obligations or as part of a public relations exercise, but for *its own sake*. For example, equal opportunities policies are practised in recruitment and selection because they are the fairest way of doing the job. Similarly, job applicants are supplied with honest and accurate job descriptions and person specifications and are trusted to have given information honestly in their application forms and during interview. Furthermore, the organisation is expected to act objectively in its dealings with

Element 4.3 Evaluate recruitment procedures, job applications and interviews

its employees, rather than on a basis of favouritism and prejudice. Ethical practices prevent distrust of the organisation from growing among employees and also encourage employees themselves to remain honest and loyal to their employer.

ACTIVITY 4.3.10

Task 1. Consider the following from the *Financial Times* article of 5 January 1994.

Small businesses place a far higher value on honesty, integrity and enthusiasm for the job when recruiting young people and are less worried about work experience or vocational and academic qualifications, stated a recent report. The study's findings, reported at the British Psychological Society's occupational psychology conference in Birmingham, appeared alongside other research which showed that managers preferred job applicants to admit their mistakes at an interview rather than blame their failings on others.

Many companies in the study were happy to recruit from initial telephone enquiries or a knock on the door, rather than insisting upon written applications. Job selection was based typically on a single unstructured interview. 'The smaller the employer, the more they seem to rely on gut reaction and first impressions,' said Professor David Bartram of Hull University, who headed the study.

Task 2. What are the main differences between the attitudes to recruitment of those companies in the survey and the attitudes you would expect from the staff of large multinational companies.

Task 3. Why do you think honesty is ranked so highly by employers?

PC
4.3.1
4.3.7
C
3.2.1
3.2.2
3.2.3
3.2.4

Self assessment questions

Questions 1–3 share answer options A to D

The persons conducting an interview will assess an interviewee by some of the following:

A assertiveness
B listening ability
C body language
D preparation

Which of these would be shown by an interviewee in the following circumstances?

1 An ability to answer precise questions accurately

2 An ability to stand up to cross-examination

3 Some knowledge of the recruiting organisation

337

4 Which of the following would need to be done before a job description is drawn up?
   a revise the level of salary
   b shortlist the candidate
   c advertise the post
   d carry out a job analysis

5 The main use of a curriculum vitae (CV) is:
   a to help candidates prepare for job interviews
   b show how suitable a candidate is for a vacancy
   c test the candidate's level of skills for a job
   d get an idea of a candidate's long term career plans

6 At a job interview a good applicant will:
   a be aware of the importance of their body language
   b avoid eye contact if they can
   c interrupt the interviewer when they feel like it
   d state that some changes need to be made to the organisation's procedures

7 Which of the following is most likely to be the first stage in the recruitment process
   a reviewing the salary
   b drawing up a job description
   c analysing the requirements of the job vacancy
   d advertising the job

8 A good letter of application should be
   a a letter written specifically for the job for which the person is applying
   b a short covering note sent with the job description
   c a general statement which can be used for any job application
   d an in-depth history of the job applicant's life, qualifications etc.

9 The main function of a job description is to provide details of
   a the salary for the post
   b the tasks and duties involved in the post
   c the person who had the post last
   d the personal attributes required for the post

10 A statement providing a profile of the 'ideal candidate' for the job is a:
   a job description
   b person analysis
   c person specification
   d job analysis

Answers to self-assessment questions

Element 4.1	Element 4.2	Element 4.3
1. a	1. a	1. b
2. a	2. d	2. a
3. a	3. a	3. d
4. b	4. c	4. d
5. b	5. b	5. b
6. a	6. d	6. a
7. a	7. d	7. c
8. a	8. a	8. a
9. b	9. c	9. b
10. a	10. c	10. c

UNIT 5

PRODUCTION AND EMPLOYMENT IN THE ECONOMY

In this unit the 'production' of goods and services will be discussed, in terms not only of manufactured output, but also of primary production (such as oil and agriculture) and services (such as banking and catering). In addition, changes in employment strategies will also be covered particularly in relation to the need for improvement in the international competitiveness of industry.

Element 5.1
ANALYSE PRODUCTION IN BUSINESS

Performance criteria

1 **Identify added value in production and ways to achieve added value.**

2 **Explain why businesses aim to add value.**

3 **Identify and give examples of factors which can contribute to change in production.**

4 **Analyse improvements in production.**

Introduction

The concept of added value is central to any study of business and the workings of the market. In this element we discuss ways to achieve added value and why business seeks to add value and we analyse the factors affecting the ability of a business to do so. Improvements in production are identified and their effects analysed.

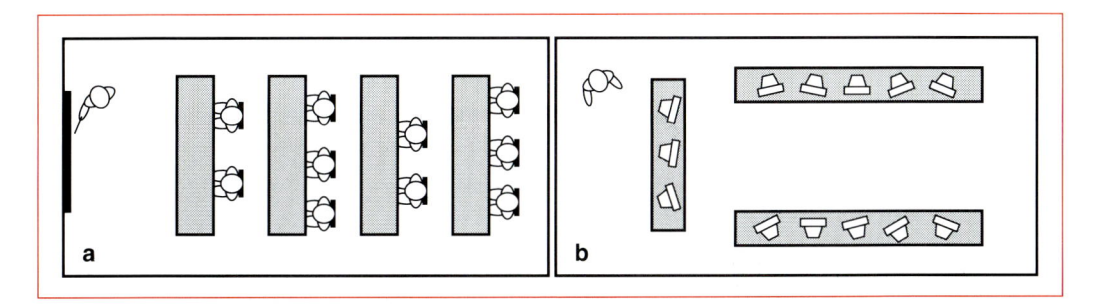

Fig 5.1 (a) Old technology – where is the learning? (b) New technology – where are the students?

THE PURPOSE OF ORGANISATIONS

Organisations only exist to fulfil human needs. If they fail to serve people, they are irrelevant. Different types of organisation exist to satisfy differing human needs. It is only their success at doing so that ensures their survival. To make life more complicated, human needs (and wants) change over time. There are many types of wants and many forms of organisation have developed to meet these wants. These range from governments to satisfy the wants of security and co-ordination, to hospitals that satisfy our need for health care, to commercial organisations that provide for our material desires.

Organisations arrange themselves to best fulfil these demands. They are not always successful, nor do they always respond quickly enough to changes in wants. In these instances they are replaced.

It is difficult, however, for organisations to have 'satisfying human wants' as their central goal; they need targets that can be measured, which will reflect the success of the organisation at satisfying the wants. It is then possible to manage the organisation with the aim of achieving the measurable targets. A need for change in organisational behaviour would then be highlighted by the gap between the operating targets and actual performance.

For commercial organisations, the key target is profit. This is a measure of the success of the company in satisfying customer wants and doing so efficiently. For other organisations, different targets may be appropriate. For example, in education, the targets may relate to the number of students successfully completing their course. Other examples are: for a job centre, the number of people who become employed; for a hospital, the number of patients treated and so on. In each case there is a difference between the inputs (what goes into the organisation) and the outputs (what the organisation produces). If we can find methods of measuring these, then we can measure the value of the organisation to society. We will find that measurement is not easy, however.

THE VALUE-ADDED METHOD

One approach to measuring the performance of an organisation is the value-added method. We can define *added value* as the difference between the cost of producing a product or service and the price that the customer is willing to pay. This we cant treat as a sum (or equation):

Added value = (Revenue from sales − Cost of production) − labour costs

where   Sales revenue   = price paid by customer multiplied by quantity sold
          Costs of production = fixed costs (i.e. those that do not change as the level of production changes, e.g. buildings, management and machinery costs) plus variable costs (i.e. costs incurred directly in production, e.g. raw materials, energy and labour costs).

Another way of saying this is:

Added value = Total revenue – (Total costs – labour costs)

We can convert this to an algebraic form:

AV = TR – (TC – LC)

Figure 5.2 illustrates the concept of added value with relation to where the surplus comes from.

Raw Materials + Product Process = Value added

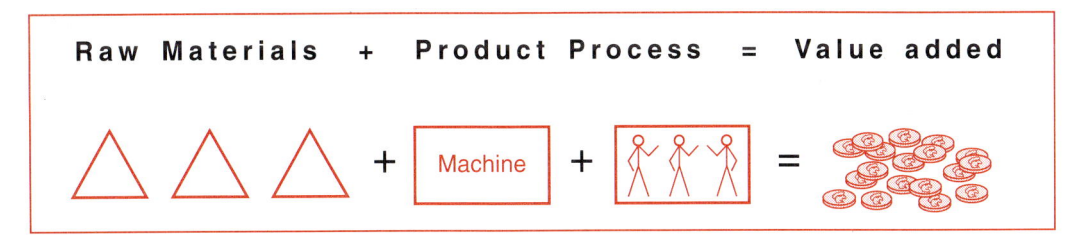

△ △ △ + [Machine] + [👥] = 🪙

Fig 5.2 Value added

There are two ways of calculating value added
1. The cost subtraction method:
   Value added = sales revenue – (bought in components + bought in materials + energy + services)
2. The appropriation model:
   Value added = wages + taxes + retained profits + distributed profits + depreciation + interest

In addition to production costs, there are additional costs associated with distributing the product. These often have the effect of raising sales revenue, however. We will consider these under marketing activities.

Added value is the source of companies' profit. In the western world, profit is the main motor of industry. Profit is necessary to provide shareholders with dividends, that is, compensation for providing the funds that industry needs. Profit also provides the money necessary for research and development. Finally, value added is the source of funds for wages and salaries. Figure 5.3 illustrates where the surplus of funds goes to.

In short, to add value, businesses must operate policies of maximising the price and/or quantity that customers are willing to pay and reducing costs. This is done by implementing some or all of the following policies.

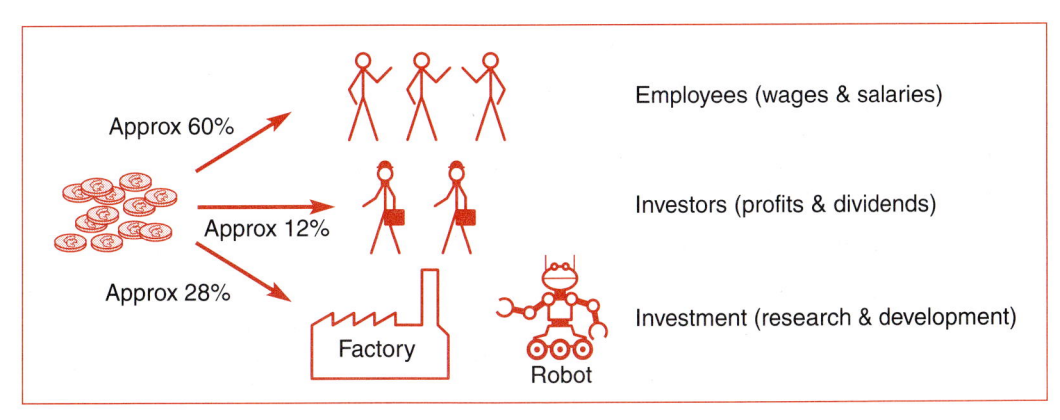

- Approx 60% → Employees (wages & salaries)
- Approx 12% → Investors (profits & dividends)
- Approx 28% → Investment (research & development)

Fig 5.3 Distribution approach to value added

Maximising price

The closer a business can match its product or service to each customer's exact wants, the more that each customer is going to be prepared to pay.

To match products to needs, it is necessary to identify what the customer, and potential customers, actually want – *market research*. After identifying consumer wants a business must design a product or service that meets those wants.

Customers do not buy a product or service simply for its apparent use. For example, the purchase of detergent is not made simply to clean clothes. There are other considerations such as the need for a consumer to maintain a satisfactory self-image. There are many aspects to the problem of maintaining self-image. Examples are:

- *Technology buffs*. Some consumers believe that it is important to own the very latest new technology. They are willing to pay very high prices if their friends are impressed. Thus it is not just 'newness' but also status that affects their purchase decisions.
- *Status concerns*. Consumers are often interested in the statement that a particular purchase makes about them as individuals. The recent increase in the demand for sports boots instead of training shoes is an example. There is a positive preference for higher priced products. Similar concerns are seen in perfumes and other items of personal grooming.
- *Conscience concerns*. Following the upsurge in interest in the environment, many consumers are now prepared to pay higher prices (premium prices) for goods that are seen as environmentally friendly (toilet rolls are the current popular example). The concerns may spread to the exploitation of third world people, however. Companies seen as unethical may suffer a consumer boycott; some already have.

Developing a positive 'corporate image'

Companies also face a problem in that consumers find it difficult to know about the advantages of products in the market. Most consumers are at a disadvantage when it comes to product knowledge. This is especially the case with long-term purchases. Since the cost of a mistake can be high, they rely on the reputation of the company as much as, if not more than, information provided. A company that loses its reputation for fair dealing, even if unjustified, is a company with major problems. Recent examples include the jewellers, Ratners, and the private pension companies.

It is the duty of the marketing and public relations departments to secure the desired perception of the organisation. There are several methods of achieving this but the most important cultivating relationships with the mass media. The process is known as *corporate advertising*.

The media are a powerful source of information for the public. Purchasing decisions are made on more than price and a firm's bad reputation can affect sales. A poor reputation can stem from many sources.

Before recent developments in South Africa, many British firms faced censure for their involvement or their employment practices in that country. In the case of Barclays Bank, this lead to a long running boycott organised by the National Union of Students. This affected Barclays recruitment of student accounts. In the early 1980s British Leyland had a reputation, spread by the media, for poor quality. Perhaps the most spectacular case was Gerald Ratner's incautious comments about the quality of his company's products that eventually lead to the name of the company being changed.

Not only the quality of the product is an issue. If a company gets a reputation for poor employee relations, either by being unfair or through reports of industrial action, this can affect its sales and hence its success. Many large companies, in particular, use corporate advertising to enhance their public image. Examples include British Telecom (BT), Hanson, National Power, and Shell.

Controlling quality

'A key development over the past 20 years has been the growing importance of the reliability of the product. Consumers now expect and demand much greater reliability than before. Companies that fail to deliver lose markets, sometimes extremely quickly. This concentration on reliability is often referred to as 'quality'. In the car industry the concept is known as 'build quality'. Currently Japanese companies in the car and consumer electronic industries have the strongest reputation for quality. The system they use is called 'kanban'; it involves not only quality assurance but also a lifetime working contract. This has enabled Japanese companies to secure the highest levels of reliability. In this respect they have even displaced some German companies.

UK firms have learned from the Japanese (as have American companies), particularly so where UK firms have acted as suppliers to Japanese car and electronics plants. The Rover Group has also learned from its extensive collaboration with Honda.

The Single European Act and quality assurance

Within the European Union there have been other developments under the Single European Act. This Act is intended to create a single market throughout the Union. One of the provisions was for the creation of a European standard for quality assurance – the IS9000 standard. The British Standards Institute developed a UK equivalent known as BS5750. If firms wish to tender for certain public sector contracts, they must have gained one of the two standards. Since 1993 there has been a recognition that BS5750 and IS9000 are not appropriate for all types of organisation (particularly those in the public sector) and the Investors in People standard has been created.

Right-first-time

Firms are realising that, if you avoid mistakes in production, then you can both increase reliability to the customer and reduce costs. The savings on repair and correction are high. Furthermore, the reputation of the company is enhanced.

Clearly it is the direct workforce that is critical in the achievement of 'quality' – it is necessary to get the workforce to seek quality. Standard motivation theory (that is, what makes people tick) tells us that involvement is the key to changing attitudes. Many companies have now involved their workforce in monitoring and improving quality of product. They often use small teams of involved workers and supervisors known as 'quality circles'. These discuss and decide what to do about problems in production that are affecting quality. Sometimes companies run suggestion boxes with prizes for ideas from staff that improve work practices.

The US giant, Microsoft, operates a suggestion system based on electronic mail. This enables employees to contact any relevant member of staff directly. It also allows ideas to be developed by added comment. Bill Gates, the founder of Microsoft, writing in the *Guardian* newspaper stated that all employees were expected to contribute ideas. Although there were not large rewards, each suggestion was recognised and, if adopted, presentations made to the employee.

Examples of companies using a quality circle approach include Nissan, Toyota, Samsung, Rover, Ford, British Gas, etc.

Supply management

The need to improve quality has lead to the development of new relationships between companies and their suppliers. It is now common for companies to both monitor and help to improve the quality of bought-in components. Although the price of components is still important, this is now seen as one item in a list of considerations which includes the following:

- specification achievement (the goods are as ordered);
- delivery schedule (the flexibility of delivery);
- response time (the ability of the supplier to react to changed orders);
- reliability (consistency);
- price.

Assembly companies, such as the car manufacturers and British Aerospace, have increasingly been moving to a system of single preferred supplier. Instead of using competition to drive down the cost of component supplies, the companies now value consistency and quality more highly. In many respects this is a reversal of the doctrine of the 1960s and 1970s when the rule for purchase managers was never to become dependent on a single supplier. At the time there were more significant problems with industrial disputes and over-reliance did present real dangers. The diminished power of trade unions to inflict damage on customers of firms in dispute has made the system of single preferred supplier possible.

Given the importance of reliability, companies must take responsibility both for their own production and for that of their suppliers. A customer is not impressed by excuses like 'It was not our fault'. Even rigorous testing of goods received does not always expose problems. This has led to companies that trade on reliability introducing customer surveys. They then use the reports they receive to identify and cure problem components.

In 1994 Jaguar cars found that their headlight bulbs had a high failure rate once the cars were in use. Even though the headlights were supplied by a components company, Jaguar's management decided that it was 'their problem'. To solve the problem, Jaguar seconded a team of engineers to the supplier who helped to redesign both the product and the manufacturing process.

Many companies have now changed from a contractual to a relationship base for their dealings with suppliers. This involves granting long-term contracts. Suppliers then have certainty of orders and this means that it is worthwhile for them to concentrate on improving production facilities. There is some assurance that the investment will not be wasted by the loss of a contract.

Marks and Spencer, the retail giant, now has joint access to its clothing suppliers' computers. This enables M&S to know whether they can meet additional contracts. The information system allows Marks and Spencer to access sales data on a daily basis and use this to establish re-order quantities. Instant reaction to changing sales patterns is possible. This means that M&S does not carry unsaleable stock; suppliers do not continue to produce unsaleable stock; and suppliers' production lines can be varied to produce the goods that are selling. This more efficient use of stock and sales area allows M&S to be more competitive on price.

Controlling costs

Across UK industry 64 per cent of all costs are labour costs. This is, therefore, the area of cost that is most critical to control. In the majority of industries, reducing wage costs is the only effective way to reduce costs. (Some firms have a lower proportion of labour costs and for these there are other issues, notably the control of capital costs or the issue of controlling raw materials usage which includes energy use.)

Labour costs have two components:

- number of employees, and
- average salary (or wage).

The number of employees in an organisation is determined by the complex relationship between the demand for the product of the company and the structure of the company. The company structure itself will be a response to the operating conditions of the market and of local customs.

Reducing wage rates

Wage costs can be brought down by *either* reducing wage rates or by increasing the amount produced by each worker, or by implementing some combination of the two. An example of introducing lower wage rates is the privatisation of public sector manual jobs, especially in the semi-skilled and unskilled areas, such as cleaning, refuse collection, etc. Alternatively, some employees have been willing to accept wage freezes or even cuts to help stave off redundancies or even the bankruptcy of the firm. One example of this was Leyland Daf trucks in March 1994.

Wage rate cuts must be introduced with caution. A firm attempting to impose wage cuts is likely to lose goodwill and motivation, which in turn lead to lower productivity.

Any attempt unilaterally to vary the conditions of employment of an employee leaves a firm open to charges of 'constructive dismissal'. In such a case an employee is entitled to redundancy payment. The loss of key workers could lead the firm to even greater problems.

In the long run, wage cuts are unlikely to secure a firm's competitive position. For example, wage rates in newly industrialising countries (NICs) and eastern Europe are far below those in the UK.

Improving productivity

The two major sources of increases in productivity are *training* (discussed later in this unit) and *the introduction of new machinery* to increase output – i.e. investment. One of the notable features of new machinery since 1980 has been the application of information technology (computers) to control machine processes, e.g. the so-called robots in car manufacture. Microelectronics has had far-reaching effects in a whole range of industries. For example, in the tourist industry the use of computers allows hotels and airlines to monitor 'real-time' occupancy rates. This enables them to offer discounts on a case-by-case basis to make sure that all seats or rooms are booked. Computer technology has revolutionised the banking industry, and the developments are continuing with the growth of 'telephone' and 'home' banking. Stock control in the retail sector has also been transformed with the use of bar code readers at checkouts which allow instant analysis of sales patterns and the automatic re-ordering of goods. These are noticeable at any large supermarket and all goods are now produced with a bar-code strip regardless of whether the shop has a reader.

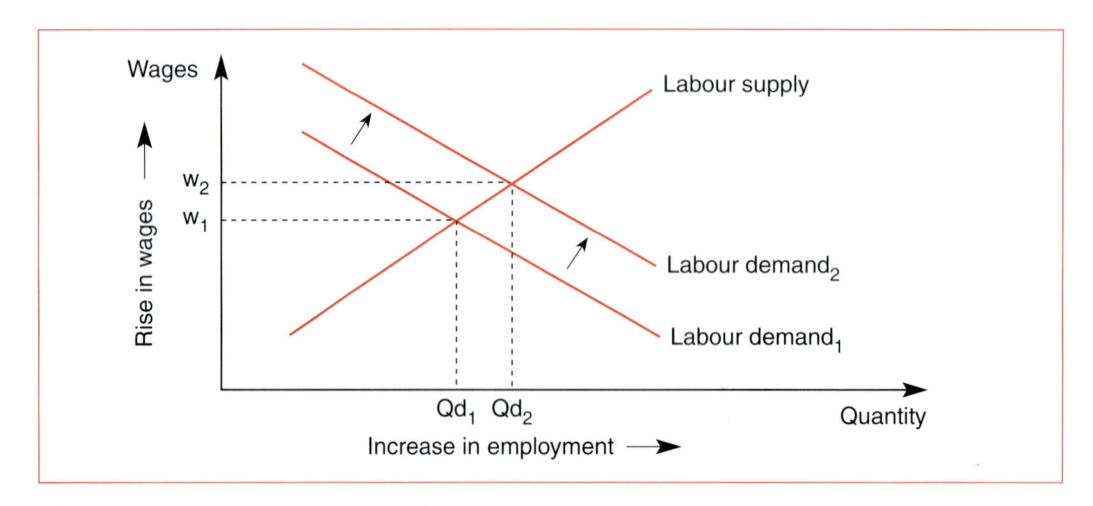

Fig 5.4 Effect of increased labour productivity

Just-in-time production

In manufacturing the use of computers has encouraged the growth of the system known as 'Just-in-time' production (JIT). The falling cost of computer memory has enabled even the smallest firms to use computers. The main advantage is the ease of information storage, processing and retrieval, allowing the more efficient use of resources. Previously stocks of raw and semi-processed materials had to be kept as an insurance against 'unforeseen' occurrences. Now, business is more predictable, not only within the firm but also outside it. Companies can now access information from both their suppliers and customers. This in turn means that firms can manage their delivery flow to meet individual customers' requirements just when they want them.

The savings to suppliers arise from the reduced need for 'working capital'; that is resources tied up in stock. This saves on borrowing charges and means that financial resources are working, not lying about as idle stock. Another feature of JIT is the use of computer-aided design and manufacture (CAD/CAM) to reduce the period from conception of a product to actual production. The Japanese car firm, Honda, reduced the time for model changes from the industry average of four-plus years to two-minus years by the use of these techniques.

JIT and CAD/CAM also enable flexible production. It becomes possible to vary the output of mass production facilities, unlike the early days of Henry Ford when customers could have any colour car so long as it was black – there is now much greater capacity for individualisation. This flexibility of production has led management and economic theorists to coin the term, *post-Fordism*.

A closely related issue is the ability of large-scale manufacturers to co-ordinate production across national frontiers. This permits firms to locate production facilities in areas that have cost advantages. For labour-intensive operations, firms locate processes in low-wage countries; high-technology operations may be situated near universities, for example, 'Silicon Valley' (near the University of California) and the Cambridge Science Park.

Labour productivity is essential to long-term success. The process of improving productivity requires constant innovation in production methods which in turn requires the adoption and adaptation of new technology. There are implications for both employees and managers: for the former, old skills and habits become obsolete, old jobs disappear and there is a constant pressure to update and develop new skills; for the latter, the need is to scan constantly the wider environment both of competitors and technology for innovations that can lead to advantage. There is also the need to change relationships with employees, especially in the case of 'quality' issues.

Maximising quantity sold

Increasing the number of units sold of a product can clearly be achieved in some cases by reducing the price of the product. Depending on the elasticity of demand (*see* Unit 1), however, this may reduce revenue not increase it.

An important issue for customers is the ability to buy *what* they want *when* they want. This requires that companies offer a wide range of products. By offering the consumer a choice of options a company increases the probability that the consumer will buy. Range here covers both specification (colour, performance, etc.) and price. Even if a company produces the required product or service, it may lose the sale if the product or service is not immediately available. It is possible that customers will wait but the risk of losing the sale is not to be taken lightly. Companies have two ways of ensuring products are available:

- Holding large stocks of finished goods so that they are always ready for the customer;
- Ensuring flexibility of production so that rises in demand can be monitored and reacted to before stocks run out.

In either case the company must control the flow of goods to the buyer, that is, it must have a distribution network.

The Ford Motor Company operates a system of licensed dealers. These are franchised operations. The dealers – the people who acually sell the cars – usually have an exclusive contract with Ford. They are computer linked to Ford's system which allows them to order both from Ford and from any other dealer in the network that has the required car. This means, if a customer wants a metallic green Escort 1.6 Injection model, the dealer can have it delivered in days, not weeks. Large supermarket chains, such as Tesco and Sainsbury's, operate central warehousing facilities capable of 24-hour (or less) response to orders from branches.

An additional advantage to the company of increasing quantity of sales is that the fixed costs of production are spread over more items reducing the average fixed cost per item. This gives firms an extra benefit: the reduction in average unit cost, if not reflected in a reduction in price to the customer, leads directly to higher profits. In the jargon of business it 'feeds straight through to the bottom line'.

Remaining competitive

Competition is defined as the actions of rival firms in the same market. In the short run, competition may mean price cutting behaviour by rival firms. Unless the price cuts are supported by lower costs of production, however, they cannot last. Only if the price reductions force some firms out of the market, so that the survivors have a larger market, share, can they be sustained. Pricing designed to ruin competitors is subject to regulation by the Monopolies and Mergers Commission in the UK and by the European Commission in the European Union. If firms are found guilty of such practices, known as *predatory pricing*, they can be ordered to pay compensation and/or be fined.

Competition is a process of product and process innovation. What is true for one firm is true for all. It is irrelevant whether the competitor firm is based in the UK or overseas – competition is competition. It is of significance only if a foreign company has some additional advantages, such as access to cheap labour.

The product life cycle is covered in detail in Unit 3. With the introduction of new technologies, the lifespan of any existing product, i.e. the period in which the product sells, is shortened. In each case, the length of time from introduction to withdrawal is reduced. Figure 5.5 shows the product life cycle of various forms of music software and highlights the changeover from one type of music software to another. 'Vinyl' LPs were dominant for 30 years. Cassettes lasted approximately 15 years and CDs have only existed for the last ten years. The diagram shows the period from introduction to maturity. As each new product is introduced, there is a decline in sales of 'older' products. The decline in sales motivates companies to introduce new goods.

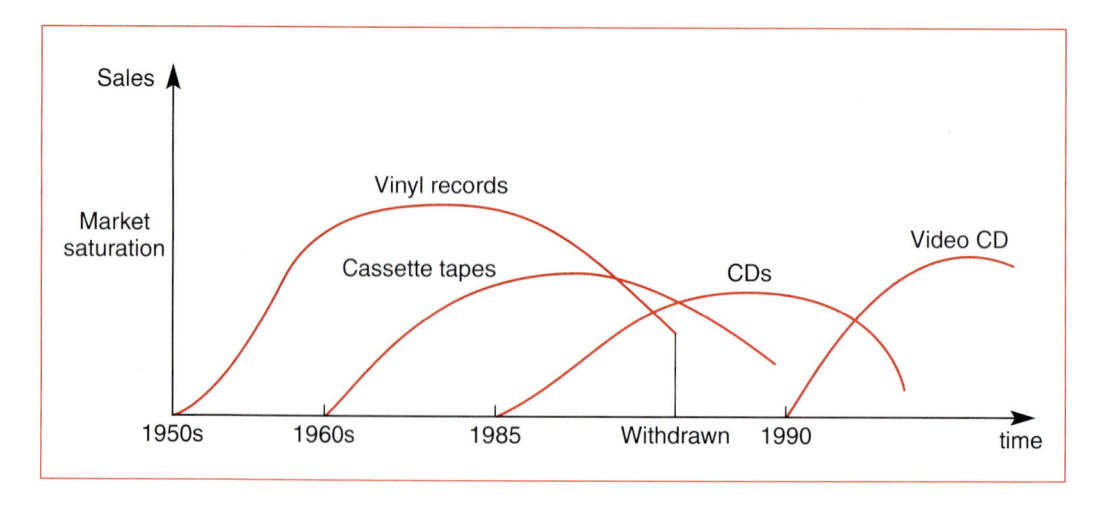

Fig 5.5 Product life cycles for consumer music software

Element 5.1 Analyse production in business

ADDED VALUE AS A MEASUREMENT OF PERFORMANCE

The success of various industries in generating value added is shown by the diagram in Fig. 5.6. Oil and gas are by far the most effective but this is misleading. Both these industries have very high levels of capital investment and the major period of employment lies in the exploration and development phase. Once constructed, the level of employment falls. The ratios for more labour-intensive industries are more relevant. Note the low added value for textiles and construction.

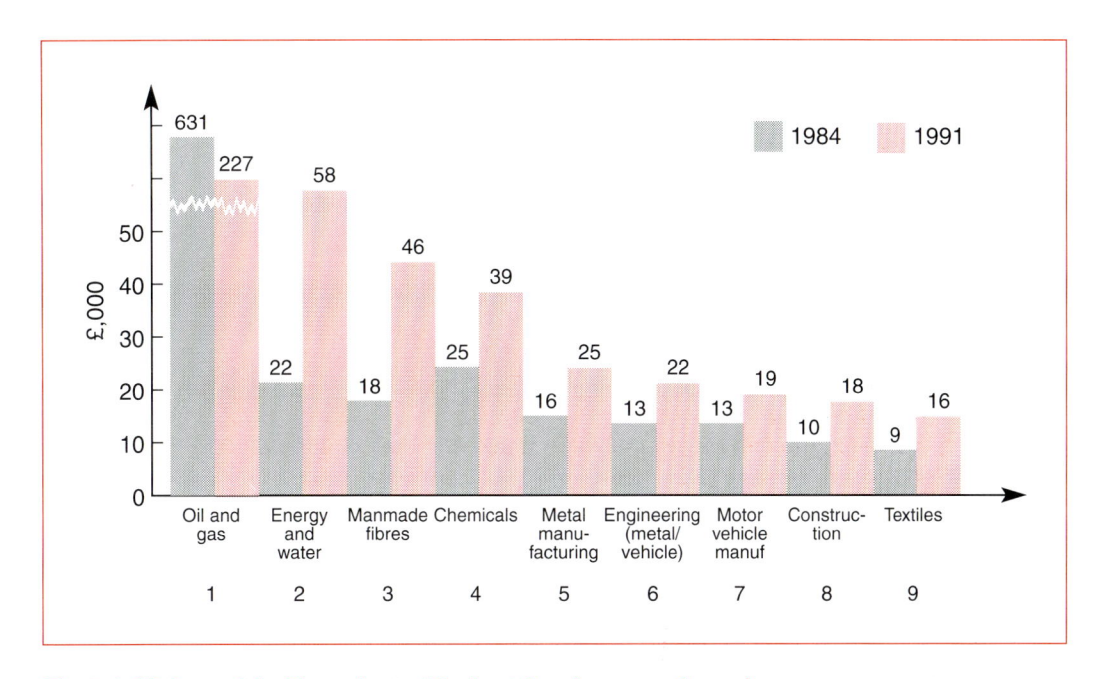

Fig 5.6 Value added in selected industries (per employee)
Source: Annual Abstract Statistics 1994, CSO

Industry	1984 (£,000)	1991 (£,000)
1 Oil and gas	631	227
2 Energy and water	22	58
3 Manmade fibres	18	46
4 Chemicals	25	39
5 Metal manufacturing	16	25
6 Engineering (metal/vehicle)	13	22
7 Motor vehicle manuf	13	19
8 Construction	10	18
9 Textiles	9	16

ACTIVITY 5.1.1

Task 1. Find the average wages for each of the industries shown in Fig. 5.6. How do the rankings compare?

Task 2. Research the level of imports in each of the industries; does this correlate with the value added rankings?

Task 3. Choose one industry and show how increases in added value per employee were achieved in the period covered.

PC
5.1.1
5.1.2
5.2.1
5.3.3

Self assessment questions

1. What are the two main approaches to calculating value added?
2. Identify three strategies used by firms to increase value added.
3. What factors influence the price consumers are willing to pay for a product?
4. Identify three companies that have suffered corporate image problems and state the nature of their problem.
5. Are there products which you purchase because of the 'brand name'? If so identify the importance to you of the brand name.
6. Under which European Treaty was there a 'quality standard' developed and what is the name of the standard?
7. Explain the importance of 'right-first-time' to companies.
8. List the key factors influencing supplier selection to a modern company.
9. What are the advantages of long-term supply contracts to both purchasing and supplying companies.
10. Explain the importance of information technology in modern materials management.
11. Identify two methods of reducing labour costs.
12. Identify four companies that use just-in-time production methods.
13. Explain the differences between mass and flexible production.
14. Draw and explain a product life cycle for a typical consumer good.
15. Identify three low value added industries.
16. Explain why these industries have low value added output.
17. How can marketing create added value? Give examples.
18. Identify and explain Government legislation that has affected supplier relationships.
19. In order of importance, identify the key costs that organisations must control.
20. What developments in European legislation have affected the adoption of the value added approach in the UK.

Element 5.2
INVESTIGATE AND EVALUATE EMPLOYMENT

Performance criteria

1 **Identify and explain types of employment.**

2 **Evaluate the effects of changes in types of employment.**

3 **Identify implications of employment trends in the local economy.**

4 **Evaluate the implications of employment trends in the local and national economy.**

Introduction

This element focuses on employment. Issues raised regarding production in general can only be tackled after changes in the labour market have been identified and their implications understood.

BUSINESS SECTORS

There are three main sectors of industry:

1 *Primary.* This refers to the food, fishery, forestry and mineral extraction industries (oil, coal and aggregates). In short, this sector provides the raw materials that are later processed to produce goods.

2 *Secondary.* This is the processing sector of the economy. An important constituent is 'Manufacturing'. This sector also includes energy and construction. In short this sector is responsible for the production of real goods either for domestic (within the UK) or export consumption.

3 *Tertiary.* This is the sector that comprises the distribution and financing of goods within the economy. It also includes the servicing of personal needs such as hotels and tourism. A large part of this sector is under the ownership of the government, for example, schools and hospitals. It is important to remember that repairs to cars or electrical equipment are part of the tertiary sector. The services under government ownership are sometimes referred to as the *quaternary sector*.

Trends

Current trends in these sectors of industry are examined below.

Figure 5.7 shows the trend in employment since the Industrial Revolution. As a band widens, there is an increase in the share of employment. This type of graph does not show increases in population, however. As such, even though the share of employment may have been falling the absolute numbers may have risen. There are also problems with the data over long periods (for instance, contracting-out employees previously classed as 'secondary' may now be classed as 'service').

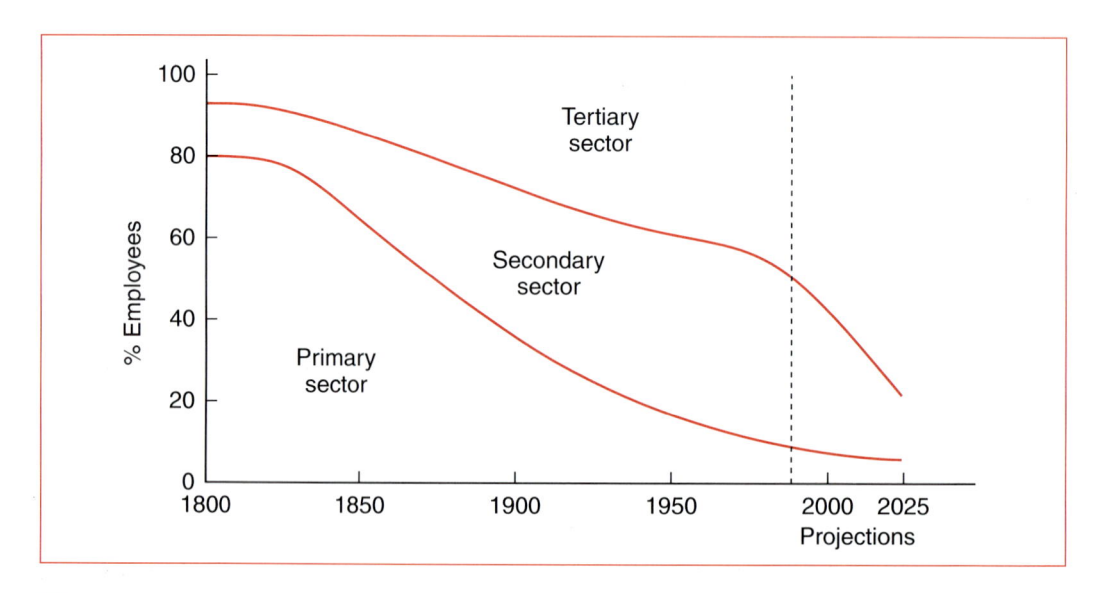

Fig 5.7 Trends in sectoral employment. *Source:* Adapted from Hurst (1974)

Element 5.2　Investigate and evaluate employment

PC 5.2.2

ACTIVITY 5.2.1

Consider Fig. 5.7. Collect figures for the population of working age and the participation rate. Combine these with percentages read from the graph to calculate the absolute number of employees in each sector.

The primary sector

This sector has shown a decline in employment ever since the Industrial Revolution in approximately 1750. The major sources of the reduction, until 1945, were the farming and forestry subsectors. Since 1945 there has been a rapid reduction in the number of people employed in the extraction industries, especially coal. Only for a brief period in the late 1970s and early 1980s was there an increase in employment in the extraction industries. This was caused by the exploitation of North Sea Oil. The development and expansion of the oil fields created several thousand jobs. By 1986, however, the amount of oil being extracted had already started to decline.

The main reason for the long-term decline of this sector has been the increased use of mechanised equipment in the agricultural sector. Labour has been displaced by machines, e.g. the labourer with a scythe has been displaced by the combine harvester. Furthermore, since the eighteenth century, there has been a move towards larger and larger farms. This has allowed farmers to benefit from economies of scale. In more recent times, following the experience of two World Wars this century, the government has given large capital grants to encourage farmers to become more productive. This has been associated with government intervention in the food markets to guarantee farmers' income. This happened before the UK joined the European Economic Community in 1973, and since that time the European Common Agricultural Policy (CAP) has been a major source of subsidies. The reasons government gave for these subsidies referred to 'food self-sufficiency'. The overall effect was to encourage farmers to become more productive and to provide them with finance for mechanisation.

The other main loss of employment occurred in the coal industry. In the period 1945 to 1974 the main cause was the displacement of coal by oil as a source of energy. This in turn was due to the falling cost of oil. Between 1951 and 1973 the real price of oil fell by 75 per cent. The electricity generating industry reacted to this by building more oil-fired power stations and by closing coal-powered stations.

In the period 1974–80 this trend was temporarily reversed following the sharp rise in oil prices. In 1984 the National Coal Board (now called British Coal) attempted to close Cortonwood Colliery in South Yorkshire and this lead to a major strike. Since 1985 there has been a very rapid decline in the number of both collieries and miners. It is noticeable that over the same period both the price of oil and the cost of imported coal have fallen. On current projections there will only be 15 to 17 collieries left in operation by the time of privatisation in 1995, employing some 15 000 men. (Compare this to a figure of over 900,000 in 1949.)

The secondary sector

Employment in this sector peaked (reached its highest share) in 1966 at 46 per cent . For the subsector, manufacturing, the peak year was much earlier; in 1955 the share of total employment was 36 per cent. Since then, there has been a reduction in both the absolute number of people and the proportion of the workforce employed in this sector. The subsector, manufacturing, has experienced an even greater decline in employment.

The secondary sector is the most complicated sector to analyse. Its analysis often varies according to the (vested) interests of the parties concerned. This is not surprising since this sector is the main wealth-creating part of the economy. Our standards of living depend more on this sector than on any other area of industry. Success or failure here is connected, therefore, to the perceived success or failure of the government.

This sector, being a varied sector, is easier to analyse if we look at important and identifiable subunits.

Construction

This sector's absolute level of employment has not significantly altered since 1945. The sector is labour intensive. Even the development of industrialised building methods, using precast concrete, etc., in the 1960s did not reduce employment. In any given year the level of employment is determined more by the demand for buildings, which in turn depends on the level of overall economic activity, than on changes in technology or productivity. Over the economic cycle employment can vary by as much as 300 000.

Energy

As we noted above, the key change in this sector has been the development and subsequent decline of oil production. The sector has also been affected, however, by the continuous rise in the demand for energy. This rise in demand is a function of increased industrial output and increased domestic usage (energy used in the home). The former depends on rising demand for industrial goods both at home and overseas and the increasing level of services. The level of domestic demand rises as incomes improve.

The trend was interrupted by the 'oil shocks' of 1974 and 1979, which led to an awareness of the volatility of energy prices. Since the mid-1980s there has been growing concern over the effect of energy production on the environment – the *'Greenhouse effect'*. Since 1984 the government has operated a policy of raising the real cost of energy through taxation. This causes a reduction in the growth rate of demand and has forced the electricity and other industries to reduce employment levels to hold down otherwise large price increases.

Manufacturing (also known as the traded goods sector)

This sector is heavily involved in international trade. As such its success is dependent on its performance relative to the same sector in other industrialised countries. To understand the changes in output and employment we need to compare UK manufacturing with American, German and Japanese industries. It is clear, however, that the UK has experienced a more severe decline in both output and employment.

The tertiary sector

Since the early years of this century this sector has seen an increase in the number of employees. The rate of increase has been faster than the growth in population and so the share of total employment has also grown. Unlike the secondary sector, prior to the 1989 recession, this sector had not been much affected by economic downturns. The pattern had been one of uninterrupted growth. Since 1990, however, this sector has also suffered employment losses. As one would expect, these have been concentrated in a particular subsector, namely financial services.

CAUSES OF DECLINE IN INDUSTRIAL OUTPUT AND EMPLOYMENT

Many explanations have been put forward for the UK's decline in industrial output, particularly in manufacturing.

1 North sea oil. Prior to 1979, the UK imported oil. We had to spend our overseas earnings on the purchase of oil. Following the oil price rise in 1974, the exchange rate (the value of the pound as measured by other currencies) fell. This made UK exports relatively less expensive, thus demand for manufactured goods tended to rise. Unfortunately, the oil price rise also created a worldwide recession. Other countries reduced the amount of UK goods they purchased. With lower demand there was a decline in both output and employment. In 1979 the UK became a major producer of oil. This reduced the level of oil imports. In the same year there was the second 'oil shock'. With the start of the Iranian Revolution, oil exports from Iran fell, the supply of oil was reduced and the price rose.

The UK now not only exported oil but at a higher price. The effect of this was to raise the value of the pound. This made our exports more expensive. The exchange rate rose from £1 = $1.60 to £1 = $2.40. Some people in the City of London argued that sterling had become a petro-currency, that is, the exchange rate depended more on the price of oil than any other factor. The demand for manufactured goods fell by over 20 per cent between 1979 and 1981. This loss of overseas markets resulted in the closure of 25 per cent of UK manufacturing capacity over the same period. To sum up, the peak year for manufacturing output was 1973. There followed a rapid decline until 1982. It was not until 1988 that manufacturing output recovered to its 1973 level. This explanation is associated with the names Eltis and Bacon who produced several articles arguing the case.

2 Natural development. This explanation depends on the theory that, as economies develop, the composition of output changes. For a period of over a century the share of manufacturing in UK output had been falling. There was nothing new about the decline. As the world's oldest industrial economy it was natural that the UK would be the first to become a post-industrial economy. The UK was comparatively better at service sector industries and the rise in output of these, including exports, would offset the fall in manufacturing. This approach was associated with the view that 'Manufacturing does not matter'. Indeed the decline in manufacturing far from being a problem was an indicator of the UK leading the world.

3 Economic failure. These approaches argue that the decline in manufacturing in particular is symptomatic of problems in the way that the UK economy is organised. The issue of industrial decline is of major political significance. Once the term failure is used, the next consideration is usually, 'Who is to blame?'

Managers. The first approach associated with trades union supporters, argues that the cause of the decline is poor management. According to this argument, the UK, unlike our European competitors, has a confrontational style of management. UK managers, it is argued, generally come from a different social background to their employees. They tend to go to different schools. There is a social divide. This leads to a 'them and us' attitude. Compared with our trading rivals who have recognised the importance of teamwork, this makes UK industry less effective. Industrial relations are viewed from a class perspective.

City of London. A related version of this approach is that the nature of company ownership obliges managers to go for short-term profit. Only if managers achieve profits is the company safe from take-over. In comparison, in continental countries such as Germany, companies are not as susceptible to changes of ownership because it is not as easy to trade shares. In other words the strength of the UK Stock Exchange, which is the largest in Europe, is a cause of industrial decline. High short-term profits can damage companies because they lead to lower levels of long-term investment. This means that in the long run UK companies are competing using out-of-date technology. Evidence for this theory is that the UK is good at inventing new products and services but that the crucial development to market product is completed overseas.

Trade unions. An alternative argument is that the decline in UK competitiveness is due to restrictive working practices, that is, the power of trades unions to prevent the implementation of new, more efficient, working methods and their reluctance to agree to new technology especially where this involves job losses. For most of the 1980s, the Conservative government accepted this view. Legislative changes were implemented to reduce the power of trades unions to prevent change. Compared to overseas, we were seen as having powerful and militant trades unions. Trades unions were compared to the Luddites of the early Industrial Revolution who smashed new machinery rather than lose their jobs. A typical example is the print industry where computer typesetting was not introduced until ten years after the USA. The television industry is a further example, where electronic news gathering requiring far fewer people was delayed for over five years.

The education system. Following the work of the American economist, Wassily Leontieff, in the 1950s there has been a belief that successful industrial economies rely on the quality of their workforce. The level of skills and education is crucial to success. This is sometimes known as the 'Human Capital' approach. In the modern world the pace of change is greater than in the past. New products are brought to the market more often than before. Products are superseded, become obsolete much more quickly. For a country

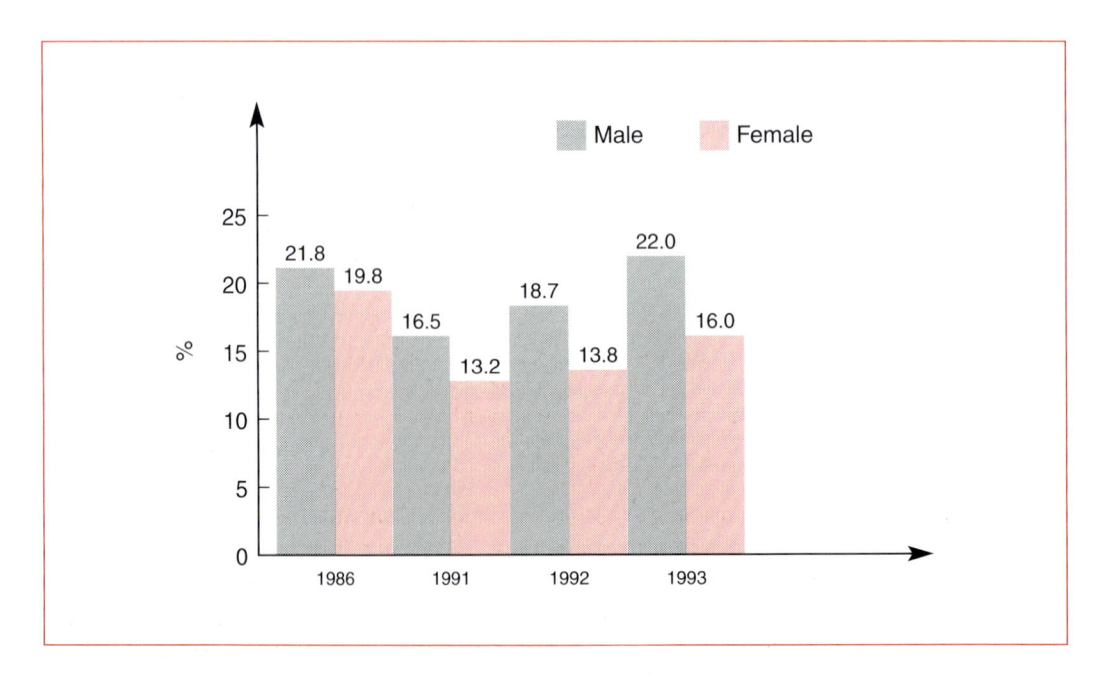

Fig 5.8 Youth (16–19) unemployment rates 1986–1993.
Source: *Social Trends* 1994, CSO

to be successful, it is necessary to innovate constantly. Innovation requires research and development, however. This in turn requires skilled and educated researchers, technicians and managers.

Unemployment is not equally distributed in the working population as can be seen in Fig. 5.8. Rates for young workers tend to rise sooner and higher than those for older workers. Note that male youth unemployment is higher than that for females in every year, and also that male unemployment rises faster than female.

The problem in the UK (and the USA) is that the education and training system has not delivered workers with the necessary skills. This includes basic literacy and numeracy, but extends to scientific and technological knowledge. An undercurrent is that schools and colleges have not prepared students for the world of work, in terms of attitude. School and college leavers have not learned the importance of 'hard work' and obeying orders (following the rules). If this is a correct understanding of our current decline, then clearly 'someone', the government, should do 'something' about it. The government has responded by taking more control over the actions of schools and colleges – the national curriculum and the introduction of GNVQ and NVQ courses like this one. It has also acted to encourage the take up of science and engineering courses in higher education and at the same time restricted the number of business and social science places.

ACTIVITY 5.2.2

Complete a similar graph to that shown in Fig. 5.8 showing rates of ethnic unemployment. Account for the differences.

PC
5.2.2
5.2.3
5.2.4

WOMEN AND EMPLOYMENT

Figure 5.9 shows that the rise in female employment has mainly occurred in the past five years. The relative share of employment is caused more by the decline in male, full-time jobs.

Manufacturing jobs tend to be full-time and mainly occupied by men. In many of the older industries, such as steel, shipbuilding and engineering, physical strength was required. Women were often excluded from such employment on the basis of prejudice. In the case of coal mining, legislation was passed in the nineteenth century barring women from working underground. This was only repealed in 1992. The social expectations of 'men's' and 'women's' work acted to prevent women from both obtaining and even wanting many secondary sector jobs. The major job losses over the past 20 years, therefore, have mainly affected men. On the other hand, the newly created jobs have been more appropriate for women. Indeed the effect of the feminist movement has been to change our perceptions of women's capabilities. Although prejudice and discrimination still exist, the main beneficiaries of the growth in service sector employment have been women.

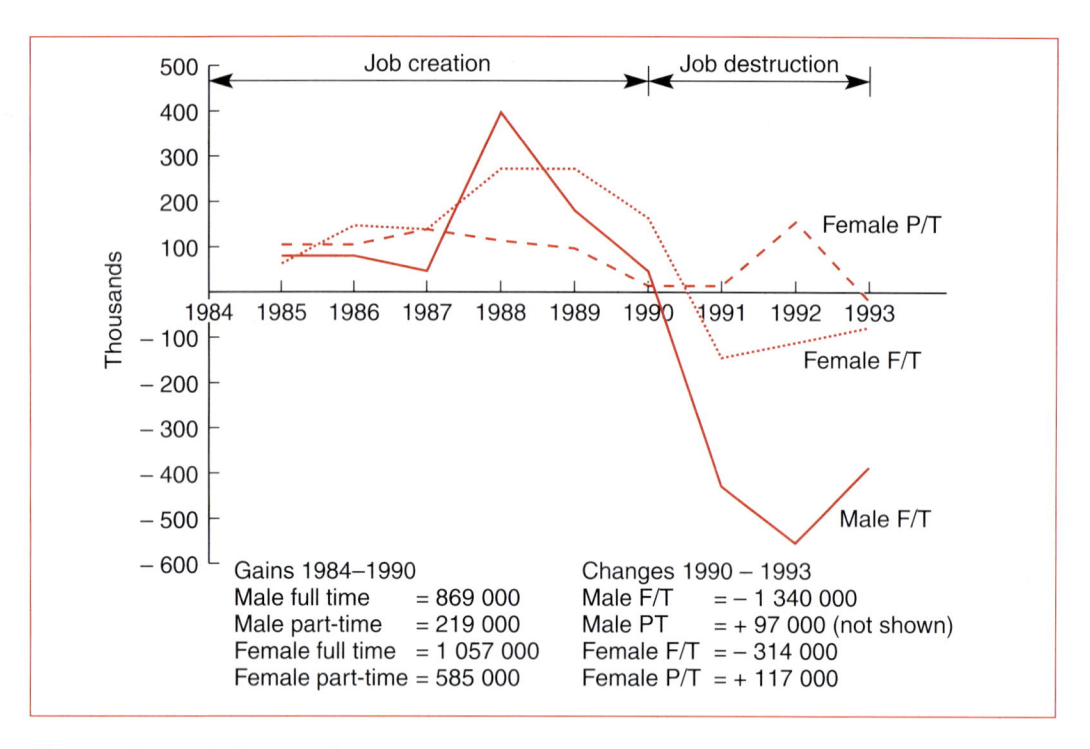

Fig 5.9 Annual changes in employment 1984–1993
Source: Social Trends 1994, CSO

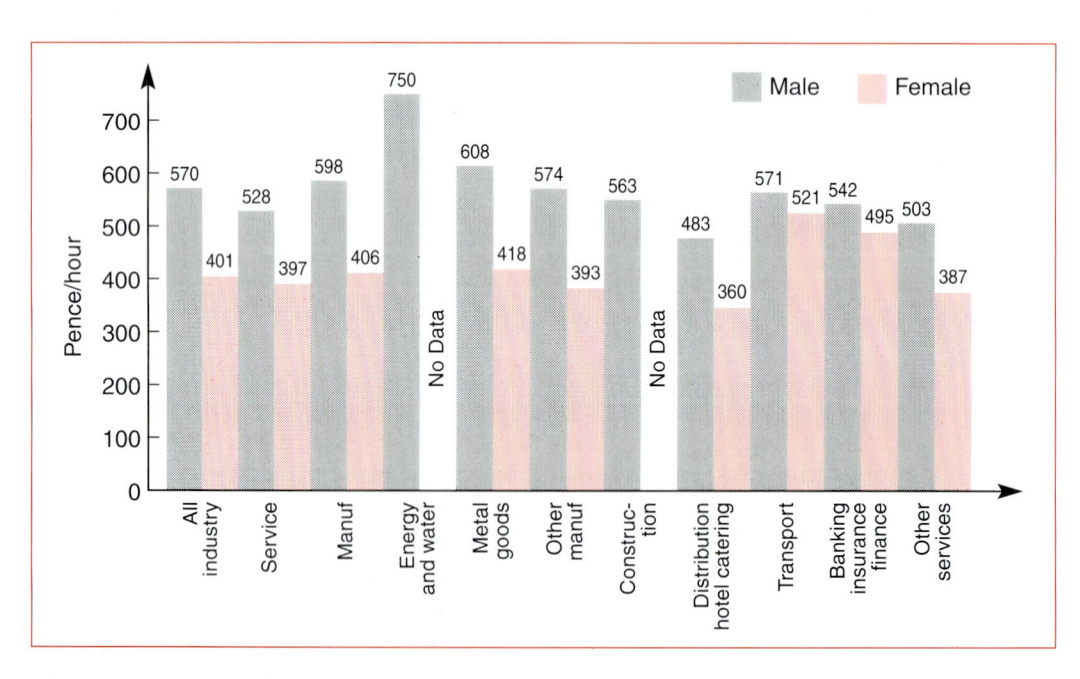

Gains 1984–1990
Male full time   = 869 000
Male part-time   = 219 000
Female full time = 1 057 000
Female part-time = 585 000

Changes 1990 – 1993
Male F/T   = – 1 340 000
Male PT   = + 97 000 (not shown)
Female F/T = – 314 000
Female P/T = + 117 000

Fig 5.10 Male and Female average earnings by industrial group. Full-time employees on adult rates 1991. Source: Annual Abstract of Statistics 1994, CSO

Industry	Male	Female
All industry	570	401
Service	528	397
Manuf	598	406
Energy and water	750	No Data
Metal goods	608	418
Other manuf	574	393
Construction	563	No Data
Distribution hotel catering	483	360
Transport	571	521
Banking insurance finance	542	495
Other services	503	387

Element 5.2 Investigate and evaluate employment

PC
5.2.2
5.2.3

ACTIVITY 5.2.3

Figure 5.10 shows the average hourly earnings of males and females in selected industries in 1991.

Task 1. Which three industries have the lowest female to male wage ratio?

Task 2. Offer explanations as to the lack of data for the energy, water and construction industries.

Task 3. In the light of the data, which industrial sector would you consider working in? Justify your answer.

EFFECTS OF CHANGES IN CONTRACTS OF EMPLOYMENT

A contract of employment is a legally binding agreement between an employer and an employee. It differs from commercial contracts in that it is subject to both statutory and common law restrictions. This means that there are certain duties and conditions that are held to be incorporated in the contract even if both parties attempt to agree otherwise. For example, an employer has a duty of care to an employee over and above any specific Health and Safety Act requirements. Equally an employee has an unconditional duty to 'obey a lawful command' and to act in 'good faith', that is, not damage his or her employer's reputation.

A standard contract of employment has the following features:

1 It is of unlimited duration.

2 It is for over sixteen hours per week.

As the economy has shifted from secondary to tertiary employment there has been increasing use of non-standard contracts (not only in the UK, but also in Europe and the USA). The following list indicates the major changes.

- *Part-time contracts.* Defined in the UK as a contract for less than sixteen hours per week, this type of contract offered until 1994 significantly reduced protection against dismissal. Further, if earnings are less than £57 per week (as at 1 January 1994), then neither the employer nor the employee are liable to pay National Insurance contributions. In March 1994, the House of Lords ruled that the lack of employment protection was in breach of European law. This was because employees were only eligible to go to an Industrial Tribunal if they had been in employment for five successive years compared to only two years for a full-time employee. This was held to be unfair.

- *Temporary contracts.* The defining feature of a temporary contract of employment is that it is time limited, that is, there is a finishing date. Temporary contracts may be either full- or part-time.

- *Home working (or telework) contracts.* The defining feature here is that the employees operate from their own homes. Traditionally, this work was low skill, for example, packing or stuffing soft toys, and the pay method was piece rate (people got paid for each item produced). Teleworking more often refers to employment that involves the

363

use of telecommunications and often computers, for example, many BT telephone operators now work at home.

- *Agency contracts.* In this case the employee is hired by a specialist company that in turn hires them to other companies. The agency pays one wage rate but charges the hiring company a higher rate. This is often called 'temping', but should not be confused with temporary contracts (*see* above). Examples are typists, nurses and truck drivers.

- *Job share contracts.* In this case there is one contract of employment but it is shared between two people. Professional jobs that attract women employees are the most common. This is most often the case in the public sector, e.g. local government. The posts often involve people-oriented occupations, such as personnel officers or training officers.

- *Self-employment.* There was a rapid growth in this sector of employment in the 1980s. The recession of the early 1990s, however, caused many of the self-employed to go bankrupt. There has been some argument as to whether self-employment happened from choice or if it was the lack of alternatives that lead to this growth. It is noticeable that the growth in self-employment occurred mainly in the construction and related industries. There was even the case of the 'self-employed' waiter; he paid a restaurant to serve at a group of tables and collected the tips.

- *The underground economy.* This relates to work that is undertaken on a 'cash only' basis to avoid the declaration of the income to the government, either via the Department of Social Security or the Inland Revenue. This type of employment is sometimes called 'the black economy'. It is not clear how large the underground economy is, nor how many people work in it. Some City economists have estimated the size at 7 per cent of Gross Domestic Product which in 1994 would have amounted to approximately £42 billion per year. In the main it is skilled tradesmen that are more likely to be involved since they have marketable skills; any low-wage sector, such as agriculture and distribution, however, will tend to attract such practices.

The flexibility these types of employment offer is attractive to some employees, especially women. However surveys have shown that most male employees have accepted non-standard contracts only because they could not gain permanent full-time employment. It is a feature of these types of employment that they are not very secure.

All the above developments make it easier for companies to reduce their staff in times of economic recession. If additionally redundancy entitlement is reduced, then it is less expensive to sack workers. If workers have reduced rights to appeal to Industrial Tribunals pleading unfair dismissal, then it is less difficult to dismiss them. The benefits of this to employers are obvious.

It is argued, however, that flexible contracts also benefit employees. If it is easier to reduce workforces, then it is less costly to expand them. This means firms are more likely to employ extra people in an upturn and as a result more people will benefit from employment. This is, in essence, the UK government's case for reducing employment protection.

An alternative view is that the insecurity of employment is damaging to both the employee and the economy. For the employee there is constant worry and stress and he or she is more likely to suffer exploitation by managers. For the economy, people in insecure employment are less likely to commit themselves to major purchases and as a result there is less demand. If there is less demand, there is less that firms can sell. Low-wage insecure employment can, therefore, damage companies' profitability. This argument is often deployed by trade unions.

Element 5.2 Investigate and evaluate employment

FLEXIBILITY AND SOCIETY

Recently there has been growing concern that approximately one third of the workforce is either in non-standard employment or unemployed, while the other two thirds is in more or less secure employment. There is a widening gap between the incomes of the two. For example, the after-tax real earnings (those adjusted for inflation) of the top 10 per cent of income earners has risen by over 60 per cent since 1979; for the bottom 10 per cent there has been no real increase and for those on statutory benefits there has been a reduction. This could lead to 'social tensions' often in the forms of crime or riots. This is now referred to as the 'underclass thesis', arguing that there is a sector of society, often associated with low skills and low educational achievement levels, that will never gain secure employment.

A recent approach to staffing organisations stresses that most companies can best operate with a limited number of key staff. Any remaining jobs can be bought in from one of the non-standard sources. It is a more than just coincidence that the usual ratio is one third core (essential) to two thirds periphery (non-essential).

Self assessment questions

1. Explain the terms primary, secondary and tertiary industry. Give two examples of each.
2. Identify the industrial sector of each of the following: construction; mining; motor repairs; hotels; chemicals.
3. In which decade did manufacturing peak?
4. In which year was the highest level of manufacturing output achieved?
5. What are the main changes in female employment since 1970?
6. Which changes in industrial structure have most affected male employment?
7. What are the three main attempts to explain manufacturing decline in the UK?
8. Explain the term 'human capital'.
9. Identify the age groups with the highest levels of unemployment.
10. What strategies has the government used to combat youth unemployment.
11. Identify the differences between 'standard' and 'non-standard' contracts of employment.
12. Explain the rise in self-employment in the UK in the 1980s.
13. What is the 'underground economy'?
14. List three advantages, to employers, of non-standard employment contracts.

15 In what ways does the development of non-standard employment influence the national economy?

16 Differentiate between 'core' and 'periphery' employment.

17 What problems may occur for society from the recent trends in employment patterns?

18 Explain the difference between 'temps' and 'temporary work'.

19 List three government initiatives designed to improve education and training.

20 What problems occur for the Government from the growth of the 'underground economy'?

Element 5.3
EXAMINE THE COMPETITIVENESS OF UK INDUSTRY

Performance criteria

1. **Compare performance of the UK economy with major competitors.**

2. **Describe business strategies intended to improve competitiveness.**

3. **Describe government strategies intended to improve competitiveness of UK industry.**

4. **Evaluate business and government strategies intended to improve competitiveness.**

Introduction

This element looks at ways to improve the competitiveness of industry, with particular reference to UK businesses operating in the world market.

Unit 5 Production and employment in the economy

GOVERNMENT ECONOMIC POLICIES

The influence of governments on business is pervasive. Governments enact legislation that set safety and product liability standards, e.g. the requirement to fit catalytic converters. Foreign governments set import restrictions that limit market opportunity. Governments set labour laws regulating working hours and conditions. In this section, however, we look at the impact of government economic policy.

Government policy may either be explicitly designed to improve the competitiveness of the UK economy or the impact of policy may have unintended effects on competitiveness.

Since the end of the Second World War, governments have accepted that they have a role to play in the management of the economy. Famously, this was exemplified in the *Beveridge Report* that committed governments to . . . maintain a high and stable level of employment'. Classically, there have been four objectives of government economic policy:

1 to maintain a high and stable level of employment;
2 to maintain stable prices;
3 to achieve rising levels of output;
4 to maintain a satisfactory balance of payments position.

These are often shortened to the following:

1 Full employment
2 Low inflation
3 Growth
4 Balance of Payments (constraint)

It is often the case that these objectives are in conflict, i.e. the achievement of one interferes with the achievement of others. It has been necessary, therefore, for governments to prioritise the objectives.

Combating unemployment

Until 1970 full employment was clearly the highest priority. Even in this period, however, the commitment was limited by the state of the balance of payments, in particular, deficits on the current account creating problems with the exchange rate. Under international agreements (The Bretton Woods Treaty), the UK government was committed to maintaining a fixed rate of exchange against the dollar. At times this required the government to raise interest rates or even tax rates to reduce a balance of payments deficit. These actions (as we shall explain) had the effect of increasing unemployment.

Combating inflation

In the period since 1970, governments, both UK and overseas, have become more concerned with the effects of inflation. Since 1979 inflation has been the primary concern of the UK government. Many government actions that have affected employment have been related to the control of inflation. Following the 'oil shocks' of the 1970s governments increasingly came to believe that high and rising inflation damaged the productive capacity of the economy – a belief supported by the work of the 'monetarist' economists.

It was believed that inflation distorted the relationship between investment and borrowing, often leading to wasteful investment that only worked because rising prices hid the mistakes. Furthermore, the people who paid the price for the mistakes were the lenders (savers) who did not receive a fair return for their thrift. In many periods the return on savings after allowing for inflation was negative.

Inflation is defined as a condition of generally rising prices, or equivalently a fall in the purchasing power of money. There are several competing explanations of the causes of inflation. Briefly, these are:

- *Demand pull inflation* – Excess spending power in the economy leads to rising prices as firms respond.
- *Cost push inflation* – Increasing costs of production, either wage costs or raw material costs force firms to raise prices to cover the increased costs.
- *Monetary inflation* – Since people only buy goods, if they have money (or credit facilities) then prices can only increase if the amount of money in the economy increases. Further the creation of money, in the final analysis, is the responsibility of government; therefore, inflation is caused by governments creating too much money.

Remedies for inflation and their effects

The actions government take to reduce or cure inflation depends on which of the above explanations they believe. Each remedy will have a particular effect on the demand for a firm's output and hence the firm's demand for labour.

Demand pull inflation

Solution. *Reduce the level of demand in the economy.*
Method. *Reduce consumers' spending power, i.e. increase taxes on consumer incomes thus leaving them with lower after-tax, or disposable, income.*

Effects. With less income, consumers spend less.

Any firm operating in the consumer goods sector will quickly notice a decline in sales. Even firms that supply goods to this sector will notice a fall in demand. Indeed the fall in demand to companies supplying capital goods (machinery, buildings, etc.) will suffer a relatively larger decline in sales.

Over a period of time, from 6 to 18 months, all sectors of the economy will feel the effects. The consumer durable sector will experience the sharpest and quickest effects. This means that the following goods will be affected: televisions, hi-fi, washing machines, cookers and other home electrical goods. New car sales will also be affected. In the medium term (6 to 12 months) there is likely to be a decline in the number of people moving house. This will affect the sales of household goods, such as furniture and carpets. This decline in demand will translate into a decline in the demand for labour. This may manifest itself as redundancies, as reduced real wages, or as a combination of the two.

Evaluation. The damaging effects of fluctuations in demand on the consumer durable sector (which is crucial to exports) is now believed to outweigh the benefits. The impact of this form of policy leads to distortion in the most important sector of the economy for export performance. Furthermore, the cumulative effect on the infrastructure of the economy has been serious. The current orthodoxy is that demand-pull inflation can be self-correcting, if the economy is open to external competition. Domestic inflation can be cured by allowing market forces to 'price' domestic demand out of the market. UK firms that allow wages to rise too quickly will become uncompetitive in both the home and export markets. Insofar as there is a cause of excess demand, it is to be found in the monetary sector, not the goods market. Apparent excess demand is a symptom not a cause of inflation. (*See* section on monetary inflation.)

Cost push inflation

Solution. *Reduce cost factors.*

Method. *Reduce ability of trades unions to successfully increase wages; either directly by passing laws (a statutory incomes policy) or indirectly. If push factors are increasing raw materials costs, most of which are imported, then action is taken to raise the exchange rate. A higher exchange rate makes imported goods cheaper in UK currency. To raise the exchange rate a government raises interest rates.*

Effects. *Statutory wages (or incomes) policy.*

In this instance the firm will not be allowed to award pay increases above a government defined limit (or 'norm'). For some firms that are in declining markets, this may make life easier. They will be able to control wages costs and blame the government. If inflation continues at a higher rate than the pay norm, then costs of production will decline. This will enable firms to become more cost-competitive.

One firm's employees are another firm's customers, however. If wages are reduced in real terms, then spending power is also reduced. In the long term, there will be a fall in domestic demand. Only if firms can increase their export sales to offset this decline can future problems be averted. Incomes policies create additional problems for successful firms. These firms with growing markets will need to attract additional workers, but they are not allowed to signal to potential employees their success because they are not allowed to increase wages. They will find it more difficult to attract workers, therefore, with the requisite skills and their expansion may be checked by (skilled) labour shortages.

In the long term, therefore, incomes policy may prevent the economy from growing, thus stifling rises in living standards and the related growth in demand.

Evaluation. It is now commonly agreed that the distortion effects of pay policy particularly over a long period, outweigh the temporary gains in inflation reduction. The evidence suggests that pay policy only affects the timing of wage increases. Worse it provokes a 'pay explosion', whenever it is relaxed. Since the election of the Conservative government in 1979 there has been no private sector incomes policy, although the government has limited and controlled public sector pay.

Effect. *Rise in interest rates.*

If the source of cost push inflation is import prices then the government will attempt to raise, or at least stabilise the exchange rate, with the effect of reducing import prices, thus reducing the pressure at source. In the short run, this can be achieved by raising interest rates. This is because raising interest rates makes it more attractive for foreigners to hold their wealth in UK assets, thus the demand for sterling rises and with a given supply, the price (exchange rate) rises. Interest rates are the cost of borrowing money.

Apart from influencing the exchange rate, other immediate effects of higher interest rates are:

1 *The cost of people's mortgages rises.* This reduces the amount of money they have to purchase other goods. In the short term this is probably the most powerful effect (an example of the 'income effect').

2 *Credit becomes more expensive.* Goods that are bought using credit become relatively more expensive. There is a decline in the sales of 'big-ticket items'.

3 *Firms find that the cost of their bank loans, especially overdrafts, increase.* They respond by cutting back on stock levels. Investment in new machinery and buildings is delayed.

Figure 5.11 shows how government policy may lead to the death of enterprises. It is not just employees who lose out in a recession; both companies and shareholders are also at risk.

After a period of six months or so the following happens:

1 *As existing export orders are exhausted, firms find that their export prices have risen.* This is due to a rise in the exchange rate. This means that they either have to accept reduced profit margins, reduced sales or find ways to reduce their costs of production.

2 *Imported goods become cheaper (exchange rate effect).* In the domestic market firms find stronger competition from foreign firms. They face the same problems as in 1 above.

Remembering that labour costs account for over 60 per cent of total costs of production, on average, clearly firms can only respond by reducing this element of cost. They must either reduce real wages or use labour in a more productive manner.

Monetary inflation

Solution. *Control rate of growth of money supply.*
Method. *Reduce demand for money by raising interest rates. Control government contribution to growth in money supply by reducing the government's need to borrow, that is, reduce the Public Sector Borrowing Requirement (PSBR).*

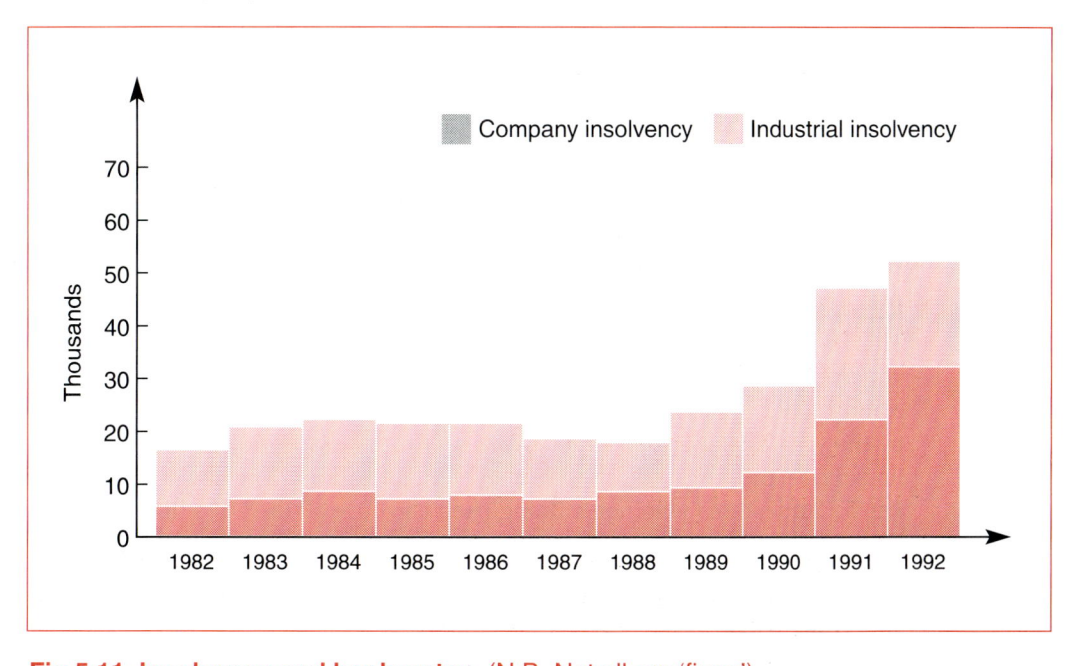

Fig 5.11 Insolvency and bankruptcy. (N.B. Not all are 'firms')
Source: Annual Abstract of Statistics 1994, CSO. Tables 17.26, 17.27

Effect. The government may either raise interest rates, in which case the effects are as above, or reduce the PSBR. In the latter case the main effect is felt by companies supplying the government with goods (and to a lesser extent services). This is because the fastest way a government can reduce its spending is by deferring capital projects. This means not building new roads, hospitals, schools and other infrastructure projects. The government can prevent the remaining nationalised industries such as British Rail and the Royal Mail from borrowing. Clearly the immediate sufferers will be the construction and capital goods industries. It is significant that these two sectors suffer the largest swings in total employment.

If, as in 1993, the government decides to reduce the PSBR by increasing taxes, then the effects are the same as demand pull remedies.

Evaluation. Government action to reduce inflation always has an effect on employment – only the immediate impact differs. Over a period of years the effects become more similar.

GOVERNMENT GROWTH POLICIES

Governments may attempt to increase the level of output in an economy in two ways.

- Supply-side measures
- Demand-side measures.

Supply-side measures

The government attempts to make the economy more productive, by making markets more efficient.

Labour market policies

The labour market is the key market. The government can intervene in this market in a number of ways.

1 *Reduce bottlenecks in the labour market by increasing the supply of skilled workers.*
This implies government action to improve training and education. In 1993 the government published National Education and Training Targets (NETTs) which committed it to increasing the number of school leavers with recognised qualifications by the year 2000. Further targets were set for the proportion of the workforce receiving 'in-service' training and for higher level qualifications. The newspaper article in Fig. 5.12 questions whether training itself can cure all the UK's ills.

2 *Reduce the power of trades unions to block (beneficial) change* (*see* section on legislation).
This has been the main focus of government activity since 1979 although the 1970–1974 government also attempted such legislation. There has been a marked reduction in the number of days' production lost to industrial action. It is not clear that this is *entirely* due to legislation, however. The effectiveness of the government's industrial relations

Element 5.3 Examine the competitiveness of UK industry

Is training the answer?

Human capital investment may be everybody's favourite economic cure-all, but applying the prescription to the UK seems an increasingly thankless task. Attacked from all sides, the government's training policy is partly the victim of a long-standing ambivalence about the state's role which has yet to be resolved.

Mr Michael Portillo, the new UK employment minister, was widely criticised last month for proposing to halve the £4 billion his department spends on training. Yet the two central ingredients of training policy hardly received ringing endorsements in the weeks that followed.

The Training and Enterprise Councils, established in 1990 to implement much of the government's training programme, are ill-managed squanderers of public funds, according to an Unemployment Unit study of London Tecs. And as for the much-fanfared system of National Vocational Qualifications, an article published in the National Institute's latest Quarterly review found them an 'inappropriate' and 'inequitable' response to the UK's training problems.

Fig 5.12 *Source:* The *Financial Times*, August 1994

legislation is challenged by Fig. 5.13. Note that although the average level of disputes has fallen apparently markedly (average lines for 1970s, 1980–85 and 1986–92) the underlying trend, if we ignore major disputes such as the miners' strikes, was in any case on a decline. All the figures are distorted by just four individual years.

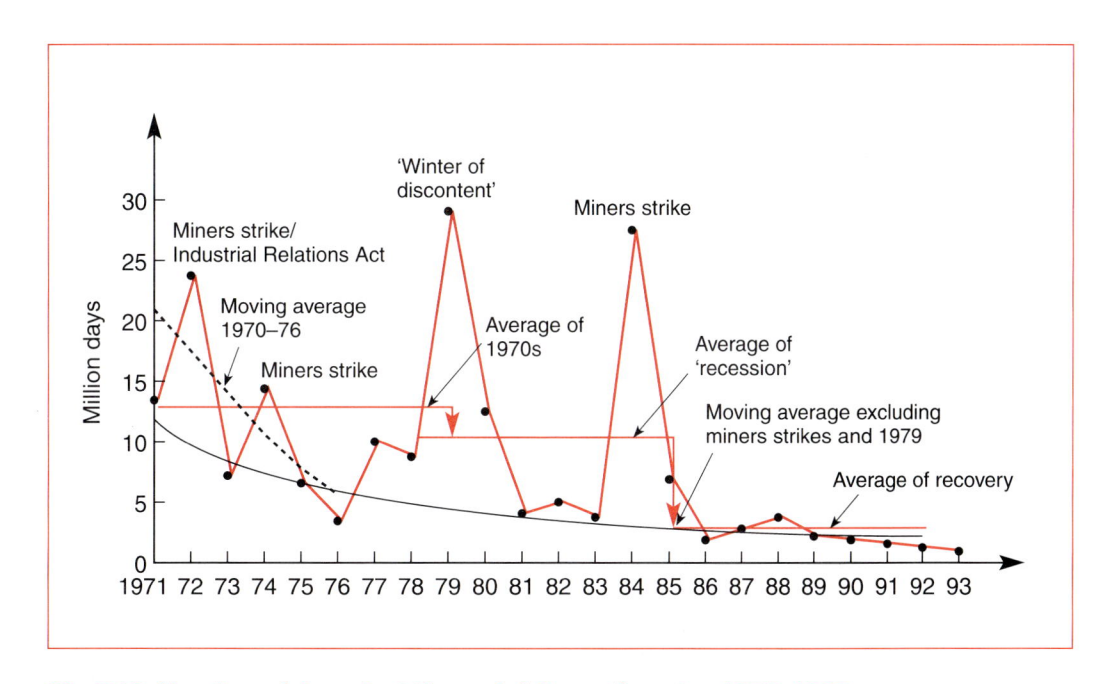

Fig 5.13 Number of days lost through labour disputes 1971–1992
Source: Social Trends 1994, CSO

ACTIVITY 5.3.1

Consider Fig. 5.13. Identify periods of 'pay policy'. Do these correlate with disputes?

3 *Improve labour market flexibility by enabling firms to increase and decrease their workforces more easily in response to changes in demand for their products.* This is marked by the steady erosion of labour market protection, e.g. extending the qualifying period for cover by employment protection legislation plus the reduced capacity of workers/ trades unions to oppose closures.

4 *Improve incentives to work by reducing marginal rates of taxation and widening the gap between wages and social security benefits.* This has been achieved first by breaking the link between social security benefits and average earnings. As a proportion of average earnings, benefits have fallen since 1981. Taxation changes have reduced the marginal rate of taxation from 33p in the pound in 1979 for basic-rate payers to 25p in the pound since 1987. For higher-rate payers the reduction has been greater; the top rate of tax has been reduced from 86p to 60p and eventually to 40p in the pound. For every pound earned over £100 000 per annum, the net improvement in incentives is 46p.

Alternative strategies to the labour market

The liberal approach to management of the labour market states that the role of training and the welfare state is a task for individual governments. They are in a position to choose among elements of liberal and corporatist approaches to reform. The *liberal approach*, often labelled the 'Anglo-Saxon model', would be based on labour market deregulation and lower taxes. Its main benefit is likely to be greater growth of part-time service sector jobs. Its main defect is likely to be less overall investment in skills and greater inequality in pay. The *corporatist approach*, sometimes called the 'Rhine model', would emphasise a shift in the tax burden from unskilled to skilled labour, combined with subsidies to unskilled labour and training, and an effort to keep the growth of real wages below the growth of labour productivity. The main benefit of this approach is likely to be more investment in skills and greater equality among working people. The main drawback is likely to be less job creation.

Policies relating to other markets

Improving the efficiency of other markets is primarily achieved by reducing government regulation, e.g. the deregulation of the stock market in 1986, or the deregulation of the financial markets in 1980 (abolition of exchange control regulations). Since late 1993, the government has begun a new campaign to reduce health and safety regulations. It has also simplified the tax and national insurance regimes for small businesses. It has been remarked that the Government has not been very active in the field of controlling private sector monopolies, even though these are potentially a key factor in market inefficiency.

Privatisation policies

The government has also *privatised* many industries. This involves selling off state-owned assets to the private sector, either by offering shares (a flotation) or by selling direct to some existing company. Some of the companies sold are:

British Telecom, British Gas, British Steel, British Coal, Rover, the electricity companies, the water companies, British Shipbuilders.

The intention was that, by exposing these companies to the discipline of the market, they would become more efficient. There would be much greater pressure on managers to run their organisations effectively for fear of either insolvency or take-over. There would be an incentive, therefore, to shed surplus labour, to reduce costs and improve profit (and value added). Although the majority of these companies have become extremely profitable, there are some doubts as to whether it is privatisation or market power that is the source of their success. In many instances the companies are 'natural monopolies'.

Policies towards small and medium-sized enterprises

Government industrial assistance, with a few notable exceptions (e.g. Nissan) has moved away from the largest firms to those employing between 1 and 500 workers. The government has introduced policies to encourage small and medium-sized enterprises (SMEs) to promote competition. These measures range from the creation of Enterprise Zones to the development of Training and Enterprise Councils (Tecs) and the emphasis of the Department of Trade and Industry on the welfare of these firms. The Treasury, through the Inland Revenue and the Department of Employment, has co-ordinated action to reduce the burden of red-tape on these firms. For example, these firms have lower rates of corporation tax; they do not have to make monthly returns to Customs and Excise for VAT purposes. Small employers are also exempt from the effect of disability legislation, etc. The present government believes that a successful SME sector is vital to economic success.

As can be seen Fig 5.14, however, it is not clear that SMEs are necessarily a good thing. In terms of value added, small employers are less productive than large. Figure 5.14 shows the ratio of value added to employment in firms of various sizes. 1 indicates both the average for the economy and that employees generate the same percentage of total added value that they account for as a percentage of total population. Small firms are relatively inefficient at creating added value, whereas the largest firms are significantly above the average. It is not clear whether this is due to economies of scale or other factors. Recent work in the USA has questioned the sense of relying on SMEs. Indeed the evidence suggests that SMEs are themselves dependent on the success of the largest firms since, in many cases, they are suppliers to the large firms.

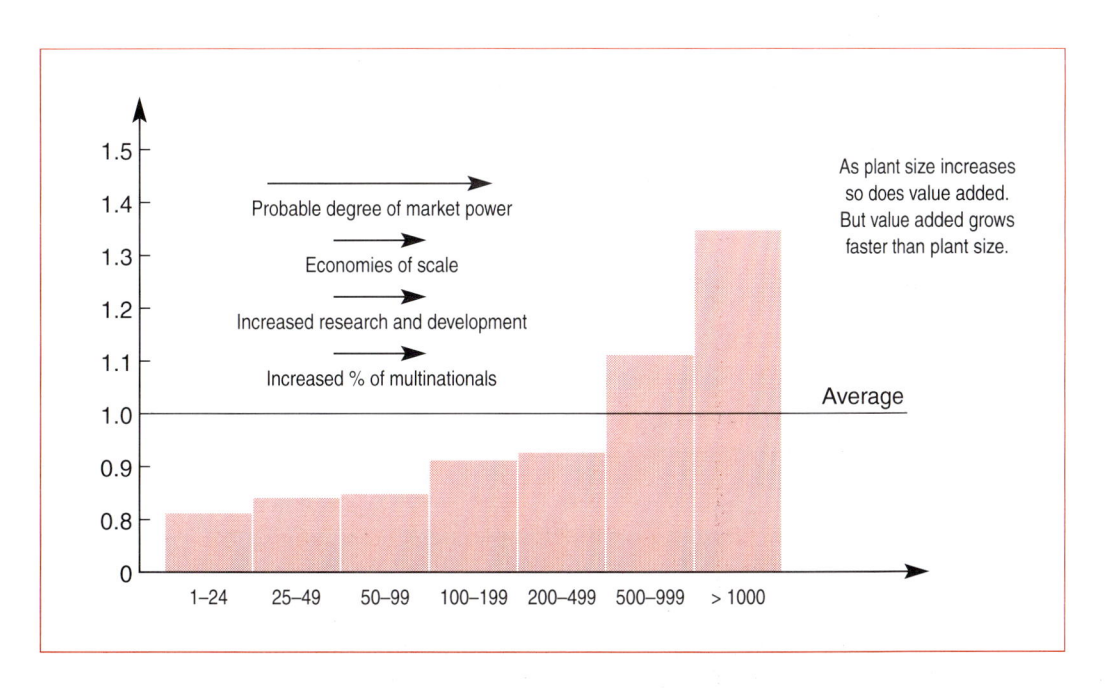

Fig 5.14 Value added share/employment share by size of unit in manufacturing (1990)
Source: Based on *Regional Trends* 1994, CSO

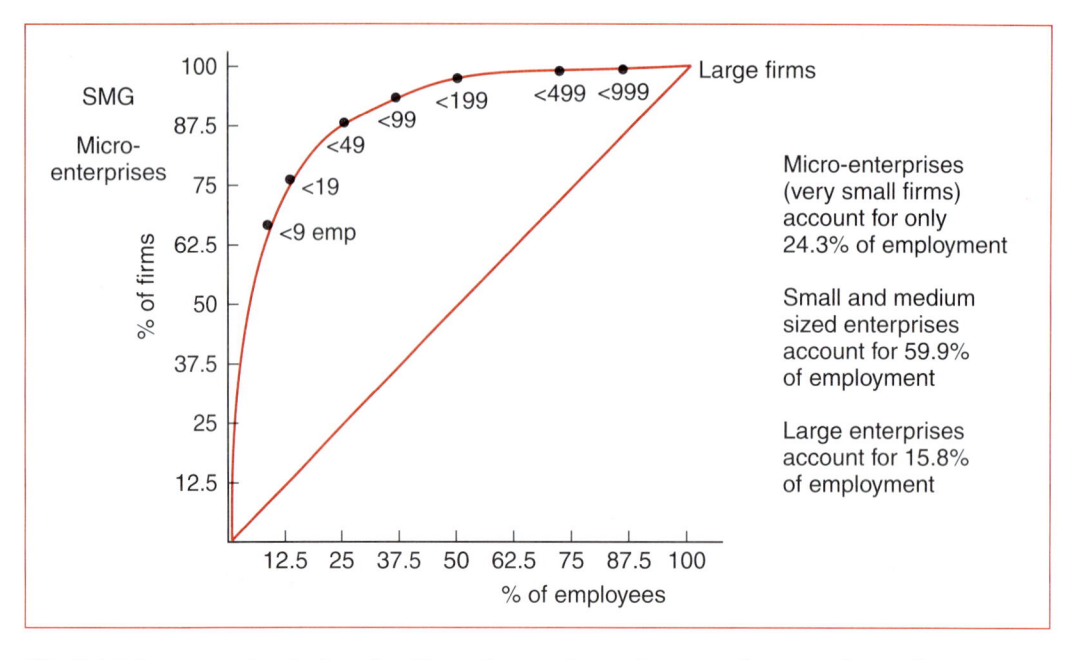

Fig 5.15 Lorentz chart showing firm size and employment in manufacturing

Ernst Schumacher wrote a book entitled *Small is Beautiful*, it was a bestseller in the 1960s. Unfortunately, small may be beautiful but ineffective. Figure 5.15 shows a Lorentz curve indicating that large firms, employing over 1000 employees, each account for only a small percentage of firms, but a large percentage of employment. (A Lorentz chart shows the relationship between cumulative percentages. If both variables are distributed evenly then we would expect the curve to lie on the straight line. The greater the 'bow' in the curve the more uneven the distributions.)

Economies of scale

Economies of scale arise when the average unit cost of production falls with plant size, that is, the production of larger amounts is associated with reduced costs. This effect has several causes. For example:

1. *Technical efficiencies.* Large scale use of energy is often more efficient than small scale (this is particularly true of heating). There may also be discontinuities, that is, the use of a single large plant or machine may be cheaper (and often is) than two or three smaller plants for the same level of production.

2. *Marketing economies.* Large firms with a nationwide (or European-wide) market find it cheaper per customer to use TV for advertising.

3. *Specialisation.* Unlike small firms it is efficient for large firms to employ specialist marketers, accountants, production planners, etc. A small firm would not have sufficient work to justify the time for such people. Large firms have sufficient need. Similarly with production workers, large firms with a known staff absence ratio can employ enough extra workers to cover at no additional cost because they know the probability of staff absence to a high degree of accuracy.

4 *Research and Development.* Although small firms do invest in R&D, it is nevertheless true that large firms with their access to capital invest proportionately more. They are more likely, therefore, to have use of the most modern and effective production processes.

5 *Market power.* Large firms tend to operate in 'oligopolistic' markets (that is markets with few competitors) which allows them more freedom in price setting than small firms which often have to accept what larger firms are willing to pay.

6 *Pecuniary (money) economies.* Large firms often have 'buying power' which enables them to force down the cost of materials.

ACTIVITY 5.3.2

Task 1. Read the article from the *Financial Times* of 17 January 1994 in Fig. 5.16.

Task 2. Discuss whether the article suggests that Tecs are effective in their role? Give examples to support your views.

PC 5.3.3

By LISA WOOD, Labour Staff

Tecs warned over role in economic activity

Training and Enterprise Councils must define more sharply their own role in local economic development, an employment research centre has warned. Tecs' work in the economic development of their areas is 'strong in aspiration but modest in effort', says a report prepared for the Tecs' national council by Professor Amin Rajan of the Centre for Research in Employment and Technology in Europe (Create). The report, published today, calls for action by government and Tecs. Its findings will be considered at the employer-led bodies' national conference in July. Tecs were set up by the government to improve training in England and Wales, as well as to be strategic bodies for local economic development. Professor Robert Bennett of the London School of Economics last week published a book that highlighted the organisations' lack of progress in a number of areas, including playing a role in local economic development. He called for a number of institutional changes, including the merging of Tecs with chambers of commerce. The Create report is neither as prescriptive nor as ambitious, but it calls for an acceleration of Tecs' activities, including the establishing of viable partnerships with other local bodies. The report urges tax relief for companies participating in the Investors in People programme, which seeks to link the training and development of employees more effectively to their companies' business needs. The scheme is the Tecs' main programme for improving training of people in work.

Fig 5.16 *Source: The Financial Times*, January 1994

Regional policies

Between 1932 and the present, the UK government has attempted to influence the location of businesses within the United Kingdom. It has done this for two reasons:

1. to attract new or expanding firms to areas of high unemployment (especially areas that are undergoing structural decline such as the North-east shipbuilding areas);

2. to steer firms away from 'overdeveloped' regions such as London and the South-east, thereby reducing the inflationary pressures in these areas which arise from intense competition for land use.

Each of these goals could be interpreted as supply-side measures that improve the overall capacity of the economy. They were seen as primarily employment policies, however, until the mid-1980s. To achieve these goals the government used a mixture of incentives and regulation: incentives in the form of subsidies for building and equipment; regulation in the form of planning permission to prevent new developments in certain areas. The most famous example of an incentive was the offer of a £200 million subsidy to Nissan to locate in the Sunderland area.

If location is not a vital consideration for a firm, then these inducements can be very powerful. The Department of Trade and Industry estimates that in 1992 they were responsible for the creation of 21 000 jobs and the safeguarding of a further 9000 jobs. Local government often supplements the grants available from central government, for example, through 'Economic Development Units'. In Scotland there are additional funds available through the Highlands and Islands Development Board. In Wales aid is also available through the Welsh Development Office.

Demand-side measures

Sometimes referred to as stabilisation policy, demand-side measures are a very controversial area of government policy. The key proposition is that firms and managers do not like uncertainty, that is, they prefer to know what the future will be like. The purpose of stabilisation policy is to counteract external shocks to the economy and reduce the fluctuations in demand.

The proponents of measures to stabilise and encourage the growth of demand in the economy argue that training, deregulation and other government actions do not create extra demand in the economy. Indeed a more efficient labour market is just another way of saying reduced wages, which, as explained above, transforms into lower demand. Fewer people work more effectively; unemployment gets worse. The problem with the UK economy is that due to a lack of stable demand, firms are unwilling to invest. We have a crisis of underinvestment which leaves the productive capacity of the economy stunted. The government, by undertaking stabilisation of demand, could guarantee firms markets for their output, which would encourage firms to increase investment in the UK. By varying government spending to offset the peaks and troughs in private-sector expenditure, the government could reduce a key area of uncertainty. Increased government investment leads to increased private-sector investment. Investment is 'crowded in'. This is in essence the 'Keynesian' case for government spending.

The alternative view is that government spending has to be paid for. If it is funded by taxes, then the private sector has fewer funds for its investment. Given the record of failures in government investment, this merely leads to inefficient use of scarce investment. Alternatively, the government borrows to fund its investment. In this case the increased demand for borrowed funds increases the interest rate, which means that private sector companies find it harder to attract investment funds at a viable rate. Therefore, they cannot invest as much as otherwise. Private sector investment is 'crowded out'. In this case, the best a government can do is to limit its use of funds to the minimum. This leads to distortions in the capital markets being as small as possible.

OTHER GOVERNMENT ECONOMIC OBJECTIVES

Assistance for industrial sectors

The main beneficiaries of this form of government subsidy have been 'high technology' industries, e.g. British Aerospace, GEC and Ferranti in the aerospace and information technology industries. In the past ICL and Inmos received help in the computer sector. These types of industry are often referred to as 'sunrise', that is, growth industries. A key feature is their strategic importance to the future success of other areas of industry. Information technology, in particular, is an 'enabling' technology, that is, its effects are felt throughout UK industry. The intended effect of these subsidies was to enhance the growth rate of these industries, increasing employment faster than would otherwise have been the case. The government has also participated in European Union high technology research programmes, such as Esprit for information technology.

Promoting free trade and competitiveness

The UK government has believed in the benefits of free trade, that is, trade without customs and excise tariffs or other barriers, since the nineteenth century. To cut a long story short, however, we will look at the impact of the EU and the GATT programmes.

GATT

This stands for the General Agreement on Trade and Tariffs. Since the end of the Second World War, there have been many agreements, the latest of which is the 'Uruguay Round' – so called because the set of negotiations took place in Uruguay. This Agreement has reduced significantly the level of tariffs and subsidies allowable on food products and standardised the treatment for the export of services. It has also liberalised (over a period of years) trade in textiles. The expectation is that there will be growth in world trade and that this will lead to an increase in living standards. The Agreement also created the 'World Trade Organisation' to act as a policeman on trade disputes. The UK is expected to benefit particularly from the liberalisation in services since we have a very large and internationally competitive financial services sector. The picture may not be so rosy for the textile sector.

European Union Programme

Single European Act

The UK government was instrumental in the formulation of the Single European Act. This is designed to create an economic space in Europe that allows the free movement of:

1 *Goods* – by standardising safety and technical specifications throughout the EU – further by opening up protected sectors such as government and public sector tenders to all EU firms (not defence goods).

2 *People* – the abolition of frontier posts and the removal of the need for passport controls. The UK government appears to be having second thoughts, however. The 'Schengen Group' of countries has progressed much faster on this issue.

3 *Services* – the introduction of home country regulation which means that (say) a bank or insurance company once authorised in one country is then free to operate in any EU country.

4 *Capital* – requiring the abolition of all 'exchange control' regulations. Now all firms and individuals are able to transfer funds to any member state. The UK achieved this in 1980; Italy not until 1992.

The Maastricht Treaty

This commits the member states to the creation of economic and monetary union, in theory by 1999 at the latest. It has caused many political difficulties for the UK government.

Monetary union would require three conditions:

1 *Currency stability for two years* – that is, all member states remaining within their ERM bands for this period;

2 *Fixed exchange rates for an indefinite period;*

3 *Creation of a European currency unit* that would replace all national currencies.

Alongside this, there are economic and monetary conditions to be achieved before member states can join. Economic union requires the convergence of indirect taxes within the EU; otherwise, with free movement there is the temptation to transport goods from low-tax areas to high-tax zones as is happening with alcohol and tobacco. For the UK government the creation of greater competition is seen as the spur to improve competitiveness.

BUSINESS STRATEGIES TO IMPROVE COMPETITIVENESS

These strategies have been dealt with throughout this text. They include:

1 marketing activities to improve market share and raise price customers are willing to pay;

2 Research and Development to ensure a constant supply of new products;

3 quality enhancement and related working practices;

4 improved customer and supplier links and relationships.

Mergers and acquisitions

In the UK there has been another major strategy – mergers and acquisitions – this has been a particular response to the development of the Single Market but has also been a long-term feature of business behaviour.

Firms attempt to derive economies of scale by increasing their size. If they do this, by improving market share or developing new products, we call it 'organic growth'. This has not been the preferred growth method for UK companies, rather there has been a tendency to gain market share by the purchase of other firms. UK firms have been the most active in this area in the whole of Europe. If a company cannot be bought, then 'alliances' have been formed and joint ventures created.

In response to competitive pressure from German and American companies operating in the EU, GEC formed a joint venture with the French company CGE to form GEC-Alsthom, to protect their market share in the production of power station generators and control systems.

Demergers

Other strategic responses include the demerger of non-core businesses; this allows managers to concentrate on those markets and production processes they understand best. Demerger has been a response to the failure to gain 'synergy' from previous acquisitions. Synergy is defined as the whole being greater than the sum of its parts, that is, there were expected to be additional gains from creating conglomerate firms, whereby one section of the business would benefit from the experience/expertise/market advantage of another.

De-layering, downsizing, empowerment and other euphemisms

With the impact of information technology firms have realised that they do not need as many middle managers. These are acting as a drain on profitability. In the brave new world of the 1990s there have been moves to excise whole layers of managers, a striking example being the experience of the large banks. Since middle managers are no longer necessary for information processing, it becomes possible to empower the direct workforce. This means giving them the relevant information directly and then allowing them to identify and solve problems. This, it is held, encourages employees by giving them more responsibility; work becomes 'more meaningful'.

In order that people can take more responsibility it is necessary for them to acquire new skills; this in turn leads to the 'multiskilling' approach. Furthermore, because no single person is competent at everything then it is sensible to organise people into teams. All of the above, it is held by human resource managers, leads to a more creative, lean and efficient organisation. More cynical and less committed observers have pointed to the lengthening dole queues.

Performance-related pay

A recent development in the UK has been the adoption of performance-related pay (PRP). This is designed to tie pay and bonuses to the achievement of agreed goals. Initially, it was implemented for senior managers but subsequently has been more widely extended. Major problems have been encountered with its implementation. Several firms have tried and dropped the idea. PRP is an individual motivator. In many organisations, however, it has led to charges that it allows managers to reward individuals for being compliant not for achievement. The degree to which goals are achieved is often a matter of judgement; the charge is that the judgement is biased, intentionally or not, by other factors.

As a result employees have regarded the system as inequitable and overall performance has declined. Furthermore, there are examples of the implementation leading to industrial conflict such as at the BBC. PRP can lead to conflicts within an organisation, if it is individually based. PRP, if team based, can lead to relationship problems if team members view their lack of achievement as being the responsibility of one team member.

Counted among learning experiences is a clearing bank which based the pay of branch managers on the branch performance, only to discover that cross-referrals to other parts of the bank – such as investment management – dried up because they were not included in the performance targets.

The unexpected results of PRP may be understandable if we consider the work of Vroom. He argued that it is not enough to set goals and rewards. To be effective, rewards must be seen as being achievable. Under PRP, the targets are sometimes seen as movable goalposts; they are, therefore, inherently unattainable. Similar effects occur if an employee is given a task that appears to be beyond his or her competence. In such situations employees are not motivated, rather they are demotivated.

Motivation also rests on ability and competence. To achieve high levels of output it is necessary to enhance the capabilities of employees which means training and development.

Globalisation

Globalisation is one of the buzzwords of the 1990s. Although it is bringing profound changes to national economies, the way companies conduct their business and the world of work, nobody seems to know how to measure it. What constitutes globalisation is fairly clear. The Paris-based Organisation for Economic Co-operation and Development (OECD) says it is a widening and deepening of companies' operations across borders to produce and sell goods and services in more markets. Globalisation's most dynamic element since the mid-1980s has been foreign investment, although it can also take the form of trade and collaboration for purposes such as product development, production and sourcing. This has been a major strategy for multinational companies.

Element 5.3 Examine the competitiveness of UK industry

EUROPE'S TOP COMPANIES

The data presented in Table 5.1 appeared in the *Financial Times* of 27 June 1994 and was based on interviews with senior industrialists throughout Europe.

Table 5.1 Europe's most respected companies: top companies by sector

Automobiles/Auto trucks & parts
1	Bayerische Motoren Werke	Germany
2	Bosch (Robert)	Germany
3	Peugeot	France

Banks & financial institutions
1	Deutsche Bank	Germany
2	Union Bank of Switzerland	Switzerland
3	Lloyds Bank	UK

Beverages & tobacco
1	LVMH Moet Hennessy Louis Vuitton	France
2	Heineken	Netherlands
3	Guinness	UK

Chemicals, paper & packaging
1	Ciba-Geigy	Switzerland
2	Air Liquide	France
3	ICI	UK

Construction & building materials
1	Holzmann, Philipp	Germany
2	RMC Group	UK
3	Pilkington	UK

Diversified holding companies
1	BTR	UK
2	Rentokil	UK
3	Hanson	UK

Electricity & water
1	RWE	Germany
2	Powergen	UK
3	National Grid	UK

Electronics & electrical components
1	Siemens	Germany
2	Alcatel	France
3	Nokia	Finland

Engineering
1	ABB Asea Brown Boveri	Sweden/Switzerland
2	Rolls-Royce	UK
3	Linde	Germany

Media
1	Reuters	UK
2	Reed Elsevier	UK
3	Bertelsmann	Germany

Table 5.1 Europe's most respected companies: top companies by sector (continued)

Oil, gas & mining
1	Royal Dutch/Shell	Netherlands/UK
2	Repsol	Spain
3	British Gas	UK

Pharmaceuticals & healthcare
1	Roche	Switzerland
2	Astra	Sweden
3	Glaxo	UK

Retail
1	Marks & Spencer	UK
2	Sainsbury's	UK
3	John Lewis	UK

Telecoms & communications
1	British Telecom	UK
2	PTT Nederland	Netherlands
3	Vodafone	UK

Transport
1	British Airways	UK
2	BAA	UK
3	Swire (John) & Sons	UK

Source: Financial Times/Price Waterhouse
© Financial Times

ACTIVITY 5.3.3

Identify local subsidiaries (or the nearest plant) of any of the companies in Table 5.1. How have local employment changes reflected the esteem of the company?

INTERNATIONAL COMPARISONS OF COMPETITIVENESS

The article from the *Financial Times* in Fig 5.17 paints a roser picture of the UK's competitive position in Europe.

The data in Table 5.2 appeared in the *Financial Times* of 6 December 1994. The following definitions may be helpful:

1 *Consumer prices.* This is a measure of the rate of consumer or retail inflation. In the UK we use the Retail Price Index (RPI) which is published monthly.

2 *Producer prices.* A measure of the change in factory gate prices. Important because changes in this measure tend to lead changes in RPI by approximately six months. It is also an indicator when compared with other countries of changes in price competitiveness of industry.

Element 5.3 Examine the competitiveness of UK industry

Britain "Booming"

Britain's exports are set for strong growth as the rest of Europe moves into economic recovery, according to two reports published in 1994. The Lloyds Bank *Quarterly Economic Bulletin* said that falling relative labour costs mean UK companies are well placed to take advantage of stronger European Union markets. Mr Trevor Williams, Lloyds' senior economist, said: 'Prospects for UK export growth seem to be the best for a decade. Relative unit labour costs improved by about 15 per cent in 1993, a much better gain than for the 1980s. After jumping 10 per cent last year, export price growth is expected to be barely positive in the next two years, helped by low domestic inflation.' This optimism, ahead of Friday's trade figures, is shared by Professor Douglas McWilliams in the quarterly economic report of the Chartered Institute of Marketing. He says: 'Surveys show a powerful growth in export orders and it would be reasonable to expect continued sales growth as the world's economic revival spreads.' The report forecasts the UK current account falling from a deficit of more than £11 billion this year to £5.6 billion in three years time.

Fig 5.17   *Source:* The *Financial Times*, January 1994

3 *Unit labour costs*. In essence a measure of the changes in wage costs per unit of production.

4 *Real exchange rate*. A weighted average of the value of a currency in terms of other major currencies. This measure allows us to track the underlying movement of a currency.

ACTIVITY 5.3.4

PC
5.3.3
5.3.4

Task 1. Using information from the Table 5.2 create graphs showing how the variables have changed for each country.

Task 2. Answer the following questions:

a What is the significance of rising unit labour cost?
b What relationship do you see between the real exchange rate and the measures of inflation?
c How do you account for the low levels of German and Japanese inflation?
d What else could the UK Government do to improve our inflation performance?

Table 5.2 International economic indicators (1994)

(a) UNITED STATES

	Consumer prices	Producer prices	Earnings	Unit labour costs	Real exchange rate
1985	100.0	100.0	100.0	100.0	100.0
1986	101.9	98.6	102.3	99.4	85.0
1987	105.6	100.7	103.9	96.7	76.2
1988	109.9	103.2	107.0	99.1	71.0
1989	115.2	108.5	110.1	101.1	74.9
1990	121.5	113.9	113.6	104.3	73.4
1991	126.6	116.3	117.3	107.8	74.2
1992	130.4	117.7	120.2	108.4	74.2
1993	134.3	119.2	123.1	107.7	76.6

(b) GERMANY

	Consumer prices	Producer prices	Earnings	Unit labour costs	Real exchange rate
1985	100.0	100.0	100.0	100.0	100.0
1986	99.9	97.5	103.4	103.8	107.4
1987					
1988	101.4	96.2	112.3	106.9	110.0
1989	104.2	99.3	117.3	108.0	107.8
1990	107.0	101.0	123.5	110.3	110.7
1991	110.7	103.4	131.2	115.0	106.2
1992	115.1	104.9	138.0	121.5	108.7
1993	119.8	104.9	145.7	125.9	110.2

(c) JAPAN

	Consumer prices	Producer prices	Earnings	Unit labour costs	Real exchange rate
1985	100.0	100.0	100.0	100.0	100.0
1986	100.8	95.3	101.4	103.4	118.4
1987	101.2	92.5	103.1	100.6	122.9
1988	102.2	92.3	107.8	96.2	131.0
1989	104.9	94.2	114.0	96.1	123.5
1990	108.2	95.7	120.1	98.3	108.3
1991	111.8	96.8	124.3	101.8	114.8
1992	113.9	95.9	125.6	111.0	116.3
1993	115.3	94.3	125.8	116.9	134.0

(d) UNITED KINGDOM

	Consumer prices	Producer prices	Earnings	Unit labour costs	Real exchange rate
1985	100.0	100.0	100.0	100.0	100.0
1986	103.4	101.4	107.7	104.1	94.2
1987	107.7	104.9	116.3	106.6	94.6
1988	113.0	108.7	126.2	109.5	102.3
1989	121.8	113.9	137.2	114.4	101.3
1990	133.3	121.0	150.1	122.7	102.8
1991	141.2	127.5	162.4	131.3	106.6
1992	146.4	131.5	173.1	133.9	103.5
1993	148.7	136.7	180.9	134.7	95.7

Notes to tables

Statistics for Germany apply only to western Germany. Data supplied by Datastream and WEFA from national government and IMF sources, and by JP Morgan, New York. *Consumer prices:* not seasonally adjusted. *Producer prices:* not seasonally adjusted, US – finished goods, Japan – manufactured goods, Germany – industrial products, UK – manufactured products. *Earnings index:* not seasonally adjusted, refers to earnings in manufacturing. Hourly except Japan (monthly) and UK (weekly). *Unit labour costs:* seasonally adjusted, measured in domestic currencies. Germany – mining and manufacturing, other countries – manufacturing industry.
© The *Financial Times*

UK UNEMPLOYMENT 1984–90

Figure 5.18 shows how employment increased throughout the period 1984 to 1990. Notice the particularly rapid rise in the boom year 1988. This followed two years of income tax reductions. These produced a fiscal stimulus. Unfortunately inflation started to rise and eventually peaked in 1990 at 10 per cent. In response to rising inflation (demand-pull) the government raised interest rates and this led to a fall in the rate of job creation and eventually the period of job destruction in the early 1990s.

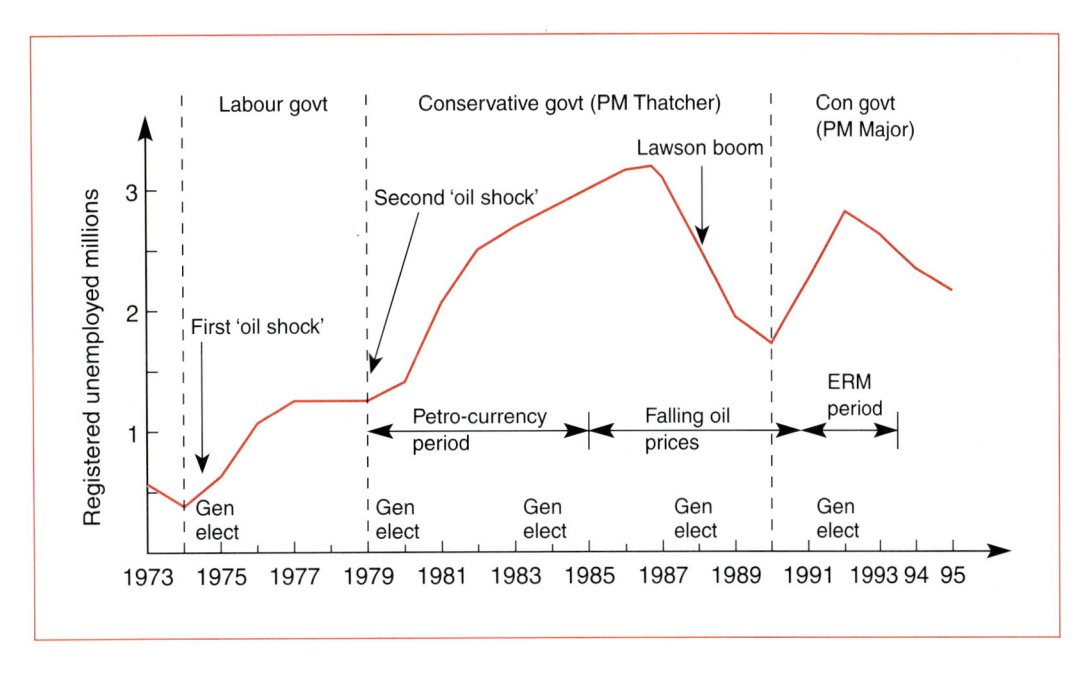

Element 5.3 Examine the competitiveness of UK industry

Fig 5.18 UK Unemployment (claimant count) *Source: Social Trends 1994*

Figure 5.19 shows an international comparison of unemployment rates. We can see that the UK has the worst record on unemployment in the period covered. This is followed by the USA.

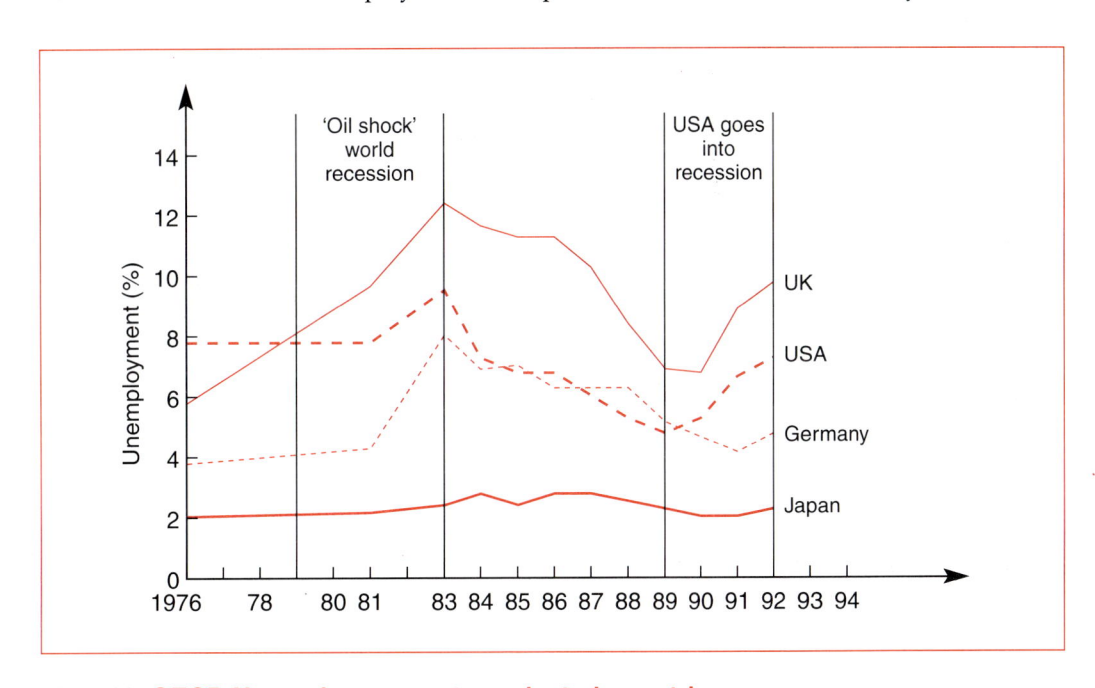

Fig 5.19 OECD Unemployment rates selected countries *Source: Social Trends 1994*

ACTIVITY 5.3.5

Obtain most up-to-date figures available and complete graph in Fig 5.19. How does the UK compare in this later period?

PC 5.2.4

387

Unit 5 Production and employment in the economy

Self assessment questions

1 What is the difference between temporary work and temping?

2 What proportion of workers are expected to be peripheral?

3 Give four strategies used by businesses to improve performance.

4 Define 'regional policy'.

5 Explain the term 'industrial policy'.

6 Give examples of 'underground-economy occupations'.

7 How has UK unemployment compared to that of the USA and Japan over the past ten years?

8 What are the benefits of free trade for competitiveness?

9 Define unit labour costs.

10 Explain the term 'relative labour costs'.

11 Give examples of exchange rates.

12 If £1=Dm 2.20, what is the cost in pounds of a car retailing at DM 24 200?

13 Give three advantages of a high exchange rate policy.

14 Give three disadvantages of a high exchange rate policy.

15 Explain the following terms: OECD, GATT, WTO, EU.

16 Identify two 'quality standards'.

17 Name five industries or firms that have been privatised.

18 Explain the terms 'Anglo-Saxon' and 'Rhine' model when applied to labour markets.

19 What is meant by the term 'human capital'?

20 Give three examples of industries where high expenditures on R&D is the norm.

Element 5.3 Examine the competitiveness of UK industry

Additional activities

ACTIVITY 5.3.6

In groups of three, you are to research the competitiveness of three separate industries. You are required to identify key indicators using government and industry statistics. Examples are average wages, value added per employee, profitability, earnings per share ratios. You will find it useful to refer back to Element 5.1.

Task 1. Identify sources of information.

Task 2. Identify relevant differences between industries.

Task 3. Answer the following questions in relation to the industries studied.
  a What external changes have the industries had to face over the past five years?
  b How has total employment in the industry changed since 1990? (What are the problems with finding this information?)

Task 4. Give examples of how these industries are improving their productivity and competitiveness. Identify and comment on additional methods they could adopt to improve their competitiveness.

You are to submit both a written report and a verbal report lasting ten minutes.

PC
5.1.3
5.1.4
5.1.5
C
3.1.1
3.1.2
3.1.3
3.1.4
3.1.5
3.2.1
3.2.2
3.2.3
3.2.4
3.2.5
AN
3.1.1
3.1.2
3.1.3
3.1.4
3.1.5
3.1.6
3.2.1
3.2.3
3.2.4
3.3.1
3.3.2
3.3.3
3.3.4
3.3.5

ACTIVITY 5.3.7

Research a company of your own choice. You are to report on external forces operating on the company that have obliged it to alter/change its behaviour. The time period to be considered will be not less than five years and may be longer if you believe it relevant. You are specifically requested to illustrate a relevant set of three of the following external forces:

1 technological changes
2 green issues
3 political/legal changes
4 economic changes (e.g. the current state of the economy)
5 social/cultural changes (e.g. status of women/children/men)
6 competitors especially from overseas.

You are advised to consider each heading separately detailing first the nature of the external change, second the impact on your chosen organisation and finally how the organisation changed. Remember that organisations may adapt by changing their product range, production methods or staffing arrangements. Try to cover the issues/forces more difficult to achieve. Finally you are required to give an evaluation of the effectiveness of your chosen organisation in adapting to the need to implement change. Your report should be in formal report format and be approximately 700 words long.

PC
5.1.1
5.1.2
5.1.3
5.1.4
5.1.5
5.3.2
5.3.4
C
3.1.1
3.1.2
3.1.3
3.1.4
3.1.5
3.2.1
3.2.2
3.2.3
3.2.4
3.2.5

389

Unit 5 Production and employment in the economy

PC
5.2.1
5.2.2
5.2.3
C
3.3.1
3.3.2
3.3.3
3.3.4
3.3.5
3.4.1
3.4.2
3.4.3
3.4.4
3.4.5

ACTIVITY 5.3.8

In the UK and throughout Western Europe there have been many changes in the organisation of work. Most notable has been the growth of non-standard employment.

Task 1. Explain the meanings of the following terms and give two examples of each:

   a Part-time
   b Temporary
   c Fixed-term
   d Job-share
   e Agency
   f Self-employment
   g Tele-work (home working)

Task 2. The conditions of service (pay, holiday entitlement, sickness benefit, etc.) are affected by the nature of the contract of employment. Using three of the above as examples show how the conditions differ.

Task 3. When you have completed your education, which type of employment do you wish to obtain ? Give reasons for your answer.

Task 4. Answer the following questions:

   a Some people may prefer one or other of the above non-standard forms. Why may this be the case ?
   b Is the development of non-standard work to be encouraged ?
   c Who does it benefit ?
   d What disadvantages are there ?
   e Who is disadvantaged ?

ACTIVITY 5.3.9

Bradford is a mature industrial city. It carries the legacy of its development. It has been a textile area specialising in woollen goods since the late seventeenth century, but its main phase of growth occurred during the nineteenth century. Following local government reorganisation in the early 1970s, it now includes Ilkley and other towns in the Wharfe Valley. In its heyday over 60 000 people were employed in the textile industry.

Since the early 1980s the local council has made strenuous efforts to increase the number of visitors to the area. A key attraction is the village of Howarth, the home of the world-famous Brönte sisters. There has also been the development of the National Museum of Film and Photography. Other local sights include Ilkley (which dates back to Roman times) and the Yorkshire Dales.

There has also been the growth of the chemical industry and the service sector. This latter growth has been limited by the nearby city of Leeds which is the regional financial centre. Nevertheless three major building societies have headquarters in the

Element 5.3   Examine the competitiveness of UK industry

ACTIVITY 5.3.9 continued

city: Huddersfield & Bradford, National Provincial and the Bradford & Bingley. It is also the home of one of the largest independent supermarket groups, Wm. Morrison's. Its current unemployment rate is 8.4 per cent.

Research and answer the following questions.

a To what extent can Bradford still be categorised as a textile town ?
b What difficulties are created by the decline of manufacturing industry in established areas ?
c Is there a connection between the rise of crime and violence and the decline of the inner cities following the change in employment patterns?
d What options are available to local governments to deal with declines in traditional employment, as exemplified by Bradford ?
e In your own town or city, what sources of information are available about the changing patterns of employment?
f How has the pattern of employment changed in your area? Which are the major job-shedding industries and which are the ones that are employing more people?

Assignment 1

PC
5.1.3
5.2.1
5.2.2
5.2.3
5.2.4
C
3.2.1
3.2.2
3.2.3
3.2.4
3.2.5
3.4.1
3.4.2
3.4.3
3.4.4

In 1984 new federal environment protection laws were passed in the USA. These forced the closure of two thirds of all the land-fill sites in that country. As a result the disposal of toxic waste became significantly more expensive. Between 1984 and 1987 the cost trebled. As a result the companies resorted to incinerating their waste.

One British firm was a major beneficiary – Rechem Environmental Services. This company specialised in the incineration of toxic wastes. From a loss of £112 000 in 1985 the company went to profits of £4.5 million in 1988. In the latter year the company had a turnover of £13.4 million.

The company had two plants for waste incineration at Pontypool in South Wales and Fawley in Hampshire. These are high-temperature plants capable of dealing with the most toxic wastes such as PCBs. Very few firms throughout the world are capable of dealing with these products and hence Rechem had the opportunity to exercise a significant mark-up.

In 1989 Rechem made a profit of £8.8 million on a turnover of £19.5 million. The share price rose from 195p in 1988 to 725p in late 1989.

In 1989 there was a rise in the prominence of environmental issues, and of the Green Party, which took 15 per cent of the vote in that year's European Parliamentary elections vote. Journalists began to write about green issues concerning pollution. Rechem was often prominent in these reports. The company benefited from support given by Conservative politicians. For example, Virginia Bottomley, then a junior environment minister praised the company as true friends of the environment. Rechem was widely acknowledged as the world leader in the safe incineration of toxic waste.

Clouds were on the horizon, however. For many years there had been stories of children born with eye defects and of diseased cattle near to the Rechem plants. In February 1989 a local action group petitioned the High Court for a declaration that Rechem was not obeying environmental legislation, and further that the local authority was failing in its statutory duty of licensing the plant. The effect of the court case was to close the plant, at least for an indefinite period.

Required:

- A report detailing other pollution incidents.
- An evaluation of the risk to the public of pollution.
- An evaluation of the adverse effects on companies of becoming associated with anti-environmental activities. (Give examples.)
- A review of UK and European Union legislation in the field.
- A report covering the impact of pollution incidents on the workers in a plant (or industry).
- An explanation of which employment laws are breached in such instances.

Assignment 2

You are a finance assistant working for Gercars PLC. The company imports cars from Germany and distributes them in the UK. It has averaged 5000 cars annually since 1987, although this figure hides the fact that sales rose from 3500 in 1987 to 7000 in 1990 and has since fallen to 2400 in 1995.

The company takes delivery of cars evenly throughout the year. For example in 1987 it imported at a rate of approximately 300 per month. Any unsold cars are held in stock. Payment to the German supplier occurs three months after delivery. Contracts are negotiated six months in advance. The most recent contract was settled in December 1994 for 1800 cars. The cars are charged in Deutschmarks, but sold in Sterling (£). In December the Deutschmark price was DM 16 310 at an exchange rate of £1 = DM2.33. The cars retail in the UK at £8000. Following a dollar currency crisis, the pound now trades at £1 = DM2.22.

Task 1. You have been asked to draft a report showing the effect of the change on the company's financial position.

Task 2. The Finance Manager has to present a recommendation as to the future pricing strategy of the company to the board of directors and has asked for a briefing paper outlining the dangers to the company if the UK government changes its exchange rate policy. The paper is for non-specialists and needs to be in plain English. He instructs you to prepare the paper considering two scenarios:

1 Britain rejoins the ERM in June 1995 at a new central rate of £1 = DM 2.20.

2 Britain remains outside the ERM and the pound depreciates by 5 per cent over the forthcoming twelve months, although there is instability in the foreign exchange markets during the period.

In each case you are to explain the advantages and disadvantages to the company, given that each scenario will affect the freedom of the UK Government to set interest rates and the level of domestic (UK) demand.

Self assessment questions

1. What is the difference between vocational and academic education?
2. What proportion of workers are expected to be peripheral by the end of the century?
3. Give four strategies used by businesses to improve performance.
4. Define 'regional policy'.
5. Explain the term 'industrial policy'.
6. Give examples of 'underground-economy occupations'.
7. How has UK unemployment compared to that of the USA and Japan over the past ten years?
8. What are the benefits of free trade for competitiveness?
9. Define unit labour costs.
10. Explain the term 'relative labour costs'.
11. Give examples of exchange rates.
12. If £1=Dm 2.20, what is the cost in pounds of a car retailing at DM 24,200?
13. Give three advantages of a high exchange rate policy.
14. Give three disadvantages of a high exchange rate policy.
15. Explain the following terms: OECD, GATT, WTO, EU.
16. Identify two 'quality standards'.
17. Name five industries or firms that have been privatised.
18. Explain the terms 'Anglo-Saxon' and 'Rhine' model when applied to labour markets.
19. What is meant by the term product innovation?
20. Give three examples of industries where high expenditures on R&D is the norm.

Unit 5 Production and employment in the economy

Answers to self-assessment questions

Element 5.1

1. The appropriation and the cost subtraction method.
2. a) quality assurance; b) increased customer satisfaction; c) reduced production costs. There are others.
3. a) availability; b) satisfaction; c) individuality; d) status concerns; e) degree of fit to consumer wants.
4. Examples include; Esso, BP, Ratners, British Gas, Regional Electricity Companies, McDonalds, Body Shop, etc.
5. Self answer
6. Single European Act initially ISO 9000 now known as BS IS EN 9000.
7. Cost reduction, improved reliability, increased consumer satisfaction.
8. Price, delivery, product specification, quality, flexibility of supply, reliability.
9. Stability, long-term planning, increased investment. 'Learning by doing' cost reductions. Security of orders and supply.
10. Stock control, stock management, introduction of 'Just in Time'. Reduction of materials inventory.
11. a) Increased productivity; b) reduced wage rates.
12. Self answer; but could include BAE, Rover, Nissan, Toyota, Ford, etc.
13. Mass production aims at producing standardised output at least cost production. Flexible production aims at satisfying individual customer needs. More market responsive.
14. See diagram page 352.
15. Examples include: textiles, catering, distribution, bulk chemicals.
16. Combination of low customer specificity, competition, low labour skill input and declining markets (see PLC).
17. Marketing helps firms to produce to meet customer (consumer) wants. Improves consumer appreciation of product. Affects corporate image increasing 'reputation' especially for big-ticket items e.g. BMW.
18. This requires appreciation of the impact of labour legislation affecting 'secondary picketing' and the reduction in the incidence of labour disputes. Thus improving security of supply.
19. Note these costs depend upon the individual organisation but include: a) labour costs, materials, machinery (capital) costs.
20. Requires answer relating to Maastricht Treaty.

Element 5.2

1. Examples include: primary, coal, quarrying, agriculture, fishing, etc.; secondary, chemicals, power generation, car manufacturers, office equipment, printing, etc.; tertiary, hotels, distribution, repairs, banking, etc.
2. Secondary, primary; tertiary; tertiary; secondary.
3. 1950s
4. 1973 (but decline on meaning of peak).
5. Increases of both full- and part-time married women's employment.
6. Decline of manufacturing employment. Also decline in primary sectors such as extraction and fishery.
7. a) failure theories; b) natural development theories; c) North Sea oil based theories.
8. The increase of productivity is due to education and training.
9. Under 24s especially males. Also over 55s but this is hidden as they often take 'early retirement'.
10. YTS, Modern apprenticeship, increased training, compulsory training. development of 'vocational' education.
11. Standard requires full-time unlimited duration any other contract is non-standard.
12. Two possible answers a) increased incentives and change to enterprise culture; or b) increased unemployment leading to self-job creation.
13. Non-registered output and employment.
14. a) flexibility easier to dismiss; b) cheaper lower social costs; c) easier to match employment to exact requirements.
15. Influences on consumption (spending) patterns. Influences on family life. Psychological and social influences of insecurity. Affects on social security budget.
16. Core equals essential. Periphery equals sub-contractable.
17. See recent 'disturbances'. Family breakdown, suicide rates. Also productivity growth low inflation and hence rising living standards?
18. Temps = Agency staff: temporary = fixed term contract (usually short).
19. Examples include GNVQ, NVQ, Modern Apprenticeship, National Curriculum, TECs, growth of Higher Education.
20. Loss of tax revenue, increased social security spending, inability to manage economy.

Element 5.3

1. Vocational education is designed to be of direct usefulness to the work situation. Academic education does not have this aim.
2. Approximately two-thirds.
3. Examples include, 'just-in-time production', flexible production, delayering, employee empowerment, the introduction of new technology, closer supplier and customer liaison,
4. Regional policy is government action that is designed to reduce the geographical inequality of unemployment.
5. Industrial policy is the action of government that is designed to improve industrial (especially manufacturing) competitiveness.
6. Typical examples include building trades and domestic service together with unskilled agricultural.
7. Much worse.
8. The existence of free competition forces firms to improve their competitiveness just to survive. Further the existence of imports prevents employees from making inflationary wage demands.
9. Unit labour costs equal wages divided by the quality (volume) of production.
10. RULC allows the international comparison of wages. Each countries' labour costs are converted to some common currency at some Exchange Rate (either current or adjusted).
11. See next question.
12. Divide 24,200 by 2.2. This gives £11,363.
13. Reduced inflationary pressures, cheaper raw materials, better terms of trade.
14. Increased unemployment, bigger balance of payments deficit, increased imports. Often needs high interest rates to support with the consequent effects on the domestic economy.
15. Check in text.
16. BS 5750, ISO 9000.
17. Choose from; gas, electricity, coal, docks, Amersham International, British Aerospace, British Steel, Property Services Agency, etc.
18. Anglo-Saxon refers to de-regulated labour markets without minimum wages, etc. Usually decentralised wage bargaining. Rhine model refers to the European practice of government intervention with centralised bargaining and additional social protection.
19. Innovation is the bringing to market of new inventions. e.g. compact discs were the product that arose from the invention of lasers.
20. Pharmaceuticals, electronics, bio-technology, computers, etc.

UNIT 6

FINANCIAL TRANSACTIONS, COSTING AND PRICING

This unit aims to give an introduction to the processes of selling and purchasing and the financial documentation and information that support those transactions. The link between the costs of providing goods and services and the determination of prices through the concept of the break-even point is also covered.

Element 6.1
EXPLAIN ADDED VALUE, DISTRIBUTION OF ADDED VALUE AND MONEY CYCLE

Performance criteria;

1. **Explain the trading cycle of goods or services in a business and their added value.**
2. **Explain the distribution of added value.**
3. **Explain the money cycle.**
4. **Explain factors for consideration when selling.**
5. **Explain factors for consideration when buying.**

CONSIDERATIONS FOR THE SELLER

When a business is in a position to sell goods or services, it needs to take a number of factors into consideration.

Payment terms

What payment terms is the business prepared to offer when selling goods or services? In other words, when does the business want the customer to pay for the goods or services? Although a business could insist on cash payments in return for the sale of its goods and services, this is normal only in certain sectors, e.g. retailing. Usually business transactions are conducted on credit. The amount of credit offered and the length of the credit period could influence the decision of a customer to buy goods or services from a supplier. How long should the credit period be? 30 days? 60 days?

Credit

How much credit should be extended to that customer? Should there be a credit limit on the customer's account, say £10 000? £20 000?

Discounts

Should the customer wish to purchase large volumes of goods or services – bulk purchases – should a discount be offered? Large customers, such as Marks and Spencer's or Sainsbury's, purchase their goods from their suppliers in such vast quantities that they are able to negotiate substantial discounts with those suppliers! It could be that some customers may prefer to settle their accounts early in return for a *cash discount*. Should the business therefore offer an incentive to its customers to settle their accounts early? If so, what should that incentive be? Cash discounts usually take the form of a certain percentage that can be deducted from the amount outstanding, if paid within a certain period of time, e.g. 5 per cent if paid within ten days. A business therefore needs to consider how much cash discount to offer and how quickly it wants the outstanding bill to be settled in return! An extreme example is payment on receipt. How much of a discount should such customers receive?

Creditworthiness

Before offering any credit to any future customer, a business must in the first instance consider very carefully that customer's creditworthiness. In other words, the business should check on the customer's ability to pay its debts. This can be done in a number of ways: the customer can be asked to forward a number of trade references; a credit check could be requested from certain credit agencies to see if anything such as a court judgement has been awarded against the customer; bank references can be requested and even the customer's last set of accounts can be considered, if available. Assessing a customer's creditworthiness is of the utmost importance as failure to take reasonable precautions could result in a *bad debt*.

Credit control

A business should also examine its debt collection procedures – its credit control – to see if it is effective enough to ensure that amounts outstanding are collected as quickly and efficiently as possible. A good credit control department is crucial in any business if the cash is to be collected promptly. Any delays in the cash collection process could have detrimental effects on the cash position of the business!

The quality of the good or service

A business should consider the good or service it offers. For example, is the service fast, friendly, efficient? How quickly can the business respond to an order? Can the business deliver the goods at all?

CONSIDERATIONS FOR THE BUYER

A customer would be interested in a number of factors when considering purchasing goods or services from a supplier.

- *Supplier assessments.* The supplier should be assessed in the first instance as a business. Is the supplier a financially stable and reputable business. This information can be obtained by analysing a recent final set of accounts, if available, assessing the reputation of the supplier in the trade or industry and maybe even requesting trade references.
- *Specification.* It would be particularly important to examine the specification of the goods offered to see if they meet the necessary requirements. Can the supplier cope with the *quality* being asked of it? Indeed, do they have the experience of coping with similar orders?
- *Delivery dates.* Can the supplier deliver to the deadlines required? What assurances can the supplier give that these delivery dates will be met? This is obviously important in that the delivery dates have a direct effect on the customer's business.
- *Financial considerations.* Perhaps the most obvious financial consideration is the *price* itself. Is it competitive? Is there room for further negotiation? The customer must also consider other factors, e.g. *credit terms* and *payment terms*. How much credit is being offered – in terms of monetary value and the length of time given. Are any *discounts* offered, e.g. cash discounts for early settlement or bulk discount if large quantities are being considered.

All of the above factors will influence a customer's decision whether or not to buy from a particular supplier. It is not a single factor that affects that decision but a combination of all factors!

Self assessment questions

1 Consider the following statements:
    i) cash discounts are offered to encourage early settlement of a debt
    ii) offering credit facilities will ensure that a potential customer will buy goods from a business.

    a (i) True, (ii) False   c (i) False, (ii) True
    b (i) True, (ii) True   d (i) False, (ii) False

2 i) the amount of credit offered could influence the decision of the customer whether or not to buy.
   ii) the payment terms offered to a customer could influence the decision of a customer whether or not to buy.
   a (i) True, (ii) False
   b (i) True, (ii) True
   c (i) False, (ii) True
   d (i) False, (ii) False

3 Consider the following:
   A business purchased goods on credit on the 20th January for £125. A cash discount of 5% is offered if the businesses pays the outstanding amount within 10 days. How much discount and by which date should the business pay the amount outstanding if it wishes to take advantage of the cash discount offer?
   a (i) £6.25 (ii) 31st Jan
   b (i) £6.25 (ii) 30th Jan
   c (i) £12.50 (ii) 29th Jan
   d (i) £6.50 (ii) 30th Jan

4 Assuming the business took full advantage of the cash discount in Question 3. How much would the net amount payable be?
   a £112.50
   b £118.48
   c £106.25
   d £118.75

5 Which of the following factors should a business consider before purchasing goods/services from a potential supplier.
   i) specification of goods
   ii) quality of goods
   iii) delivery dates
   iv) price of goods
   a (i) and (ii)
   b (i), (ii) and (iii)
   c (i) and (iii) only
   d All of them

6 A good credit control dept. in any business is crucial if the cash is to be collected as quickly as possible.
   a True
   b False

7 Which of the following should a business check when assessing a potential customers creditworthiness?
   i) trade references
   ii) credit check with a credit agency
   iii) the name of the financial acountant
   iv) bank references
   a (i) and (ii) only
   b (i), (ii) and (iii) only
   c All of them
   d (i), (ii) and (iv) only

8 Assessing a customers' creditworthiness is of the utmost importance, as failure to take reasonable precautions could result in a bad debt.
   a True
   b False

9 How would you assess the financial stability of a potential supplier?
   a by examining the specifications of the goods
   b by asking for trade references
   c by analysing a recent set of accounts
   d by asking the suppliers' Managing Director

10 A thorough credit assessment of a potential customer will ensure that that particular customer will never become a bad debt.
   a True
   b False

Element 6.2
EXPLAIN FINANCIAL TRANSACTIONS AND COMPLETE SUPPORTING DOCUMENTS

Performance criteria

1 Explain the purposes of financial transactions and documentation.

2 Explain the use of purchases documents and complete them clearly and accurately.

3 Explain the use of sales documents and complete them clearly and accurately.

4 Explain the use of payments documents and complete an example clearly and accurately.

5 Explain the use of receipts documents and complete an example clearly and accurately.

6 Explain why it is important to complete documents correctly and give possible consequences of incorrect completion.

7 Identify and explain security checks for business documents.

PURPOSES OF FINANCIAL TRANSACTIONS AND DOCUMENTATION

Every business should keep clear and accurate records of its financial transactions for the following reasons.

1 The business knows exactly what the financial position is at any point in time with regards to its bank/cash balance: for example, how much it owes its suppliers (creditors), how much it is owed by its customers (debtors) and so on. The careful monitoring of the bank/cash, creditors and debtors balance of a business will also ensure that mistakes and omissions are kept to a minimum.

2 The business has a source from which to prepare a set of accurate and periodic management accounts, e.g. monthly/quarterly final accounts or year-end/statutory accounts.

3 The business can monitor its progress or performance regularly through financial analysis (e.g. by making appropriate comparisons with last month's/year's results, with a forecasted set of results or maybe with another business operating in the same field), so that the decision-making process within the organisation can be as effective as possible. Information gained from such analysis could also form the basis of future budgets and forecasts

4 The business can see how profitably it is operating.

5 The owners of the business – shareholders in the case of a company – can judge the effectiveness of the management.

6 Any legal requirements are met, e.g. to enable the business transactions to be audited by an independent firm of accountants so that annual statutory accounts may be filed at Companies House (in the case of a company), the Customs & Excise for VAT calculations or the Inland Revenue for any other tax calculations.

7 Other interested parties can be given the correct financial information, e.g. bank manager, financial institutions, potential investors, financial analysts, etc.

PURCHASES AND SALES DOCUMENTS

Table 6.1 is a list of the large number of business documents which are in constant use in organisations involved in the buying and selling of goods and services.

This will be useful as a reference when the individual forms of business documentation are discussed later in this element.

Element 6.2 Explain financial transactions and complete supporting documents

Table 6.1 The business documentation cycle

Document	Supplier (Seller)	Customer (Buyer)
Enquiry by phone, fax or letter	Received by	Sent by
Quotation by letter or fax	Sent by	Received by
Purchase order	Received by	Sent by
Acknowledgement of order	Sent by	Received by
Action to despatch goods (e.g. requisition to stores raised, stock records altered)	Actioned by	---
Advice note	Sent by	Received by
Delivery note	Sent by	Received by
Goods received note	---	Issued by
Sales invoice (a sales invoice issued by the supplier will be the purchase invoice to the customer)	Sent by	Received by
Statement of account	Sent by	Received by
Credit control documentation	Sent by	Received by
Settlement of account	Received by	Sent by

Initial contact

The purchasing process begins with a *letter of enquiry*. This is sent by the potential customer (buyer) to the potential supplier (seller) in the initial stages of a trading relationship. An individual or a business wishing to purchase goods or services will probably issue letters of enquiry to a number of suppliers (sellers) requesting certain information (e.g. prices, delivery times, various specifications of the goods in question, etc.). It should be noted that an enquiry could take the form of a formal letter (individual or standard), a fax or even a simple telephone conversation.

A *quotation* is issued by the supplier (seller) on receipt of the above enquiry from the potential customer (buyer). This clearly indicates the details requested (e.g. a price, availability, etc.). Again a quotation could take the form of a formal, standard or bespoke letter headed quotation or simply the despatch of a price list or catalogue.

Order and delivery

If the quotation is to the potential customer's (buyer's) satisfaction, the individual or the buyer within a business will issue an official *purchase order*, which is sent to the supplier (seller). A typical purchase order is shown in Fig. 6.1.

```
┌─────────────────────────────────────────────────────────────┐
│                                                              │
│             PURCHASE ORDER                    No. 589        │
│                                                              │
│                 RIVERSIDE CLOTH HOUSE                        │
│                    4, Riverside Walk,                        │
│                       Pepperfield,                           │
│                         PE1  4XN                             │
│                                                              │
│            Tel. (0967) 75789   Fax. (0967) 81461             │
│                                                              │
│   To:   Mahmood Enterprises,                  Date 1/10/94   │
│         Unit 6,                                              │
│         Bingford,                                            │
│         BC2 3PX                                              │
│                                                              │
│   Please supply the following goods to the above address     │
│   within 5 days receipt of this order.                       │
└─────────────────────────────────────────────────────────────┘
```

Quantity	Catalogue No.	Description	Price £
2	A/123	Cloth	250.00 plus VAT

Signed: *S. Pidgeon*   S. PIDGEON – BUYER

Fig 6.1 Purchase order

It can be noted from Fig. 6.1 that Riverside Cloth House is ordering certain items from Mahmood Enterprises and the purchase order clearly shows the goods that are being ordered, the amount, the price, when the order is required – in this case within five days of receipt of the order – and the delivery address.

On receipt of the purchase order in Fig. 6.1, the seller or supplier (Mahmood Enterprises) will send an *acknowledgement of order* to the buyer or customer (Riverside Cloth House) confirming receipt of the purchase order and that the goods ordered can indeed be supplied by the required date. The acknowledgement of order can be in the form of a standard or bespoke letter headed 'Acknowledgement' or even a fax. Riverside Cloth House should at this stage check the contents of the acknowledgement to ensure that it meets with its approval.

An advice note is then sent by Mahmood Enterprises (the seller), when the goods have been despatched, to inform Riverside Cloth House (the buyer) that the ordered goods are on the way and that they should be expected imminently. The advice note is effectively a copy of the *delivery note* which accompanies the goods, a copy of which is shown in Fig. 6.2.

When the goods have arrived, the Riverside Cloth House should check what has actually been received against the delivery note. Any discrepancies should be noted, the delivery note signed and given to the Mahmood Enterprises' driver. As can be seen from Fig. 6.2, the delivery note (or the advice note for that matter) is simply a list of the goods being delivered which 'advises' the buyer (Riverside Cloth House) of that fact. It also acts as proof that the goods were actually delivered and it should be filed by the seller (Mahmood Enterprises).

If a carrier had been used that did not belong to the supplier (i.e. Mahmood Enterprises) then a *consignment note*, which is similar to the delivery note, would need to be signed.

DELIVERY/ADVICE NOTE   No. 1234

MAHMOOD ENTERPRISES,
Unit 6, Eccleshall Mills,
Bingford,
BG2 3PX

Tel. (05912) 5652496
Fax. (05912) 589093

Deliver to:

Riverside Cloth House,
4, Riverside Walk,
Pepperfield,
PE1 4XN.

Your Order No.	Invoice No.	Date	Account No.
589	1234	4/10/94	ME 146

Quantity	Catalogue No.	Description	
2	A/123	Cloth	

Proprietor: ADIL MAHMOOD   Received: *S. Pidgeon*

Fig 6.2 Delivery note

```
┌─────────────────────────────────────────────────────────────┐
│           RIVERSIDE CLOTH HOUSE            No. 589          │
│         GOODS RECEIVED NOTE                Date 4/10/94     │
│                                                             │
│  Supplier                 Mahmood Enterprises               │
│  Delivery Note No.        1234                              │
│  Our Purchase Order No.   589                               │
├──────────────┬──────────────────────────────────────────────┤
│  Quantity    │  Description of goods                        │
├──────────────┼──────────────────────────────────────────────┤
│      2       │  Rolls of cloth – type A/123                 │
│              │                                              │
├──────────────┴──────────────────────────────────────────────┤
│  Accepted by:  K Eaves                                      │
│  Details of any damage:  Damage to one roll agreed with driver │
└─────────────────────────────────────────────────────────────┘
```

Fig 6.3 Goods received note

Riverside Cloth House should now issue a *goods received note* (GRN) which is an internal document and is proof that the given goods have actually been received. The difference between a goods received note and a delivery note is that a goods received note is proof to the buyer (Riverside Cloth House) that the goods have actually been received, whereas a delivery note, once signed by the buyer (Riverside Cloth House), is proof of delivery to the seller (Mahmood Enterprises). The goods received note is shown in Fig. 6.3. A goods received note contains the name of the supplier, date received and a note of any damages.

Payment

Mahmood Enterprises now issues an *invoice* to Riverside Cloth House, assuming that Mahmood Enterprises has granted Riverside Cloth House credit facilities (i.e. Riverside Cloth House pays for the goods on a given date) e.g. 30 days from receipt not immediately. This is probably the most important document in the transaction. As can be seen from Fig. 6.4, it is prepared by the seller (Mahmood Enterprises) and is sent to and received by the buyer (Riverside Cloth House). As far as the seller is concerned a *sales invoice* has been raised, but, as far as the buyer or purchaser is concerned, a *purchase invoice* has been received. It is important that students realise that a sales invoice and a purchase invoice is the same document; its interpretation and treatment depend on who is considering it, i.e. the buyer or the seller!

The invoice clearly shows the following:

a details of the goods supplied to Riverside Cloth House;
b the individual prices of the goods supplied – £250.00;
c the VAT charged – £87.50;
d the total amount that is owing by Riverside Cloth House – £587.50;
e the terms of trade, i.e. when the amount outstanding (£587.50) should be paid – within 30 days;

Element 6.2 Explain financial transactions and complete supporting documents

---

INVOICE

No. 1234

MAHMOOD ENTERPRISES,
Unit 6, Eccleshall Mills,
Bingford,
BG2 3PX

Tel. (05912) 5652496
Fax. (05912) 589093

VAT Reg. No. 123 896011

To: Riverside Cloth House,
4, Riverside Walk,
Pepperfield,
PE1 4XN.

Your order No.	Invoice No.	Date/Tax point	Account No.
589	1234	4/10/94	RCH 146

Quantity	Catalogue	Description	Price	VAT	Total
2 rolls	A/123	Cloth	250.00	87.50	500.00

Terms: Nett 30 days
E & OE

Proprietor: ADIL MAHMOOD

Amount	500.00
Plus VAT @ $17\frac{1}{2}$%	87.50
Total Payable	587.50

Fig 6.4 Invoice

f name and address of the seller – Mahmood Enterprises;
g name and address of the buyer – Riverside Cloth House;
h VAT registration number mechanism – a VAT registered business must print this number;
i an invoice number – 1234 which provides Mahmood Enterprises with a 'control';
j the date of sale or the tax point – 4/10/94;
k purchase order number – so that Riverside Cloth House can easily identify the original order;
l an account number in the books of Mahmood Enterprises;
m E and OE – which is an abbreviation for 'Errors and Omissions Excepted' found on invoices, credit notes and statements, meaning that the seller can rectify at a later date any mistakes which may have occurred on the original invoice, either in the text or in the arithmetic. If this does not appear, the customer (Riverside Cloth House) could claim a final contractual price for the goods they received.

Let us now examine the invoice in Fig. 6.4 to see what Riverside Cloth House has been charged for two rolls of cloth type A/123. This is indeed what was signed as having been received on the delivery note and what Riverside Cloth House has documented on its goods received note. Let us assume for a moment, however, that one of the rolls was damaged in transit. Riverside Cloth have should not have to pay for two rolls of cloth; the damaged roll should be returned to Mahmood Enterprises. This should have been recorded as such on the delivery note, of course, and Riverside Cloth House's goods received note. If this is the case the invoice received by Riverside Cloth House is clearly wrong as it is being charged for two rolls of A/123 cloth.

In order to rectify the situation, Mahmood Enterprises (seller) must now issue Riverside Cloth House (buyer) with a *credit note* for the amount overcharged, i.e. £293.75. The Credit Note is shown in Fig. 6.5.

CREDIT NOTE

No. C004

MAHMOOD ENTERPRISES,
Unit 6, Eccleshall Mills,
Bingford,
BG2 3PX

Tel. (05912) 5652496
Fax. (05912) 589093

VAT Reg. No. 123 896011

To: Riverside Cloth House,
     4, Riverside Walk,
     Pepperfield,
     PE1 4XN.

Your order No.	Invoice No.	Date/Tax point	Account No.
589	1234	4/10/94	RCH 146

Quantity	Catalogue	Description	Price	VAT	Total
1 roll	A/123	Cloth	250.00	43.75	293.75

Reason for Credit:
Damage to cloth in transit
E & OE
Proprietor: ADIL MAHMOOD

Amount — 293.75
Plus VAT @ $17\frac{1}{2}$% — 43.75
Total Payable — 293.75

Fig 6.5 Credit note

Note that the credit note details are almost identical to that of an invoice; for this reason the credit note is issued in 'red' to clearly distinguish it from an invoice. As with the invoice, the credit note is prepared by the seller (Mahmood Enterprises) and is sent and received by the buyer (Riverside Cloth House) – that is, from the seller's point of view a *sales credit note* has been issued, whereas from the buyer's or purchaser's point of view a *purchase credit note* has been received. It is important that students realise that a sales credit note and a purchase credit note are the same document; its interpretation and treatment again depending on who is considering it.

A credit note would also have been issued if, for example, one roll of cloth was not of the type ordered, only one roll was despatched by mistake, or if there was an error on the invoice with the result of overcharging the customer (Riverside Cloth House). The effect of the credit note is therefore to reduce the amount outstanding to the correct amount!

Sometimes an error can be made on the invoice in the customer's favour with the result that the buyer or customer has been undercharged. In this instance, the seller or supplier

STATEMENT OF ACCOUNT

MAHMOOD ENTERPRISES,
Unit 6, Eccleshall Mills,
Bingford,   BG2 3PX

Tel. (05912) 5652496
Fax. (05912) 589093

VAT Reg. No. 123 896011

To: Riverside Cloth House,
     4, Riverside Walk,
     Pepperfield,
     PE1 4XN. A/C No. RCH 146

Date	Invoice credit note no.	Dr	Cr	Balance
30.9.94	Bal b/fwd	1250.00		1250.00
4.10.94	1234	587.50		1837.50
21.10.94	C004		93.75	1543.75
31.10.94	1259	990.00		253.75

E & OE

REMITTANCE ADVICE

MAHMOOD ENTERPRISES,
Unit 6, Eccleshall Mills,
Bingford,   BG2 3PX

Tel. (05912) 5652496
Fax. (05912) 589093

VAT Reg. No. 123 896011

To: Riverside Cloth House,
     4, Riverside Walk,
     Pepperfield,
     PE1 4XN. A/C No. RCH 146

Date	Invoice credit note no.	Dr	Cr	Balance
30/9	Bal	1250.00		1250.00
4/10	1234	587.50		1837.50
21/10	C004		93.75	1543.75
31/10	1259	990.00		2533.75

E & OE

Fig 6.6 Statement of account

issues the buyer or customer with a *debit note*. This will have the effect of rectifying the situation and will also be clearly shown on any statement of account as a charge; it therefore has the same effect as an invoice. Not surprisingly, the debit note will look much the same in content as an invoice, with the exception that the debit note (like the credit note) shows some reference to the original invoice.

At the end of each month, the seller or supplier (Mahmood Enterprises) should issue a *statement of account* to each one of its customers. A copy of the one sent to Riverside Cloth House is shown in Fig. 6.6.

As can be seen, the statement of account is simply a record of all the transactions between the buyer (Riverside Cloth House) and the seller (Mahmood Enterprises) including all invoices and credit notes issued and cheques received by the seller during the month, showing the amount currently owing to the seller (Mahmood Enterprises) – i.e. £2533.75. The invoice number 1234 and the credit note number C004 can clearly be seen together with a further invoice number 1254 which was issued on the 31 October 1994. The sum of these three transactions are then added to the balance still outstanding (if any) at the end

Fig 6.7

of last month, i.e. the balance brought forward. The statement usually takes the form of three columns: debit, credit and balance. All invoices are debited and all credit notes issued and cheques received by the seller credited. Note the balance column provides a 'running balance' total, i.e. debits are added to previous amounts outstanding, while credit notes and cheques are deducted. A debit balance means that the seller is owed money, or conversely the buyer owes money to the seller.

ACTIVITY 6.2.1

Follow the logic of the last paragraph through the statement of account issued to Riverside Cloth House in Fig. 6.6, and note the contents.

Statements of account would probably be generated by a computer, but they could be raised and issued manually, i.e. typed on a printed form.

The buyer (Riverside Cloth House) should now pay the amount outstanding on the statement of account and return with the payment (remittance) the attached *remittance advice* which informs the seller (Mahmood Enterprises) of the invoices that are being settled.

It should also be noted that a buyer could issue his or her own remittance advice based on the buyer's records, which should be, but may not necessarily be the same as the seller's (for reasons which will be dealt with later).

Credit control

Before an account is actually settled by a buyer, the seller may, in addition to the statement of account, issue further *credit control documentation* in order to prompt, remind and encourage payment if payment has not already been made within the specified terms as agreed, e.g. nett 30 days. This could take the form of a simple 'reminder', a letter phrased in such a way so as not to unduly upset the buyer (as he or she may already have paid or may be in the process of paying) or a much more strongly worded letter outlining specific threats that will be implemented if payment is not forthcoming:

- no further supplies of goods until payment is received;
- withdrawal of credit facilities;
- referral of the account to a credit collection agency, or;
- legal action.

Those threats may have to be implemented in more extreme cases, which will of course generate appropriate documentation, e.g. credit letters, solicitor's letters, court proceeding agency, etc.

It must be appreciated that credit control documentation should only be issued by the seller if the amount outstanding is overdue, i.e. the terms of payment have been broken by the buyer and that 'reminder' letters or requests for payment should be progressive in content, i.e. follow-up letters should be more strongly worded than initial ones.

PAYMENTS AND RECEIPTS DOCUMENTS

Methods of payment

By far the most common method of payment in the commercial world is by cheque, although cash payments do of course occur. Other forms of payment include postal orders, money orders, banker's drafts (effectively, a bank's cheque that guarantees payment, i.e. it cannot bounce), direct debit, standing order, credit cards, charge cards, bank, credit or credit transfer.

Fig 6.8

A cheque can be made out for any amount as long as there are sufficient funds in the account. If there are not sufficient funds in the account and no overdraft facilities have been agreed with the bank, the cheque will 'bounce' and will be returned to the payee marked 'refer to drawer'. It should be noted that a cheque can act as proof of payment and from a security point of view is much safer than cash. A sample cheque is shown in Fig. 6.9.

A cheque must be signed by an authorised cheque signatory (sometimes two signatories are required to minimise the possibility of embezzlement). It should be dated no later than six months ahead, the amounts in words and figures should agree and for added security should be crossed with the words 'account payee' (thus only allowing the cheque to be paid into the payee's account – in fact cheques may now only be paid into the named person's account, i.e. the payee, whether they are crossed or not).

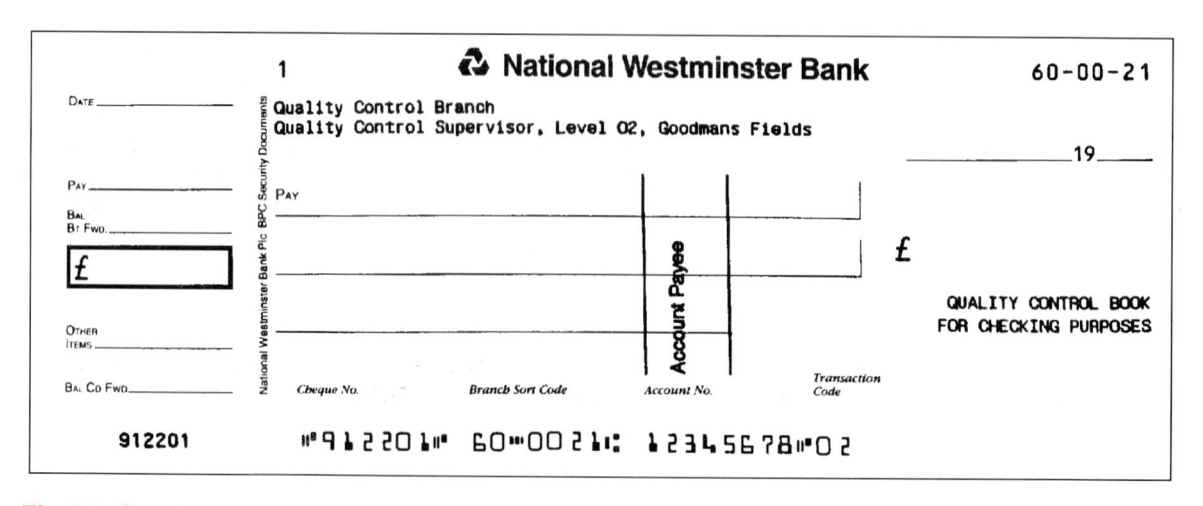

Fig 6.9 Specimen cheque

Some businesses insist on cheques being supported by a cheque card, which effectively guarantees payment by the bank up to and including a set amount, e.g. £50, or in some cases £100.

Once a cheque has been received by a business from a customer, the customer may ask for *a receipt* which clearly acknowledges receipt of payment. This may be needed for security reasons (particularly for cash payments) or simply to act as proof of expenditure in the customers' accounts. Receipts can be raised manually, e.g. receipt book, by machine issue or typed.

The Cash Book

Each business develops its own method of handling its receipts and payments. All receipts and payments must be entered into what is called the *Cash Book* which will be discussed later as part of 'recording sales' and 'recording purchases'. A typical Cash Book is shown below.

Debit (Dr)   Credit (Cr)

Date	Details	Bank £	Cash £	Date	Details	Bank £	Cash £

The left-hand side of the Cash Book is known as the debit side (Dr) and the right-hand side the Credit side (Cr). There are two columns on each side: one for bank transactions and one for cash transactions.

The rules for entering receipts and payments in the Cash Book are simple:

> All receipts are debited and all payments are credited.

Therefore, clearly, at any point in time the balance of the account can be calculated by comparing the total receipts with total payments and extracting the difference. If the total receipts exceed total payments (including any balances brought forward), then there is a balance in hand or a *debit balance*. Conversely, if the payments exceed the receipts, then an overdrawn situation occurs or a *credit balance*. It must be appreciated that, although it is possible to be overdrawn in the bank column, the same cannot be said of the cash column, i.e. a business can be overdrawn at the bank but cannot have a negative amount of cash.

Example

The following receipts and payments occurred at Andrew Stephens during the first week of February. Debit balances brought forward were bank £500 and cash £50.

Feb 1   Paid J Hains £259 by cheque
Feb 3   Paid A Singh £40 cash
Feb 4   Received from CF Taylor £895 cheque

413

Feb 5   Paid the electricity bill by cheque – £205
Feb 6   Received £250 for cash sales
Feb 7   Paid wages £225 cash

At the end of the first week of February, the two columns of the Cash Book were written up and balanced off as below.

Andrew Stephens
Cash Book at 7.2.94

Debit (Dr)   Credit (Cr)

Date	Details	Bank £	Cash £	Date	Details	Bank £	Cash £
1994				1994			
Feb 1	Bal b/f	500	50	Feb 1	J Hains	259	
Feb 4	CF Taylor	895		Feb 3	A Singh		40
Feb 6	Sales		250	Feb 5	Electricity	250	
				Feb 7	Wages		225
				Feb 7	Bal c/f	931	35
		1395	300			1395	300
Feb 8	Bal b/f	931	35				

From the above example, we can see that the bank and cash transactions have been kept completely separate, enabling two balances carried forward to be calculated: one for the bank and one for cash. The business should have £931 in the bank account and £35 in the cash account as at 7 February. The two columns are balanced off and the appropriate

Fig 6.10

opening balances brought forward are shown on 8 February as bank £931 debited and cash £35 debited.

Accounts can be closed off in this manner by following the instructions below.

1 Add up each side of the account (Dr=bank £1395, cash £300; Cr = bank £464, cash £265).

2 Subtract the smaller side from the larger side (bank £1395 – £464; cash £300 – £265).

3 Record the difference on the smaller side as balance carried forward usually abbreviated as c/f or c/fwd (bank £931, cash £35).

4 Add up both sides again – both sides should now agree (bank £1395, cash £300).

5 Write the totals on each side opposite each other and close the account off by underlining the totals twice.

6 Bring forward any outstanding balance on the first day of the following week or month, i.e. bring forward the balance carried forward figure, but now call it the balance brought forward (bank £931 and cash £35).

ACTIVITY 6.2.2

The following receipts and payments occurred at Andrew Stephens during the remainder of the month of February. Complete the cash book for the month of February, balance off the two columns and bring forward any balances at 1 March.

Feb 8	Paid an outstanding bill by cheque £100 to A Webb
Feb 9	Received a cheque from a customer Richards & Co. of £625
Feb 11	Cash sales £300
Feb 13	Paid Lister & Co. a supplier – £525
Feb 16	Paid wages £235 in cash
Feb 18	Paid the rent £300 by cheque
Feb 20	Cash sales £240
Feb 22	Paid wages £200 in cash
Feb 23	Received from S Happin cheque to the value of £200
Feb 24	Received a cheque value £500 from SG Ltd
Feb 26	Cash sales £220
Feb 27	Paid £100 cash into the bank
Feb 28	Paid wages £210 in cash

PROCESSING CASH AND CHEQUES

Most businesses bank their takings (both cash and cheques) on a daily basis, but this obviously depends on the volume of transactions and indeed the amounts involved. Any monies (either cash or cheques) are be paid into the bank either personally or by means of a night-safe after the completion of a *paying-in slip* (see Fig. 6.11). A business will normally be issued with its own book of paying-in slips with its own details clearly printed on each slip.

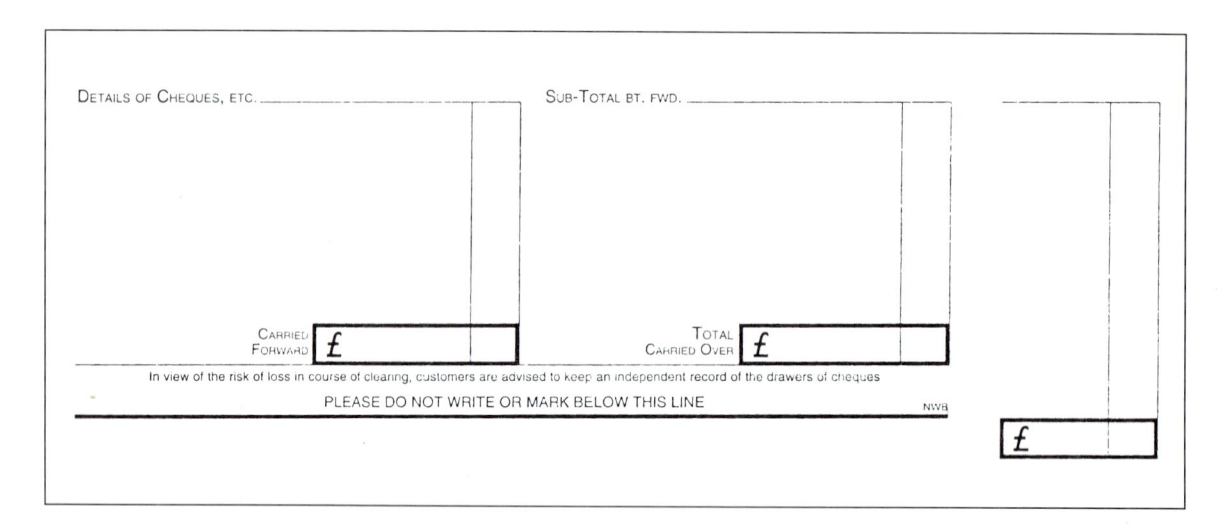

Fig 6.11 Bank paying-in slip (both sides)

You will see from Fig. 6.11 that on the reverse side of a paying-in slip, *all* cheques being deposited at the bank must be listed and the total should be shown on the front of the paying-in slip under 'cheques'. The cheques total is then added to the cash total to arrive at the total being banked. It is this total that will appear on the next *bank statement* that will be sent to the business by the bank. A typical bank statement is shown in Fig. 6.12.

A bank statement is sent to both individuals and businesses on a regular basis. Most bank statements are sent out monthly, but the frequency depends on the volume of transactions. For example, large companies with large turnovers or businesses simply with a lot of transactions will receive daily bank statements, or a customer may simply request more frequent bank statements.

The bank statement's last three columns – debit, credit and balance – are now usually substituted by payments, receipts and balance to help the customer in his or her understanding of the statement. As can be seen from Fig. 6.12, the bank statement shows all monies coming into the account and all monies going out of the account.

Element 6.2 Explain financial transactions and complete supporting documents

BANK STATEMENT
Statement No 122/1

Account 227291
Dates 3 Nov 19 _ _

	Date	Details			Dr	Cr	Balance
	1 Oct	Brought forward					5320.00
✓	4 Oct	Cheque	001090	CHQ	127.82		5192.18
✓	7 Oct	Royal Her 473512		DDR	20.00		5172.18
✓	8 Oct	Electric 4121372290X		STO	100.00		5072.18
✓	9 Oct	Scot Awareness 22501CW		DDR	22.50		5049.68
✓	10 Oct	Cheque	001092	CHQ	1200.50		3849.18
✓	14 Oct	Water 332467839		STO	150.00		3699.18
✓	14 Oct	Gas CX220625		DDR	200.00		3499.18
✓	16 Oct	Cheque	001093	CHQ	50.43		3448.75
✓	16 Oct	Wescliffe		CASH		150.00	3598.75
✓	21 Oct	Borough of Wescliffe		DDR	350.00		3248.75
✓	21 Oct	BT 6231 721G		DDR	40.00		3208.75
✓	24 Oct	Cheque	001099	CHQ	15.28		3193.97
✓	28 Oct	Chelsea		CHQ		258.00	3451.47
✓	31 Oct	Cheque	001094	CHQ	42.50		3408.97
	1 Nov	NET INTEREST PAID				65.00	3473.97
	1 Nov	ACCOUNT CHARGES			120.00		3353.97

Fig 6.12 A typical bank statement

Each transaction is clearly dated and identified as to the method of payment or receipt, e.g. standing order, direct debit, bank giro credit, etc. Note that a balance in hand would appear as a credit balance (Cr) and an overdrawn balance a debit balance (Dr). This is the reverse of the Cash Book because the bank statement is showing the customer account from the bank's point of view: a debit balance signifies a debtor, i.e. the customer owes the bank money as the customer is overdrawn; a credit balance signifies a creditor, i.e. the bank owes the customer money as the customer has money in the account.

RECORDING SALES

A 'sale' can be defined as 'that which forms part of the normal business activities'. If a furniture shop sells a piece of furniture from the showroom that is regarded as a sale, but if it sold an ageing company car, then this would not be regarded as part of its normal business activities – its normal trade – and would therefore not be regarded as a 'trade sale'.

Assuming that a sale has been made to a customer on credit (i.e. the customer has made no payment for the goods, as he/she has been granted credit terms, e.g. 30 days from the date of invoice), then a proper record of this transaction must be made.

In the first instance, the sale must be recorded in the *Sales Day Book* – sometimes called the *Sales Journal*. This and other day books which we will discuss later are known as 'Books of Original Entry' as these books are the first to have information entered into them. All the information is obtained from the sales invoice and a typical Sales Day Book is shown below.

Sales Day Book

Date	Invoice No.	Account No.	Customer	Goods amount £	VAT amount £	Total amount £

A customer that has not paid for goods immediately but has been granted credit terms, is known as a debtor. If the sale was a credit sale, then a record of that fact (i.e. that monies are owing from the customer) must be made. The debt is recorded in the *Sales Ledger* and remains there until the debt (the amount outstanding) has been paid. A typical Sales Ledger is shown below.

Debit (Dr)   **Sales Ledger Account**   Credit (Cr)

Date	Details	£	Date	Details	£

The left-hand side of the ledger is known as the debit side (Dr) and the right-hand side the credit side (Cr). An individual account is opened for each customer that has bought goods on credit, i.e. for each debtor. The rule for entering details on to a sales ledger account is.

All credit sales (credit sales invoices) are entered on the debit side of the Sales Ledger.

Cash sales, i.e. those sales for which immediate payment is received, are entered straight into the *Cash Book* as no record is needed of the amount outstanding as there isn't one – the customer has paid in full immediately on receipt of goods (*see* earlier example of typical Cash Book).

As already mentioned, the left-hand side of the Cash Book is the Debit side (Dr) and the right-hand side the credit side (Cr) and there are two columns depending on how monies are received or paid, bank and cash. Care must be taken as to which column monies are entered into – bank or cash. The rules for entering sales details in the Cash Book are:

All receipts (i.e. monies received) are entered on the debit side (Dr) of the Cash Book.

All payments are entered on the credit side of the Cash Book.

All cash sales are entered on the debit side of the Cash Book.

When the customer, who received goods on credit, i.e. the debtor, eventually pays the amount owing, the debtor's account is cleared.

All receipts from credit sales are entered on the credit side of the Sales Ledger and then they are also debited in the Cash Book as a receipt.

This has the effect of clearing the debtor's account and also recording the fact that monies have been received by the business.

We have up to this point looked at how we should record sales, i.e. record sales invoices. Not all sales will be acceptable to customers, however, e.g. some goods may arrive damaged or simply not be in working order, or there may be a short delivery. In these instances the amount outstanding by the customer needs to be altered to arrive at the 'correct' amount outstanding. This is done by issuing a credit note which has the effect of reducing the amount that is owed by the customer.

Assuming that a sales credit note has been issued to a customer, then, just as in the case of a sales invoice, a proper record of the transaction must be made.

In the first instance, the sales credit note must be entered in the *Sales Returns Day Book* – sometimes called the *Sales Return Journal*. This is also a book of original entry and a typical Sales Returns Day Book is shown below:

Sales Returns Day Book

Date	Credit Note No.	Account No.	Customer	Goods amount £	VAT amount £	Credit Note amount £

The Sales Returns Day Book again provides a comprehensive list, this time of all sales returns that were made in a business in a given accounting period.

Once the transaction has been recorded in the Sales Returns Day Book, it must then be recorded in the relevant debtor's account in the Sales Ledger in order to reduce the amount outstanding.

All sales credit notes are entered on the credit side of the Sales Ledger.

RECORDING PURCHASES

A 'purchase' can be defined as those goods that have been bought with the intention to sell. For example, if a furniture shop buys furniture from a manufacturer with the full intention of reselling it to a future customer, that is regarded as a purchase. If the furniture shop bought a car or van to be used as a company car, it would not be regarded as 'part of its normal business activity', i.e. it is not in the business of selling cars, and this would therefore not be regarded as a purchase.

Assuming that a purchase has been made from a supplier on credit (i.e. no payment has been made to the supplier for the goods as credit terms have been granted, e.g. 30 days from the date of invoice), then, just as in the case of sales, a proper record of this transaction must be made.

In the first instance, the purchase must be recorded in the *Purchase Day Book* – sometimes called the *Purchase Journal*. The Purchase Day Book is a book of original entry and is normally used only for credit purchases. It can be used for cash purchases as well, however. A typical Purchase Day Book is shown below.

Purchase Day Book

Date	Invoice No.	Account No.	Customer	Goods amount £	VAT amount £	Total amount £

All the information is obtained from the purchase invoice and, when complete, the Purchase Day Book provides a comprehensive list of purchases made by a business, thus enabling easier identification of transactions.

A supplier who has not been paid by the purchaser for goods received, due to having granted credit terms, is known as a *creditor*. If the purchase was a credit purchase, then a record of that fact (i.e. monies that are owing to the supplier) must be made. The debt is recorded in the *Purchase Ledger* – sometimes known as the *Bought Ledger*, and remains there until the debt has been paid. A typical Purchase Ledger is shown on page 421.

Element 6.2 Explain financial transactions and complete supporting documents

Debit (Dr) **Purchase Ledger Account** Credit (Cr)

Date	Details	£	Date	Details	£

As always, the left-hand side of the ledger is the debit side and the right-hand side the credit side. Just as in the Sales Ledger, an individual account is opened for each supplier from whom goods have been bought on credit, i.e. for each creditor.

All credit purchases (credit purchases invoices) are entered on the credit side of the Purchase Ledger.

Cash purchases, i.e. those purchases for which immediate payment is made, are entered straight into a Cash Book. No record is needed of the amount outstanding as there isn't one – the supplier has been paid in full, immediately on purchase of the goods.

All cash purchases are entered on the credit side of the Cash Book.

Care should be taken as to which column monies are entered into – bank or cash.

When the supplier is eventually paid, the amount owing is cleared from the creditor's account.

All payments for credit purchases are entered on the debit side of the Purchase Ledger and then are also credited in the Cash Book as a payment.

This has the effect of clearing the amount outstanding in the creditors' accounts and also recording the fact that monies have been paid out of the business.

Up to this point we have looked at how we should record purchases, i.e. record purchase invoices. Just as some sales may not always be acceptable to customers, some purchases may also need to be returned to the supplier, e.g. goods damaged, broken, etc. The amount outstanding to the supplier needs to be altered, therefore, as some of the goods are being returned. The supplier must therefore issue a credit note to 'correct' the amount outstanding.

Assuming that a purchase credit note has been received by a customer, then again a proper record of the transaction must be made.

In the first instance, the purchase credit note must be entered in the *Purchase Returns Day Book* – sometimes known as the *Purchase Returns Journal*. This again is a book of original entry and a typical Purchase Returns Day Book is shown on page 422.

As in the case of the day books already discussed, the Purchase Returns Day Book provides a comprehensive list – in this case of all purchase returns that were received by a business in a given accounting period.

Once the transaction has been recorded in the above Purchase Returns Day Book, it must then be recorded in the relevant creditor's account in the Purchase Ledger in order to reduce the amount outstanding.

Purchase Returns Day Book

Date	Credit Note No.	Account No.	Customer	Goods amount £	VAT amount £	Credit Note amount £

All purchases credit notes are entered on the debit side of the Purchase Ledger.

An example of recording sales and purchases

Bronowski and Borkowski started in business in January of this year as a supplier of stationery. During the first month the following transactions occurred:

Folio	1994	
A	Jan 3	Purchase £1000 worth of goods on credit from M & M Supplies.
B	Jan 4	Sold goods for cash to SG Traders – £300.
C	Jan 6	Received a credit note from M & M Supplies – £100.
D	Jan 10	Purchased goods for cash from Higginbottom & Co. – £200.
E	Jan 14	Sold goods on credit to Hainsworth & Co. for £500.
F	Jan 19	Issued a credit note to Hainsworth & Co. for £50.
G	Jan 25	Paid M & M Supplies £900 by cheque.
H	Jan 28	Sold goods on credit to Pidgeon & Co. for £300.
I	Jan 30	Received a £450 cheque from Hainsworth & Co.
J	Jan 31	Purchased further goods on credit from M & M Supplies – £1200.

The following accounts have been set up:

PURCHASE LEDGER K

M & M Supplies	MM001
Higginbottom & Co.	HB001

SALES LEDGER L

Hainsworth & Co.	1HC
Pidgeon & Co.	1PC
SG Traders	1SG

GENERAL LEDGER M

Purchases	P100	Returns In	R100	Debtors	D100
Sales	S100	Returns Out	R200	Creditors	C100

The business has negotiated overdraft facilities with its bank of £1000.

Ignoring VAT, the above transactions would be entered in the appropriate Day Books, Ledgers and Accounts as shown on page 423.

Bronowski & Borkowski

Purchase Day Book for the month ended 31.1.94

Date	Invoice No.	Account No. K	Supplier	Amount £
Jan 3	P001	MM001	M & M Supplies	A 1000.00
Jan 10	P002	HB001	Higginbottom & Co.	D 200.00
Jan 31	P003	MM001	M & M Supplies	J 1200.00
				2400.00

Sales Day Book for the month ended 31.1.94

Date	Invoice No.	Account No. L	Supplier	Amount £
Jan 4	S001	1 SG	SG Traders	B 300.00
Jan 14	S002	1H	Hainsworth & Co.	E 500.00
Jan 28	S003	1P	Pidgeon & Co.	H 300.00
				1100.00

Purchase Returns Day Book for the month ended 31.1.94

Date	Credit Note No.	Account No. K	Supplier	Amount £
Jan 6	PC001	M001	M & M Supplies	C 200.00
				200.00

Sales Returns Day Book for the month ended 31.1.94

Date	Credit Note No.	Account No. K	Supplier	Amount £
Jan 19	SC001	1H	Hainsworth & Co.	F 50.00
				50.00

Unit 6 Financial transactions, costing and pricing

Bronowski & Borkowski

Debit (Dr)   Credit (Cr)

Date	Details	£	Date	Details	£
	Purchase Ledger for the month ended 31.1.94				
	M & M Supplies (a/c. no. MM0001) K				
Jan 6	Credit Note PC001 C	100.00	Jan 3	Invoice P001	A 1000.00
Jan 25	Cheque G	900.00	Jan 31	Invoice P003	J 1200.00
Jan 31	Balance c/fwd	1200.00			
		2200.00			2200.00
			Feb 1	Bal b/fwd	1200.00
	Sales Ledger for the month ended 31.1.94				
	Hainsworth & Co (a/c no. 1HC) L				
Jan 14	Invoice S002 E	500.00	Jan 19	Credit note SC001	F 50.00
			Jan 30	Cheque	I 450.00
		500.00			500.00
	Pidgeon & Co (a/c no. IPC) L				
Jan 28	Invoice S003 H	300.00	Jan 31	Bal c/fwd	300.00
		300.00			300.00
	Balance b/fwd	300.00			
	General Ledger for the month ended 31.1.94				
	Purchase (a/c P100)				
Jan 6	Goods – M & M Supplies	1000.00			
	Goods – Higginbottom	200.00			
	Goods – M & M Supplies	1200.00	Jan 31	Bal c/fwd	2400.00
		2400.00			2400.00
	Balance b/fwd	2400.00			
	Sales (a/c No. S100)		Jan 3	Goods – SG Traders	300.00
			Jan 14	Goods – Hainsworth	500.00
Jan 31	Balance b/fwd	1100.00	Jan 28	Goods – Pidgeon + Co	300.00
		1100.00			1100.00
			Feb 1	Bal b/fwd	1100.00
	Creditors a/c (C100)				
Jan 31	PRDB – January	100.00	Jan 31	PDB – January	2400.00
Jan 31	January Cash	200.00			
Jan 31	January Bank	900.00	Jan 31		2400.00
Jan 31	Bal c/fwd	1200.00			
		2400.00			
			Feb 1	Bal b/fwd	1200.00
	Debtors a/c (D100)				
Jan 31	SDB – January	1100.00	Jan 31	SRDB – January	50.00
			Jan 31	January Cash	300.00
			Jan 31	January Bank	450.00
			Jan 31	Bal c/fwd	300.00
Feb 31	Bal b/fwd	1100.00			1100.00
		300.00			
	Returns In a/c (R100)				
Jan 31	Bal b/fwd	100.00	Jan 6	M & M Supplies	100.00
		100.00			100.00
			Feb 1	Bal b/fwd	100.00
	Returns Out a/c (R200)				
Jan 19	Hainsworth & Co	50.00	Jan 31	Bal c/fwd	50.00
		50.00			50.00
Feb 1	Bal b/fwd	50.00			

Element 6.2 Explain financial transactions and complete supporting documents

Bronowski & Borkowski
Cash Book at 21.1.94

Debit (Dr) / Credit (Cr)

Date	Details	Bank	Cash	Date	Details	Bank	Cash
Jan 4	SG Traders		300.00	Jan 10	Higginbottom C & Co		200.00
Jan 30	Hainsworth & Co	450.00		Jan 25	M&M Supplier	900.00	
Jan 31	Bal c/fwd	450.00		Jan 31	Bal c/fwd		100.00
		900.00	300.00			900.00	300.00
Feb 1	Bal b/fwd		100.00	Feb 1	Bal b/fwd	4500	

Notes to the example

1. Organisations use computerised accounting systems that identify accounts by an account number which can be numeric or alphanumeric. Depending on the system, any number of 'identifying' account numbers can be given. In the example alphabetics precede numerics in the Purchase Ledger to distinguish from Sales Ledger accounts. General Ledger accounts have been given one alphabetic to distinguish them from Purchase Ledger accounts.
2. Sales invoice numbers are preceded by the letter S. Purchase invoice numbers are preceded by the letter P. Sales credit notes numbers are preceded by the letters SC. Purchase credit notes numbers are preceded by the letters PC. Again, a number of other quite acceptable sequential numbering systems could have been adopted. Much depends on what is meaningful to the business.
3. Note that the example clearly shows the name of the business, the title of the ledger or book and the date, e.g. Bronowski and Borkowski, Purchase Ledger for the month ended January 1994.
4. Each transaction is identified with an alphabetic folio, A–N, which should make it easier to follow each of the transactions through the ledgers/books.
5. Each account is balanced off and the appropriate opening balance (if any) brought forward on the first day of the following month. Each and every account should be closed off in this manner.
6. The following steps should be taken in balancing off accounts (details refer to the extract from a purchase ledger shown below).
    - Add up each side of an account (Dr = £1000, Cr = £2200).
    - Subtract the smaller side from the larger side (£2200 – £1000).
    - Record the difference on the smaller side as 'balance carried forward,' abbreviated as c/f or c/fwd, and usually dated the last day of the month (£1000).
    - Add up both sides again – both sides should now agree!
    - Write the totals on each side opposite each other and close the account off by underlining the total twice.
    - Bring forward any outstanding balance on the first day of the following month, i.e. bring forward the balance carried forward figure (if any) but now call it balance brought forward.
7. Note that the Creditors and Debtors Accounts are summary or control accounts. Their totals should equal of all of the individual creditors and debtors respectively, i.e. Creditors equals M&M Supplies £1200 outstanding and Debtors equal Pidgeon & Co £300 outstanding.

Purchase Ledger (Extract)
M & M Supplies A/C (MM001) at 31.1.94

Date	Details	£	Date	Details	£
Jan 6	Credit note PC001	100	Jan 3	Invoice P001	1000
Jan 25	Cheque	900	Jan 31	Invoice P003	1200
Jan 31	Balance c/f	1200			
		2200			2200
			Feb 1	Balance b/f	1200

Element 6.2 Explain financial transactions and complete supporting documents

ACTIVITY 6.2.3

The following transactions occurred at C Stajkowski & Co. during the first month of trading.

Feb 1	Purchased £1500 worth of goods on credit from Mahmood Enterprises.
Feb 4	Sold goods on credit to A Smith – £1200.
Feb 8	Sold goods on credit to C Everard – £300.
Feb 11	Issued a credit note to A Smith & Co. – £200.
Feb 14	Purchased a further £900 worth of goods on credit from Mahmood Enterprises.
Feb 18	Received a cheque from A Smith for £1000.
Feb 21	Received a credit note from Mahmood Enterprises for £100.
Feb 23	Sold Goods to B Jones for £400 cash.
Feb 25	Purchased goods for cash from Dabrowski Bros. – £100.
Feb 27	Paid Mahmood Enterprises £1500 by cheque.

Ignore VAT.

Task 1. Charles Stajkowski asks you to open the following accounts, using whatever logic you see fit.

Purchase Ledger
Mahmood Enterprises

Sales Ledger
A Smith
C Everard

General Ledger
Purchases	Returns In	Debtors
Sales	Returns Out	Creditors

Task 2. Charles Stajkowski has decided that he wishes to enter only credit transactions in the Day Book and asks you to record the relevant transactions (in the day books).

Task 3. You are now asked to enter all of the transactions in the appropriate ledgers and books opening whatever accounts you see fit.

All invoices and credit notes must be properly numbered. Use whatever sequential identification you feel appropriate.

ACTIVITY 6.2.4

Singh & Co. was involved in the following transactions during the month of March.

March 3	Credit purchases from K Eaves £200.
March 6	Credit sales to C Greaves £125.
March 8	Credit purchases from L Pilsudski £100.
March 10	Cash sales to A Billington £75.
March 13	Credit note received from L Pilsudski £10.
March 16	Credit purchases from S Patel £150.
March 19	Cash sales to D Edwards £50.
March 21	Credit sales to K Dennison £75.
March 24	Cash purchases from B Jones £50.
March 26	Credit note issued to K Dennison £25.
March 29	Cheques sent to L Pilsudski – settling outstanding account in full.
March 30	Cheque received from C Greaves £125.

Task Enter the above transactions in the relevant Books and Ledgers, balancing off any accounts and where appropriate ensure any outstanding are brought forward accordingly.

STATEMENTS AND REMITTANCE ADVICES

Assuming a purchaser has brought goods from a supplier during the month, that supplier will send the purchaser a statement at the end of the month, detailing all the invoices with which you the purchaser have been charged during that month and those invoices that still remain outstanding, i.e. unpaid. The final total, represents the amount that the supplier says that the purchaser, as a customer, still owes.

The remittance advice is attached to the statement, and is sent back by the purchaser to the supplier together with payment (remittance) with appropriate adjustments. This informs the supplier of the invoices for which the purchaser is now paying, which should agree with the amount on the purchaser's Purchase Ledger account.

At the end of each month, a statement should be reconciled with the purchaser's own Purchase Ledger account to see if both agree. The chances are that they do not, for the following reasons.

1 Invoices may not as yet be entered on the Ledger due to delays in the post or the invoice may be held back pending arrival of a credit note, etc.

2 Payments which the purchaser has made, but as yet have not been received or are not recorded by the supplier.

3 There may be allocation errors in the purchase ledger.

4 Credit notes may not have been received yet and therefore have not been entered on the Purchase Ledger account.

The purchaser will in turn send statements to its customers, and they in turn will also reconcile them with their Purchase Ledger accounts!

Example

An accounts clerk at Fred White PLC is asked to pay the appropriate amount to Joe Bloggs Ltd. The most recent statement received from Joe Bloggs (*see* Fig. 6.13) and its account on the Fred White Purchase Ledger is shown below:

STATEMENT

JOE BLOGGS LTD
Bradford Road,
Keighley

Customer: Fred White PLC Keighley Road Bradley	Date	30.11.94		
	Customer Number	123		

Date	Ref	£ Debit	£ Cedit	£ Total Outstanding	Date
1.10.94	A105	105		105	1.10.94
5.10.94	A109	59		164	5.10.94
20.10.94	A151	51		215	20.10.94
30.10.94	A197	213		428	30.10.94
5.11.94	A205	197		625	5.11.94
17.11.94	A251	91		716	17.11.94
25.11.94	A259	24		740	25.11.94
30.11.94	C101		51	689	30.11.94
Totals		740	51	689	Total

Fig 6.13 Statement from Joe Bloggs

Fred White plc
Purchase Ledger – Joe Blogg Ltd Account

Date	Detail	DR (£)	CR (£)	Balance (£)
October 1	1001		105	(105)
October 5	1059		59	(164)
October 20	1071		51	(215)
October 30	1091		213	(428)
November 5	1099		197	(625)
November 17	2101		91	(716)

The clerk should first reconcile J Bloggs Ltd's statement to Fred White's Purchase Ledger. All debit items on the statement should be matched with the corresponding credit items on the Purchase Ledger, to see if the two agree. The account clerk is left with the following items missing from the Purchase Ledger:

Invoice Ref. A259	£24
Credit Note Ref. C101	£51

Both these items appear towards the end of the month of November, so it would be reasonable to assume that the reason why these two items do not appear on the Purchase Ledger may be because Fred White PLC has not yet received the invoice and credit note (i.e. they are in the post) or they may not have been entered on to the Purchase Ledger because they may be awaiting approval. In any case, the accounts clerk should really only pay what is on the Purchase Ledger and you must therefore reconcile the statement as follows:

	£
Balance as per statement	689
Less invoice not received/awaiting approval	(24)
Plus credit note not received	51
Cheque enclosed	716

*Note that the £716, i.e. the amount payable, agrees with what appears as outstanding on the Purchase Ledger!

Element 6.2 Explain financial transactions and complete supporting documents

ACTIVITY 6.2.5

Consider the following Purchase Ledger account.

Fred White plc
Purchase Ledger – Joe Blogg Ltd Account

Date	Detail	DR (£)	CR (£)	Balance (£)
Oct 1	1001		105	(105)
Oct 5	1059	59		(46)
Oct 20	1071		51	(97)
Oct 30	1091	21		(76)
Nov 5	1099		197	(273)
Nov 17	2101		91	(364)

Task From this Purchase Ledger account, work out what Joe Haines' statement should look like.

ACTIVITY 6.2.6

Consider the following Purchase Ledger account.

Tom Sweet Ltd
Purchase Ledger – John Child plc Account

Date	Detail	DR (£)	CR (£)	Balance (£)
Oct 1	111		101	(101)
Oct 7	139		51	(152)
Oct 15	151		213	(365)
Oct 30	C159	13		(352)
Nov 1	169		79	(431)
Nov 5	175		181	(612)
Nov 10	189		98	(710)
Nov 20	C195	21		(689)
Nov 30	201		113	(802)

Task Using the details in Tom Sweet's Purchase Ledger work out what John Child's statement should look like.

MAINTAINING PETTY CASH RECORDS

The *Petty Cash Book* is used to record transactions involving small payments in exchange for a service or an actual purchase of goods, e.g. window cleaning, coffee, tea, milk, sugar, taxi fares, postage stamps, petrol, entertaining, stationery, etc. This effectively prevents the main cash book being 'cluttered-up' with small payments and also allows the work of handling such small items of cash to be delegated down to a petty cashier, should the size of the organisation permit.

The *Imprest System* works on the principle that an original float is agreed (the imprest amount), e.g. £100. It could be less or more, depending on the volume and value of transactions currently being experienced. The petty cash is replenished back up to that float at regular intervals or when a shortage of money demands. The amount of money left out of the original float (usually kept in a tin, i.e. the cash box) will decrease in direct proportion to the amount spent and the amount replenished therefore, should, always equal net expenditure (payments less any income), ensuring that the float is always replenished back up to the original agreed amount. For example, if we start with a float of £100 and spend £70, we are left with £30 in cash. To bring the float back up to the original amount (i.e. £100) we need to cash a cheque for £70.

It should be noted that the float is altered at anytime; if the present float is inadequate to cope with higher levels of expenditure, the petty cashier may ask the cashier to increase the float by an appropriate amount.

With an *Analytical Petty Cash Book* the basic idea is to group together identical or similar items of expenditure under one heading, thereby analysing each item of expense in a separate column. At the end of any given accounting period, it is therefore a simple matter to extract the total amount spent on each type of expense.

The Petty Cash Book

Receipts	Date	Details	Folio	Total				

It should be noted that any payments out of the petty cash should only be made against appropriate documentation, e.g. a petty cash voucher (*see* Fig. 6.14) which has been signed and duly authorised by that person's departmental head or other designated official, with any receipts attached (e.g. petrol bill, hotel bill, etc.). It is also advisable that one member of staff be responsible for petty cash and the cash box itself where the float will be held. The cash box must be kept secure, i.e. locked and out of sight.

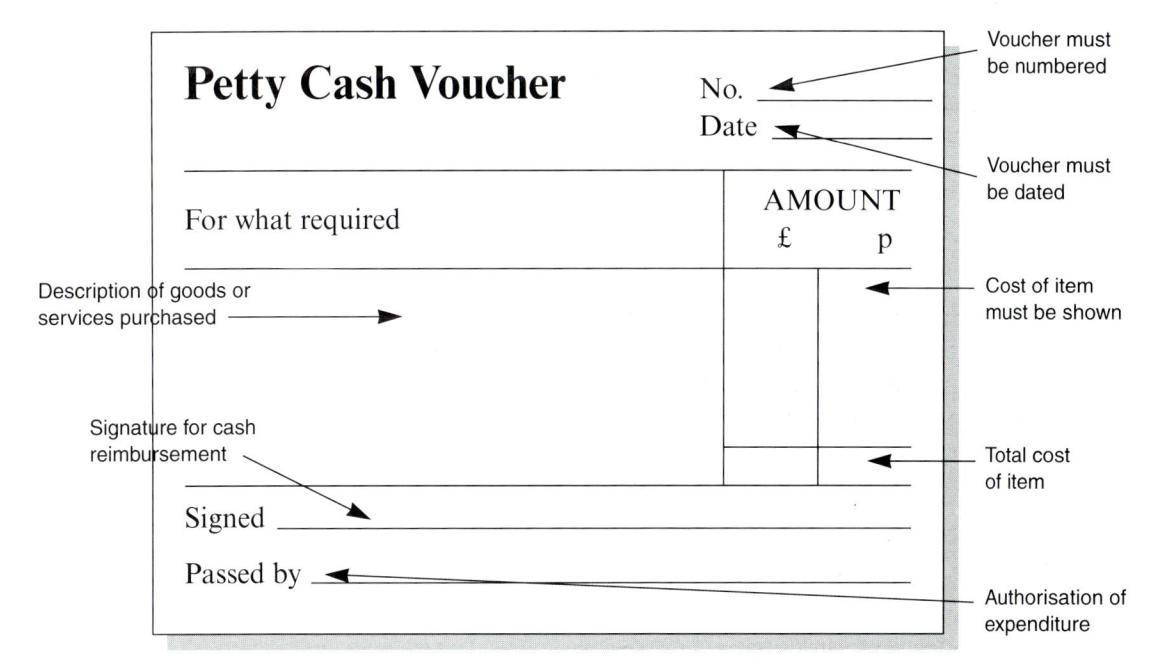

Petty Cash Voucher

- Voucher must be numbered (No.)
- Voucher must be dated (Date)
- Description of goods or services purchased (For what required)
- Cost of item must be shown (AMOUNT £ p)
- Total cost of item
- Signature for cash reimbursement (Signed)
- Authorisation of expenditure (Passed by)

Any relevant receipts or invoices must be attached to the petty cash voucher.

Fig 6.14 Petty cash voucher

Any member of staff claiming from the petty cash should obtain, wherever possible, a *VAT receipt* for the money that has been spent. The vouchers and appropriate receipts are the petty cashier's proof that the cash has been paid out of the account. Any VAT paid must be properly accounted for in the Petty Cash Book by opening a VAT column. The VAT receipt must have a proper VAT registration number, otherwise 'strictly speaking' the VAT cannot be reclaimed. VAT is chargeable on most items, but not all. For example, VAT is not charged on postage (including DataPost) but is chargeable on Red Star parcels which are treated as carriage and not postage! VAT is not charged on food but on restaurant bills for legitimate business expenses.

Operating a Petty Cash Book

1. Obtain a petty cash book.

2. Decide on approximate headings for the analysis columns, e.g. petrol, postage, stationery, etc.

3. Do not forget you must have a column for VAT (Value Added Tax). VAT is charged in the United Kingdom on goods and services at the current rate of 17.5%; some goods and services however are not liable to VAT, e.g. books, newspapers.

4 Decide on the amount of the float and subsequently record the float under cash received.

5 Payments should only be made against a VAT receipt and completion of a duly authorised petty cash voucher.

6 Record these payments at once in the 'total paid' column and again in the appropriate analysis column, separating and recording any VAT in the VAT column.

7 The Petty Cash Book should be regularly 'balanced' to determine the amount of cash actually in the cash box (and the account). The regularity depends on the volume of transactions.

Some organisations may have to balance daily and others weekly. The balance is obviously the difference between receipts in and payments out.

8 Check the balance against the actual money in the cash box. The two figures should be the same! If they are not, a mistake has been made or cash is missing!

9 When the float is low, replenish it. On the production of receipts the amount of money spent may then be reimbursed to the petty cash account, therefore bringing the float back to its original level.

The following payments were made out of the petty cash during the first week in March at Bastows Ltd. Assuming an original float of £25 at March 1, write-up, replenish and balance off the petty cash book as at 7 March.

March 1   Paid Mr Singh £5 for petrol.
March 3   Bought postage stamps for £2.
March 4   Purchased pens from M & M Supplies for £3.
March 5   Paid Mr Jennings £4 for petrol.
March 6   Purchased pencils from M & M Supplies for £4.
March 7   Paid Mr Smith £2 for petrol.

The float at 1 March was £25 and the petty cash book at 7 March, with all payments written up and balanced off and the float replenished, is shown below.

The analysis columns for the payments are created depending on need and the totals of all the analysis columns should equal the total paid column.

Note to the example petty cash book

1 It can be immediately seen how much has been spent for each item of expenditure by looking at each analysed total.

2 Balance b/fwd at 8 March is equal to original float.

3 VAT is calculated by applying the following formula:

$$\frac{17.5}{117.5} \quad \text{or} \quad \frac{7}{47}$$

For example:

$$5 \times \frac{17.5}{117.5} = 0.75$$

4 Transactions must be identified, i.e. petty cash vouchers, for audit trail purposes. Any appropriate folios can be used, e.g. M = March, A = April or 3/1 = March transaction number one, 4/2 = April transaction number two, etc.

Element 6.2 Explain financial transactions and complete supporting documents

BASTOWS LTD
Petty Cash Book for the week ended 7.3.9X

Dr — Receipts | Cr — Payments

Total Receipts (£)	Date	Details	Folio	Total Paid £	VAT	Petrol	Postage	Stationery
25	March 1	Balance b/fwd Mr Singh	1	5	.75	4.25		
	3	Stamps	2	2			2.00	
	4	M & M Supplies	3	3	.45			2.55
	5	Mr Jennings	4	4	.60	3.40		
	6	M & M Supplies	5	4	.60			3.40
	7	Mr Smith	6	2	.30	1.70		
20		Cash		20	2.70	9.35	2.00	5.95
		Balance c/fwd		25				
45				45				
25	8 March	Balance b/fwd						

ACTIVITY 6.2.8

On 1 January the petty cashier receives £50 from the cashier as a float. The following payments were made out of petty cash during the month of January:

Jan 2	Petrol – F Bloggs	£5.00
Jan 5	Postage	£2.00
Jan 6	Canteen, supplies – Food	£3.00
Jan 8	Petrol – S Hainsworth	£2.00
Jan 10	Canteen supplies – Cleaning items	£4.00
Jan 12	Postage	£1.00
Jan 15	Petrol – M Irving	£3.00
Jan 18	Cleaning expenses (VAT receipt attached)	£4.00
Jan 20	Red Star Parcels	£5.00
Jan 25	Petrol – F Bloggs	£8.00
Jan 29	Monthly bills for newspapers	£2.00
Jan 30	Carriage – Datapost	£5.00

Task. Draw up the correct entries in the Petty Cash Book and calculate how much the petty cashier needs to replenish the float. Assume all appropriate VAT receipts are attached.

Unit 6 Financial transactions, costing and pricing

ACTIVITY 6.2.9

You are presently employed in an organisation with the structure shown in Fig. 6.15.

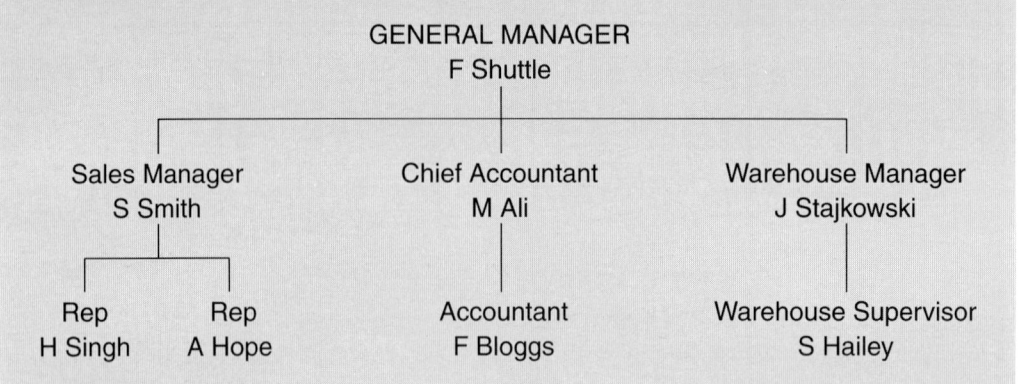

```
                        GENERAL MANAGER
                            F Shuttle
            ┌───────────────────┼───────────────────┐
      Sales Manager       Chief Accountant     Warehouse Manager
         S Smith                M Ali             J Stajkowski
        ┌────┴────┐                │                     │
      Rep       Rep            Accountant       Warehouse Supervisor
     H Singh   A Hope           F Bloggs              S Hailey
```

Fig 6.15 A typical organisation structure

It is the policy of the organisation that:

- No petty cash is to be paid out without an appropriate VAT receipt.
- The recipient signs for receipt of money.
- Each petty cash voucher is properly authorised by the appropriate Department Manager.
- All VAT is reclaimed.
- In order to control petty cash effectively, the Imprest System is to be used.

Task 1. Suggest the appropriate person to authorise each of the following payments.

Task 2. Assuming a float of £100 at 1 May and taking into consideration the organisation's policies outlined earlier, enter the following transactions into a Petty Cash Book showing as much analysis as possible. The float was replenished on 10 and 20 May. Use the sample petty cash book which appeared earlier in this unit as a guide.

May 1	Petrol for F. Bloggs	£10
May 2	Petrol for H. Singh	£20
May 3	Stationery for the Accounts Dept.	£7.50
May 5	Canteen Goods – Tea, Coffee etc.	£5.50
May 7	Travelling Expenses – A. Hope (Hotel Bills)	£25.00
May 9	Travelling Expenses – F. Bloggs (Hotel Bills)	£30.00
May 11	Postage	£5.00
May 12	Window cleaning	£25.00
May 14	Taxi fares (customers to Railway Station)	£7.50
May 15	Milk	£5.00
May 16	Flowers (for the Accountants wife after having a baby)	£10.00
May 19	Postage	£10.00
May 21	Stationery – Sales Order Book	£20.00
May 23	Coffee & Tea	£5.00
May 25	Sale of Stamps	£2.00
May 27	Travelling Expenses – H. Singh (Hotel Bill)	£20.00
May 29	Petrol for S. Hailey	£25.00
May 31	Red Star Parcels – goods for a customer	£8.50

Element 6.2 Explain financial transactions and complete supporting documents

Self assessment questions

1 Consider the following statements:
   (i) A statement of account received by a buyer is a summary of the amount outstanding to a creditor.
   (ii) An invoice is a receipt for goods received.

   Which option best describes the two statements?
   a (i) True,   (ii) True
   b (i) True,   (ii) False
   c (i) False, (ii) True
   d (ii) False, (ii) False

2 Consider the following statements.
   (i) A goods received note is sent by the supplier to the customer.
   (ii) A goods received note is sent together with the cheque by the buyer to identify what goods are being paid for.

   Which option best describes the two statements?
   a (i) True,   (ii) True
   b (i) True,   (ii) False
   c (i) False, (ii) True
   d (i) False, (ii) False

3 Which document accompanies the goods to the customer?
   a Sales invoice
   b Advice note
   c Delivery note
   d Goods received note

4 Which document should accompany a cheque and be sent to the supplier?
   a Goods received note
   b Remittance advice
   c Delivery note
   d Acknowledgement

5 Which description best describes a sales invoice?
   a A payment for goods received
   b A bill for goods or services received
   c Identical to a delivery note
   d An acknowledgement that a purchase order has been received

6 What is the primary function of a statement of account?
   a To accompany the goods to the customer
   b To inform the customer where to send payment
   c To inform the customer of the total amount outstanding
   d To identify which goods have been sent

7 If a business is VAT-registered, which document must clearly show this number?
   a An acknowledgement
   b A cheque

c A goods received note
   d An invoice

8 If a supplier sells goods on credit, to whom does the supplier send the invoice ?
   a The Sales Department
   b Creditor
   c Debtor
   d To its Head Office

9 What would be the consequence of a purchase order never being received by a supplier?
   a Goods despatched but no invoice raised
   b Goods despatched and an invoice raised
   c No goods despatched but an invoice raised
   d No goods despatched and no invoice raised

10 Business documents are raised:
   a To give accountants something to do
   b To record transactions
   c To enable bank overdrafts to be negotiated
   d To provide records for the Registrar of Companies?

Additional activities

As the subjects covered in this element are of a practical nature, some extra activities are included here to give the student practice in the bookkeeping skills described.

ACTIVITY 6.2.10

Write out the purchase orders from each of the following customers to Eaves & Hoyle, Unit 15, Pepperfield Trading Estate, Shipfield, SD7 4DT.

1 Purchase order 1245 – Westcliffe Enterprises, 25 Hill Crescent, Shipfield, SD7 1QR – 06.01.1995

   4 packs of bookkeeping paper – Type AB4
   3 packs of bookkeeping paper – Type AB5

2 Purchase order A127 – Hilton Traders, Unit 14, Listerfield Trading Estate, Canal Road, Bradfield, BR1 4QT – 07.01.1995

   5 calculators Model A100
   2 calculators Model A200

3 Purchase order 1247 – Westcliffe Enterprises, 25 Hill Crescent, Shipfield, SD7 1QR – 15.01.1995

   4 packs ball point pens Type X100 – Blue
   5 packs ball point pens Type X200 – Red
   3 packs HB pencils

4 Purchase order X456 – Greaves & Son, No. 25, The Trading Estate, Valley Road, Shipfield, SH4 4AP – 24.01.1995

   1 calculator Model A100
   1 calculator Model A200
   1 pack bookkeeping paper Type AB4
   1 pack bookkeeping paper Type AB5
   1 pack ball point pens – Blue X100
   1 pack ball point pens – Red X100

5 Purchase order A127 – Hilton Traders, Unit 14, Listerfield Trading Estate, Canal Road, Bradfield, BR1 4QT – 09.01.1995

   Correction fluid, 4 packs
   Ball point pens – Red Type X100 – 3 packs
   Ball point pens – Blue Type X200 – 2 packs
   Pencils – HB – 4 packs

6 Purchase order 1259 – Westcliffe Enterprises, 25 Hill Crescent, Shipfield, SD7 1QR – 11.01.1995

   1 calculator – Model A100
   2 calculators – Model A200

ACTIVITY 6.2.11

You have now received the above purchase orders at Eaves & Hoyle during the month of January.

Task 1. Assuming all goods were despatched within 48 hours of receipt of the purchase order and using the price list below, issue the six invoices relating to the above purchase orders to the appropriate customers:

Price List	£
Bookkeeping paper – Type AB4 (per pack)	9.50
Bookkeeping paper – Type AB5 (per pack)	10.00
Calculators – Model A100 (each)	10.75
Calculators – Model A200 (each)	17.50
Boardmarkers (per box)	7.50
Ball point pens – blue or red – Type X100 (per pack)	5.00
Ball point pens – blue or red – Type X200 (per pack)	6.00
Pencils – Type HB (per pack)	2.00
Correction fluid (per pack)	15.00

The above prices are subject to $17\frac{1}{2}$% of VAT.

Task 2. Issue a statement of account to each of the customers at the end of January. Balances outstanding from the previous month are as follows: Hilton Traders £59.50 and Westcliffe Enterprises £153.25.

Task 3. The policy at Eaves & Hoyle is to offer a cash discount of 5% to any customer that settles its account within 10 days of the date of invoice. Invoices are despatched 48 hours from receipt of the purchase orders. Assuming all your customers take advantage of the cash discount on offer, calculate how much cash discount will be taken by each customer and indicate what would be the last acceptable date that Eaves & Hoyle should accept.

Task 4. Reissue a statement of account to each of the customers at the end of January, but this time take into consideration any payments Eaves & Hoyle have received as a result of Task 3 and the following further transactions:

Date	Customer	Goods	VAT	Total
14.1.95	Hilton Traders	100.00	17.50	117.50
19.1.95	Greaves & Son	125.00	21.88	146.88
25.1.95	Westcliffe Exteriors	75.00	13.13	88.13
27.1.95	Hilton Traders	150.00	26.25	176.25
29.1.95	Westcliffe Enterprises	25.00	4.38	29.38
31.1.95	S Pidgeon & Bros	50.00	8.78	58.75

Assume, as in Task 3, that all customers take advantage of the cash discount on offer.

Task 5. Assuming all monies received are banked at the end of each week, complete separate paying-in slips to the bank at the end of weeks 1, 2, 3 and 4.

ACTIVITY 6.2.12

Task 1. Consider the document in Fig. 6.16

B CHARLTON & SON
24 Airedale Road
BRADFIELD
BR1 2AT
(Incorporating M Peters & Son)

B MOORE & CO.
18 Shipford Road
BRADLEY
BA2 5NT

Date: 31/1/1994

Date	Reference	DR (£)	CR (£)	Balance
Jan 1	Bal b/f			(125.00)
Jan 4	650	100.00		(225.00)
Jan 9	C102		50.00	(175.00)
Jan 15	658	80.00		(255.00)
Jan 21	cheque received		125.00	130.00
Jan 26	665	70.00		200.00
Jan 30	670	40.00		240.00

Part of N Stiles Group, 18 Wharfedale Road, Shipfield, SD7 1QR.

Fig 6.16 Document from B Charlton

Element 6.2 Explain financial transactions and complete supporting documents

Task 2. Answer the following questions relating to the document.

1 Is the above document:
   a an invoice
   b an advice note
   c a statement of account
   d a goods received note

2 In the above document, who is the supplier of the goods?
   a N Styles Group
   b M Peters & Son
   c B Moore & Co.
   d B Charlton & Son

3 In the above document, who is the customer?
   a H Styles Group
   b M Peters & Son
   c B Moore & Co.
   d B Charlton & Son

4 Is the document reference number C102
   a a statement of account
   b a credit note
   c an invoice
   d an advice note?

5 Assuming that $17\frac{1}{2}$% VAT was charged on the invoice reference no. 650, what was the VAT charged?
   a £17.50
   b £1.75
   c £14.89
   d £1.49

ACTIVITY 6.2.13

You are employed at Singh & Co. as a stores clerk and you have just received a consignment of goods from Patel & Edwards which was accompanied by the delivery note in Fig. 6.17.

Task 1. What should you do in the first instance?

Task 2. Complete the goods received note (GRN) based on the information given.

Task 3. What is the purpose of a goods received note?

DELIVERY NOTE

PATEL & EDWARDS
Unit 1 The Pavillion
Bradfield BR4 1AX

Singh & Co
24 Toller Drive
BRADFIELD
BR4 1AX

Date: 1/2/94

VAT Ref. No. 123–89783

Quantity	Description of goods	Catalogue No.		
2	Calculator	Type A/600		
4	Calculator	Type A/800		

Fig 6.17 Delivery note

ACTIVITY 6.2.14

You are employed at Leslie Dove Enterprises, 1 Cleckton Road, Halford, West Yorkshire and you wish to order the following goods from Black & White Ltd, 5 Helson Street, Bradfield, West Yorkshire:

4 Type AB circuit boards
5 screens – model 1A

Task 1. Write a letter of enquiry to Black & White Ltd requesting information with regards to the products' availability, prices and delivery details.

Task 2. Assuming a positive response in Task 1, issue a formal purchase order requesting delivery within 10 days to Leslie Dove Enterprises' address. The quotation you received informed you that a single Type AB circuit board would cost £28.50 and a single screen (model 1A) £21.26. Both prices are subject to VAT at $17\frac{1}{2}$%.

Task 3. Answer the following questions.

a What document would you expect to receive from Black & White Ltd in advance of receipt of the goods?
b What document would you expect to receive from Black & White Ltd together with the goods?
c What information would you expect to find on the above two documents?
d Draft the document you would expect to receive in 3 (b), showing clearly the contents.
e What should you now do with this document?

Task 4. Assume one of the screens was delivered broken; this was confirmed by the driver who was employed by Black & White Ltd. What should you now do?

Task 5. Issue a goods received note for the goods received.

Task 6. You receive an invoice from Black & White Ltd, an extract of which appears below.

Invoice date: 1/1/XX

Qty	Details	Price	Total
4	Type AB circuit boards	28.50	114.00
5	Screens – model 1A		100.63
	Total amount of goods		214.63
	VAT @ $17\frac{1}{2}$%		37.56
	Total amount due		£252.19
	Terms = Nett 30 days		

a Examine the above extract carefully. What do you think your next step should be?
b If the above invoice were paid, i.e. £252.19, what would be the consequences?
c What would be the consequences if your actions in 6(a) had not been adhered to?

Task 7. Assuming you are now satisfied that all is in order and that all the documents have been received from Black & White Ltd, issue a cheque to Black & White Ltd for the amount you think is due.

Task 8. Why are there sometimes two signatories on a cheque?

Task 9. If you have paid by cash, what should you have asked for in return and why? Draft and complete the document in question.

ACTIVITY 6.2.15

You are employed at Pigeon, Dove & Co as an accounts clerk and you receive the following cheques today.

Customer	Amount
Matthew Andrews Ltd	£125.00
Nicholas Charles & Co.	£142.95
Matthew Christopher	£194.14
Horton Enterprises	£56.20
Dennison Printworks	£19.72

In addition you have received the following cash during the course of the year for sales over the counter.

Jack Hunter	£10.50
Fred Pierce	£9.47

Unit 6 Financial transactions, costing and pricing

Task 1. Enter the above receipts on to a bank paying-in slip and issue receipts where appropriate.

Task 2. During the day you have been asked by a member of the senior management team to pay the following suppliers the amounts indicated:

Supplier	Amount
Chilvers & Greaves Ltd	£125.15
Patel & Co.	£461.04
QM Designs Ltd	£79.15

What documents should you seek so that payment can be made? Assuming approval has been given to pay the three suppliers by the appropriate authorities, issue the cheques involved.

Task 3. In addition to the duties you have performed so far, your employees bring receipts to you for items which they have purchased on behalf of the business and for which they wish to receive reimbursement.

Employee	Amount	Goods
Christina Lubelska	£25	Postage/stamps
Steven Bloggs	£30	Tea/coffee/sugar etc. (for the staff canteen)
Anthony Bell	£15	Stationery for Accounts Department
Sunita Mistry	£20	Cleaning items (e.g. washing-up liquid, detergents, etc.)

a Issue a petty cash voucher for each of the above four employees clearly showing (where applicable) any VAT paid.
b Before you pay the employees, what security should you enforce?

Assignment

Scenario 1

Paul has just been appointed 'buyer' at Supermicro Ltd, a small company based in Bradford, which manufactures computer monitors. Having only just left school, his experience of working in a commercial environment is limited. On his first day at Supermicro he finds five invoices on his desk which puzzle him, as he does not know what to do with them (*see* Fig 6.18 on pages 445, 446 and 447).

His instinct tells him to enlist the help of Sheila, the accounts clerk, who, much to his annoyance, is away sick. Undeterred, Paul seeks the advice of the Company Accountant, who, as luck would have it, was in the Bahamas for his annual holiday.

Paul, now in a near state of panic, approaches the Managing Director, who, not being fully conversant with the day-to-day routines of the company, suggests you contact Bookkeeping Personnel and seek temporary assistance.

Bookkeeping Personnel is an agency, who send YOU on your first assignment to Supermicro Ltd, initially to help Paul, but also to assume the role of temporary accounts clerk, as Sheila will probably be away for at least another two weeks.

On your arrival you find not only the five invoices on the buyer's desk, but also five completed works orders on your desk, the summaries of which appear in Fig. 6.19.

Element 6.2 Explain financial transactions and complete supporting documents

INVOICE

No. A109

From: Super Conductors Ltd.,
1, The Close, Huddersfield.
Tel (0193) 650691
Fax. (0193) 69065

To: Supermicro Ltd., Bingford

VAT Reg No. 245789

Date: 10/1/95

Your order No.	Delivery Note	Tax point	Terms
654	33	10/1/95	30 days

Qty	Description	Cat. No.	Price each (£)	Cost (£)	VAT rate	Vat amount (£)
2	Type AA	X/41	50.00	100.00	17.5%	17.50
3	Type BB	X/42	150.00	450.00	17.5%	78.75
			VAT @ 17.5%	96.25		
			TOTAL PAYABLE	646.25		

E & OE

Registered Office: 1, The Close, Huddersfield.
Directors: A. Saunders, F. Saunders, E Jaes FCA

INVOICE

No. 310H

From: Bradford Electronics PLC
Shipton Lane, Sheffield.
Tel (05942) 6913
Fax. (05942) 4146

To: Supermicro Ltd., Bingford

VAT Reg No. 245787

Date: 2.1.95

Your order No.	Delivery Note	Tax point	Terms
321	44	2.1.95	30 days

Qty	Description	Cat. No.	Price each (£)	Cost (£)	VAT rate	Vat amount (£)
1	Type BB	X/42	150.00	150.00	17.5%	26.25
3	Type CC	2/C	120.00	360.00	17.5%	63.00
			VAT @ 17.5%	89.25		
			TOTAL PAYABLE	599.25		

E & OE 6% Discount if paid within 5 days

Registered Office: 5, Shipton Lane, Sheffield.
Directors: F. Czojka, Z. Mitchell BSc, J. Billington ACIS, B. Phillips.

INVOICE

No. 0059

From: Micro Comp Ltd.,
2, Ashfield Rd., Leeds.
Tel (06413) 8165789
Fax. (06413) 6784612

To: Supermicro Ltd., Bingford

VAT Reg No. 245123

Date: 1.1.95

Your order No.	Delivery Note	Tax point	Terms
987	11	1.1.94	30 days

Qty	Description	Cat. No.	Price each (£)	Cost (£)	VAT rate	Vat amount (£)
5	Type CC	2/C	120.00	600.00	17.5%	105.00
			VAT @ 17.5%	105.00		
			TOTAL PAYABLE	705.00		

E & OE   2.5% Discount if paid within 14 days of the date of the invoice

Registered Office: as above
Directors: D. Ellis FCA, G. Medley FSc Phd, J. Aske

INVOICE

No. 1051

From: Shipfield Monitors Ltd.,
24, Bradfield Road, Halifax.
Tel (9671) 10796
Fax. (9671) 70169

To: Supermicro Ltd., Bingford

VAT Reg No. 245456

Date: 5.1.95

Your order No.	Delivery Note	Tax point	Terms
012	22	5.1.95	30 days

Qty	Description	Cat. No.	Price each (£)	Cost (£)	VAT rate	Vat amount (£)
10	Type DD	100/X	20.00	200.00	17.5%	35.00
			VAT @ 17.5%	35.00		
			TOTAL PAYABLE	235.00		

E & OE   10% Discount if paid within 14 days of the date of the invoice

Registered Office: 1, The Orchards, Halifax.
Directors: P. Hamorsen, F. Pierce ACIS, M. Eccles.

Element 6.2 Explain financial transactions and complete supporting documents

INVOICE   No. 3591

From: Computer Applications Ltd.,
101, Halifax Street, Keighley.
Tel (0365) 9071
Fax. (0365) 8145

To: Supermicro Ltd., Bingford

VAT Reg No. 245345

Date: 15.1.95

Your order No.	Delivery Note	Tax point	Terms
345	55	15.1.95	30 days

Qty	Description	Cat. No.	Price each (£)	Cost (£)	VAT rate	Vat amount (£)
15	Type DD	100/X	20.00	300.00	17.5%	52.50
			VAT @ 17.5%	52.50		
			TOTAL PAYABLE	325.50		

You are invited to claim 5% discount if you settle the outstanding amount within 10 days.

Registered Office: as above.
Directors: A. Singh, Z. Stajkowski, G. Booth

E & OE

Fig 6.18

Date	Works Order No.	Customer	Customer Order No.	Delivery Note No.	Description of Goods	Quantity (No. of Units)	Terms
Jan 1	100	Shibdon Ltd 21 Woodville Rd York	123	1001	Black & White Monitor Deluxe Model Colour Monitor Std Model Circuit Board Type C	2 2 12	30 days credit
Jan 2	101	Clacton Ltd 50 Bramer Street Leeds	234	1002	Circuit Boards Type X/2	100	30 days credit
Jan 3	102	Mitchells Ltd 40 The Rise Lancaster	456	1003	Black & White Monitor Semi Deluxe Model Colour Monitor Deluxe Model Circuit Boards Type A Circuit Boards Type B	1 2 50 60	30 days credit
Jan 4	103	Redburn Ltd 59 Stanton Drive Huddersfield	478	1004	Black & white Monitor Deluxe Model Black & White Monitor Standard Model	3 1	30 days credit
Jan 5	104	Woodview Bros. 12 Thackley Street Halifax	890	1005	Circuit Boards Type A Circuit Boards Type B Circuit Boards Type C Circuit Boards Type X/2	25 50 75 20	30 days credit

Fig 6.19 Summary of completed work orders

Unit 6　Financial transactions, costing and pricing

Task 1. Advise Paul on his course of action.

Task 2. Perform your duties as accounts clerk, making all the necessary records of the five invoices in Fig. 6.19 in the appropriate books and ledgers provided for you at the end of this Assignment. Use the following codes.

Customer account codes

Clackton Ltd	C10
Mitchells Ltd	M2
Redburn Ltd	R4
Shibdon Ltd	S21
Woodview Bros	W3

Supplier account codes

Bradford Electronics PLC	21 BE
Computer Applications Ltd	11 CA
Micro Co-op Ltd	9 MC
Shipfield Monitors Ltd	14 SM
Super Conductors Ltd	16 SC

General ledger account codes

Sales A/C	S100
Sales Ledger Control A/C (Debtors A/C)	S200
Purchase A/C	P100
Purchase Ledger Control A/C (Creditors A/C)	P200
VAT A/C	V100

Task 3. Copy the blank invoice in Fig. 6.21 five times and then complete the five invoices, based on the information in the completed works orders (Fig. 6.19) and the attached price list (Fig. 6.20).

SUPERMICRO LTD

Black and white monitor – Standard Model	£150.00
Black and white monitor – Semi Deluxe Model	£175.00
Black and white monitor – Deluxe Model	£200.00
Colour monitor – Standard model	£300.00
Colour monitor – Deluxe model	£350.00
Circuit boards – Type A	£1.25
Circuit boards – Type B	£2.75
Circuit boards – Type C	£3.25
Circuit boards – Type X/2	£4.50

All the above prices are subject to VAT at 17.5%.

Fig 6.20 Price list

Element 6.2 Explain financial transactions and complete supporting documents

		INVOICE		No.
Reg Office.	Supermicro Ltd., 50, Cottingdale Road, Bingford, BG6 1AP. Tel (05912) 5656913 Fax. (05912) 5894146		Customer:	
VAT Reg No. 245345				Date/Tax Point:

Your order No.	Delivery Note No.	Tax point	Terms
			30 days

Qty	Description	Cat. No.	Price each (£)	Cost (£)	VAT rate	Vat amount (£)

Directors:
S. Pidgeon
P. Dove
A. Robin

Goods Total
VAT @ 17.5%
Amount payable

E & OE

Fig 6.21 Blank Invoice

Task 4. How many copies of each sales invoice would you normally produce and why?

Task 5. Make the necessary records, in the appropriate books or ledgers provided for you at the end of this Assignment, of the five invoices you have issued in Task 3.

Scenario 2

You are now advised by one of your customers, Clackton Ltd, that his Order No 234 was not delivered correctly. The consignment was short by two units, which was confirmed by your driver when he delivered them.

Task 6. What should your course of action be in response to Scenario 2? Issue the appropriate documentation and make the necessary entries in the appropriate books or ledgers provided for you.

Task 7. What do you understand by the term cash discount. Assuming you wished to take full advantage of all cash discounts on offer by your suppliers, how much would you save and on what dates would you pay each supplier. (*See Purchase Invoices* at the beginning of the assignment).

Task 8. Assuming you take advantage of all cash discounts offered in Task 7, issue the necessary cheques (make copies of Fig. 6.22) and make the necessary entries in the appropriate books or ledgers provided for you at the end of this Assignment.

Unit 6 Financial transactions, costing and pricing

_____19___	**PROVINCIAL BANK PLC**	40-51-20
	21, North Street, Bingord.	_____19___
	PAY _____	
	_____	£
£_____	_____	For and on behalf of Supermicro Ltd
000014	⑈ '000014 9⑈'51201: 12345678⑉	

_____19___	**PROVINCIAL BANK PLC**	40-51-20
	21, North Street, Bingord.	_____19___
	PAY _____	
	_____	£
£_____	_____	For and on behalf of Supermicro Ltd
000015	⑈ '000015 9⑈'51201: 12345678⑉	

_____19___	**PROVINCIAL BANK PLC**	40-51-20
	21, North Street, Bingord.	_____19___
	PAY _____	
	_____	£
£_____	_____	For and on behalf of Supermicro Ltd
000016	⑈ '000016 9⑈'51201: 12345678⑉	

_____19___	**PROVINCIAL BANK PLC**	40-51-20
	21, North Street, Bingord.	_____19___
	PAY _____	
	_____	£
£_____	_____	For and on behalf of Supermicro Ltd
000017	⑈ '000017 9⑈'51201: 12345678⑉	

_____19___	**PROVINCIAL BANK PLC**	40-51-20
	21, North Street, Bingord.	_____19___
	PAY _____	
	_____	£
£_____	_____	For and on behalf of Supermicro Ltd
000018	⑈ '000018 9⑈'51201: 12345678⑉	

Fig 6.22 Blank cheques

Element 6.2 Explain financial transactions and complete supporting documents

Scenario 3

On your last day at Supermicro Ltd, you receive three cheques (*see* Fig. 6.23) from your customers.

```
┌─────────────────────────────────────────────────────────┐
│  NORDWEST BANK PLC                       29-99-94       │
│  High Street, Carlton, Leeds            Jan 17 19 95    │
│  PAY  Supermicro Ltd                                    │
│       Five Hundred and Eighteen Pounds and  £ 518.17p   │
│       seventeen Pence Only                 For and on behalf
│                                            of Clackton Ltd
│                                                S. Metcalfe
│  "'009834   9"'54509:  12345678",,                      │
└─────────────────────────────────────────────────────────┘
```

```
┌─────────────────────────────────────────────────────────┐
│  PROVINCIAL BANK PLC                     30-99-99       │
│  Main Street, Huddersfield              Jan 17 19 95    │
│  PAY  Supermicro Ltd                                    │
│       Eight Hundred and Eighty One Pounds   £ 881.25p   │
│       and 25p only                         For and on behalf
│                                            of Redburn Ltd
│                                                J. Moore  │
│  "'029996   9"'67801:  12345678",,                      │
└─────────────────────────────────────────────────────────┘
```

```
┌─────────────────────────────────────────────────────────┐
│  BORDERS BANK PLC                        29-99-94       │
│  High Street, York.                     Jan 18 19 95    │
│  PAY  Supermicro Ltd                                    │
│       One Thousand, Two Hundred & Twenty   £1220-83p    │
│       Pounds and 83p only                  For and on behalf
│                                            of Shibdon Ltd
│                                                L. Mahmood
│  "'123016   7"'51299:  121212178",,                     │
└─────────────────────────────────────────────────────────┘
```

Fig 6.23 Three cheques from customers

Task 9. Make the necessary entries in the appropriate books or ledgers provided for you of the three cheques in Scenario 3 and fill in the paying-in slip in Fig 6.26.

Task 10. Your Managing Director has been considering the possibility of selling certain of his products 'over the counter' on a strictly cash basis only. How would you account for such a transaction and how would the recording of a cash transaction differ from that of a credit transaction.

Scenario 4

A couple of weeks after you left Supermicro Ltd, Bookkeeping Personnel contact you again. Apparently the Company Accountant has decided to set up a practice in the Bahamas and will consequently not be returning, and Sheila has since left the company. Paul has settled down well, however, but is finding it difficult to cope with the workload. As you have had previous experience with Supermicro Ltd, you are sent on your second assignment.

On your arrival you meet Paul. He tells you that the following transactions have taken place in your absence.

Summary of additional invoices issued during the month of January

Date	Invoice No.	Customer	Goods amount (£)	VAT (£)	Total amount (£)
Jan 6	006	Shibdon Ltd	80.00	14.00	94.00
Jan 9	007	Woodview Bros	100.00	17.50	117.50
Jan 11	008	Clacton Ltd	350.00	61.25	411.25
Jan 13	009	Shibdon Ltd	400.00	70.00	470.00
Jan 16	010	Mitchells Ltd	275.00	48.13	323.13
Jan 18	011	Clacton Ltd	145.00	25.38	170.38
Jan 20	012	Woodview Bros	165.00	28.88	193.88
Jan 24	013	Redburn Ltd	190.00	33.25	228.25
Jan 26	014	Shibdon Ltd	105.00	18.38	123.38
Jan 28	015	Redburn Ltd	195.00	34.13	229.13
Jan 29	016	Clacton Ltd	295.00	51.63	346.63
Jan 30	017	Woodview Bros	425.00	74.38	499.38
Jan 31	018	Mitchells Ltd	225.00	39.38	264.38

Summary of additional credit notes issued during the month of January

Date	Credit note No.	Customer	Goods amount (£)	VAT (£)	Total amount (£)
Jan 10	C2	Shibdon Ltd	15.00	2.63	17.63
Jan 17	C3	Woodview Bros	25.00	4.38	29.38
Jan 25	C4	Mitchells Ltd	17.00	2.98	19.98

Summary of additional cheques received from customers during the month of February

Date	Customer	Total amount (£)
Feb 20	Clacton Ltd	581.63
Feb 28	Shibdon Ltd	669.75
Feb 28	Woodview Bros	282.00

Paul asks you to perform the following tasks based on that information.

Element 6.2   Explain financial transactions and complete supporting documents

Task 11. Make the necessary entries in the appropriate books or ledgers of the additional invoices issued and the additional credit notes issued during the month of January. Do not complete an actual invoice or credit note.

Task 12. Balance off all the books and ledgers at the end of January.

Task 13. Issue a statement of account to each of your five customers at the end of January using copies of the statement of account in Fig. 6.24.

Task 14. After clearly showing the balances brought forward in the Cash Book and in each of the customers' accounts in the Sales Ledger, enter the three cheques received during February in the appropriate book and ledger. Balance off the Cash Book and all the accounts in the Sales Ledger.

Task 15. Your Managing Director has voiced his concern over security regarding the payment of suppliers. How can you be certain you are paying the correct amount outstanding and how can you be sure that you only pay for goods that were actually ordered, received and not returned? Prepare a short report clearly outlining your recommendations in order to alleviate your Managing Director's anxieties.

You should hand in as part of your answer any documentation (e.g. invoices, credit notes, statements of account, cheques, etc.) which you have issued, together with all the appropriate books and ledgers duly totalled and balanced off where necessary. Samples of a blank credit note and a blank paying-slip are provided in Figs 6.25 and 6.26 respectively.

STATEMENT OF ACCOUNT

SUPERMICRO LTD
Reg. Office:
50, Cottingdale Rd.,
Bingford
BG6 1AP

Tel: (05912) 5656913
Fax (05912) 5894146
VAT Reg. No. 613 589103

To	Account No.
Date	Invoice, C/N Ref. Payment	Dr	Cr	Balance

E & OE

Fig 6.24 Statement of account

SUPERMICRO CREDIT NOTE No.

Reg Office. 60, Cottingdale Road,
Bingford, BG6 1AP.
Tel (05912) 5656913
Fax. (05912) 5894146

Customer:

VAT Reg No. 613589103

Date/Tax Point:

Your order No.	Invoice No.	Date of invoice	Account No.	Reason for credit

Qty	Description	Cat. No.	Price each (£)	Cost (£)	VAT rate	Vat amount (£)

Directors: S. Pidgeon P. Dove A. Robin	Goods Total VAT @ 17.5% Total		E & OE

Fig 6.25 Blank credit note

DATE ______________

Cashier's stamp

______________ 19____

Cashier's stamp

PAID IN BY ______________

bank giro credit

Provincial Bank

Notes £50		
£20		
£10		
£5		
Coins £1		
Other Coins		
Total Cash *		
Cheques, etc		
£		

A/C ______________

CASH ______________

CHEQUES ETC. ______________

£

FEE BOX

CHEQUES 3 60-60-08 16022351 84

Branch Sort Code · Account Number · Transaction Code

National Westminster Bank Plc Please do not fold this counterfoil or write or mark below this line

100091 ⑈100091⑈ 60⑆60081⑆ 16022351⑈ 84

Fig 6.26 Blank paying-in slip

Element 6.2 Explain financial transactions and complete supporting documents

Supermicro Ltd Sales Day Book   Date ....

Date	Invoice No.	Account No.	Customer	Goods amount £	VAT amount £	Total amount £
			Totals			

Supermicro Ltd Purchase Day Book   Date ....

Date	Invoice No.	Account No.	Customer	Goods amount £	VAT amount £	Total amount £
			Totals			

Supermicro Ltd Sales Returns Book   Date ....

Date	Credit note No.	Account	Customer No.	Goods amount £	VAT amount £	Total amount £
			Totals			

Supermicro Ltd
Purchase Ledger (Extract)

Debit (Dr)   Credit (Cr)

Date	Details	Amount £	Date	Details	Amount £

Element 6.2 Explain financial transactions and complete supporting documents

Supermicro Ltd
Sales Ledger (Extract)

Debit (Dr)   Credit (Cr)

Date	Details	Amount £	Date	Details	Amount £

Supermicro Ltd
General Ledger (Extract)

Debit (Dr)   Credit (Cr)

Date	Details	Amount £	Date	Details	Amount £

Element 6.2 Explain financial transactions and complete supporting documents

Supermicro Ltd
Cash Book

Debit (Dr)   Credit (Cr)

Date	Details	Bank £	Cash £	Date	Details	Bank £	Cash £

Element 6.3
CALCULATE THE COST OF GOODS OR SERVICES

Performance criteria

1. Explain direct and indirect costs of businesses.
2. Identify correctly a unit of production or unit of service from given data.
3. Calculate the direct costs of the production or service for a time period.
4. Calculate the indirect costs of the production or service for a time period.
5. Calculate the total (absorption) cost of a unit of the production or service.
6. Explain variable and fixed costs in terms of their relationship with production.
7. Calculate the variable costs of a unit of the production or service from given data.
8. Calculate the marginal cost of a unit of the production or service.

Introduction

All organisations, whatever their form of ownership, size and complexity, must seek to make the best use of their resources. The success or failure of the organisation may well depend on the ability of its management to control costs and make decisions based upon reliable information relating to existing costs and probable future costs.

Accounting objectives

All organisations have to satisfy two different sets of accounting objectives.

1 Financial accounting

This relates to the statutory obligations placed upon the organisation. The financial accountant must take into account the requirements of company law, or the law that relates to the organisation if it is not a company, plus the requirements of the major accountancy bodies. Primarily, these laws, rules and regulations relate to the calculation of profit, using trading and profit and loss accounts or income and expenditure accounts and balance sheets. These are presented to the owners of the organisation to account for the managers' 'stewardship' of the organisation's assets and activities over the previous accounting period which usually covers one year.

2 Cost accounting

The second set of objectives relates to cost accounting and management information. There are no laws that govern the production of costing information. An organisation's managers spend time, money and effort producing such accounting information because it contributes towards the more efficient management of the organisation.

Cost accounting uses the data provided by the financial accounting system together with more detailed data from the operations side of the organisation. The cost accountant will use data in both monetary and non-monetary forms. This will include the recording of such information as the quantities of materials purchased and used, the number of products made or services provided, the hours worked and costs of the various types and grade of labour, etc. The main objective is to ascertain the actual cost of products, operations, services and departments. These costs are usually compared with a predetermined budget or standard cost.

It is this second set of objectives which we will address in this element. Management need to plan, control and make decisions, and the cost accounting system provides information which helps them to do this. Although there are numerous other control systems within a typical organisation, the cost accounting system is the key financial control system and monitors the results of all the organisation's activities that involve money and the use of assets.

All systems need to change as organisations change in line with their changing environment. Like other systems a costing system can become obsolete and in need of updating. If the information produced by the cost accounts is no longer used for managerial decision making, for control purposes or for planning, it has no value and should not be prepared.

Every costing system should be unique, to a large extent, because it should have been designed to suit the needs of the individual organisation and its products, processes and personnel.

> **ACTIVITY 6.3.1**
>
> Prepare notes so that you can give a five-minute presentation to your colleagues, explaining the relationship between financial accounting and cost accounting.
>
> This activity will require you to interpret the above explanations in this element and to undertake a limited amount of research into the differences between financial and cost accounting. Your notes should be brief and to the point (no more than 250 words).

DIRECT AND INDIRECT COSTS

A *cost unit* is the cost of a unit of production, service or time. Examples of cost units include such items as a tonne of sugar, a gallon of fuel oil, a tennis racquet produced, or indeed, a unit of service such as an hour worked for a client by a lawyer or an accountant. Cost units may be identical units, such as washing machines, made on a production line or they may be individual units of production such as in a jobbing, building or engineering firm where each *job* or *batch* could be specially produced for an individual customer to the customer's specification.

A *cost centre* is an area, department or machine to which expenditure can be charged for later allocation to cost units. A cost centre usually has its own set of accounts within the cost accounting system with its own individual account code number.

Costs can be classified in numerous ways. For example, costs can be classified by functions such as production, marketing and administration. These are usually the basis of an organisation's departmental structure. The most fundamental initial classification, however, is to split an organisation's costs between *direct costs* and *indirect costs*.

Direct costs

Direct costs are costs that can be allocated to a cost centre or a cost unit. They include such items of cost as *direct materials, direct labour* and *direct expenses*. Direct costs are *allocated* or charged straight to the account to which they relate. The total of all the direct costs is known as the *prime cost*.

Direct materials

Direct materials are used in production and are either purchased through the organisation's purchase order system and the resultant invoice is charged directly to the account concerned, or materials are issued directly from the organisation's stores where the cost is charged via a stock issue note to the account concerned.

When dealing with materials charged directly through the purchase order system, the only cost that can be charged is the actual cost of the materials on the date of their purchase. The bookkeeping entries in the accounts will credit the bank account when the cheque is drawn, and debit the cost centre account.

Materials that have been issued from stock may have been in the stores for a long time and their issue price may not represent their replacement value.

There are various methods of pricing stock issues:

FIFO

This is the most common method – First In First Out. This means that the first price used for the purchase of that item of stock will be used when it is issued from stores, until all of the stock that was purchased at that price has been issued. The next price that will be used will be the next oldest, until all of the stock at that price has been issued, and so on. Thus the issues from stock, although at cost prices, are not at current cost prices.

LIFO

This uses the Last In First Out price for the stock issues.

AVCO

The average price method calculates a new average value for each item of stock each time a new stock purchase has been delivered to the store.

All of these pricing methods use actual cost and if the cost price of the stock purchases was always the same each method would give identical results. (*See* Fig. 6.27.)

Stores Ledger (LIFO System)

Description — Screws/wood/2G x 8's/steel
Commodity number — 5213
Item quantity — Box of 200

Date	Receipts	Issues	Balance
1 Jan	200 @ 4		200 @ 4 = 800
5 Jan	300 @ 5		300 @ 5 = 1500
10 Jan		200 @ 5	200 @ 4 = 800
			100 @ 5 = 500
11 Jan	300 @ 6		300 @ 6 = 1800
14 Jan		200 @ 6	200 @ 4 = 800
			100 @ 5 = 500
			100 @ 6 = 600
19 Jan	250 @ 7		250 @ 7 = 1750
24 Jan		250 @ 7	200 @ 4 = 800
		50 @ 6	100 @ 5 = 500
			50 @ 6 = 300
			1600

Fig 6.27a Bin stock cards

Stores Ledger (AVCO System)

Description — Screws/wood/2½ x 8's/steel
Commodity number — 5213
Item quantity — Box of 200

Date	Receipts	Issues	Balance
1 Jan	200 @ 4		200 @ 4 = 800
5 Jan	300 @ 5		300 @ 5 = 1500
			500 @ 4.60 = 2300
10 Jan		200 @ 4.60	300 @ 4.60 = 1380
11 Jan	300 @ 6		300 @ 6 = 1800
			600 @ 5.30 = 3180
14 Jan		200 @ 5.30	400 @ 5.30 = 2120
19 Jan	250 @ 7		250 @ 7 = 1750
			650 @ 5.95 = 3870
24 Jan		300 @ 5.95	350 @ 5.95 = 2083

Fig 6.27b Bin stock cards

There are two basic records of materials kept for stock.

1 In the store the storeman keeps a *bin card*, which records the numbers of stock receipts and issues and the balance held in stock for each commodity. Most stores have a considerable number of different stock items or commodities in stock at any one time and each is given its own commodity number.

2 The other stock record is kept by the costing section and is called the *Stock Ledger*. This contains the same information as the bin card but it also has the values of the stock in addition to the numbers involved.

Today with the increasing use of computerised stock systems and the use of bar codes to input the commodity codes there is no need for a separate bin card system as the computer keeps all records on line and each terminal within the network has access to the same up-to-date data.

Activity 6.3.2 shows the effect on the pricing of stock that each method has in times of rapid inflation.

Direct labour

Direct labour is the wages paid to the workers who make the products or provide the service. Wages can be calculated either on a *time basis*, whereby the actual time spent on making the product or service is multiplied by the agreed hourly rate paid to the employee, or on the basis of the number of units of production produced by the employee (*piecework*).

Element 6.3 Calculate the cost of goods or services

ACTIVITY 6.3.2

Task 1. From the following receipts and issues, prepare three Stores Ledger accounts using FIFO, LIFO and the Average Price methods.

Commodity No 232115
Screws/countersunk/3 in × 6's/steel
Unit = 1 box of 200 screws

Feb 1	Received 100 boxes valued at £3.00 each
Feb 5	Received 200 boxes valued at £3.10 each
Feb 6	Issued 150 boxes
Feb 10	Received 200 boxes valued at £3.20 each
Feb 11	Issued 250 boxes
Feb 15	Received 100 boxes valued at £3.30 each
Feb 16	Issued 150 boxes
Feb 20	Received 200 boxes valued at £3.40 each
Feb 21	Issued 100 boxes

Task 2. Explain in a short note why materials are a direct cost in most businesses.

Time-based labour costs

In an organisation, such as a building firm or a garage, the workers usually work on a number of different jobs in each week. They record the time spent on these jobs on *time cards* (*see* Fig. 6.28) so that at the end of each week the cost of their wages can be charged to the jobs on which they worked.

TIME CARD

Works No.	Department	Employee's Name	Week Commencing
323	*Stores*	*Susan Adams*	Mon. *12 May*

Day	Ordinary Time				Overtime		Hours		
	In	Out	In	Out	In	Out	Basic	Overtime	Saturday
Monday	0800	1200	1258	1700			8		
Tuesday	0758	1203	1306	1701	1730	1930	7.5	2	
Wednes	0759	1201	1300	1702	1730	1930	8	2	
Thursday	0807	1201	1300	1700	1731	1932	7.5	2	
Friday	0800	1200	1302	1703			8		
Saturday					0800	1200			4
					Total Hours		39	6	4

39 hours at £ 2 = 78.00
6 hours at £ 3 = 18.00
4 hours at £ 4 = 16.00
Total gross pay £ 112.00

Fig 6.28 Sample time card

Employees who work on the same job all the time, such as production line workers, do not need to keep individual time sheets; all they need is a method of recording their time at work. *Time recording clocks* that require the workers to clock in and clock out are often used.

These clocks are placed at the entrance to the factory and use two racks: an *In* and an *Out* rack. The racks hold the employee's time card and the employee on entering work takes his or her card from the Out rack, stamps it in the clock and places it in the *In* rack. The managers can see at a glance at these racks who is in work and who is not; they will also know who is late. When the employee leaves work, he or she must clock out by taking the card from the In rack, stamping it in the clock and placing it in the Out rack. The time printed on the cards can be used to calculate the hours worked so that the employees get paid and their wages are charged to the correct cost centre.

These days most of these systems are linked to computers that will automatically update the payroll system and the costing system with the data from the time clocks. If a factory has different production departments, which are also different cost centres, it will need different entrances and clocks in order to record the times of the employees in each department.

Piecework labour costs

Piecework, or payment by results, involves paying people for the quantity of acceptable work that they do. The obvious disadvantage of the system is the additional quality control that is required to maintain standards when the workers' natural reaction is to work as quickly as possible regardless of quality and even their own safety. The cost of the additional inspection systems and rectification work often outweighs the savings made in wages. The advantage that piecework is said to have is that it motivates workers to achieve higher levels of output.

Other systems can have the same effect but with less problems in quality control and health and safety. These are the various incentive bonus methods that can increase a worker's basic pay in line with increased productivity.

All of these methods of payment are illustrated in the following example.

Example

ML Ltd employs three workers: Horton, Magee and Wood. The company is investigating the effect on the total payroll cost of the firm, if different pay rates were used. Last week's pay data is shown in Table 6.2.

Table 6.2

	Horton	Magee	Wood
Price per unit	£1.15	£1.50	£1.25
Actual units produced	200	125	150
Guaranteed hourly rate	£6.00	£7.50	£5.00
Time allowed (hrs/100 units)	23 hrs	32 hrs	38 hrs
Actual time taken	40 hrs	42 hrs	39 hrs

The following report shows the amount that each worker would have been paid under the systems of hourly rates, piecework and a bonus system based on one-third of time saved.

1 **Hourly rates.**

Horton	40 hrs × £6.00 = £240
Magee	42 hrs × £7.50 = £315
Wood	39 hrs × £5.00 = £195

2 **Piecework.**

Horton	200 units × £1.15 = £230
Magee	125 units × £1.50 = £187.50
Wood	150 units × £1.25 = £187.50

3 **Bonus.**

Horton Time allowed = 23 hrs × 200 units/100 = 46 hrs
46 hrs time allowed − 40 hrs time taken = 6 hrs time saved
Bonus = 1/3 × 6 hrs time saved = 2 hrs bonus
Time paid = 40 hrs time worked + 2 hrs bonus = 42 hrs
Pay = 42 hrs × £6.00 = £252

Magee Time allowed = 32 hrs × 125 units/100 = 40 hrs
40 hrs time allowed − 42 hrs time taken = No time saved
No bonus
Pay = 42 hrs × £7.50 = £315

Wood Time allowed = 38 hrs × 150 units/100 = 57 hrs
57 hrs time allowed − 39 time taken = 18 hrs time saved
Bonus = 1/3 × 18 hrs time saved = 6 hrs
Time paid = 39 hrs time worked + 6 hrs bonus = 45 hrs
Pay = 45 hrs × £5.00 = £225

ACTIVITY 6.3.3

Task 1. The managers at ML Ltd were interested by the above illustration and have requested you to do the same calculations for three other employees:
Leake, Golab and Rooney. Their last week's pay data are shown in Table 6.3.

Table 6.3

	Leake	*Golab*	*Rooney*
Price per unit	£1.35	£1.05	£1.20
Actual units produced	260	200	180
Guaranteed hourly rate	£8.00	£6.00	£5.00
Time allowed (hours/100 units)	36 hrs	34 hr	30 hrs
Actual time taken	30 hrs	31 hr	27 hrs

Produce a working paper to show your calculations of the amount that each worker would have been paid under each of the following systems:

1 hourly rates
2 piecework
3 a bonus system based on $\frac{1}{3}$ of time saved.

Task 2. Explain in a short note why labour is considered to be a direct cost in most businesses.

Unit 6 Financial transactions, costing and pricing

Direct expenses

Direct expenses are few but can be costly and include costs like royalties and copyrights or plant hire used for a particular job. As with all direct costs the whole expense can be attributed to a particular production cost centre or job.

An example of the payment of royalties is the payment made by what was then Austin Rover to Honda in the early 1980s of £400 for each Triumph Acclaim that Austin Rover built. Honda had designed and developed the car as the Honda Ballade and sold it in markets outside Europe. Austin Rover simply made the cars to Honda's design and even included many Honda parts such as engines and dashboards that they bought in. Both parties were better off with the royalty agreement: Honda received royalty payments and sold expensive parts to Austin Rover who were saved the very expensive, time consuming and risky process of designing and developing their own new model.

Indirect costs

All material, labour and expenses that cannot easily be charged to cost units are *indirect costs*, which are often collectively known as *overheads*. Typical examples of indirect costs in a manufacturing firm are shown in Table 6.4.

Table 6.4 Indirect costs for a manufacturer

Indirect materials	Lubricating oils, stationery, consumable materials, maintenance materials, spare parts for machines, etc.
Indirect labour	Factory supervision, maintenance wages, storeman's costs, etc.
Indirect expenses	Rent, rates and insurance for the factory, plant insurance, depreciation, etc.

Indirect costs refer more to the passage of time than to the actual production of a product or the provision of a service to a customer. If you consider the expenses of rent, rates, insurance and depreciation, you will appreciate that most of these costs are based on a financial year.

Indirect costs are often separated into categories such as *production overheads*, *administration overheads*, *selling overheads* and *financial overheads*. These are costs that need *allocating* or *apportioning* to a cost centre. This means that when these overhead costs are first incurred they are initially charged to an overhead cost centre. The problem is that at some stage the costs held in the set of accounts that make up the overhead cost centre must be recharged to the firm's production, i.e. the cost units.

Some overhead costs within a firm are not related to any particular production department and relate more to the service departments which exist to support the production departments. These costs will be charged initially to a set of overhead accounts that will need to be apportioned, i.e. shared out, among the other production overhead accounts prior to their final allocation to the cost units.

The charging of overhead costs to production is known as *overhead absorption*. When deciding on which is the best method of absorption, consideration must be given to the production process: whether it is mechanised or manual, the main items and type of overheads and how they are incurred. Most overhead costs vary with time, such as rent, rates, insurances and salaries, and therefore if one job takes twice as long as another it should take twice the overhead cost.

Finding the best method of charging for overheads is not easy and most firms have their own methods that they have established over the years. When the firm's overhead costs are a small proportion of their final cost, the use of differing methods of absorption will not have a great effect on the final cost of the firm's products. When overhead costs are a substantial part of the product cost, however, the charging method will have an effect on the amount charged to the different products made by the firm. This makes it difficult to compare the cost of making similar products in different firms, if each has its own unique overhead absorption system.

Production is now becoming more capital intensive; we are replacing the use of labour with the more intensive use of machines, and this is having the effect of decreasing the products' direct costs and increasing the indirect costs through increased depreciation on the additional machinery and plant. Unlike the allocation of direct costs, where because of the direct nature of their payment there is little room for any debate over their charge to the final job for which they were incurred, indirect cost allocation can become a matter of opinion and argument within the firm. It is necessary to achieve a consensus among the firm's managers as to the best system to use for their firm. As mentioned above, different systems will allocate the same costs in different proportions to the firm's products.

Provisions for the depreciation of fixed assets

As already mentioned, the cost of depreciating fixed assets can form a large proportion of a firm's overhead costs. With the possible exception of land values, all fixed assets tend to fall in value over a period of time. The following are the main reasons for such reductions.

- *Wear and tear* – whereby the asset is gradually worn out by usage.
- *Passage of time* – whereby the asset deteriorates the older it gets (e.g. rust or oxidisation). Leasehold property runs out of value as the period of lease expires.
- *Obsolescence* – whereby the asset falls in value due to the introduction of new technology or a change in fashion or model.

If these three reasons are applied to the fall in value of a motor car, it is easier to see the need for the provision for depreciation. We have to reduce the value of the asset in the accounts and make a charge for the use of the asset to the departments or cost centres that use it.

One of the problems with depreciation is that until the asset is sold at the end of its useful life, the accountant cannot know accurately how much depreciation to charge. The accountant must guess the amount, therefore, and use such an estimate in the accounts for the year's expense. Although many systems exist to estimate the annual charge for depreciation, three systems have evolved in an attempt to standardise such estimates: these are *the straight line method*, *the revaluation method* and *the reducing balance method*. These systems of calculating depreciation are dealt with in more detail in Unit 7. We shall cover the most popular method here – the straight line method. Its calculation is divided into two steps:

- Estimate the number of years that the asset will last and its probable resale (or scrap) value at the end of that period.
- Deduct the resale value from the original cost of the asset and divide the answer by the estimated number of years.

	£
Cost	10 000
Scrap value	256
Loss	9 744
Life	4 years
Depreciation per year	£9744/4 = £2436

As it is easy to calculate, this method is used most widely by business managers. This method produces the same charge for depreciation each year and as a result it is not considered a very accurate reflection of the fall in the real value of the asset. If again you consider the fall in the value of a motor car, you will appreciate that most of the depreciation occurs in the earlier years of its useful life.

Overhead absorption methods

The principal methods of absorbing production overheads from a cost centre into a cost unit are the *labour-hour basis*, the *machine-hour basis* and the *unit basis*.

To use the *labour-hour basis*, the total estimated overhead cost is divided by the total estimated number of labour hours used in the budget period. When any employee works on a job in the department not only will his or her pay be charged to the job, but the amount of overhead cost per labour hour will also be charged. A similar system uses a percentage on cost rate for the overhead charge; that is, if the labour rate of pay for an employee is £5 per hour and the overhead recovery rate is £2.50 per hour, we can say that the percentage on cost per labour hour is 50%.

The *machine-hour basis* follows a similar pattern in that the total estimated overhead cost is divided by the estimated number of machine hours expected to run in the budget period. We then have an overhead recovery rate per machine hour, and every hour that the machines are run will generate a charge for overheads.

The *unit cost basis* is the easiest to use. The total estimated overhead cost is divided by the estimated number of units that are expected to be made in the budget period, and the resultant amount is charged to the cost of each product made. This system has the advantage of simplicity, but when differing types of products are made, it is not usually fair to charge the same amount of overhead cost. Some products cost more to make and some take longer to make than others, and as such, should take proportionately more of the overhead costs.

Overhead budgets

You will have noticed that all of the above comments relate to estimated overhead costs and estimated labour and machine hours and production units. One of the problems of dealing with overheads is that the costs are incurred throughout the year in an uneven way. Products need to be charged with their share of overhead cost as soon as they are produced in order to know the total product cost, which is needed for marketing purposes. The firm's managers do not want to set their selling price lower than their cost price. New products and jobs need careful budgeting and the managers need to be able to base their estimates on reliable current costing data for existing products.

Before the start of the financial year, the firm's accountants and managers must complete the calculation of their estimates of the likely total overhead cost for the year. It is these estimates that form the basis of the overhead recovery rates that will charge the production cost units with the overhead costs.

The cost centre for the overhead accounts will have an income account that will be credited with the amount of overhead cost charged to the production cost units. Managers hope that their estimates of costs and production levels are correct and that all of the overhead costs are charged out during the year and no balance remains on the overhead cost centre accounts at the end of the year. As you can appreciate, this is a very difficult task that is almost impossible to achieve and managers have to monitor throughout the year both the expenditure and the income that comes from charging out the overheads to production. If they think that the rates need adjusting in order to achieve a nil balance at the end of the year, then new rates will be calculated and used.

To charge out more overhead costs than are actually incurred means that the income to the overhead cost centre is greater than the expenditure on the overheads, and this is known as *overabsorption*. When more expenditure has been incurred than income generated through charges to production via the overhead recovery rate the cost centre will have underabsorbed.

An example of overhead absorption

The following example is based on a small manufacturing firm and illustrates the three stages in the charging of overhead costs to the cost units.

In our example, each job done in the factory is given a separate *job cost code* on the firm's computer system and each job is a separate *cost centre*. This is the code for the account to which all of the costs incurred by that job will be charged. In the old days of manual record-keeping, this account would have been kept on a *job cost sheet*. The direct costs of materials, labour and expenses will be charged directly to this account as indicated earlier. The indirect overhead costs of keeping the factory running cannot be charged directly and must be charged to their own set of accounts and then recharged on an overhead recovery rate.

Our factory has been organised into three different *production departments*: engineering, assembly and packaging. There are also two *service departments*, that maintain the factory buildings and machinery. Some of the indirect labour and expenses can be allocated to the production departments, such as the supervision costs and the insurance and depreciation costs on the machinery used in each department. Other indirect costs are attributable to the two maintenance departments. Table 6.5 shows the way in which the costs are attributed at present.

Table 6.5

	Production Depts			Maintenance Depts	
	Engineering £	Assembly £	Packaging £	Buildings £	Machines £
Indirect costs	000	000	000	000	000
Expenses	40	60	30	10	20
Labour	20	40	20	30	40
Total	60	100	50	40	60

The first task is to apportion the estimated cost of the two maintenance departments to the production departments.

When the firm's managers considered the way in which the costs of the two service departments were incurred, they found that the cost of the Buildings Department related to the floor space occupied by each department, whereas the Machine Maintenance Department's costs related more to the number of machines used in each department.

When the plans of the buildings were looked at, the floor space occupied by each department was calculated, as was the total floor space. The number of machines in each department was recorded on each department's inventory and checked by counting them in the departments.

Buildings Department

Apportioning the cost of the Buildings Department used the formula:

$$\frac{\text{Departmental floor space}}{\text{Total floor space}} \times \text{Building Department's total indirect cost}$$

Therefore:

Engineering Department
4000 m² ÷ 20 000 m² × £40 000 = £8 000

Assembly Department
8000 m² ÷ 20 000 m² × £40 000 = £16 000

Packaging Department
6000 m² ÷ 20 000 m² × £40 000 = £12 000

Machinery Department
2000 m² ÷ 20 000 m² × £40 000 = £4 000

                      Total   £40 000

Machinery Department

Apportioning the cost of the Machinery Department used the following formula:

$$\frac{\text{Number of machines in each department}}{\text{Total number of machines in the firm}} \times £64\,000$$

Note that the cost of the Machinery Department has increased because of the £4000 Building, Maintenance Department's costs that have been charged in the above apportionment.

Therefore:

Engineering Department
70 machines ÷ 100 machines × £64 000 = £44 800

Assembly Department
20 machines ÷ 100 machines × £64 000 = £12 800

Packaging Department
10 machines ÷ 100 machines × £64 000 = £6 400

                      Total   £64 000

Table 6.6 shows how the costs are now attributed to the individual departments.

Table 6.6

	Production Depts			Maintenance Depts	
	Engineering £	Assembly £	Packaging £	Buildings £	Machines £
Indirect costs	000	000	000	000	000
Expenses	40	60	30	10	20
Labour	20	40	20	30	40
Total	60	100	50	40	60
Building Dept	8	16	12	(40)	4
Machine Dept	12	24	28	–	(64)
Total cost	80	140	90	–	–

We have now charged out all of the costs of the two service departments to the three production departments and have completed the first part of our attempt to recharge the overhead costs. Our next task is to decide upon the most appropriate method to use to charge the above overhead departmental costs to the jobs.

The Engineering Department's overhead absorption rate

Due to the intensive usage of machinery in the Engineering Department, the managers at the factory have decided to use a machine-hour basis for the absorption rate. It is estimated that the 70 machines in the department will run for about 105 000 hours during the next year. Therefore, the calculation of the overhead charge per machine hour is:

£80 000 ÷ 105 000 hours = £0.7619 per machine hour

It should be noted that we are dealing with estimated figures, each of which may turn out to be wrong and we would be foolish to use such levels of detail on estimated figures. We will round down our machine hour absorption rate to the nearest penny, therefore, at 76 pence per machine hour.

The Assembly Department's overhead absorption rate

Although there are some machines in the Assembly Department, the managers considered that as the work of the department was essentially labour-intensive, the most suitable basis of apportionment is the labour-hour basis. There are currently 12 assembly workers who will work an estimated 24 000 hours during the next year, and therefore the calculation of the hourly rate is as follows:

£140 000 ÷ 24 000 hours = £5.833333333 per labour hour

This would be taken to the nearest penny at £5.83 per labour hour.

The Packaging Department's overhead absorption rate

Once again the managers considered that this department was labour-intensive and the best method to use is the labour-hour basis. There are four workers in the department who are estimated to work about 9000 hours during the next year. The rate per labour hour is calculated as follows:

£90 000 ÷ 9000 labour hours = £10 per labour hour

An example of a job costing system using direct and indirect costs

In order to illustrate how the above rates are used, the following jobs need to be costed. Each job has been through each department in our factory. All that we need to know are the direct material and labour costs; there are no direct expenses. The labour costs are: Engineering £8.00 per hour; Assembly £6.00 per hour; and Packaging £4.00 per hour.

Job no. 1334	£	**Job no. 1335**	£
Direct materials	345.00	Direct materials	567.00
Direct labour		Direct labour	
40 hrs Engineering @ £8.00	320.00	23 hrs Engineering @ £8.00	184.00
8 hrs Assembly @ £6.00	48.00	16 hrs Assembly @ £6.00	96.00
4 hrs Packaging @ £4.00	16.00	7 hrs Packaging @ £4.00	28.00
Overheads		Overheads	
36 Machine hrs @ £0.76	27.36	49 Machine hours @ £0.76	37.24
8 hrs Assembly @ £5.83	46.64	16 hrs Assembly @ £5.83	93.28
4 hrs Packaging @ £10.00	40.00	7 hrs Packaging @ £10.00	70.00
Total cost	£843.00	Total cost	£1075.52

ACTIVITY 6.3.4

Ivor Pain Ltd has a small factory with three production departments (Assembly, Painting and Finishing) and two service departments (Maintenance and Administration). The estimated overhead costs for the next cost period are shown in Table 6.7.

Table 6.7

	Production Depts			Service Depts	
	Assembly £	Painting £	Finishing £	Maint £	Admin £
Indirect costs	000	000	000	000	000
Expenses	50	40	40	10	20
Labour	30	50	40	30	40
Total	80	90	80	40	60

The costs of the service departments are to be allocated between the production departments on the following basis:

Maintenance 50 per cent to Assembly Dept, 20 per cent to Painting Dept, 20 per cent to Finishing Dept, 10 per cent to Administration Dept

Administration 25 per cent to Assembly Dept, 25 per cent to Painting Dept, 50 per cent to Finishing Dept

The Assembly and Finishing Departments' overhead recovery rates are based on estimated labour hours of 20 000 hrs and 16 000 hrs respectively. The Painting Department uses a machine-hour rate and the estimated number of machine hours in the next cost period is 20 000.

You are required to calculate the overhead absorption rates for the three production departments for the next cost period.

Element 6.3 Calculate the cost of goods or services

ACTIVITY 6.3.5

Using the overhead recovery rates that you have calculated in Activity 6.3.4, you are now required to complete the following job cost cards given that the direct labour rates per hour in the three departments are:

Assembly workers	£6.00 per hour
Painters	£5.50 per hour
Finishers	£5.00 per hour

Job 23789
Direct materials	£49.00
Direct labour hours	
Assembly	50 hrs
Painting	20 hrs
Finishing	12 hrs
Machine hours – Painting	16 hrs

Job 23790
Direct materials	£58.00
Direct labour hours	
Assembly	23 hrs
Painting	17 hrs
Finishing	10 hrs
Machine hours – Painting	15 hrs

Job 23791
Direct materials	£64.00
Direct labour hours	
Assembly	34 hrs
Painting	43 hrs
Finishing	34 hrs
Machine hours – Painting	40 hrs

FIXED AND VARIABLE COSTS

Earlier in this element we looked at the split of costs between direct and indirect costs. There is another way that costs can be analysed and this is to split our classification into those costs that vary with production (which are mostly direct costs) and those costs that will not change if production levels are altered (these are mostly indirect costs). The following lists show how costs can be classified between these two categories.

- *Variable costs* relate to a unit of production such as materials, wages, fuel, energy and packaging costs.

- *Fixed costs* do not relate to individual units of production. They are often in the nature of overhead costs and are more related to the passage of time, such as rent, rates, insurances, depreciation, heat, light, cleaning, maintenance, administration and selling and distribution costs.

If we want to calculate the cost of a unit of production or service our calculations must take into account the nature of the above costs. Consider the following example.

Example

A firm makes dolls and its costs for last year were:

	£
Direct materials	12 000
Direct labour	13 000
Indirect costs	50 000
Total costs	75 000

During the year it made 50 000 dolls. Its cost per doll was, therefore: £75 000/50 000 dolls = £1.50. When the firm's managers considered how the firm incurred its costs they decided that all of the materials and labour were variable costs and that £10 000 of the indirect costs were also variable. The managers wanted to know what the unit cost would be if they doubled production. The new calculation is:

	£
Variable costs:	
Direct materials	24 000
Direct labour	26 000
Indirect costs	20 000
Total variable cost	70 000
Add fixed costs	40 000
Total cost	110 000

The new unit cost is £110 000/100 000 dolls = £1.10.

These calculations can be done in a different way that will illustrate why the two answers are different.

The total variable cost of 100 000 dolls is £70 000; the variable cost per unit is £70 000/100 000 dolls = £0.70. If we want to find the total cost of any number of dolls produced we simply multiply £0.70 by the number of dolls and add on the fixed costs. For example:

40 000 dolls × £0.70 = £28 000 + £40 000 fixed cost = £68 000
50 000 dolls × £0.70 = £35 000 + £40 000 fixed cost = £75 000
60 000 dolls × £0.70 = £42 000 + £40 000 fixed cost = £82 000
70 000 dolls × £0.70 = £49 000 + £40 000 fixed cost = £89 000
80 000 dolls × £0.70 = £56 000 + £40 000 fixed cost = £96 000
90 000 dolls × £0.70 = £63 000 + £40 000 fixed cost = £103 000
100 000 dolls × £0.70 = £70 000 + £40 000 fixed cost = £110 000

From the above example you can see that at any level of production, the fixed costs will not change. In the example it was always £40 000. The cost that does change is the total variable cost. Conversely when we consider the unit cost (i.e. the cost per doll), we find that as production increases the cost per unit will fall as the fixed costs are shared out over more units.

Element 6.3 Calculate the cost of goods or services

MARGINAL COSTING

From the above example it is clear that a firm has to pay its fixed costs regardless of the number of units of production or service that it produces. Eventually there will be a point at which production cannot be increased due to either shortage of skilled labour, materials, production equipment or space. The only way to get by this limiting factor on production is to increase production capacity by either employing more people, obtaining additional materials from a new supplier or equipment or premises. Various changes to the type of product that the firm makes can also increase profits in the short term. This analysis is called *contribution per limiting factor* and is beyond the scope of the Advanced GNVQ qualification.

If we accept that fixed costs will always remain the same for any level of production, the only increase in cost will be the variable cost. This is the concept of *marginal costing*. In our example of the firm that makes dolls the marginal cost of making one more doll is £0.70.

Note that further explanations of fixed and variable costs and marginal costing is given in Unit 8 Element 2 on the completion of marketing and sales budgets.

ACTIVITY 6.3.6

M.L. Components Ltd makes parts for the motor industry. It estimates that next year's costs will be £1 000 000 of which 60 per cent is considered to be variable cost and 40 per cent is fixed costs. The total production is estimated to be 100 000 units.

Task 1. Calculate:
  (i) the total cost per unit
 (ii) the variable cost per unit
(iii) the fixed cost per unit

Task 2. Explain the difference between fixed and variable costs and give examples of each.

Task 3. If the company were to make an additional 10 000 units, what would be the increase in the total cost of production.

Task 4. If the company could save £48 000 on its fixed costs in addition to the increase in production outlined in Task 3 above, what would the following figures be:
  (i) the total cost per unit
 (ii) the variable cost per unit
(iii) the fixed cost per unit

Task 5. Why is the answer to Task 1 and Task 2 different?

Unit 6 Financial transactions, costing and pricing

Self assessment questions

1 Which of the following is usually considered to be a direct cost?
   a Materials
   b Royalties
   c Factory rent
   d Supervisors' wages

2 An organisation's costs can be divided between direct and indirect costs. Consider the following statements.
   (i) Service industries do not have direct costs.
   (ii) When the factory is closed, there will be no direct costs.

   Which option best describes these statements?

   a (i) True, (ii) True
   b (i) True, (ii) False
   c (i) False, (ii) True
   d (i) False, (ii) False

3 The total cost of a product includes both direct and indirect costs. Consider the following statements.
   (i) Factory overheads can be identified with individual products.
   (ii) Stores issues cannot be charged directly to a product.

   Which option best describes the two statements?

   a (i) True, (ii) True
   b (i) True, (ii) False
   c (i) False, (ii) True
   d (i) False, (ii) False

4 Consider the following statements.
   (i) If the cost of direct labour increases following a pay rise, the products made by the workers will earn less profit.
   (ii) If the factory overhead costs can be reduced, the reduced costs will affect all products equally.

   Which option best describes the two statements?

   a (i) True, (ii) True
   b (i) True, (ii) False
   c (i) False, (ii) True
   d (i) False, (ii) False

5–8 Questions 5, 6, 7 and 8 relate to the following information.

A clothing company has calculated the cost of making one of its garments as follows:

	£
Materials	2.50
Labour	
Cutting	1.00
Sewing	1.50
Finishing	0.50
Factory rent	0.20
Factory maintenance	0.30
Admin & marketing	3.60
Total cost	9.60

These costs can be analysed in the following ways:

a labour cost
b prime cost
c factory cost
d indirect cost

5 Which cost is calculated to be £5.50?

6 Which cost is calculated to be £3.00?

7 Which cost is calculated to be £6.00?

8 Which cost is calculated to be £4.10?

Assignment

Kray Bros & Co. Ltd make three products for the security industry – G, B, and H – the direct costs of which are:

	G £	B £	H £
Materials	45	50	55
Labour			
Machine Shop @ £8 per hr	8	16	16
Finishing Shop @ £7 per hr	14	21	28
Total direct costs	67	87	99
Machine hours required per product			
Machine Shop	8	3	6
Finishing Shop	1	1	2
Estimated production units	8000	9000	3000

Estimated overhead costs:
  Machine Shop   £58 000
  Finishing Shop   £72 000

Task 1. Calculate the overhead absorption rate for each product using the machine-hour basis and produce a total cost figure for each product.

Task 2. Calculate the overhead absorption rate for each product using the labour-hour basis and produce a total cost figure for each product.

Element 6.4
EXPLAIN BASIC PRICING DECISIONS AND BREAK-EVEN

Performance criteria

1 **Identify basic factors which determine price and describe related pricing strategies.**

2 **Explain break-even point.**

3 **Draw and label a break-even chart from given data.**

4 **Analyse the break-even chart.**

5 **Explain reasons for using a break-even chart.**

PRICING CONSIDERATIONS

There are a number of issues that need to be considered before prices for goods and services can be determined.

- *The cost of the product or service.* The cost of the product or service itself obviously affects the price. Costing was discussed in Element 1.3. The cost is determined by how much of that product or service is sold, in that the less a business sells, the higher the price will have to be if a business wants to achieve a certain level of profit. This is because the fixed costs of a business are spread over the units sold. Clearly the more that is sold, the greater the spread of the fixed costs will be; therefore, the cost will be reduced. The method chosen to cost a product can also determine the eventual price of a product (*see* Element 6.3).

- *The level of profit required.* The level of profit required will also affect the price of a product and the level of profit needed is determined by a number of issues, including investment (past and future), the policy on distribution of profit (e.g. dividends to shareholders or drawings to a proprietor), the need to attract future investment or maybe the need to expand.

- *The degree of competition.* The profit that may be required may not always be achievable, however, as the market may simply not be able to stand 'high' prices due to competition. In this instance a selling price is influenced largely by what competitors charge for this product as customers will obviously tend to buy from the supplier who provides the cheapest product. In a competitive environment therefore the related pricing strategy that would be adopted is *'market-lead pricing'*.

The selling price a business adopts therefore will depend on a number of issues, including profit required, cost structure, costing method adopted, level of output and sales and simply what the market can stand.

MARGINAL COST PRICING

Marginal costing, as already mentioned in Element 6.3, identifies two types of cost:

- *variable costs* – those that vary in line with production (output) (e.g. direct labour and direct materials); and

- *fixed costs* – those that do not vary in line with production (output) over a given period. A fixed cost will be incurred whether or not a single unit is produced or sold (e.g. rent, rates, insurance, depreciation). In other words, these costs will have to be incurred whether a business makes no units or a thousand units (however students should note that fixed costs remain fixed only up to certain levels of output).

We shall use an example to illustrate the implementation of Clayton Associates plan to produce and sell 20 000 units of product X for £5 each. Direct labour is estimated to be £25 000 and direct material £40 000 for the coming year. In addition, fixed costs of £25 000 will also be incurred. The factory will be working at 80 per cent capacity.

Element 6.4 Explain basic pricing decisions and break-even

Calculation of profit

The anticipated profit will therefore be calculated as follows:

		£
Sales (20 000 units × £5 each)		100 000
Less: Variable costs		
Direct labour	25 000	
Direct material	40 000	65 000
Total contribution		35 000
Less: Fixed costs		25 000
Profit		10 000

Marginal costing introduces the concept of *contribution*, which, as can be seen from the above example, is the difference between sales and variable costs (direct labour and direct material); this contribution goes towards covering the fixed costs. Once fixed costs have been covered, a profit is achieved (in the above example £35 000 – £25 000 = £10 000). Under marginal costing, profit is calculated as follows:

Sales – Variable costs = Contribution – Fixed costs = Profits

Calculation of break-even point

The cost structure for one unit in this example would break down as follows:

		£
Selling price		5.00
Less: Variable costs		
Direct labour	1.25	
Direct material	2.00	3.25
Contribution per unit		1.75

In other words each unit produced and sold contributes £1.75 towards the fixed costs of the business. In our example, Clayton Associates, would need to produce and sell 14 286 units to cover their fixed costs of £25 000. This is known as the *break-even point* and is calculated as follows:

$$\frac{\text{Total fixed costs}}{\text{Contribution per unit}} = \frac{25\,000}{1.75} = 14\,286 \text{ units}$$

Calculation of desired level of output

If we wanted to take the formula one stage further, we could even use it to calculate the number of units required to be produced and sold to make a given level of profit. For example, let us calculate how many units we need to produce and sell in order to make a profit of £10 000. We could then apply the following formula:

$$\frac{\text{Fixed costs + Required profit}}{\text{Contribution per unit}}$$

$$= \frac{25\,000 + 10\,000}{1.75}$$

$= 20\,000$ units

We know that this is correct as this is where we started; refer back to the beginning of this example!

Calculation of selling price

We can adapt the formula to calculate the selling price by applying the following:

$$\frac{\text{Fixed costs} + \text{Variable costs} + \text{Profit required}}{\text{Number of units produced and sold}}$$

$$= \frac{25\,000 + 65\,000 + 10\,000}{20\,000}$$

$= £5$

Again we know that this is correct as this is where we started (*see* original example)!

Calculation of viability of additional contract

Suppose Clayton Associates are now offered a contract to produce a further 5 000 units but the customer is only prepared to pay £3.75 per unit and not the full £5. At first glance it would appear that we could not possibly accept the contract as the price offered is much too low. Consider the following, however:

Existing contract	£	£	*Additional new contract*	£	£
Sales		100 000	(5000 × 3.75)		18 750
Less: Variable costs					
Direct labour	25 000		(5000 × 1.25)	6 250	
Direct material	40 000	65 000	(5000 × 2.00)	10 000	16 250
Contribution		35 000			2 500
Less: Fixed costs		25 000			–
Profit		10 000	Additional profit		2 500

If Clayton Associates take on the new additional contract (remember they are only working at 80 per cent capacity, so the additional contract can be absorbed), they will make an additional profit of £2500! Examine the above working and note that there are no fixed costs attributed to the additional new contract. This is because the fixed costs have already been covered by the existing business, i.e. the original 20 000 units producing £100 000 worth of sales. You should note, however, that if the fixed costs were not totally covered by the existing business, any additional contract would need to generate sufficient contribution to cover any outstanding fixed costs, before *any* profit is made.

Marginal costing allows a business to take on additional business at a reduced selling price as long as the selling price is sufficiently high enough to generate a contribution per unit which becomes profit if all of the fixed costs have been covered by existing business!

If a business finds itself running at less than full capacity, therefore, the related pricing strategy to be adopted should be *marginal cost/contribution pricing*.

ACTIVITY 6.4.1

Drake & Co. specialise in the manufacture of plastic ducks. Each duck incurs £1.50 of direct labour, £2 of direct material and £1 of direct expense. In addition, annual fixed costs are anticipated to be £120 000. The company hopes to sell 20 000 ducks and make around £40 000 profit in the coming year.

Task 1. What should the selling price of each duck be, if the above profits are to be achieved?

Task 2. How much should the company charge for each duck if it wished to achieve a profit of £75 000?

Task 3. If an advertising campaign were undertaken costing £20 000 which hopefully increased sales by 25 per cent, what should the selling price be if the profits are to be maintained?

Task 4. It has been suggested that a new manufacturing process be adopted. This would add a further £20 000 per year to the fixed costs, but the total variable cost per duck would fall by £1.00. Assuming the company wants to achieve a profit of £40 000, should this proposal be adopted?

DRAWING A BREAK-EVEN CHART

The break-even chart (sometimes known as the break-even graph) is a graphic representation of the relationship between the number of units of a product produced and the variable costs and fixed costs related to that product.

Once again we shall use an example to illustrate this concept.

Nicholas James and Co make Product X which sells for £16. It costs £5 of direct material and £3 of direct labour to make one unit of X. In addition it is anticipated that £100 000 of fixed costs will be incurred during the year and that the number of units produced and sold should reach 15 000. The company makes no other product.

Armed with this information it is possible to draw up a break-even chart for Product X by taking the following steps.

Step 1. The first thing that needs to be done is to separate out costs into variable costs and fixed costs. The next is to work out the sales revenue, variable cost, fixed cost and total cost on at least two levels of output so that a line can be plotted on the chart/graph. This could involve the construction of the schedule in Table 6.8.

Unit 6 Financial transactions, costing and pricing

Table 6.8

(a) No. of units	(b) Sales revenue (£) (a) × £16	(c) Variable costs (£) (a) × £8	(d) Fixed costs (£)	(e) Total costs (£) (a) + (d)	(f) Profit/ loss (£) (b) + (e)
0	0	0	100 000	100 000	(100 000)
5 000	80 000	40 000	100 000	140 000	(60 000)
10 000	160 000	80 000	100 000	180 000	(20 000)
20 000	240 000	120 000	100 000	220 000	20 000
	320 000	160 000	100 000	260 000	60 000

Table 6.9, as a result of its layout, enables the contribution to be identified.

Table 6.9

(a) No of units	(b) Sales revenue (£) (a) × £16	(c) Variable costs (£) (a) × £8	(d) Contribu- tions (£) (a) – (c)	(e) Fixed costs (£)	(f) Profit/ loss (£) (d) – (e)
0	0	0	0	100 000	(100 000)
5 000	80 000	40 000	40 000	100 000	(60 000)
10 000	160 000	80 000	80 000	100 000	(20 000)
15 000	240 000	120 000	120 000	100 000	20 000
20 000	320 000	160 000	160 000	100 000	60 000

Step 2. The chart can now be drawn! When drawing up a graph the following points should be kept in mind:

- Always use a sharp pencil.
- Head the chart/graph accordingly.
- Use an appropriate scale.
- Label both axes.
- Label each line plotted.

Step 3. Draw and label the axes, i.e. the vertical axis representing total sales in £s and the horizontal axis representing the number of units produced.

Step 4. Draw and label the fixed cost line, plotting the information found in columns (a) and (e) of Table 6.9. This will be a straight horizontal line running parallel to the horizontal axis.

Step 5. Draw and label the total cost line, plotting the information found in columns (a) and (e) of Table 6.8. This will be a straight line starting at £100 000 (the fixed costs) on the vertical axis sloping diagonally upwards from left to right on the chart.

Step 6. Draw and label the variable cost line, plotting the information found in columns (a) and (c) on either Table 6.8 or Table 6.9. This will also be a straight line, but in this

Element 6.4 Explain basic pricing decisions and break-even

instance starting at zero, i.e. the point of origin (if nothing is produced – no variable cost will be incurred) sloping diagonally upwards from left to right on the chart.

Step 7. Draw a label on the sales revenue line, plotting the information found in columns (a) and (b) on either Table 6.8 or Table 6.9. This will also be a straight line, again starting at zero, i.e. the point of origin (if nothing is sold, no sales revenue will be received) sloping diagonally upwards from left to right on the chart. The selling price will determine the slope of the sales revenue line.

The break-even chart is shown in Fig. 6.29.

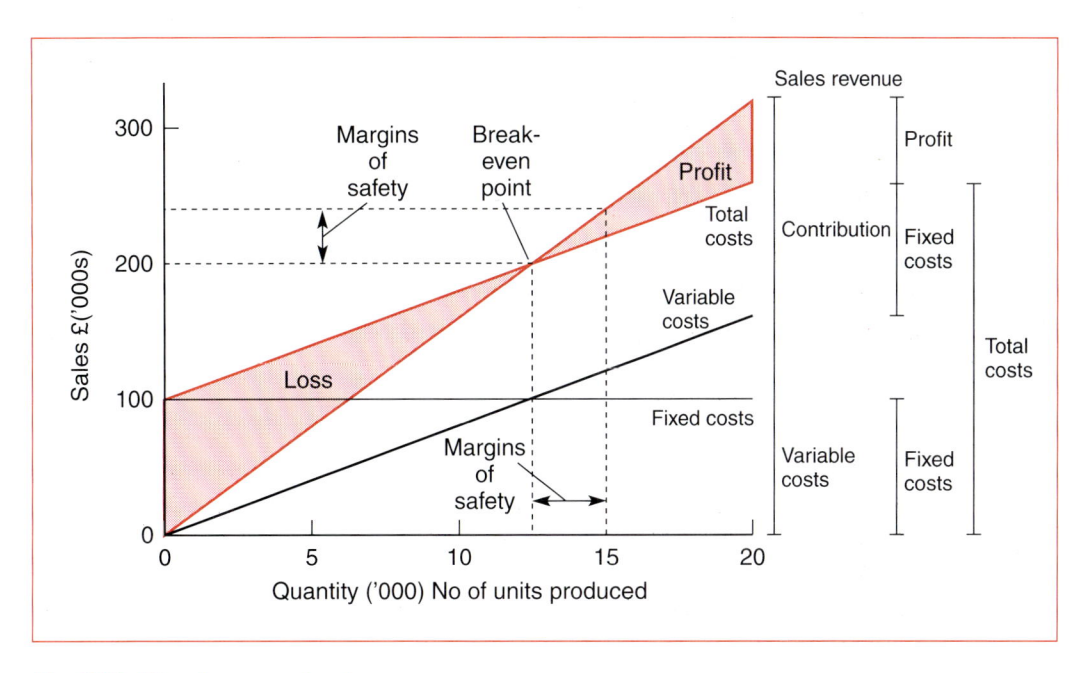

Fig 6.29 Break-even chart

The *break-even point* is where the sales revenue line crosses the total cost line on the break-even chart. At this point the business makes neither a profit nor a loss, i.e. total sales equals total costs. Above the break-even point a profit is achieved; below the break-even point a loss is made. In Fig 6.29 the break-even point for Nicholas James & Co is 12 500 units or £200 000 (in terms of sales revenue).

The *margin of safety* is the excess of the anticipated or planned level of output over the break-even point. It can be measured in either number of units or sales revenue. In the case of Nicholas James & Co, the margin of safety is 2500 units or £40 000. The margin of safety is important in that it gives an indication of the amount by which sales can fall from the planned or required operating levels before a loss is achieved. In the case of Nicholas James & Co sales can fall by 2500 units from the anticipated or planned levels, before a loss would be registered.

The *relationship* between the four lines that have been plotted on the break-even chart should be noted. The fixed cost line is a straight horizontal line signifying that £100 000 must be incurred whether no units are made and sold or 20 000 units are made and sold. Notice the variable cost line and total cost line are running parallel to each other – the difference between the two lines should always represent the fixed costs, i.e. in this example £100 000, because variable costs plus fixed costs equals total costs. The contribution can be measured by comparing the sales revenue line and the variable cost line – the difference between the two lines should always represent the contribution. The shaded area above the break-even point represents profit as it is here that the sales revenue line exceeds the total cost line. The gap between the two lines widens (therefore more profit is achieved) as more units are produced and sold. The shaded area below the break-even point represents a loss as below this point, the total cost line exceeds the sales revenue line. The gap between the two lines widens (therefore more loss is achieved) as less units are produced and sold.

You should familiarise yourself thoroughly with the break-even chart noting the relationship between the four lines plotted.

ANALYSIS OF THE BREAK-EVEN CHART

Once the chart has been drawn up, analysis can begin. We can answer the following questions by considering the break-even chart in Fig. 6.29.

1. *What is the break-even point in units and sales value?* Note the break-even point in Fig. 6.29 is where the sales revenue line crosses the total cost line, i.e. the point where total cost equals total sales revenue. In Fig. 6.29 the break-even point in units is 12 500 and in sales value terms £200 000.

2. *What is the margin of safety in units and sales value?* The margin of safety is the difference between the planned level of output and the break-even point, i.e. in effect the excess! In Fig. 6.29 the margin of safety is 2500 units or £40 000. In other words, sales can fall by 2500 units before a loss is achieved!

3. *How many units would need to be produced and sold to make a profit of £40 000?* The shaded area above the break-even point between the sales revenue line and the total cost line represents profit, i.e. the difference between these two lines at any given level of output above the break-even point represents the profit achieved. Where the difference reads £40 000, 17 500 units will need to be produced and sold.

4. *How much profit/loss would be made if the anticipated production and sales figure of 15 000 is reached?* Follow the principle as in (3), i.e. read from the point where 15 000 units meets the total cost line until the sales revenue line is reached – the difference between the total cost line and the sales revenue line at 15 000 units. The profit achieved at this level of sales is £20 000.

5. *What would be the profit/loss if 7500 units were produced?* Again, following the same principles as outlined in (3) and (4) read the difference between the sales revenue line and the total cost line at 7500 units. The first thing that you should notice, is that the total cost line is now above the sales revenue line and not below as was the case in (3) and (4) and that we are now below the break-even point. The shaded area shown below the break-even point represents a loss, i.e. the difference between the sales revenue line and the total cost line at any given level of output below the break-even point represents the loss achieved. If Nicholas James & Co only produce and sell 7500 units a loss of £40 000 will be recorded.

6 *How many units would the firm need to produce and sell to make a loss of £80 000?* Following the same principles as outlined in (3) to (5) above, an output level of 2500 units would produce a loss of £80 000.

7 *What would be the contribution at the break-even point and at the planned level of output of 15 000 units?* The contribution figure is determined by measuring the difference between the variable cost line and the sales revenue line and will be £100 000 at the break-even point, i.e. just enough to cover the fixed costs of £100 000 and £140 000 at the planned level of output of 15 000 units. The difference between the £140 000 contribution at the planned level and the £100 000 contribution at the break-even point is of course the profit at the planned level of 15 000 units, i.e. £40 000 as £100 000 of fixed costs have to be covered.

8 *What is the variable cost at the break-even point?* The variable cost at the break-even point is £100 000 – simply read along the variable cost line at the break-even point of 12 500 units.

REASONS FOR USING A BREAK-EVEN CHART

1 As an aid to management, break-even charts can help the decision-making process of a business in that they can be used to determine the levels of output necessary to break even, the margin of safety offered at any given planned level of activity, the effects on profitability, etc. This is particularly useful when starting a business, maybe as part of the business plan or on an ongoing basis as the business grows.

2 Break-even charts are useful when examining 'what-if' situations, e.g. determining profitability at any given level of output other than the planned level, or when examining the effects of changes in revenues and costs.

3 Break-even charts are useful when comparing production strategies and considering the effect the choice of strategy would have on the break-even point, margin of safety, profitability, etc., e.g. comparing a labour-intensive operation with low fixed costs to a machine intensive operation with high fixed costs.

4 Break-even charts are easy and simple to follow and understand, offering a pictorial or graphical representation which would be particularly welcomed by persons from a non-financial background.

5 The visual impact of a break-even chart can be very useful for illustrative purposes and can often say more than a numerical/financial approach. This would not only be welcomed by persons from a non-financial background, but also by management perhaps as part of a report.

6 Break-even charts offer a clear and concise view of the position of a business, particularly where a simple overview is all that is necessary.

7 Finally, break-even charts are actually easy to construct.

Self assessment questions

1. Which of the following correctly calculates contribution?
   a Sales – fixed costs
   b Fixed costs – variable costs
   c Sales – variable costs
   d Profit + variable costs

2. Which one of the following formulae would calculate the break-even point?
   a Sales revenue/contribution per unit
   b Variable costs/contribution per unit
   c Fixed costs/contribution per unit
   d Profit/contribution per unit

3–5 Consider the following information relating to product X:

   Selling price £12.50
   Direct labour £4.25
   Direct materials £5.00
   Direct expenses £1
   Fixed costs £450 000
   Number of units produced and sold 250 000

3. What is the contribution per unit?
   a £22.50
   b £3.25
   c £8.25
   d £2.25

4. What is the break-even point?
   a 2000 units
   b 200 000 units
   c 20 000 units
   d 200 units

5. What profit is achieved?
   a £11 250
   b £1250
   c Nil
   d £112 500

6. On a break-even chart, which two lines should intersect so that a break-even point can be identified?
   a Sales and fixed cost lines
   b Fixed cost and variable cost lines
   c Sales and variable cost lines
   d Sales and total cost lines

Element 6.4 Explain basic pricing decisions and break-even

7 What is the margin of safety?
   a The point where neither a profit nor a loss is made
   b The profit margin
   c The excess of the planned level of output over the break-even point
   d The break-even point

8 Which of the following correctly describes the horizontal (x) and vertical (y) axis of a break-even chart?
   a Sales revenue and total costs
   b Sales revenue and number of units produced
   c Total costs and number of units produced
   d The number of units produced and the sales revenue

9–10 Questions 9 and 10 relate to the break-even chart shown below:

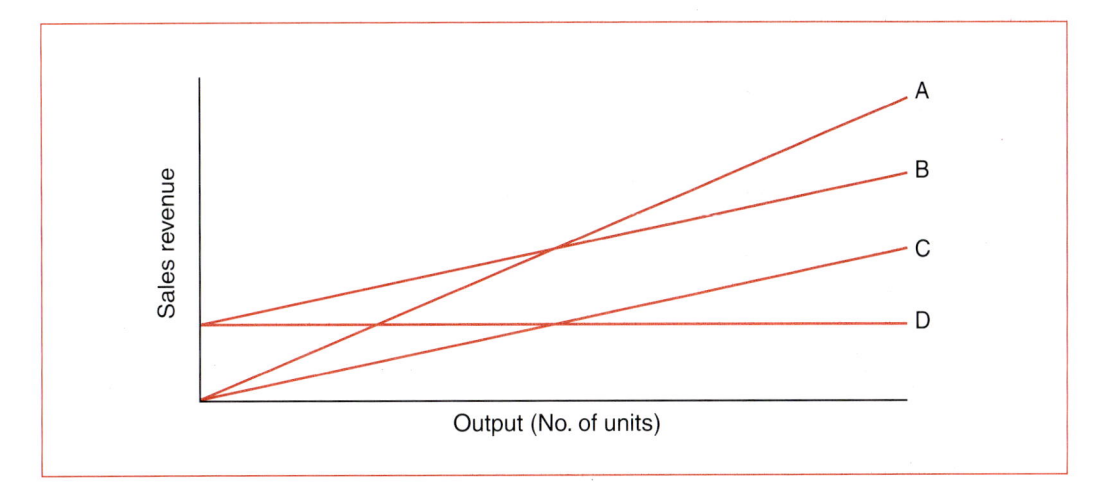

Fig 6.30 Break-even chart

9 Which of the four lines are (i) fixed costs and (ii) total costs?
   a A and D
   b B and A
   c C and D
   d D and B

10 Which of the four lines are (i) sales revenue and (ii) total costs?
   a A and C
   b A and B
   c A and D
   d B and C

Unit 6   Financial transactions, costing and pricing

Additional activities

Due to the practical nature of this element, some additional activities have been included at this point to give students more practice in the skills involved.

ACTIVITY 6.4.2

Both the Accountant and Sales Manager are rather concerned at Nicholas James & Co. at the £100 000 fixed costs: £50 000 is for rent and £25 000 is for rates. Both these figures have been based on the previous year.

> The Accountant asks, 'What if our landlords want to renegotiate the terms of the contract and increase the rent for the coming year by 20 per cent in line with our experience at our other factory?'
>
> She continues, 'What if the local council increases the business rates by as much as 24 per cent, a figure which was reported in the local press recently?'
>
> The Sales Manager states, 'The £16 selling price for product X was very difficult to achieve last year. Market research indicates, that if we reduce our selling price to £15, we should increase our sales by 20 per cent!'

Task 1. Redraw the break-even chart for Nicholas James & Co., taking into consideration the points discussed in the above conversation between the Accountant and the Sales Manager, clearly identifying the break-even point and the margin of safety. Compare the break-even point, margin of safety and profitability with the original break-even chart (Fig. 6.29). How does it compare?

Task 2. The original break-even chart in Fig. 6.29 was analysed using eight questions. Answer these questions again, basing your answers this time on your new redrawn break-even chart.

Task 3. Use the break-even chart to determine the anticipated profits at the new level of production.

ACTIVITY 6.4.3

Examine the break-even chart in Fig. 6.31 and identify the following:

1 the break-even point (in both units and sales value);

2 assuming a planned production of 124 000 units, the margin of safety (in both units and sales value);

3 the sales revenue, variable cost, fixed costs and total cost lines;

4 the area where profit would be achieved;

5 the area where a loss would be achieved;

6 the axes.

'000s (y-axis)

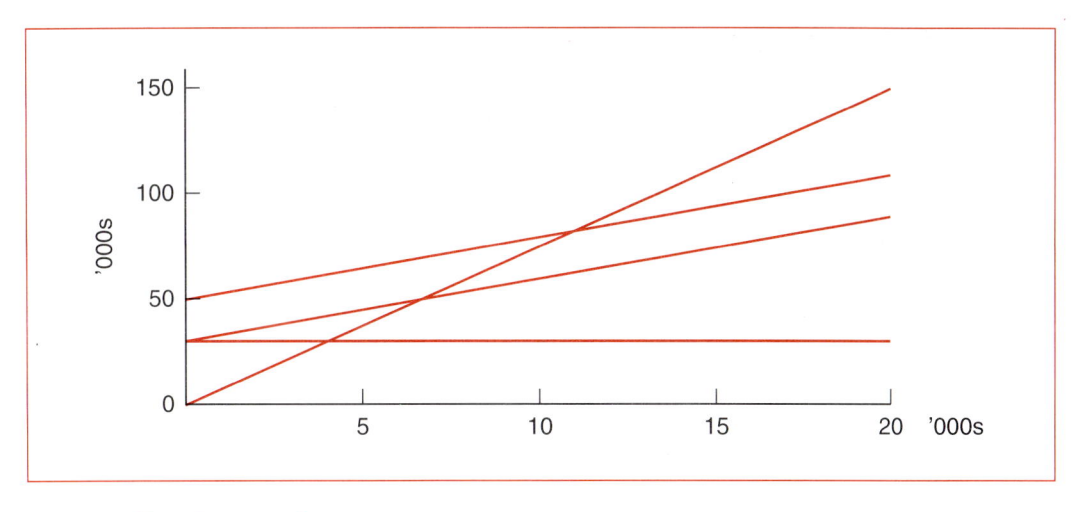

'000s (x-axis)

Fig 6.31 Break-even chart

ACTIVITY 6.4.4

A business manufactures a single product – the 'blob' – and has a total capacity to make 30 000 blobs per annum. The business expects to make 25 000 blobs in the coming year and the fixed costs are anticipated to be around £150 000. You are provided with the following additional information:

	£ per blob
Selling price	16.50
Direct labour	4.50
Direct material	3.00
Direct expenses	1.50

Task 1. Draw a break-even chart showing the likely profit at the planned level of production.

Task 2. Use the break-even chart to find:

a the break-even point in number of blobs;

b the break-even point in sales value;

c the margin of safety in number of blobs;

d the margin of safety in sales value;

e the amount of profit made at the expected level of output;

f the amount of profit made assuming the business works at full capacity.

Task 3. Redraw the break-even chart assuming that the fixed costs increased to £200 000, the selling price increased to £18 and the direct labour reduced by £1.

Task 4. Use your break-even chart in Task 3 to answer Task 2 (a) to (f) again.

ACTIVITY 6.4.5

Hainsworth & Co. presently employs 10 people, all of which are directly involved in the manufacture of a single product called the 'blib'. The total wages bill for the above 10 people averages £1500 per week and in addition the firm usually spends an average of £10 000 per month on direct material with the exception of December which usually averages at £12 000. The firm expects to produce and sell 40 000 blibs this year for £12 each and incur £140 000 of fixed costs.

The management is presently considering investing £100 000 of new machinery which would reduce the direct labour bill to £18 000 for the year but increase the fixed costs to £70 000. The direct material cost would probably remain the same but £20 000 would be incurred for direct expenses. The purchase of the new machines would increase the firm's capacity to produce blibs by at least 25 per cent but the management does not expect production and sales to exceed 40 000 blibs this year. As a result of the probable savings made by the introduction of the new machines, the selling price could probably be reduced to £11.

Task 1. Write a report to the board of management advising them as to whether or not Hainsworth & Co. should invest in the new machinery.

Task 2. Would your answer have been any different if the selling price remained at £12 after the purchase of the new machinery?

Your report should include break-even charts to help illustrate your answers and it should take into consideration anticipated profits, effect on profits, break-even points, margins of safety, cash flows, future plans, capital outlay, etc.

Assignment

Nevin & Wine Ltd produced 20 000 lawn-mowers last year and the following costs were incurred:

	£	
Direct materials	350 000	
Direct labour	290 000	
Indirect expenses	110 000	(of which £50 000 were fixed)
	750 000	
Selling and distribution expenses	190 000	
Administrative expenses	80 000	
Total cost	1 020 000	

All the lawn-mowers produced were sold for £75 each and the selling and distribution expenses and administrative expenses were all considered fixed costs.

Scenario 1
The Sales Manager at the company expects to produce and sell 25 000 lawn-mowers this coming year. The Accountant, on the other hand, thinks that there will be an overall increase of 5 per cent on all variable costs.

Element 6.4 Explain basic pricing decisions and break-even

Task 1. Prepare a break-even chart for Scenario 1 clearly identifying each line that you have plotted and the break-even point and the margin of safety. Use the chart to determine the following:

a the break-even point (in both units and sales value);
b the margin of safety (in both units and sales value);
c the profit, if the company achieves its planned level of output.

Task 2. Indicate the area on your chart where a profit and a loss might be achieved.

Scenario 2
The Sales Manager is considering running an advertising campaign costing £50 000, which he anticipates will increase the number of lawn-mowers sold by 2500. If the company wishes to maintain the anticipated profits in Scenario 1, what should the new selling price be for each lawn-mower?

Scenario 3
Part way through the year, Nevin & Wine Ltd are offered a contract to supply 1000 lawn-mowers to a new customer who is willing to pay only £40 for each lawn-mower. Should the above contract be accepted?

(Assume you are in Scenario 1, i.e. the advertising campaign was *not* initiated.)

Answers to self assessment questions

Element 6.1	Element 6.2	Element 6.3	Element 6.4
1. a	1. b	1. a	1. c
2. b	2. d	2. c	2. c
3. b	3. c	3. d	3. d
4. d	4. b	4. b	4. b
5. d	5. b	5. b	5. d
6. a	6. c	6. a	6. d
7. d	7. d	7. c	7. c
8. a	8. c	8. d	8. b
9. c	9. d		9. d
10. b	10. b		10. b

UNIT 7

FINANCIAL FORECASTING AND MONITORING

This unit introduces the standard formats used for financial information in business and the finance needed to set up and run a business. Sources of finance, the use of cash flow forecasts, business plans and budgeting are all discussed. The importance of ratios as a tool for the analysis of financial information is also covered.

Element 7.1
EXPLAIN SOURCES OF FINANCE AND FINANCIAL REQUIREMENTS OF BUSINESS ORGANISATIONS

Performance Criteria

1. **Explain the financing requirements of a business.**
2. **Explain assets and working capital.**
3. **Explain common methods of finance appropriate to the financing requirements.**
4. **Explain usual sources of finance appropriate for different methods of finance.**
5. **Explain characteristics of common methods of finance.**
6. **Explain usual sources of finance for different types of business organisations.**

Introduction

There are two sides to any business: the first is represented by the assets and working capital of the business and the second is represented by the sources of finance that enable the business to acquire them. In this element we discuss these two sides of the business and introduce the balance sheet which brings these two sides together.

ASSET TYPES

Assets are things that a person or an organisation owns. In a business these are used to help to produce products or services. In accounting and finance we split assets into two distinct types: fixed and current.

- *Fixed assets* are held in the business for use rather than resale and cover such items as land, buildings, production machinery, office machines, vehicles, furniture and fittings.

Fig 7.1 The fixed assets of Manville Ltd include their vehicles

- *Current assets* which are those assets that are constantly changing on a daily basis such as stock, debtors, prepayments, cash at the bank and cash in hand.

Each of these types of assets is now explained in greater detail.

Fixed assets

Fixed assets can be said to cost a lot of money and last a long time. Most fixed assets are described as *tangible assets*, that is, they can be seen and they physically exist. There are other fixed assets, however, which are described as *intangible assets*, for example, goodwill, copyrights, patents and trademarks. Although intangible assets exist as concepts, they do not physically exist and cannot therefore be seen.

- *Goodwill* is the difference between the value of the tangible assets of a business and the value that someone will pay to purchase them. This usually represents the value of the existing customer base of the business.
- *Copyrights* grant the owner legal protection against their work being copied, e.g. books, records, videos and computer software. Copyrights can be sold and can have considerable value.

Element 7.1 Explain sources of finance and financial requirements of business organisations

- *Patents* stop the copying of products or ideas or manufacturing processes. An example is the Pilkington Glass manufacturing process for making float glass which gives Pilkington's a considerable income from licensing the process to other firms.
- *Trademarks* are brand names that cannot be copied by others. These intangible assets can often have great value and many take-over battles have been fought to acquire them.

Fig 7.2 The Cadburys logo is an intangible asset which adds enormous value to a product

The most common types of tangible fixed assets that you will need to know about are included in the following list.

- *Land.* Land is of course the most fixed asset of all. All businesses need to be located somewhere. The land that they occupy can either be owned outright and is therefore an asset of the business or it can be rented or leased from another person or business. Clearly a business that rents an asset from another cannot claim ownership of that asset.
- *Buildings.* When a business owns its own premises or buildings they will usually be one of its more costly fixed assets. Many businesses value their land and buildings together. It is possible, however, to purchase buildings that have been erected on leased land.
- *Production machinery.* Production machinery is often called plant and machinery and refers to the cost of acquiring all of the machines, robots and systems necessary to make the products of the business. This also includes the installation costs of setting up the production processes.
- *Office machinery.* If you work in a large office you will be familiar with these assets. They include such items as computers, printers, typewriters, postal franking machines and any other type of equipment.
- *Vehicles.* Under this heading we can include such assets as lorries, cars and vans. Quite often we need another category for items of plant such as tractors, excavators, compressors, cranes, concrete mixers, etc.
- *Furniture and fittings.* These items are usually obvious to us all. Some business fittings can be very costly, however. If you consider the cost of fitting out a large shop, you will appreciate the problem. Similarly, modern offices require modular furniture, air conditioning and ducting for computer networks.

Provisions for the depreciation of fixed assets

A definition of a provision is the setting aside of profits to meet a known future liability, and in this case the future liability is the fall in value of a fixed asset. With the exception of land values, all fixed assets tend to fall in value over a period of time, usually for one of the following reasons:

- *Wear and tear*. This is where the asset is gradually worn out by its everyday use.
- *Passage of time*. This is where the asset deteriorates, the older it gets (perhaps due to rust or oxidisation). Leasehold property runs out of value as the period of lease expires.
- *Obsolescence*. This is where the asset falls in value due to the introduction of new technology or a change in fashion or model.

Making a provision for depreciation in the accounts of a business involves making the following entries in the ledgers:

1 Debit profit and loss account (creating an expense).

2 Credit the provision for depreciation account.

The latter account is deducted from the fixed asset account in the balance sheet so that a more realistic current value of the asset is shown. This is usually known as the *book value*.

One of the problems with depreciation is that, until the asset is sold at the end of its useful life, the accountant cannot know accurately how much depreciation to charge. It is necessary to estimate the amount and use such an estimate in the accounts for the year's expense. Although many systems exist to estimate the annual charge for depreciation, in an attempt to standarise such estimates, three systems have evolved.

1 Revaluation

Each year the fixed asset is valued by an expert and the fall in the asset's value from one year to the next is the amount of depreciation for that financial year. This is the most accurate method of estimating depreciation but it can be expensive if the firm has to pay for the annual valuation.

2 Straight-line method

The number of years that the asset will last and its probable resale (or scrap) value at the end of that period are estimated. The resale value is deducted from the original cost of the asset and the answer is divided by the estimated number of years. For example:

Cost	£10 000
Scrap value	£256
Loss of value through depreciation	£9 744
Life	4 years
Depreciation per year	£9744 ÷ 4 = £2436

As it is easy to calculate, this method is used most widely by business managers. This method produces the same charge for depreciation each year and as a result it is not considered a very accurate reflection of the fall in the real value of the asset.

3 Reducing-balance method

Using a formula that goes beyond the needs of this course, a percentage figure is calculated. This figure is applied to the *book value* of the asset in calculating the annual charge for depreciation. For example:

Percentage Depreciation Charge	60%
Cost	£10 000

	£
Depreciation Year 1 (60% x 10 000)	6 000
Net book value – Year 1	4 000
Depreciation Year 2 (60% x 4 000)	2 400
Net book value – Year 2	1 600
Depreciation Year 3 (60% x 1 600)	960
Net book value Year 3	640
Depreciation Year 3 (60% x 1 600)	384
Net book value – Year 4	256

This method is considered to be more realistic than the straight-line method, as the fall in the book value of the asset corresponds more closely to the values that result from the revaluation method.

ACTIVITY 7.1.1

Your firm is about to purchase a new car for the Production Director that costs £26 000. The car will be kept at the firm for the next three years and is estimated to be worth about £8000 at the end of that time. Write a short report to the Production Director explaining how the car's depreciation can be dealt with in the accounts and compare these costs to the cost of heating and hire purchse.

Note: The best way to find out about the cost of leasing and hire purchase is to ask a Sales Assistant at your local car salesroom.

PC
7.1.1
7.1.2

Current assets

As mentioned earlier, current assets include such items as stock, debtors, prepayments and cash at the bank and cash in hand. These assets constantly change as the affairs of the business are conducted.

Stock

We sell stock usually on credit to other businesses or to consumers. In doing this we create *debtors*, that is, people or organisations that owe our business money for the goods that they purchased. When we collect the money from our debtors we can either keep it as *cash in hand* or pay it into the *bank*. All of these assets are clearly of worth in that they either represent cash or can be converted into cash in the short term. These assets represent the bulk of our *working capital*.

Prepayments

These are another common current asset and represent the business expenses that have been paid in advance. The most common types of expense that have to be paid in advance are insurances and most payments for rental agreements. Obviously, if a business does not pay its insurance bills in advance, it is not insured. Such prepaid expenses have value. Had these not been paid, the bank balance would have been bigger. Prepayments are adjustments to the end-of-year expense account totals that reduce the expense to represent that value that has been incurred during the year rather than the amount that was actually paid during the year. This value is transferred to next year's expense account. In carrying out this adjustment, we create a prepayment.

CURRENT LIABILITIES

Current liabilities represent the amount of money that a business owes to other businesses. The amount owed must be paid to them within the next twelve months. Clearly, if these sums had already been paid, they would not be owed. Because they have not been paid, the bank balance of the business is bigger. Current liabilities include such amounts owing as creditors, accruals, interest and dividends due for payment, business taxation due for payment, bank overdrafts and other short-term loans.

- *Creditors* are amounts due to businesses resulting from our purchase of stock for resale.
- *Accruals* are in fact the opposite of prepayments, in that they are expenses that have not been paid during the year and are still owing. The year-end adjustment for them is to increase the expense account for their value and to transfer the debt from one financial year to the next. In doing this we create an account for the accrued expense.

PC 7.1.2

ACTIVITY 7.1.2

Define the current assets and liabilities of a typical small business.

WORKING CAPITAL

When we deduct the total current assets from total current liabilities, we arrive at the value of working capital. In all organisations this figure is probably the most important figure in the financial management of the business. Put simply, it represents the amount of money that can be readily made available to the business for the payment of its future bills. If this value is insufficient to pay all of the future expenditures of the business it must find sufficient money from others, usually by borrowing.

Element 7.1 Explain sources of finance and financial requirements of business organisations

If the business cannot find such money, its creditors and/or its bank will start court proceedings to have the business wound up and its assets sold off to raise funds to pay its debts. This process is called *insolvency*. It is also known as bankruptcy, although only individuals can be made bankrupt and this term should not be used in connection with insolvent companies.

A business will not become insolvent immediately, when it starts making losses. So long as the business can continue to pay its debts, it will remain in existence. Indeed, some firms have remained in business for many years while making losses. It is only when the firm's creditors think that they may not get paid that they will initially stop all further credit sales to the business and eventually take court proceedings to obtain monies due. As most business is conducted on credit, a withdrawal of credit facilities to a business usually has dire consequences.

Businesses must, therefore, not only have sufficient money to purchase fixed assets, but, more importantly, they must have sufficient money tied up in working capital in order to pay their way. Many profitable businesses have gone out of existence because they tried to grow too fast, spent too much money on fixed assets and ran out of money to pay their creditors.

Element 7.2 of this unit will show you how to project the cash flow requirements of a business into the future so that it can control its income and expenditure in order to allow it to continue in business and make the best use of its cash resources.

ACTIVITY 7.1.3

PC 7.1.1

Write a short report explaining how an apparently profitable firm can be put into receivership. Use the following extract from such a company's balance sheet.

	£	£
Fixed assets		100 000
Current assets	30 000	
Less Current liabilities	29 000	
Working capital		1 000
Net assets	101 000	101 000
Less Long-term loans	40 000	40 000
	61 000	61 000
Financed by:		£
Share capital		30 000
Profit and loss account balance		31 000
		61 000

SOURCES OF BUSINESS FINANCE

Now that we know the nature of business assets and the importance of working capital we can relate them to a given business plan.

It is necessary to know more than just the type of fixed assets that a business will need; there are other considerations to take into account. The most important of these is, whether or not the business has sufficient finance to fund its operations.

If we were to set up in business as a building company we would need certain fixed assets, such as a small van, plant such as a concrete mixer. In addition to these fixed assets we will also require working capital in the form of stocks of bricks, cement and the like, plus sufficient cash to pay for expenses like advertising, petrol for the van, plus all of the additional costs of insurance, road tax, printing and stationery, telephone and postage. We will also need to locate our business somewhere. This may be in the garage or spare room at home at very little cost to the business. With luck, the business will grow sufficiently well for it to justify its own premises in the near future.

At this stage it would be necessary to work out how sufficient money to finance these activities could be raised. We could use our own money – *Capital*. We could borrow from our friends – *long- and short-term loans* – or we could ask the bank for help in the form of *bank overdrafts* or *mortgage loans* based upon the value of our other assets, usually our property. If we enquired through government agencies or the banks we might be eligible for some form of *grant* towards our venture, particularly if our firm is located in a government-sponsored *development area*, or a local authority *assisted area*. If we have been unemployed for a number of years, we may be eligible for assistance from the *Department of Employment*. We could acquire our van and our equipment through *hire purchase* or *leasing agreements*. All of these are examples of sources of business finance.

Fig 7.3 A form of transport can sometimes be a fixed asset of primary importance

Element 7.1 Explain sources of finance and financial requirements of business organisations

THE BALANCE SHEET

As mentioned in the introduction to this element, there are two sides to any business: the assets and working capital on the one hand and the sources of finance on the other. In business accounting we always record two sides to any transaction.

If we start business with £1000 in a business bank account, we would record not only the money in the bank – our business asset – but also the source of the money which in this case is our own capital investment. We could at this stage produce a balance sheet which would show £1000 on each side as follows:

Capital	£1000	Cash at bank	£1000

If we were to borrow a further £500 from the bank, our balance sheet would look like this:

Capital	£1000	Cash at bank	£1500
Loan	£500		
	£1500		£1500

If we purchased an old van for £800 and a carpet cleaning machine for £200, our balance sheet would look as follows:

Capital	£1000	Fixed assets (Van and machine)	£1000
Loan	£500	Cash at bank	£500
	£1500		£1500

Fig 7.4 Balance sheet

In the above balance sheets you should have noticed that the left-hand list of balances shows where the money came from that financed the assets listed on the right-hand list. In a modern balance sheet we list the assets and working capital first and then show where the money came from in the last part of the statement which is called the *financed* by section.

As you have learned in Unit 6, business is more complex than the above example and many transactions have to be recorded in many different types of account. Annual statements of profit and loss are required and all asset and liability balances are listed in a balance sheet that shows all of the sources of finance used by the business.

A typical balance sheet is shown on page 546 for G. Wood's business.

SOURCES OF ASSET FINANCE

Capital

Sole traders and partnerships are the more usual form of small firm. When a business expands, there is usually an increased requirement for capital to finance the increase in the demand for fixed assets and working capital. The ability to raise this amount of additional cash is often beyond the resources of the owners of the business, and banks and other institutional lenders seldom lend more than an amount that is equivalent to the value of the owners' capital. The most common way to increase the capital invested in a business is to form either a partnership with others, or a limited company which will increase the number of owners. These are, of course, the company's shareholders.

Share issues

When companies are formed, they must state in their memorandum and articles of association how many shares of each type and value that they wish to issue. There are in fact many different types of share and a company can choose any value that it wants. There is no need for the company to issue all of its shares at the same time, quite often a proportion of the company's shares remain unissued. This is why companies have to state in their balance sheets how many shares have been authorised and how many have been issued. The most common types of company share are listed below.

Ordinary shares (or equity)

An ordinary share gives its holder the right to a share of the profit or loss and the return of capital in the event of the winding up of the business. When a business ceases trading, the assets of the business are sold off and the moneys raised are then used to repay the liabilities of the business. The remaining cash (if any) is then paid out to the shareholders.

The term 'equity shares' means ordinary shares. Most ordinary shares carry the right to attend and vote at all meetings of the company. The shareholders elect the board of directors and the company's auditors. They also have the right to vote to accept or reject a take-over offer made by another company.

Anyone who possesses over 50 per cent of the voting shares is said to have a *controlling* interest in a company, while the other shareholders are known as the *minority interest*. In a public limited company (PLC) the ordinary shareholder has a right to sell his or her shares on the market and the company has a duty to record this transfer in its share register and issue the appropriate share certificate.

Element 7.1 Explain sources of finance and financial requirements of business organisations

Advantages and disadvantages of ordinary shares

Advantages	Disadvantages
■ The ordinary shareholder possesses the right to all profits remaining after preference share dividends have been paid. ■ The shareholder has the right to the potential capital growth from profits retained in the business.	■ The shareholders could lose their investment should the firm fail. ■ The firm has no obligation to pay any dividend at all. ■ If profits are poor then either no dividend will be paid or the rate of the dividend payable will be low and the value of the shares will fall.

The main disadvantage to a company of issuing more ordinary shares is that the creation of extra votes may change control in a company. It may also give more investors the chance to join in the distribution of the same amount of profit and therefore each shareholder would get less dividend.

When an issue of ordinary shares is floated on the market it is first advertised in what is called a *prospectus*. The investor will apply for shares which are to be issued, sending in his or her application money at the same time. The terms of issue of a £1 share may be 25p on application and 25p on allotment, with two calls thereafter. This means that when a potential shareholder applies for shares in the issue he or she must send application money of 25p per share for all the shares required. The board of the company will review the applications for their issue and, if it is oversubscribed (i.e. number of applications for the shares exceeds number of shares available) they will scale down applications by lottery or selection, selecting only those potential shareholders whom they wish to be members of the company.

If a share issue is likely to be popular with the investing public, it is possible to issue it at a premium (e.g. a £1 share can be issued for £1.50). If 10 000 such shares are issued, the ordinary share capital of the company is increased by £10 000 and a share premium of £5000 is also created. This is a capital reserve and is credited to an account called the share premium account.

Preference shares

Preference shares are so called because holders of preference shares have a preferential right both to receive their dividend (if profits exist) before the ordinary shareholders and to repayment of capital before ordinary shareholders. The exact rights of preference shareholders will be found in the articles of association of the company. The dividend on such shares is limited, however, to a fixed percentage of the *face value* (*nominal* or *par* value) which is stated on the share certificate. We can speak, therefore, of 8% preference shares, that is shares whose owner has a right to a dividend of 8 per cent each year, but no more.

If a company has issued 10 000 8% £1 preference shares and has made a profit of only £800 then the preference shareholders will have a right to receive their dividend before any payment is made to the ordinary shareholders, who in this case will receive nothing. The same rule applies in the event of a winding up: the preference shareholders are repaid the face value of their shares before any money is paid to ordinary shareholders. The ordinary shareholders have a right, however, to divide equally among themselves the entire value of the business on a winding up after the preference shareholders have received the face value of their shares. The ordinary shareholders take the greater risk, therefore, since they are the last group to receive their share or profit or their money back on a winding up. They do have a right to all the surplus that is earned, however. This is why ordinary shares are often referred to as *risk capital*.

Preference shareholders also suffer due to restriction of their voting rights. Normally they carry no right to vote at a general meeting of the company but if an extraordinary meeting is called to discuss matters which prejudice their preferential rights (e.g. a capital reorganisation scheme), then preference shareholders are usually allowed to vote.

Cumulative preference shares

Some companies will issue cumulative preference shares to avoid the difficulty which occurs in a year when profits are too small to pay either the preference or ordinary share dividends. In this case a normal preference shareholder will receive nothing and will have to wait until the following year for his or her normal fixed percentage dividend. The holder of a cumulative preference share will receive, in a subsequent year, his or her arrears of dividend which have accumulated in the past, before any dividend is paid on the ordinary shares. The preference shareholders are, therefore, in a safer position than the ordinary shareholders because they take less risk.

ACTIVITY 7.1.4

Go to any large high street bank and ask the receptionist or counter clerk for information on how a member of the public can purchase shares in a PLC, such as ICI. Use the financial pages of a national newspaper to find the current market price of an ordinary share and make notes so that you can give a short presentation to your group at school or college on how to invest on the stock exchange and how much it will cost you to purchase 1000 ordinary shares in a company such as ICI.

Retained profits

For most businesses there is the need to keep back some of the profits earned in each year in order to help finance future growth and expansion. Indeed, if a business did not do so, the capital held in the business would actually reduce in real terms in times of inflation, as the value of the working capital of the business declines. If a company were to issue as dividend all of its annual profit, its dividends would obviously be higher and at first glance you may think that the shareholders would be pleased. If it did this on a regular

Element 7.1 Explain sources of finance and financial requirements of business organisations

Fig 7.5 'Falling share prices'

basis, its share price would fall as the market would consider that the future earning potential of the company would be reduced. Companies are expected to keep a proportion of their profits in the firm in order to finance future growth and to pay large dividends with the firm's cash would lead to cash flow problems. More important than the amount of dividend to most shareholders is the market value of their shares.

Loans

A loan is a sum of money borrowed by a borrower. This is called the *principal* part of the loan. There is almost always a charge made for borrowing money and this is called *interest*. The rate of interest charged on a loan depends on many factors, the most important of which are the influence of government policy on the bank rate, the state of the market in which the company operates and the creditworthiness of the company itself.

When companies are expanding, they should borrow to invest in more fixed assets and working capital. When times are bad and the companies' markets are contracting the smaller the amount of debt held the better as interest still has to be paid even if profits and cash flow are poor. It is the art of management to try to achieve these conflicting goals and stay in business. A company's managers need only get this balance wrong once, however, and the company can be put into receivership, or it can be taken over by another company. Either way, the managers are likely to lose their jobs and the shareholders may lose a lot of money.

Debentures

These are in fact loans that a company can issue in small denominations, often of £1000 each. They are bought and sold on the stock market like shares but they do not have any rights at shareholders' meetings nor are they eligible for dividends. Like any other type of loan they receive interest at half-yearly intervals. The rate of interest payable on debentures is fixed at the time of their issue and must be paid by the company whether the company makes a profit or loss. Most debentures have a guaranteed repayment date. Debentures are long-term loans.

Long-term loans

Companies can borrow money from other sources than debenture holders. Such loans can come from banks, building societies, finance companies, insurance companies and indeed any other organisation that is willing to lend money for the required length of time at an acceptable rate of interest. Like debentures, loan interest must also be paid whether the company makes a profit or a loss. Long-term loans are loans that are repayable in more than one year.

Short-term loans

These are loans that are repayable in less than one year, and include bank overdrafts. Although short-term loans can be required to be repaid with just a few days' or weeks' notice, many of them can exist for a considerable length of time, sometimes for a number of years. The point to remember is that the lending organisation if it wishes, can require repayment within the time of the notice stated on the loan agreement. The best example of this type of loan is a *bank overdraft*. These are usually stated to be at one month's notice, but many firms treat them as long-term finance because the bank will only request repayment if it thinks the company is likely to fail. Obviously, in these circumstances, the withdrawal of overdraft facilities by the bank will put most companies into receivership. Bank overdrafts are the most favoured form of borrowing. The reason for this is the interest on the loan is only charged when the bank account is overdrawn, and it is charged on the actual overdrawn balance each day. Businesses are seldom overdrawn up to their limit for long periods of time, so although the rate of interest charged may be slightly higher than other short-term loans, the actual amount charged is less. The effect of unpresented cheques on your current account and the fluctuations in the firm's receipts and payments will usually keep the actual overdraft at a lower level than your estimate.

Other sources of finance

Renting, leasing and hire purchase

If an organisation wants to acquire the use of a fixed asset, it does not need to purchase it. It can rent the asset, lease it or it can acquire its use by hire purchase.

Rental agreements and *leasing agreements* are very similar in that the asset can be used at the cost of paying rent. Rental agreements are usually taken out with the firm that supplies the asset. With leasing agreements, it is often a finance company that provides the money to purchase the asset and the organisation using the asset pays rent to the leasing company. The asset cannot become the property of the organisation using it. It is usually sold off to a third party at the end of the lease period.

Hire purchase on the other hand is a deferred method of purchase in that at the end of the repayment period the asset becomes the property of the organisation using it.

Trade credit

Most organisations purchase their goods and services on credit. Clearly, if they pay their debts early, it will please their suppliers but it will also reduce the organisation's bank balance. By paying late, the organisation will be able to use this money to finance other

Element 7.1 Explain sources of finance and financial requirements of business organisations

projects, or repay other debts. Late payment of debts cannot be taken too far, however, as the creditors may refuse future credit and this would lead to severe cash flow problems and production difficulties. It would be self-defeating. This source of finance, if used wisely, will not cost anything at all. There is no interest to pay on outstanding creditor accounts, only a loss of reputation within the business community. If your business sells its goods or services to others on credit, it is in your interest to collect your debts as soon as possible.

ACTIVITY 7.1.5

Comment on the implications of the following statement:

Our company is undercapitalised; we need more long-term finance to underpin our future expansion.

PC
7.1.1
7.1.3
7.1.5

ACTIVITY 7.1.6

Compare the sources of finance that are available to organisations in the voluntary sector with those available to a small business.

PC
7.1.6

Self assessment questions

1 Which is a fixed asset?
   a Stock of goods for resale
   b Cash at bank
   c Advertising
   d Land and buildings

2 Which is a current asset?
   a Capital
   b Furniture and fittings
   c Stock of goods for resale
   d Motor vehicles

3 Which is a current liability?
   a Cash
   b Bank overdraft
   c Bank mortgage
   d Shop fixtures

The following data relates to Questions 4, 5 and 6 below.

A company has four methods of raising finance:
a grants
b mortgage
c leasing
d shareholders' funds.

Which is the most appropriate method for each of the following?

4 To purchase land and buildings

5 To raise money to purchase another company

6 To acquire new computer hardware

7 A company has obtained an overdraft facility from its bank.

Consider the following statements.
 (i) This is an inexpensive method of borrowing money.
 (ii) The company only borrows money when it needs it.

Which option best describes the two statements?
a (i) True   (ii) True
b (i) True   (ii) False
c (i) False   (ii) True
d (i) False   (ii) False

8 A company needs additional cash for a short period of time.

Consider the following statements.
 (i) It can make its debtors pay up faster.
 (ii) It can pay its creditors as soon as possible.

Which option best describes the two statements?
a (i) True   (ii) True
b (i) True   (ii) False
c (i) False   (ii) True
d (i) False   (ii) False

9 In order to expand a company needs more working capital.

Consider the following statements.
 (i) The company can buy more stock.
 (ii) The company can issue more shares.

Which option best describes the two statements?
a (i) True   (ii) True
b (i) True   (ii) False
c (i) False   (ii) True
d (i) False   (ii) False

Element 7.1 Explain sources of finance and financial requirements of business organisations

10 A company is thinking of opening a new warehouse in a development area of high unemployment.

Consider the following statements.
 (i) It can get a bank loan more easily.
(ii) It can get a government grant.

Which option best describes the two statements?
- **a** (i) True (ii) True
- **b** (i) True (ii) False
- **c** (i) False (ii) True
- **d** (i) False (ii) False

Assignment

PC
7.1.1
7.1.2
7.1.3
7.1.4
7.1.5

Prepare a financial plan for the start of a new business that buys and sells garden furniture. The business will need to rent premises, and purchase, lease or hire fixtures and fittings, a van and office equipment. Additionally, it will need sufficient working capital to finance its operations during the start up-period, including the purchase of stock. Your plan should indicate how the above assets are to be financed and where you are likely to obtain such finance.

In order to find out how much the fixed assets will cost you will have to undertake some research. Look in the local paper or an estate agent's window to find the cost of premises. Consult local dealers about the cost of purchasing, leasing or hiring the other fixed assets. Estimate the amount of money that you will need to finance the purchase of stock and the initial payment of expenses. You will need sufficient cash to pay your way until your customers start to pay you.

Element 7.2
PRODUCE AND EXPLAIN FORECASTS AND A CASH FLOW FOR A SMALL BUSINESS

Performance criteria

1. Explain the purposes and components of forecasts.
2. Produce a capital budget and trading forecast for a twelve-month period for a small business.
3. Explain capital budget headings and trading forecast headings.
4. Explain the purpose of a cash flow as a component of a forecast to a business seeking finance.
5. Explain the significance of timing in a cash flow forecast.
6. Explain cash in-flow and cash out-flow headings.
7. Collect data for each heading to support informed forecasts.
8. Produce feasible forecasts of cash in-flow and cash out-flow for one twelve-month period.
9. Produce monthly and cumulative net balances for a twelve-month period.
10. Explain the consequences of incorrect forecasting.

Introduction

In Element 7.1, you were introduced to the concept of planning. This element requires you to produce an acceptable cash budget – also known as a cash flow statement – which represents one of the most important activities in financial and business planning. Today these plans are usually produced using a computer spreadsheet system. It is important, therefore, to learn how to use these packages in constructing a series of cash budgets. First, however, it is necessary to understand the need for cash budgets in business and how they are produced manually.

There are many different types of computers now available for office or personal use. The computers referred to in this text are called *personal computers*, usually referred to as PCs. The systems that enable us to use them are called software systems that have been programmed to do different types of functions. These include word processing, databases, spreadsheets, graphics and accounting. Quite often the first four of these programmes are linked together into an integrated office suite, such as *Microsoft Office*.

WORKING CAPITAL

The importance of cash flow to a business has already been highlighted (in Unit 6 and Element 7.1). Cash flow is usually discussed under the general description of *liquidity*. A business needs sufficient cash to pay its debts and when it cannot do so, it will be wound up. It is not the lack of profits that will end a business but a lack of money to pay the creditors. Business is seldom so simple, however.

A business does not have to rely on its own cash to pay its debts; it can borrow money, or with the bank's permission it can become overdrawn and use the bank's money, for which it will of course have to pay interest and bank charges. Almost all firms exist on trade credit and pay for their goods and services at a later date. They are, therefore, using the late payment of debts as a source of funds. This reduces their need for cash to pay their debts. Similarly, with the exception of items sold in shops and cash-and-carry warehouses, most sales are made on credit. These periods of credit can be manipulated to a firm's advantage. Customers can be asked to pay early and the firm's bills can be paid late. This practice can, if taken to excess, result in the business losing some customers and in credit purchases being difficult to obtain due to a poor payment reputation with suppliers.

The working capital cycle

Goods are bought in advance and may have to be held in stock for a period of time prior to being sold on credit. This effect is known as the *working capital cycle* and firms need sufficient funds to be able to finance the next turn of the cycle and purchase more stock for resale (*see* Fig. 7.6).

Cash is also needed to pay for overheads and fixed assets. Many profitable firms have gone out of business due to their overinvestment in fixed assets for long-term growth and their inability to generate sufficient cash income in the short term in order to pay their immediate bills.

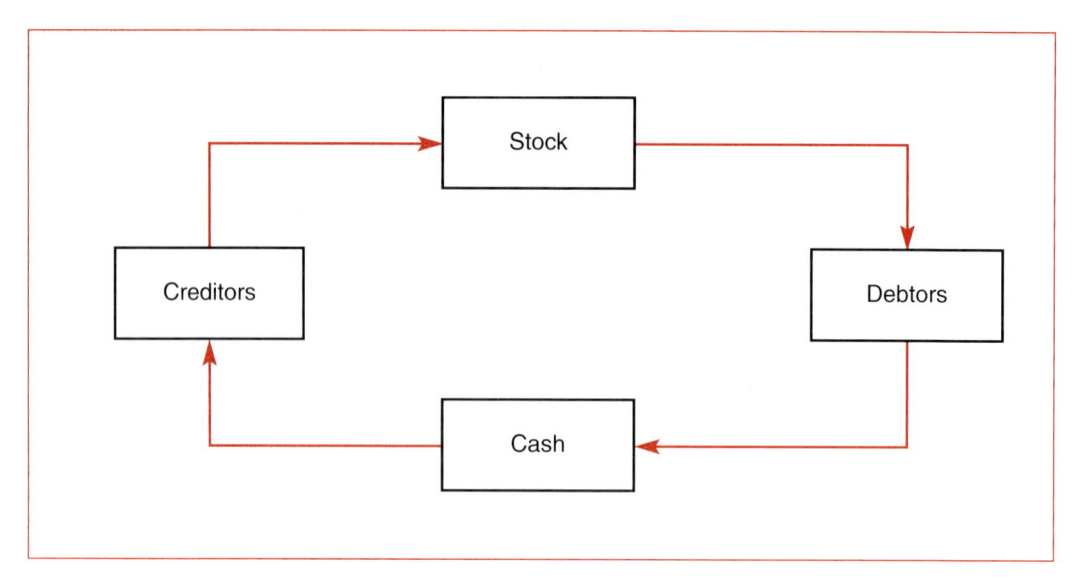

Fig 7.6 The Working Capital Cycle

CAPITAL BUDGETS

The largest amount of expenditure that a firm is likely to have involves the purchase of fixed assets. The main problem facing the firm is its ability to raise sufficient cash in its bank account in order to make these payments. There are various sources of finance open to most businesses (*see* Element 7.1) and the main purpose of a capital budget is to make sure that there is sufficient finance available from whatever source to support the payments required. Making the arrangements to obtain such finance can involve many weeks or months. Additionally, it can take a long time to negotiate the purchase of fixed assets, such as new plant and machinery and especially new premises. Budgets of these cash in-flows and cash out-flows need to be carefully drawn up in order to plan and control these events.

The headings used in a capital budget for a small firm usually relate to the type of asset being acquired and the nature and timing of the payments of cash and the receipt of funds into the bank account. The purchase of many large fixed assets involves stage payments to the firm contracted to do the work, be it the construction of a new item of machinery or a new building, or extension to an existing building. Quite often these payments are spread over one or more financial years for large projects. Clearly, firms need to have the money available to finance these payments, but it would be wasteful if they obtained this amount of money in advance of their need to pay it out, due to the loss of interest involved in having money lying about in a bank current account gaining little or no interest. The downfall of most new and expanding firms is their failure to plan the acquisition of expensive fixed assets and to obtain sufficient finance to fund them. The word used to describe this lack of capital is *undercapitalised*.

Element 7.2 Produce and explain forecasts and a cash flow for a small business

TRADING FORECASTS

In addition to the initial capital budget for fixed assets and the finance required to fund their purchase, any firm, and particularly any new firm, should try to estimate the financial effects of their likely trading activity over the next six- or twelve-month period. The format for these estimates or budgets should follow the format used for the firm's accounts so that during the year the firm's managers can monitor the firm's actual income and expenditure against the budget.

Contribution analysis

To calculate a trading budget using contribution analysis, the following format is used:

Formula	Example
Selling price per unit	£20
Less	
Variable cost per unit	£12
= Contribution per unit	£8
Multiplied by	
The estimated number of units sold	800
= Total contribution	£6400
Less	
Estimated total fixed costs	£4000
Estimated net profit	£2400

The above type of budgets can be calculated on a weekly, monthly or annual basis. What makes them most useful is the ease of recalculation should any of the figures have to be changed.

Try the following calculations.

a Alter the estimated number of sales to 1000.

b Alter the estimated number of sales to 600.

c Alter the variable cost per unit to £13 keeping the number sold at 800 and the selling price at £20.

d Alter the selling price to £22, keeping the variable cost per unit at £12 and the number sold at 800.

e Alter the total fixed cost to £4200, keeping the number sold and the selling price and variable cost per unit as in the example.

The net profit figures that you should have calculated are:

a £4000
b £800
c £1600
d £4000
e £2200

The drawback with this type of budget is that it is often quite difficult to split a firm's costs between fixed and variable costs. Remember, however, all budgets involve a great deal of estimation which can best be described as intelligent guesswork. By their nature they are not entirely accurate so do not spend too much time on what can be said to be spurious accuracy, i.e. a great deal of analysis that has no impact on the final solution.

Budgets should be accurate enough to give the firm's managers a good idea of the likely outcomes of their actions. All of the managers should agree with the assumptions that were built into the budget because they will be made responsible for attaining the levels of output stated in the budget, its income and its expenditure. If the actual results are different from the budget, the firm could be put into a difficult financial position. If the sales forecast, for instance, were to be unattainable, the firm's income would be down below expectation. The firm would also be overstocked as it would have purchased too many stock items, produced too many products and have an increased storage requirement. All of these conditions would mean that too much money was spent at a time when the firm's income from sales was lower than expected. The net result is a fall in working capital and possible insolvency.

All budgets should be used to check on the firm's actual activity levels throughout the financial year in order to make adjustments to the budgeted activity levels before things get too bad. This is called *budgetary control*. The budget should be altered to fit reality when the managers find that market conditions have changed from those that formed the basis of the budget forecasts.

CASH BUDGETS

In order to control the flow of cash, management must produce and keep up-to-date a system of cash budgets so that any shortage of cash can be spotted in advance and action can be taken to cover the deficit. Bank managers resent customers who overdraw without prior notice. The finance needed may well be long term and require additional capital such as a new issue of shares or debentures. Such issues need planning well in advance, and a cash budget will show how much will be needed and when it will be needed.

The following example shows how to construct a cash budget for a small manufacturing firm.

Cash budget for six months to end of July

	Feb £	Mar £	April £	May £	June £	July £
Receipts						
Cash sales	2 000	3 400	3 400	3 400	3 100	3 100
Debtors	13 000	14 000	17 000	16 000	16 000	16 000
1 Total receipts	15 000	17 400	20 400	19 400	19 100	19 100
Payments						
Wages	8 000	8 000	8 000	8 800	8 800	8 800
Creditors	2 000	2 100	2 200	2 200	2 200	2 200
Variable overheads	1 000	800	800	1 000	800	800
New equipment			14 000	6,000	10 000	
Loan interest		400			400	
Drawings	800	800	800	800	800	800
2 Total payments	11 800	12 100	25 800	18 800	23 000	12 600
3 **Receipts less payments**	3 200	5 300	(5 400)	600	(3 900)	6 500
4 **Bank balance** (£4 000 b/fwd)	7 200	12 500	7 100	7 700	3 800	10 300

All of the receipts are listed for each month and a total receipts row is produced (Row 1). These receipts do not differentiate between cash or bank as it is assumed that all cash takings will be banked within a few days at the most. Similarly the payments are listed for each month and a monthly total of payments out of the bank is produced (Row 2).

The next step is to produce Row 3 by deducting the total payments from the total receipts. This represents the change in the bank balance for each month. In February, therefore, the bank balance should increase by £3200 while in April it will decrease by £5400.

The final row (Row 4) represents the estimated bank balance at the end of each month. At the beginning of February the balance was £4000 and by the end of February it is estimated to be £7200 in hand (£4000 + £3200 = +£7200). In March the bank balance is estimated to increase by £5300 to +£12 500.

The main problem in constructing such an analysis is usually determining the month to which the receipts and payments relate. For example, if faced with a statement such as 'Debts are collected in the second month after the sale', it is tempting to say that January's sale will produce receipts in February because it is the second month, but if you think about it more closely, the receipts of January's sales will appear in March, i.e. two months after January.

The technique to adopt in producing cash budgets is to complete the figures a row at a time and only add them up when all of the figures have been entered. To construct the budget a column at a time (i.e. January, February, etc.) will take much longer.

Having constructed a cash budget we must now consider the implications of the figures contained in it. In the above example, the firm never became overdrawn at the bank (i.e. Row 4 is never a negative figure) and no action is needed, therefore, to arrange overdrafts or delay either payments or purchases, or raise new loans or capital.

To have money in the bank for long periods of time is very wasteful as the firm could repay any existing loans, spend it on expanding its existing business, or it could lend it to other organisations and gain interest. If the firm has sufficient surplus cash, it could use it to purchase other businesses and expand through take-overs and acquisitions.

The owner of the firm may of course take all surplus cash for his or her own personal use as either drawings or dividends. Should the firm's owner decide to expand the business then the cash could be used to increase the firm's trading activity or new fixed assets could be purchased to increase its efficiency.

To increase its trading activity, more cash could be spent on extra purchases of stock, additional marketing activities such as more advertising, more sales personnel, warehousing space and delivery costs and the firm would then need to finance more debtors due to its increase in credit sales.

The purchase of new fixed assets could well involve the expansion of production facilities through the purchase of new land and buildings and new plant and machinery. Cash could be spent on upgrading the firm's warehouse and storage areas or its delivery and distribution systems. New vehicles could be purchased. New sales showrooms could be bought or existing facilities could be refurbished. Office furniture and fittings could be upgraded and new computer equipment could be bought.

All of the above decisions stem from the knowledge gained from cash budgets. We live in changing times, however, and the assumptions made when producing a cash budget may change due either to changing economic circumstances or perhaps errors in the collection of data that went into the cash budget in the first place. A twelve-month cash budget is not done once a year; it should be redrafted at least once a month and more often in times of uncertainty and more often for large organisations where the volume of transactions is greater and the amounts involved are greater. One per cent of the turnover of Sainsbury's, for example, is a lot of money.

Cash budgets should be done on a rolling basis whereby when the first month is completed the budget is recalculated for a further twelve months. This does not mean that the first month is simply deleted and another is added on at the end. A complete review of the actual results should be made and these should be compared to the estimated activities in the initial cash budget. New forecasts should then be made for all activities that affect the flow of cash, and a new cash budget should be drawn up.

Element 7.2 Produce and explain forecasts and a cash flow for a small business

An example of typical cash budget calculation

Alf Hall is going to set up a new business on 1 January, supplying schools with imported gymnastic equipment. He estimates that his first six months in business will be as follows:

1. He will put £50 000 into a bank account for the firm on 1 January.

2. He will receive a loan of £60 000 on 6 January. This will be paid into the business bank account immediately. Interest is to be paid quarterly at 12 per cent per annum.

3. On 1 January, he will buy machinery (£4000), a motor vehicle (£15 200) and premises (£88 000) paying for them immediately out of the business bank account.

4. All purchases will be effected on credit. He will buy £4500 of goods on 1 January and he will pay for these in February. Other purchases will be for the rest of January (£3000) and February, March, April May and June will be £4000 each month. Other than the £4500 worth bought in January, all other purchases will be paid for two months after the goods were received.

5. Sales (all on credit) will be £4000 for January and £12 000 for each month after that. Debtors will pay for the goods in the third month after purchase.

6. He will purchase a new machine costing £2000 and pay for it in March.

7. Salaries will be £1000 per month and will be paid on the last day of each month starting in January.

8. General expenses will be £300 per month, payable in the same month following that in which they were incurred.

9. Insurance, covering the 12 months, will be paid for by cheque on 3 February, costing £640.

10. Rates will be as follows: for the three months to 31 March, £300 by cheque on 28 February; and £900 for the 12 months ended 31 March next year by cheque on 30 June.

11. He will make drawings of £650 per month by cheque.

Alf Hall has asked you to construct a cash budget for the six months to 30 June so that he can take this with him to see his bank manager.

In addition he wants you to tell him why the cash budget is so important, how often it should be done and what he should do if he thinks that he might exceed the overdraft limit that he is hoping to get from the bank.

The cash budget which was calculated for Alf Hall is shown on page 524.

The comments that should be made to Alf Hall on the above cash budget are:

1. Alf needs to know in advance the likely balance on his bank account at the end of each month if he pays his bills monthly, or at the end of each week if he pays them weekly.

2. Any budgeted overdraft has to be within the bank's agreed overdraft limits. If the budget shows that this limit will be exceeded he must do one or all of the following:

   - *Reduce his payments* for the month either by paying late or by not incurring the expenditure in the first place, i.e. the machine purchased in March.
   - *Increase his income* by selling more or by borrowing more money. Both of these activities will probably reduce his profits as he may have to cut prices and advertise more to increase his sales and any additional loans will increase his interest payments.

Cash budget for six months to 30 June

	Jan £	Feb £	Mar £	April £	May £	June £
Receipts						
Sales				4 000	12 000	12 000
Loan	60 000					
Total Receipts	60 000	–	–	4 000	12 000	12 000
Payments						
Loan Interest				1 800		
Machine	4 000		2 000			
Vehicle	15 200					
Premises	88 000					
Purchases		4 500	3 000	4 000	4 000	4 000
Salaries	1 000	1 000	1 000	1 000	1 000	1 000
General exps	300	300	300	300	300	300
Insurance		640				
Rates		300				900
Drawings	650	650	650	650	650	650
Total Payments	109 150	7 390	6 950	7 750	5 950	6 850
Receipts less payments	(49 150)	(7 390)	(6 950)	(3 750)	6 050	5 150
Balance at bank (£50 000 b/fwd)	850	(6 540)	(13 490)	(17 240)	(11 190)	(6 040)

- *Go to the bank* and negotiate a temporary increase in the overdraft limit in the light of the figures in the cash budget.

3 If Alf does not do a cash budget and update it every month he may find that his overdraft gets out of control and the bank will eventually stop his cheques. This will stop his suppliers selling stock to him on credit and will lead eventually to bankruptcy proceedings.

Notes on completing spreadsheet activities for cash budgets

Photocopy the blank spreadsheet template in Fig. 7.7 and fill in the missing cells from the following data. Do what all accountants do and use a pencil so that you can easily alter your answer should you make a mistake. Use a calculator and find out how to use the constant (k) facility for making repetitive multiplications. For example, in Activity 7.2.2 you have to multiply different production and sales volumes by the same values. This involves inputting into your calculator the same number and multiplying it by a different number of units. To use the constant enter into your calculator the value, for instance, of sales at £35 and press the multiply button twice. You should then see on the calculator a small (k) to denote constant. Some calculators do not show this but still do the same calculations. Next, you must enter the units sold for the month and press the equals button. Do not press any other function key or you will lose the constant. If you enter the next month's units sold and press equals the calculator will continue to perform multiplication of £35 until you either clear the machine or press any of the other function keys.

ACTIVITY 7.2.1A

The following data must be put into the format of a cash budget so that the owner of the firm can appreciate the likely financial consequences of the decisions that have been made. Using one the blank forms taken from the template in Fig. 7.7, fill in the detail from the estimated receipts and payments.

Receipts

Cash sales	£5000 in January and £10 000 per month thereafter.

Payments

Staff	Staff wages total £1200 per month
Rent	£2500 per quarter, payable in January, April, July and October
Rates	£2000 per annum (£1000 payable in April and £1000 payable in October)
Electricity	£500 payable in March, £450 payable in June, £350 payable in September and £600 payable in December.
Telephone and Postage	January £500, April £300, July £350 and November £400.
Insurance	£600 payable in February
New purchases of stock	£6000 per month payable one month in arrears, i.e. the first payment will be paid in February.
New purchases of Fixed assets	£5000 in February, £5000 in March.

ACTIVITY 7.2.1B

Present the above cash budget to your tutor and explain the purposes and components of the forecasts contained in the budget. Note the effect on finance of the capital expenditure on fixed assets in February and March.

PC
7.2.1
7.2.2
7.2.3
7.2.4
7.2.5
7.2.6
7.2.8
7.2.9

CASH FLOW FORECAST

FOR: _____

(Name of Company, Partnership)

FOR PERIOD FROM: _____ TO: _____

HOW TO COMPLETE THE FORM:
1. Insert the date in the month when your cash position is likely to be at its lowest (A).
2. Enter the Opening Bank Balance on that date in (B). This is the balance at the Bank - not in the Company's/Firm's etc., books. Receipts paid in but not credited to the Bank Account or Cheques Issued, but not debited to the Bank Account should be included in the Income/Expenditure column.
3. Income/Expenditure includes all items which pass

		Projected	Actual	Projected	Actual	Projected	Actual	Projected	Actual	Projected	Actual	Projected	Actual
ENTER THE DATES CHOSEN (A)													
OPENING BANK BALANCE CREDIT/DEBIT (B)													
INCOME	Cash Sales												
	Debtors												
OTHER INCOME (Please Specify)													
TOTAL INCOME (C)													
EXPENDITURE	Cash Purchases												
	Creditors												
	Wages and Salaries												
	P.A.Y.E.												
	Heat, Light & Power												
	Rent												
	Rates												
	Bank Charges (Quarterly)												
	Interest Charges (Quarterly)												
	H.P. Payments												
	Loan Repayments												
	V.A.T. (Payments)												
	Tax												
	Dividends												
OTHER EXPENDITURE (Please Specify)													
TOTAL EXPENDITURE (D)													
CASH INCREASE/DECREASE (E)													
CLOSING BANK BALANCE CREDIT/DEBIT (F)													
ACTUAL BANK BALANCE IN QUESTION													
VARIATION FROM FORECAST FAVOURABLE/ADVERSE													

Fig 7.7 Cash template

through the Bank Account. Enter each item in the column under the date by which it is expected to be debited/credited. (Note likely variations, Bank Holiday short weeks etc.).

4. The difference between Total Income (C) and Total Expenditure (D), representing the net cash flow for the period, should be entered on line (E), in the column for the relevant date, as an increase or (decrease) whichever is applicable.

5. As a final step, the amount of the difference (E) between Total Income and Total Expenditure should be added to, or subtracted from, the Opening Bank balance (B) to arrive at the figure representing the Closing Bank balance to be inserted on line (F) in the appropriate date column. The Closing Bank balance (F) at the end of any given period should be carried forward as the Opening Bank balance (B) for the subsequent period.

														TOTAL	
Actual	Projected	Actual	Projected	Actual	Projected	Actual	Projected	Actual	Projected	Actual	Projected	Actual	Projected	Projected	Actual

Unit 7   Financial forecasting and monitoring

PC
7.2.1
7.2.2
7.2.3
7.2.4
7.2.5
7.2.6
7.2.7
7.2.8
7.2.9

ACTIVITY 7.2.2

Before attempting a question like Activity 7.2.2 you must read it carefully all the way through and make notes on how you will deal with each part. You will need to know, for instance, how many lines to create to record the receipts in your spreadsheet before you can go on to write out your payments. Some information may not be relevant, such as expenditure on items like depreciation which does not involve a cash payment. Some items of information are best dealt with on two lines, such as raw materials and (item d) and variable overheads (item f).

For raw materials, you have been told that one third of the £6 per unit is to be paid one month before production, and two thirds in the same month. One third of £6 is £2, and January's production is 700 units, therefore £1400 is payable in December and £2800 in January. December is of course prior to the time of this budget and is not required. February's one third, £1280 (£2 x 640 units), is payable in January. The easiest way to deal with raw materials is to have one line for the one third and another for the payment of the remaining two thirds. Thus, you will use two lines.

Similarly, variable overheads, are payable three quarters in the same month and one quarter in the following month. Three quarters of £16 is £12, and one quarter is £4. January's production is 700 units, therefore, one line will show a payment for January of £8400 (£12 x 700 units). The other quarter is shown on a separate line and January's production of 700 units will result in a payment of £2800 (£4 x 700 units), in February. Do not forget that at the start of this line the payment for January relates to December's production (£4 x 540 units).

Required

Task 1. Draw up a cash budget for James Plant's business from the following information for the six months ended 30 June.

a Opening bank balance £25 000
b A loan of £20 000 will be received in February.
c Production in units

Dec	Jan	Feb	Mar	Apr	May	June	July	Aug	Sept	Oct	Nov	Dec	Jan
540	700	640	560	500	420	380	400	400	440	460	480	600	720

d Raw materials used in production cost £6 per unit: of this one third is paid one month before production and two thirds in the same month as production.
e Direct labour costs of £8 per unit are payable in the same month as production.
f Variable overheads are £16 per unit payable three quarters in the same month as production and one quarter in the month following production.
g Sales are at an average of £35 per unit and the number of units sold is estimated as follows:

Nov	Dec	Jan	Feb	Mar	Apr	May	June	July	Aug	Sept	Oct	Nov	Dec
460	480	580	620	620	680	520	360	360	380	400	420	440	480

Debtors pay their accounts two months after the goods were sold.

h Fixed overheads are £2500 per month payable each month.
i Extensions to the premises costing £35 000 are to be paid £15 000 in February, £10 000 in April and £10 000 in June.
j Taxation and dividends will be paid as follows:

        August   £10 000   Dividend
        October   £ 5 000   Taxation

Task 2. Comment on the financial position shown in the cash budget and explain the purpose of your cash budget as a component for seeking additional finance.

Element 7.2   Produce and explain forecasts and a cash flow for a small business

ACTIVITY 7.2.3

Task 1. Draw up a cash budget for Pete Robinson and Co. Ltd from the following information for the six months ended 31 December.

a Opening bank balance £10 000 overdrawn.
b Will receive £5000 in June and December for rent from subletting part of the premises.
c Production in units:

Dec	Jan	Feb	Mar	Apr	May	Jun	Jul	Aug	Sept	Oct	Nov	Dec
300	320	270	250	240	270	300	320	350	370	380	360	340

d Raw materials used in production cost £10 per unit. Of this 80 per cent is paid in the month of production and 20 per cent in the month after production.
e Direct labour costs of £16 per unit are payable in the month of production.
f Variable expenses are £14 per unit, payable one half in the same month as production and one half in the month following production.
g Sales are at an average value of £65 per unit and the following units are estimated to be sold:

Nov	Dec	Jan	Feb	Mar	Apr	May	Jun	July	Aug	Sept	Oct	Nov	Dec
320	310	300	280	260	250	250	290	320	340	360	380	390	360

Debtors will pay their accounts two months after that in which sales are made.

h Fixed overheads of £4200 per month payable each month.
i Machinery costing £9000 to be paid for in October, and a further £11 000 in November.
j Directors' remuneration to be £2000 per month.
k Dividend of £15 000 to be paid in March.
l Taxation of £25 000 to be paid in October.
m Robinson's overdraft limit at the bank is £40 000.

Task 2. Comment on the significance of the timing of payments and receipts as shown in your cash budget.

The cash flow forecast in Fig. 7.8 has been reproduced by kind permission of Lloyds Bank PLC. This form is used by the bank's customers to keep track of their cash flow and is a part of the bank's service to its customers who manage small firms. The form itself can be used by the bank's customers when they request additional overdraft facilities from the bank.

Unit 7 Financial forecasting and monitoring

I do not believe it!

I cannot escape this stupid 3 letter word.

Cashflow Forecast

Business name: FOX ENTERPRISES

Period covered:

Period (eg 4 weeks/Month)	FIRST YEAR			
	BUDGET	ACTUAL	BUDGET	ACTUAL

TOTAL RECEIPTS (Enter these in the month when you actually receive your money. Your cashflow forecast will show the effect...)

Cash sales		30,000			
From debtors		53,625			
Other income (eg from capital introduced)		—			
TOTAL RECEIPTS	A	83,625			

PAYMENTS (This shows when you have to pay for the goods you buy-in rather than when you receive them and the effect...)

Cash purchases		61,000			
To creditors		—			
Wages/salaries/PAYE/NICs/other		—			
Rent/rates		7,800			
Light/heat/power		600			
Maintenance		500			
Bank/finance charges & interest		300			
HP payments/leasing charges		—			
Insurance		600			
Drawings/fees		10,000			
VAT-net					
Tax					
Loan repayments					
Capital expenditure (purchase of equipment, vehicles etc.)					
Professional fees (eg solicitors, accountants, surveyors)		500			
Advertising		1,000			
TOTAL PAYMENTS	B	82,300			

A-B (net inflow) or B-A (net outflow)	C	*	1,325		
Balance at end of previous period brought forward	D	*			
Balance at end of period carried forward (aggregate of C+D)		*			

Agreed overdraft					

*If a deficit – please enclose in brackets

Fig 7.8

Element 7.2 Produce and explain forecasts and a cash flow for a small business

COMPUTER SPREADSHEETS

What is a spreadsheet?

A spreadsheet is a tool for manipulating numerical data. In its manual form, as you have seen earlier, a spreadsheet is usually set up on analysis paper and is used in the preparation of cash budgets, operational budgets and also financial forecasting.

The spreadsheets that we will now look at are expandable computerised versions of our piece of financial analysis paper. A spreadsheet consists of many rows and columns which divide the paper into boxes (known as 'cells') and each box contains data in one form or another. The rows and columns each have headings, so that you can work out what the information in each cell refers to. The number of rows and columns are flexible, and data is entered into, and calculations performed in individual cells on a worksheet in the form of a matrix or grid. The total number of rows and columns available varies from package to package. A typical spreadsheet displays over 250 rows and 60 columns, although some of the more powerful packages can have over 16 000 rows and 256 columns. You can therefore use as many or as few rows and columns as needed.

When a spreadsheet is prepared manually, any calculation (e.g. totalling the rows or columns) have to be done by hand. Obviously this is time-consuming and as each calculations is open to human error, the possibility of mistakes creeping into the spreadsheet is always something that has to be seriously considered. Additionally, any alteration to the numbers within the spreadsheet will involve changing the totals and calculations within it which is very time-consuming and, unless it is done carefully, can result in arithmetical errors. One of the main benefits of using computer spreadsheet systems is their ability to recalculate automatically the arithmetical functions following any change to the numbers within the columns.

The following activities require you to use a computer spreadsheet to produce a series of cash budgets. The data for these budgets is that used earlier in the text for the manual budgets prepared in Activities 7.2.1 and 7.2.2. Use your answers to these activities to check that your spreadsheet works correctly. In order to help you do this, the answers to these questions have been produced showing both the text, formula and numbers used to set up the budget and also the final completed answer.

ACTIVITY 7.2.4

Task 1 Using the data given in Activity 7.2.1, produce a computer spreadsheet and print it out.
Task 2 Explain the consequences of incorrect forecasting.

ACTIVITY 7.2.5

Using the data given in Activity 7.2.2, produce a computer spreadsheet and print it out.

PC
7.2.1
7.2.2
7.2.3
7.2.4
7.2.5
7.2.6
7.2.7
7.2.8
7.2.9
7.2.10

Unit 7 Financial forecasting and monitoring

Instructions for inputing a spreadsheet in Excel

These instructions relate to the completion of Activity 7.2.5 – the cash budget for James Plant, the data for which is given in Activity 7.2.2.

1. Log on to the Excel spreadsheet program.
2. Excel already creates a blank worksheet for you to work on.
3. In column A, row 1, key in the heading:

    'JAMES PLANT'S CASH BUDGET '

    Press the Enter key. (Don't worry that it goes across into column B as you can widen the column later.)

4. In column B row 2, type 'JAN', then press the right arrow key to take you across to cell C2.
5. In column C2, type 'FEB', and again, press the right arrow key to take you to the next column. (If, by mistake, you press the Enter key, the cursor stays in the cell you have just input into.)
6. Continue entering the months across row 2.
7. In column A3 type the word 'RECEIPTS', then press the right arrow key to take you to cell B3.
8. In column B3 type the '£' sign. This time instead of entering the £s individually into each column across the spreadsheet, you can use the Copy command and Fill Right to do it for you as follows:

    - Make sure the cursor is in cell B3, then position the mouse arrow on the Edit menu and click.
    - From the Edit menu, choose the Copy command.
    - Holding the left-hand mouse button down, drag the mouse across row 3 as far as the DEC column, then release the mouse button. Row 3 should now be highlighted (i.e. row 3 should be blacked out as far as column M).
    - From the Edit menu, choose Fill Right. (The £ sign should now have been copied across the spreadsheet.)

9. Position the cursor in A4 and enter the subheadings down the left-hand column starting with Debtors (g). (This time use the down arrow to take you to cell A5.)
10. Continue entering the subheadings down column A.
11. Now widen column A to show the headings fully, as follows:

    - Position the cursor anywhere in column A.
    - From the Format menu, choose Column Width.
    - In the Column Width box, type 25.
    - Click on OK with the mouse.

12. At this point save the spreadsheet as follows:

    - From the File menu, choose Save As.
    - Click on the down arrow under the heading 'Drives' and choose A.
    - In the Filename box, type the filename (must be eight characters or less), then click OK.

13 Key in the numbers along rows 4 and 5. Check the figures and save the spreadsheet (File, Save).

14 In cell B7 calculate the formula of B4+B5 as follows:

= SUM(B4:B5)

15 With the cursor in B7, copy the formula across row 7 as follows:

- Edit, Copy.
- Highlight row 7 across to the DEC column.
- Edit, Fill Right.

16 Key in the numbers for payments along rows 10 to 17.

17 In cell B19, calculate the formula of B10 to B17 as follows:

= SUM(B10:B17)

18 Repeat instruction number 15 to copy the formula for B19 across row 19.

19 In cell B20, calculate the formula to take RECEIPTS from PAYMENTS, as follows:

= B7-B19

20 With the cursor in cell B20, copy the formula across the spreadsheet as previously instructed.

21 To find the Bank balance, calculate the formula as follows:

= A21+B20

(Do not worry that this should be a minus sign. The computer will recognise cell B20 as a minus value and automatically deduct it from A21.)

22 Copy the formula in B21 across the row to the DEC column.

23 Save the spreadsheet and print a copy out.

Self assessment questions

1 In a cash budget depreciation is:
   a a payment
   b a receipt
   c either a receipt or a payment
   d neither a receipt nor a payment?

2 In a cash budget interest is:
   a a payment
   b a receipt
   c either a receipt or a payment
   d neither a receipt nor a payment?

3 In a cash budget the purchase of stock is:
  a a payment
  b a receipt
  c either a receipt or a payment
  d neither a receipt nor a payment?

4 Consider the following statements.
  (i) Cash budgets are used to predict profits.
  (ii) Cash budgets are completed once a year.

  Which option best describes the statements?
  a (i) True   (ii) True
  b (i) True   (ii) False
  c (i) False   (ii) True
  d (i) False   (ii) False

Questions 5, 6 and 7 relate to the following information.

B Soon's Cash Budget for the four months to the end of July

	April £000	May £000	June £000	July £000
Total receipts	50	45	30	60
Payments				
Wages & salaries	10	10	10	10
Purchases	14	15	16	16
Variable expenses	10	18	8	8
Fixed expenses	8	8	8	8
Fixed asset purchase			12	
Total payments	42	51	54	42
Receipts less payments	8	(6)	(24)	18
Bank balance £10	18	12	(12)	6

If April is Month A, May is Month B, June is Month C and July is Month D, which month's figures show the following?

5 A bank overdraft will be required.

6 Wages and salaries can only just be paid without help from the bank.

7 The fixed asset payment should be delayed by one month.

Element 7.2 Produce and explain forecasts and a cash flow for a small business

Assignment

PC
7.2.1
7.2.2
7.2.3
7.2.4
7.2.5
7.2.6
7.2.7
7.2.8
7.2.9
7.2.10

Task 1. Using the data given in Activity 7.2.3, produce a computer spreadsheet for Pete Robinson and Co. Ltd and print it out.

Task 2. Write a report to Pete Robinson outlining:

a The benefits of using spreadsheets to complete regular cash budgets.

b The points to note in the cash budget that you have produced and any action that Mr Robinson ought to take based upon your figures.

c The use of a cash budget in an application to a bank for a loan.

d The consequences of incorrect forecasting and assumptions within a budget.

Include your spreadsheet completed in Task 1 as an appendix to your report.

Element 7.3
PRODUCE AND EXPLAIN PROFIT AND LOSS STATEMENTS AND BALANCE SHEETS

Performance criteria

1 **Explain a basic accounting system suitable for a small business.**

2 **Identify and explain accounting periods.**

3 **Extract a trial balance from given accounting records.**

4 **Identify each account on the trial balance correctly in relation to profit and loss or balance sheet.**

5 **Produce and explain profit and loss account and balance sheet in vertical form from the trial balance.**

6 **Explain the purposes of balance sheets and profit and loss statements.**

Introduction

The financial accountant's main job is to close the accounts of an organisation by producing the year-end accounting statements. For private sector firms, these are the *trading and profit and loss account* and *the balance sheet*. For most public sector organisations these statements are called the *revenue account* or *income and expenditure account* and *the balance sheet*.

During the year all organisations keep financial records of one type or another. Mostly these records are kept according to *double-entry bookkeeping* techniques. All other less sophisticated systems require the accountant to generate the same information that would have been produced using the double-entry system. Although the double-entry system is shown in outline, it is not the intention of this unit to teach the details of bookkeeping. You simply have to be aware how the records in the accounts are recorded so that you can appreciate the year-end accounting requirements needed to produce the final accounts and balance sheet. (*See* Unit 6 for a more detailed explanation of bookkeeping.)

DOUBLE-ENTRY BOOKKEEPING

This system is now about 500 years old and is capable of infinite expansion and use by any organisation. All computer accounting systems use it although this may not be apparent at a superficial level. The basis of the system is that for all transactions there are two aspects. If you were to give me £500, I would receive £500; the bookkeeping system would record both the giving and the receiving.

Within the same set of bookkeeping records there would be an account for you to record the giving of value and an account for me to record the receiving of value. The terms *debit* and *credit* are used to denote each side of the transactions. In the above example the account that gave value, i.e. your account, would be credited, while the account that received value, i.e. my account, would be debited. Obviously, if each transaction produces a debit and a credit entry in the accounts there should be the same value of debits as there are credits in any accounting system.

The ledgers

In any accounting system there will be many different types of accounts. Some will record what the firm owns (assets); others will record what the firm owes (liabilities). Other accounts will record the firm's income and expenses. Some of these categories of account may have many individual accounts. The firm's expenses will be recorded in different accounts such as rent, rates, insurances, wages, salaries, depreciation of fixed assets, vehicle running costs etc. If the firm sells on credit terms it will need one account for each customer in order to record the amount owed by that customer. Similarly, if the firm purchases goods from different suppliers, it will need one account for each supplier in order to record the amount that it owes to that supplier. It is not unusual for small firms to have hundreds of accounts and for larger firms to have many thousands of accounts. This is one of the reasons why it is usual to group the accounts into different *Ledgers*.

A ledger is a set of accounts of a similar type. Most firms subdivide their accounting system into a minimum of three ledgers: the Nominal or General Ledger, the Purchases Ledger and the Sales Ledger.

The *Nominal Ledger* contains the firm's asset and liability accounts and its income and expense accounts. It does not contain the accounts of the suppliers from whom the firm purchased goods. These accounts are known as *creditors* as each will have a credit balance that denotes the amount of money owed to the creditor. These creditor accounts are kept in the *Purchases Ledger*.

The Nominal Ledger does not contain the accounts of the firm's customers who owe the firm money following credit sales. The balances on these accounts are all debit balances and the customers' accounts are known as *debtors*. All of the firm's debtor accounts are kept in the firm's *Sales Ledger*.

Note that neither the sales account nor the purchases account are in their named ledgers; they are both in the Nominal Ledger.

It is common practice for both the Sales and Purchases Ledgers to have a control account that simply records the total of all debits and credits in the accounts within their ledgers. The balances on these accounts gives us the total figures that we need at the year-end in our trial balance and subsequently the balance sheet.

The rules of double entry

It has already been stated that every transaction entered into by a business requires two entries in the financial records of that business. The following rules apply:

- A debit balance in the financial books represents either:
  1. an expense incurred by the business; or
  2. an asset of the business.

- A credit balance in the financial books represents either:
  1. income of a business;
  2. a provision against a known future liability;
  3. a liability;
  4. capital.

Recording transactions

With these points in mind we can start to record transactions in the ledger of a business. (Note that the illustration of bookkeeping records shown below differs in its presentation to those shown in Unit 6. Unit 6 used the traditional debit and credit side layout of the accounts.) The layout in this unit is more like that shown on a computer system (such as that which a bank might use) and it obviates the need to balance the accounts at the end of the month. Compare the two methods.

Example

P Rooney has just set up new retail business. Consider the following transactions:

April 1	Started business with £20 000 in the bank.
April 3	Rented shop premises for £2000 per month paying the first instalment of £2000 by cheque.
April 4	Purchased shop fittings on credit from A Smith for £5000.
April 7	Purchased goods for resale (stock) for £2500 paying by cheque.
April 12	Purchased a van for £10 000 from Cars and Vans Ltd on credit.
April 13	Paid A Smith £5000 by cheque.
April 21	Purchased more goods for resale (stock) for £2000 on credit from T D Jones Ltd.
April 28	Paid Cars and Vans Ltd £10 000 by cheque.

These transactions should be recorded in the ledgers of the business as below.

Element 7.3 Produce and explain profit and loss statements and balance sheets

P Rooney's Ledger

Date	Details	Debit £	Credit £	Balance £
Capital account				
Apr 1	Bank		20 000	20 000 Cr
Bank account				
Apr 1	Capital	20 000		20 000
Apr 3	Rent		2 000	18 000
Apr 7	Purchases		2 500	15 500
Apr 15	A Smith		5 000	10 500
Apr 28	Cars & Vans Ltd		10 000	500
Rent account				
Apr 3	Bank	2 000		2 000
Shop Fittings account				
Apr 4	A Smith	5 000		5 000
A Smith's account				
Apr 4	Shop Fittings		5 000	5 000 Cr
Apr 15	Bank	5 000		nil
Purchases account				
Apr 7	Bank	2 500		2 500
Apr 21	T D Jones Ltd	2 000		4 500
Van account				
Apr 12	Cars & Vans Ltd	10 000		10 000
Cars and Vans Ltd account				
Apr 12	Van		10 000	10 000 Cr
Apr 28	Bank	10 000		nil
T D Jones Ltd account				
Apr 21	Purchases		2 000	2 000 Cr

The following general rules apply:

- *Credit entries are in accounts that give value. Debit entries are in accounts that receive value, e.g. Bank pays £10 000 (credit) Cars and Vans Ltd receive £10 000 (debit).*
- *Debit balances are in accounts that are assets or expenses or purchases. Credit balances are in accounts that are either liabilities (i.e. the firm owes something), income or capital.*

Now look back over the example for Rooney and try to relate either one or both of the above rules to each transaction.

ACCOUNTING DOCUMENTATION

In Unit 6, Financial Transactions, costing and pricing, you were introduced to basic bookkeeping and the documentation that the system used. There is little point in repeating the same information here and you are referred back to Unit 6 for the details that you are required to know for this Unit.

THE TRIAL BALANCE

We have now reached the end of April and Mr Rooney wants to know if the accounts have been kept correctly. If we have always made a debit entry and a credit entry for each transaction, we should have the same value of debits as credits. We can prove this by listing all of the accounts and adding up the debit balances and the credit balances. Compare the following list of balances with the accounts shown earlier. Accounts with a nil balance are not shown.

P Rooney
Trial Balance as at 30 April

Account	Debit	Credit
	£	£
Capital		20 000
Bank	500	
Rent	2 000	
Shop Fittings	5 000	
Purchases	4 500	
Van	10 000	
T D Jones Ltd		2 000
	22 000	22 000

As you can see, the two credit balances of capital and T D Jones Ltd add up to the same figure as the total of all of the debit balances. The accounts are therefore in balance and can be assumed to be correct, subject to the following types of error:

- *Compensating errors* whereby there are two different errors for the same amount and they cancel each other out.
- *Errors of omission* whereby no transaction has been entered into the books at all (either debit or credit).
- *Errors of commission* whereby a transaction has been entered into the wrong account.

- *Errors of original entry* whereby the wrong amount has been entered (e.g. £78 instead of £87).
- *Reversed entries* whereby the debits and credits have been entered into the opposite columns of the accounts (e.g. crediting purchases rather than debiting them).
- *Errors of principle* whereby a transaction has been entered correctly in the financial books but has been treated in a fundamentally incorrect manner, e.g. treating the purchase of shop fittings as a purchase for resale.

The single-column trial balances

Many bookkeeping systems, particularly those used by computers, do no show the trial balance as two columns: debit and credit. Instead, all of the account balances are listed together and the system treats the debit balances as pluses and the credit balances as minuses. These balances are listed and totalled and, if the accounts balance, the total should be zero. If we use Mr. Rooney's trial balance as an example, it would show the following balances.

P Rooney
Trial Balance as at 30 April

	£	
Capital	20 000	Cr
Bank	500	
Rent	2 000	
Shop Fittings	5 000	
Purchases	4 500	
Van	10 000	
T D Jones	2 000	Cr
	0	

ACTIVITY 7.3.1

Task 1. Define the following terms: debtor; creditor; liabilities; ledger.

Task 2. Answer the following questions:

a If an account gives value, is it debited or credited?
b What is the purpose of a trial balance?
c Are asset balances in the accounts debits or credits?
d Why are accounts produced for the financial year?

Task 3. Using the example accounts of Mr. Rooney, make an oral presentation to your tutor explaining the accounting system used. Identify and explain accounting periods and the use of the trial balance.

PC
7.3.1
7.3.2
7.3.3

Unit 7 Financial forecasting and monitoring

PC
7.3.1
7.3.2
7.3.3

ACTIVITY 7.3.2

The following are the transactions for I Shipley for her first month's trading.

June 1	Started business with £5 000 in a business bank account.
June 2	Received a loan from M Bingley of £4000 and paid the cheque directly into the bank.
June 3	Rented an industrial unit at a quarterly rent of £3000, paying the first quarter's rent by cheque.
June 4	Purchased goods for resale from an importer costing £4000, paying by cheque.
June 5	Paid advertising bill, costing £350, by cheque.
June 10	Purchased fittings on credit from Stackit Ltd, for £2000.
June 11	Sold goods to the value of £1300 on credit to M Baildon.
June 13	Paid advertising bill, costing £300, by cheque.
June 15	Sold goods on credit to D Bradford for £650.
June 18	Sold goods for cash £250.
June 19	Paid insurance, by cheque £680.
June 25	Purchased more goods on credit costing £3 000.
June 27	Paid advertising bill, costing £300 by cheque.
June 28	Paid printing bill, £460 by cheque.
June 29	Received a cheque for £1300 from M Baildon.
June 30	Paid Stackit Ltd, £2000

Task 1. You are required to enter the above transactions in the accounts of I Shipley and extract a single-column trial balance as at 30 June.

Task 2. Write a short note to Miss Shipley to explain the double-entry system using your accounts from Task 1 as an example.

FINAL ACCOUNTS AND BALANCE SHEETS

One of the main subjects of this element is the year-end analysis of the data collected in the accounts as shown by the trial balance at the end of the year. These statements are known as the final accounts (i.e. trading and profit and loss account) and balance sheets (a list of asset and liability balances left in the ledgers after the production of the final accounts). This is where bookkeeping ends and accountancy begins.

The trading account

At the end of the year all accounts that relate to the purchase and sale of goods or services are transferred to this account in order to find the difference between the cost of the goods and their total selling price or sales revenue. This figure is the firm's *gross profit* and is one of the most important business considerations. If the manager of the business gets gross profit wrong, the business is likely to fail. Gross profit is calculated by deducting the cost of purchasing the goods that were sold, from their total sales value.

If a firm has no stock at the start and end of the year and has neither issued nor received any credit notes (returns in and outwards) gross profit will simply be the difference between the total of the sales account and the total of the purchases account.

If, as is more usual, the firm has balances of stock at the start and end of the year, the trading account will look like this example:

G Wood
Trading account for the year ending 31 December

	£	£
Sales (net)		80 500
Less Cost of sales		
Stock b/fwd	2 500	
Add Purchases (net)	37 000	
	39 500	
Less Stock c/fwd	3 000	36 500
Gross profit		44 000

In this example we could not simply deduct purchases from sales as the firm had some unsold stock brought forward from last year to the start of this year. This figure will not appear in this year's purchases account, as it was bought last year. Similarly, the firm did not sell all of its stock by the end of the year of account. £3,000 of stock included in the purchases account total was not sold and it did not affect the sales total. We must, therefore, deduct this value of unsold stock from the purchases total in order to arrive at the value at cost price of the goods shown in the sales account at selling price. It will, of course, be sold next year and will be in next year's trading account as the value of stock brought forward.

These adjustments are required in order to work out the gross profit on the items of stock that have been sold in this year of account. The adjustments for stock at the start and end of a financial year illustrate one of the main accounting principles, the *matching principle*, whereby the income due in the year is matched against the cost incurred in achieving that income.

The Profit and Loss Account

The next stage in the accounting process is to deduct from the Gross Profit all of the costs that have been incurred in helping to create it. These are the firm's business expenses. Many business people refer to them as overhead costs and the following list shows some typical examples:

- *Administrative Expenses*
  - Salaries and wages
  - Rent and Rates and Insurance
  - Depreciation (explained later)
  - Heating and Lighting
  - Repairs
- *Selling and Distribution*
  - Delivery costs (or carriage outwards)
  - Salesmen's salaries and commission
  - Advertising
  - Rent, Rates and Insurance (of sales office etc.)
  - Depreciation of salesmen's cars, delivery vans, etc.
- *Financial Expenses*
  - Interest on Loans

The above list of expenses is not exhaustive and different firms call the same types of account by different names (e.g. Heating and Lighting may be split into separate accounts for Gas, Electricity, Solid fuel and Oil) it is up to you as the accountant to understand the nature of the expense and treat it accordingly.

When the expenses are deducted from the gross profit, we arrive at the net profit. This represents the earnings of the firm and it belongs to the firm's owner and is therefore added to his or her capital account at the end of the year.

G Wood
Trading and Profit and Loss Account for the year ended 31 Dec

	£	£	£
Sales (net)			80 500
Less Cost of sales:			
Stock b/fwd		2 500	
Add Purchases (net)		37 000	
		39 500	
Less Stock c/fwd		3 000	36 500
Gross profit			44 000
Less Expenses:			
Admin expenses			
Salaries and wages	12 500		
Rent, rates and insurance	12 000		
Depreciation	1 000		
Heating & lighting	2 500		
Repairs	300		
		28 300	
Selling and distribution expenses			
Motor expenses	2 900		
Postage and packing	200		
Advertising	1 400		
		4 500	
Financial expenses			
Interest on loans		1 200	34 000
Net profit			10 000

Element 7.3 Produce and explain profit and loss statements and balance sheets

The balance sheet

A balance sheet is a list of assets and liability balances left in the accounts after the revenue account balances have been transferred to the trading and profit and loss account. The layout or presentation of the account balances in a balance sheet can be shown in many different styles but the following two types of presentation predominate in the UK.

G Wood
Balance Sheet as at 31 December

Liabilities	£	£	Fixed Assets	Cost	Dep'n	Book Value
Capital		25 000	Shop Fittings	10 000	1 000	9 000
Add net profit		10 000	Van	10 800	5 800	5 000
		35 000		20 800	6 800	14 000
Less drawings		9 000				
		26 000	Current Assets			
			Stock		16 000	
			Debtors		3 000	
Long term liabilities			Bank		4 800	
Bank Loan		10 000	Cash		200	
						24 000
Current liabilities						
Creditors	1 400					
Accrued expenses	600	2 000				
		38 000				38 000

The same account balances can also be shown in the more usual vertical presentation of a balance sheet as shown overleaf.

G Wood
Balance Sheet as at 31 December

	Cost £	Depreciation to date £	Book value £
Fixed assets			
Shop fittings	10 000	1 000	9 000
Van	10 800	5 800	5 000
	20 800	6 800	14 000
Current assets			
Stock		16 000	
Debtors		3 000	
Bank		4 800	
Cash		200	
		24 000	
Less Current liabilities			
Creditors	1 400		
Accrued expenses	600	2 000	
Working capital			22 000
Total assets *less* Current liabilities			36 000
Less Long-term liability			
Bank loan			10 000
			26 000
Financed by		£	£
Capital			25 000
Add Net profit		10 000	
Less Drawings		9 000	1 000
			26 000

Compare both types of balance sheet and note the differences and similarities.

1 The sections of the balance sheet are not changed.

2 The main difference is the treatment of current liabilities that are deducted from the total of the current assets in vertical format in order to show the total for working capital.

3 The balance sheet totals are different (the difference being the total of current and long term liabilities). The two-side format shows the total of current and fixed assets while the more informative vertical presentation shows the book value of the firm (net asset value).

4 The vertical presentation shows where the money came from (the financed by section) to pay for the above assets (i.e. what the owner's capital was spent on).

An example of the preparation of final accounts.

Consider the following trial balance of R Dunn's retail firm.

R Dunn
Trial balance as at 31 December

Account	Debit	Credit
General expenses	4 380	
Advertising	1 640	
Postage and telephone	1 025	
Lighting and heating	2 595	
Insurance	490	
Rent and rates	16 860	
Salaries and wages	22 840	
Motor expenses	11 616	
Printing and stationery	1 360	
Bank Interest charges	1 540	
Sales		179 805
Purchases	80 144	
Stock b/fwd	30 140	
Debtors	20 314	
Commission received		1 000
Creditors		16 100
Fixtures and fittings	10 400	
Motor vehicles	16 400	
Drawings	16 000	
Capital		38 000
Cash in hand	453	
Bank overdraft		3 292
	238 197	238 197

Note stock at 31 December was valued at £25 091 (i.e. no stock carried forward).

A trading and profit and loss account for the year ended 31 December and a balance sheet as at that date can now be prepared.

R Dunn
Trading and profit and loss account for the year ended 31 December

	£	£
Sales		179 805
Less Cost of sales:		
Stock b/fwd	30 140	
Add Purchases	80 144	
	110 284	
Less Stock c/fwd	25 091	85 193
Gross profit		94 612
Add Other operating income:		
Commission received		1 000
		95 612
Less Expenses:		
General expenses	4 380	
Advertising	1 640	
Postage and telephone	1 025	
Lighting and heating	2 595	
Insurance	490	
Rent and rates	16 860	
Salaries and wages	22 840	
Motor expenses	11 616	
Bank interest and charges	1 540	
Printing and stationery	1 360	64 346
Net profit		31 266

Notes

1. In this example the firm had income other than sales in the form of commission received (i.e. another organisation had paid Dunn £1000 commission for helping to sell their own goods). All income received other than sales forms part of the profit and loss account and is added to gross profit before the expenses are deducted.

2. This example also had a bank overdraft rather than cash in the bank. Obviously, an overdraft is a liability rather than an asset and as such it is shown as a current liability in the balance sheet. Even if the description of the bank account had not said that it was an overdraft you should have been able to deduce this from the fact that the balance is a credit balance and therefore a liability rather than a debit balance indicating an asset.

R Dunn
Balance Sheet as at 31 December

	£	£	£
Fixed assets			
Fixtures and fittings			10 400
Motor vehicles			16 400
			26 800
Current Assets			
Stock		25 091	
Debtors		20 314	
Cash		453	
		45 858	
Less **Current liabilities**			
Bank overdraft	3 292		
Creditors	16 100	19 392	
Working capital			26 466
			53 266

	£	£
Financed By		
Capital		38 000
Add Net profit	31 266	
Less Drawings	16 000	15 266
		53 266

Unit 7 Financial forecasting and monitoring

ACTIVITY 7.3.3

Extract a trading and profit and loss account for the year ended 31 March and a balance sheet as at that date from the following trial balance at 31 March.

	£	
Rent and rates	2 560	
Insurance	305	
Lighting and heating	1 516	
Motor expenses	1 960	
Wages	10 100	
Sales	61 200	Cr
Purchases	21 650	
Trade expenses	806	
Motor vans	8 000	
Creditors	6 250	Cr
Debtors	6 810	
Shop fixtures	3 960	
Shop buildings	40 000	
Stock b/fwd	9 320	
Cash at bank	1 134	
Drawings	10 000	
Capital	50 671	Cr

Stock at 31 March was £9960.

YEAR-END ADJUSTMENTS

Before a business prepares its year-end final accounts and balance sheet there are several adjustments to be made to the figures in the accounts in the trial balance. The reason for this is an attempt to make the financial statements show a truer view of the profit for the period and also give a more accurate account of the assets and liabilities at the balance sheet date.

Accruals

These are expenses incurred during an accounting period which are still outstanding at the date of the trial balance and they have not been recorded in the firm's accounts. We have had the benefit of the expense, however. We must make the following adjustments for this type of outstanding expense.

1 Add the amount outstanding to the appropriate expense shown in the trial balance. This will increase the debit values.

2 Make a new credit entry in the trial balance called Accruals for the same value.

Because you have made entries for the same amount in the Debit and Credit columns of your trial balance, the two totals will still be equal (the totals will have changed, but they should all agree).

When preparing the profit and loss account, you will now enter the new increased expense figure from your trial balance and on the balance sheet under the heading 'Current liabilities', you will show the accrued expenses. There may be several of these accruals but add them together and show only the total figure.

ACTIVITY 7.3.4

Task 1. Answer the following questions:
a What effect will an accrual have on the net profit?
b What effect will an accrual have on the balance sheet?

Task 2. Name four types of expenses likely to be unpaid at the end of the financial year.

Prepayments

These are expenses which have been paid during the financial year but some part of the payment relates to the next accounting period. For example, if a business pays for 12 months' insurance on 1 July, and the year end is 31 December, the business has only had the benefit of six months' insurance despite having paid for 12. Six months' insurance premium has therefore been prepaid. You should

1 Deduct the amount prepaid from the expense in the trial balance.
2 Make a new debit entry in the trial balance called Prepayments.

You have made an equal deduction from and an addition to the debit values in your trial balance. When preparing the profit and loss account, enter the reduced expense, and on the balance sheet, under the heading Current assets, you will show the total of the prepaid expenses.

ACTIVITY 7.3.5

Task 1. What effect will prepayments have on net profit?

Task 2. What effect will it have on the balance sheet?

Task 3. Why are prepayments an asset?

Provision for bad debts

Bad debts are an expense and the management must decide the value of any debts which they think are irrecoverable. The entries in the accounts will be to credit the debtors account, thus bringing it to a zero balance and to debit the new expense account called Bad debts. If, after the trial balance has been extracted from the accounts, the managers decide to write off some bad debts all we need to do is to reduce the value of the Debtor's figure in the debit column of the trial balance and increase the debit balance for the Bad debts account. Remember that the Debtors figure represents the total value of all of the firm's Debtors rather than just one account.

Fig 7.9 'Bad debt'

ACTIVITY 7.3.6

Task 1. What effect will a bad debt have on net profit?

Task 2. What effect will it have on current assets?

Provision for doubtful debts

Some debts may be recoverable either in part or whole and therefore should not be treated as bad debts and a provision should be made against the possible loss, however. The doubtful debts should be added to the bad debts account, thus creating an additional expense, i.e. a debit entry, then another new credit account should be opened called the Provision for doubtful debts and enter the same estimated amount. The balance sheet will show the provision for doubtful debts as a deduction from Debtors as follows:

Element 7.3 Produce and explain profit and loss statements and balance sheets

	£	£
Current assets		
Stocks		35 000
Debtors	25 000	
Less Provision for doubtful debts	1 000	24 000
Bank and cash		1 000
		60 000

The most accurate method of assessing doubtful debts is to look carefully at each debtor's account and decide upon those who may not pay all or part of the balance that they owe. In a larger firm with many hundreds of debtors accounts, this may be impracticable and the firm will have to use its managers' experience and estimate a reasonable figure. Quite often a simple percentage of the total debtors value is used.

Most firms do not bother to identify individual doubtful debts in the following year's accounts. When they eventually become bad debts they simply write the balance off to the bad debts account in the normal way. Therefore, at the end of the next year, there will be a credit balance on the provision for doubtful debts account that should be used to reduce the value of the actual bad debts written off. After that has happened a new provision for doubtful debts should be created in the manner described above.

Fig 7.10 'Doubtful debt'

Provision for depreciation

The definition of a provision is the setting aside of profits to meet a known future liability. In the case of the provision for doubtful debts the future liability was the potential bad debt. With the provision for depreciation, however, the future liability is the fall in value of a fixed asset. A description of the methods used to estimate the annual provision for depreciation was given in Element 7.1.

The accounting entries are:

1 Debit profit and loss account (creating an expense).

2 Credit the provision for depreciation account.

Note that neither of the above entries involves either cash or money in the bank. The provision for depreciation is simply an accounting entry in the firm's books and is deducted from the fixed asset account in the balance sheet in order to show the asset's book value. This should approximate to the market value of that asset but many firms use methods to calculate depreciation that give inaccurate values during the early years of the asset's life. One of the problems with depreciation is that until the asset is sold at the end of its useful life the accountant cannot know accurately how much depreciation to charge. It is necessary, therefore, to include an estimate in the accounts for the year's expense (*see* Element 7.1).

To illustrate the treatment in the final accounts and balance sheets of the effect of accruals, prepayments and the provision for bad debts and depreciation, the following example is used.

An example of year-end adjustments

The following trial balance was extracted from the records of P Horton, a trader as at 31 December.

The following matters are to be taken into account at 31 December.

a Stock £32 429.
b Expenses owing: Sundry expenses £82; Motor expenses £88.
c Prepayment: Rates £266.
d Provision for doubtful debts to be reduced to £580.
e Depreciation for motors to be £2400 for the year.
f Part of the premises were let to a tenant who owed £250 at the 31 December.
g Loan interest owing to M Leake £4000.

P Norton
Trial balance at 31 December

	Debit £	Credit £
Discounts allowed	1 410	
Discounts received		506
Carriage inwards	309	
Carriage outwards	4 218	
Sales		138 936
Purchases	73 480	
Stock b/fwd	30 816	
Motor expenses	4 917	
Repairs to premises	1 383	
Salaries and wages	26 184	
Sundry expenses	5 807	
Rates and insurance	2 896	
Premises at cost	50 000	
Motor vehicles at cost	11 160	
Provision for depreciation Motors b/fwd		3 860
Debtors and creditors	41 640	34 320
Cash at bank	4 956	
Cash in hand	48	
Drawings	8 736	
Capital		50 994
Loan from M Leake		40 000
Bad debts	1 314	
Provision for doubtful debts b/fwd		658
	269 274	269 274

The following trading and profit and loss account and balance sheet can now be prepared based on the preceding trial balance.

P Norton
Trading and profit and loss account for the year ended 31 December

	£	£	£
Sales			138 936
Less Cost of sales:			
Stock b/fwd		30 816	
Add purchases	73 480		
Add carriage inwards	309	73 789	
		104 605	
Less Stock c/fwd		32 429	72 176
Gross profit			66 760
Add Other operating income:			
Discount received		506	
Rent due		250	756
			67 516
Less Expenses:			
Discount allowed		1 410	
Carriage out		4 218	
Motor expenses (4 917 + 88)		5 005	
Repairs to premises		1 383	
Salaries and wages		26 184	
Sundry expenses (5 807 + 82)		5 889	
Rates and Insurance (2 896 − 266)		2 630	
Loan interest owing		4 000	
Bad debts	1 314		
Less reduction in provision (658 − 580)	78	1 236	
Depreciation of motors		2 400	54 355
Net profit			13 161

P Norton

Balance sheet as at 31 December

	Cost £	Depreciation to date £	Book value £
Fixed assets			
Premises	50 000		50 000
Motors	11 160	6 260	4 900
	61 160	6 260	54 900
Current assets			
Stock		32 429	
Debtors	41 640		
Less Provision for bad debts	580	41 060	
Other debtors (Rent due)		250	
Prepaid rates		266	
Bank		4 956	
Cash		48	
		79 009	
Less Current liabilities			
Creditors	34 320		
Loan interest due	4 000		
Accruals (88 + 82)	170	38 490	
Working capital			40 519
Total assets Less Current liabilities			95 419
Less Long-term liability			
Loan from M Leake			40 000
			55 419
Financed by			
Capital			50 994
Add Net profit		13 161	
Less Drawings		8 736	4 425
			55 419

ACTIVITY 7.3.7

The trial balance shown below was extracted from the books of Alf Hall as at 31 December.

The following are to be taken into account as at 31 December:

a Stock-in-trade £38 610.
b Insurance prepaid £240.
c Salaries outstanding £1030.
d The new provision for bad debts is to be increased to £900.
e Provide for depreciation for the year: fixtures £2200: Motor vans £4850.
f Loan interest of £2000 is still to be paid at 31 December.

Task. You are required to prepare a trading and profit and loss account for the year ended 31 December and a balance sheet as at that date.

Alf Hall
Trial balance at 31 December

	Debit £	Credit £
Purchases	99 450	
Sales		170 200
Delivery expenses	760	
Motor expenses	1 864	
Salaries	25 310	
Discounts allowed	309	
Discounts received		210
Rent and rates	9 810	
Insurance	1 204	
Bad debts	1 516	
Provision for bad debts b/fwd		805
Stock b/fwd	41 630	
Debtors	22 460	
Creditors		21 960
Drawings	17 155	
Cash in hand	150	
Cash at bank	5 850	
Fixtures at cost	21 000	
Motor vans at cost	19 400	
Provision for depreciation b/fwd		
Fixtures		4 400
Motor vans		4 850
Capital		45 443
Long term loans		20 000
	267 868	267 868

Element 7.3 Produce and explain profit and loss statements and balance sheets

Self assessment questions

1. Which of these is a business expense?
   a. Motor vehicles
   b. Rent
   c. Debtors
   d. Drawings

2. Which of these figures should appear in the balance sheet?
   a. Bank
   b. Purchases
   c. Stock brought forward
   d. Insurance

3. Which of the following items of information will appear in a company's profit and loss account?
   a. The company's liabilities
   b. The owner's drawings
   c. The company's cash and bank balances
   d. The depreciation charged in the year

4. Which of the following will appear in a company's balance sheet?
   a. Cash flow
   b. The market value of the company
   c. The book value of the company's assets
   d. The company's turnover

5. Which of the following will appear in a sole trader's balance sheet?
   a. The year's expenses
   b. The annual sales
   c. The share capital
   d. The owner's capital

6. Consider the following statements.
   i) A trial balance can detect addition errors in the accounts.
   ii) A trial balance can show that the wrong account has been used.

   Which option best describes the two statements?
   a. (i) True,   (ii) True
   b. (i) True,   (ii) False
   c. (i) False, (ii) True
   d. (i) False, (ii) False

7. Which of the following will be shown in a trial balance?
   a. The working capital
   b. The current assets
   c. The net profit
   d. The balances on the accounts

Unit 7   Financial forecasting and monitoring

Assignment

You are Mr Wise's accountant and you must use this information for Task 1 and 2 of this assignment.

The trial balance shown below was extracted from the books of B Wise as at 31 December.

B Wise
Trial balance at 31 December

	Dr £	Cr £
Stock-in-trade b/fwd	49 900	
Purchases	196 450	
Sales		361 800
Bank charges	2 100	
Carriage outwards	14 760	
Motor expenses	11 864	
Salaries and wages	41 800	
Discounts allowed	10 300	
Discounts received		2 210
Rent and rates	29 810	
Insurance	9 204	
Bad debts written off	2 100	
Provision for doubtful debts b/fwd		750
Debtors	31 000	
Creditors		50 100
Drawings	28 000	
Cash in hand	250	
Bank overdraft		20 100
Plant and equipment at cost	80 000	
Motor vans at cost	30 000	
Provision for depreciation b/fwd:		
Plant and equipment		16 000
Motor vans		22 500
Capital		64 078
	537 538	537 538

Element 7.3 Produce and explain profit and loss statements and balance sheets

The following are to be taken into account at 31 December:

a Stock-in-trade £45 900.
b Insurance prepaid £1800, Rent and rates £4900.
c Salaries outstanding £4000.
d The new provision for doubtful debts will be £1000.
e Provide for depreciation for the year: plant and equipment 10 per cent (straight-line method); motor vans 50 per cent (reducing balance method).

Task 1. You are required to prepare a trading and profit and loss account for the year ended 31 December and a balance sheet as at that date.

Task 2. You must write a report to Mr Wise that explains the use and purpose of the profit and loss account and balance sheet that you produced in Task 1 above.

Element 7.4
IDENTIFY AND EXPLAIN DATA TO MONITOR A BUSINESS

Performance criteria

1 **Identify users of accounting information.**

2 **Explain the reasons for monitoring a business.**

3 **Explain the use of comparisons and variance in monitoring a business.**

4 **Identify and explain key components of information required to monitor a business.**

5 **Explain the implications for the performance of a business from a given set of accounting information.**

6 **Explain the use of solvency ratios, profitability ratios and performance ratios in the interpretation of accounting information.**

Element 7.4 Identify and explain data to monitor a business

USERS OF ACCOUNTING INFORMATION

A number of users of accounting information can be identified.

Internal users

Internal users are those people working within an organisation, more specifically, the directors and managers of an organisation. Financial information is required by managers of an organisation for a number of reasons:

1 to plan and control the business;

2 to aid decision-making;

3 to obtain information for third parties, e.g. banks, shareholders, employees, etc.;

4 to formulate policies.

External users

From an 'external' point of view, there are a number of people, groups of people, organisations, institutions, etc. who would be interested in the accounting information of various businesses.

1 *Owners, proprietors, shareholders* – both actual and potential. Clearly owners of a business would wish to know not only how profitable their business is, but also how efficiently it is performing. By the same token, both actual and potential shareholders would also be interested in the profitability of the company and of course the ability to pay present and future dividends, as well as future objectives and aspirations, in order to assess the scope for capital growth of their shareholdings. Although accounting information clearly cannot forecast the future it can help in forming judgements on what is likely to happen based on the past and present performance of a company. The amount of information required would depend on the size of the investment in the business.

2 *Providers of finance* – i.e. lenders of the business and its creditors. In all cases the providers of finance will want to satisfy themselves that they are likely to have their money repaid! The question of risk will also be analysed, i.e. will the organisation be able to repay its debts? If not, what could be the consequences?

3 *The government*, under its many guises, would also be interested in the accounting information of organisations, e.g. Inland Revenue for tax purposes, Customs and Excise for value added tax, the Department of Trade and Industry for its highly comprehensive periodic compilation of statistics, local authorities for social and economic reasons and, in the case of companies, Company House for annual returns.

4 *Employees and trade unions.* As far as employees are concerned, both present and potential, they would be interested in the finances of a business in order to assess the stability of their employers and in turn the security of their employment. Trade unions would like to see the accounting information of a business for much more

sophisticated reasons and would be seeking answers to the following questions: What is the future demand for employment and indeed the future demand for skills? What are the prospects of the business? What kind of wage increases can be realistically expected? What is management performance like and is there an indication of the future aspirations and goals of the business?

5 *Business contacts* which would include suppliers, customers, and competitors. Suppliers would be interested in the financial stability of the business and would want to ensure that the business has sufficient cash to pay for its goods or services sold on credit (included under point 2 above). Customers would obviously be interested in a business if they had entered into a long-term business relationship with them, or if they were dependent on the business for a substantial part of their supplies. The ability to make continued supplies at competitive prices would be of paramount importance.

Competitors and other business rivals would be very keen to know of any new products, market shares, prices, etc. and may even be interested in mergers and amalgamations or take-overs (as potential investors).

6 *Analysts and advisors* from a number of backgrounds and for a variety of reasons actively research various forms of accounting information on all sorts of businesses. This grouping would include financial analysts, the financial press, stockbrokers, economists, researchers (e.g. government, academic, etc.), insurance companies and credit-rating agencies. The accounting information researched could be for themselves or for their clients or potential clients or simply for public consumption in the case of government statistics.

7 *The public itself* may also be interested in the accounting information, e.g. taxpayers, council tax payers, political parties, consumers, various consumer groups, pressure groups and even environmental groups.

Fig 7.11 Trade unions will also be interested in the finances of the company in as far as they affect the interests of the employees

Element 7.4　Identify and explain data to monitor a business

> **ACTIVITY 7.4.1**
>
> *Task 1.* List the reasons why the following users would need financial information:
> - a manager of a business;
> - a potential shareholder;
> - a bank manager;
> - a customer;
> - trade unions;
> - competitors;
> - a credit-rating agency;
> - a stockbroker.
>
> *Task 2.* Assume a small local business has approached you and has asked you to deliver goods to its premises on 30 days' credit. You have never had any business dealings with it and all you know is that it started trading some $3\frac{1}{2}$ years ago. Write a report to your accounts supervisor, clearly outlining the information you would require before making your decision as to whether or not you should give the business the credit it is asking for.

PC
7.4.1
7.4.2

REASONS FOR MONITORING A BUSINESS

To evaluate and assess the performance of the business

Every business should have goals and objectives that it aims to achieve and as a result there is a need to measure the performance of the business in order to establish whether or not those objectives are being achieved. The persons who effectively run the business, i.e. the management, are also being assessed, therefore, as it is through their policies that ultimately the goals of the business will be achieved.

Performance is measured by comparing actual results against predetermined targets that reflect those objectives. These targets are formalised in what are called forecasts and budgets and we will be examining these in much more detail later. Actual performance is therefore compared to targeted or budgeted performance and any differences closely investigated so that performance may ultimately be improved.

The ultimate objective of a business may not necessarily be 'high profits'. For example, it could be planning to increase sales or to produce environmentally friendly goods and so on. The achievement of reasonable profits is necessary for future investments, however, (and ultimately the future survival of the business) or, in the case of a company, for the payment of dividends. We also need to monitor a business in order to measure its profitability to ensure that it remains in business!

To establish the financial position of the business

A business should not only be profitable, but also have sufficient working capital, i.e. liquid funds (put simply, cash), to meet any short-term obligations, e.g. creditors. The business should also have the ability to maintain that capability and to be able to acquire any future fixed assets that may be required.

The liquidity position of any business needs constant monitoring in order to assess not only present but future working capital requirements. An assessment of its ability to attract future finance is also based on its financial position. Is it financially stable? Is it likely to survive? Is it likely to expand? If so, are its finances in order? Is it likely to be taken over?

To adhere to government regulations

Businesses need to adhere to many government regulations, e.g. Inland Revenue for taxation purposes, Customs and Excise for value added tax purposes and for company law and other legal reasons.

To summarise, therefore, a business needs to be monitored for the following reasons:

- to meet management needs – planning and control, decision-making, policy determination, etc.;
- to measure performance of the management;
- to measure performance of the business;
- to measure profitability of the business;
- to measure liquidity of the business;
- to assess financial position of the business;
- to assess future prospects of the business;
- to adhere to government regulations.

Every business needs regular and periodic monitoring simply to ensure that the business is progressing along satisfactory lines. If it is established that it is not, then corrective action can be taken in order to improve the performance of the business.

ACTIVITY 7.4.2

Task 1. Give six reasons why you think we need to monitor a business.

Task 2. Why do you think it is so important to regularly monitor a business?

Task 3. Why does the management of a business need to be monitored?

Task 4. What do you understand by the term 'financial stability'?

KEY COMPONENTS OF ACCOUNTING INFORMATION

As we have already established businesses need to produce periodic accounting information in order that its performance, most notably its profitability, and its solvency can be monitored. A number of financial statements are prepared periodically, usually monthly (with much more detailed versions annually), so that constant checks on the performance of a business can be made. We will now examine each of these statements in turn.

The trading and profit and loss account

You have learned much of the relevant accounting statements in the previous element 7.3. However we will look again at the profit statement which is called the trade and profit and loss account, which is a historical document for the previous accounting period, e.g. month or year, and shows results over that period of time. It clearly identifies sales and expenses and the gross profit and the net profit.

M Ali
Trading and profit and loss account for the year ended 31 December

	£	£
Sales		100 000
Less Cost of sales:		
Opening stock	25 000	
Add Purchases	45 000	
	70 000	
Less Closing stock	25 000	45 000
Gross profit		55 000
Less Expenses:		
Gas and electricity	5 000	
Wages	20 000	
Rent and rates	10 000	
Insurance	2 500	
Stationery	2 500	
Advertising	5 000	
Provision for depreciation	5 000	50 000
Net profit		5 000

An example is shown below.

This financial statement is in fact broken down into two distinct parts:

- *the trading account*, where the *gross profit* is calculated, i.e. sales less cost of sales; and
- *the profit and loss account* where all of the expenses or costs of the business are identified and subtracted from the gross profit to arrive at the *net profit*.

The trading and profit and loss account is a revenue account and tells the owners of a business (and other interested parties for that matter) how much profit or loss has been made through either its trading or manufacturing operations. The expenses that are itemised in the trading and profit and loss account have been incurred in order to achieve the given amount of sales, and subsequently the profit, for that accounting period, e.g. a year. These expenses are known as *revenue expenses*.

The layout of this particular type of financial statement can vary depending on the approach taken. For example, if the business uses the marginal costing approach, the layout would look slightly different to the account just shown, as can be seen from the account below.

As you would probably expect, the final net profit is exactly the same, but the layout is completely different. This is because a profit statement based on marginal costing assumes that expenses or costs behave in a certain manner. The theory is sometimes called the *contribution theory* and it believes that costs behave in one of two ways: there are those that vary directly in line with output (for example, direct material, direct labour, etc.) and there are those that remain fixed or static irrespective of output (in other words, those costs that have to be incurred no matter what happens). Good examples of fixed costs are rent, rates, insurance, provision for depreciation, etc. It is not always possible to

M Ali
Profit statement – (marginal costing approach) for the year ended 31 December

	£	£
Sales		100 000
Less Variable costs		
Direct material	45 000	
Direct labour	20 000	
Gas and electricity	5 000	
Stationery	2 500	72 500
Total contribution		27 500
Less Fixed costs		
Rent and rates	10 000	
Insurance	2 500	
Advertising (assume all fixed)	5 000	
Provision for depreciation	5 000	22 500
Net profit		5 000

class costs in convenient 'black' and 'white' compartments as we have done. There are many 'grey' areas and some costs may be classed as semi-variable or semi-fixed! This is outside the scope and level of this unit, and we will stick with variable and fixed costs.

You may also have noticed the term *'contribution'*. This was discussed in Unit 6. It is calculated by deducting all our variable costs from our sales. The contribution then goes on to cover any fixed costs and once the fixed costs are covered, net profit is generated! So we have the following:

Sales – Variable costs = Contribution – Fixed costs = Net profit

Therefore, contribution can be calculated in one of two ways:

Contribution = Sales – Variable costs

Contribution = Fixed costs + Net profit

If we now apply the figures from our example, the concept will probably become clearer:

Contribution = 100 000 – 72 500 = 27 500

Contribution = 22 500 + 5 000 = 27 500

We can now take the theory one stage further. If we assume that M Ali produced 1000 units and sold all of them for £100 each, he would have made a total of £100 000 in sales, according to the accounts. We can now work out what we call the break-even point – the point at which he neither makes a profit nor a loss. This is calculated as follows:

$$\text{Break-even point} = \frac{\text{Fixed costs}}{\text{Contribution per unit}}$$

We therefore need to calculate the contribution per unit and this is done as follows:

$$\frac{\text{Total contribution}}{\text{No. of units}}$$

$$= \frac{27\ 500}{1\ 000} = £27.50$$

It is now possible to calculate the break-even point:

$$\frac{22\ 500}{27.50} = 819 \text{ units}$$

We can now say that M Ali must produce and sell 819 units at £1000 each in order to simply break even!

The balance sheet

Having examined two types of profit statements, which as we have seen, are historical as they are reporting past events, we should now move our attention to what is called the *balance sheet*, an example of which is shown over the page.

M Ali
Balance sheet as at 31 December

	Cost £	Depreciation to date £	Net book value £
Fixed assets			
Land and buildings	50 000	5 000	45 000
Plant and machinery	40 000	10 000	30 000
Motor vehicles	30 000	15 000	15 000
Fixtures and fittings	20 000	10 000	10 000
	140 000	40 000	100 000
Current assets			
Stock		25 000	
Debtors		30 000	
Bank		10 000	
Cash		5 000	
		70 000	
Less Current liabilities			
Creditors		40 000	
Working capital			30 000
Total net assets			130 000
Less Long-term loans			27 500
			102 500
Financed by			
Capital			100 000
Plus Net profit for the year		5 000	
Less Drawings		2 500	2 500
			102 500

Whereas the trading and profit and loss account was historical, (note the title refers to 'for the year ended'), the balance sheet is a financial statement which is not for a period of time but 'as at' (note the title) a particular point in time, i.e. the year-ended. A balance sheet refers to a specific point in time and is dated as such.

As you learned in element 7.1 there are traditionally five components to a balance sheet which we now re-examine briefly:

- *Fixed assets*. Whereas revenue expenses were dealt with in the profit and loss account, expenditure assets on capital (i.e. those that will help to make a profit for more than one year) are dealt with in the balance sheet. Fixed assets have a relatively long life, usually cost a lot, are relatively fixed in nature and purchased by a business so that it may perform its operations, e.g. land and buildings, plant and machinery, etc.

- *Current assets*. These differ from fixed assets in that they are constantly changing on a daily basis and are much more easily liquidated, e.g. stock debtors, bank and cash. (Note that these are presented in a balance sheet in that order, known as the *order of liquidity*.)

- *Current liabilities*. These represent the amount of money that a business owes to other people or organisations. The liabilities are referred to as 'current' because they must be repaid within a period of twelve months. Typical examples include trade creditors and a bank overdraft.

- *Capital*. This is the amount the owners or proprietors of the business have invested out of their own pockets into the business. This figure should hopefully be increased by subsequent years' profits being made.

- *Long-term liabilities*. This is a term used to refer to loan or borrowed capital, i.e. what the owners or proprietors have borrowed in order to finance the business effectively.

Whereas the trading and profit and loss account showed us the profitability of a business, the balance sheet shows us the financial position of the business, e.g. its liquidity position – the working capital, i.e. the amount of liquid funds available to the business.

You should be made aware at this stage that the format of a set of final accounts – i.e. the trading and profit and loss account and the balance sheet – varies according to the type of organisation in question, e.g. sole trader, partnership, manufacturer, company, etc. In essence they all follow the same fundamental principles, however.

A cash flow forecast

Now that we have looked at the past and the present, we should look or try to look into the future! A *cash flow forecast* was outlined in detail in element 7.2 and it attempts to assess our future cash needs. A typical cash flow forecast is shown on the next page.

A cash flow forecast attempts to establish if there are any future cash flow problems! If a problem is identified, then management must ask how large that potential problem is and how long that potential problem will last.

If a business can establish potential cash flow problems then corrective action before the event can be taken, e.g. the borrowing of temporary funds, the postponing of certain projects, etc. Effective working capital management (or, put simply, cash management) is crucial to any business as there must be sufficient cash to pay creditors; otherwise the creditors may refuse to supply goods and services which the business needs to maintain the operation and to ultimately make a profit!

Aged debtors and aged creditors reports

An 'ageing schedule' for both debtors and creditors should be prepared by all businesses trading on credit. An aged debtors schedule tells a business precisely how old debts owing to it by customers actually are; 'chasing' debts is therefore made easier. As far as creditors are concerned, an ageing schedule would also be useful in that it would tell a

M Ali
Cash flow forecast for the six month period from January to end of June

	Jan £	Feb £	March £	April £	May £	June £
Cash and bank balance b/fwd	15 000	16 250	17 550	16 350	15 150	16 450
Receipts						
Debtors	9 000	9 000	9 000	9 000	9 000	9 000
Total receipts	9 000	9 000	9 000	9 000	9 000	9 000
Payments						
Trade Creditors	5 000	5 000	5 000	5 000	5 000	5 000
Wages	1 700	1 700	1 700	1 700	1 700	1 700
Stationery	200	200	200	200	200	200
Gas and electricity	450	400	400	400	400	400
Rent and rates			2 500			2 500
Insurance				2 500		
Advertising	400	400	400	400	400	400
Total payments	7 750	7 700	10 200	10 200	7 700	10 200
Bank balance c/fwd	16 250	17 550	16 350	15 150	16 450	15 250

business precisely how much needs to be paid in the following month, for example, and total outstanding debts. Ageing both debtors and creditors is a significant aid to cash management and therefore complements the preparation of a cash flow forecast. The ageing of debtors also assists in identifying potential or possible bad debts, or in the creation of a provision for bad debts.

The budget

So far we have discussed financial statements that provide a business with actual accounting information and we have mentioned 'targets', 'forecasts' and 'budgets'.

As we have seen, every business has goals and objectives and they are implemented through the policies as directed by the management. The budget is the final piece in the jigsaw, as it is the plan or forecast to implement those policies expressed in financial terms. Most businesses will prepare an annual budget which will be further split into months. There are many types of budgets which we should now identify.

1 *The master budget*. When all the budgets described below are completed and accepted by the business, they will be incorporated into what is known as the master budget which will also include a budgeted trading and profit and loss account, a budgeted balance sheet and a budgeted or forecasted cash flow statement. This is because these

statements represent the 'summary' of all the other budgets and their contents. The contents and presentation of these statements will be identical to those described earlier. A budgeted trading and profit and loss account will look identical in appearance and content to an actual trading and profit and loss account. These budgeted financial statements give the business direction and targets to aim for so that management will know whether or not the business is on course to achieve the desired objectives. The budget therefore offers a business a yardstick against which it can measure its performance.

2 *The sales budget* gives a detailed breakdown of planned sales, i.e. by product, area, etc.

3 *The production budget* will, of course, mirror the sales budget as it will be based on the information in the sales budget, i.e. assuming the business is a manufacturer, it can only sell what it produces. It will therefore contain quantities of products to be produced, together with costs such as direct materials, labour and overheads.

4 *Departmental budgets* clearly detail specific expenses for each department, e.g. accounts, marketing, sales, works, personnel, etc. These will be revenue expenses as summarised in the final budgeted trading and profit and loss account.

5 *Capital expenditure budgets* will include capital expenditure for things such as plant and machinery, fixtures and fittings, computers, motor vehicles, i.e. any fixed assets which may need to be purchased in order to fulfil the objectives of the business.

6 *Cash budgets*. We discussed the need for a cash budget earlier in this Unit and its part in the master budget. The business will need to know its future working capital requirements, in order to achieve its desired goals!

The budget will therefore provide targets for the management to achieve. Periodically, probably monthly, actual results will be compared to budgeted targets and the variances obtained (the difference between the two) will have to be investigated and explained. Any corrective action necessary can therefore be taken.

ACTIVITY 7.4.3

PC 7.4.4

Task 1. Match the following financial statement to the corresponding descriptions:

Profit and loss account	Present
Balance sheet	Historical
Trading account	Future
Cash flow forecast	Historical

Task 2. Explain the differences between the following terms:
- a capital expense and a revenue expense;
- a fixed asset and a current asset;
- a variable cost and a fixed cost;
- sales and cost of sales;
- a sales budget and a production budget.

Unit 7 Financial forecasting and monitoring

> **ACTIVITY 7.4.4**
>
> *Task 1.* If a business sold a unit for £10 which had a variable cost of £6, what would be the break-even point of the business if its fixed costs averaged £50 000 per year?
>
> *Task 2.* Define the following terms: working capital; a budget; an aged debtors report; a master budget.

RATIO ANALYSIS

Ratio analysis is a technique used to interpret a set of accounts so that comparisons can be made between different accounting periods (e.g. months, years, etc.), between different businesses, between forecast or targeted figures and actual, and so on. Through these comparisons and the identification of further trends the performance of a business can be assessed.

Profitability ratios

Profitability ratios attempt to measure the profitability of a business.

1 *The gross profit percentage* is calculated as follows:

$$\text{Gross profit percentage} = \frac{\text{Gross profit}}{\text{Net sales}} \times 100$$

2 The *net profit percentage* is calculated as follows:

$$\text{Net profit percentage} = \frac{\text{Net profit}}{\text{Net sales}} \times 100$$

Both the above ratios are usually referred to as 'profit margin' ratios and attempt to measure the profitability of a business in relation to its sales. In other words, they calculate the profit in £s for every £100 of sales made. These ratios are excellent for comparative purposes, e.g. comparing this year's profit with last year's, or with the forecast or with other businesses in the same industry.

3 *The return on capital employed* (ROCE) is a much better indicator, however. This is calculated by:

$$\text{ROCE} = \frac{\text{Net profit}}{\text{Capital employed}} \times 100 \quad or \quad \frac{\text{Net profit}}{\text{Net assets}} \times 100$$

This ratio is sometimes referred to as the 'prime ratio' and is perhaps the 'best' performance indicator as it measures net profit against actual capital employed by the business. Capital employed is the *total* capital being used by the business, i.e. owners' capital, loan capital, profits reinvested, etc.

4 *The return on owners' equity (ROE)* is similar to ROCE but differs in that it relates the net profit to the amount actually invested by the owners of the business, i.e. proprietors or shareholders, and is thus calculated as follows:

$$\text{ROE} = \frac{\text{Net profit}}{\text{Owners' equity}} \times 100$$

Before we move on to liquidity ratios it is worth noting two further ratios which are complementary to those so far discussed

5 **Expenses ratio** = $\dfrac{\text{Expenses}}{\text{Net sales}} \times 100$

6 **Cost of sales ratio** = $\dfrac{\text{Cost of sales}}{\text{Net sales}} \times 100$

It should be noted that whereas for profitability ratios 1 to 4 in the list we were looking for as high a return as possible – the higher the ratio, the better – with ratios 5 and 6 in the list the reverse is true, as we are now talking about expenses, i.e. costs. Therefore, the lower the percentage, the better!

Liquidity ratios

Liquidity ratios measure the liquidity or solvency of a business. It is not sufficient for a business to be merely profitable as it must also have sufficient short-term liquid funds to meet any financial obligations as they fall due, e.g. creditors requesting payments.

A business should not only be profitable, therefore, but also liquid. If there are insufficient liquid funds available (put simply, cash) to meet suppliers' demands, then profits will never materialise. Students must appreciate the close relationship between profitability and liquidity – they are of equal importance!

There are a number of ratios that test solvency which we should now examine and we will start with:

7 *The Current ratio* (sometimes referred to as the *liquidity ratio*) which is calculated as follows:

$$\text{Current ratio} = \frac{\text{Current assets}}{\text{Current liabilities}}$$

This ratio is *not* expressed as a percentage but as a ratio of one, i.e. x:1 and it simply measures the ability of a business to meet its short-term obligations, i.e. its debts. It seeks to establish whether or not a business has sufficient current assets to meet its current liabilities. The ratio effectively measures the number of times the current assets of a business cover its current liabilities and is, therefore, an extremely important ratio to potential and existing creditors as well as the business itself. A 2:1 ratio is normally regarded as the 'textbook,' most appropriate, 'optimum' ratio.

Great care should be taken, however, as differences will occur depending on the nature of the business and indeed the industry within which it operates. For example, a retailer who transacts most of its business on a cash basis (but still has the luxury of trading on credit with its suppliers) can trade very successfully on a much lower ratio than 2:1, e.g. Marks and Spencer PLC. Furthermore in present times of recession even the manufacturing sector has had to survive and trade on a much lower ratio than 2:1. Clearly, if the ratio falls too close to 1:1, where current assets barely cover current liabilities, the business is in danger of not being able to meet its financial obligations, i.e. its debts, as they fall due. If the ratio falls below one, then the firm will have insufficient liquid funds to stay in business for very long!

It should also be noted that a current ratio very much higher than 2:1 can be 'too good'. It means that the business is not utilising its financial resources efficiently and should, therefore, transfer its funds into more profitable investments! Clearly, a balance to achieve an optimum ratio is what is called for.

8 *The acid or quick test* is calculated as follows:

$$= \frac{\text{Current assets} - \text{Stock}}{\text{Current liability}}$$

Again expressed as a ratio, the acid test also measures the liquidity position of a business and is perhaps a better measure than the current ratio, as it omits or does not recognise (for the purposes of liquidity) stock – hence the name 'acid test'! The reason for not recognising stock in the calculation is that the stock of a business is usually the most difficult to liquidate as the stock could be old, obsolete, slow moving, or there could simply be a lack of demand for it! The other current assets are already liquid, e.g. cash and bank, or are easier to liquidate, e.g. debtors. In this instance a ratio of less than 1:1 would signify a liquidity problem and this situation will not be sustained for a prolonged period of time, as the business will simply not have the necessary liquid funds to survive.

As the acid test obviously relates closely to the current ratio, comments mentioned earlier also apply in this instance.

9 *Average Debtors Collection Period* measures how quickly the business debtors pay on average and is calculated as follows:

$$\frac{\text{Average debtors}}{\text{Credit sales}} \times 365 = \text{number of days}$$

It can also be expressed in terms of weeks or months by multiplying by 52 or 12 instead of 365, but the number of days is probably the most popular. In this instance it is preferable to collect your outstanding debts as quickly as possible but only up to the point where your customer legitimately finds it reasonable. You should ask yourself a simple question, 'Could your customers obtain better credit terms elsewhere?' If your customer could obtain better credit terms elsewhere and you value the business, you should not be overzealous in that you obtain your outstanding debts so quickly that you may lose the business. Clearly an optimum credit facility agreed between yourselves and your customer should be aimed at.

The ratio is useful, therefore, to measure the efficiency of the collection process and for comparability with previous accounting periods (months or years), or with other businesses particularly in the same industry. As a rule the quicker you collect your debts the better but this general rule should be applied with caution. If the number of days rises to 'unacceptable' levels (this could depend on the policy of the business and indeed the industry itself), the credit collection procedures, the staff implementing them or the policies of the business itself, should be examined.

10 *Average Creditors Payment Period* measures how quickly the business pays its creditors on average and is calculated as follows:

$$\frac{\text{Average creditors}}{\text{Credit purchases}} \times 365 = \text{number of days}$$

This ratio can also be expressed in terms of weeks and months by multiplying by 52 or 12, respectively, instead of 365, but, again the number of days is probably the most popular. In this instance it is clearly preferable to withhold payment to your creditors for as long as possible and, therefore, obtain maximum credit facilities. You should again be cautious, however, as refraining from payment for too long would more than likely upset your supplier with the probable result of having your credit facilities withdrawn, preventing future deliveries until payment is made (thus disrupting your work schedule) or ultimately suppliers simply not wishing to trade with you. Trying to obtain 'too much' credit could be to your detriment, therefore. As in the previous ratio, an optimum situation where both you and your supplier are happy should be sought.

This ratio is related to the debtors ratio above in that if a business does not collect its outstanding debtors quickly enough there will be insufficient cash to pay the creditors on time! Therefore the ability to pay creditors is dependent on cash availability which in part is affected by debtors paying their debts on time.

Average stock turnover ratio

Average stock turnover ratio measures how efficiently a business turns over its stock and is calculated as follows:

$$\frac{\text{Cost of sales}}{\text{Average stock held}} = \text{number of times turned over}$$

Clearly the faster stock is turned over, i.e. the quicker a business despatches its goods to customers out of its warehouse, the better. This means stock is not lying around in the warehouse, not only incurring additional warehousing costs (wages, rent, heat, etc.) but also, perhaps more importantly, having working capital tied up in the assets which could be released and used more efficiently elsewhere. Good stock management is therefore crucial! The higher the number of times turnover, the better.

Capital ratios

Gearing Ratio attempts to measure the amount of loan capital against the equity of a business, i.e. proprietors' funds. In other words, it measures the relationship between the amount a proprietor has borrowed (on a long-term basis) to set up and run his or her business and the amount the proprietor has invested in the business out of his or her own pocket and eventually generated by the business itself.

A number of methods of calculation exist. The most popular is probably:

$$\frac{\text{Loan capital}}{\text{Total capital employed}} \times 100$$

where the percentage calculated represents the proportion of borrowed funds, i.e. loan capital, as opposed to total capital employed within the business as a whole. Too high a ratio here would inevitably lead to vast amounts of profits having to be used to pay out interest charges, thus limiting funds for investment or for paying out dividends (in the case of companies) to existing and potential shareholders. A good example of too much borrowed money being used to finance a business was the Maxwell Empire! Obviously potential investors (shareholders) and money lenders (banks and other financial institutions) would find this ratio of great interest in that, if too much of the future profits of the business are already accounted for in future interest payments, there will be less available to pay any future dividends and additional interests charges.

Interest Cover Ratio is calculated by the following formula:

$$\frac{\text{Profit before interest}}{\text{Interest charges for the year}} = \text{number of times cover}$$

This ratio measures how well placed a business is to cover its interest payment on its loans. In other words, by how much can profits go down before the business is unable to meet interest payments on its loans? Clearly, the higher the cover, the better. Obviously, this ratio would be of considerable interest to present and potential lenders.

Other supporting ratios

There are many ratios we have not discussed as they are outside the scope of this course and this level of study. We should perhaps look at one further type of ratio – asset turnover ratios.

Asset turnover ratios

Asset Turnover Ratios measure how efficiently the assets have been used to generate the given amount of sales. Clearly the higher the turnover, the better. The 'overall' asset turnover ratio is calculated as:

$$\frac{\text{Sales}}{\text{Total net assets}} = \text{number of times turned over}$$

However, each asset or group of assets can be broken down in turn to pinpoint particular areas of weaknesses or strengths. For example:

$$\frac{\text{Sales}}{\text{Fixed assets}} \qquad \frac{\text{Sales}}{\text{Current assets}}$$

$$\frac{\text{Sales}}{\text{Plant and machinery}} \qquad \frac{\text{Sales}}{\text{Stocks}}$$

$$\frac{\text{Sales}}{\text{Land and buildings}} \qquad \frac{\text{Sales}}{\text{Debtors}}$$

Element 7.4 Identify and explain data to monitor a business

The limitations of ratio analysis

Ratio anaylsis can be used as an effective tool to measure the performance of a business through the calculation of ratios, measuring or identifying trends and comparing with previous accounting periods or standards, i.e. budgeted or forecasted figures, or with other businesses in the same field, i.e. industrial averages or norms published by various agencies. The technique does have its limitations, however.

The important point to remember is that for any comparison to be meaningful and credible, you must compare like with like and be consistent in the basis of your comparisons.

1. One should really only compare figures between two businesses within the same industry (e.g. textile industry, food industry) as comparisons across the economy as a whole may give misleading interpretations.

2. One should ensure that the accounting periods cover the same time span, i.e. one month compared to one month, and one year to one year. This is particularly important when comparing one business with another – the accounting periods may not always coincide.

3. Beware of changes in accounting policies or indeed differences in accounting policies from one business to another, e.g. a change in the method of calculating depreciation from straight-line one year to the reducing-balance method the following year.

4. Another problem is the distorting effect of inflation. Sales and profits may have increased, but the monetary value of one year's figures as compared to, say, the preceding year's figures may be considerably less due to the ravages of inflation. The ratio calculated could be painting a much improved picture!

5. Remember much of the information on which you are basing your ratios is historical, e.g. the trading and profit and loss account. The information is last year's figures – not present-day figures!

6. The ratios that you calculate are only as good as the figures on which you base them. In some organisations, management information systems may be poor! Some ratios are open to manipulation and should be interpreted with great care, e.g. cash at bank could be held artificially high by management by simply withholding payment to suppliers immediately before the year end!

7. The nature of the business of the organisation may change, e.g. the sales mix or different markets.

8. The final problem is one of 'statistics'. Consider the scenario outlined in Table 7.1.

Table 7.1

	Business A		Business B	
	Yr 1	Yr 2	Yr 1	Yr 2
Sales	£100	£150	£100	£150
Net profit	£5	£15	£15	£30
Net profit (%)	5%	10%	15%	20%

579

Although Business B is far more profitable, both actually and from a net profit percentage point of view, one could argue that Business A's profits have increased threefold and its net profit percentage doubled, whereas Business B's profit have 'only' doubled and its net profit percentage increased by 'only' a third!

Put that way, it would sound as if Business A had outperformed Business B! You must therefore beware how ratios have been interpreted and presented to you!

Although ratio analysis does have its limitations, it does not mean that it is in any way devalued as a technique. An awareness of those limitations, however, should make the user of those ratios more cautious in assessing financial information.

The important point for you to realise is that ratio analysis is an effective tool in measuring the performance of a business, providing that you appreciate the limitations outlined above. You should also realise that any analysis of a business should include all possible accounting information on which you can make judgements, e.g. forecasts, budgets, trends, etc. as well as ratio analysis.

Presentation of the interpretation of calculated ratios

The ratios which are to be calculated at any time will depend entirely on the task in hand. For example, if you are asked to comment on the liquidity position of a business, ratios which are pertinent to that subject should be calculated and applied. It is not necessary, therefore, to calculate all of the ratios you have learned to every problem. You should always read the question very carefully and consider which ratios you need apply. Once you have decided on which ratios you will need, follow this procedure:

1 Calculate the identified ratios and show *all* workings.

2 If a report is asked for, do not forget to head up the report appropriately. Even if a formal report is not asked for, you should keep the following in mind when preparing your commentary:

   a Include summary of all calculated ratios and any other supporting yardsticks which may be given in the task, e.g. targets, industrial norms, etc. – making a comparison easy and straightforward.
   b Identify your objectives in your introduction clearly – these are usually given to you in your task;
   c Make appropriate comments on the ratios calculated plus any other trends and comparisons you can identify. You may find it useful to use headings (depending on your objectives above). Refer to the original task for your main headings.
   d Offer firm conclusions, recommendations and answers to your objectives in a, which should answer the task in question.

Particularly in 2 and a, it is important that you do not simply describe the figures you have calculated throughout the entire commentary. All you are doing is repeating yourself – in the first instance numerically and in the second (in the commentary) alphabetically. You should be analytical in your thoughts, whenever possible, and offer possible reasons for the said ratios being what they are and the consequences if appropriate action is not taken. Proper recommendations and suggestions for alternative action should be offered with firm conclusions in the final analysis, together with any advice you find appropriate to help answer the problem you have been set.

Remember your presentation should be neat, tidy and pleasing to the eye. Many people are wary of figures so it does not help if your findings are not presented in a professional manner.

An example of ratio analysis

Now that we have discussed ratios analysis, their calculation, application, limitations and interpretation, we can now work through an example.

You are employed as an accounting assistant at James Matthews, a trader who imports much of its goods, and Mr Matthews himself asks you to:

1 calculate as many accounting ratios as you can; and

2 compile a report for Mr Matthews on the financial performance of his business, taking into consideration the ratios you have calculated in 1 above.

You are provided with the last two years' trading and profit and loss accounts and balance sheets, together with the following additional information.

James Matthews & Co.
Trading and profit and loss accounts for the years ended 31.12.92 and 31.12.93

	31.12.92 £	31.12.92 £	31.12.93 £	31.12.93 £
Sales		170 000		195 000
Less Returns in		10 000		5 000
		160 000		190 000
Less Cost of sales				
Opening stock	20 000		30 000	
Plus Purchases	90 000		155 000	
Less Closing stock	30 000	80 000	75 000	110 000
Gross profit		80 000		80 000
Less Expenses		40 000		50 000
Net profit		40 000		30 000

James Matthews & Co.
Balance sheets as at 31.12.92 and 31.12.93

	31.12.92 £	31.12.92 £	31.12.93 £	31.12.93 £
Fixed assets				
Buildings		60 000		70 000
Plant and machinery		30 000		40 000
Motor vehicles		20 000		25 000
		110 000		135 000
Current assets				
Stocks	30 000		75 000	
Debtors	30 000		60 000	
Bank	14 000		–	
Cash	1 000		5 000	
	75 000		140 000	
Less **Current liabilities**				
Creditors	30 000		55 000	
Bank overdraft	–		45 000	
	30 000	45 000	100 000	40 000
Net assets		155 000		175 000
Financed by:				
Capital		85 000		125 000
Net profit		40 000		30 000
Long-term Loan		30 000		20 000
		155 000		175 000

The following additional information should also be noted.

1 The total sales after any returns are broken down as follows:

    1992 Cash sales   £10 000
                Credit sales £150 000

    1993 Cash sales   £30 000
                Credit sales £160 000

2 All purchases were on credit.

3 Debtors at 31.12.91 amounted to £20 000.

4 Creditors at 31.12.91 amounted to £20 000.

5 Interest charges included in the expenses figure for 1992 were £3000 and 1993 was £2000.

Element 7.4 Identify and explain data to monitor a business

Based on the following information provided, your findings should be presented in the following way.

James Matthews & Co – Workings

1 *Gross profit percentage* = $\dfrac{\text{Gross profit}}{\text{Net sales}} \times 100$

1992 $\dfrac{80\,000}{160\,000} \times 100 = 50\%$ **1993** $\dfrac{80\,000}{190\,000} \times 100 = 42.1\%$

2 *Net profit percentage* = $\dfrac{\text{Net profit}}{\text{Net sales}} \times 100$

1992 $\dfrac{40\,000}{160\,000} \times 100 = 25\%$ **1993** $\dfrac{30\,000}{190\,000} \times 100 = 15.8\%$

3 *Return on capital employed* (ROCE) = $\dfrac{\text{Net profit}}{\text{Capital employed}} \times 100$

1992 $\dfrac{40\,000}{155\,000} \times 100 = 25.8\%$ **1993** $\dfrac{30\,000}{175\,000} \times 100 = 17.1\%$

4 *Return on (owner's) equity* (ROE) = $\dfrac{\text{Net profit}}{\text{Owner's equity}} \times 100$

1992 $\dfrac{40\,000}{125\,000} \times 100 = 32\%$ **1993** $\dfrac{30\,000}{155\,000} \times 100 = 19.4\%$

5 *Expenses percentage* = $\dfrac{\text{Expenses}}{\text{Net sales}} \times 100$

1992 $\dfrac{40\,000}{160\,000} \times 100 = 25.1\%$ **1993** $\dfrac{50\,000}{190\,000} \times 100 = 26.3\%$

6 *Cost of sales ratio* = $\dfrac{\text{Cost of sales}}{\text{Net sales}} \times 100$

1992 $\dfrac{80\,000}{160\,000} \times 100 = 50\%$ **1993** $\dfrac{110\,000}{190\,000} \times 100 = 57.9\%$

7 *Current ratio* = $\dfrac{\text{Current assets}}{\text{Current liabilities}}$

1992 $\dfrac{75\,000}{30\,000} = 2.5:1$ **1993** $\dfrac{140\,000}{100\,000} = 1.4:1$

8 $\text{Acid test} = \dfrac{\text{Current assets} - \text{Stock}}{\text{Current liabilities}}$

1992 $\dfrac{75\,000 - 30\,000}{30\,000} = 1.5:1$ **1993** $\dfrac{140\,000 - 75\,000}{100\,000} = 0.65:1$

9 $\text{Average debtors collection period} = \dfrac{\text{Average debtors}}{\text{Net credit sales}} \times 365$

1992 $\dfrac{(20\,000 + 30\,000)/2}{150\,000} \times 365$ = 60.8 days

1993 $\dfrac{(30\,000 + 60\,000)/2}{160\,000} \times 365$ = 102.7 days

10 $\text{Average creditors payment period} = \dfrac{\text{Average creditors}}{\text{Credit purchases}} \times 365$

1992 $\dfrac{(30\,000 + 30\,000)/2}{90\,000} \times 365$ = 101.4 days

1993 $\dfrac{(30\,000 + 55\,000)/2}{155\,000} \times 365$ = 100 days

11 $\text{Stock turnover ratio} = \dfrac{\text{Cost sales}}{\text{Average stock held during the year}}$

1992 $\dfrac{80\,000}{(20\,000 + 30\,000)/2} = 3.2 \text{ times}$

1993 $\dfrac{110\,000}{(30\,000 + 75\,000)/2} = 2.1 \text{ times}$

12 $\text{Gearing} = \dfrac{\text{Loan capital}}{\text{Total capital employed}} \times 100$

1992 $\dfrac{30\,000}{155\,000} \times 100 = 19.4\%$ **1993** $\dfrac{20\,000}{175\,000} \times 100 = 11.4\%$

13 $\text{Interest cover ratio} = \dfrac{\text{Profit before interest}}{\text{Interest charges for period}}$

1992 $\dfrac{43\,000}{3\,000} = 14.3 \text{ times}$ **1993** $\dfrac{32\,000}{2\,000} = 16 \text{ times}$

14 $\text{Asset turnover} = \dfrac{\text{Sales}}{\text{Net sales}}$

1992 $\dfrac{160\,000}{155\,000} = 1:1$ **1993** $\dfrac{190\,000}{175\,000} = 1.1:1$

Ratio summary

Ratio	1992	1993
Gross profit percentage	50%	42.1%
Net profit percentage	25%	15.8%
ROCE	25.8%	17.1%
ROE	32%	19.4%
Expenses percentage	25%	26.3%
Cost of sales ratio	50%	57.9%
Current ratio	2.5:1	1.4:1
Acid test	1.5:1	0.65:1
Average debtors collection period	60.8 days	102.7 days
Average creditors payment period	101.4 days	100 days
Stock turnover ratio	3.2 times	2.1 times
Gearing	19.4%	11.4%
Interest cover ratio	14.3 times	16 times
Asset turnover ratio	1.1	1.1:1

REPORT

To   Mr J Matthews
From Yourself
Date 1 December 1994

Subject: Financial Performance of James Matthews & Co. 1992–3

The object of this report is to analyse the financial performance of the business over the last two years.

Profitability

From a profitability point of view there certainly appears to be a marked deterioration in the second year. All profitability ratios have decreased quite substantially! The net profit percentage has fallen over 9 per cent representing a 37 per cent reduction in the net profit percentage. The primary cause for this appears to be an increase in the cost of sales ratio up 7.9 per cent. The causes of this must be investigated but could possibly be: an increase in suppliers' prices, thus increasing our raw material cost; a drop in value of the pound; a high degree of theft from stores; or a reduction in our selling prices. Expenses have also played their part – increased by 1.3 per cent – although to a much smaller degree. A much higher control over expenses should be exercised. The ROCE and ROE figures have also both dramatically decreased with falls of 34 per cent and 40 per cent respectively. This is as a direct result of profitability decreasing by 25 per cent and the capital base increasing by 13 per cent. In other words more assets have been used to generate less profits.

Liquidity

From a liquidity point of view, the position is no better! Both the current ratio and the acid test have fallen dramatically – down from 2.5:1 and 1.5:1 to 1.4:1 and 0.65:1 respectively. Both decreases are alarming and point to imminent cash flow problems if the situation is not rectified immediately. All the supporting liquidity ratios have deteriorated and in fact point to the cause of the problem. For example, debtors seem to be out of control – up from 60.8 days to 102.7 days – an increase of 41.9 days. We are not given any indication that it was the policy of the business to offer extended credit facilities to stimulate sales, therefore, we can only assume that ineffective debt collection procedures or the failure of the staff to implement them have caused this massive increase in the number of days' credit given.

We should also look at our buying policies and the management of our stock, as our stock levels have increased 2.5 times, with the result that our stock turnover ratio has fallen 34 per cent to 2.1 times. Both our debtors and our stock have cash tied up in them unnecessarily and this should be released through the implementation of much tighter credit control procedures and more efficient stock management so that the liquid position could be improved and the cash put to more effective use.

The movement of the bank balance at the beginning of 1993 of £14 000 to the overdraft position at the end of 1993 of £45 000 has effectively been financing the increase in our stock levels, the extension of credit facilities being given to our customer and the purchase of additional fixed assets to the tune of £25 000. This position must be reversed! The dramatic fall in the profitability of the business has also had a marked effect on the liquidity of the business, i.e. no profits, no cash.

Capital ratios

The gearing of the business has decreased due to the repayment of part of the loan – £10 000 and an increase in the capital (equity) base of the business. The interest cover ratio has improved as the interest repayments have been lower due to a repayment of part of the loan, despite the reduction in net profit. At 11.4 per cent the business is therefore 'lowly geared' which offers scope for the possibility of attracting prospective lenders – a possibility if an immediate injection of additional working capital is called for if the liquidity position does not improve immediately!

Conclusion

The business seems to have hit problems in 1993 from both a profitability and liquidity point of view. The decreases in the ratios have been both dramatic and alarming and I suggest the implementation of the following advice in an attempt to rectify the position as quickly as possible.

1 Identify reasons for the sudden increase in cost of sales ratio and take appropriate action, e.g. change of supplier, increases in selling prices, if possible etc.
2 Greater control over future expenditure.
3 Implement more effective credit control procedures and/or look at skills of staff in the Credit Control Department.
4 Reduce stock to manageable levels.
5 You may need an immediate injection of working capital to tide you over this imminent crisis. The gearing and the interest cover ratio give plenty of scope for the eventuality.

Finally, the situation the business finds itself is not irredeemable. Through careful management of the working capital and a more efficient use of the asset base a return to more profitable and solvent days is possible.

Element 7.4 Identify and explain data to monitor a business

ACTIVITY 7.4.5

Singh & Co. are traders, who are wholesalers dealing in a popular range of goods. You are presented with the following summarised forecast and actual (respectively) profit and loss accounts and balance sheets as at 31 December 1993.

Task. Compare the actual set of final accounts of Singh & Co. against the forecast and comment as to whether or not in your opinion the business has performed better or worse than predicted. You should support your comments with appropriate ratios and mention what further information you would require before reaching any firmer conclusions.

PC
7.4.3
7.4.4
7.4.5
7.4.6

Profit and loss accounts for the year ended 31.12.93

	Forecast £000s	Forecast £000s	Actual £000s	Actual £000s
Sales		1 200		1 600
Cost of sales		900		1 248
Gross profit		300		352
Administration expenses	138		156	
Selling & dist. expenses	66		100	
		204		256
		96		96

Balance sheet as at 31.12.93

	Forecast £000s	Forecast £000s	Actual £000s	Actual £000s
Fixed assets				
Motor Cars		124		152
Fittings		58		94
		182		246
Current assets				
Stock	112		104	
Debtors	150		134	
Bank	16		–	
	278		238	
Less current liabilities				
Creditors	76		156	
Bank OD	–		8	
	76		164	
Working capital		202		74
Total net assets		384		320

Self assessment questions

1. How is net profit calculated?
   a Sales – Cost of sales
   b Gross profit – Cost of sales
   c Sales – Expenses
   d Gross profit – Expenses

2. Which of the following is a revenue expense?
   a Debtors
   b Creditors
   c Cost of sales
   d Wages and salaries

3. Which of the following is a current asset?
   a Debtors
   b Creditors
   c Cost of sales
   d Wages and salaries

4. What does the acid test evaluate?
   a Liquidity
   b Profitability
   c Capital structure
   d Cash availability

5. Is the return on capital employed (ROCE) a measure of a firm's:
   a Sales
   b Liquidity
   c Profitability
   d Solvency?

6. To calculate the current ratio, current liabilities are compared to:
   a Current assets
   b Fixed assets
   c Total assets
   d Net assets?

7. When calculating the acid or quick test, what is deducted from current assets before comparing to current liabilities?
   a Opening stock
   b Debtors
   c Closing stock
   d Creditors

8. Is the gross profit percentage ratio a measure of a return on:
   a Sales margin
   b Cost of sales
   c Sales
   d Credit sales?

Element 7.4 Identify and explain data to monitor a business

9. Gearing attempts to relate:
   a. Loan capital to shareholders' funds
   b. Profitability to liquidity
   c. Capital to profitability
   d. Profit to sales?

10. The net profit percentage measures:
    a. Return on capital employed
    b. Return on sales
    c. Return on total net assets
    d. Return on assets?

11. The average debtors collection period is calculated by:

    $\dfrac{\text{Debtors}}{X} \times \text{No. of days.}$ What is X?

    a. Cash sales
    b. Cash and credit sales
    c. Credit sales
    d. Total sales

12. The average creditors payment period measures how quickly it takes a business to pay its:
    a. Credit sales
    b. Purchases
    c. Creditors
    d. Cost of sales?

13. What does capital employed equal?
    a. Total current assets
    b. Total net assets
    c. Total fixed assets
    d. Total assets

Unit 7 Financial forecasting and monitoring

PC
7.4.3
7.4.4
7.4.5
7.4.6

Assignment

Nichols and Myers Trading and profit and loss accounts for the years ended

	Nichols 31.12.92 £	Myers 31.12.92 £	Nicols 31.12.93 £	Myers 31.12.93 £
Sales	200 000	250 000	250 000	280 000
Cost of sales	100 000	180 000	125 000	190 000
Gross profit	100 000	70 000	125 000	90 000
Expenses	50 000	20 000	70 000	40 000
Net profit	50 000	50 000	55 000	50 000

Balance sheet as at

	Nichols 31.12.92 £	Myers 31.12.92 £	Nichols 31.12.93 £	Myers 31.12.93 £
Fixed assets (net book value)				
Buildings	50 000	80 000	60 000	90 000
Motor vans	20 000	30 000	25 000	30 000
Fixtures and fittings	5 000	5 000	5 000	5 000
	75 000	115 000	90 000	125 000
Current assets				
Stocks	60 000	30 000	65 000	80 000
Debtors	70 000	60 000	35 000	70 000
Bank and cash	–	50 000	30 000	5 000
	130 000	140 000	130 000	155 000
Less Current liabilities				
Creditors	(45 000)	(60 000)	(50 000)	(65 000)
Working capital	85 000	80 000	80 000	90 000
Net assets (i.e. Fixed assets and working capital)	160 000	195 000	170 000	215 000
Financed by:				
Capital	65 000	100 000	115 000	150 000
Net profit for the year	50 000	50 000	55 000	50 000
Less Drawings	(10 000)	(5 000)	(20 000)	(10 000)
Long-term Loans	55 000	50 000	20 000	25 000
	160 000	195 000	170 000	215 000

Further information

1. During 1992 Nichols sold 90 per cent of his goods on credit whereas Myers sold 95 per cent on credit. By the end of 1993 Nichols' proportion of credit sales had increased to 94 per cent and Myers' had dropped to 90 per cent.

2. The cost of sales figures comprised the following:

	Nichols 1992	Nichols 1993	Myers 1992	Myers 1993
Opening stock	340 000	60 000	60 000	30 000
Plus Purchases	130 000	130 000	156 000	240 000
	160 000	190 000	210 000	270 000
Less Closing stock	60 000	65 000	30 000	80 000
	100 000	125 000	180 000	190 000

All purchases of stock were bought on credit.

3. Creditors at the end of 1991 were as follows:

Nichols   £30 000
Myers   £30 000

and debtors were:

Nichols   £30 000
Myers   £65 000

4. Interest payments were as follows:

Nichols   £5000 (1992)   £2000 (1993)
Myers   £4500 (1992)   £2000 (1993)

Task 1. Nichols and Myers are both in the same business as James Matthews who is considering purchasing one of the businesses. Mr Matthews asks you for advice as to which, in your opinion, is the better performing business over the two-year period.

You should support your answer with the calculations of whatever ratios you see fit, together with a detailed report clearly advising the course of action Mr Matthews should take.

Task 2. Mr Matthews has obtained from both Mr Nichols and Mr Myers detailed forecast profit and loss accounts and balance sheets for 1994. Taking these figures into consideration, would your advice to Mr Matthews be the same as in Task 1 or different?

Forecast summarised profit and loss accounts for the year ended 31.12.94

	Nichols £	Myers £
Sales	280 000 (95% on credit)	300 000 (96% on credit)
Less Cost of sales		
Opening stock	65 000	80 000
Plus Purchases	150 000 (all on credit)	180 000 (all on credit)
Less Capital stock	70 000	55 000
	145 000	205 000
Gross profit	135 000	95 000
Less Expenses	70 000	50 000
Net profit	65 000	45 000

Forecast Summarised Balance Sheets as at 31.12.94 (Extracts)

	Nichols £	Myers £
Fixed Assets (NBV)	95 000	130 000
Current assets		
Stocks	70 000	55 000
Debtors	50 000	80 000
Bank and cash	5 000	5 000
	125 000	140 000
Less Current liabilities		
Creditors	(30 000)	(70 000)
Working capital	105 000	70 000
Net assets	200 000	200 000

UNIT 8

BUSINESS PLANNING

This unit covers how to produce a business plan with all of its supporting documentation, so that it can be presented to a potential provider of finance. It should be studied last as it represented the culmination of all the other units of the programme and work produced in the other units should be used to produce the plan.

Unlike the other mandatory units of the GNVQ this unit has no external test, nor is it suitable for the other types of assessment used in the other units. The assessment of this unit is best organised around the business plan which is itself more in the nature of a project.

The unit allows a basic business idea to be considered prior to the risking of financial and time resources in setting up an actual business. A rationale and factual details must be supplied to support an application for a loan to fund either a new business start-up or a projected business purchase and the student should show how the plan will be monitored and implemented. Business scenarios should be considered from the human, marketing, production, timing and financial points of view and the presentation of the information should be such that it persuades providers of finance to support the business. In doing this, students must analyse their own strengths and weaknesses with regard to employment and self-employment.

Students may do the basic research for their plan in groups but the final plan must be an individual piece of work.

Element 8.1
PREPARE WORK AND COLLECT DATA FOR A BUSINESS PLAN

Performance criteria

1 **Explain the purposes of a business plan.**

2 **Identify the business objectives and collect supporting information for the business activity for which a plan is to be prepared.**

3 **Identify the legal and insurance implications of the business objectives.**

4 **Discuss the feasibility of proposals with others.**

5 **Estimate resource requirements to design, produce, promote and sell the goods or services.**

6 **Produce a flow chart illustrating estimated time scales.**

7 **Identify potential support for the plan.**

8 **Prepare an action plan identifying actions to be taken to finalise the business plan for presentation.**

Introduction

At the end of this element you will be asked to draft an outline of a business plan that will show your understanding and application of the above criteria. The draft plan should set out:

- the planned time scales;
- legal and insurance implications;
- first estimates for resource requirements;
- possible support for the plan from financial, legal, marketing or production specialists;
- action points identifying next steps to complete the business plan.

Before tackling the performance criteria for this element, however, the student may find an insight into the background and academic input into planning helpful.

INTRODUCTION TO PLANNING

Planning, when used in a business context, can be defined as the establishment of business objectives and the evaluation and selection of strategies and actions needed to achieve the objectives. Business plans are often split into three parts – long-term strategic plans, medium-term tactical plans and short-term operational plans that are often expressed as budgets and targets set for the activities of the organisation's individual departments and managers. The concepts of financial budgeting were covered in Unit 7 and these activities are closely connected with an organisation's operational planning and control functions.

Table 8.1 illustrates the various levels and activities that are often found in an organisation's planning systems.

Table 8.1 An organisation's planning system

Time	Activity

Long-term planning (strategic planning)

Five years or more	• What business should the organisation be in?
	• What is its best structure?
	• How should its activities be financed?
	• How should its resources be allocated?

Medium term planning (tactical planning)

One to five years	• What products or services should the business produce?
	• What production facilities should be used?
	• What capital expenditure is required on new or changed production facilities?
	• What prices should be charged?

Short-term planning (operational planning)

Annual budget Less than 12 months	• What is the best marketing plan?
	• What is the best production plan that meets the needs of the marketing plan?
	• What are the material, labour and other production costs needed to meet the targets in the production plan?
	• What is the effect on the organisation's cash flow of the above activities?
	• What is the expected profit resulting from these activities?

The planning activities of any organisation are entirely dependent upon the needs of the organisation, its managers, owners and customers. The managers can do as little or as much planning as they like and the systems and routines used are entirely at their discretion. This unit describes ideas for business planning requirements for medium-

Element 7.4   Identify and explain data to monitor a business

Answers to self-assessment questions

Element 7.1	Element 7.2	Element 7.3	Element 7.4
1. d	1. d	1. b	1. d
2. c	2. c	2. a	2. d
3. b	3. a	3. d	3. a
4. b	4. d	4. c	4. a
5. d	5. c	5. d	5. c
6. c	6. a	6. b	6. a
7. a	7. c	7. d	7. c
8. b			8. c
9. b			9. a
10. c			10. b
			11. c
			12. c
			13. b

sized to large organisations. Larger organisations may use much more sophisticated systems and smaller organisations will not need the same complexity of analysis.

Business existence is subject to various degrees of uncertainty. Your studies in all of the preceding units of this course should have alerted you to these uncertainties. The individual markets in which a firm trades are subject to many influences that can affect its performance. Businesses use a variety of forecasting techniques and methods to anticipate these changes in market conditions. These forecasts form the basis of the plans and budgets that control the activities of the business. In this way the managers of the business try to maximise any favourable market conditions and minimise any unfavourable occurrences.

No matter how much effort is devoted to business planning activity, however, things can still go disastrously wrong for the firm.

Between 1960 and 1985, one of the stars of the business world was IBM, the American computer giant. Recent history has shown that even such firms can base their plans and activities on the wrong assumptions.

Even governments can get their plans wrong, the consequences of which can be economically painful for most of us.

After the stock market crash of 'Black Monday' in the late 1980s, the then Chancellor, Nigel Lawson, was told by his advisors to increase the money supply in the economy in order to avoid a 1930s type slump. This he did with the immediate effect of creating the 'Yuppie' boom which had to be corrected by John Major's subsequent budgets.

Strategic planning

A business should always keep its long-term strategy in mind and review it periodically. The first questions that it must consider are:

- What is the business environment likely to be in the future?
- How should the business be organised to take account of the threats and opportunities present in that environment?

Without the aid of a crystal ball, business managers have to evaluate the various indicators that can provide some idea of future trends in the economy as a whole and the markets of the business in particular. They will take notice of the following.

1 *Economic forecasts of the level of activity in the global and domestic economies.* There are a number of econometric computer-based models that supply this information, the most important being that used and published by the UK Treasury.

2 *Either domestic or foreign political interference in trade.* This could either affect the ability of the business to purchase goods from abroad, or to sell goods and services abroad. The main problem here is not so much the barriers to trade that exist at the moment, but the barriers that may be introduced in the future. No one would have foreseen a few years ago any problem in importing Yugo cars from what is now Serbia, or of selling goods to Malaysia during 1994.

3 *Changes in technology.* A firm may have invested heavily in new production facilities which due to changes in technology are now obsolete. This may not matter as long as

its competitors are also using out-of-date methods or materials, but as soon as a major competitor changes the firm will be forced to do likewise. Failure to do so may save money in the short term but, in the medium to long term, will lead to a loss of market share and profitability.

4 *Social changes* in lifestyles, age groups, income levels and tastes may affect product sales. In the 1980s everyone wanted a Porsche sports car and some could even afford them! In the early 1990s people still wanted them, but few could afford them and the sales of Porsche cars collapsed.

Considering the above examples, it is obvious that things can and do go wrong for businesses. It is the job of the managers of each business to anticipate and respond to changing conditions in order to ensure the survival of the business and, if all goes well, its continued growth.

Many large firms have grown to the extent that their managers and owners have decided to split them into smaller more manageable units. In the UK, one of the largest companies was ICI, the drugs and chemical giant. In 1993 it was split into two separate companies: ICI retained the traditional chemical divisions while a new company, Zeneca was created out of ICI's drugs businesses. In this way, the managers of each company can concentrate on the core activities of their organisations.

This trend to create more smaller independent business units has also affected management in the public sector. The Civil Service is being broken down into agencies such as the Benefits Agency that has taken on the role of paying and assessing people's rights to social security benefits. Schools can opt out of local authority control. Hospitals can form trusts to manage their own affairs. In the language of business strategy they have become semi-autonomous business units run by their governors or trustees.

When considering strategic planning it has become common for business managers to resort to methods of analysis developed by researchers and academics that are often expressed as acronyms. These are simply ways of organising information in order to help decision making.

SWOT

This means analysing one's business in terms of its perceived *strengths, weaknesses, opportunities* and *threats*.

If we use British Telecom as an example, we could say that its strength was its size and monopoly position in the market when it was privatised. Its weaknesses were its inappropriate organisation structure, obsolete systems and overmanning. Its opportunities were the anticipated boom in communications due to new technology. The threats that it faced related to the break up of its monopoly and the entry into the market of new competitors.

SOFT

This is a refinement of the above and requires the analysis to be carried out under the headings of *strengths, opportunities, failures* and *threats*.

Using the same example of British Telecom, this method of analysis would use the same list of strengths, opportunities and threats but would substitute the firm's perceived failures for its weaknesses. Failures relate more to past actions that can be more easily identified, while weaknesses can be difficult to identify.

Whatever system is used to list those external and internal influences that affect or may affect the future performance of the business, all planning activities must start with their consideration. From this analysis the managers can decide the future strategy of the business: what business the organisation should be in, what its best structure is, how it should be financed and how its resources should be allocated.

Tactical planning

Once the business strategy is accepted, it is the managers' responsibility to plan its implementation. This often involves making decisions that may take a number of years to carry out. New products may have to be developed, existing products may have to be repositioned in the market and future production facilities will have to be planned. The consequent effect on finance will have to be calculated both in terms of the cost of the products and services but also in terms of the capital cost of changed production systems and distribution networks.

Operational planning

The routines involved in setting and controlling the implementation of financial plans expressed in the form of budgets were covered in Unit 7. These are the main expression of a firm's operational plans, but some targets relate to non-financial outcomes and these must have equal importance in the planning systems used by the firm. Many of these targets are used in the formulation of the figures in the budget, however, and include such items as labour hours, material quantities and numbers of products. These figures are often derived from and are used in the firm's costing systems.

Marketing plans were introduced in Unit 3 and these, together with finance and production plans, form the basis of the business plan.

BUSINESS OBJECTIVES

Within our economy there are many types of organisation, each one with different objectives. Some organisations may want to make profits, others may want to break even and make neither a profit nor a loss; while others may have to be subsidised.

Most firms in the private sector have as their main objective the need to make a profit. It may well be the case that, given certain circumstances, this is not attainable in the short term, but their overall objective is to make sufficient profits to reward owners, pay managers and debts and finance future growth.

Organisations in the voluntary sector and some parts of the public sector have as their objective the need to break even; that is they attempt to match their income to their expenditure. Once again this may not be attainable in the short term, but only over an acceptable period of time.

Most public sector organisations exist to provide services to the community and it is either too complicated to charge directly for the service (e.g. the provision of roads) or it is socially unacceptable to do so (e.g. the provision of welfare benefits or state education). The organisations providing these services have an objective to provide the best service for the amount of subsidy that they receive.

A limited company must include in its Memorandum and Articles of Association an objectives clause, which states the company's main reason for existence. In order not to tie the company down to a very limited range of objectives, most companies keep this statement as general as possible, because to act outside these objectives is unlawful. The doctrine of *ultra vires* means beyond the powers and this is applied to the company's actions and its objectives clause.

Public sector organisations, such as local authorities, are also subject to *ultra vires* in that they can only spend money on the services that they are empowered by statute to provide. Their objectives are contained in the acts of parliament that created them.

LEGAL IMPLICATIONS

All organisations are subject to the law. The law affects business in the areas of employment, health and safety, environmental protection, trades descriptions, age limits, asset insurance, public liability and product liability. The most important part of the law, however, relates to contracts and the sale of goods.

The Sale of Goods Act 1979 regulates the rights of buyers and sellers where the seller transfers or agrees to transfer the property in goods to the buyer for a consideration called the price. *Property in goods* means ownership and goods relate to all assets other than land and buildings and patents and copyrights. A *contract of sale* includes *express terms* that are either expressed in writing or by word of mouth. *Implied terms* relate to terms that have been established either through custom or by statute or the courts. The major terms in a contract are called *conditions* and the minor terms are called *warranties*. The implied conditions covered by the Act include the following:

- the seller has the right to sell the goods;
- the goods are of merchantable quality;
- the goods are fit for the purpose intended;
- the goods must correspond to their description.

The implied warranties covered by the Act include the following:

- the buyer shall have and enjoy quiet possession of the goods;
- the goods are free from any charge or incumbrance not disclosed or known to the buyer before or at the time of the contract of sale.

It is the seller's duty to deliver the goods and the buyer's duty to pay for them. An unpaid seller, however, has the right to hold on to the goods until the debt is paid. Furthermore, the goods can be stopped in transit if the buyer becomes insolvent. The buyer can be sued for non-payment and, if the buyer has refused to accept and pay for the goods, the seller can sue for damages due to breach of contract. The buyer can sue for damages due to non-delivery by the seller and can also claim specific performance of the contract if the courts consider that monetary damages are an insufficient remedy. The buyer can also sue for breach of warranty.

The Supply of Goods and Services Act 1982 covers sales that fall outside the scope of the Sale of Goods Act. These include such contracts as hire agreements, contracts of exchange or barter and contracts for the supply of services. The detailed workings of this Act are similar to the Sale of Goods Act but this Act implies the use of reasonable care and skill in the performance of the service and also a reasonable time scale for completion. Hire purchase agreements are not sales agreements and come under the provisions of the **Supply of Goods (Implied Terms) Act 1973**. Such contracts are for hire and the last payment by the user of the goods constitutes an option to buy them. These agreements also come under the terms of the **Consumer Credit Act 1974**. A consumer credit agreement is a personal agreement where the borrower is an individual or a partnership and the amount of the loan does not exceed £15 000. The Act requires that loan agreements for the supply of goods contain consumer protection, impose trading standards and give the consumer adequate and accurate information. The Director of Fair Trading is responsible for the supervision of the Act. The Director's office administers a licensing system and issues and enforces regulations to those organisations giving consumer credit.

The Unsolicited Goods and Services Act 1971 states that the recipient need not pay for or return the goods. If the sender of the goods does not collect them within six months of delivery, or within 30 days of receiving notice of where the goods can be collected, the goods become the property of the recipient.

The Trades Descriptions Acts 1968 and 1972 apply to sales which are made for business purposes (private sales are not covered). It covers both oral and written descriptions made by the seller to the buyer. These descriptions include information written on the packaging relating to size, ingredients and fitness for purpose, and make it an offence to apply a false trade description or to supply or knowingly or recklessly make false statements about the provision of service accommodation or facilities. The Act is enforced by local authority trading standards officers.

The Food Safety Act 1990 contains a number of offences governing the sale of food and drink for human consumption. The Act covers the sale of food that is unfit for consumption, is sub-standard or is incorrectly labelled. The Act is enforced by the local authority environmental health and trading standards officers.

The Consumer Protection Act 1987 makes it an offence to give any misleading information as to the price of goods, services, accommodation or facilities and to this end a code of practice on price indications was published in 1988 which provides traders with guidelines on acceptable pricing practices. The Act additionally introduced the concept of product liability which makes the producer liable for any injury resulting from defects in the product, without the injured party having to show fault. As with the Trades Descriptions Act, the Act is enforced by the trading standards officers.

The Restrictive Trade Practices Acts 1976 and 1977 cover agreements between suppliers, distributors and retailers to make sure that such agreements are in the best interest of the consumer. **The Resale Price Act 1976** stopped the practice whereby suppliers could dictate prices to retailers, and the **Competition Act 1980** stopped anti-competitive practices in the supply of goods and services such as price fixing by cartels operating against the public interest. These Acts empower the Director General of Fair Trading to investigate and report his findings and, where necessary, refer matters to the Monopolies and Mergers Commission.

INSURANCE IMPLICATIONS

All businesses should have some form of insurance against potential, uncertain events that could prove to be very costly. The business, *the insured*, takes out a policy with an insurance company, *the insurer*, that will *indemnify* the insured against any loss suffered (that is pay the insured the cost incurred in rectifying any loss) due to an event that was the subject of the insurance *policy*. A policy is a contract that is a written agreement that lists the terms and conditions of the insurance. These contracts are based on the principles of *insurable interest* and *utmost good faith*. Insurable interest means that the insured must suffer a loss before the insurer will pay out. Utmost good faith requires all parties to the agreement to state all relevant facts that affect the policy. Non-disclosure by the insured will result in non-payment by the insurance company following any claim.

An insurance company will take premiums from many firms and individuals in the hope that the premium income will exceed any liability arising from claims. If the company calculates that it is paying out more than it is collecting it could increase the premiums, reduce the risks covered or refuse to insure against certain events. All of these points have been used in recent years to combat the increased risks involved in insuring certain cars that have proved to be popular with car thieves. Certain locations attract greater premiums for insurance against burglary and vandalism.

The usual risks that a business will insure against are:

- destruction of buildings and contents by fire;
- loss of goods and property by theft;
- loss of motor vehicles following accidents;
- third-party claims arising from accidents;
- death, disability or sickness of key members of staff;
- marine losses.

THE FEASIBILITY STUDY

If you have a business idea and have started to form a draft business plan, it is wise to discuss its proposals with other people whom you think can help. You should seek answers to the following points.

- Is there likely to be a demand for the product?
- Who are the likely customers?
- What are the start-up requirements?
- How will the first year's expenses be financed?
- What is the level of sales and profitability needed to ensure survival?
- What is the number and the degree of expertise of the active participants in the business?

- What are the levels of stock and the amount of associated equipment and fixtures and fittings that are required?

In conducting your research into the above points, you could consult teaching staff and external experts from other organisations such as banks, building societies, estate agents, insurance company representatives. By discussing your plans with others you will be able to gauge its feasibility – is it likely to work?

EXTERNAL SUPPORT

There are many agencies that exist to support business activity. Such support may come from within other parts of the same organisation (such as other divisions of the company or other subsidiary firms owned by the company owners). Many medium-sized and large companies today are part of larger groups of companies owned by a holding company.

Support may be required in product design, manufacturing techniques, supplies of materials or components, distribution systems, marketing and finance. If the required expertise is not available within the organisation, it can be bought in from external agencies or individuals. Individuals can be appointed as *consultants* or as executive directors, and other firms can be employed to complete tasks required by the company. Such subcontracting of work from one firm to another is a very common occurrence.

Most small firms have at least three people from whom they can request assistance in the running of their business: *the firm's bank manager*, *its solicitor* and *its accountant* – all will know the firm, its products and organisation structure, its strengths and weaknesses. Many managers do not make sufficient use of the expertise available to them, mistakenly thinking that it will cost them too much to ask, that help will not be forthcoming, or that it will be seen as a sign of weakness on their part. Solicitors, bankers and accountants deal with many other clients and are able to pass on their experience when asked. It is in all their interests for their client to succeed. As the business grows, so will the work that they will be required to perform for their client and, correspondingly, their fees. Obtaining advice from professionals has the safeguard that if that advice is faulty, the person giving it can be sued for negligence and the courts could award damages to the firm.

All firms need insurance cover for the risks outlined earlier. External help in this area is essential and is relatively easy and inexpensive to acquire through the use of either an *insurance broker* or by dealing directly with an *insurance company* through one of its representatives. The latter, of course, will not provide unbiased information and will only offer the services of one insurance company.

When a new firm is established, or an existing firm requires new production assets, there are various sources of information that can help in the choice of which assets to acquire, and how to finance their purchase. *Trade journals* exist for almost every type of business and they contain articles on the reviewers' opinions of all current methods of production, production machinery, distribution systems and the latest marketing information. Access to this data is best sought through the local library system. The librarians will find the relevant articles from the back issues of the journals in their possession. If the local library cannot help, the journals' publishers will be willing to provide copies of articles for a small charge.

Details of products can be obtained from a *supplier's representative* or salesperson. This advice will cost nothing, of course, but it will not be unbiased – it is their job to sell you something. If your earlier researches have led you to investigate a range of products from one or more supplier, however, this should be your next step. You should be careful to evaluate the claims of each representative prior to placing an order. Most suppliers will provide finance for the sale of their products but the cost of such finance should be compared to that offered elsewhere. Ask your bank manager, or your accountant.

RESOURCES REQUIREMENTS

Resources can be split into the following categories:

- human resources,
- physical resources,
- financial resources and
- time.

Time is obviously a resource that is in short supply and we all have to work to deadlines that we set ourselves or are set by others. All of the other resources have been covered by other parts of this book.

THE NEW BUSINESS PROPOSAL

If we decide to start a new business, we will clearly need a product or service to sell. We shall use the following example to illustrate how a new business proposal is put together.

A modern printing and graphic design service has been set up by Adrian, a graphic designer, who three years ago completed his National Diploma in two-dimensional design and has since been working as a desk-top publishing technician at the college. He has recently received a legacy of £10 000 from a deceased relative and has decided to set up his own firm. Prior to doing this, he has made use of the expertise of his colleagues in the Business Studies Department at the college. He has consulted lecturers in finance and marketing and has had long discussions over coffee with his former mentors in the printing section of the Art Department.

The result of these discussions has been written down as a draft feasibility proposal that he intends to take to his local bank manager in order to start his new venture. The following are included in his notes:

- a concise description of the services that he intends to offer and the type of client that he intends to target,
- a list of the equipment that he will need and its cost,

- the working capital requirements that will see him through his start-up period until his clients start to pay their bills and provide him with sufficient income to pay his way.

From your studies in the previous units of this book you will appreciate Adrian's efforts.

In our example Adrian listed the fixed assets that he needed to start his print design business. This included a new computer, a laser printer, a second-hand printing machine, binder and collator. The cost of all of these assets amounted to £12 000 and he thinks that he will also need a further £3000 working capital. He is about to ask the bank manager to allow him a £5000 overdraft. He also acquired an old van on hire purchase, and rented business premises on a monthly basis from the local council at a subsidised rent, with rates combined. His total monthly payments amount to an average of £800.

Assignment

PC
8.1.1
8.1.2
8.1.3
8.1.4
8.1.5
8.1.6
8.1.7
8.1.8

Draft a *business plan* that outlines the goods or services to be provided and the relevant supporting marketing and financial information. The draft plan should set out:

- the planned time scales;
- its legal and insurance implications;
- first estimates for resource requirements;
- possible support for the plan from financial, legal, marketing or production specialists;
- action points identifying next steps to complete the business plan.

The draft business plan should be supported by a statement which explains the objectives of the business and the purpose of producing a business plan.

Element 8.2
PRODUCE AND PRESENT A BUSINESS PLAN

Performance criteria

1. Describe and explain business objectives for a business enterprise.
2. Outline a marketing plan for a business enterprise.
3. Outline a production plan for a business enterprise.
4. Outline the resource requirements for marketing and production.
5. Produce financial data and forecasts to support the business plan.
6. Identify monthly profit and loss and balance sheet monitoring and review procedures for the business plan.
7. Present and explain a business plan to an audience.

Introduction

You are required to produce a business plan for an organisation that has one product or one service. Your plan should be in the following format:

1. introduction and objectives;
2. an outline marketing plan;
3. an outline production plan;
4. resource requirements;
5. financial support data.

Note that much of the above detail will already have been covered in other parts of the course – business objectives (Element 8.1), marketing (Unit 3), resource requirements (Unit 7). We will cover most of these areas again in this element, however, and, where appropriate, refer you back to previous parts of the book when greater detail is required.

Element 8.2 Produce and present a business plan

At the end of the element you should be capable of presenting your business plan to other interested people, both in written and oral forms, in order to interest a potential provider of finance. Your presentation should cover the above five points and the oral presentation should be supported by relevant visual aids and be addressed to an individual or group representing a potential provider of finance. This presentation should be followed by a question-and-answer session that allows you to demonstrate an understanding of the marketing, production and financial implications of the plan in greater depth.

THE PURPOSES OF PRODUCING A BUSINESS PLAN

Obviously, if you are starting a new business, you should have some idea as to what that business is. The simple desire to be your own boss, or to be a business tycoon, is not enough. The first and most important concept in your business is, What business are we in?

This is a deceptively difficult question. Do you provide a service, and if so, what type of service? What type of market does it operate in and how is that service seen by your customers and competitors? You may find that others see your business in a different light to you. Similarly, if you make and sell a particular product, your own view of it may be different to that of people outside your firm. For example, you may think that you provide a personal planning and information system, others may think that you print diaries.

The following questions must be kept in mind when planning all business ventures.

- What business were we in?
- What business are we in now?
- What business do we want to be in?
- How will we change our business strategy and policies to achieve our new business aspirations?
- Who are our present customers?
- What are their future needs?
- Will our future customers change?
- What are our current products?
- How should we adapt our products or services to meet future customer needs?
- What will our future costs be?
- What sales revenue will we generate?
- What will our profitability be?
- What is our cash flow likely to be?
- Can we generate sufficient funds to finance future growth?
- Will we have to attract more capital or increase borrowings?
- Have we the physical and manpower resources to achieve our plans?

When most of the above questions can be answered by the firm's managers and owners, the drawing up of a business plan can be a simple operation as everyone involved in running the firm will understand the need to work together to help achieve the firm's objectives. However, very few firms ask these questions and even fewer have answers to them.

Objectives

The setting of business objectives and the formulation of strategies and policies was dealt with at the beginning of this unit. A list of a firm's objectives will often include statements on the firm's target return on capital employed, its supply of goods or services, sales volumes and values, time scales, profits and its market share. Further details of these concepts can be found in Unit 6, (Financial transactions, costing and pricing) and Unit 3 (Marketing).

In addition to a firm's stated objectives, many have a *mission statement*, which tells the firm's employees and shareholders what the firm hopes to achieve in the near future. It is usually a concise statement of the firm's goals, and is an attempt to keep everyone in the firm working towards the same set of objectives.

The questions that are stated above are an attempt to keep the firm's managers' and employees' attention on the things that matter most to the firm's success. Many new firms fail because their managers cannot provide adequate answers to these questions, and indeed, have never even thought about most of them. Research has shown that up to 80 per cent of new firms fail in the first two years of existence. Anyone can start a business, often with very little capital. Many are potentially very good businesses that are doomed to fail due to poor management. Common errors that lead to business failures include:

1. *A desire to grow too fast* – an overestimate of the qualities of the firm's services or its products, or an inability to convince potential customers of their value.

2. *Undercapitalised and poor credit control* – not enough working capital and a failure to understand the working capital cycle whereby stock is sold on credit, debtors are slow to pay up and creditors demand payment for the initial credit purchase of stock. The failure of debtors to pay their debts is the most common reason why new small firms go bankrupt; if one firm fails, then because it owes money to other firms they in turn will also fail.

3. *Marketing* – overestimating the size of the market and/or overestimating the size of the market share that the firm could expect to win.

4. *Costing* – poor control over costs and/or poor profit margins due to competitive market conditions.

5. *Economic conditions* – failure to respond quickly enough to changes in external economic conditions, particularly the effects of government monetary policy on economic demand and the firm's own interest costs on its debts.

6. *Product and production* – insufficient expertise with regard to product design and production systems and techniques.

PC 8.2.1

ACTIVITY 8.2.1

Write a mission statement for a proposed small limited company that will employ 10 people, have a turnover of £100 000, and an intended market in the wholesale bakery industry. Its main product lines will be frozen gateaux that will be sold to wholesale, cash-and-carry firms and supermarkets.

THE MARKETING PLAN

In today's complex economic environment it is essential that the firm's managers are aware of the external threats and opportunities that can and will affect its ability to generate sales and profits. The most sensible way to achieve this is to have some system of planning that will ensure that the firm is made aware of factors that are likely to influence the purchasing decisions of the firm's current and potential customers. Marketing plans can be split into *strategic* and *operational*.

- The *strategic plan* will place greater emphasis on scanning the external environment to gain an earlier appreciation of the forces that are most likely to affect the markets in which the firm operates. This should then lead to the development of strategies to respond to any identifiable trends or changes in market conditions. The strategic plan should cover a period of between two and five years.
- The *operational plan* should provide targets and allocate resources in both physical and budgetary values. At no time should the operational plan be considered before the strategic plan has been agreed.

Figure 8.1 illustrates the individual components of the marketing planing cycle. A *position audit* requires the firm to analyse the market in which it operates and to find out as much as it can about its customers' and competitors' opinions of its products and services. *SWOT* was outlined in Element 8.1, and it requires the analysis of the firm's strengths, weaknesses, opportunities and threats. Knowing these concepts and their application to the firm's products and services will help to establish the firm's *marketing objectives*, which should of course coincide with the firm's mission statement, its business strategies and its overall objectives. (These again were covered earlier in this unit.) *Planning activities* are described below. The *control* and *feedback* elements relate to the firm's review and evaluation processes that establish whether its marketing activities are worthwhile. Such data will be available from the firm's marketing information systems and its management accounting system. This process will influence the firm's future marketing plans and it should provide a systematic way of continuously refining its marketing objectives.

The firm's marketing objectives could be stated in terms of its targets in the following areas:

- profit
- market share and penetration
- total sales and sales revenue
- corporate image.

If the firm is not achieving its targets, as laid down in the above objectives its managers should investigate further to find out why this has happened and make alterations to either the personnel involved and its organisation, or to the resources allocated, or to make an adjustment to the objectives themselves. You are referred back to Unit 3 (Marketing) for comments on the marketing mix and how it affects the attainment of the above objectives. Additionally, you are asked to investigate the concept of market segmentation and product positioning.

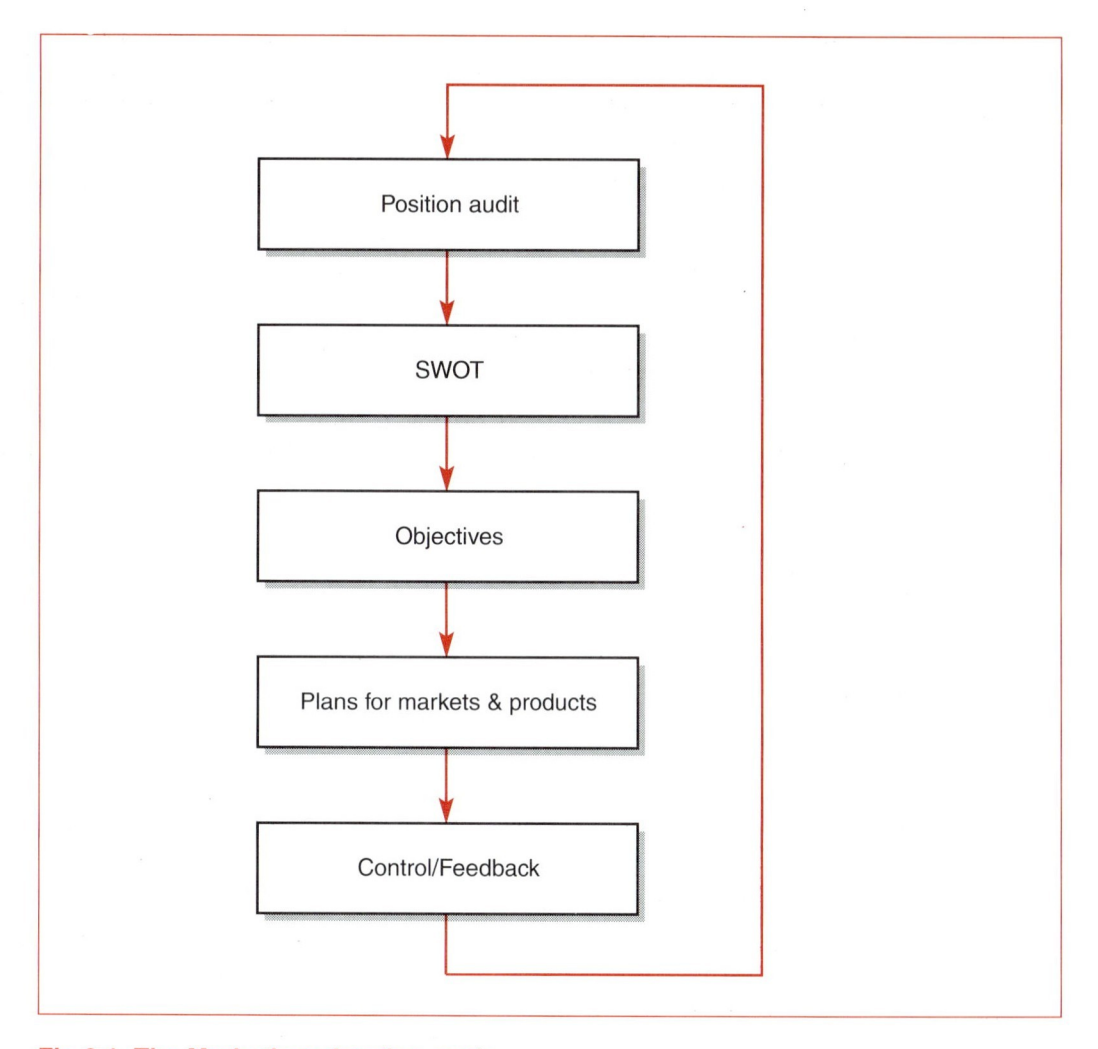

Fig 8.1 **The Marketing planning cycle**

Planning activities

Most new firms are either local to a particular geographical area, such as a new retail business, or they are specialist firms that offer a limited range of services or products in a specialised national market, such as a specialised computer software firm. To be successful the firm must be able to produce a marketing plan. In a small owner–manager firm it need not always be formally written as long as it is understood by all of its senior staff, while a large firm will need a formal set of plans and objectives that are written and effectively communicated to all of its managers. In particular all of the firm's managers should have a full knowledge of the markets that the firm operates in.

The management should undertake further market research into the following areas:

1 the size and extent of the market available to the firm;

2 the market dominance of existing firms, the degree of unsatisfied demand in the market, and the degree of price sensitivity of the firm's products or services within the market;

3 the spending power of the firm's potential customers (in the 1990s many Western European firms were attracted to the hugh potential demand existing in the former communist countries of Eastern Europe, but the customers in these countries had no money to pay for expensive imports from the West);

4 the external economic conditions that will affect the market in which the firm will operate.

The above research must come up with an estimate of the likely demand for the product or service, a range of prices that will attract potential customers and the probable cost of production. The last point will be tied in with the firm's production plan and its financial forecasts and budgets. If the firm is satisfied with the potential for growth and profitability shown in its marketing research, it will produce its marketing plan.

In addition to all of the market research, pricing, costing and budgeting, the marketing plan must contain details of marketing expenditure on promotion and advertising and distribution systems.

Promotion and advertising

Unless potential customers know and appreciate the benefits offered by a firm's products or services, they will not buy them. Advertising and other promotional and public relations (PR) activities are intended to gain the attention of the type of customer with whom the firm wants to do business. An example of PR activities in the 1980s and 1990s has been Richard Branson and his exploits in seeking publicity for his various businesses under the name of Virgin. He has crossed the Atlantic Ocean by hot air balloon and by speed boat and has led various charitable ventures and good causes, such as cleaning up Britain and setting up a new firm to produce cheap condoms to help fight the AIDS virus.

Publicity and PR exercises can sometimes be seen as an attempt to get a message across to potential and existing customers without directly purchasing media time to do so. It can go wrong, however, in that the wrong messages are in many cases given to the public. The organisation seeking the publicity has no control over how the media report on their activities.

Other types of promotional activities are intended to maintain or increase sales by offering the customers various inducements to purchase or continue purchasing the firm's products. For example, petrol companies often give tokens that can be saved up in order to claim free gifts, detergents offer money off the next purchase and many firms offer free tokens towards 'airmiles'.

Sponsorship of well reported events, such as football fixtures and other sporting activities, can give the sponsor a very wide exposure. A good example of this is the sponsorship of England's cricket test matches by the previously little known Cornhill Insurance company.

Advertising is used to inform potential customers of the benefits offered by a service, product or simply a firm's name. It involves the purchase of time on radio and television, the placing of material in books, newspapers and magazines and the display of material on posters.

The purchasing of advertising space and advice on advertisements and promotional activities is usually undertaken by specialist advertising agencies, such as Saatchi and Saatchi. Such firms will offer advice on the type and quantity of advertising material and the best media format to choose.

Unit 8 Business planning

PC 8.2.2

ACTIVITY 8.2.2

To emphasise the requirements of a marketing plan, we will continue to use as an example the firm that produces cakes for sale to a number of wholesale outlets and supermarkets (*see* Activity 8.2.1).

You are now required to list and describe a range of promotional activities and advertising promotions that would be suitable for the size and market in which the firm operates.

Storage and distribution

This involves the storage and movement of goods to customers once they have left production. For a small retail shop this will be no problem: goods are purchased from suppliers and placed on display in the shop for the customers to purchase. Larger retail organisations either need a store or a warehouse of some size, or they need to invest in complex just-in-time delivery systems, whereby the firm's suppliers are informed electronically of the firm's orders and guarantee almost instant delivery. The supplier firms have to keep large amounts of stock to be able to respond in time. If your firm sells to such organisations, it will need a series of distribution warehouses and an efficient transport system if it deals in large quantities of goods or of goods of a substantial size. Other smaller quantities or sizes can be dispatched by mail or by an independent carrier.

PC 8.2.2

ACTIVITY 8.2.3

List and describe the types of storage and distribution facilities that would be appropriate to the cake-making firm mentioned in Activities 8.2.1. and 8.2.2.

PC 8.2.1
8.2.2

ACTIVITY 8.2.4

Present your findings from Activities 8.2.1, 8.2.2 and 8.2.3 to either your colleagues at work or your fellow students at college. Make use of all relevant audiovisual aids as appropriate, such as handouts and overhead projector slides.

Estimating the marketing budget

One of the most powerful financial tools that can be used in the preparation of the marketing plan is that of *contribution* or *break-even analysis*.

This analysis attempts to put into practice the economists' theories of price elasticity, whereby the volume of sales is dependent upon the selling price of the product or service. As discussed earlier, some products are price inelastic in that a change of selling price will not unduly affect the number of items sold. In markets like this the firm will want to charge as high a price for its goods as the market will allow. Some products or services exist in markets that are said to be elastic, in that any change of price will affect the number of products sold. If a firm charges more, it will make more profit per product but will sell fewer of them, while if it charges less it will make less profit per unit but will sell more of them.

Contribution analysis will help a business to maximise its total profit by indicating the price that will generate the optimum sales volume. It should be noted, however, that if a business changes its prices, so will its competitors, and the business may not achieve its intended sales volumes.

Although contribution analysis is a powerful tool and a quick method of calculating profit, it depends on the individual firm's ability to control its own pricing structure. In most markets it is the market mechanism that determines prices. Additionally, the analysis depends upon the firm's ability to split its costs into fixed and variable costs.

A product's contribution is the difference between its selling price and the variable costs involved in making that product. It is the contribution that the product makes towards fixed costs and profits, that is just another way of looking at the calculation of profit. It uses all of the same expenses and costs that go into the trading and profit and loss account but analyses them between fixed and variable costs. The following example relates to the making of cakes.

	£	£
Selling price		£1.25
Less Variable costs:		
Ingredients	£0.35	
Electricity	£0.10	
Wages	£0.30	
		£0.75
Contribution		£0.50

The firm has estimated its fixed costs to be £2000 per month and its normal production is 5000 cakes. We can calculate the firm's profit or loss by multiplying the contribution per unit (£0.50), by the number of units made and sold in the month to get the total contribution and then deduct the month's fixed costs.

    5000 cakes × £0.50 contribution per unit
= £2500 total contribution minus £2000 the month's fixed costs
= £500 net profit.

We can in fact do this calculation for any number of cakes produced and sold in a month. Use a calculator and check the following calculations:

1000 cakes	=	£1500	loss		4500 cakes	=	£250	profit
1500 cakes	=	£1250	loss		5000 cakes	=	£500	profit
2000 cakes	=	£1000	loss		5500 cakes	=	£750	profit
2500 cakes	=	£750	loss		6000 cakes	=	£1000	profit
3000 cakes	=	£500	loss		6500 cakes	=	£1250	profit
3500 cakes	=	£250	loss		7000 cakes	=	£1500	profit
4000 cakes	=	£0						

You will have seen from the above figures that at 4000 cakes made and sold in the month the firm makes neither a profit nor a loss. This volume of sales is called the *break-even point*, and is a very important figure to the firm's managers. They must always try to sell more that 4000 cakes in a month in order to remain profitable.

The break-even point can easily be calculated using the formulae:

Fixed costs / Contribution per unit

In our example this would be £2000 divided by £0.50, which is 4000 cakes. This volume of sales can be expressed as sales revenue if we multiply the number of cakes by the selling price.

4000 cakes × £1.25 = £5000 sales per month

Thus in order to survive this firm must generate more than £5000 sales income per month.

We can do other budgets using contribution. If the owner of the above business demands a minimum profit of £300 per month we can calculate the sales volume required and also the sales revenue:

cakes sold to achieve £300 profit per month
= fixed costs + profit / contribution per unit
= £2000 + £300 / £0.50 = 4600 cakes
4600 cakes x £1.25 = £5750 sales revenue

The above calculations are shown in the break-even chart in Fig. 8.2.

The above analysis is entirely dependent upon the managers' ability to split the firm's costs between fixed and variable costs.

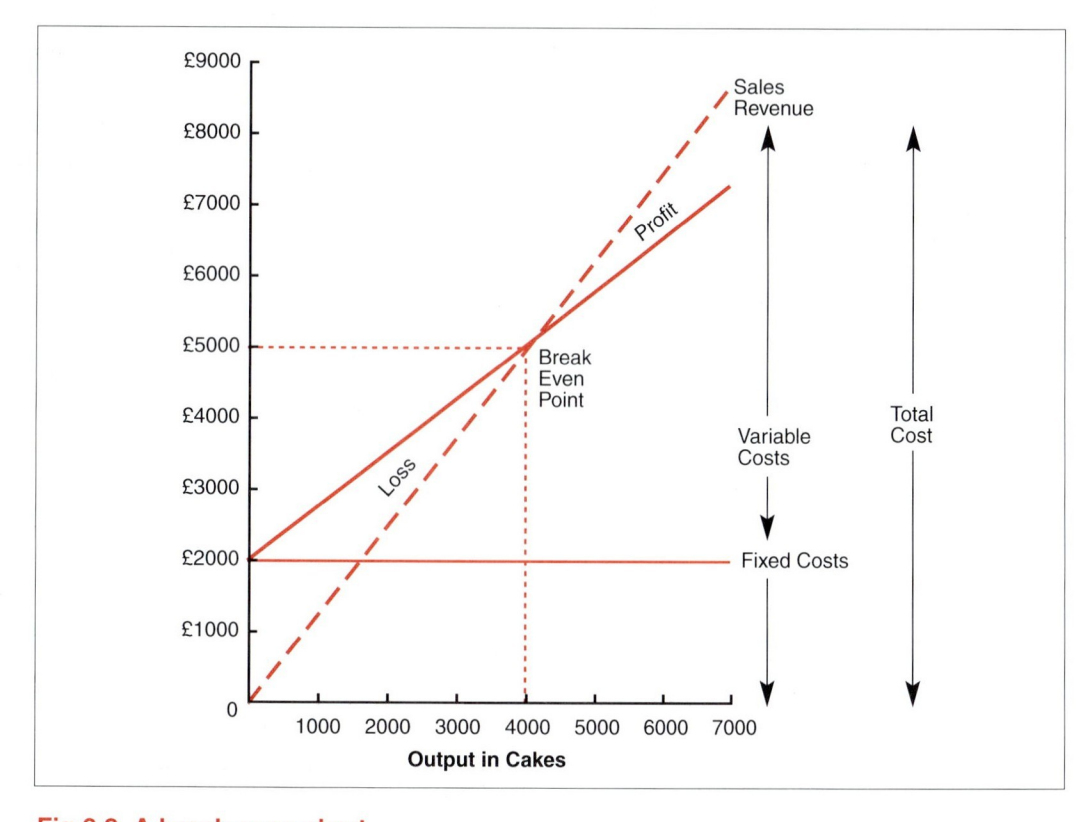

Fig 8.2 A break-even chart

ACTIVITY 8.2.5

PC 8.2.2

Calculate the profit for the cake making business based on the following calculations and present your findings to the Marketing Director in the format of a written report using a break-even chart to illustrate your comments.

The selling price and production costs of a new type of cake are as follows:

	£	£
Selling price		£2.00
Less Variable costs:		
Ingredients	£0.48	
Electricity	£0.15	
Wages	£0.62	£1.25
Contribution		£0.75

The firm's fixed costs are now estimated to be £2625 per month and its normal level of sales and production is estimated to be 4500 cakes.

The timing of sales and marketing activities

Earlier in this element we split the planning activities for marketing into strategic and operational plans: the first involving a time span of more than two years, while the latter effectively allocates finance and targets that will control the firm's marketing activities in the forthcoming year. The planning and control of sales and marketing activities is an essential part of the operational plan of the firm.

It is important that all of the managers involved in sales and marketing activities are fully conversant with the key objectives of the strategic marketing plan prior to drawing up their activities in the operational plan. Their effectiveness should be measured against the achievements of those strategic objectives. For this reason these marketing managers should have helped to produce the strategic marketing plan and it should contain sales and profit levels that are attainable rather than, as sometimes happens, a case of wishful thinking by those at head office who have no responsibility for its achievement.

As the external marketing environment is forever changing, so should the operational marketing plan. Regular meetings should be held during the year to monitor the achievement of the targets in the plan. Contingency actions should be planned in advance if targets become unattainable.

The marketing managers should not only forecast the quantities and values for the sales of each product in each geographical area but they must also state how many of each product are likely to be sold in each sales period. Such sales are estimated on either a weekly basis or a monthly basis. The timing of these sales must be linked with the production and storage facilities of the firm so that the firm does not overproduce slow moving stock, thus filling warehouses with goods that it may never sell. Conversely, it can be very dangerous for a firm to run out of products to sell to its customers who will then buy alternatives from the firm's competitors. Indeed, the firm may lose its customers altogether once they become used to buying elsewhere.

Unit 8   Business planning

An example of a sales and marketing plan

Figure 8.3 shows the layout and style of a marketing plan that has been used for a small firm in West Yorkshire that was attempting to introduce South Asian sweets into the UK. Its layout follows that adopted by the Department of Trade and Industry when considering bids for financial and managerial assistance and is suitable for use by small firms.

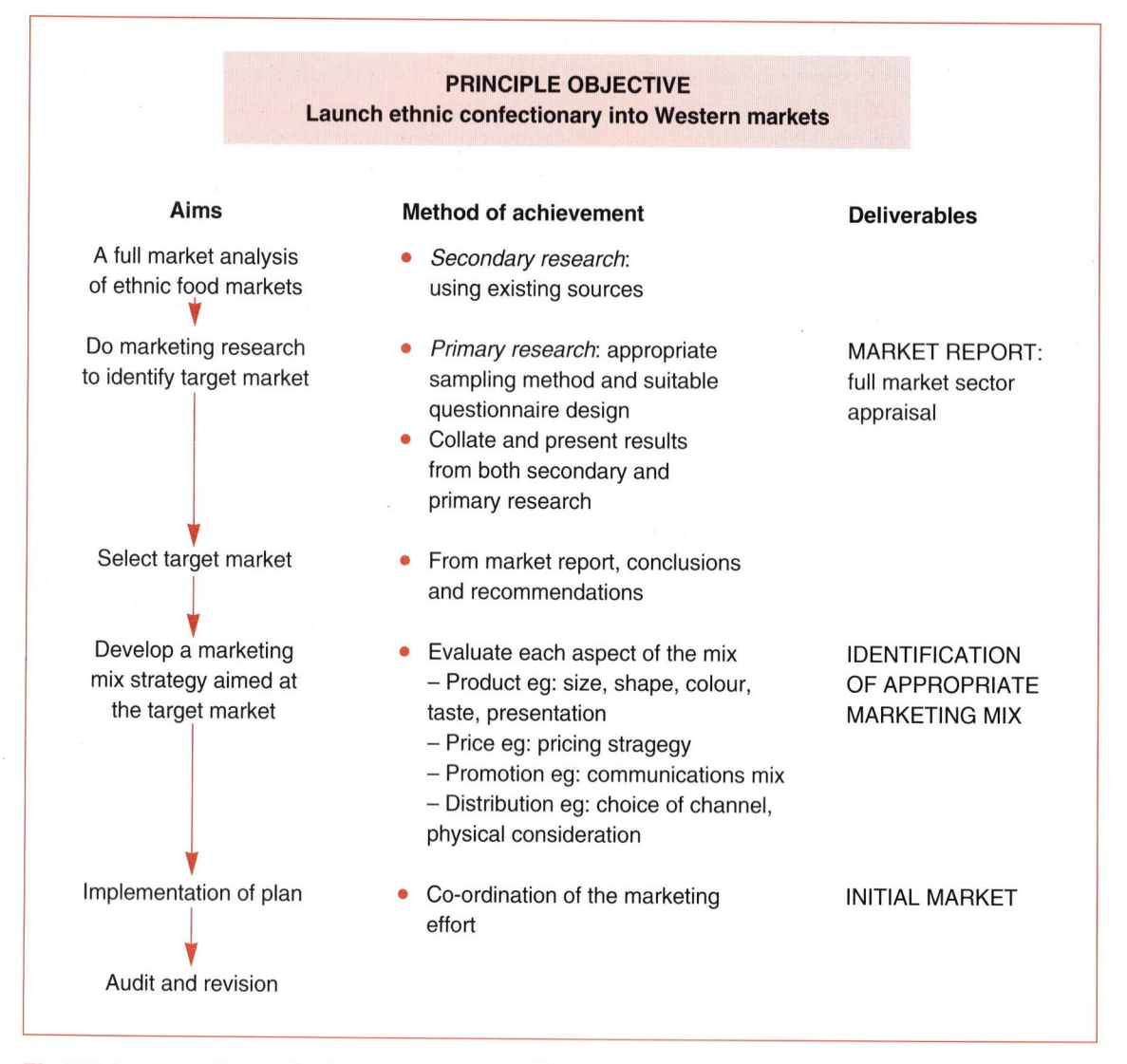

PRINCIPLE OBJECTIVE
Launch ethnic confectionary into Western markets

Aims	Method of achievement	Deliverables
A full market analysis of ethnic food markets	• *Secondary research*: using existing sources	
Do marketing research to identify target market	• *Primary research*: appropriate sampling method and suitable questionnaire design • Collate and present results from both secondary and primary research	MARKET REPORT: full market sector appraisal
Select target market	• From market report, conclusions and recommendations	
Develop a marketing mix strategy aimed at the target market	• Evaluate each aspect of the mix – Product eg: size, shape, colour, taste, presentation – Price eg: pricing stragegy – Promotion eg: communications mix – Distribution eg: choice of channel, physical consideration	IDENTIFICATION OF APPROPRIATE MARKETING MIX
Implementation of plan	• Co-ordination of the marketing effort	INITIAL MARKET
Audit and revision		

Fig 8.3 Layout of a marketing plan for a small firm

PC 8.2.2

ACTIVITY 8.2.6

Produce a full marketing plan for the cake-making business and present your proposals to your teacher in both written and oral forms. You should use your previous work from the other activities to support your presentation.

THE PRODUCTION PLAN

Once the management and the marketing people have decided upon the quantities and products that the firm's customers are likely to demand, it is up to the firm's production managers to make them to the required specification and quality at the lowest cost. There is usually a dilemma facing the firm's managers in that the demand for most products is to some extent seasonal while the most efficient production methods require a steady output. How this is resolved is up to the firm's managers but additional labour can be employed at busy times and staff can work longer hours, and conversely, the factory can be put on shorter shifts or closed during the periods of low demand.

Once the number of products to be produced and the times of their delivery and completion schedules have been agreed with the Marketing Department, the Production Department has to determine the work schedules in the factory. It must also determine the volume of labour, the materials required and when they are required, the usage of plant and machinery and the storage space for materials, work in progress and finished goods.

Orders have to be placed with the firm's suppliers and delivery times and places agreed. If new plant or machinery is needed, or alterations to the production systems, then the production managers must arrange for the work to be carried out with as little disruption to the working environment as possible.

One of the main problems in British industry is the availability of adequate numbers of trained workers when a firm is expanding its production. Most firms can only afford to keep adequate numbers of such workers on their payroll to see them through the periods of low demand. They will make all of their surplus workers redundant in order to keep their costs down and stay in business. When the next upturn in the economy comes, they then have insufficient workers to increase production and meet additional orders. This is made worse by a general failure to invest in training for their remaining workers, and the workers made redundant soon lose their former skills, particularly when new equipment is being used in the factories. It is, therefore, one of the production manager's main tasks to find and train sufficient workers to keep production at the levels demanded by the Marketing Department. A similar problem also arises with materials and component supplies, in that a shortage of supplies when demand has increased often stops the firm expanding as fast as it needs to in order to meet its new customer orders. Close liaison between the Production Department and the firm's Purchasing Department is essential if the right materials and supplies of the required quality are to be available at the right time.

Production budgets

These budgets are usually completed in two stages: one being in units of production and the other in monetary values. The former is the budget that is the most important to the Production Department in that it will provide the basis for all of its production activities. The main input to this budget is the number of units that are estimated to be sold throughout the forthcoming months. If the firm keeps a stock of its completed products in order to respond quickly to its customers' demands, then the effect on the stock levels of the estimated sales will determine the numbers of products to be produced in the budget period. As you can see from the following budget, the calculation and completion of a production budget is well suited for the use of a computer spreadsheet package (*see* Element 7.2 on the use of such systems).

Production budget for the next six months (units)

	Jan	Feb	Mar	Apr	May	Jun
Opening stock	120	140	140	130	110	90
Add Production	70	70	70	70	70	70
	190	210	210	200	180	160
Less Sales	50	70	80	90	90	80
Closing stock	140	140	130	110	90	80

As you can see the Production Manager has opted for a level production schedule of 70 units per month, while the volume of sales has varied. This has led to a variety of stock levels ranging from 80 units to 140 units. It may be the case that the firm does not have the storage facilities to keep 140 units and will have to alter its production levels down to an appropriate number. Such alterations to the budget will be made and the managerial consequences considered and agreed until everyone is content that the best compromise has been reached. These alterations and amendments to the budget can easily be done on a spreadsheet which will automatically recalculate the opening and closing stock figures.

Having agreed the production levels for each week the next stage is to produce the materials budget and the labour budget. The system for doing this is identical to the production budget.

FORECASTING

Forecasts are prepared prior to the organisation's budget. The most important of these is the forecast of likely future demand for the organisation's products or services. A wide-ranging list of factors needs to be taken into account when producing this forecast.

- Is there a trend or seasonal effect in the historical pattern of demand?
- To what extent is demand influenced by economic conditions outside the organisation's control?
- Does the organisation intend to try to influence demand directly through advertising or price variations, etc.?
- How will the difference between providing for specific customers' demands and satisfying demand from stock affect demand forecasts?

Once the basic forecast of sales demand has been produced, other forecasts will be derived such as specifying the materials' quality and quantity purchases and stock levels, the volume and type of labour required and the production facilities needed. When predicting material requirements, it is necessary to know how long it takes to either purchase them or manufacture them. Careful scheduling of production requirements will show the need for plant, labour and materials. Various statistical techniques exist to quantify forecasts and stock levels such as moving averages and computer simulations. These lie beyond the scope of this text.

Element 8.2 Produce and present a business plan

PC 8.2.3

ACTIVITY 8.2.7

Produce a production budget for the cake-making company mentioned in earlier activities. It estimates that it will produce and sell 100 000 cakes in the next financial year but its sales in each month will be:

January	9 600
February	9 400
March	9 000
April	8 600
May	8 000
June	7 600
July	6 600
August	6 600
September	6 800
October	7 800
November	9 200
December	10 800

The Production Manager is concerned that with the current production workers and plant he cannot produce more than 8400 cakes per month. The deep freeze is full at a stock level of 6000 cakes. The Marketing Manager insists that the stock levels must not fall below 1400 cakes so that all customers can be supplied from stock. The company does not keep stock for longer than three months.

You are required to produce your production budget and comment on the viability of next year's production plan. If you have access to a computer spreadsheet package, produce your plan on your computer.

DEPARTMENTAL BUDGETS AND THE BUSINESS PLAN

An organisation will produce a budget for each of its activities or for each operating department. The various budgets have to be linked together and a business plan and a Master Budget are produced. Often this is really a budgeted set of final accounts, plus a list of target outcomes and activities. The following list includes the budgets which are typically required by most small to medium-sized manufacturing firms.

- Sales budget
- Production budget
- Cash budget
- Selling expense budget
- Administration expense budget
- Direct labour budget
- Purchases budget

It is probable that when all the budgets have been brought together, the Master Budget shows a smaller profit than the firm's management expected in their business plan. This will usually lead to a change in the activity levels in the budgets to see whether a greater profit can be earned and the budgets will then be altered. There could be many such amendments before a Master Budget can be agreed.

An example of a business plan

Consider the following example of a firm that is drawing up its business plan for the next trading period. It is working from its current position and its forecasted activities will conform to its operational plan.

Current Position Balance Sheet as at 31 December

	Cost £	Depreciation to date £	Net book value £
Fixed assets			
Land and buildings	100 000	–	100 000
Equipment and machinery	50 000	25 000	25 000
Motor vehicles	10 000	5 000	5 000
	160 000	30 000	130 000
Current assets			
Stocks:			
Finished goods (120 units)		14 400	
Raw materials		4 000	
Debtors (Nov £16 200 + Dec £10 800)		27 000	
Cash and bank balances		5 000	
		50 400	
Less Current liabilities			
Creditors for raw materials			
(Nov £3500 + Dec £4000)	7 500		
Creditors for fixed expenses (Dec)	2 500		
Taxation due	3 000		
Dividend payable	10 000	23 000	27 400
			157 400
Financed by:			
Share capital 100 000 shares of £1 each			100 000
Profit and loss account balance			57 400
			157 400

The plans for the six months ended 30 June are as follows:

1 Production will be 60 units per month.

2 Production costs will be (per unit):

	£
Direct materials	50
Direct labour	40
Variable overhead	30
	120

3 Fixed overhead is £2500 per month payable one month in arrears.

4 Sales at a price of £180 per unit are expected to be:

Jan	Feb	Mar	Apr	May	Jun
50	50	60	90	90	70

5 Purchases of direct materials (raw materials) will be £3000 per month to April and £4000 per month for May and June.

6 The creditors for raw materials bought are paid two months after purchase.

7 Debtors are expected to pay their accounts two months after they have bought the goods.

8 Direct labour and variable overhead are paid in the same month as the units are produced.

9 A new vehicle costing £10 000 will be bought and paid for in March.

10 Taxation will be paid in January and the dividend in March.

11 Depreciation for the six months: Plant machinery £2500, Motor vehicles £1000.

The detailed operational plan

We must first of all draw up the various budgets and incorporate them into the Master Budget.

Production budget (units)

	Jan	Feb	Mar	Apr	May	Jun
Opening stock *(Note 1)*	120	130	140	140	110	80
Add Produced	60	60	60	60	60	60
	180	190	200	200	170	140
Less Sales	50	50	60	90	90	70
Closing Stock	130	140	140	110	80	70

Materials budget

	Jan £	Feb £	Mar £	Apr £	May £	Jun £
Opening stock *(Note 2)*	4000	4000	4000	4000	4000	5000
Add Purchases	3000	3000	3000	3000	4000	4000
	7000	7000	7000	7000	8000	9000
Less Used in production *(Note 3)*	3000	3000	3000	3000	3000	3000
Closing stock	4000	4000	4000	4000	5000	6000

Note 1: This is the figure in the opening balance sheet for stock of finished goods.

Note 2: This is the value of the stock of raw materials in the opening balance sheet.

Note 3: Production per month is 60 units costing £50 each in raw material costs.

Creditors budget

	Jan £	Feb £	Mar £	Apr £	May £	Jun £
Opening balance	7 500	7 000	6 000	6 000	6 000	7 000
Add Purchases (Note 4)	3 000	3 000	3 000	3 000	4 000	4 000
	10 500	10 000	9 000	9 000	10 000	11 000
Less Payments (Note 5)	3 500	4 000	3 000	3 000	3 000	3 000
Closing balance	7 000	6 000	6 000	6 000	7 000	8 000

Debtors Budget

	Jan £	Feb £	Mar £	Apr £	May £	Jun £
Opening balances (Note 6)	27 000	19 800	18 000	19 800	27 000	32 400
Add Sales	9 000	9 000	10 800	16 200	16 200	12 600
	36 000	28 800	28 800	36 000	43 200	45 000
Less Received (Note 7)	16 200	10 800	9 000	9 000	10 800	16 200
Closing balance	19 800	18 000	19 800	27 000	32 400	28 800

Note 4: These are the same figures as in the purchases in the materials budget.

Note 5: The first two payments come from the creditors listed in the balance sheet at the start of the year. The payment made in March relates to the materials purchased in January.

Note 6: The opening debts balance comes from the balance sheet and represents November sales of £16 200 and December sales of £10 800; customers pay two months after purchase

Note 7: January receipts represent November sales.

Cash budget

	Jan £	Feb £	Mar £	Apr £	May £	Jun £
Receipts						
Debtors	16 200	10 800	9 000	9 000	10 800	16 200
Payments						
Creditors	3 500	4 000	3 000	3 000	3 000	3 000
Fixed overheads	2 500	2 500	2 500	2 500	2 500	2 500
Direct labour	2 400	2 400	2 400	2 400	2 400	2 400
Variable overheads	1 800	1 800	1 800	1 800	1 800	1 800
New vehicle			10 000			
Taxation	3 000					
Dividend			10 000			
Total payments	13 200	10 700	29 700	9 700	9 700	9 700
Receipts less Payments	3 000	100	(20 700)	(700)	1 100	6 500
Balance at bank (£5000 b/fwd)	8 000	8 100	(12 600)	(13 300)	(12 200)	(5 700)

Master Budget
Forecast operating statement for the six months ended 30 June

	£	£	£
Sales (410 units)			73 800
Less Cost of goods sold:			
Opening stock of finished goods (120 units)		14 400	
(Note 8) Add Cost of goods completed (360 units)		43 200	
		57 600	
Less Closing stock of finished goods (70 units)		8 400	49 200
Gross profit			24 600
Less			
Fixed overhead (2 500 × 6 months)		15 000	
Depreciation: Machinery	2 500		
Motors	1 000	3 500	18 500
Net profit			6 100

Note 8: This figure includes Direct Materials, Direct Labour and Variable Overheads at £120 per unit.

Forecast balance sheet as at 30 June

	Cost £	Depreciation to date £	Net book value £
Fixed assets			
Land and buildings	100 000	–	100 000
Plant and machinery	50 000	27 500	22 500
Motor vehicles	20 000	6 000	14 000
	170 000	33 500	136 500
Current assets			
Stocks: Finished goods		8 400	
Raw materials		6 000	
Debtors		28 800	
		43 200	
Current liabilities			
Creditors for goods	8 000		
Creditors-overheads	2 500		
Bank overdraft	5 600	16 200	27 000
			163 500
Financed by			
Share Capital			100 000
Profit and Loss Account (57400 + 6100)			63 500
			163 500

Unit 8   Business planning

PC
8.2.4
8.2.5
8.2.6
8.2.7

ACTIVITY 8.2.8

Margaret Dean is to open a shop on 1 January. She will put in £60 000 cash into a business bank account as Capital, she will also borrow £30 000 from the Bank. In addition she is allowed an overdraft of £20 000. Her financial plans are as follows:

1. Bank interest and charges are estimated to be £2000 payable 31 May.

2. On 1 January to buy and pay for Premises £70 000, Shop Fixtures £9000, Motor £11 000.

3. She will employ two assistants, each to get a salary of £600 per month, to be paid at the end of each month.

4. She will buy the following goods on one month's credit from a range of wholesale outlets.

Jan	Feb	Mar	Apr	May	Jun
£5000	£3000	£3000	£3500	£3500	£3500

5. Her average mark up will be 60% and she expects to have an average value of stock in the shop of £2000 at cost prices.

6. The other expenses of the shop will be £400 per month payable in the month following that in which they were incurred.

7. Margaret's cash drawings will amount to £1000 per month.

8. Depreciation is to be provided on Shop Fixtures at 10% per annum and on the Motor van at 20% per annum (note: your budget is for 6 months).

Task 1. Prepare a cash budget for the six months ended 30 June.

Task 2. Construct a forecast Trading and Profit and Loss Account for the six months ended 30 June and a Balance Sheet as at that date.

Monitoring and Review of Business Plans

Unless the organisation is prepared to spend valuable management time on looking at both current and past performance its planning activities will be worthless. Departmental managers must be made accountable for their performance and this must be measured against the targets that they set for themselves when they agreed the budget at the start of the financial period. Although many of the planned outcomes stated in the budget may have been outlined in financial terms most of the important figures for individual managers in the plan will probably be in volumes such as units of production or sales, labour hours or kilos of raw material consumed.

Managers must make weekly or monthly reports on how their outcomes compared to their original budget. Often these reports are on an exceptions basis whereby only the items that are not near their targeted output levels will be reported. There is no need to report that all is going to plan, the firm's managers will assume that this is happening unless told otherwise. If the firm's planned activities are not being attained management must take action and they can only do so effectively if they are told immediately. There is for instance no point in continuing to produce to planned production levels if sales are lower than those planned levels.

ACTIVITY 8.2.9

PC
8.2.4
8.2.5
8.2.6
8.2.7
8.2.8

I. Khan is going to set up a new business on 1 January. He estimates that his first six months in business will be as follows:-

1. He will put £10 000 into a bank account for the firm on 1 January.
2. He will receive a loan of £10 000 on 1 January. This will be paid into the business bank account immediately. Interest is charged at 2% per month and is taken out of the bank by direct debit.
3. On 1 January, he will buy machinery £2000 and a Van £1600, Premises £5000, paying for them immediately out of the business account.
4. He will rent premises costing £4000 per quarter. His first payment being 1 January.
5. All purchases will be effected on credit. He will buy £2000 goods on 1 January and he will pay for these in February. Other purchases will be the rest of January, £3200, and for February, March April, May and June £4000 each month. Other than the £2000 worth bought in January all other purchases will be paid for two months after purchase.
6. Sales (all on credit) will be £4000 for January and £5000 for each month after that. Debtors will pay for the goods in the third month after purchase by them.
7. Stock-in-trade on 30 June is estimated to be £2000.
8. Wages and Salaries are estimated to cost £1500 per month and will be paid on the last day of each month.
9. General expenses will be £100 per month payable in the month following that in which they were incurred.
10. Insurance covering the 12 months from 1 January will be paid for by cheque on 30 January, £240.
11. Rates will be paid as follows: for the three months to 31 March, by cheque on 28 February, for the 12 months ended 31 March next year, by cheque on 31 July. Rates are £2400 per annum.
12. He will make drawings of £800 per month by cheque.
13. His bank manager will give him an overdraft of up to £10 000.
14. Depreciation: Motors 20% per annum, Machinery 10% per annum. (Note you are dealing with 6 months.)

Task 1. Prepare a cash budget for the six months to the end of June.

Task 2. Construct the forecast Trading and Profit and Loss Account for the first six months' trading and a Balance Sheet as at 30 June.

Task 3. Comment in the format of a report to Mr Khan on your findings as shown in the foregoing plans.

Unit 8 Business planning

PC
8.2.1
8.2.2.
8.2.3
8.2.4
8.2.5
8.2.6
8.2.7

Assignment

You must produce a written business plan for a one product or service firm of your own choice. You must undertake all of the necessary research into the business objectives, administration, marketing, production, resource requirements and the financial consequences of your proposed business. Your plan must be presented to your tutor who will act the part of a bank manager who can offer financial support. You must convince the 'Bank Manager' that your business is worthy of the bank's support.

Element 8.3
PLAN FOR EMPLOYMENT OR SELF-EMPLOYMENT

Performance criteria

1. **Identify and give examples of types of employment and self-employment.**
2. **Identify statutory requirements for employment or self-employment.**
3. **Identify sources of information and collect information for employment or self-employment.**
4. **Identify opportunities for employment or self-employment.**
5. **Analyse and discuss skills to support employment or self-employment.**
6. **Propose a personal plan for employment or self-employment.**

TYPES OF EMPLOYMENT AND SELF-EMPLOYMENT

About half of the UK's economic activity relates to the various organisations in the public sector. It is clear, therefore, that a similar proportion of job opportunities will occur in the public sector. Element 2.1 of Business Organisations and Systems explains the types of public sector organisations that are likely to provide employment opportunities. The main employers in this sector are: central government (i.e. the Civil Service and its related agencies), public corporations, local authorities and the National Health Service.

As you are aware, the private sector is made up of firms whose ownership can be categorised into sole traders, partnerships, private limited companies and public limited companies (*see* Element 2.1).

A Department of Trade and Industry report, published in July 1994, stated that in the previous year 96 per cent of all firms in Britain employed fewer than 20 people. Note that this statistic relates to the number of firms and not people in employment. Some firms in Britain are very large employers who employ many thousands of people. One trend in employment patterns is clear, however: large firms are shedding labour as the impact of new technology and work practices progresses. These organisations are also adopting different approaches to work where their employees are more likely to be working from home and where individuals are required to take more responsibility for their own actions in their workplace. Some firms have hived off parts of their structure and formed semi-autonomous work groups of former employees who subcontract for work from the firm. If these groups are not competitive in comparison to outside firms then they will lose their work. The aim is to make them more effective by bringing decision making down to the lowest level and make them more efficient and responsible for their own actions.

STATUTORY REQUIREMENTS

The following sections relate to the various statutes and regulations that can have an effect on both self-employed people who employ others and those in work who are employees. In other words, these regulations will affect most people in employment, either directly or indirectly. Some are specific to certain types of ownership; others have a general effect on us all. In most cases you need to know that they exist and that you can get help should you need to know more. This help usually comes from accountants or solicitors and all firms should appoint such firms in order to be able to ring an expert up for advice should it be necessary. You will be charged for this service, of course, but it is cheaper to do things right in the first place than to have to go back to a problem in order to make it right later on. This is particularly true of financial matters that can waste a lot of time if not done properly from the start. PAYE, National Insurance Contributions, VAT, bookkeeping, etc. are enough to give anyone sleepless nights, if not carried out correctly. Furthermore, many owners of firms pay too much tax because they do not seek advice during the year from their accountants.

Accounting requirements

All organisations have to produce some form of accounts to indicate to the owners, government or other interested parties how the management of the organisation dealt with the organisation's assets in the period of account.

Sole traders are people who own a firm that is neither a partnership nor a limited company. They own it outright, in that they own all of the firm's capital. In order to be assessed for income tax, the sole trader must produce a full and acceptable set of final accounts and a balance sheet for the year of account. The tax inspectors at the Inland Revenue assess the amount of income tax that has to be paid according to the accounts submitted by the sole trader. In order to present an acceptable set of accounts that show the most advantageous position for tax purposes, the sole trader will usually appoint an accountant to prepare the accounts and balance sheet and audit the firm's transactions. The accountant, if satisfied with the accounts after the audit, will give a certificate that states that in his or her view the statement shown by the accounts and balance sheet show a true and fair view of the financial affairs of the firm at the balance sheet date. Furthermore, the accountant will prepare a tax computation that shows how much tax the sole trader should pay. The Inland Revenue will either agree or negotiate with the accountant for the correct tax due.

Legally, partnerships are dealt with on the same basis as sole traders in that their accountant audits the accounts, produces the final accounts and balance sheet and negotiates with the Inland Revenue for the amount of income tax that each partner owes.

Whereas sole traders and partnerships produce final accounts and balance sheets in order to satisfy the demands of the Inland Revenue, limited companies must produce these statements by law. The various Companies Acts require companies to publish accounts and financial information that informs the shareholders who own the company how the company has been managed by the directors who run it on their behalf.

ACTIVITY 8.3.1

Your friend is planning to start a new business and you have told him that he ought to appoint an accountant before the business starts trading. Write a letter to your friend giving reasons to back up your advice.

PC 8.3.2

Legal requirements

Various other legal requirements are placed upon businesses that are of a financial nature, such as those involving Value Added Tax (VAT), National Insurance and Pensions.

Value Added Tax

With the exception of food, children's clothing, books, magazines and housing costs, most expenditure items in the UK and in most of the countries in the European Union attract value added tax. In theory, its operation is simple: a percentage tax on cost is added to the cost of goods and services at the point of sale. The firm that charges VAT must pay over to Customs and Excise the amount of tax charged to its customers, not the amount collected. It may deduct from this figure the amount of VAT that it had to pay to others during the same period. The effect of these regulations is that the final consumer pays the whole of the tax, which at the moment stands at 17.5 per cent.

Income Tax

Every person in the country has his or her own individual National Insurance number that will identify them for both National Insurance and taxation purposes.

All individuals must pay income tax if their income exceeds the lower limit for tax purposes. This and other taxation limits, rates and allowances can, and often are, altered each year in the Chancellor's budget. The basis of the system of income tax is that each person is given a tax code that relates to his or her tax allowance, i.e. the income upon which no tax is paid. For most of us in employment this is calculated on a weekly or a monthly figure using tax tables published by the Inland Revenue, table A. All income that is received over this tax-free limit is taxed at rates set by the government – the more you receive, the more tax you should pay. The tax payable for those in employment is again worked out on tax tables published by the Inland Revenue, table B. It is the employer's responsibility to deduct the correct amount of tax and to pay it over to the Collector of Taxes.

National Insurance contributions

Every person in employment in this country must, if he or she earns more than the statutory minimum wage, pay National Insurance contributions. Originally, these contributions were intended to fund the National Health Service and provide pensions and national assistance payments to the poor and the unemployed. This earmarking of income to expenditure never in fact took place and today the National Insurance contributions can simply be considered as another form of taxation. Unlike most superannuation and private pension schemes, these contributions are not invested in order to fund future pensions. State pensions are paid out of the income generated from current taxation. During the 1980s and 1990s it has become increasingly apparent that the future cost of state pensions cannot be funded from reasonable levels of taxation and the government has sought ways to minimise its liability for the payment of state pensions. As more people live longer, the cost of state pensions increases each year, and these costs have to be borne by an ever-decreasing proportion of the population that is in paid employment.

National Insurance contributions are collected from employees at the same time as income tax is deducted from their pay through the *Pay As You Earn* income tax system. As well as the amount of money deducted from a person's wage or salary, the employer has to pay over the employer's National Insurance contribution for each employee. The rates of income tax and both employees' and employer's contributions can be changed by the Chancellor of the Exchequer in the annual Budget.

Figures 8.4 and 8.5 have been reproduced by permission of the Inland Revenue and show how an employer has to deal with the administration of the Pay As You Earn income tax system and the National Insurance system.

Thinking of taking someone on?

You may be thinking of taking on an employee because your business is expanding and needs another pair of hands. If so, read this leaflet. It answers some of the questions you may have about Pay As You Earn (PAYE).

What is PAYE?

Under the Pay As You Earn system employers deduct tax from their employees' pay on the weekly or monthly payday, and send it to the Inland Revenue.

To save costs, National Insurance Contributions are also collected in the same way.

Do I have to operate PAYE for every employee?

You have to deduct tax from all employees who are paid at more than a certain rate, which is set each year. Employer's and employee's NIC also have to be paid once the employee's earnings reach a certain amount each week or month.

You may also have to pay Statutory Sick Pay (SSP) in certain circumstances. SSP is treated in the same way as pay and you have to charge tax and NICs on it.

If I decide to take on an employee, what should I do first?

Tell the tax office which already deals with your business. You will then be told which office will be your PAYE tax office – it may be a different one. The PAYE tax office will send you the instructions, tables and forms you need to operate PAYE and NICs. They will also give you a PAYE tax reference. You should use this reference if you have any PAYE problems you need to ask them about.

What do I do?

There are five main things you need to do:

- Tell the tax office when an employee starts to work for you.
- Work out the tax and NICs due each payday.
- Pay this over to the Accounts Office each month (the Accounts Office is part of the Inland Revenue that collects or receives your payments).
- Tell the tax office when an employee leaves.
- Tell the tax offfice at the end of each tax year how much each employee has earned and how much tax and NICs you have deducted. (The tax year runs from 6 April of one year to 5 April of the next year. Your PAYE instructions include an income tax calendar showing how the tax year is divided into tax weeks and months.)

So you can see the only regular jobs are working out the tax and NICs each payday and sending them in each month. You will soon get into the routine.

What do I do when an employee starts?

Ask your new employee for form P45, and NI number if it is not shown on the form. The P45 is a leaving certificate given by the last employer. You send part of it to your tax office and keep the other part. If the employee doesn't have a P45, you give him or her a starting certificate (form P46) to sign. You complete the rest of it and where appropriate send it to the tax office. These forms contain information which you need to work out PAYE for the employees.

How do I work out the tax and NICs?

To do this you need

- a PAYE code for each employee
- tax tables and NIC tables
- A Deductions working sheet for each employeee.

What is a PAYE code?

A PAYE code is usually a number and a letter. It represents the amount of the employee's tax allowances – that is, tax-free pay – for the year. You use it with the tax tables to find out how much pay is tax-free each payday.

When an employee starts, the code to use is shown on the P45 given to you. If the new employee doesn't have a P45, your instructions tell you which code to use. This will depend on which part of the P46 is signed.

The tax office will let you know if the code has to be changed.

Fig 8.4 PAYE and NIC extracts from explanatory leaflets

Unit 8 Business planning

Deductions working sheet P11 (New)

Employer's name	Employee's surname in CAPITAL LETTERS	First two forenames		Year to 5 April 1987
JOHN KNIGHT	WILLIAMS	GEORGE ALBERT		

Tax District and reference	National Insurance no.	Works no. etc	Date of birth in figures Day Month Year	Date of leaving in figures Day Month Year	Tax Code †	Amended code †	Week/Month in which applied
WATFORD 2 728/K52	YP 37 20 18 A	W 4	13 04 47	15 08 86	233 L		

National Insurance Contributions*

	Total of Employee's and Employer's Contributions payable	Employee's contributions payable	Employee's contributions at Contracted-out rate included in Col 1b	Statutory sick pay in the week or month included in Col 2		WEEK number	MONTH number	Pay in the week or month including statutory sick pay	Total pay to date	Total free pay to date as shown by Table A	Total taxable pay to date	Total tax due to date as shown by Taxable Pay Tables	Tax deducted or refunded in the week or month † Mark refunds "R"	For employer's use
	1a	1b	1c	1d				2	3	4a	4	5	6	7
						1	6 April to 5 May							
						2								
						3								
						4								
						5	6 May to 5 June							
						6								
11 24	5 62			245.86	7	2	6 June to 5 July	490 00	314 93	175 07	50 25	10 15
11 24	5 62			80 00	8			570 00	359 92	210 08	60 90	10 15
11 24	5 62			80 00	9			650 00	404 91	245 09	71 05	10 15
11 24	5 62			80 00	10	3	6 July to 5 Aug	730 00	449 90	280 10	81 20	10 15
11 24	5 62			80 00	11			810 00	494 89	315 11	91 35	10 15
11 24	5 62			80 00	12			890 00	539 88	350 12	101 50	10 15
11 24	5 62			80 00	13	4	6 Aug to 5 Sept	970 00	584 87	385 13	111 65	10 15
11 24	5 62			80 00	14			1050 00	629 86	420 14	121 80	10 15
11 24	5 62			80 00	15			1130 00	674 85	455 15	131 95	10 15
11 24	5 62			80 00	16	5	6 Sept to 5 Oct	1210 00	719 84	490 16	142 10	10 15
11 94	5 97			85 00	17			1295 00	764 83	520 17	153 70	11 60
11 94	5 97			85 00	18	6	6 Oct to 5 Nov	1380 00	809 82	570 18	165 30	11 60
11 94	5 97			85 00	19			1465 00	854 81	610 19	176 90	11 60 Leaver
					20								
					21	7							
					22								
					23								
					24								
					25								
					26								
					27								
					28								
					29								
					30								

| Total carried forward | Total carried forward | Total carried forward | | | | | | Total carried forward | | | | | |
| 136 98 | 68 49 | | | | | | | | | | | | |

▼ A

*NI Contribution Table letter must be entered overleaf beside the NI totals boxes – see the note shown there
This box may be used if the employer wishes to record the NI letter while this side of the sheet is in use

† If amended cross out previous code
Ø If in any week/month the amount in column 4 is more than the amount in column 3, make no entry in column 5

P11 (New)

Fig 8.5 A deductions working sheet (Crown copyright is reproduced with the permission of the Controller of the HMSO)

636

> **ACTIVITY 8.3.2**
>
> In Activity 8.3.1, you wrote to your friend advising him to appoint an accountant prior to starting his own business. Your friend has thanked you on the telephone but has told you that he cannot see the reason for doing so. You have told him that at your next meeting you will tell him about VAT, National Insurance and income tax and how it could affect his business, particularly as he intends to employ others in his new venture. Draft some notes to help you in your discussion.

The Office, Shops and Railway Premises Act, 1963

This Act requires all employers to provide the minimum working conditions for their employees. Its provisions include the following:

- minimum temperature of 16 degrees centigrade;
- minimum 400 cubic feet of space per employee;
- a fire certificate;
- once-a-week cleaning of floors;
- first-aid boxes and trained first aider;
- sanitary conveniences and wash basins;
- drinking water and suitable and sufficient eating facilities.

Employment law

Under the Employment Protection (Consolidation) Act 1978, employers are required to give written information to their employees of the terms of their employment within 13 weeks of their commencing work. The information which must be supplied relates to the parties to the contract, the date employment began, the notice required by the employee to terminate the contract, pay, hours of work, holidays, incapacity for work, pensions and the employee's job title. Furthermore, a statement must be included specifying any disciplinary rules, the person to whom application for redress of grievances may be made and notification of any change in the terms must be provided within one month of the change.

If the employee is to serve a trial probationary period, this should also be included in the contract. The length of the trial period is negotiable but is usually six or twelve months. The employer with the consent of the employee, can extend the trial period, but the employee can be dismissed within the trial period at the employer's discretion.

The method and frequency of payment of the employee will be laid down in the contract and the employee is entitled to receive a pay slip showing the total wages or salary payable, the amount of any deduction and the net payment.

During employment there are a number of circumstances that could lead to disciplinary action, such as incompetence, misconduct, time-wasting or poor time-keeping and problems between individual employees. Problems involving incompetence should be dealt with during the initial trial period of employment where the employee can be warned that its effect will lead to dismissal. Incompetence can be difficult to prove once the trial period has elapsed.

The usual procedure adopted in a disciplinary process involve a verbal warning to the employee and if that warning has no effect, a written warning. The latter should be delivered as part of a formal interview and a statement of its delivery and an acknowledgement of receipt should be kept in the employee's personal file. This warning represents a final warning and any recurrence of the problem within the stated time limit given with the warning will result in dismissal. The period of notice given to the employee and the notice itself should conform to the requirements of the Employment Protection Act 1975. Alternatively, it is often decided that payment in lieu of notice is a more preferable method. In some cases instant dismissal will be used in cases of gross misconduct. Instant dismissal without the statutory period of notice can be given for the following reasons:

- disobedience to orders given by a responsible superior (the orders must be lawful and within the terms of the contract of employment);
- gross negligence;
- dishonesty;
- drunkenness or drug-taking which interferes with the employee's duties;
- wilful misconduct at work;
- immorality which is interfering with the employee's duties;
- disclosure of business secrets.

Unfair dismissal legislation

The Employment Protection Consolidation Act 1978 contains provisions regarding constructive dismissal:

where the employee terminates the contract, with or without notice, in circumstances that he is entitled to terminate it without notice by reason of the employer's conduct.

This means that an employer may unilaterally change the terms of employment in some way, presenting the employee with virtually no choice but to resign.

An employee may be dismissed on the following grounds:

- capability or qualification of the employee;
- conduct of the employee;
- redundancy.

If the employee considers that he or she was unfairly dismissed the onus of proof is on the employee to prove that the dismissal was constructive. The employer must prove that the dismissal was fair and reasonable and that proper and adequate procedures had been followed.

The remedies for unfair dismissal are reinstatement in the old job, re-engagement in a comparable job or compensation for loss of past and future earnings, pension rights and reputation.

The Redundancy Payments Scheme

Started under the 1965 Redundancy Payments Act, the provisions have been included in the 1978 Consolidation Act and require an employer to make a lump sum payment to an employee who is dismissed because of redundancy. The amount of the payment is related to the employee's age, pay and length of service. Employers have to pay the required sum but can reclaim 41 per cent of the cost from the government's Redundancy Fund.

Element 8.3 Plan for employment or self-employment

The Employment Protection Act 1975

The main purpose of this act is to encourage collective bargaining. Employers who are planning redundancies must consult the appropriate trade union via the union's representatives. Employees may appeal to a tribunal following unfair dismissal for any reason connected to trade union membership. One of the most far reaching consequences of the Act was the establishment of ACAS, the Advisory, Conciliation and Arbitration Service, which offers industrial relations advice and provides a conciliation service between employees and employers who are in dispute.

ACTIVITY 8.3.3

Write a guide to advise the supervisors at your place of work on correct procedures regarding the disciplining of their workers. Within the guide, make reference to the various acts outlined above.

PC 8.3.2

OPPORTUNITIES FOR EMPLOYMENT OR SELF-EMPLOYMENT

Very few people are in a position to set up in business on their own immediately on leaving school or college. Although they may have learned a lot about business, they lack the detailed knowledge and skills about a sector of business that in most cases can only be acquired from experience. You need to know the products and the market in which you will operate in order to succeed. You also need to know your potential customers and in most cases they need to know and trust you.

Once you have the required experience you may want to start your own firm. Many people cannot raise the necessary capital to enable them to do this. Many others cannot take the career risk of leaving a good, well paid job for a venture that initially is not likely to provide much remuneration and may fail leaving them owing a lot of money. Furthermore, the hours of work required are usually much greater, as is the responsibility and worry. The rewards of being self-employed, however, can be great both in financial terms and in job satisfaction. The taxation system in particular favours the self-employed, as tax is paid in arrears and there are legal ways of avoiding tax liabilities in the first place.

If you know the type of job that you want to do, you should seek out as much advice as possible during your years in education. Obtaining the correct qualifications is usually the first step into a successful career – ask your careers tutors. Better still, talk to the people who actually do the type of job that you would like to do. If, for instance, you want to be an accountant, ask an accountant how to enter the profession, what qualifications are needed both to get a job and, just as important, to become a registered student of one of the professional bodies such as ACA, ACCA, CIMA or CIPFA. Do you need a degree? If so, does it matter about the subject of the degree or the level of pass awarded? People will always spend time giving advice to those who want to do similar work to themselves. Do not be afraid to ask.

There are many organisations that exist to help people into either employment or self-employment. The Careers Service, run by the local education authority, is for people under the age of 19. The *Training and Enterprise Councils* assist all age groups with both advice and finance. The *job centres* offer advice and help to find paid employment and have schemes to help people start to be self-employed. *Private employment agencies* offer employment opportunities. Most *local authorities* provide an advice service and grants and loans for new businesses. There are various *voluntary sector organisations* that provide financial help and advice, such as the Prince's Trust, or you can do charitable work overseas with the Voluntary Service Overseas (VSO) organisation.

THE SKILLS REQUIRED

Knowing your own strengths and weaknesses is one of the most important aspects of success in both working for someone else and working for yourself. Although this may seem self-evident, many of us seldom admit our weaknesses to ourselves and, just as important, many of us are unaware of our own strengths. Our egos often lead us to want to achieve levels in our careers that are impractical. Many people have ambitions beyond their capabilities. Many others underachieve through lack of ambition or self-belief.

If you are good at something and interested in it, you will probably succeed in a career that is connected with it. If you are not interested in your job, you will probably not succeed. If you are the type of person that does not like to study and would prefer to go to the pub every night, then you should look for a job in that type of business and aim to run your own pub in the long term when you can get the finance together and have the necessary experience to succeed. There are a lot of business skills needed in such a job and the contents of this book will help to develop them and will provide much of the knowledge required. Business is business and it is preferable to get into the business that interests you most.

One thing you will have to find out about yourself is, Are you a good team player or do you work best on your own? In Element 2.3 working with others was discussed. If you like to work alone, you can seek out jobs where such group work is at a minimum, but almost all jobs need some skills in team work and there is help available to increase your skills in this area. Consult your local library and college.

Planning, time measurement, setting targets and reviewing progress are disciplines that we can all develop if we are systematic in our approach to work. It is always tempting to jump into any situation without thought or self-control and it is almost always a mistake. This unit aims to encourage people to plan their actions and monitor their actions against their plans.

AN ACTION PLAN FOR EMPLOYMENT

When trying to gain employment you should set yourself a personal plan. Refer back to Unit 4 and in particular, the sections on the recruitment of staff. Study how job descriptions and personnel specifications are used in the recruitment and selection of staff. The key to getting an interview is to complete your job application on the basis of the personnel specification – that tells you the type of person that the firm is looking to employ. When you get to an interview try to relax and talk. If you do not understand a question, ask the questioner to elaborate. Arrive early for the interview and dress according to the type of employment that you are seeking. Do not turn up at an interview for an articled clerk's job at a solicitor's firm in jeans, T shirt and trainers.

Evidence of previous employment is important, even if it is only stacking supermarket shelves. The prospective employer wants to know if you are employable. For example, do you turn up to work on time? Do you have unexplained absences? Will you do as you are told? Do you get on with your colleagues?

You can seek advice from job centres, careers advisors, private employment agencies and the local and national press when looking for job advertisements. Some jobs are only advertised in trade magazines or professional journals. You have to ask advice from those people in the type of job that you are looking for in order to make sure that you are looking in the correct places. Do not become disheartened if you do not get many replies or interviews – keep at it!

AN ACTION PLAN FOR SELF-EMPLOYMENT

The following checklist is for you to follow when you start up in business for the first time. If you cannot follow all of the points, then you should seek help. They may not all be relevant to the firm that you want to start, but it is better to have considered these points prior to starting your business.

Fig 8.6 Make sure you are looking in the correct places for your type of job

- What is your business idea?
- What are the advantages and disadvantages of buying an existing business, buying a franchise or starting from scratch?
- Does your idea stand a good chance of success?
- Are you aware of the common mistakes that new self-employed people make?
- Have you prepared your business plan?
- Do you know your market?
- Do you know your potential customers' requirements?
- Can you expand on this number of customers?
- What assets will you require and can you raise the required finance?
- Will you make sufficient profit?
- Have you done a realistic cash budget?
- Can you do the firm's accounts or can you get someone else to do them?
- Can you deal with VAT, National Insurance Contributions and Taxation? If not, have you appointed an accountant?
- Are you going to form a sole trader, partnership or a limited company?

All of these points have been covered in this book; use the index and contents pages to find them.

Fig 8.7 'Have you done a realistic cash budget?'

SOURCES OF INFORMATION

This section is intended to direct you to the type of information that is available to you as an employee and, more particularly, as a self-employed person. It is essential to all aspects of business planning that you know where information can be found or how you can set up systems to collect and analyse information.

Primary sources of information are those that provide original data that is specific to the organisation's needs and as such they are usually confidential to the organisation and represent the latest data available.

Secondary sources of information are those that provide information that is obtained and compiled by others. Much useful information can be collected from such sources and many large firms keep their own libraries which stock standard reference books, journals, computer databases and information systems like Excel and McCarthy. Many works of reference are now available on CD ROM for quick access on personal computers. These include the McCarthy cards, articles from newspapers like *the Times*, *the Financial Times* and the *New York Herald Tribune*. The government publishes a great number of indices and statistics that illustrate the country's economic activity: the best known of these is the Index of Retail Prices that is used as the main indicator of inflation. Many other statistics are published by the various government departments, particularly the Department of Trade and Industry. This data is collected by the Central Statistical Office and is also available in various quarterly and annual abstracts. The most useful secondary sources of information for your needs are listed below.

Databases

- Secos. European and UK statistics package. Has a variety of tables.
- Census 1991. Currently being produced with a wealth of material on employment income, etc. Use a mapping package, for example, Supermap.
- CD-ROMS. The *Financial Times*, *Guardian* and *Times* are now available. Others will no doubt follow.
- Internet sources. Try the EC Cordis database.

Newspapers

- *The Financial Times* excellent for the economic data. Read also S. Brittan and Joe Rogally.
- *The Guardian*, particularly Monday's Economic Page. Other articles by Will Hutton and Larry Elliot.
- *The Times*, *the Independent* and *the Daily Telegraph* also have regular articles.
- Sundays: *the Independent, Sunday Times, Observer, Sunday Telegraph*.
- Magazines such as *the Economist*.
- Bank reviews particularly Barclay's Lloyd's, Royal Bank of Scotland, Natwest. These are usually free to customers so ask at your branch. Lloyd's Bank also produces an annual survey of the UK economy; it is normally available from late October or early November.

Government sources

There are many hundreds of government publications, including:

- *Key data.* A special student edition containing extracts from other sources.
- *Annual Abstract of Statistics.* More detailed tables taken from government publications.
- *Regional Trends.*
- *Social Trends.*
- *Business Monitor.*
- *National Income Accounts.*

Local sources

Clearly these will vary depending on which part of the country you live in, but should include:

- Chamber of commerce
- Tec
- Local council
- Economic development unit.

Desk research refers to information that is generated within the organisation. All organisations have to produce and keep certain types of information, mostly of a financial or a technical nature, such as final accounts and balance sheets and plans, designs and specifications of products. Furthermore, employee records are kept for personnel purposes and inventories of plant and equipment are kept for audit purposes. All of this information can be of use to the organisation and, should it be required, looking it up in existing and archived records is called desk research.

The sources of information required by the different sections of a company are given below.

Marketing

- Customer details
- Customer buying trends
- Product test results
- Information on competitors

Sales

- Sales volumes by area
- Value of sales by area
- Information on customer reaction to new products
- Customer reaction to competitor products
- Customer preferences
- Customer complaints and warranty work

Production

- Details of customer orders and probable future sales
- Costing data on current and estimated future costs

Accounts

- Financial accounting data
- Cost accounting data
- Budgets and budgetary control details

ACTIVITY 8.3.4

You are required to do a five-minute presentation to your teacher on how you would do the research required for the assignment at the end of this element.

PC 8.3.3

Assignment

PC
8.3.1
8.3.4
8.3.5
8.3.6

Task 1. Make notes on three types or areas of employment that interest you.

Task 2. Choose one of the above types of employment (or self-employment) and list the opportunities that are available in either the United Kingdom, European Union or any other international location.

Task 3. Discuss with your tutor your own strengths and weaknesses in relation to the skills needed for your selected employment or self-employment opportunity and propose a personal plan for employment or self-employment.

INDEX

absenteeism 294–5
ABTA (Association of British Travel Agents) 250
ACAS (Advisory, Conciliation and Arbitration Service) 276, 278, 639
accountants 605
accounts
  ageing schedules 571–2
  balance sheets 507–8, 545–6, 557, 569–71
  cash flow 505, 517, 530, 571
  departments 106
  double-entry bookkeeping 537–9
  final accounts 547–9
  information requirements 644
  legislation 633
  objectives 461
  policy changes 579
  profit and loss 543–4, 556, 567–9
  trading accounts 542–3
  trial balances 540–1, 555
  users of 563–4
  year-end adjustments 550–4
  see also ratio analysis
accruals 504, 550–1
acid rain 47
acid test ratio 576
ACORN (A Classification Of Residential Neighbourhoods) 240, 242
acquisitions 381
added value 344–5
  as a performance measure 353
administration systems
  health and safety 117–18
  information technology 107
  job evaluation 108–10
  management stucture 101–6
  systems description 112–17
  systems evaluation 110–11

advertising
  agencies 613
  by oligopolists 34
  corporate 346
  costs 34, 228
  and demand 9
  recruitment 324
  and sales promotions 182
  test surveys 209
  see also marketing
Advertising Standards Authority (ASA) 250
advice notes 404–5
Advisory, Conciliation and Arbitration Service (ACAS) 276, 278, 639
age analysis 235–6
ageing schedules 571–2
agency contracts 363–4
agendas of meetings 126
agents 255
aggregate demand 53
Amway 256
Ansoff's product-market matrix 195–6
answering machines 135
ASA (Advertising Standards Authority) 250
assets
  current 500, 503–4, 571
  fixed 469–70, 500–3, 570–1
  ratio analysis 578
  sources of finance for 508–13
Association of British Travel Agents (ABTA) 250
Austin Rover 468
average creditors payment period ratio 577
average debtor collection period ratio 576
Avon 184

Index

bad debts 552–3
balance sheets 507–8, 545–6, 557, 569–71
bank managers 605
banker's drafts 411
bankruptcy 505
banks
   cheques 411–13, 415–17
   statements of account 416, 417
bar codes 107, 210, 350
Barclays Bank 346
BBC (British Broadcasting Association) 91
Benetton 89, 249
Bensons Crisps 8
Beveridge Report 368
bin stock cards 463, 464
Boddington 246
Body Shop 89
Boots 166
brands 32, 167–8, 177–8, 184
   loyalty to 244–5
Branson, Richard 613
break-even charts 485–8, 614, 616
   analysing 488–9
   use of 489
Bretton Woods Treaty 368
British Aerospace 348
British Broadcasting Association (BBC) 91
British Coal 357
British Gas 34, 36
British Leyland 346–7
British Standards Institute (BSI) 347
brokers 255
BT 33, 34, 44, 600
   Confertel 136
   Datel 136
   PBX exchange systems 134–5
Budget, The 56–7
budgets 470–1, 625–6
   capital 518
   cash 520–5
   departmental 621–2
   marketing 614–16
   production 619–20
   trading forecasts 519–20
   types of 572–3
building societies 78
Burger King 166

business analysis 193
business plans
   example 622–3
   monitoring 628–9
   purpose 609–10
   see also planning
business sectors
   primary 26, 356, 357
   quarternary 356
   secondary 26, 356, 357–8
   tertiary 26, 356, 358
businesses
   competition strategies 380–2
   Europe's top companies 3 83–4
   industrial sector 25–6
   monitoring 565–6
   objectives 78–81, 601–2, 611
   private sector 26
      objectives 79–81
      ownership 81–90
   public sector 26, 90–3
      objectives 78–9
   start-up proposal 606–7
   structure 94–8
   see also organisations

cable TV 140
CAD (Computer Aided Design) 350–1
Cadbury 194
CAP (Common Agricultural Policy) 66, 357
capital budgets 518
capital ratios 577–8
Careers Service 639–40
cash books 413–15
cash budgets 520–5
cash flow 505, 517, 530, 571
Catalina system 210
CATI (Computer Assisted Telephone Interviewing) 208
cellular mobile telephones 135–6
Central Statistical Office (CSO) 201
centralised organisational structures 96–7
chairmen 101–2
change management 183–92
   competitor analysis 185
   economic change 186–90
   political change 186

societal change 191–2
technological change 192
working conditions 305–6, 311–13
charities 26, 80–1
marketing objectives 170–1
cheques 411–13, 415–17
circular flow of income 52
Citizens' Advice Bureaux 250
cluster sampling 205
co-operatives 78, 87–8
coal industry 357
collective bargaining 285
command economies 23, 48–9
commercialisation 195
Common Agricultural Policy (CAP) 66, 357
communication
channels 121–2
with employees 292–3
equipment 134–9
changes to 139–40
and organisational structure 96
sales conferences 259–60
verbal 123–30
visual 123
written 123, 130–4
Companies Acts 85
Companies House 85, 86
company secretaries 102–3
competition 31–2, 44, 181
business strategies 380–2
competitor analysis 185, 234
international comparisons 384–6
legislation 603
and pricing 482
remaining competitive 352
complaint handling 259
complement goods 7
Computer Aided Design (CAD) 350–1
Computer Assisted Telephone Interviewing (CATI) 208
computer spreadsheets 531–3
Confertel 136
construction industry 358
constructive dismissal 280
consultants 605
consultative committees 293
Consumer Credit Act (1974) 603
Consumer Protection Act (1987) 603

consumers
co-operatives 87
conscience concerns 346
demand 191
demographic variables 235–9
geographic variables 240
loyalty 14–15
motives and lifestyle 240–1
socio-economic variables 239–40, 242
sovereignty 31–2
status concerns 346
targeting 243–4
see also customers
contracts of employment 272–3, 311
effects of changes in 362–4
and grievance procedures 276
contracts of sale 602
contribution analysis 614, 615
copyrights 468, 500
corporate image 346
corporation tax 45, 58
cost centres 462, 471
cost push inflation 56, 370–1
costs
accounting system 461
advertising 34, 228
controlling 349–51
depreciation 469–70, 502–3, 553–4
direct 462–8
economies of scale 20–1, 376–7
externalities 24
fixed 18, 475–6, 482
indirect 468–74
labour 349, 464–7
marginal costing 477, 482–5
of materials 462–4
overhead absorption 470–4
overheads 468–9
of packaging 179
and pricing 180, 482
of production 344, 352, 470
in profit and loss accounts 568–9
ratio to sales 575
social costs 40
of supply 18–19
variable 18, 475–6, 482
Council of Ministers 64
Council Tax 93
craft unions 283

Index

credit cards 137, 411
credit control 398–9, 411, 512–13
credit notes 408–9
creditors 504
  ageing schedule 571–2
  average creditors payment period ratio 577
crisp business 8
CSO (Central Statistical Office) 201
cumulative preference shares 510
current assets 500, 503–4, 571
current liabilities 504, 571
current ratio 575–6
curriculum vitae (CV) 326–7
customer focus 171–3
customer service 172–3
  and sales staff 258–9
customers
  analysing 234
  maintaining self-image 346
  marketing and needs of 164–5
  purchasing considerations 399
  see also consumers
CV (curriculum vitae) 326–7

Dalgety 8
data
  coding 217
  collection 211
  dispersion 219–21
  editing 217
  preparation 216–21
  summarising 218–21
  tabulating 217–18
databases 202, 643
Datel 136
de-layering 381–2
debentures 511
debit notes 410
debtors 552–3
  ageing schedule 571–2
  average debtor collection period ratio 576
delegation 96
delivery notes 405
DeLorean Motor Company 172
demand
  and advertising 9
  aggregate demand 53

complement goods 7
conditions of 5–11
cross elasticity of 15
excess demand 22
and expectations 10
and green products 10
and income 9, 11
income elasticity of 15–16
interaction with supply 21–5
law of 4–5
market demand 4
price elasticity of 12–15
and prices 6–7, 22–4
and quality of goods 9
substitute goods 6–7
and tastes and fashion 10
demand management 52–5, 378–9
demand pull inflation 56, 369–70
demergers 381
departmental budgets 621–2
departmental managers 103–6, 300–1
depreciation 469–70, 502–3
  provisions for 553–4
design of packaging 179
devolved organisational structures 96–7
dichotomous questions 212
direct costs 462–8
direct mail 247
direct marketing 247–50
  legislation 249–50
direct selling 256
directors 101–2, 103
  job roles 300
  worker directors 293
disciplinary procedures 278–81
discounts 398
discrimination 274–5
  lawful 336
dismissal 279–81, 638
distribution 182–3, 614
  channels 254–6
documentation
  advice notes 404–5
  bank statements 416, 417
  bin stock cards 463, 464
  cash books 413–15
  credit notes 408–9
  cycle 403
  debit notes 410

delivery notes 405
goods received notes 114, 115, 406
ledgers 418, 420–1, 537–8
paying-in slips 415, 416
petty cash records 432–5
purchase orders 113, 403–4
purchase records 420–2
   example 422–6
purchase requisition 112, 113
purpose of 402
remittance advices 409, 411, 428, 430–1
sales records 418–20
   example 422–6
statements of account 409, 410–11, 416, 417
supplier's invoices 114, 115, 406–7
time cards 465
double-entry bookkeeping 537–9
downsizing 381–2
dynamic organisational structures 97–8
economic price 179
economies
   command economies 23, 48–9
   demand management 52–5, 378–9
   forecasting 599
   free markets 23, 49
   government policies 51–2, 368–72, 379–80
   growth in 44
   international indicators 386
   mixed economies 49
   multiplier effect 54–5
   supply-side economics 55–6, 372–9
   underground economy 364

economies of scale 20–1, 376–7
education 360–1
   see also training
EFTA (European Free Trade Association) 62
elasticity of demand 12–16
employees
   absenteeism 294–5
   career path 270–1
   civil legal action by 276–7
   communication 292–3
   consultative arrangements 285–6
   contracts of employment 272–3, 276, 311, 362–4
   dismissal 638
   equal opportunities 274–5
   equal pay 275
   involvement 290–1, 292
   job roles 301
   motivation 287–90, 313, 347, 382
   redundancy 281–2, 311, 638
   representative roles 302
   rights 273–4
   staff turnover 296
   staff welfare 104
   unfair dismissal 279–81, 638
   use of company accounts 563–4
   worker representation 293
employment
   application letters 323–5
   causes of decline in 359–60
   flexibility 365
   as a government priority 44, 368
   information sources 643–5
   legislation 637–8
   opportunities 639–40
   planning for 640–1
   skills required 640
   statistics 189–90, 360, 361, 632
   trends 356–8
   of women 191–2, 362
   see also self-employment
Employment Act (1989) 280
Employment Protection Act (1975) 638, 639
Employment Protection (Consolidation) Act (1978) 272, 280, 281, 335, 637, 638
empowerment 381–2
energy industry 358
environmental issues 346
   government policies 46–7
EPOS (Electronic Point Of Sale) systems 210
equal opportunities 274–5, 336
Equal Pay Act (1970) 275
equity shares 508–9
ERM (Exchange Rate Mechanism) 69–70
ethnicity 238–9
European Commission 64, 352
European Council 64
European Court of Justice 65
European Free Trade Association (EFTA) 62

Index

European Parliament (Assembly) 64
European System of Central Banks (ESCB) 63
European Union
  Common Agricultural Policy 66, 357
  development 61–3
  institutions 63–5
  Maastricht Treaty 61, 63, 380
  Single Market 36
  Social Charter 61
Europe's top companies 383–4
Exchange Rate Mechanism (ERM) 69–70
exchange rates 67–70, 359, 368
  abolition of exchange controls 374
  floating 66, 68
  government influences on 69–70
extraction industries 357

facsimile machines 137
Fair Trading Act (1973) 250
Family Expenditure Survey 189
feasibility studies 604–5
final accounts 547–9
finance sources 506, 508–13
financial accounting 461
financial economies of scale 21
fixed assets 469–70, 500–3, 570–1
fixed costs 18, 475–6, 482
fixed-term contracts 311
flat organisational structures 95–6
focus group interviews 209
Food Safety Act (1990) 603
Ford Motor Company 351
  product mix 174–6
forecasting 222–3, 599, 620
franchises 88–90, 256
free markets 23, 49
Friedman, Milton 56
functional specialisation 96

Gallagher Tobacco 34
Gates, Bill 289, 348
Gateway Principle 138
GATT (General Agreement on Trade and Tariffs) 379
Gaulle, Charles de 62
gearing ratio 577–8
GEC 381
General National Vocational Qualifications (GNVQs) 309

geo-demographic factors 240
Germany, economic indicators 386
Gillette 184
globalisation 382
GNVQs (General National Vocational Qualifications) 309
Golden Wonder crisps 8
goods received notes 114, 115, 406
goodwill 500
Gorbachev, Michail 48
government
  Chancellor's budget 56–7
  economic objectives 51–2, 379–80
  economic policies 368–72
  environmental policies 46–7
  expenditure 45, 54
  growth policies 372–9
  labour market policies 372–4
  market intervention 45–7, 51–2
    reasons for 44–5
  privatisation policy 58–9, 91, 374–5
  publications 201–2, 644
  regional policies 378
  small business policies 375–7
  social policies 46
  structure 92
  subsidies 379
  taxation policy 57–8, 374
  use of company accounts 563
Green, Howard 306
grievance procedures 276–7, 311
Gross Domestic Product (GDP) 188–9
gross misconduct 279
Gross National Product (GNP) 25–6, 37, 188–9
groups 124–5, 301–2, 306–7

Häagen Dazs 180
Hanson 32
health and safety 117–18
  and personnel departments 104
Health and Safety at Work Act (1974) 44–5, 117–18, 275
Heath, Edward 62
Heinz 177–8
Herzberg, Frederick 289
hierarchical structures 95–6
hierarchy of needs 287–9
hire purchase 512

holiday pay 311
Holsten 231
home-working contracts 363
homogenous markets 234
Honda 468
Hoover 34
housing associations 78
human resource management
   absenteeism 294–6
   disciplinary procedures 278–81
   employee communication 292–3
   employee involvement 290–2
   employee motivation 287–90, 347
   employee representation 293
   employers and employees rights 272–5
   grievance procedures 276–7, 311
   industrial relations 104, 282–6
   and job roles 302–3
   redundancy 281–2, 311, 638
   responsibilities 270–1
Hurd, Douglas 66
hygiene factors 289

IBA (Independent Broadcasting Authority) 250
ICI 600
idea generation 193
IIP (Investors in People) 309
income tax 634
incomes
   circular flow of income 52
   definition 186
   and demand 9, 11
   discretionary income 187
   disposable income 187
   distribution 188
   targeting market segments by 239
   see also wages
indirect costs 468–74
industrial relations 104, 282–6
Industrial Tribunals 280, 281
inflation 44, 55–6
   and accounting ratios 579
   cost push 56, 370–1
   demand pull 56, 369–70
   monetarist 56, 371–2
   and purchasing patterns 186
   remedies and effects 368–72

information flows 121–2
information technology 107
insolvency 505
insurance 604, 605
interest cover ratio 578
interest rates 46
internal audits 111
Internet 202–3
interviews 328–32
   focus group interviews 209
   interviewee techniques 333–4, 641
   in market research 208–9
   performance appraisals 305
   recruitment 328–32
      techniques 330–1
inventory management 183
Investors in People (IIP) 309
invoices 114, 115, 406–7

Jaguar 348
Japan, economic indicators 386
job centres 640
job descriptions 110, 319–20, 321
job design 313
job enlargement 291
job enrichment 291
job evaluation 108–10
job extension 290–1
job roles 300–2
job rotation 291
job-share contracts 364
journals 202, 605
just-in-time production 350–1

'kanban' 347
Keynes, John Maynard 52–3
Kimberley-Clark 245
Kotler, Philip 164
KP crisps 8
Kwiksave 239

labour
   costs 349, 464–7
   government policies 372–4
   mobility 312
   productivity 351
Lamont, Norman 66, 69
lateral communication channels 121–2
Lawson, Nigel 599

leasing agreements 512
ledgers 418, 420–1, 537–8
legislation
   accounting 633
   Companies Acts 85
   Competition Act (1980) 603
   Consumer Credit Act (1974) 603
   Consumer Protection Act (1987) 603
   on direct marketing 249–50
   Employment Act (1989) 280
   employment law 637–8
   Employment Protection Act (1975) 638, 639
   Employment Protection (Consolidation) Act (1978) 272, 280, 281, 335, 637, 638
   Equal Pay Act (1970) 275
   Fair Trading Act (1973) 250
   Food Safety Act (1990) 603
   Health and Safety at Work Act (1974) 44–5, 117–18, 275
   Local Government Acts 79
   Office, Shops and Railway Premises Act (1963) 104, 637
   Partnership Act (1894) 83
   Race Relations Act (1976) 274
   Redundancy Payments Act (1965) 638
   Resale Price Act (1976) 603
   Restrictive Trade Practices Acts 603
   Sale of Goods Act (1979) 602–3
   Sex Discrimination Act (1975) 274
   Single European Act (1987) 62, 347, 380
   Supply of Goods (Implied Terms) Act (1973) 603
   Supply of Goods and Services Act (1982) 603
   Trade Descriptions Acts 603
   on trade unions 372–3
   Unsolicited Goods and Services Act (1971) 603
Leontieff, Wassily 360
letters 131–2
   application for employment 323–5
   letters of enquiry 403
   sales 261
   written offer of employment 273, 335
Likert, Rensis 214
limited liability 85

liquidity ratios 575–7
loans 511–12
local government 93
   legislation 79

Maastricht Treaty 61, 63, 380
McCarthy's database 202, 643
McDonalds 89, 166, 168
McGregor's Theory X and Theory Y 290
mail panels 207
Major, John 66, 599
management
   as a cause of falling employment 359
   chairmen 101–2
   company secretaries 102–3
   departmental managers 103–6, 300–1
   directors 101–2, 103, 300
   job roles 300–2
   managing directors 102
   motivating 97
   span of control 96
   supply management 348–9
   see also change management; human resource management
management by objectives 304
managerial economies of scale 21
managing directors 102
manufacturing industry 358, 359
marginal cost pricing 477, 482–5
market research
   data preparation 216–21
   experimentation 203–4
   Internet 202–3
   interviews 208–9
   marketing contribution 224
   observation 204
   presenting findings 223–4
   primary data 203–10
   publications 201–2
   questionnaires 211–15
   research stages 215–16
   sampling 204–6
   secondary data 201–3
   surveys 206–10
   trend analysis 221–3
marketing
   achieving aims 171
   budgets 614–16
   channels 254

co-operatives 88
and corporate image 168–9
and customer focus 171–3
and customer needs 164–5
departments 105–6
direct 247–50
economies of scale 21, 376–7
information requirements 644
and market share 166–7
marketing mix 106, 170, 173–83
network marketing 256
and non-profit organisations 170–1
objectives 165–71, 180
   of charities 170–1
and place (distribution) 182–3
planning 612–13, 614–16, 618
and price 179–81
principles 164–5
and products 167–8, 174–9
and quality assurance 170
and sales and profits 165–6
test marketing 194
timing 617
see also advertising
markets
   concentration ratios 31, 33
   consumer 233
   defining 231–2
   developing new 195
   domination 80
   elastic and inelastic 14
   equilibrium 18, 23
   geographic location 240
   government intervention 44–7, 51–2
   industrial 233
   monopolies 32, 34–6, 44
   oligopolies 33–4, 44
   perfect competition 31–2
   price competition 181
   segmenting 233–5
Marks & Spencer 32, 239, 349
Maslow's hierarchy of needs 287–9
materials
   costs 462–4
   handling 183
mean values 219
median values 219
meetings 125–8
memorandum 131

Mercury 33, 34, 137
mergers 381
merit goods 25
method study 111
Microsoft 348
minimum efficient scale of production (MES) 20
minutes of meetings 126–7
mission statements 303, 611
mixed economies 49
mobile telephomes 135–6
mode values 218
monetarist inflation 56, 371–2
money orders 411
monopolies 32, 34–6, 44
Monopolies and Mergers Commission (MMC) 36, 352
multiple-choice questions 213
multiplier effect 54–5

National Education and Training Targets (*NETT*s) 372
National Health Service (NHS) 78, 79, 91, 92–3
National Insurance Contributions 634
National Vocational Qualifications (NVQs) 309
nationalised industries 58–9, 91
Netto 239
network marketing 256
newspapers 643
Nissan 378
nominal ledgers 537
North Sea Oil 357, 359
note taking 130–1
NVQs (National Vocational Qualifications) 309
office services 104
Office, Shops and Railway Premises Act (1963) 104, 637
OFGAS 181
OFTEL 44
OFWOT 59
oil industry 357, 359
oligopolies 33–4, 44
omnibus surveys 210
open-ended questions 214
operatives *see* employees
order processing 183

ordinary shares 508–9
Organisation and Methods (O&M) systems 111
organisational structure 94–8
   centralised and devolved 96–7
   hierarchical and flat 95–6
   static and dynamic 97–8
organisations
   growth 192–6
   purpose 344
   see also businesses
overdrafts 512
overhead absorption 470–4
overheads 468–9

PABX (Private Automatic Branch Exchanges) 134
packaging 178–9
pagers 135
Pareto optimality 38, 40
part-time contracts 363
partnerships 26, 82–4, 508
   accounting requirements 633
   legislation 83
patents 501
PAYE 57, 634, 635
payment terms 398
PBX exchange systems 134–5
penetration pricing 181
pensions 634
PepsiCo Foods International 8
performance appraisals 305
performance measurement 304–5, 353, 565
performance-related pay 382
periodicals 202
person specifications 110, 320–3
personal interview surveys 208–9
personnel departments 103–4, 115
   responsibilities 271
personnel functiom, *see* human resource management
petty cash records 432–5
phonecards 137
piecework labour costs 466–7
pilot studies 215
planning
   for employment 640–1
   information sources 643–5

marketing 612–13, 614–16, 618
operational 598, 601, 624
production 619–20
strategic 598, 599–601
tactical 598, 601
see also business plans
plant hire 468
PMBX (Private Manual Branch Exchanges) 134
postal orders 411
postal surveys 207–8
predatory pricing 352
preference shares 509–10
prepayments 504, 551
presentations 257
Prestel 138
price
   competing on 181
   and demand 6–7, 22–4
   and marketing 179–81
   maximising 346
   skimming 181
   and supply 18, 22–4
price wars 34
   crisp business 8
pricing 179–81, 180, 482
   break-even charts 485–8, 614, 616
      analysing 488–9
      use of 489
   and competition 482
   considerations 482
   marginal cost pricing 477, 482–5
   predatory pricing 352
primary business sector 26, 356, 357
Prince's Trust 640
print industry 360
private limited companies 26, 85–6
private sector businesses 26
   objectives 79–81
   ownership 81–90
privatisation 58–9, 91, 374–5
Procter & Gamble 34
   postal surveys 207
production
   budgets 619–20
   costs 344, 352, 470
   information requirements 644
   planning 619–20

productivity 110–11, 312–13, 349–50
  labour productivity 351
products
  brands 32, 167–8, 177–8, 184, 244–5
  definition 174
  developing new 192–5
  differentiation 244
  image 167–8
  life cycle 176–7, 345–6, 352
  and marketing 174–9
  maximising quantity sold 351–2
  merit goods 25
  packaging 178–9
  product mix 174–6
  product concept 172
  product-market matrix 195–6
  public goods 24–5
  range 351
  storage and distribution 614
  test surveys 209
profit and loss accounts 543–4, 556, 567–9, 568–9
profit-sharing schemes 292
profits
  calculating 542–3, 574
  maximising 79–80
  and pricing 482
  ratio analysis 574–5
  re-investing 510–11
  target for organisations 344
promotions 182, 229–30, 613
Prontaprint 89
prospecting 257
PSBR (Public Sector Borrowing Requirement) 187
public goods 25
public limited companies (PLCs) 26, 86
public relations 229, 613
public sector businesses 26, 90–3
  objectives 78–9
publications
  government 201–2, 644
  newspapers 643
  trade journals 202, 605
purchasing
  departments 104–5
  documentation 402–11, 420–2
    example 422–6
  economies of scale 20–1, 376–7

ledgers 537
  systems 113–15, 116

qualitative data 216
quality assurance 170
quality circles 291, 347
quality control 347–9
quantitative data 216
quarternary business sector 356
questionnaires 211–15
quick test ratio 576
quota sampling 205–6
quotations 403

Race Relations Act (1976) 274
radiopaging 135
radiotelephone services 137
random sampling 204–5
range of data 219–21
ratio analysis 574–8
  example 581–6
  limitations 579–80
  presentation 580–1, 585–6
Ratner, Gerald 347
Ratners 346
recruitment
  CV (curriculum vitae) 326–7
  advertising 324
  interviews 328–32
  job descriptions 319–20
  letters of application 323–5
  person specifications 110, 320–3
  and personnel departments 104
  procedure 318
  selection decision 332
  sources of 318–19
redundancy 281–2, 311
  legislation 638
regional policies 378
Registrar of Companies 85, 86
remittance advice notes 409, 411, 428, 430–1
remuneration see incomes; wages
rental agrements 512
reports 132–4
Resale Price Act (1976) 603
resource allocation 234–5
Restrictive Trade Practices Acts 603
retailers 255

return on capital employed (ROCE) 574
return on equity (ROE) 575
Rolls Royce 170
Rover 468
royalties 468

Sainsbury 167–8, 239
Sale of Goods Act (1979) 602–3
sales
   administration 260–2
   communication methods 259–60
   conferences 259–60
   customer service 172–3, 258–9
   departments 105
   direct selling 256
   distribution channels 254–6
   documentation 402–11, 418–20
      example 422–6
   information requirements 644
   ledgers 418, 537
   letters 261
   presentations 257
   promotions 182, 229–30, 613
   staff responsibilities 257–9
   timing of marketing 617
sampling 204–6
satellite TV 140, 256
Schumacher, Ernst 376
screening new products 193
secondary business sector 26, 356, 357–8
segmentation
   benefit 240–1
   lifestyle 241
self-employment 364, 632
   information sources 643–5
   opportunities 639–40
   planning 641–2
   skills required 640
Sex Discrimination Act (1975) 274
share issues 508–10
share premium accounts 509
share-option schemes 292
share-saving schemes 292
shareholders
   appointing of board members 101
   use of company accounts 563
shift patterns 311
ships radiotelephone services 137
shop audits 210

sick pay 311
Sinclair, Sir Clive 194, 289
Single European Act (1987) 62, 347, 380
Single Market 36
skimming 181
Smith, W.H. 166
Social Charter 61
social costs 40
socio-economic groupings 239, 242
SOFT (Strengths, Opportunities, Failures
    and Threats) analysis 600–1
sole traders 26, 81–2
   accounting requirements 633
solicitors 605
Soviet Union 48
specialisation 244
spending patterns 189
sponsorship 34, 613
spreadsheets 531–3
staff associations 286
staff turnover 296
staff welfare 104
statements of account 409, 410–11, 416, 417
static organisational structure 97–8
Stella Artois 180–1
stock control 107, 463–4, 503
   turnover ratio 577
Stock Exchange 360
stratified sampling 205
subcontracting 605
subjective forecasting 223
subsidies 379
suppliers 605
   assessing 399
supply
   and costs 18–19
   determinants 18–19
   excess supply 22
   and government influence 19–20
   interaction with demand 21–5
   management 348–9
   and price 18, 22–4
   and technology 19
Supply of Goods (Implied Terms) Act
    (1973) 603
Supply of Goods and Services Act (1982)
    603
supply-side economics 55–6, 372–9
surveys 206–10

switchboards 134–5
SWOT (Strengths, Weaknesses, Opportunities and Threats) analysis 243, 600
systematic random sampling 205
systems analysis 111

targeting consumers 243–4
taxation
　corporation tax 45, 58
　Council Tax 93
　government policy 57–8, 374
　income tax 634
　indirect 58
　National Insurance Contributions 634
　PAYE 57, 634, 635
　payment for public goods 25
　and purchasing patterns 187
　Value Added Tax (VAT) 433, 633–4
team briefings 292–3
teams 124–5, 301–2, 306–7
technical economies of scale 20
technology 139–40, 313
TECs (Training and Enterprise Councils) 309, 375, 377, 640
telemarketing 247
telephones 128–30
　mobile 135–6
　surveys 208
　switchboards 134–5
teleprinters 138
Teletex 138
television 140
telework contracts 363
Telex 138
temporary contracts 363
tertiary business sector 26, 356, 358
test marketing 194
test surveys 209
Theory X 290
Theory Y 290
time cards 465
time-based labour costs 465–6
trade associations 202
trade credit 512–13
Trade Descriptions Acts 603
trade journals 202, 605
trade references 398
trade unions 283–6, 297
　as a cause of falling employment 360
　legislation 372–3
　single union deals 284
　types of 283–4
　use of company accounts 563–4
trademarks 501
trading accounts 542–3
trading forecasts 519–20
Trading Standards Department 250
training 360–1
　induction 308
　qualifications 308–9
　types of 307–8
Training and Enterprise Councils (TECs) 309, 375, 377, 640
Treaty of Rome (1957) 61–2
trend analysis 221–3
trial balances 540–1, 555

ultra vires doctrine 602
underground economy 364
unemployment
　distribution 361
　statistics 386–7
unfair dismissal 279–81, 638
Unilever 33, 34
United Biscuits 8
United Kingdom
　decline in industrial output 359–61
　economic indicators 386
　EEC membership 62, 66
　unemployment statistics 386–7
United States, economic indicators 386
Unsolicited Goods and Services Act (1971) 603
utility of demand 4

value added, *see* added value
Value Added Tax (VAT) 433, 633–4
variable costs 18, 475–6, 482
verbal communication 123–30
vertical communication channels 121
video conferencing 139
video printers 138
videophones 139
Viewdata 138
visual communication 123
Voluntary Service Overseas (VSO) organisation 640

wages
- average earnings 363
- and job evaluation 109–10
- performance-related pay 382
- and personnel departments 104, 115
- reducing rates 349
- systems 115–17
- *see also* incomes

Walkers Smiths crisps 8
warehousing 183
warranties 602
water boards 59
wealth of countries 37, 38
welfare of countries 37–8
wholesalers 255
Wilson, Harold 62
women, and trade unions 284
women in employment 191–2, 362
work study 110–11
worker co-operatives 87–8
worker directors 293
worker representation 293
working capital 504–5, 517–18
working conditions 305–6, 311–13
World Trade Organisation 379
written communication 123, 130–4

Yeltsin, Boris 48
youth unemployment rates 360

Zeneca 600